k

Y

D0953987

THE CULTURE AND PSYCHOLOGY READER

GN 502 .C87 1995
The culture and psychology
                        211603

DATE DUE

BRODART   Cat. No. 23-221

THE SOCIAL AND POLITICAL THOUGHT

Contents

Acknowledgments

First of all we would like to acknowledge The Fielding Institute for providing a setting which encourages the exploration of new ideas and new theories. Fielding's guiding values—among them collaborative interaction among faculty and students and the development of a critical global perspective—guided us as we undertook this project.

We would especially like to acknowledge the ongoing encouragement and intellectual contributions of our students who have shared their experience, knowledge, and scholarship with us. Our dialogues with them have influenced our understandings and continuously challenged us.

Our husbands—Joe and Leo—have been very important to us in this process. At the times when we did not want to talk about anything else than the issues in this book, they both patiently listened and helped us clarify our thinking. They further nurtured our project by cooking delicious meals when we were too busy or preoccupied to do it ourselves.

We would like to thank all the staff of NYU Press who have assisted us in the preparation of this book. Tim Bartlett, our editor, Kathe Sweeney, who obtained permissions from the contributing authors to this volume, and Despina Papazoglou Gimbel, who managed the details of production, have been most attentive and enthusiastic in their work with us.

Finally, we want to thank each other. Collaboration that includes full sharing of each step of a project like ours is not always easy to achieve. As we learned from each other and shared our excitement, our intellectual connection and friendship has grown. Ending this project is both bittersweet and a source of pride.

PART I

The Politics of Difference

1. What's in a Name? The Case for "Intercultural" Psychology

Jody Bennet Veroff and Nancy Rule Goldberger

A multicultural perspective in studying and understanding human behavior has become essential in the waning days of the twentieth century. John Donne's declaration four hundred years ago that "no man is an island" has become an inescapable reality for most individuals, for all of the societies that make up the global community, and for culturally distinctive enclaves within any given society. The interconnectedness of the fate of all people is increasingly difficult to ignore. The enormous social problems—poverty and hunger, environmental degradation, population expansion, epidemic disease, human rights abuses—that threaten the lives and well-being of many members of our society and most citizens of the world cannot be resolved by simplistic application of interventions based on understandings or expectations of any one culture. Rather we must begin to take into account the different circumstances, different needs, different values, different constructions of reality, and different worldviews and belief systems that significantly shape the experience and behavior of all cultural groups. It seems imperative that we—as students, educators, researchers, and practioners of Western social sciences whose theories and practices have implications for the lives of so many people well beyond our own cultural milieu—begin to put our own value assumptions, methods, and constructs to the test: Are we culture sensitive? Are we culturally competent? This volume of readings, we hope, will both challenge old ideas and expand understanding.

THE SEARCH FOR DEFINITIONAL FOOTING AND ESSENTIAL PAPERS

Our interest in putting together a collection of papers relevant to psychology and culture came from several sources. Perhaps most compelling was our concern about the mounting social problems that seemed in part a consequence of conflicts between "cultures in collision." Although such conflicts have multiple causes, we believe that they are often fueled at the individual level by a pervasive lack of knowledge of cultures other than one's own. With the absence of knowledge comes distrust and prejudice between culturally different groups and widespread failures in understanding and appreciation of cultural differences.

Secondly, we were aware of how little attention psychology has given to the role of culture in human behavior and development. Historically, psychologists have been somewhat indifferent to culture and context as they went about their business of looking for universal laws of human behavior. Even those psychologists interested in cultural differences marginalized themselves (or were marginalized) into a special interest group: cross-cultural psychology. Their research, which primarily involves comparative culture studies, has had surprisingly little influence on mainstream psychological theory. Most psychological theorists, compared with theorists from other social science disciplines, have been late coming to the recognition that we need to expand our understanding of how persons and cultures "construct" each other (Gergen 1985; Sampson 1989). It is only recently that psychologists, especially those practitioners working in culturally diverse communities, have begun to promote the need to become culturally competent.

Thirdly, our work with our students had informed us that many articles and books relevant to important issues in culture and psychology were widely scattered, not always easy to locate. The old and new writing that links psychology and culture is plentiful in its variety, but it is often garnered away in special corners of the professional journals and libraries, embedded in first-person narratives or culture tales (Howard 1991), marginalized in interdisciplinary journals and books outside the purview of mainstream psychology and anthropology. How useful, we thought, if some of the articles we had found most valuable were collected in one place.

Finally, we wanted to extend our own knowledge and understanding of psychology and culture and welcomed a project that would focus our efforts on doing that. We had already tasted the excitement of feminist challenges to mainstream psychology and their exhilarating effects on our ways of thinking. We rightly anticipated that our learning in this area would similarly challenge and excite us. We especially welcomed the opportunity to extend our understandings of the issue of power as it affects groups living in close proximity and of the structural inequalities that maintain differences in power, opportunity, and access to resources.

Despite our sense of mission and intellectual excitement, we must acknowledge that we also experienced a strong undertow of anxiety provoked by the task of assembling the most useful papers in this area. Not only did this concept stir up uneasiness about the presumption of deciding what papers in this broad and diverse area are most useful, but also we were aware that our own particular cultural locations inevitably shaped our perceptions of what ideas were important. Thus, in our very desire to extend general awareness of issues we believed were critically important, we knew our judgments were vulnerable due to our own parochialisms and inevitable blind spots. Our omissions would undoubtedly offend some; our inclusions might offend others. Yet, all of the risks seemed worth it.

As we began our efforts we quickly realized that we had undertaken a review of a vast area where anthropology, sociology, psychology, and linguistics intersect. We needed to narrow our focus at least a little to make our project feasible. The process of setting boundaries around an area as diffuse and intrinsically complex as "culture and psychology" turned out to be a daunting and challenging task. Struck by the inherent interdisciplinarity of an enterprise which attempts to address the relationship between everyday experience and culture, we read broadly across feminist texts, critical theory, linguistics, third-world literature, and what has come to be called culture theory (Shweder and LeVine 1984). As do many who teach, we began to integrate into our seminars the articles that most perplexed or enchanted us; we engaged our students in our deliberations about the history and elusive center of the study of culture and psychology. We enlisted our students as co-sleuths in our quest for provocative and informed writing that best illustrated what we were coming to believe were central questions and themes in the juncture of anthropology and psychology, of persons and cultures. Together with our students we began to wander through autobiographies and personal narratives—that is, the lived experiences of individuals in their cultural context—once we realized how much these stories illuminated culture theory. The list of possible essential papers grew as we expanded our vision of the territory appropriate for the student of culture and psychology.

With the expansion of the list came an explosion of terms and constructs to be unpacked before we could proceed with the task of selection. We ran into semantic peculiarities arising out of different discipline-based language communities with very different histories and scientific values. It became apparent that terms indigenous to one discipline were sometimes co-opted by the other with a subtle change in meaning and theoretical relevance, making cross-discipline translation difficult.

In addition, as we wandered back and forth between the popular and academic literature, we began to feel that an admixture of pop and academic language had so invaded the fields of both anthropology and psychology that buzzwords such as "multiculturalism," "cultural diversity," "essentialism," and "postmodernism" carried tremendous affective power and had the ability to short-circuit any calm evaluation or meaning-making intention of the curious student. Like Shweder (chapter 3 in this volume), we began to ask "What is it?"

When Shweder asked, "What is it?" he was referring to the particular approach to studying psychology and culture which he calls *cultural psychology*. In the process of explaining what cultural psychology is, he first addresses what it is not by drawing differentiating boundaries around various other disciplines—such as general psychology, psychological anthropology, cross-cultural psychology, and ethnopsychology—which are also concerned about relationships between culture and human behavior. Closely allied terms which Shweder did not include in his definitional index are "multicultural psychology" and "indigeneous psychology," terms which have gained in popularity recently and are contributing to definitional confusions. We have discovered that many writers use some of these labels generically. Thus, individual writers may identify their work and interest in the relationship between culture and human behavior as falling into the general realm of cross-cultural psychology or cultural psychology or multicultural psychology, without being aware of the implications of the discipline boundaries described by Shweder.

THE CASE FOR INTERCULTURAL PSYCHOLOGY

In our own attempts to describe this large field, we have found it useful to make differentiations based on the principal focus of study and research and have identified three major categories:

1. the study of particular cultures or groups to determine the relationship between the structure, values, belief systems, myths, language, and practices of the culture and the behavior of individuals living in the culture;
2. the comparison of characteristics of human behavior in different cultures;
3. studies of the interactive effects between cultures that coexist in a larger societal context.

The first category describes the general content and focus of cultural anthropology, cultural psychology, indigenous psychology, psychological anthropology, and, in some instances, multicultural psychology. The second category is represented by cross-cultural psychology, transcultural psychiatry, and comparative psychology. Representatives of the third category seem limited to intercultural psychology and those aspects of multicultural psychology that focus on understanding the pluralistic nature of many societies in our world today.

Each of these foci of study yields important insights about the effects of culture on human behavior. Ideally, an integration of the studies associated with each could greatly accelerate progress in developing more complete psychological understandings. As a discipline, mainstream psychology has been faulted both politically and scientifically for its traditional exclusion of diverse groups from study and its claim to have discovered universal laws governing human behavior based on a limited sample of the world's population. The ethnocentrism in identifying one small group of human beings as the "real" people of the world whose ways of behaving have become the standard for understanding all of human behavior is challenged by all of the varieties of cultural study; their scholarship cannot help but move psychology toward more global perspectives.

We have been surprised, however, by the relative lack of attention that psychologists interested in culture have paid to intercultural effects. The technological miracles that permit frequent and often almost immediate communication between the most remote corners of the world by satellite transmission of images, telecommunication networks, and air transportation systems guarantee that most cultures in the world can and inevitably will have increasing interaction with each other. It is becoming increasingly difficult to imagine understanding human behavior without reference to the interactive cultural contexts in which it occurs.

At the most innocuous level, cultures living contiguously are altered by the exchanges of cultural aspects such as language, customs, material commodities, technologies, cuisines, and art forms. These exchanges can mutually enrich neighboring cultures and lead to distinctively new cultural forms. However, contiguous cultures rarely achieve a mutually rewarding, harmonious, and equitable coexistence. Issues of power, issues of domination and subordination, and issues of superiority and inferiority almost inevitably arise because of competing economic and political interests.

The interactive effects of cultures living side-by-side, thus, typically include the maintenance of differentials in the rights, opportunities, and access to resources for members of each culture as well as the ways in which members of each culture evaluate and respond to their "neighbors" and the way individuals from each culture adapt to their particular location in "the neighborhood." Although the lives of individuals belonging to groups designated as subordinate or inferior may be most negatively affected by the dominant culture's appraisals and practices, it can be argued that the context of life in the dominant culture is also affected.

Understanding these interactive, culture-shaping forces and their effects seems to require a psychology that is *intercultural.* Increased knowledge of different cultural groups by itself is unlikely to dispel parochial assumptions, especially those supported by the values of the dominant culture. Only when this knowledge leads to a fuller understanding of the interactive effects of one culture on another and an awareness of the systemic interdependence of all groups living within a society can psychologists begin to develop the intercultural perspectives that seem required to inform both theory and practice. Prilleltensky (1990) recommends what he calls a "macro-sociopolitical" approach for "understanding the impact of societal structures on the human experience." He not only suggests that a full understanding of the psychological problems of humans requires an understanding of the existing social systems and political arrangements, but also argues that meaningful therapeutic or ameliorative interventions must often involve efforts to empower oppressed individuals and to change social systems.

The current emphasis on diversity and multiculturalism in this society has created new cultural icons on a par with apple pie and motherhood, exemplified by a proliferation of images of beautiful children of all colors singing and playing together. It has also spawned a frightened, hostile backlash among many "mainstream" Americans. No better example of this paradox has come to our attention than a recent account of the new school board policy in a small Florida town (*New York Times,* May 15, 1994). The school board has adopted Florida's multicultural education policy, but has also voted to require teachers to teach their students that American culture, values, and political institutions are inherently superior to other foreign or historic cultures. Contradictions as extreme as this may arise out of the lack of dominant-culture awareness of the systemic relationships between dominant and subordinate groups. To the extent that institutions in this society are inspired by the appealing values of diversity and multiculturalism to take action to address existing and historic inequalities between groups, life will change for at least some members of the dominant culture in ways which will alter their entitlements and privileges.

Resolving the dilemmas that may be stimulated by a focus on the interdependence of coexisting cultures may be an issue not only for small-town school boards but also for those scholars and practitioners concerned with human behavior who have made significant contributions to the existing body of psychological knowledge. Thus, we expect that the intercultural approach to studying the relationship between psychology and culture may be less warmly embraced than other approaches since it may represent a particularly troublesome challenge to existing psychological knowledge and traditional research methodologies. Because its implications are ultimately political as well as scientific, they provide a radical challenge to existing approaches to practice as well. Yet, the survival of our own society which encompasses so much diversity of cultures, orientations, and concerns, as well as the survival of what is fast becoming the global community of our world, seems to us to depend greatly on increasing knowledge of the ways in which cultures are inevitably interdependent.

This conviction has guided our selection of papers for this volume. We have chosen papers representing many of the approaches to understanding the relationship between culture and psychology we have discussed because we believe their insights inform this area of study in general and contribute, either directly or indirectly, to an argument for an intercultural perspective. We have also included personal reflections and stories of people whose experiences are shaped and influenced by the interfaces between their own culture and the dominant culture. We hope that these will be as effective in stimulating intercultural perspectives for our readers as they have been for us.

BASIC ISSUES

In addition to representing a variety of approaches to cultural study, the papers we have collected also illuminate some of the more abstract and overarching debates in this general area. Different positions about these issues are to some extent associated with the various disciplines encompassed in the study of culture and psychology, but the themes we have noted are of concern not only to proponents of all approaches to study in this area, but also reflect debated issues in psychology in general.

What Is Culture?

Perhaps the first and most basic issue surrounds the very definition of culture. Kroeber and Kluckhohn (1963) collected 157 definitions of culture in their classic content analysis study completed during the early 1950s. They offered a comprehensive definition of culture that they believed embodied most of the implications inherent in the various definitions:

Culture consists of patterns, explicit and implicit, of and for behavior acquired and transmitted by symbols, constituting the distinctive achievement of human groups, including their embodiments of artifacts; the essential core of culture consists of traditional (i.e., historically derived and selected) ideas and especially their attached values; culture systems may, on the one hand, be considered as products of actions, on the other as conditioning elements of further action. (357)

More useful definitions, perhaps, are less encompassing and more accessible, but most support the usage of the word "culture" as referring to a collectivity of people who share a common history, often live in a specific geographic region, speak the same or a closely related language, observe common rituals, beliefs, values, rules, and laws, and which can be distinctively identified according to culturally normative practices such as child-rearing, kinship arrangements, power arrangements, ascribed roles that make up the fabric of how a society functions. More emphasis has been given of late to the concept of culture as a system of shared meanings that grow out of the cultural qualities detailed above and provide a common lens for perceiving and structuring reality for its members.

The concept of culture, especially within pluralistic societies, has come recently to include an additional component that recognizes the extent to which groups of people sharing some characteristics may be viewed by others as members of a group. When such groups of "marked" people either elect to join together in more or less formal association or are compelled to do so by the response of the larger society to them, the identity of members is often strongly influenced by both the assumptions of the outer society and by the group members' chosen or compulsory association with each other and the actions and goals that are collectively undertaken. Thus, in our society today it is not uncommon for groups identified by race, gender, class, ethnicity, sexual orientation, disability, or age to call themselves "cultures" and to be so called by others, despite the fact that their members also reside in and partake in the "culture" of the larger society and despite the fact that members of these groups do not necessarily share distinctive histories, languages, rules, beliefs, or an inclusive array of cultural practices. Considerable debate exists as to whether this extension of the concept of culture is warranted. Our own orientation toward intercultural psychology makes us favor this extension which permits attention to the possibility that "a culture" is always in part created by the recognition of outsiders that the group is "different" and separate from the outside observers on one or many dimensions. Because this demarcation of a group that results in its being both inside and outside the larger society often involves issues of power and privilege and marginalization, these "cultures" are particularly illuminating in understanding intercultural processes.

"Early Entry" vs. "Late Entry" of Culture in Academic Study and Discourse

Van de Vijver and Hutschemaekers (1990) have identified two different approaches to the theory and study of culture and psychology, differentiated by whether "culture" as a theoretical construct, variable, or focus of study is included early or late in the conceptualizing process. We understand the meaning of early or late entry as referring to the degree of centrality and importance of culture as a primary or secondary structuring factor that affects the whole enterprise of the cultural study.

According to these authors, the "late entrance" approach is typified by universalism, by implicit emphasis on cultural similarities, by an emphasis on explaining behavior, by an interest in comparison of a phenomenon as it might be observed in various cultural groups or historical periods, by an effort to "decontextualize" behavior, by a view of culture as a "set of behavior-inducing conditions" and by experimental or quasi-experimental research methodologies.

By contrast, the "early entrance" approach is characterized by relativism, implicit emphasis on cultural differences, by an emphasis on understanding behavior, by an interest in studying many interrelated phenomena in a single group, by an effort to "contextualize" behavior, by a view of culture as a system and by a hermeneutic, interpretive research methodology.

Van de Vijver and Hutschemaekers's analysis sums up a number of the "hot" debates in the general domain of psychology and culture that we will cover in more detail below. Additionally, it suggests that positions on various debated topics tend to cluster together.

Universalism vs. Relativism

Perhaps the most fundamental of these debates has revolved around the question of whether there are universal laws that govern human behavior that can be applied in any context, any time, any culture. The efforts of research psychologists have traditionally been fueled by the assumption that such universal laws do exist and by the desire to identify and verify them. Indeed, many psychologists have contended that the development of a truly scientific psychology with the rigor of "hard sciences" like physics requires a search for universal principles.

At the opposite extreme are challenges from relativists and social constructionists who adhere to a more pluralistic, contextual view of knowledge and the postmodernists who question the whole notion of objective invariant truth.

While this debate flourishes throughout the general discipline of psychology, it is particularly central in the study of culture and its relationship to human behavior. If the significance and meaning of a behavior or a trait depends on its context and/or on the whole complex system of meanings of the culture in which it occurs, the task of demonstrating invariant commonalities becomes mind-boggling in its complexity; the goal of finding fundamental relationships that might hold across all situations is both questionable and probably unattainable. Critics of relativism, especially in its more radical form represented by postmodernism, contend that it implies giving up science altogether "as an evidential, public, self-critical social enterprise" (Smith 1994) and threatens to put in its place a kind of demoralized and amoral chaos in which no theory or belief has any greater truth claim than any other. Other critics point to the essential biological sameness of humans that guarantees a sameness of survival needs and at least the logical possibility that these commonalities also result in humans' sharing many ways of responding to similar situations regardless of specific context or culture.

The debate between universalism and relativism sometimes leaves out consideration of the issue of the power relationships that are usually involved in who is studying whom by what method, for what purpose, and with what already embedded assumptions about the nature of truth. Perhaps if all groups of people shared equally in defining truth and in profiting from the generation of knowledge, there could be a universal cocreation of knowledge that sufficiently represented the diversity of ways of being and knowing within different cultural circumstances so as to reconcile the cultural specifics with the universal similarities humans share as a species.

Essentialism vs. Deconstructionism

Some of the other issues that characterize this area of study are related to the universalism/relativism debate. For example, essentialism and deconstructionism are similarly opposed. On the one side stand theorists who propose innate distinguishing characteristics that describe groups of people and account for their differences from other groups of people who also have innate distinguishing characteristics. The other side is represented by those who contend that apparent differences among groups are socially constructed and need to be understood within the context of the whole milieu in which the groups exist.

This debate has been particularly acrimonious among feminists. It has divided those who have attempted to increase understanding of women's "psychology" by identifying ways of responding, thinking, and relating that typify women in contrast to men and those who have contended that observed differences between women and men are not innate, are unsubstantial, and have been primarily constructed by the genderized arrangements in which women and men live. The poignance of this debate among feminists resides for us in the fact that feminists on either side of the fence are struggling to combat the sexist bias of traditional psychological research and theory in which women were essentially left out of study or were studied by comparing them with men who represented the standard.

Those who have emphasized the ways in which women's being is different from men's have attempted to redress the omissions of traditional psychology by demonstrating and often valorizing qualities that women have and men presumably do not. Those who have challenged the existence or importance of gender differences have attempted to dispel the "difference as deficiency" model that characterized prior gender research.

The hazards of the "alpha bias" in which differences between groups are exaggerated and the "beta bias" in which they are minimized or ignored (Hare-Mustin and Marecek 1990) lie at the boundaries of this debate and can characterize the studies of different cultural groups as well as women and men. It is of interest to note that a member of any particular group or culture is likely to be highly aware of the individual differences that exist in the group and the extent to which some members of the group are as much like people from other groups as they are like their own. By contrast, an outsider is likely to attend to the similarity of members of a group or culture. This may suggest that studies which attempt to describe a culture in terms of identifying characteristics of its members are most likely to be carried out by outsiders. This debate seems to exist in dialectic tension: the farthest reaches of essentialism seem perilously akin to the stereotyping that maintains prejudice and intergroup hostility, while the farthest reaches of deconstruction may obscure evidence that objective differences in the ways societies or cultures are structured influence the lives of individuals by limiting or facilitating what is possible.

Otto Rank (1941) spoke of a profound paradox in the way psychology has dealt with the issue of difference and offered an explanation for the difficulties in resolving the paradox. He observes that

psychology, by its very nature is ambiguous in explaining all men as fundamentally alike and yet stressing their differences as personalities. As an explanatory science, psychology shows every individual to be a unique entity in and by himself; whereas the ideology represented by every psychological theory assures the individual of his fundamental likeness to his fellowmen, thereby guaranteeing self-perpetuation regardless of social and political differences. (61)

His comments, although focused on the individual within a society, can well be applied to this debate as it is carried on in the study of culture.

Emic-Etic Debate

The emic-etic distinction (Pike 1954) refers to different views about the proper standpoint for studying human behavior. Pike described "the etic viewpoint [as studying] behavior from outside of a particular system, and as an essential initial approach to an alien system" and "the emic viewpoint [as resulting] from studying behavior as from inside the system." Although this distinction can be seen as essentially a methodological difference, it carries implications of more critical assumptive differences.

The etic approach assumes that the variables of interest to the researcher and the ways of assessing these are not so embedded in the researcher's own culture or value system as to be inappropriate, inapplicable, or meaningless in a different culture. Such assumptions inherently run the risk of importing theories and values from one culture to another and "measuring" the culture under consideration by comparing it with the researcher's culture. Both the aspects of behavior that are under study and the ways of assessing them can be seen as arising from the "emics" of the researcher's own culture. Proponents of the etic approach argue that the study of a culture within the terms of its own system does not permit a more overarching study of differences between cultures that might enhance understanding of the influence of cultural practices on behavior.

The development of indigenous psychology as a defined discipline has been fueled in part by the awareness of social scientists, particularly in Asia and Africa, of the extent to which their own approaches and theories in studying their own cultures have been shaped by Western theorists and researchers whose teachings have dominated their own understandings. Additionally, their call for indigenization of social science within their countries reflects a growing concern about misrepresentation and inadequate understanding of their people that have resulted from studies conducted by Western social scientists in the "etic mode" and by what some have viewed as the exploitative practices of Western researchers whose studies in their countries have been undertaken to promote the development of essentially Western theories; such studies, it is claimed, have been so detached from practical application that no benefit accrues to the country being studied (Jahoda 1973; Bonifacio 1977; Sampson 1988; Enriquez 1990).

Subjectivity vs. Objectivity

Closely related to the emic-etic debate is an epistemological debate concerning subjectivity versus objectivity of knowledge. The debate boils down to several issues:

1. Who is entitled to know?
2. Is the outside observer's "objective" knowledge privileged over the insider's "subjective" knowledge with regard to truth claims?
3. Can individuals' accounts of their experiences constitute acceptably valid data for scientific understanding or, instead, does subjectivity necessarily introduce unacceptable bias?

Traditionally, the scientist or researcher has enjoyed the privileged position of knower, explorer, and discoverer of knowledge. This privilege has been bestowed with the implicit assumption that knowing requires both distance and difference from that which is to be known in order to avoid contamination from biasing self-interests or personal needs. There has been growing recognition that no matter how distanced they may be, researchers themselves cannot be free of self-interests or values that may influence the questions they seek to understand and the evidence they gather and the way they collect it. Because they have claimed both objectivity and also the power of knowers and discoverers, they may be even less likely than others to be able to recognize their own biases. It can be argued that the very distance assumed to convey objectivity may actually imperil it in a particularly resistant way.

Countering the prevailing "scientific" distrust of subjectivity, some have argued that no one can know the nature and meaning of an individual's experience more fully and accurately than the person who is actually living it. By this analysis the "subjects" of study are in a unique position to inform the researcher about themselves and their lives. The penchant in experimental or quasi-experimental research to make "subjects" the objects of study by subjecting them to experimental treatments or by scrutinizing their responses as if they were static organisms viewed under a microscope may not only deprive researchers of full knowledge but also constitute a dehumanizing orientation to the phenomena to be studied. Although the elevation of "subjects" to the status of uniquely informed knowers may disrupt the accustomed authority and power of the scientist, the benefits of potentially discovering relationships that the researcher could not even have conceived of may enrich knowledge and lead to a more complete understanding of human behavior.

Honoring the value of subjectivity is not a necessary component of cultural study, even when the researcher has chosen an emic approach to understanding a culture, since it is certainly possible for the researcher who is exploring behavior within the context of a specific culture to employ methods which essentially convert subjects to objects. However, to the extent that the concept of subjectivity can be extended beyond the individual informant, a culture can be studied either "objectively" (that is, from an authoritative position of distance and difference) or "subjectively" through the study of the meaning-making of the members of the culture.

Standpoint Theory

The subjectivity/objectivity debate has been taken to a different level in standpoint theory. Although this theory has been most prominently developed by feminist theorists (Smith 1977; Jaggar 1983; Hartsock 1983), the basic tenets can be applied to differences in knowledge bases between any two groups in which one group is in a position of dominance over the other. This theory (or theories) stress the centrality of understanding the epistemological "standpoint" of the knower in any analysis of knowledge claims. Most standpoint theorists claim that the research "subject" is, in fact, a knower in a privileged position to know about her own life and experience. They also propose that generally people who possess less power in the structure of a society are in a unique position to know a great deal about the powerful group in the society and the structures of the society that sustain the power relationships and power differential. Although the state of subjugation often has implications for access to education and knowledge which are usually considered the domain of the more powerful group in a society, standpoint theorists argue that subjugated people may have special knowledge because, in order to survive, they are required to be aware and sensitive to the perspective of those who hold power over them. Potentially, thus, they can know themselves in the context of their social circumstance, they can know intimately the characteristics and ways of being of their oppressors, and they have a unique opportunity to understand the ordinarily less visible societal structures which maintain inequality.

By contrast, those who are most powerful in the society can be seen as strongly motivated not to know a lot about the people they dominate and not to develop a sensitive understanding of the structures that preserve their power. Their knowledge can thus be seen as "partial and perverse" (Hartsock 1983).

Standpoint theories have been criticized on several grounds: (1) these theories may be seen as honoring naive theorizing over "scientifically" assembled evidence; (2) an oppressed person who has not developed any political awareness of being oppressed may be unable to speak of the knowledge that oppression has created; (3) these theories lead to the problematic political implication that oppression is required for full knowledge; (4) by claiming standpoint knowledge as superior to previous objectivist science, the problem of what kind of evidence can demonstrate the superiority of one set of truth claims over another is not resolved, but simply reframed. Despite these criticisms, standpoint theories bring important epistemological challenges to the study of cultures as well as gender, because they make clear the ideological basis of knowledge and its relationship to power. They too, like other gender and culture theorists, raise serious questions about the adequacy of androcentric, Eurocentric understandings of human behavior.

Does Culture Create the Individual or Do Individuals Create the Culture?

We have saved for the end the "cart and horse" debate as to whether culture creates individuals or individuals create culture (also see Shweder, chapter 3 in this volume). From our intercultural perspective, we are tempted to give a knee-jerk response: that individuals and their cultures are so intimately interrelated that the creation of one or the other is necessarily an outcome of the interaction between the culture and the individual. However, the debate deserves more attention, if only to spell out the opposing poles.

"Culture" has often been treated as if it were an invariant, static variable which, depending on the predilection of the theorist or researcher, is seen either to play a major formative role in shaping human experience or instead is assigned a relatively minor role, except perhaps for the special case in which two cultures under consideration differ profoundly. The view of culture as an unchanging entity (especially in the case of so-called "primitive cultures") has permitted generalizations about different groups of people and societies that tend not to be subjected to much review or revision even in the wake of dramatic social and technological changes. This static view of "culture" is often associated with understandings of a culture that emphasize the similarities of members of the culture and leads to generalizations such as "The Navahos are an x type of people or a people characterized by x, y, and z." In this view "culture" creates and seems exclusively to determine the nature of individual members.

At the most extreme opposite pole defined by deconstructionism, culture exists only in the minds of individuals as a construction derived from individuals' processes of meaning-making about the conditions and structures of the world they live in. Although cultural elements, such as laws, customs, belief systems, and other structures may be identified by an outsider, their relevance to the meaning-making of individuals is seen as so highly variable as to make it reasonable to conclude that each individual creates his or her own "culture." Although this view represents perhaps the most radical form of relativism, it is also one that is endorsed by people who dismiss the importance of culture in shaping human behavior because they believe that human beings are essentially the same "under the skin." It is of interest that the most decontextualized view of human behavior as well as the most radically relativist can come to the same conclusion that individuals are the authors of their lives and their contexts.

If one grants that entities commonly identified as cultures do, in fact, exist as identifiable societal units, there seems merit in a middle-ground position that acknowledges the powerful shaping effects of culture on its members in their ways of being, ways of knowing, ways of construing reality, ways of relating as well as their fundamental assumptions about the outer world and that can at the same time encompass both the slow and rapid changes in cultures that may be a function of technological developments, natural disasters and other environmental changes, political movements or revolution, war and other conflicts between cultures. In this sense individuals can and do create culture and all cultures must be seen as the consequence of the array of solutions the members of a collectivity have devised over time to the problems and circumstances confronting them. That this array of solutions is codified in a more enduring form that influences individual members, and at the same time is in some degree of constant flux, suggests a continuous interaction between a culture creating the individual and individuals creating cultures.

This systemic view of the relationship between the individual and culture parallels our view of the systemic interrelationships between coexisting cultures and between their members. Thus, we return to our initial theme of the ultimate interdependence of all people and all cultures. We hope that the papers we have collected will both enhance understanding of that interdependence and also represent the diversity of approaches and points of view that characterize the study of culture and psychology.

REFERENCES

Bonifacio, M. F. 1977. Ethical issues influencing the acceptance and rejection of cross-cultural researchers who visit various countries. In *Issues in cross-cultural research (Annals of the New York Academy of Sciences)*, ed. Lenore Leob Adler, 295: 185–202. New York: New York Academy of Sciences.

Enriquez, V. G., ed. 1990. *Indigenous psychology: A book of readings*. Quezon City, Philippines: Akademya Ng Sikolohiyang Pilipino.

Gergen, K. J. 1985. The social constructionist movement in modern psychology. *American Psychologist* 40: 255–65.

Hare-Mustin, R. T., and J. Marecek. 1990. *Making a difference: Psychology and the construction of gender*. New Haven: Yale University Press.

Hartsock, N. C. M. 1983. The feminist standpoint: Developing the ground for a specifically feminist historical materialism. In *Discovering reality*, ed. S. Harding and M. B. Hintikka, 283–310. Dordrecht, Holland: D. Reidel Publishing.

Howard, G. S. 1991. Culture tales: A narrative approach to thinking, cross-cultural psychology, and psychotherapy. *American Psychologist* 46: 187–97.

Jaggar, A. M. 1983. *Feminist politics and human nature*. Sussex, England: The Harvester Press.

Jahoda, G. 1973. Psychology and the developing countries: Do they need each other? *International Social Science Review* 25: 461–74.

Kroeber, A. L., and C. Kluckhohn 1963. *Culture: A critical review of concepts and definitions*. Cambridge, Mass.: Harvard University Press.

Pike, K. L. 1954. Emic and etic standpoints for the description of behavior. In K. L. Pike, *Language in relation to a unified theory of the structure of human behavior* (preliminary edition). Glendale, Calif.: Summer Institute of Linguistics.

Prilleltensky, I. 1990. The politics of abnormal psychology: Past, present and future. *Political Psychology* 11: 767–85.

Rank, O. 1941. *Beyond psychology.* New York: Dover Publications.

Sampson, E. E. 1988. The debate on individualism: Indigenous psychologies of the individual and their role in personal and societal functioning. *American Psychologist* 43: 15–22.

———. 1989. The challenge of social change for psychology: Globalization and psychology's theory of the person. *American Psychologist* 44, no. 6: 914–21.

Shweder, R. A. 1991. *Thinking through cultures: Expeditions in cultural psychology.* Cambridge, Mass.: Harvard University Press.

Shweder, R. A., and R. A. LeVine, eds. 1984. *Culture theory: Essays on mind, self, and emotion.* New York: Cambridge University Press.

Smith, D. E. 1977. Some implications of a sociology for women. In *Woman in a man-made world,* ed. N. Glazer and H. Y. Wachere, 15–29. Chicago: Rand McNally.

Smith, M. B. 1994. Selfhood at risk: Postmodern perils and the perils of postmodernism. *American Psychologist* 49: 405–11.

Van de Vijver, F. J. R., and G. J. M. Hutschemaekers. 1990. Introduction. In F. J. R. Van de Vijver and G. J. M. Hutschemaekers, *The investigation of culture: Current issues in cultural psychology.* Tilburg, Holland: Tilburg University Press.

A. HISTORICAL ANTECEDENTS AND SOME CURRENT POSITIONS

The anthropologist Clifford Geertz's classic essay (chapter 2 in this volume) raises the important questions of how we are to know the other—as he puts it, to see things "from the native's point of view"—and, even more importantly, is it even possible to enter into another's subjective world? The first question is framed as a question of method and implies there may be more than one approach to knowing another person or another culture from which we may choose. However, the second question gets at the basic assumption behind the first, which is that it is indeed possible to "know" the other. Of course, both psychology and anthropology have a great deal at stake in a positive response to this second question, since both disciplines are in the business of studying, describing, classifying, naming, and explaining various facets of human behavior and human institutions. Geertz, with his usual flair, argues that "you don't have to be one to know one," but that the trick for the student of cultural and human otherness is to "figure out what the devil they think they are up to."

This phrase "what they *think* they are up to" becomes focal for Richard Shweder, a central figure and explicator of the new interdisciplinary force linking psychology, anthropology, philosophy, and linguistics which he and others call cultural psychology. In his now famous essay included as chapter 3 in this volume (in which he spends as much time on what cultural psychology is not as what it is), he explains that cultural psychology is the study of intentional worlds, that is, the study of how meanings and intentions are products of the inevitable interdependence of psyche and culture. He argues that, in fact, psyche and culture "make each other up." Human beings seize meaning from the sociocultural environment in which they are born and grow up while at the same time no sociocultural environment exists independently of the way human beings seize meanings from it. This revolutionary idea requires that we let go old ways of thinking about the separation of persons from their environments or analyzing either as dependent and independent variable. They are, says Shweder, inextricably intertwined.

Hector Betancourt and Steven López, in their essay in chapter 4, bring us back to psychology's history in its study of culture. First pointing to the marginalization of and disinterest in culture among most mainstream psychologists, they also criticize cross-cultural psychologists, who do comparative studies of cultural differences and similarities, for failing to recognize and study the very thing that would seem vital to an understanding of persons in their cultural context — that is, exactly how culture or aspects of culture influence behavior. They also address and try to clarify some of the conceptual confusion that pervades the field in its use and understanding of concepts such as race, ethnicity, and culture. Although Betancourt and López might be considered traditionalists alongside such a theorist as Shweder, they do provide a new outlook on ways to improve and enhance psychologists' understanding and study of culture.

We chose the last essay in this section — the one by David Ingleby (chapter 5) — for two reasons: we wanted to include work by someone outside the American academic community, and we liked Ingleby's analysis of how psychology is not just embedded in its own culture, but creates its own reality. Ingleby's ideological analysis of psychological epistemology, method, and practice will be echoed in essays appearing later in this volume. However, his sharp and potent critique leads us to the possibility that psychology, in the way it has constituted itself and assumed authority, operates much as a religion does. Ingleby challenges psychology's claim of scientific objectivity and asks, can there be a nonethnocentric cross-cultural psychology?

2. "From the Native's Point of View": On the Nature of Anthropological Understanding

Clifford Geertz

Several years ago a minor scandal erupted in anthropology: one of its ancestral figures told the truth in a public place. As befits an ancestor, he did it posthumously, and through his widow's decision rather than his own, with the result that a number of the sort of right-thinking types who are with us always immediately rose to cry that she, an in-marrier anyway, had betrayed clan secrets, profaned an idol, and let down the side. What will the children think, to say nothing of the layman? But the disturbance was not much lessened by such ceremonial wringing of the hands; the damn thing was, after all, already printed. In much the same fashion as James Watson's *The Double Helix* (1968) exposed the way in which biophysics in fact gets done, Bronislaw Malinowski's *A Diary in the Strict Sense of the Term* (1967) rendered established accounts of how anthropologists work fairly well implausible. The myth of the chameleon fieldworker, perfectly self-tuned to his exotic surroundings, a walking miracle of empathy, tact, patience, and cosmopolitanism, was demolished by the man who had perhaps done most to create it.

The squabble that arose around the publication of the *Diary* concentrated, naturally, on inessentials and missed, as was only to be expected, the point. Most of the shock seems to have arisen from the mere discovery that Malinowski was not, to put it delicately, an unmitigated nice guy. He had rude things to say about the natives he was living with, and rude words to say it in. He spent a great deal of his time wishing he were elsewhere. And he projected an image of a man about as little complaisant as the world has seen. (He also

Reprinted by permission of the author and American Academy of Arts and Sciences from *American Scientist* 63 (1975): 47–53 © American Academy of Arts and Sciences.

projected an image of a man consecrated to a strange vocation to the point of self-immolation, but that was less noted.) The discussion was made to come down to Malinowski's moral character or lack of it, and the genuinely profound question his book raised was ignored; namely, if it isn't, as we had been taught to believe, through some sort of extraordinary sensibility, an almost preternatural capacity to think, feel, and perceive like a native (a word, I should hurry to say, I use here "in the strict sense of the term"), how is anthropological knowledge of the way natives think, feel, and perceive possible? The issue the *Diary* presents, with a force perhaps only a working ethnographer can fully appreciate, is not moral. (The moral idealization of fieldworkers is a mere sentimentality in the first place, when it isn't self-congratulation or a guild pretense.) The issue is epistemological. If we are going to cling — as, in my opinion, we must — to the injunction to see things from the native's point of view, where are we when we can no longer claim some unique form of psychological closeness, a sort of transcultural identification, with our subjects? What happens to *verstehen* when *einfühlen* disappears?

As a matter of fact, this general problem has been exercising methodological discussion in anthropology for the last ten or fifteen years; Malinowski's voice from the grave merely dramatizes it as a human dilemma over and above a professional one. The formulations have been various: "inside" versus "outside," or "first person" versus "third person" descriptions; "phenomenological" versus "objectivist," or "cognitive" versus "behavioral" theories; or, perhaps most commonly, "emic" versus "etic" analysis, this last deriving from the distinction in linguistics between phonemics and phonetics, phonemics classifying sounds according to their internal function in language, phonetics classifying them according to their acoustic properties as such. But perhaps the simplest and most directly appreciable way to put the matter is in terms of a distinction formulated, for his own purposes, by the psychoanalyst Heinz Kohut (1971), between what he calls "experience-near" and "experience-distant" concepts.

An experience-near concept is, roughly, one which someone — a patient, a subject, in our case an informant — might himself naturally and effortlessly use to define what he or his fellows see, feel, think, imagine, and so on, and which he would readily understand when similarly applied by others. An experience-distant concept is one which specialists of one sort or another — an analyst, an experimenter, an ethnographer, even a priest or an ideologist — employ to forward their scientific, philosophical, or practical aims. "Love" is an experience-near concept, "object cathexis" is an experience-distant one. "Social stratification," or perhaps for most peoples in the world even "religion" (and certainly "religious system"), are experience-distant; "caste" or "nirvana" are experience-near, at least for Hindus and Buddhists.

Clearly, the matter is one of degree, not polar opposition — "fear" is experience-nearer than "phobia," and "phobia" experience-nearer than "ego dyssyntonic." And the difference is not, at least so far as anthropology is concerned (the matter is otherwise in poetry and physics), a normative one, in the sense that one sort of concept is to be preferred as such over the other. Confinement to experience-near concepts leaves an ethnographer awash in immediacies, as well as entangled in vernacular. Confinement to experience-distant ones leaves him stranded in abstractions and smothered in jargon. The real question, and the one Malinowski raised by demonstrating that, in the case of "natives," you don't have to be one to know one, is what roles the two sorts of concepts play in anthropological analysis. Or, more exactly, how, in each case, ought one to deploy them so as to produce an interpretation of the way a people lives which is neither imprisoned within their mental horizons, an ethnography of witchcraft as written by a witch, nor systematically deaf to the distinctive tonalities of their existence, an ethnography of witchcraft as written by a geometer.

Putting the matter this way — in terms of how anthropological analysis is to be conducted and its results framed, rather than what psychic constitution anthropologists need to have — reduces the mystery of what "seeing things from the native's point of view" means. But it does not make it any easier, nor does it lessen the demand for perceptiveness on the part of the fieldworker. To grasp concepts which, for another people, are experience-near, and to do so well enough to place them in illuminating connection with experience-distant concepts theorists have fashioned to capture the general features of social life, is clearly a task at least as delicate, if a bit less magical, as putting oneself into someone else's skin. The trick is not to get yourself into some inner correspondence of spirit with your informants. Preferring, like the rest of us, to call their souls their own, they are not going to be altogether keen about such an effort anyhow. The trick is to figure out what the devil they think they are up to.

In one sense, of course, no one knows this better than they do themselves; hence the passion to swim in the stream of their experience, and the illusion afterward that one somehow has. But in another sense, that simple truism is simply not true. People use experience-near concepts spontaneously, unselfconsciously, as it were colloquially; they do not, except fleetingly and on occasion, recognize that there are any "concepts" involved at all. That is what experience-near means—that ideas and the realities they inform are naturally and indissolubly bound up together. What else could you call a hippopotamus? Of course the gods are powerful, why else would we fear them? The ethnographer does not, and, in my opinion, largely cannot, perceive what his informants perceive. What he perceives, and that uncertainly enough, is what they perceive "with"—or "by means of," or "through" . . . or whatever the word should be. In the country of the blind, who are not as unobservant as they look, the one-eyed is not king, he is spectator.

Now, to make all this a bit more concrete, I want to turn for a moment to my own work, which, whatever its other faults, has at least the virtue of being mine—in discussions of this sort a distinct advantage. In all three of the societies I have studied intensively, Javanese, Balinese, and Moroccan, I have been concerned, among other things, with attempting to determine how the people who live there define themselves as persons, what goes into the idea they have (but, as I say, only half-realize they have) of what a self, Javanese, Balinese, or Moroccan style, is. And in each case, I have tried to get at this most intimate of notions not by imagining myself someone else, a rice peasant or a tribal sheikh, and then seeing what I thought, but by searching out and analyzing the symbolic forms— words, images, institutions, behaviors—in terms of which, in each place, people actually represented themselves to themselves and to one another.

The concept of person is, in fact, an excellent vehicle by means of which to examine this whole question of how to go about poking into another people's turn of mind. In the first place, some sort of concept of this kind, one feels reasonably safe in saying, exists in recognizable form among all social groups. The notions of what persons are may be, from our point of view, sometimes more than a little odd. They may be conceived to dart about nervously at night shaped like fireflies. Essential elements of their psyche, like hatred, may be thought to be lodged in granular black bodies within their livers, discoverable upon autopsy. They may share their fates with *Doppelgänger* beasts, so that when the beast sickens or dies they sicken or die too. But at least some conception of what a human individual is, as opposed to a rock, an animal, a rainstorm, or a god, is, so far as I can see, universal. Yet, at the same time, as these offhand examples suggest, the actual conceptions involved vary from one group to the next, and often quite sharply. The Western conception of the person as a bounded, unique, more or less integrated motivational and cognitive universe, a dynamic center of awareness, emotion, judgment, and action organized into a distinctive whole and set contrastively both against other such wholes and against its social and natural background, is, however incorrigible it may seem to us, a rather peculiar idea within the context of the world's cultures. Rather than attempting to place the experience of others within the framework of such a conception, which is what the extolled "empathy" in fact usually comes down to, understanding them demands setting that conception aside and seeing their experiences within the framework of their own idea of what selfhood is. And for Java, Bali, and Morocco, at least, that idea differs markedly not only from our own but, no less dramatically and no less instructively, from one to the other.

In Java, where I worked in the fifties, I studied a small, shabby inland county-seat sort of place; two shadeless streets of whitewashed wooden shops and offices, and even less substantial bamboo shacks crammed in helter-skelter behind them, the whole surrounded by a great half-circle of densely packed rice-bowl villages.[1] Land was short, jobs were scarce, politics was unstable, health was poor, prices were rising, and life was altogether far from promising, a kind of agitated stagnancy in which, as I once put it, thinking of the curious mixture of borrowed fragments of modernity and exhausted relics of tradition that characterized the place, the future seemed about as remote as the past. Yet in the midst of this depressing scene there was an absolutely astonishing intellectual vitality, a philosophical passion really, and a popular one besides, to track the riddles of existence right down to the ground. Destitute peasants would discuss questions of freedom of the will, illiterate tradesmen discoursed on the properties of God, common laborers had theories about the relations between reason and passion, the nature of time, or the reliability of the senses. And, perhaps most importantly, the problem of the self—its nature, function, and mode of operation—was pursued with the sort of reflective intensity one could find among ourselves in only the most recherché settings indeed.

The central ideas in terms of which this reflection proceeded, and which thus defined its boundaries and the Javanese sense of what a person is, were arranged into two sets of contrasts, at base religious, one between "inside" and "outside," and one between "refined" and "vulgar."[2] These glosses are, of course, crude and imprecise; determining exactly what the terms involved signified, sorting out their shades of meaning, was what all the discussion was about. But together they formed a distinctive conception of the self which, far from being merely theoretical, was the one in terms of which Javanese in fact perceived one another and, of course, themselves.

The "inside"/"outside" words, *batin* and *lair* (terms borrowed, as a matter of fact, from the Sufi tradition of Muslim mysticism, but locally reworked), refer on the one hand to the felt realm of human experience and on the other to the observed realm of human behavior. These have, one hastens to say, nothing to do with "soul" and "body" in our sense, for which there are in fact quite other words with quite other implications. *Batin,* the "inside" word, does not refer to a separate seat of encapsulated spirituality detached or detachable from the body, or indeed to a bounded unit at all, but to the emotional life of human beings taken generally. It consists of the fuzzy, shifting flow of subjective feeling perceived directly in all its phenomenological immediacy but considered to be, at its roots at least, identical across all individuals, whose individuality it thus effaces. And similarly, *lair,* the "outside" world, has nothing to do with the body as an object, even an experienced object. Rather, it refers to that part of human life which, in our culture, strict behaviorists limit themselves to studying—external actions, movements, postures, speech—again conceived as in its essence invariant from one individual to the next. These two sets of phenomena—inward feelings and outward actions—are then regarded not as functions of one another but as independent realms of being to be put in proper order independently.

It is in connection with this "proper ordering" that the contrast between *alus,* the word meaning "pure," "refined," "polished," "exquisite," "ethereal," "subtle," "civilized," "smooth," and *kasar,* the word meaning "impolite," "rough," "uncivilized," "coarse," "insensitive," "vulgar," comes into play. The goals is to be *alus* in both the separated realms of the self. In the inner realm this is to be achieved through religious discipline, much but not all of it mystical. In the outer realm, it is to be achieved through etiquette, the rules of which here are not only extraordinarily elaborate but have something of the force of law. Through meditation, the civilized man thins out his emotional life to a kind of constant hum; through etiquette, he both shields that life from external disruptions and regularizes his outer behavior in such a way that it appears to others as a predictable, undisturbing, elegant, and rather vacant set of choreographed motions and settled forms of speech.

There is much more to all this, because it connects up to both an ontology and an aesthetic. But so far as our problem is concerned, the result is a bifurcate conception of the self, half ungestured feeling and half unfelt gesture. An inner world of stilled emotion and an outer world of shaped behavior confront one another as sharply distinguished realms unto themselves, any particular person being but the momentary locus, so to speak, of that confrontation, a passing expression of their permanent existence, their permanent separation, and their permanent need to be kept in their own order. Only when you have seen, as I have, a young man whose wife—a woman he had in fact raised from childhood and who had been the center of his life—has suddenly and inexplicably died, greeting everyone with a set smile and formal apologies for his wife's absence and trying, by mystical techniques, to flatten out, as he himself put it, the hills and valleys of his emotion into an even, level plain ("That is what you have to do," he said to me, "be smooth inside and out") can you come, in the face of our own notions of the intrinsic honesty of deep feeling and the moral importance of personal sincerity, to take the possibility of such a conception of selfhood seriously and appreciate, however inaccessible it is to you, its own sort of force.

Bali, where I worked both in another small provincial town, though one rather less drifting and dispirited, and, later, in an upland village of highly skilled musical instruments makers, is of course in many ways similar to Java, with which it shared a common culture to the fifteenth century.[3] But at a deeper level, having continued Hindu while Java was, nominally at least, Islamized, it is quite different. The intricate, obsessive ritual life, Hindu, Buddhist, and Polynesian in about equal proportions, whose development was more or less cut off in Java, leaving its Indic spirit to turn reflective and phenomenological, even quietistic, in the way I have just described, flourished in Bali to reach levels of scale and flamboyance that have startled the world and made the Balinese a much more dramaturgical people with a self to match. What is philosophy in Java is theater in Bali.

As a result, there is in Bali a persistent and systematic attempt to stylize all aspects of personal expression to the point where anything idiosyncratic, anything characteristic of the individual merely because he is who he is physically, psychologically, or biographically, is muted in favor of his assigned place in the continuing and, so it is thought, never-changing pageant that is Balinese life. It is dramatis personae, not actors, that endure; indeed, it is dramatis personae, not actors, that in the proper sense really exist. Physically men come and go, mere incidents in a happenstance history, of no genuine importance even to themselves. But the masks they wear, the stage they occupy, the parts they play, and, most important, the spectacle they mount remain and comprise not the facade but the substance of things, not least the self. Shakespeare's old-trouper view of the vanity of action in the face of mortality—all the world's a stage and we but poor players, content to strut our hour, and so on—makes no sense here. There is no make-believe; of course players perish, but the play doesn't, and it is the latter, the performed rather than the performer, that really matters.

Again, all this is realized not in terms of some general mood the anthropologist in his spiritual versatility somehow captures but through a set of readily observable symbolic forms; an elaborate repertoire of designations and titles.[4] The Balinese have at least a half-dozen major sorts of labels, ascriptive, fixed, and absolute, which one person can apply to another (or, of course, to himself) to place him among his fellows. There are birth-order markers, kinship terms, caste titles, sex indicators, teknonyms, and so on and so forth, each of which consists not of a mere collection of useful tags but a distinct and bounded, internally very complex, terminological system. When one applies one of these designations or titles (or, as is more common, several at once) to someone, one therefore defines him as a determinate point in a fixed pattern, as the temporary occupant of a particular, quite untemporary, cultural locus. To identify someone, yourself or somebody else, in Bali is thus to locate him within the familiar cast of characters—"king," "grandmother," "thirdborn," "Brahman"—of which the social drama is, like some stock company roadshow piece—*Charley's Aunt* or *Springtime for Henry*—inevitably composed.

The drama is of course not farce, and especially not transvestite farce, though there are such elements in it. It is an enactment of hierarchy, a theater of status. But that, though critical, is unpursuable here. The immediate point is that, in both their structure and their mode of operation, the terminological systems conduce to a view of the human person as an appropriate representative of a generic type, not a unique creature with a private fate. To see how they do this, how they tend to obscure the mere materialities—biological, psychological, historical—of individual existence in favor of standardized status qualities would involve an extended analysis. But perhaps a single example, the simplest further simplified, will suffice to suggest the pattern.

All Balinese receive what might be called birth-order names. There are four of these, "firstborn," "secondborn," "thirdborn," "fourthborn," after which they recycle, so that fifthborn child is called again "firstborn," the sixth "secondborn," and so on. Further, these names are bestowed independently of the fates of the children. Dead children, even stillborn ones, count, so that in fact, in this still high-birthrate, high-mortality society, the names don't really tell you anything very reliable about the birth-order relations of concrete individuals. Within a set of living siblings, someone called "firstborn" may actually be first, fifth, or ninth born, or, if somebody is missing, almost anything in between, and someone called "secondborn" may in fact be older. The birth-order naming system does not identify individuals as individuals, nor is it intended to; what it does is to suggest that, for all procreating couples, births form a circular succession of "firsts," "seconds," "thirds," and "fourths," an endless four-stage replication of an imperishable form. Physically men appear and disappear as the ephemerae they are, but socially the acting figures remain eternally the same as new "firsts," "seconds," and so on emerge from the timeless world of the gods to replace those who, dying, dissolve once more into it. All the designation and title systems, so I would argue, function in the same way: They represent the most time-saturated aspects of the human condition as but ingredients in an eternal, footlight present.

Nor is this sense the Balinese have of always being on stage a vague and ineffable one either. It is, in fact, exactly summed up in what is surely one of their experience-nearest concepts: *lek*. Lek has been variously translated or mistranslated ("shame" is the most common attempt); but what it really means is close to what we call stage fright. Stage fright consists, of course, in the fear that, for want of skill or self-control, or perhaps by mere accident, an aesthetic illusion will not be maintained, that the actor will show through his part. Aesthetic distance collapses, the audience (and the actor) lose sight of Hamlet and gain it, uncomfortable for all concerned, of bumbling John Smith painfully miscast as the Prince of Denmark. In Bali, the case is the same: what is feared is that the public performance to which one's cultural location commits one will be botched and that the personality—as we would call it but the Balinese, of course, not believing in such a thing, would not—of the individual will break through to dissolve his standardized public identity. When this occurs, as it sometimes does, the immediacy of the moment is felt with excruciating intensity and men become suddenly and unwillingly creatural, locked in mutual embarrassment, as though they had happened upon each other's nakedness. It is the fear of faux pas, rendered only that much more probable by the extraordinary ritualization of daily life, that keeps social intercourse on its deliberately narrowed rails and protects the dramatistical sense of self against the disruptive threat implicit in the immediacy and spontaneity even the most passionate ceremoniousness cannot fully eradicate from face-to-face encounters.

Morocco, Middle Eastern and dry rather than East Asian and wet, extrovert, fluid, activist, masculine, informal to a fault, a Wild West sort of place without the barrooms and the cattle drives, is another kettle of selves altogether.[5] My work there, which began in the midsixties, has been centered around a moderately large town or small city in the foothills of the Middle Atlas, about twenty miles south of Fez. It's an old place, probably founded in the tenth century, conceivably even earlier. It has the walls, the gates, the narrow minarets rising to prayer-call platforms of a classical Muslim town, and, from a distance anyway, it is a rather pretty place, an irregular oval of blinding white set in the deep-sea-green of an olive grove oasis, the mountains, bronze and stony here, slanting up immediately behind it. Close up, it is less prepossessing, though more exciting: a labyrinth of passages and alleyways, three-quarters of them blind, pressed in by wall-like buildings and curbside shops and filled with a simply astounding variety of very emphatic human beings. Arabs, Berbers, and Jews; tailors, herdsmen, and soldiers; people out of offices, people out of markets, people out of tribes; rich, superrich, poor, superpoor, locals, immigrants, mimic Frenchmen, unbending medievalists, and somewhere, according to the official government census for 1960, an unemployed Jewish airplane pilot—the town houses one of the finest collections of rugged individuals I, at least, have ever come up against. Next to Sefrou (the name of the place), Manhattan seems almost monotonous.

Yet no society consists of anonymous eccentrics bouncing off one another like billiard balls, and Moroccans, too, have symbolic means by which to sort people out from one another and form an idea of what it is to be a person. The main such means—not the only one, but I think the most important and the one I want to talk about particularly here—is a peculiar linguistic form called in Arabic the *nisba*. The word derives from the triliteral root *n-s-b*, for "ascription," "attribution," "imputation," "relationship," "affinity," "correlation," "connection," "kinship." *Nsīb* means "in-law"; *nsab* means "to attribute or impute to"; *munāsaba* means "a relation," "an analogy," "a correspondence"; *mansūb* means "belonging to," "pertaining to"; and so on to at least a dozen derivatives, from *nassāb* ("genealogist") to *nīsbīya* ("[physical] relativity").

Nisba itself, then, refers to a combination morphological, grammatical, and semantic process which consists in transforming a noun into what we call a relative adjective but what for Arabs is just another sort of noun by adding *ī* (f. *īya*): *Sefrū/Sefrou—Sefrūwī/*native son of Sefrou; *Sūs/*region of southwestern Morocco—*Sūsī/*man coming from that region: *Beni Yazğa/*a tribe near Sefrou—*Yazğī/*a member of that tribe; *Yahūd/*the Jews as a people, Jewry—*Yahūdī/*a Jew; 'Adlun/*surname of a prominent Sefrou family—*'Adlūnī/* a member of that family. Nor is the procedure confined to this more or less straightforward "ethnicizing" use, but is employed in a wide range of domains to attribute relational properties to persons. For example, occupation (*hrār/*silk—*hrārī/*silk merchant); religious sect (*Darqāwā/* a mystical brotherhood—*Darqāwī/*an adept of that brotherhood or spiritual status) (Ali/The Prophet's son-in-law—*'Alawī/*descendent of the Prophet's son-in-law, and thus of The Prophet).

Now, as once formed, nisbas tend to be incorporated into personal names—Umar Al-Buhadiwi/Umar of the Buhadu Tribe; Muhammed Al-Sussi/Muhammed from the Sus Region—this sort of adjectival attributive classification is quite publicly stamped onto an individual's identity. I was unable to find a single case where an individual was generally known, or known about, but his or her nisba was not. Indeed, Sefrouis are far more likely to be ignorant of how well-off a man is, how long he has been around, what his personal character is, or where exactly he lives, than they are of what his nisba is—Sussi or Sefroui, Bhuadiwi or Adluni, Harari or Darqawi. (Of women to whom he is not related that is very likely to be all that he knows—or, more exactly, is permitted to know.) The selves that bump and jostle each other in the alleys of Sefrou gain their definition from associative relations they are imputed to have with the society that surrounds them. They are contextualized persons.

But the situation is even more radical than this; nisbas render men relative to their contexts, but as contexts themselves are relative, so too are nisbas, and the whole thing rises, so to speak, to the second power: relativism squared. Thus, at one level, everyone in Sefrou has the same nisba, or at least the potential of it—namely, Sefroui. However, within Sefrou such a nisba, precisely because it does not discriminate, will never be heard as part of an individual designation. It is only outside of Sefrou that the relationship to that particular context becomes identifying. Inside it, he is an Adluni, Alawi, Meghrawi, Ngadi, or whatever. And similarly within these categories: There are, for example, twelve different nisbas (Shakibis, Zuinis, etc.) by means of which, among themselves, Sefrou Alawis distinguish one another.

The whole matter is far from regular: What level or sort of nisba is used and seems relevant and appropriate (to the users, that is) depends heavily on the situation. A man I knew who lived in Sefrou and worked in Fez but came from the Beni Yazgha tribe settled nearby—and from the Hima lineage of the Taghut subfraction of the Wulad Ben Ydir fraction within it—was known as a Sefroui to his work fellows in Fez, a Yazghi to all of us non-Yazghis in Sefrou, an Ydiri to other Beni Yazghas around, except for those who were themselves of the Wulad Ben Ydir fraction, who called him a Taghuti. As for the few other Taghutis, they called him a Himiwi. That's as far as things went here, but not as far as they can go, in either direction. Should, by chance, our friend journey to Egypt, he would become a Maghrebi, the nisba formed from the Arabic word for North Africa. The social contextualization of persons is pervasive and, in its curiously unmethodical way, systematic. Men do not float as bounded psychic entities, detached from their backgrounds and singularly named. As individualistic, even willful, as the Moroccans in fact are, their identity is an attribute they borrow from their setting.

Now as with the Javanese inside/outside, smooth/rough phenomenological sort of reality dividing, and the absolutizing Balinese title
systems, the nisba way of looking at persons—as though they were
outlines waiting to be filled in—is not an isolated custom but part of
a total pattern of social life. This pattern is, like the others, difficult
to characterize succinctly, but surely one of its outstanding features
is a promiscuous tumbling in public settings of varieties of men kept
carefully segregated in private ones—all-out cosmopolitanism in the
streets, strict communalism (of which the famous secluded woman is
only the most striking index) in the home. This is, indeed, the
so-called mosaic system of social organization so often held to be
characteristic of the Middle East generally: differently shaped and
colored chips jammed in irregularly together to generate an intricate
overall design within which their individual distinctiveness remains
nonetheless intact. Nothing if not diverse, Moroccan society does not
cope with its diversity by sealing it into castes, isolating it into
tribes, dividing it into ethnic groups, or covering it over with some
common-denominator concept of nationality, though, fitfully, all
have now and then been tried. It copes with it by distinguishing,
with elaborate precision, the contexts—marriage, worship, and to an
extent diet, law, and education—within which men are separated by
their dissimilitudes, and those—work, friendship, politics, trade—
where, however warily and however conditionally, they are connected by them.

To such a social pattern, a concept of selfhood which marks public
identity contextually and relativistically, but yet does so in terms—
tribal, territorial, linguistic, religious, familial—which grow out of
the more private and settled arenas of life and have a deep and
permanent resonance there, would seem particularly appropriate.
Indeed, the social pattern would seem virtually to create this concept
of selfhood, for it produces a situation where people interact with
one another in terms of categories whose meaning is almost purely
positional, location in the general mosaic, leaving the substantive
content of the categories, what they mean subjectively as experienced
forms of life, aside as something properly concealed in apartments,
temples, and tents. Nisba discriminations can be more specific or less,
indicate location within the mosaic roughly or finely, and they can
be adapted to almost any changes in circumstance. But they cannot
carry with them more than the most sketchy, outline implications
concerning what men so named as a rule are like. Calling a man a

Sefroui is like calling him a San Franciscan: It classifies him, but it doesn't type him; it places him without portraying him.

It is the nisba system's capacity to do this—to create a framework within which persons can be identified in terms of supposedly immanent characteristics (speech, blood, faith, provenance, and the rest)— and yet to minimize the impact of those characteristics in determining the practical relations among such persons in markets, shops, bureaus, fields, cafés, baths, and roadways that makes it so central to the Moroccan idea of the self. Nisba-type categorization leads, paradoxically, to a hyperindividualism in public relationships, because by providing only a vacant sketch, and that shifting, of who the actors are—Yazghis, Adlunis, Buhadiwis, or whatever—it leaves the rest, that is, almost everything, to be filled in by the process of interaction itself. What makes the mosaic work is the confidence that one can be as totally pragmatic, adaptive, opportunistic, and generally *ad hoc* in one's relations with others—a fox among foxes, a crocodile among crocodiles—as one wants without any risk of losing one's sense of who one is. Selfhood is never in danger because, outside the immediacies of procreation and prayer, only its coordinates are asserted.

Now, without trying to tie up the dozens of loose ends I have not only left dangling in these rather breathless accounts of the senses of self-hood of nearly ninety million people but have doubtless frazzled even more, let us return to the question of what all this can tell us, or could if it were done adequately, about "the native point of view" in Java, Bali, and Morocco. Are we, in describing symbol uses, describing perceptions, sentiments, outlooks, experiences? And in what sense? What do we claim when we claim that we understand the semiotic means by which, in this case, persons are defined to one another? That we know words or that we know minds?

In answering this question, it is necessary, I think, first to notice the characteristic intellectual movement, the inward conceptual rhythm, in each of these analyses, and indeed in all similar analyses, including those of Malinowski—namely, a continuous dialectical tacking between the most local of local detail and the most global of global structure in such a way as to bring them into simultaneous view. In seeking to uncover the Javanese, Balinese, or Moroccan sense of self, one oscillates restlessly between the sort of exotic minutiae (lexical antitheses, categorical schemes, morphophonemic transformations) that make even the best ethnographies a trial to read and the sort of sweeping characterizations ("quietism," "dramatism," "contextualism") that make all but the most pedestrian of them somewhat implausible. Hopping back and forth between the whole conceived through the parts that actualize it and the parts conceived through the whole that motivates them, we seek to turn them, by a sort of intellectual perpetual motion, into explications of one another.

All this is, of course, but the now familiar trajectory of what Dilthey called the hermeneutic circle, and my argument here is merely that it is as central to ethnographic interpretation, and thus to the penetration of other people's modes of thought, as it is to literary, historical, philological, psychoanalytic, biblical, or for that matter to the informal annotation of everyday experience we call common sense. In order to follow a baseball game one must understand what a bat, a hit, an inning, a left fielder, a squeeze play, a hanging curve, or a tightened infield are, and what the game in which these "things" are elements is all about. When an *explication de texte* critic like Leo Spitzer (1962) attempts to interpret Keats's "Ode on a Grecian Urn," he does so by repetitively asking himself the alternating question "What is the whole poem about?" and "What exactly has Keats seen (or chosen to show us) depicted on the urn he is describing?" emerging at the end of an advancing spiral of general observations and specific remarks with a reading of the poem as an assertion of the triumph of the aesthetic mode of perception over the historical. In the same way, when a meanings-and-symbols ethnographer like myself attempts to find out what some pack of natives conceive a person to be, he moves back and forth between asking himself "What is the general form of their life?" and "What exactly are the vehicles in which that form is embodied?" emerging in the end of a similar sort of spiral with the notion that they see the self as a composite, a persona, or a point in a pattern. You can no more know what *lek* is if you don't know what Balinese dramatism is than you can know what a catcher's mitt is if you don't know what baseball is. And you can no more know what mosaic social organization is if you don't know what a nisba is than you can know what Keats's Platonism is if you are unable to grasp, to use Spitzer's own formulation, the "intellectual thread of thought" captured in such fragment phrases as "Attic shape," "silent form," "bride of quietness," "cold pastoral," "silence and slow time," "peaceful citadel," or "ditties of no tone."

In short, accounts of other peoples' subjectivities can be built up without recourse to pretensions to more-than-normal capacities for ego effacement and fellow feeling. Normal capacities in these respects are, of course, essential, as is their cultivation, if we expect people to tolerate our intrusions into their life at all and accept us as persons worth talking to. I am certainly not arguing for insensitivity here, and hope I have not demonstrated it. But whatever accurate or half-accurate sense one gets of what one's informants are, as the phrase goes, really like does not come from the experience of that acceptance as such, which is part of one's own biography, not of theirs. It comes from the ability to construe their modes of expression, what I would call their symbol systems, that such an acceptance allows one to work toward developing. Understanding the form and pressure of, to use the dangerous word one more time, natives' inner lives is more like grasping a proverb, catching an illusion, seeing a joke—or, as I have suggested, reading a poem—than it is like achieving communion.

NOTES

1. For a full description of the town, see Geertz (1965).
2. For a fuller discussion of these concepts, see Geertz (1960).
3. For the town, see Geertz (1963): for the village, Geertz (1966).
4. For these see Geertz (1973). A few sentences in following paragraphs have been taken verbatim from that essay.
5. The Moroccan work is in process of completion. For a general characterization of the country, see Geertz (1968).

REFERENCES

Geertz, Clifford. 1960. *The Religion of Java*. Glencoe, Ill.: Free Press.
———. 1963. *Peddlers and Princes*. Chicago: University of Chicago Press.
———. 1965. *The Social History of an Indonesian Town*. Cambridge, Mass.: MIT Press.
———. 1966. Tihingan: A Balinese village. In Koentjarahingrat, ed., *Village Communities in Indonesia*. Ithaca, N.Y.: Cornell University Press.
———. 1968. *Islam Observed*. New Haven, Conn.: Yale University Press.
———. 1973. Person, time and conduct in Bali. In Clifford Geertz, *The Interpretation of Cultures*. New York: Basic Books.
Kohut, Heinz. 1971. *The Analysis of the Self*. New York: International Universities Press.
Malinowski, Bronislaw, 1967. *A Diary in the Strict Sense of the Term*. New York: Harcourt, Brace and World.
Spitzer, Leo. 1962. *Essays on English and American Literature*. Princeton, N.J.: Princeton University Press.
Watson, James. 1968. *The Double Helix*. New York: Atheneum.

3. Cultural Psychology: What Is It?

Richard Shweder

A discipline is emerging called cultural psychology. It is not general psychology. It is not cross-cultural psychology. It is not psychological anthropology. It is not ethnopsychology. It is cultural psychology. And its time may have arrived, once again. This essay is a preliminary attempt to say, taxonomically and narratively, what the discipline of cultural psychology was, is, and ought to be about.[1] Ultimately it is a story of cyclical return.

In the short run, however, the essay is a story of one of the pitfalls of the "cognitive revolution" of the 1960s, of its failure to develop an adequate theory of the "person," because of the prevailing Platonism implicit in its scientific agenda. It is also a scouting expedition across the boundaries of some very treacherous disciplinary territories in the search to recover an important interdisciplinary identity.

Cultural psychology is the study of the way cultural traditions and social practices regulate, express, and transform the human psyche, resulting less in psychic unity for humankind than in ethnic divergences in mind, self, and emotion. Cultural psychology is the study of the ways subject and object, self and other, psyche and culture, person and context, figure and ground, practitioner and practice, live together, require each other, and dynamically, dialectically, and jointly make each other up.

Cultural psychology is premised on human existential uncertainty (the search for meaning) and on an "intentional" conception of "constituted" worlds. The principle of existential uncertainty asserts that human beings, starting at birth (and perhaps earlier), are highly motivated to seize meanings and resources out of a sociocultural environment that has been arranged to provide them with meanings

Reprinted by permission of the authors and Cambridge University Press from *Cultural Psychology: Essays on Comparative Human Development* © 1990 Cambridge University Press.

and resources to seize and to use. The principle of intentional (or constituted) worlds asserts that subjects and objects, practitioners and practices, human beings, and sociocultural environments, interpenetrate each other's identity and cannot be analyzed into independent and dependent variables. Their identities are interdependent; neither side of the supposed contrast can be defined without borrowing from the specifications of the other.

The basic idea of cultural psychology is that, on the one hand, no sociocultural environment exists or has identity independently of the way human beings seize meanings and resources from it, while, on the other hand, every human being's subjectivity and mental life are altered through the process of seizing meanings and resources from some sociocultural environment and using them.

A sociocultural environment is an intentional world. It is an intentional world because its existence is real, factual, and forceful, but only so long as there exists a community of persons whose beliefs, desires, emotions, purposes, and other mental representations are directed at, and thereby influenced by, it.

Intentional worlds are human artifactual worlds, populated with products of our own design. An intentional world might contain such events as "stealing" or "taking communion," such processes as "harm," or "sin," such stations as "in-law" or "exorcist," such practices as "betrothal" or "divorce," such visible entities as "weeds" and invisible entities as "natural rights," and such crafted objects as a "Jersey cow," an "abacus," a "confessional booth," a "card catalogue," an "oversize tennis racquet," a "psychoanalytic couch," or a "living room."

Such intentional (made, bred, fashioned, fabricated, invented, designated, constituted) things exist only in intentional worlds. What makes their existence intentional is that such things would not exist independently of our involvements with and reactions to them; and they exercise their influence in our lives because of our conceptions of them (Schneider 1968, 1984; D'Andrade 1981, 1984, 1986). Intentional things are causally active, but only by virtue of our mental representations of them.

Intentional things have no "natural" reality or identity separate from human understandings and activities. Intentional worlds do not exist independently of the intentional states (beliefs, desires, emotions) directed at them and by them, by the persons who live in them.

Thus, for example, a weed is an intentional thing. It is an intrusive, interfering, or improper plant that you do not want growing in your garden. Consequently, a daisy, sunflower, a foxglove, or perhaps even a thorny rose that turns up in your vegetable patch might be plucked out as a weed, while one can find intentional worlds in which crabgrass, marijuana, or dandelions are not constituted as weeds at all. Instead they are cultivated as cash crops.

Because a weed is a weed is a weed, but only in some intentional world, there is no impersonal, neutral, "objective," "scientific," independent-of-human-response, botanical, genetic, or "natural kind" definition of plants that can specify *in the abstract* or *in general* which ones count as weeds. The botanical capacity to self-seed bestows on a plant the power to be a nuisance, if the plant is unwanted. Yet the same plant, if it is wanted, has the power to produce abundant harvests. And there are other routes by which a plant might make itself troublesome or become misplaced in your garden, ultimately to be weeded out.

It would seem to follow that in some fascinating and important sense, the weeds in our gardens achieve their reality because we are implicated in their existence, and we achieve our reality, at least in part, by letting them become implicated in ours. Our identities interpenetrate and take each other into account. Without us nature knows little of the existence of weeds. Without the existence of weeds and of all the aims, activities, and practices (Wittgenstein's "forms of life") presupposed by their existence and constitutive of it, there would be less to us worth knowing.

And because a weed is a weed is a weed, but only in some intentional world, what is truly true (beautiful, good) within one intentional world (for example, "That is a 'weed'; therefore, it ought to be plucked out of the ground and discarded") is not necessarily universally true (beautiful, good) in every intentional world; and what is not necessarily true (beautiful, good) in every intentional world may be truly true (beautiful, good) in this one or in that one.

According to the principle of intentional worlds there is no logical requirement that the identity of things remain, fixed and universal, across intentional worlds; while within any particular intentional world (for example, the twentieth-century intentional world of American baseball, or the sixteenth-century intentional world of English witchcraft) the identity of a thing (for example, a "foul ball" or a "witch") can be real and the question of its real identity (for example, was that a "foul ball"? or is she a "witch"?) can be a subject for rational and objective dispute.[2]

Cultural psychology is the study of intentional worlds. It is the study of personal functioning in particular intentional worlds. It is the study of the interpersonal maintenance of any intentional world. It is the investigation of those psycho-somatic-socio-cultural and, inevitably, divergent realities in which subject and object cannot possibly be separated and kept apart because they are so interdependent as to need each other to be (see Kleinman 1986; Shweder 1986).

Finally, cultural psychology is an interdisciplinary human science. It aims to develop several companion disciplines, especially an anthropology (reunited with linguistics) suitable for the analysis of sociocultural environments (meanings and resources; "forms of life") in all their intentionality and particularity, and a psychology (reunited with philosophy) suitable for the analysis of persons in all their intentionality and historicity.

ANSWERING A "WHAT IS IT?" QUESTION

It is a principle of cultural psychology—the principle of intentional worlds—that nothing real "just is," that instead realities are the product of the way things get re-presented, embedded, implemented, and reacted to in various taxonomic or narrative contexts or both. The reality of cultural psychology is no exception to the principle. As a constructed intellectual discipline cultural psychology has a taxonomic and narrative identity whose reality is not independent of our sharing with each other, debating, and acting upon our conception of it.

To say what something is, taxonomically, is to say what it is not, to say what it is a kind of, and to point to instances of it. It is to subsume it as a particular example of something more general and to generalize it, so as to turn something more particular than it into its example.

To say what something is, narratively, is to describe its origination ("once upon a time") and its density (its aim, purpose, or function) and to comprehend its current status, in the here and now, as part of a longer story of strivings, achievements, obstacles, growth, adaptations, failures, dormancy, or never-ending cyclical return.

Placed in its taxonomic context an ideal cultural psychology has qualities that distinguish it from general psychology, cross-cultural psychology, psychological anthropology, and ethnopsychology.

It Is Not General Psychology

First cultural psychology must be distinguished from general psychology.

"People are the same wherever you go" is a line from the song "Ebony and Ivory," by Paul McCartney and Stevie Wonder; that line describes pretty well a basic assumption of general psychology. The assumption is sometimes referred to as the principle of psychic unity of humankind.

General psychology assumes that its subject matter is a central (abstract and transcendent = deep or interior or hidden) processing mechanism inherent (fixed and universal) in human beings, which enables them to think (classify, infer, remember, imagine), experience (emote, feel, desire, need, self-reflect), act (strive, prefer, choose, evaluate), and learn. The aim of general psychology is to describe that central inherent processing mechanism of mental life. Since the central processing mechanism is presumed to be a transcendent, abstract, fixed, and universal property of the human psyche, general psychology has the look, taste, and smell of a Platonic undertaking. For it is that presupposed central and inherent processing mechanism that is the true object of fascination in general psychology and not all the concrete, apparent, variable, and particular stuff, substance, or content that is operated upon by the processor or may interfere with its operation.

It is a necessary step in the general psychology enterprise to distinguish intrinsic psychological structures and processes from extrinsic environmental conditions, to procedurally abstract and analytically withdraw the knower from what he or she knows, and to insist on a fundamental division between the processing mechanism of the person versus his or her personal or group history, context, stimulus and task environment, institutional setting, resources, beliefs, values, and knowledge.

Of course, people are not the same wherever you go. Not even Paul McCartney and Stevie Wonder are the same. And no general psychology is so unworldly as to overlook that fact.

General psychology may be Platonic but it is certainly not thoughtless. The principle of general psychology that "people are the same wherever you go" does not mean that people are the same in *every* respect. It means that transcendently, "deep down" or "inside," where the central processing mechanism lives, people are the same (or, alternatively, what gives people "psychic unity" is what makes them all the same "deep down" or "inside").

All the other stuff—stimuli, contexts, resources, values, meanings, knowledge, religion, rituals, language, technologies, institutions—is conceived to be external to or outside of the central processing mechanism. Observations on Rajput widows in India, motivated by special beliefs and desires, immolating themselves along with their deceased husband on his funeral pyre; or observations on Chinese abacus experts, assisted by special mental representational techniques, solving arithmetic problems "in their head" at a speed several orders of magnitude faster than the rest of humanity—all that may be rich material for humanistic inquiry, journalistic reporting, and literary representation, yet all of it must, given the Platonist impulse, be viewed, in and of itself, as incidental or secondary to the aim of general psychology.

The aim, as noted: to get behind superficial appearances, local manifestations, and external resources to isolate the intrinsic central processing mechanism of the mental life and describe the invariant laws of its operation.[3]

It is that Platonic impulse, one suspects, that was behind the memorable remark from an anthropologist who, upon hearing about Mike Cole and John Gay's research in Liberia (1972), argued to the effect that the thinking processes of West African tribesmen do not differ from our own; only their values, beliefs, and classifications differ, which is why the Kpelle perform so differently on psychological tests (see Cole and Gay 1972, p. 1066).

It is that same impulse, one suspects, that once led Melford Spiro (1955), with his interest in group differences in personality, to express the methodological concern that in demonstrating emotional and behavioral differences across different sociocultural contexts, anthropologists had not demonstrated the existence of *genuine* personality differences at all. They "have merely demonstrated that different stimuli evoke different responses" (p. 257).

The methodological "merely" in Spiro's analysis is revealing. For one might have argued, methodologically and non-Platonically, that the power of a particular stimulus to evoke a particularizing response is not independent of the way a person or people get particularly involved with it psychologically—classify it, reason about it, tell stories about it, appropriate it to their purposes—and that that is what *genuine* personality differences are about. In intentional worlds "stimuli" are not external to or independent of our understanding of them, and those understandings are a large part of what we mean by "personality" (see, for example, Mischel 1973).

In other words, one might have argued, from the point of view of intentional worlds, that the study of genuine psychological differences between ethnic groups should be conceived as the study of how different sociocultural environments become different *by virtue of* the ways they are differently constituted psychologically by different peoples so as to possess different response evocation potentials.

Platonism is an ancient and formidable school of interpretation. It is crucial to recognize that the long-lived and imaginative idea of an inherent (fixed, universal) and central (transcendent, abstract) processing mechanism, a psychic unity to humankind, will never be seriously threatened by the mere existence of performance differences between individuals or populations. Those performance differences can always be interpreted, and should be interpreted, as the consequence of incomparabilities, incommensurabilities, or just some plain differences in all the other stuff; which leaves permanently unsettled and eternally unsettlable the question whether there really is, deep down, an inherent and central processing mechanism hidden behind all the other stuff. Platonism and its alternatives will always be with us, offering different interpretations and competing visions of the nature of the human psyche.

It is equally crucial to recognize that general psychology with its Platonic imagery and premises is not the only imaginative and interpretative game in town for understanding the mental life. If one subscribes to an alternative, non-Platonic principle of intentional worlds, that nothing in particular exists independently of our involvement with it and interpretation of it, it is possible to conceive of the mental life as variable and plural and substantive and constructively stimulus bound.

And it is possible to characterize a large part of the mental life in terms of the particularizing ways peoples constitute and get involved with particulars, thereby giving to those constructed stimuli, task environments, and sociocultural contexts the powers they have to evoke the special responses they evoke.

Nevertheless the aim of general psychology is Platonic, and its

Platonic aim is to seek out a presumed central processing mechanism of human beings and to isolate it from all the other stuff.

Given that aim, it is not surprising that general psychology has constructed its own special intellectual standards for knowledge representation (its preferred ontology) and knowledge seeking (its preferred epistemology). Ontologically speaking, knowledge in general psychology is the attempt to imagine and characterize the form or shape of an inherent central processing mechanism for psychological functions (discrimination, categorization, memory, learning, motivation, inference, and so on). Epistemologically speaking, knowledge seeking in general psychology is the attempt to get a look at the central processing mechanism untainted by content and context, and so on.

The main force in general psychology is the idea of that central processing device. The processor, it is imagined, stands over and above, or transcends, all the stuff upon which it operates. It engages all the stuff of culture, context, task and stimulus material as its content.

Given that image, the central processor itself must be context and content independent. That means, in effect, that the processor must be describable in terms of properties that are either free of context/content (abstract, formal, structural properties) or general to all contexts/contents (invariant, universal properties).

Still speaking ontologically, it is that image of an inherent (fixed, universal) and central (abstract, transcendent) processing mechanism—a context/content-independent and omnipresent mental unity—that is the explanation for the great esteem conferred in general psychology upon accounts of the mental life in terms of universal mathematical functions and invariant formal limits or constraints (for example, exponential decay functions mapped in an abstract psychological space for representing the probability of generalization between pairs of stimulus events in any domain for any sensory modality for any species, as in Shepard 1987; or magical numbers, seven plus or minus two, to represent the maximum capacity of the central processing mechanism for distinguishing values, whatever the values, along any single dimension, whatever the dimension, in any single instant, wherever and whenever the instant, as in G. Miller 1956).

Great esteem is also conferred within general psychology upon certain ways of seeking knowledge. Knowledge seeking in general psychology is the attempt to gain direct access to the central processing mechanism without having to become quagmired in all the other stuff.

General psychologists *qua* general psychologists are typically wary of rain forests, swamps, and the complex textures and tones of everyday life, language, and institutional settings. They take comfort in a radically simplifying (some would call it a radically "surreal") article of faith, namely, that the central processor is most likely to reveal its pristine form when lured by meaning-free or unfamiliar or novel stimulus items into a context-free environment.[4]

Nonsense syllables, white coats, and darkened bare rooms may be misguided or monstrous anachronisms for serious researchers in general psychology, yet the experimental lab is still treated as a privileged space, where, quite fantastically and against much evidence, it is conveniently assumed that we can physically enter a transcendent realm where the effects of context, content, and meaning can be eliminated, standardized, or kept under control, and the central processor observed in the raw. The image of a central processing mechanism and the search for a window or a peephole through which to view it naked and pure may explain why in general psychology there has become entrenched the intuition that real scientists do experiments in a lab.

Unfortunately, even if the presumed inherent but hidden central processing mechanism does exist, the psychological laboratory is probably not the mythical enchanted doorway through which we can step straight away into a more fundamental reality. Indeed, one suspects that the sociocultural environment of lab life is not even plausibly equivalent to the physicist's vacuum or the physiologist's X-ray for directly accessing things that are basic, deep, or hidden from view. The ideas of a context-free environment, a meaning-free stimulus event, and a fixed meaning are probably best kept where they belong, along with placeless space, eventless time, and squared circles on that famous and fabulous list of impossible notions. For when it comes to the investigation and examination of psychological functioning, there probably is no way to get rid of all the other stuff, even in the lab.

Of course, nothing I have said argues against studying "stuff" in a lab. If the stuff brought into the lab (or simulated there) is interesting enough stuff to study, and if one can bring it into the lab (or reproduce it there) without spoiling it (those are big "ifs"), then one can certainly study it there, and there may even be very good reason to (see, for example, Milgram 1974). Whether there is a royal road running through the lab to the land of the central processing mechanism of the mental life is, however, quite another issue.

Roger Shepard's recent discussion (published, appropriately, in *Science* magazine) (1987) of "a universal law of generalization for psychological science" is a revealing illustration of Platonist presuppositions in general psychology and the way they guide a research enterprise and structure the interpretation of evidence by even the most brilliant practitioners.

Shepard begins and ends by holding out Newton's mathematical and universal law of gravitation as the standard by which to judge the success or failure of the discipline of psychology. Psychology, Shepard avers, should strive to be the science of the invariant mathematical forms underlying psychological functioning. Three hundred years after the publication of Newton's *Principia* Shepard thinks psychology can finally point to a success, a mathematical law of stimulus generalization which "is invariant across perceptual dimensions, modalities, individuals and species" and which shows that psychology "may not be inherently limited merely to the descriptive characterization of the behavior of particular terrestrial species" or the properties of particular stimulus domains (pp. 1317–18, 1323).

Shepard's "universal law" is basically an abstract spatial representation of an exponential decay function for stimulus generalization likelihoods between pairs of stimuli. The exponential decay function is detectable in several data sets from humans and pigeons, which record for selected domains (for example, consonant phonemes, triangles of different sizes and shapes) the probability that a response learned to any one stimulus within the domain will generalize to any other stimulus within the domain. Shepard believes that this exponential decay function is the central processing mechanism for stimulus generalization in its pristine form—abstract and transcendent (= deeply interior), fixed, and universal (p. 1318).

To have a glimpse at this abstract transcendent processing function Shepard is quite prepared—indeed, feels compelled—to exteriorize, treat as illusory, and withdraw his attention from several levels of reality that play a major part in human classificatory behavior.

First he must withdraw his attention from measurable similarities and differences in the stimulus materials themselves. For it has been shown—he views the relevant findings as "troublesome" and "discouraging"—that there exists no universal mathematical function for predicting the probability of a generalization response from measurable physical characteristics of pairs of stimuli; those mathematical functions seem to vary by stimulus domain (p. 1317). For example, the mathematical function for the color space may differ from the function for tonal scales, and these may differ by species or individuals; and within a particular stimulus domain, such as the color space, a response to a particular color chip may generalize to a distant hue at the opposite end of the spectrum. So if there is to be a universal law of generalization it is not going to be a law of the stimulus environment. It must be a pure psychological function, not a psychophysical function (p. 1318). It cannot tell us which stimulus items in any domain will be generalized to, only that the likelihood of generalization across pairs of stimulus items (whichever they should turn out to be) will decay exponentially. To reach the central processing mechanism of stimulus generalization Shepard must get beyond the stimulus environment.

Then he must also get beyond learning processes. For he does not expect his universal law of generalization to describe generalization behavior under multiple learning trials, because "differential reinforcement could shape the generalization function and contours around a particular stimulus into a wide variety of forms" (p. 1322).

Finally he must get beyond reconstructive memory processes. For it is known that the universal law is *not* descriptive of generalization behavior when learning trials are delayed. This Shepard interprets as a failure of the law because of interfering " 'noise' in the internal representation of the stimuli" (p. 1322).

At this point a reader of *Science* interested in similarity and difference judgments might be tempted to ask what we have learned about human classificatory behavior. Having withdrawn his attention from the stimulus environment and from processes of learning and memory, why does Shepard think he is looking at something fundamental such as a central processing mechanism of mind?

The answer is clear and Platonic. Late in his article Shepard points out that, strictly speaking, his universal law is descriptive of stimulus generalization behavior *only* when "generalization is tested immediately after a single learning trial with a novel stimulus" (p. 1322).

Here we come to the great and unbreachable divide between general psychology and cultural psychology. Moved by the Platonic impulse (and perhaps by the prestigious image of Newton's gravitational forces operating in a vacuum), Shepard seems to think that something truly fundamental about the mind—an inherent central processing mechanism—can be divined only if we can transcend the noise and clutter of the environment by bleaching it of familiar things and impoverishing it of feedback, and by isolating the mind from its own mental supports.

The alternative interpretation—that of cultural psychology—is that the mind left to its own devices is mindless. From that perspective, Shepard's proposed "universal law of generalization for psychological science" is little more than an extremely unqualified description of the special, restrictive (and, we might add, rather peculiar) effects on similarity and difference judgments of unfamiliar stuff (novel stimuli) examined in one-trial learning environments.

According to the principles of cultural psychology the effects of stuff will not go away, even in the lab, for there is no context-free environment. We are intentional beings who live in an intentional world of constituted and re-presented particulars—domain-specific, concrete, subject-dependent artifactual things. Absolute transcendence is a great and marvelous thing, but not if we want to keep the psyche in psychology.

The implication, of course, is that genuine success for psychological science will come when we stop trying to get beyond the "noise" and start trying to say interesting things about some of the more robust and patterned varieties of it.[5]

That is the challenge for cultural psychology. But I am getting ahead of my story. First we must consider cross-cultural psychology (not to be confused with cultural psychology), which can be very "noisy," perhaps too noisy.

It Is Not Cross-Cultural Psychology

One of the hazards of general psychology as a Platonic undertaking is the inherent difficulty of distinguishing statements about a presumed inherent central processing mechanism from statements about all the other stuff. It is that difficulty that has kept the discipline of cross-cultural psychology in business.

Cross-cultural psychology is a subdiscipline of general psychology that shares with it the Platonic aim of characterizing the inherent central processing mechanisms of the mental life. Practitioners of the subdiscipline carry the general psychologist's tests and research procedures abroad.

Occasionally cross-cultural psychological research replicates some regularity observed in Western-educated subjects (Ekman 1989). The main discovery of cross-cultural psychology, however, is that many descriptions of mental functioning emerging from laboratory research with Western-educated populations do not travel very well to subject populations in other cultures. Thus, although almost all adults in Geneva, Paris, London, and New York display so-called concrete operational thinking on Piaget's conservation of mass, number, and liquid quantity tasks, many adults in many Third World capitals do not (Cole and Scribner 1974; Hallpike 1979).

The definitive problematic of cross-cultural psychology is the struggle, fought in Platonic terms, over how to interpret population-based differences in performance on psychological tests and tasks. Within the framework of Platonic thinking there are only two possibilities. The first possibility is that the performance differences exist primarily because the central processing mechanism inherent in the mind has not yet become fully developed among certain peoples of the world (Hallpike 1979; see Shweder 1982 for a critique). The second possibility is that the performance differences exist primarily because the psychologist's tests and tasks baffle and bewilder certain peoples of the world and deny them a fair opportunity to put on display the extant central processing mechanisms of the mind (Cole and Scribner 1974).

Both interpretations presuppose the principle of psychic unity. According to the first interpretation, psychic unity is the anticipated result of central processor development, but the universal and uniform structures inherent in the mind will mature only under ideal environmental conditions. This leads some cross-cultural psychologists to become concerned with possible external stimulators of growth of the central processing mechanism — literacy, schooling, toys, Socratic dialogue, and so on. According to the second interpretation psychic unity is not just a potential inherent in the mind. Psychic unity has already been achieved. It is there, waiting to be revealed. This leads other cross-cultural psychologists to become concerned with "etics" and "emics" and with the incommensurateness or inappropriateness across cultures of test materials and research tasks; and it leads them to search for more "natural" or "realistic" settings, activities, and institutions in everyday life where central processor functioning goes on unimpeded by the artificial or unfamiliar conditions of psychological task environments.

Cross-cultural psychology has lived on the margins of general psychology as a frustrated gadfly, and it is not too hard to understand why. For one thing, cross-cultural psychology offers no substantial challenge to the core Platonic principle of general psychology (the principle of psychic unity). Moreover, if you are a general psychologist cum Platonist (and a principled one at that) there is no theoretical benefit in learning more and more about the quagmire of appearances — the retarding effects of environment on the development of the central processing mechanism, the "noise" introduced by translation or by differences in the understanding of the test situation or by cultural variations in the norms regulating the asking and answering of questions. Rather, if you are a general psychologist, you will want to transcend those appearances and reach for the imagined abstract forms and processes operating behind the extrinsic crutches and restraints and distortions of this or that performance environment.

Perhaps that is why, in general psychology, cross-cultural psychology has diminutive status, and why its research literature tends to be ignored. Not surprisingly, developmental psychology — the study of age-graded differences in performance on psychological tests and tasks — has suffered a similar fate, and for similar reasons.

It is doubtful that anyone is going to divest general psychology of its fascination with the imaginative idea of an inherent central processing mechanism. And certainly this disenchantment is not going to be produced by merely showing that the regularities observed in the Western lab do not travel well to other contexts, or generalize to subjects from other cultures (or age levels) or to stimulus materials from everyday life (see LeVine n.d.). The Platonist framework for interpretation is likely to remain enshrined in general psychology and definitive of its intellectual agenda. Like the scripture of some great religion of the world, it sets the terms for its own assessment, and it has enormous appeal, especially for those devoted to it to whom it appeals.

A problem with cross-cultural psychology is that it is not heretical enough, even as it raises its serious concerns. It would not be too great an exaggeration to assert that so-called method effects (major variations in research findings as a result of slight variations in research procedure, elicitation technique, wording of questions, description and representation of problems, expectation of examiners, subject population, and so on) are the main effects to emerge out of decades of laboratory research in general psychology. The method effect phenomenon (see Campbell and Fiske 1959; Cronbach 1975; Fiske 1986) is quite consistent with the discovery that generalizations from psychological research on one population do not travel very well across cultural, historical, and institutional boundaries.

Unfortunately, in the face of that evidence most cross-cultural psychologists have been unable to free themselves of the hegemony of Platonistic presuppositions in general psychology. They have continued to assume a psychic unity to humankind and to search for the presumed central processing mechanism in growth-stimulating environments (literate, Western industrialized urban centers) or through culture-fair or everyday stimulus materials.

Cultural psychology is far more heterodox vis-à-vis the canon of psychic unity. For cultural psychology is built out of a fundamental skepticism concerning all those fateful and presupposed distinctions: intrinsic properties of mind versus extrinsic properties of environments, form versus content, the "deep" versus the "superficial," the inherent central processing mechanism (psychic unity) versus all the other stuff.

Cultural psychology offers an alternative discipline of interpretation of the fundamentals of the mind. The mind, according to cultural psychology, is content driven, domain specific, and constructively stimulus bound; and it cannot be extricated from the historically variable and cross-culturally diverse intentional worlds in which it plays a co-constituting part. Consequently, cultural psychology interprets statements about regularities observed in a lab or observed anywhere else, on the street or in a classroom, in Chicago or in Khartoum, not as propositions about inherent properties of a central processing mechanism for human psychological functioning but rather as descriptions of local response patterns contingent on context, resources, instructional sets, authority relations, framing devices, and modes of construal.[6]

It is the aim of cultural psychology to understand the organization and evocative power of all that stuff, to study the major varieties of it, and to seek the mind where it is mindful, indissociably embedded in the meanings and resources that are both its product and its components.

It Is Not Psychological Anthropology

Whereas cross-cultural psychology is a subdiscipline of psychology, psychological anthropology is a province of anthropology; which means that psychological anthropology is less concerned with behavior in laboratories or on standardized tests or with novel stimulus materials and more concerned with other kinds of stuff. The stuff of anthropology includes rituals and folk tales, games and art forms, family life practices and religious doctrines, kinship categories and inherited systems of knowledge. Anthropologists in general like to muck around in the stuff of everyday life and language, and psychological anthropologists are no exception.

It should come as no surprise that psychological anthropology is psychological. Its proper and excellent aim is to understand the way ritual, language, belief, and other systems of meaning function or are put together in the lives and experiences and mental representations of persons.

In recent years many psychological anthropologists have turned to the study of cultural psychology and have revised some of the classic assumptions of the discipline. What I write here applies to psychological anthropology before its more recent reincarnation as cultural psychology.

Classically, psychological anthropology has tended to conceive of the psychological in the general psychology sense, which means that when psychological anthropologists have mucked around in classic form in their favorite anthropological stuff (for example, initiation ceremonies, kinship classifications, origin stories, conceptions of the gods) they have done so with the idea of psychic unity in mind.

Psychological anthropologists of the classic form have gone searching for the transcendental in the world of appearances. They have tried to explain the stuff of culture by reference to the workings of a central processing mechanism underlying psychological functioning. They have tried to use the stuff of culture to characterize or discover a central processing device. Whereas general psychologists search for the central processor by trying to eliminate the "interfering" effects, the "noise" and "distortion" produced by any meaningful stimulus environment, psychological anthropologists have looked for the central processor in the stimulus environment, on the assumption that there is something about long-surviving sociocultural environments that makes them relatively noiseless and distortion free.

The hallmarks of classical psychological anthropology are the sanguine premises that there exists an inherent central processing mechanism for individual psychological functioning and that its powers and influences extend into the sociocultural environment. Therefore, to remain viable any sociocultural environment must be adapted to or expressive of the central processing mechanism's abstract form and invariant constraints.

Psychological anthropology can be taxonomized along received fault lines (body versus mind; affect and motivation versus thought) into two subfields: "culture and personality" and "cognitive anthropology."

Before the recent reemergence of a cultural psychology the subfields of classical psychological anthropology were united with each other, as well as with general psychology and cross-cultural psychology, by the now familiar assumption of the psychic unity of humankind.

The central problematic for general psychology, as we have seen, is to characterize the central processing mechanism inherent in mental functioning by isolating it from the environment and from all the other extrinsic stuff upon which it operates. The central processor is abstract, transcendent (interior, deep, hidden, beyond, somewhere else), fixed, and universal. The central problematic for cross-cultural psychology is to explain the noteworthy performance differences on psychological tests between human populations without renouncing the idea of an inherent psychic unity. Performance differences exist, it is argued in cross-cultural psychology, either because the cultural environment has slowed the full maturation of the central processor in some populations, or because the performance environment of psychological testing has inhibited the central processing mechanism from going on display.

The central problematic of classical psychological anthropology, however, is more imperial—to find expanded into the territory of sociocultural environments the central authority of the psychological processing machine. The imperial premises: that the stuff of sociocultural environments gets shaped or molded by the dictates and constraints of the central processing mechanism into a limited number of possible designs for living; that the central processing mechanism gives structure to a sociocultural environment, either by mediating the relationships between its stuff or by impressing its abstract form upon it.

Thus, in classical psychological anthropology sibling terminological systems might be interpreted as revelatory of a universal and inherent disinclination of the central processing mechanism to engage in disjunctive reasoning (Nerlove and Romney 1967). Cultural origin stories might be interpreted as revelatory of an inherent preference of the human mind for dichotomous categories (Lévi-Strauss 1963). And almost everything, from myths to patterns of kinship avoidance and joking to adolescent circumcision ceremonies, might be interpreted as revelatory of that famous presumptive psychic universal known as the Oedipus complex (Stephens 1962; Spiro 1983).

Psychological anthropology, classically practiced, is a reductionist enterprise. Unlike Shepard (1987), who searches for the abstract central processing mechanism for stimulus generalization behavior by trying to reach beyond the "noisy," autonomous, and resistant physical constraints of any concrete stimulus domain, principled psychological anthropologists assume that the substantive domains of a sociocultural environment are a relatively pliant content operated upon by, or expressive of, deep and invariant psychological laws or processes of motivation, affect, and intellect.

Cultural psychology is not psychological anthropology.

Psychological anthropology assumes that there is an inherent central processing mechanism.

Psychological anthropology assumes that the central processing mechanism not only stands outside the sociocultural environment as an independent, fixed, and universal given of the human psyche; the central processor also reaches in to the sociocultural environment, leaving its indelible stamp.

Psychological anthropology assumes that the structure and functioning of the central processing mechanism is not fundamentally altered by the content, stuff, material, or sociocultural environment on which it operates.

Psychological anthropology assumes that whatever the differences are between populations in all the other stuff (in religious beliefs, in ceremonial life, in mythology, and so on), those differences can and should be interpreted as just so many products of the deep operations of a psychically unifying central processing device.

Cultural psychology is dubious of all those assumptions; indeed, cultural psychology is psychological anthropology without those assumptions. Many psychological anthropologists today are in fact doing cultural psychology.

It Is Not Ethnopsychology

If cultural psychology is psychological anthropology without the premise of psychic unity, then ethnopsychology is cultural psychology without a psyche at all.

Ethnopsychology is the study of ethnic variations in theories of the mental life. It is the investigation of indigenous representations of mind, self, body, and emotion. Such representations might include biochemical theories linking black bile or tired blood or sluggish neurotransmitters to depression. They might include interpersonal theories of guilt and possessive states conceiving of the mind as populated with the unplacated spirits or shadows of one's ancestors. They might include lay classifications of subjective states (thinking, feeling, willing). They might even include Platonistic theories positing a psychic unity to humankind.

There are many points of similarity between cultural psychology and ethnopsychology, especially a common concern for the psychological categories of indigenous folk. The major point of difference is that ethnopsychology is a subdiscipline of ethnosemantics or ethnoscience. It is primarily concerned with the investigation of mind, self, body, and emotion as topics (along with, for example, botany or kinship) in the ethnographic study of folk beliefs.

Ethnopsychology is thus less concerned with the actual psychological functioning and subjective life of individuals in the cultures whose doctrines about mind, representations of emotions, formal texts about the self, and gender ceremonies are under examination. Ethnopsychology is cultural psychology without the functioning psyche.

For some general anthropologists, especially those who are psychophobic, the focus in ethnopsychology on folk beliefs and doctrines sanitizes its subject matter (mind, self, emotion) and makes it more acceptable for investigation. The person is allowed in to general ethnography safely contained in the form of an idea or an ideology.

Cultural psychology is more person centered and a bit less cerebral; for it is the ethnopsychology of a functioning psyche, as it actually functions, malfunctions, and functions differently, in different parts of the world. Many ethnopsychologists today are in fact doing cultural psychology.

AN ORIGIN STORY FOR CULTURAL PSYCHOLOGY

Taxonomically, as presented so far, cultural psychology is the plural, variable, domain-specific, and constructively "stimulus-bound" psychology of intentional worlds. It is psychological anthropology without the premise of psychic unity. It is the ethnopsychology of the functioning psyche as it actually functions, malfunctions, and functions differently in the different parts of the world.

Cultural psychology tries to synthesize, or at least combine, some of the virtues of general psychology, cross-cultural psychology, psychological anthropology, and ethnopsychology while seeking to disencumber itself of their vices. It should come as no surprise that a vice in the intentional world of cultural psychology turns out to be a Platonist's virtue, and vice versa.

Viewed from the intentional world of cultural psychology, the virtue in general psychology is its concern with the organized nature of the mental life. Its vice is its conception of the mental as a central processing mechanism—abstract, interior (transcendent), universal, fixed, and content free.

The virtue in cross-cultural psychology is its concern with performance differences between ethnic groups. Its vice is its orthodox adherence to the premise of psychic unity.

The virtue in psychological anthropology is its focus on psychological functioning in sociocultural context. Its vice is its subordination of the sociocultural environment to the postulated directives of a central processing device.

The virtue in ethnopsychology is its attention to indigenous or local conceptions of mind, self, body, and person. Its vice is its psychophobia.

There is, of course, much more that needs to be said and worked out about each of those points. Yet there is also another way to "thicken" (Geertz 1973) our appreciation of cultural psychology, which is to treat it not only in a taxonomic context of definition but also in a narrative one.

There are many stories that can be told, at varying orders of magnitude of historical time depth, about ups and downs in the life of cultural psychology. The following tale is a short and very contemporary one, selected from the many that could be told. It is the story of a pitfall of the "cognitive revolution" of the 1960s.

It is probably no accident that the current renewal of interest in cultural psychology is occurring after thirty years of intellectual fragmentation in both general anthropology and general psychology. That fragmentation can be interpreted as a salutary reaction against the Platonism hidden in the agenda of the so-called cognitive revolution of the 1960s (see Shweder 1984, pp. 7–8).

The cognitive revolution got off to a promising start. Many (and I am one of them) welcomed it as the obvious and necessary corrective to the radical behaviorism that preceded it. The revolution seemed to address a rather serious shortcoming in psychology and anthropology, namely, the lack of a notion of mental representations and intentional states (mind, self, and emotion) in theories of the person and the lack of a notion of mental representations and intentional worlds (subject-dependent objects embedded in constituted "forms of life") in theories of the sociocultural environment.

Unfortunately, the cognitive revolution turned out to be far less than the rediscovery of intentionality and mental representations, and far more than just the displacement of behaviorism. Along with the cognitive revolution came an uninvited *Geist*—the spirit of Platonism—which aroused in psychology, and even in some corners of anthropology, that ancient fascination with formal, mathematical, structural models and an inherent central processing mechanism.

As the cognitive revolution spread through the disciplines, so did Platonism. Although some cognitivists (for example, Roy D'Andrade, George Lakoff, Catherine Lutz) sought to develop the idea of intentionality and mental representations by investigating the specifics of indigenous conceptions of physical, biological, social, and psychological things as those conceptions have a bearing on people's lives (Schank and Abelson 1977; Holland and Quinn 1986), for the most part content got set aside in favor of process, the particular in favor of the general, the substantive in favor of the abstract and the formal. The person and his or her intentional worlds, meanings, and sociocultural resources, like all concrete particulars, somehow got lost in the search for the inherent central processing mechanism of the mind.

Today, thirty years into the cognitive revolution, psychology and anthropology are more fragmented than before. In 1959 it was possible to point to experimental work on animal learning or psychophysics as "real" psychology or to ethnographic field work on social organization, ritual, and kinship as "real" anthropology, and to have some agreement about it. But no longer. When, in 1987, Shepard reported the discovery of a universal law of generalization and compared it favorably with Newton's laws of gravitation, relatively few hearts skipped a beat, and many heads shook in dismay.

To everyone's surprise—some scholars react with delight, others with despair—in 1989 it has become increasingly difficult for leading scholars to reach consensus about the specifications for an excellent psychological research project, or an excellent anthropological one. The criteria for identifying the intellectual core of each discipline have become freely contestable. With the breakup of general psychology and general anthropology, the usual definitional exercises have become strenuous and fruitless. Now when one asks scholars within the respective disciplines to name the prototypical psychologist or the prototypical anthropologist, opinions scatter, with every school of thought fancying a claim to a nonexistent center stage.

Even the recent Platonist nostalgia in some areas of psychology for something abstract and bleached and really real, and the diffuse distraction of attention to the latest intellectual fashion in reductionism and formalism, known as artificial intelligence, has proved to be short-lived. Already other reductive and nonreductive varieties of cognitive science (for example, neural nets and parallel distributed process models) are screaming like demons for their equal time (see the special winter 1988 issue of *Daedalus* on artificial intelligence).

For the sake of developing and liberating a cultural psychology all the commotion and fragmentation has probably been for the good. Too often in the past the wrong hegemonic general psychology has conspired with the wrong hegemonic general anthropology to divide and conquer the realm. General psychology played its part by reducing and diminishing our conception of the person or of psyche to a transcendent and abstract and fixed and universal central processing mechanism. General anthropology, fascinated by all the historical and ethnographic variations and diffusional clusterings of concrete sociocultural institutions, practices, and beliefs, played its part by taking no interest in the person or psyche at all. The two hegemonic intellectual regimes preserved and deserved each other's disciplinary parochialism. Both research traditions made it difficult even to conceive of a meaningful collaboration between anthropologists and psychologists. Culture and psyche were made to keep their distance by defining what they had in common, the person and his or her intentionality, out of both.

Under a Platonist influence most high-status research in the psychological sciences during the 1960s came to be guided by five maxims or research heuristics. Modest exposure to those heuristics produced an instant indifference to the kinds of phenomena (meaning systems, institutional settings, rituals, artifacts, modes of representation, interpersonal power orders, conflicts of motives, goal-setting) of interest to cultural psychology. Those five prescriptions/proscriptions for research went something like this (see Shweder 1984, pp. 3–4):

Heuristic 1. Search for a central processing system and represent it as an abstract structure or as a pure mathematical form; mere content can be ignored.

Heuristic 2. Language use is epiphenomenal to the true causes of behavior; what people actually say to each other can be ignored. (Note: Grammar and phonology remained legitimate topics for investigation, for they were abstract and structural and perhaps even deep; see heuristic 1).

Heuristic 3. What is really real (the central processing mechanism) is hidden and interior, and exists solely inside the skin of individuals; exterior and extrinsic macrounits such as the sociocultural environment can be ignored.

Heuristic 4. Search for universal (timeless and spaceless) laws of nature; the organization of knowledge in Newtonian physics is the ideal form for all true understanding.

Heuristic 5. Do not think about anything that cannot be controlled and measured in a lab, for the lab is the royal road to the central processing mechanism.

Those were, of course, not the only heuristics widely and wildly promoted by Platonism in psychology during the cognitive revolution. And I would not want to deny that there exists at least one research topic, and perhaps even two or three, for which those heuristics were, and continue to be, quite useful.

During the cognitive revolution, however, those heuristics became reigning ones. Their overextension and prevalence lent credence to epithets defining psychology as the "nonsocial social science." Ironically, right in the thick of the cognitive revolution, the psyche and the person were nowhere to be found in psychology; the discipline designed to study the soul, the subjectivity, the person, the rational strivings of human beings for dignity and self-esteem had turned away from those themes and returned to the mechanistic investigation of automatic processes and deep abstract mathematical forms.

Quite predictably, during the cognitive revolution the person did not succeed at gaining a foothold in anthropology. The local representatives of the revolution, the structural anthropologists (Claude Lévi-Strauss, Sir Edmund Leach), searched for the abstract universal principles of organization (for example, class inclusion, binary opposition) of the central processing mechanism. The ethnosemanticists and ethnoscientists studied classifications of flora and fauna; later they became ethnopsychologists and studied classifications of ideas about emotional states, without studying functioning (or malfunctioning) emotions at all. The culture and personality theorists—the ones who were really supposed to care about the lived experiences of persons in society—either felt disgruntled by the lack of concern for motivation and emotion or played possum; yet they could offer no compelling alternative to the Platonism of the times, since they fully endorsed Platonism's central theme—deep psychic unity. Most anthropologists, however, simply carried on as usual, just more so, documenting ethnographically and historically the diversity of exotic human institutions, practices, and beliefs and taking no interest in the person at all.

Indeed, as if to return (with a vengeance) the compliment of psychology's indifference to the "extrinsic" stuff of culture, society, meaning and context, the hegemonic prototype for research in general anthropology induced among (too) many a motivated state of psychophobia. The more psychology conceived of the person or the psyche as fixed, interior, abstract, universal, and lawful, the more anthropology chose to interpret sociocultural environments as exterior, historically variable, culture specific, and arbitrary and to renounce any interest in psyches or persons, or in the general causes of anything.

The person disappeared from ethnography. The question of why people believe the things they believe or practice what they practice was either begged, tabooed, or trivialized. The question was reduced to questions of conformity or indoctrination or some other variation on the metaphorical theme of robotics or social pressure (see Obeyesekere 1981).

For three decades a person-free psychology of an abstract invariant human nature conspired with a person-free anthropology of local systems of arbitrary, socially sanctioned coercive practices and meanings to keep a cultural psychology of intentional states and intentional worlds off the center stage.

Fortunately for cultural psychology there were many sideshows, and those sideshows drew an exciting and excited countercultural crowd. If you knew where to look or had the right friends, you could find cultural psychology there all along, doing its unorthodox things outside the main pavilions and the center rings.

Some of the sideshows were dazzling.[7] There was the tent of Lucien Lévy-Bruhl (1910), where exotic ethnic mentalities were put on display in defiance of psychic unity. There was the tent of Ludwig Wittgenstein (1968 [1953]), where Platonism was turned sour and transmuted into a "form of life." There was the tent of Aaron Cicourel (1974) and the "ethnomethodologists," where realities were dissolved, contextualized, infinitely regressed yet still apparently able to reconstruct themselves out of themselves. There was the tent of Roy D'Andrade (1981) and other psyche-sensitive ethnographers of mental representations, where anthropology resisted the Platonism implicit in the cognitivist agenda, on a platform of local or domain-specific territories of meaning.

There was the tent of Clifford Geertz (1973), where there was magic in words and reality in rhetoric, and where manner matters were discussed with such sophistication that the same became the different, the formal became contentful, and the fixed began to move.

There was the tent of Arthur Kleinman (1986) and the "medical anthropologists," where soma revealed psyche and the body exposed its intentionality, and where all could see that there was more to a "splitting head" or a "broken heart" or "frayed nerves" than the matter of disease. There was the tent of Edward Sapir and the "linguistic relativity" hypothesis, where the barker spoke the ultimate mystery (of cultural psychology): "the worlds in which different societies live are distinct worlds, not merely the same world with different labels attached" (Sapir 1929, p. 209).[8]

SO WHAT IS IT?

It still remains to be seen what this new age in anthropology and psychology of seeking to conflate ancient antimonies (form/content, process/content, person/environment, interior/exterior, subjective/objective, psyche/culture) will bring.

Cultural psychology, properly understood and practiced, is heretical. Its central theme is that you cannot take the stuff out of the psyche and you cannot take the psyche out of the stuff. Cultural psychology does not presume that the fundamentals of the mental life are by nature fixed, universal, abstract, and interior. It presumes instead intentionality—that the life of the psyche is the life of intentional persons, responding to, and directing their action at, their own mental objects or representations and undergoing transformation through participation in an evolving intentional world that is the product of the mental representations that make it up. Cultural psychology assumes that intentional persons change and are changed by the concrete particulars of their own mentally constituted forms of life.

Those who labor for a cultural psychology must address many difficult analytic, methodological, and substantive issues and overcome many old habits of thinking. Betwixt and between anthropology and psychology in the reoccupied zone of cultural psychology the main agenda item these days is how to minimize, fill in, or bridge the gap created by the Platonist separation of an inherent central processing mechanism from all the other extrinsic stuff. There have been many types of attempts.

First, among those who study formal norms for reasoning (for example, philosophers of science), the Platonist search has largely been abandoned for a universally binding inductive "logic" or "formal scientific method" that might operate on its own or mechanically to draw sound inferences, free of entrenched local systems for encoding and representing and "abducting" events (Putnam 1981).

There is also the emergence among psychologists of an interest in "expertise." Among those who study problem solving, the cognition of virtuosos has become a central topic of investigation, and exemplary cognition is increasingly talked about in non-Platonic ways, as knowledge based, constructively stimulus bound, and domain specific or modular. The current turn toward "content" is significant and widespread. Indeed what seems to differentiate an expert from a novice (chess player, abacus user, medical diagnostician, and so on) is not some greater amount of content-free pure logical or psychological power. What experts possess that neophytes lack is a greater quantity and quality of domain-specific knowledge of stimulus properties, as well as dedicated mastery of the specialized or parochial tools of a trade (see Stigler 1984; Stigler, Chalip, and Miller 1986; Stigler and Baranes 1988). It is thus no coincidence that those who study expertise do not equate the mental with the abstract. Instead they interpret the mind as it is embodied in concrete representations, in "mediating schemata," "scripts," and well-practiced "tools for thought."

The idea of tools for thought is an apposite (and self-referring) metaphor for thinking about thinking. It says that thinking is fundamentally interdependent with the traditional intellectual artifacts, representational schemes, and accumulated knowledge of some cultural or subcultural community. It says that as thinking becomes, as it must, metaphorically displaced from the operations of any fixed and central processing mechanism, the life of the mind becomes an extension or an analogue of, or an appendage to, cultural artifacts and their built-in design features.

Jerome Bruner (1966, p. 56), speaking in resistance to the Piagetian notion of a deeply interior and abstract central processing mechanism undergoing progressive development, used to talk of cultural "amplifiers" of thought. His idea was that what we think with (and about) can be decisive for how we think; and that those amplifiers or collective modes of representation, and the role they play in formal and informal education, are proper topics for the psychology of thought.

Of course it is hardly news to point out that one cannot be indifferent to content and still make sense of everyday cognitive, emotional, and conative functioning. From a Platonist point of view everyday cognitive, emotional, and conative functioning is "noise" laden and stimulus bound, which is, of course, precisely why the Platonists believe that the stimulus and task environment must be transcended if pure "psychological" laws are to be discovered (see the discussion of Shepard, above).

What is new (and renewing) in anthropology and psychology is a return of a this-worldly interest in the study of actual functioning and the reemergence of a genuine respect for all that psychocultural, psychophysical, psychosomatic "noise."

Indeed, in the land of cultural psychology all of the action is in the "noise." And the so-called noise is not really noise at all; it is the message.

Notably, in the language of cultural psychology there are no pure psychological laws, just as there are no unreconstructed or unmediated stimulus events. There are intentional persons reacting to, and directing their behavior with respect to, their own descriptions and mental representations of things; and there are intentional worlds, which are the realities we constitute, embody, materialize out of our descriptions and representations of things. Indeed, according to the premises of cultural psychology, even the transcendent realities portrayed by scientists are part of intentional worlds and cannot really take us beyond our mental representations of things.[9] In the world of cultural psychology transcendence and self-transformation are possible but only through a dialectical process of moving from one intentional world into the next, or by changing one intentional world into another.

Every person is stimulus bound, and every stimulus is person bound. That is what it means for culture and psyche to make each other up. That is why a cultural psychology signals an end for the purely psychological in psychology, an end to the quest for the inherent central processing mechanism of mental life, and an end to the Platonist legacy of the cognitive revolution. Cultural psychology is a return to the study of mental representations (emotions, desires, and beliefs and their intentional objects) without the presumption of fixity, necessity, universality, and abstract formalism. And while it may well be true that the constitutive and meaning-laden act of scientific comparison may require the postulation of a standard or universal Archimedean point of view from which to spot differences and talk sensibly about them (difference does presuppose likeness), it should be remembered that such posits of a universal grid for comparison are constructed and deconstructed by us, so as to make our intentional world intelligible. One of the hazards of comparison may be the ease with which the universals that we posit as part of our own intentional activities, in maintaining and enriching our own intentional world, get projected onto some imagined deep and essential structure of the mind.

As interpretative frameworks change, so do perceptions. Thus it is also a sign of the times that the "fundamental" Platonist distinction between "higher"-order and "lower"-order systems (between "deep" structure and "surface" structure) no longer seems quite so easy to sustain.

It is not just that there exist content-rich mediating schemata that bridge the gap between supposed abstract structures and the real-life instances to which they apply. (Platonists have no trouble with that.

They view the application of abstract principles to concrete cases as either beside the point or as rulelike and mechanical.) The more difficult problem for Platonism is that once the gap between abstraction and case has been filled in, a general and rulelike distinction between a central processor and its content is not so readily defined.

A deep suspicion has arisen in cultural psychology that so-called strict or intrinsic dispositions for behavior (Putnam 1987) and neat linear relationships between things are the exceptions in a world of local nonlinear dynamic processes with circular or dialectical feedback loops between so-called (and once Platonically conceived) levels of analysis, and between subject and object, text and context, manner and matter, content and form, fact and value, belief and directive force. There seems to be far less distinction in those famous old distinctions than there used to be.

At forums in anthropology and psychology these days someone is bound to say "not so fast" if you blithely presuppose a central processing mechanism consisting of abstract universal underlying structures or laws that impose form on any substance that happens to come along; or if you casually presume a self-evident division between an interior psyche and an exterior sociocultural environment.

Indeed, with the reemergence of a cultural psychology a new aim has been defined for anthropologists and psychologists: to find ways to talk about culture and psyche so that neither is by nature intrinsic or extrinsic to the other.

That aim for cultural psychology is to conceive imaginatively of subject-dependent objects (intentional worlds) and object-dependent subjects (intentional persons) interpenetrating each other's identities or setting the conditions for each other's existence and development, while jointly undergoing change through social interaction. That aim is to develop an interpretative framework in which nothing really real is by fundamental nature fixed, universal, transcendent (deep, interior), and abstract; and in which local things can be deeply embedded, but only for a while; and then, having developed the framework, the aim is to see how far it will go. (It may not go everywhere, but that remains to be seen.) That aim is to bridge the gap between psyche and culture by talking about them in new (or is it in very old?) ways. Here is one new (and very old) way of talking about psyche and culture.

Psyche refers to the intentional person. Culture refers to the intentional world. Intentional persons and intentional worlds are interdependent things that get dialectically constituted and reconstituted through the intentional activities and practices that are their products, yet make them up (see the discussion of weeds, above). Psyche animates her vessels and turns them into persons, leaving them mindful, soulful, willful, and full of goals and judgments.

The breath of psyche is the stuff of intentional states, of beliefs and desires, of fears and fancies, of values and visions about this or that. Psyche refers to patterns of motivated involvement, subjective states responsive to and directed at our mental representations of things. The breath of psyche is the stuff of intentional processes: goal setting, means-ends calculation, reality testing, embodied emotional reactiveness, self-monitoring and self-regulation in the pursuit of personal dignity, and so on. Psyche refers to "already-there" intentional states and processes distributed and organized within a person or across a people, and undergoing change, reorganization, and transformation across the life cycle.

In thinking about culture in new (or very old) ways it is crucial to remind ourselves again and again that a sociocultural environment is a world constituted, occupied, and used by intentional beings (see Sahlins 1976 on the symbolic or intentional uses of food and clothing). For psyche imparts to her vessels that charmed and spiritual quality of intentionality (and the teleology and pursuit after mental objects and final causes that accompanies it): psyche's vessels strive always to keep up appearances, to remain visibly dignified and exemplary of their imagined kind, and to express through their social actions a conception of themselves and of their place in the constituted scheme of things.

Culture is the constituted scheme of things for intending persons, or at least that part of the scheme that is inherited or received from the past. Culture refers to persons, society, and nature as lit up and made possible by some already there intentional world, an intentional world composed of conceptions, evaluations, judgments, goals, and other mental representations already embodied in socially inherited institutions, practices, artifacts, technologies, art forms, texts, and modes of discourse.

It is those inherited conceptions, evaluations, judgments, and goals embodied in cultural things (institutions, artifacts, discourse) about which the intending think, out of which the intending build their lives, and with respect to which the intending give substance to their minds, souls, wills, and directed actions.

Psyche and culture are thus seamlessly interconnected. A person's psychic organization is largely made possible by, and is largely expressive of, a conception of itself, society, and nature; while one of the very best ways to understand cultural conceptions of self, society, and nature is to examine the way those conceptions organize and function in the subjective life of intending individuals (see D'Andrade 1984).[10]

It cannot be repeated enough that a cultural psychology aims to develop a principle of intentionality—action responsive to and directed at mental objects or representations—by which culturally constituted realities (intentional worlds) and reality-constituting psyches (intentional persons) continually and continuously make each other up, perturbing and disturbing each other, interpenetrating each other's identity, reciprocally conditioning each other's existence.

The aim of cultural psychology is to examine the different kinds of things that continually happen in social interaction and in social practice as the intentionality of a person meets the intentionality of a world and as they jointly facilitate, express, repress, stabilize, transform, and defend each other through and throughout the life of a person or the life of a world. There are histories (narratives) that can be written about each, or both—the history of lives and the history of practices and institutions.

Most of the work of cultural psychology is still ahead of us. To achieve its aims cultural psychology must develop an analytic framework for characterizing the relationships between reality-constituting psyches (intentional persons) and culturally constituted realities (intentional worlds) that is at least as rich as the framework developed by behavioral geneticists for characterizing so-called genotype-environment correlations (Scarr and McCartney 1983; Plomin 1986, chapter 6).

As ethnographers, economists, and experimental social psychologists have known for a long time, intentional worlds can be strongly disposing and powerfully promoting of certain intentional states and not of others. They prompt and dispose in a variety of ways—by the way objects and events are represented and described by local guardians of the intentional world (parents, teachers, leaders, experimenters), by the way resources and opportunities are arranged and managed, by the way rituals and routines are performed, by the way sanctions are allocated (see B. Whiting and J. Whiting 1975; Ochs and Schieffelin 1984; Miller and Sperry 1987; Whiting and Edwards 1988).

Here is a simple yet vivid example of a strongly disposing (micro) intentional world: an alarm clock ringing loudly from where it was deliberately placed the night before, on the other side of the room, tends to stimulate an intense desire to turn it off, which gets us out of bed (see Schelling 1984, chapters 2 and 3).

For a moment let us borrow from the behavioral geneticists (Scarr and McCartney 1983; Plomin 1986) their analytic framework for talking about genotype-environment interactions, and let us transmute it a bit. Since genotype is irrelevant to the logic of the analytic framework, let us drop it and talk instead about person-environment interactions. Using the Scarr and McCartney framework one can imagine at least six types of relationships between reality-constituting psyches (intentional persons) and culturally constituted realities (intentional worlds). The relationship can be either *positive* (when the intentionality of the world amplifies or supports the intentionality of the person) or *negative* (when the intentionality of the world diminishes or contravenes the intentionality of the person). And the relationship can be either *active* (when the target person himself creates or selects his intentional world), *reactive* (when other persons create or select an intentional world for the target person in the light of that person's intentionality or the intentionality that others anticipate in the target person), or *passive* (when a target person ends up living in an intentional world created or selected by others for others or for themselves). That gives us six types: positive (active, reactive, passive) and negative (active, reactive, passive).[11]

The alarm clock arranged to go off just out of reach is a negative active relationship. The reality-constituting person constructs an intentional world using collective resources to contravene his or her own anticipated preference to stay in bed and go back to sleep. Whistling a happy or confident tune in the dark to alleviate one's fear is a second example of a negative active relationship. Hiding one's face from, or not looking at, or avoiding seductive or attractive things that might tempt you to transgression is a third example. Rituals of transcendence or detachment, such as Buddhist meditative exercises through which a reality-constituting person strives to make his or her own body ego alien by conceiving of it as a bag of feces (Obeyeskere 1985), provide a fourth example.

It is characteristic of the negative *active* relationship that the psyche creates or selects an intentional world to protect itself against itself, often by means of so-called culturally constituted defenses (the alarm clock, the happy tune, and so on).

The negative *reactive* relationship is one in which others intervene to protect you against your own intentionality. The institution of purdah for adolescent females is an example of a negative reactive relationship. Thus, in some intentional worlds girls are not permitted to do at age thirteen what they were permitted to do at age five; whatever desire they may have for autonomy in decision making becomes dangerous with the onset of puberty. Menstruating daughters are kept off the street in that intentional world, for the sake of what is good and true and beautiful in that intentional world. Purdah, too, is a culturally constituted defense, but a reactive one, choreographed by others for the self rather than written by the self for itself.[12]

In contrast, in the negative *passive* relationship the reality-constituting person experiences the meanings and resources of an intentional world created or selected by others for others or for themselves. For example, during the ten to twelve days of death pollution in orthodox Hindu communities in India, family members assist the soul of the deceased in detaching from its corpse and in proceeding on its eternal transmigratory journey. The pollution in the corpse is believed to burden the soul of the deceased and keep it bound to its material vessel. So to assist the deceased his or her living relatives absorb the pollution in the corpse into their own bodies. To facilitate the absorption of death pollution, family members are careful to avoid other kinds of pollutants ("hot" foods, "hot" activities such as sex, and "hot" emotions). They fast. They are abstinent. They stay at home. The mourning period is over when the soul of the deceased has successfully detached itself from its dead body. Family members then cleanse their own bodies of the death pollution they have absorbed. They do so by shaving their hair, cutting their nails, and taking a special bath. They put on new clothes and return to life in the outside world.

It seems likely that for some members of the family, at some point in the life cycle, the experience of the mourning ritual is a negative passive one. Children or other family members may want to go out, play, or eat "hot" foods. Adults may want to have sex. There probably does occur some transgression of the requirements of the intentional world of the funeral practice. Yet because children participate passively and vicariously in the practice and experience its meanings, resources, and sanctions, the intentional world of mourning customs (including the end at which it is aimed—salvation of an eternal transmigrating soul through the help of loyal, devout, and self-sacrificing relatives) comes to be upheld and pursued by precisely those reality-constituting persons whose intentions came to be formed through participation in those very practices.

I will not illustrate or examine all the positive types of relationships between reality-constituting psyches and culturally constituted realities, although instances are not difficult to bring to mind—for example, to mention a positive active type, the gregarious youth who creates dance parties at school.

The main reason for reviewing here a logical scheme for types of person-environment interactions is to suggest that it might be fruitful in cultural psychology to conceive of socialization processes in terms of *at least* those six forms of relationship between intentional persons and intentional worlds. There is a reciprocal and dynamic relationship between intentional persons and intentional worlds, each setting conditions for the other's existence and development. All the relationships are self-transforming and dialectical. At stake in these relationships are both the cultivation of a human psyche suited to the historical context of some intentional world, and the cultivation of an intentional world, capable of cultivating and supporting the human psyche in one of the various forms of its nobility.

The three negative relationships describe "defensive" engagements. Making use of the resources from an already-there intentional world, an already-there personal intention becomes attenuated, modified, or hidden, either through direct self-regulation (active) or through direct or vicarious interpersonal regulation (reactive, passive). The three positive relationships describe "expressive" engagements. Making use of the resources from an already-there intentional world, an already-there personal intention is amplified, reproduced, and displayed, either through direct self-promotion (active) or through direct or vicarious interpersonal subsidization (reactive, passive).

In some orthodox Brahman communities in Orissa, India, for example, there is a positive reactive ritual that takes place in the context of joint family living arrangements the day after a marriage is consummated. Everyone in the extended household knows that the bride has lost her virginity the night before. (Indeed, some of them may have been listening and giggling at her door). She knows that everyone knows it. Everyone knows that she knows that everyone knows it. She feels embarrassed to show her face the next morning; she wants to hide. So she is made to hide. They feel embarrassed to face her. So they are not allowed to face her. The day-after-the-fateful-night-before is explicitly labeled the "day of embarrassment." That day the bride is expected to stay secluded in her room all day or to go away to visit a friend. By means of a positive reactive relationship between a reality-constituting person (yesterday's virgin) and a culturally-constituted world (the "day of embarrassment") the young Hindu bride is protected from humiliation and permitted safely to dramatize her state of mind and realize her intention to hide.

It is tempting but not feasible in this preliminary scouting expedition to view or review the key analytic and empirical contributions of the various intellectual communities that have so much to contribute to a cultural psychology. The territory is too vast.[13] The many insights and refigurations that emerge from those various intellectual communities are stimulating (perhaps even breathtaking) in their own terms. Yet they are also suggestive of a possible unification of intellectual agendas under the banner of a cultural psychology. Even a very brief consideration of the several varieties (positive versus negative; active, reactive, passive) of continual engagement between intentional persons and intentional worlds should make it apparent that neither psyche nor culture can long be denied by anyone genuinely curious about the functioning and development of either.

The challenge before us is to define more precisely this promising new discipline. How far can we go with an interpretative framework within which, and in whose terms, nothing is by fundamental or intrinsic nature fixed, universal, transcendent, and abstract? What kind of knowledge can we expect from a cultural psychology?

Those are questions for other occasions. They call for deep rethinking and broad discussion across intellectual communities sympathetic to the general framework and aims of a cultural psychology.

It does seem likely, however, that our received images of "real" or honorific science will have to be revised.

A cultural psychology studies precisely those causal processes that go on because of our understanding of and involvement with them. It would seem to follow that the truths to be formulated in cultural psychology are typically going to be restricted in scope, because the causal processes they describe are likely to be embedded or localized in particular intentional worlds. What we are likely to discover are patches of institutionalized regularities, stabilized within culture areas during certain historical epochs, perhaps even for centuries, yet subject to change (see Gergen 1973).

It would also seem to follow that if realities are not independent of our representations of them and involvement with them, then the raising of questions, even "scientific" questions, is no innocent act. Asking people what they want to do is a way of promoting autonomous decision making. Asking about the potential uses of something is a way of constituting it as instrumental. The world of cultural psychology is a world of dialectical feedback loops and dynamic nonlinear relationships between things undergoing transformation. Given such a world, many of our received expectations for, and models of, successful research are going to make less sense. For example, we may not be able to fix or standardize the definitions of concepts. We can do that in a unitary, homogeneous, linear world where things stay put, permitting their presumed essences to be interdefined, but not in the world of cultural psychology.

And we should not expect that the same truths will reappear in every intentional world, or that something more wonderful and fundamental and revelatory has been discovered when and if they do, as sometimes they will.

Most important, we should not expect reality to be independent of our participation in it. The likelihood that an event will occur in an intentional world is not independent of the confidence we have that it will occur.

Most normative models for decision making have not yet taken account of that simple truth. There are good metaphors and bad metaphors for the actions of intentional persons in intentional worlds. Most normative models for rational choice are metaphorical variations on the properties of roulette wheels, random-number tables, dice games, and coin flips. Those rather special, peculiar (and ethically controversial) cultural artifacts and technologies have been deliberately designed by us so that their behavior is independent of our attitudes toward them; as a result, they are among the most inappropriate metaphors for intentional action in general. The intentional world is not typically the world of a coin flip. It is more often a world in which our confidence in an event influences the likelihood of its occurrence and in which we not only monitor but also regulate and control deviations from expectation. It is a world in which if we did not have the confidence we have in things occurring, then they might not occur, just because of us! Patterns of decision making that are irrational in Las Vegas may well be rational and constructive in most other intentional worlds.

THINKING THROUGH OTHERS: CULTURAL PSYCHOLOGY AS AN INTERPRETATIVE DISCIPLINE

Among the most celebrated collections of anthropological essays on intentional worlds is Clifford Geertz's *Interpretation of Cultures* (1973). Cultural psychology is an interpretative enterprise in Geertz's senses. Yet just what is it one actually does in the interpretation of (intentional) worlds and (intentional) lives?

The answer to that question has much to do with the process of "thinking through others" (thinking through other cultures, thinking through other lives, thinking through India, thinking through Plato) in at least the four senses discussed in the Introduction: (1) thinking by means of the other; (2) getting the other straight; (3) deconstructing and going beyond the other; and (4) witnessing in the context of engagement with the other.

First, there is "thinking through others" in the sense of using the intentionality and self-consciousness of another culture or person — his or her or its articulated conception of things—as a means to heighten awareness of our less conscious selves.

Orthodox Hindus in India, to select a not so random example, have, as intentional beings, for thousands of years reflected on the relationship between moral action and outcome, on hierarchy, on patronage and paternalism, on sanctity and pollution. The more we try to conceive of an intentional world in their intentional terms, the more their doctrines and rituals and art forms and other modes of representation come to seem like sophisticated expressions of repressed, dormant, and potentially creative and transformative aspects of our own psyche pushed off by our intentional world to some mental fringe. We do not know how to talk about karma or how to comprehend an occasional dread that if we do something bad something bad may happen to us; yet we experience it. We do not know how to justify status obligations and hierarchical relationships, but we live them. We do not quite know how to acknowledge the presence of personal sanctity, yet we feel it.

"Thinking through others" in the first sense is to recognize the other as a specialist or expert on some aspect of human experience, whose reflective consciousness and system of representations and discourse can be used to reveal hidden dimensions of our selves. Some cultures of the world are virtuosos of grief and mourning, others of gender identity, and still others, of intimacy, eroticism, ego striving, and so on.

Ruth Benedict, an ancestral spirit of cultural psychology, with her conception of cultures as selections from the arc of human possibilities, understood well the first sense of "thinking through others."

Then there is "thinking through others" in the sense of getting the other straight, of providing a systematic account of the internal logic of the intentional world constructed by the other. The aim is a rational reconstruction of indigenous belief, desire, and practice. The assumption is that the organization of the psyche is based on a reality principle, whereby culturally constituted realities and reality-constituting psyches are mutually adjusted to one another until some attractive equilibrium is reached—a graceful or proportionate fit between the world as the other has made it out/up and the other's reactions to the world made out and up.

Freud is one of the great champions of the reality principle and the second sense of "thinking through others." In his inspiring defense of nonbiomedical healing practices, "The Question of Lay Analysis" (1962 [1929]), he notes that "if a patient of ours is suffering from a sense of guilt, as though he had committed a serious crime, we do not recommend him to disregard his qualms of conscience and do not emphasize his undoubted innocence; he himself has often tried to do so without success. What we do is to remind him that such a strong and persistent feeling must after all be based on something real, which it may perhaps be possible to discover" (p. 190).

The process of "thinking through others" in its second sense is a process of representing (and defending) the other's evaluations of and involvements with the world—such as a taboo against eating meat or a prohibition against remarriage—by tracing those evaluations and modes of involvement to some plausible alternative intentional world and conception of reality, which, in the ideal case, no rational person, not even Freud, can defeat.

Then there is "thinking through others" in the sense favored by Jacques Derrida and other postmodern deconstructionists. It is the sense of thinking one's way out of or beyond the other. It is the sense of passing through the other or intellectually transforming him or her or it into something else—perhaps its negation—by revealing what the life and intentional world of the other has dogmatically hidden away, namely, its own incompleteness.

It is a third sense, for it properly comes later, after we have already appreciated what the intentional world of the other powerfully reveals and illuminates, from its special point of view. "Thinking through others" is, in its totality, an act of criticism and liberation, as well as of discovery.

And then there is "thinking through others" in the sense of a situated perspectival observer, thinking *while there* in an alien land or with an alien other, trying to make sense of context-specific experiences. It is the sense of Geertz's "I-witnessing" author trying to turn a personal field experience into a "they-picturing" account of the other (Geertz 1988).

In this fourth sense of "thinking through others," the process of representing the other goes hand in hand with a process of portraying one's own self as part of the process of representing the other, thereby encouraging an open-ended self-reflexive dialogic turn of mind.

It seems to me that a genuine cultural psychology, the one we can feel proud of, is the cultural psychology that strives to think through others in all four senses, and more.

Finally, we come to the ultimate question: How far can we go with a cultural psychology? Can it take us all the way?

It is always a good idea to leave ultimate questions for some other occasion. Still, I will express my doubts. I think cultural psychology will take us very far, but not all the way.

I do not think it will take us as far as Nirvana, if there is such a place or state of mindlessness. I think there is such a place. And I think that if we get there we won't have the slightest need for a content- and context-dependent this-worldly cultural psychology. I certainly hope we won't.

Yet who knows; perhaps even Nirvana is really a special state of mind in a special intentional world, which it is the proper business of a cultural psychology to understand.

NOTES

1. I am uncertain of the origin of the expression *cultural psychology.* It appears and reappears with varying meanings in the writings of nineteenth- and twentieth-

century social and psychological theorists, including those of Michael Cole (1989), Alan Howard (1985), and James Peacock (1984).

In defining cultural psychology I shall assume, as did the ancients, that a proper appreciation of a thing integrates its taxonomic and narrative contexts (its being with its becoming). That assumption is characteristic of teleological approaches to definition and understanding, and it is associated with the following conception of reality or nature: what is real or in the nature of things is what a thing of a certain kind strives to become so as to realize its identity and become excellent, developed, and exemplary of its kind.

The teleological approach to definition may sound old-fashioned or premodern, which is not surprising, since teleology, and all that it implied about nature, society, and persons, was one of the casualties of modern thinking in the West. It was replaced in the Enlightenment by a positive science conception: the natural order as unanimated, deterministic, and indifferent to human affairs and to all other mental events. Thus, in modern consciousness, the idea of what was proper or excellent or elevated or cultivated became detached from the idea of what was natural. One consequence of that separation was that all the traditional and central normative ideals for human functioning and development—ideas of the good, the right, the beautiful, etc.—were deprived of natural or objective force, while the idea of a natural norm was reduced to a nonevaluative statistical notion, the so-called value-neutral positive science idea of regularly occurring or repetitive events. Natural science and normative ethics, is and ought, got in the habit of moving through modern times in entirely divorced ways, and social science suffered for it.

Yet teleology still has some things to recommend it, not the least of which is the opportunity it affords to move seamlessly back and forth between descriptions of what something is and descriptions of what something ought to be; to see an as-yet-unrealized regulative ideal immanent and active in the development of instances of its kind; and to promote what is natural in the light of what is.

Hence this essay, which is itself part of a teleological process, lending assistance, quite purposefully, to the discipline of cultural psychology in an attempt to help it discover, and hence realize, its nature.

2. At any historical moment, of course, what has been constituted as true, beautiful, or good within some one, then existing, intentional world might also happen, as a matter of contingency, to have been constituted that way within each of all the then-existing intentional worlds. In other words, there may well be some intentional truths that are true universally.

However, since an intentional truth becomes true only by virtue of its embeddedness in some particular intentional world, it follows that there is no sense of necessity associated with a universal intentional truth.

A universal intentional truth is universally true because it has been constituted as true within each of the then-existing particular intentional worlds, which is no guarantee that it must of necessity be true within every existing intentional world, past or future, or within every imaginable one.

3. For those general psychologists who are, by metaphysical choice or second nature, materialists, reductionists, and incorrigible utopians, there is also an additional aim, someday to locate Plato's transcendent realm of fixed ideas in some physical realization in the brain or the nervous system, or on chromosome 11.

It may well have been René Descartes, a latter-day Platonist, who interiorized the ancient search for the transcendent, and first tried to postulate a physical realization—localized in the pineal gland—for an abstracted central processor of the mind, the "I".

4. Descartes, of course, tried an alternative Platonist route to the central processor, the route of rationalism (deductive reasoning from undeniable premises, for example, "I think, therefore I am") rather than the route of empiricism (inductive reasoning from sense data or observations). Adhering to his principle of radical doubt, Descartes treated as deceptive or illusory or exterior all sensations and stimulus materials and tried to reconstruct the logically necessary features of the central processing mechanism through deductive reasoning alone.

Both rationalism and empiricism are the offspring of the Platonic imagination, which fancies routes of direct access to a fixed and uniform reality. General psychology is the empiricist child of Platonism, while its rationalist sibling lives on in the philosophy of mind and language, in normative ethics, and in the field of artificial intelligence.

If there is to be a cultural psychology it will have to synthesize rationalism and empiricism into something else or provide an alternative to both. C. S. Peirce's (1940) notion of abductive reasoning as the indispensable assistant to the "unaided rationality" of logic and sense data is a promising starting point. One version of Peirce's notion, if I understand it, is this: transcendent realities can be imagined but never seen or deduced, for they are constructions of our own making, which sometimes succeed in binding us to the underlying reality they imagine by giving us an intellectual tool—a metaphor, a premise, an analogy, a category—with which to live, to arrange our experience, and to interpret our experiences so arranged. In other words, the abductive faculty is the faculty of imagination, which comes to the rescue of sensation and logic by providing them with the intellectual means to see through experience and leap beyond empty syllogisms and tautologies to some creative representation of an underlying reality that might be grasped and reacted to, even if that imagined reality cannot be found, proved, or disproved by inductive or deductive rule-following.

The fact that you cannot get beyond appearances to reality with the methods of science or the rules of logic (or, for that matter, through meditative mysticism) does not mean that you should stop trying to imagine the really real, or that the imagination *must* be disrespectful of sense data or deductive logic, or that "anything goes."

Of course there are times and places when it makes good sense to be disrespectful of sense data and of logical deductions, especially when they lead you places where there is good reason not to go.

5. For a discussion of how the field of geophysics had to get free of the standards of Newtonian mechanics in order to gain some self-respect and make progress see Richter (1986) on the topic of plate tectonics. For a discussion of the importance in the social sciences of not waiting around for our Newton see Converse (1986).

6. From the interpretative framework of cultural psychology researchers in general psychology might be construed as participant observers in the special sociocultural and procedural world of laboratory life, where they talk to and observe the reactions of informants—most often college-age students—from some specific cultural and historical tradition, typically their own.

7. Of course I am being very selective and contemporary here. Cultural psychology has many ancestral spirits, including Abelard, Herder, Hegel, Heidegger, and Brentano. A short list of important contemporary texts critiquing one aspect or more of the Platonist conception of a central processing mechanism includes Lévy-Bruhl (1910), Wittgenstein (1968 [1953]), Kuhn (1962), Garfinkle (1967), Toulmin (1972), Geertz (1973), Goodman (1968), MacIntyre (1981), Fish (1980), Lakoff (1987), and Putnam (1987).

8. One of the great ancestral spirits of cultural psychology, whose work deserves to

be honored and revived, is Edward Sapir, who tried to define an interdisciplinary agenda for anthropology, psychology, and linguistics.

Hardly anyone in the social sciences (historians are an exception) reads things more than ten years old these days, let alone a poetic, Aristotelian essay from 1924 written by an anthropological linguist and published in a sociology journal. The anthropological linguist in question is Edward Sapir, the less honored, though more formidable, intellectual figure behind the so-called Sapir-Whorf "linguistic relativity" hypothesis. Yet in 1924, just before joining the University of Chicago, Edward Sapir published an article in the *American Journal of Sociology* entitled "Culture: Genuine and Spurious," in which he conceived of the way traditions and individuals, cultures and psyches, might conspire to make each other up and excellent. Sections of the essay could well have been subtitled "A Manifesto for a Cultural Psychology." A genuine culture, Sapir argued, is not an externally imposed set of rules or forms or a "passively accepted heritage from the past," but rather a "way of life" (p. 321), gracefully proportioned to the beliefs, desires, and interests of its bearers, with which it is indissociably linked. A genuine culture consists of institutions, resources, and ideals that assist individuals in cultivating precisely those reactions, skills, and mental states that have "the sanction of a class and of a tradition of long standing" (p. 309). In a genuine culture there are processes at work aimed at the achievement of a harmonious, interdependent balance between psyche and culture. Traditional ideals for a good and proper life are made salient through diverse forms of representation—art, artifacts, ritual, language, folklore, mundane practice—and individuals deliberately and creatively come to terms with and use those ideals to refashion their selves, thereby revivifying and confirming the tradition. In a genuine culture, processes of cultural maintenance and personal maintenance serve each other. The tradition gives to the self "the where-withal to develop its powers" and "a sense of inner satisfaction, a feeling of spiritual mastery" (p. 323).

Sapir was concerned that the alienation of culture from psyche had, in modern times, become real and pervasive. He held out as a mission for anthropology the examination of the processes by which genuine or unalienated cultures integrate cultural and personal symbols. Cultural psychology promises to carry on where Sapir left off.

9. Relevant here is the work of the so-called Edinburgh school (Woolgar, Pinch, Collins, Barnes, and others) in the sociology of science, as well as the work of Donald McCloskey and Allan Megill on the rhetorics of science. See, for example, Barnes and Shapin (1979), Latour and Woolgar (1981), McCloskey (1985), and Collins (1981).

10. It has become increasingly recognized among anthropologists that speculative ontologies and other cultural "texts" can be misleading guides to operative beliefs, which is one reason that the idea of "metaphors we live by" (Lakoff and Johnson 1980) in our personal and interpersonal functioning has taken hold.

11. My use of the Scarr and McCartney framework to talk about person-environment interactions should not imply that those authors are engaged in an exercise in cultural psychology, or that my appropriation and extension of their logical scheme is a comment, one way or the other, upon behavioral genetics. The framework of positive (active, reactive, passive) versus negative (active, reactive, passive) relationships is totally detachable from any concern with the genetic determination of behavior.

I might add that the behavioral geneticists seem all too fascinated with, indeed overjoyed by, the idea of positive person-environment relationships and far too little concerned with the ubiquity of negative ones. At its core the field of behavioral genetics displays strong Platonist tendencies and is relatively innocent of the idea of intentional persons and intentional worlds. Robert Plomin (1986) and Daniel G. Freedman (1974) are exceptions.

12. Of course, in some other intentional worlds parents react to the onset of maidenhood by encouraging their teenage daughters to date, go to parties, and get out of the house.

If I had to divide all the cultures of the world into two types, putting aside everything else, I would partition them into those in which boys and girls are pushed together at puberty and those in which they are kept apart—kissing-game cultures versus purdah cultures. I suspect that many other aspects of value and practice are associated with that division.

13. Such a review would include philosophical work on intentionality and partial translatability (Brentano, Derrida, Gadamer, Goodman, Heidegger, MacIntyre, Manicus, Rorty); linguistic work on discourse processes, performative utterances, and the pragmatics of language use (Austin, Dunn, Grice, Haviland, Heath, Labov, Peggy Miller, Much, Fred Myers, Ochs, Schieffelin, Searle, Silverstein, Slobin); cognitive work on framing effects, construal, and the representation of knowledge (D'Andrade, Holland, Ed Hutchins, Kahneman, Kempton, Nisbett, Charles Nuckolls, Quinn, Ross, Schank, Siegler, Trabasso, Tversky); literary work on rhetoric inside and outside of science (Booth, Clifford, de Man, Fish, Geertz, McCloskey, Barbara H. Smith); sociological work on situated meanings and the construction of realities, including scientific realities (Cicourel, Latour, Mehan, Pinch, Woolgar); critical interpretative work on social and psychological theory (Bernstein, Bloor, Bourdieu, Mike Cole, Gergen, Goodnow, Lave, Haskel Levi, Tambiah); medical work on "placebo," psychosomatic effects, and the body as an intentional system (Csordas, Gendlin, Good, Kleinman); developmental work on social referencing and the socialization of emotions (Campos, Camras, Dunn, Emde); clinical work on the role of cultural myths and stories in the self-regulation of emotional states (Doi, Herdt, Kakar, Spiro, Zonis); anthropological work on person-centered ethnography (Gregor, LeVine, Robert Levy, Obeyesekere, Scheper-Hughes, Whiting and Whiting); ethnographic work on the socialization of motivations, attitudes, and subjective states in institutional settings—families, schools, military units (Bletso, Csikszentmihaly, Edgerton, Alan Fiske, Phil Jackson, Ogbu, Lois Peak, G. W. Skinner, Stodolsky, Weisner); psychological and anthropological work on narrative and dialogue (Bruner, Cohler, Crapanzano, Nancy Stein); and ethno-psychological work on the representation of self and subjective states (Michael Bond, Fogelson, Paul Harris, Heelas, Karl Heider, Lutz, Joan Miller, Triandis, Geoffrey White).

REFERENCES

Barnes, B., and S. Shapin. 1979. *The Natural Order: Historical Studies of Scientific Culture.* Beverly Hills: Sage.

Bruner, J. S. 1966. On cognitive growth II. In J. S. Bruner, R. R. Olver, and P. M. Greenfield, eds., *Studies in Cognitive Growth.* New York: Wiley.

Campbell, D. T., and D. W. Fiske. 1959. Convergent and discriminant validation by the multitrait-multimethod matrix. *Psychological Bulletin* 56:81–105.

Cicourel, A. V. 1974. *Cognitive Sociology.* New York: Free Press.

Cole, M. 1989. Cultural psychology: A once and future discipline? Manuscript. [Available from Michael Cole, Department of Communication, University of California at San Diego.]

Cole, M., and J. Gay. 1972. Culture and memory. *American Anthropologist* 74:1066–84.

Cole, M., and S. Scribner. 1974. *Culture and Thought: A Psychological Introduction.* New York: Wiley.

Collins, H. M. 1981. Stages in the empirical programme of relativism. *Social Studies of Science* 11:3–10.

Converse, P. E. 1986. Generalization and the social psychology of "other worlds." In D. W. Fiske and R. A. Shweder, eds., *Metatheory in Social Science: Pluralisms and Subjectivities.* Chicago: University of Chicago Press.

Cronbach, L. J. 1975. Beyond the two disciplines of scientific psychology. *American Psychologist* 30:116–127.

D'Andrade, R. G. 1984. Cultural meaning systems. In R. A. Shweder and R. A. LeVine, eds., *Culture Theory: Essays on Mind, Self, and Emotion.* New York: Cambridge University Press.

———. 1986. Three scientific world views and the covering law model. In D. W. Fiske and R. A. Shweder, eds., *Metatheory in Social Science: Pluralisms and Subjectivities.* Chicago: University of Chicago Press.

Ekman, P. 1989. The argument and evidence about universals in facial expressions of emotion. In H. Wagner, ed., *Handbook of Social Psychophysiology: Emotion and Social Behavior.* London: Wiley.

Fish, S. 1980. *Is There a Text in This Class?* Cambridge, Mass.: Harvard University Press.

Fiske, D. W. 1986. Specificity of method and knowledge in social science. In D. W. Fiske and R. A. Shweder, eds., *Metatheory in Social Science: Pluralisms and Subjectivities.* Chicago: University of Chicago Press.

Freedman, D. G. 1974. *Human Infancy.* Hillsdale, N.J.: Lawrence Erlbaum Associates.

Freud, S. 1962 [1929]. The question of lay analysis. In James Strachey, ed., *The Standard Edition of the Complete Psychological Works of Sigmund Freud.* Vol. 20. London: Hogarth Press.

Garfinkle, H. 1967. *Studies in Ethnomethodology.* Englewood Cliffs, N.J.: Prentice-Hall.

Geertz, C. 1973. *Interpretation of Cultures.* New York: Basic Books.

——— 1988. *Works and Lives.* Stanford: Stanford University Press.

Gergen, K. J. 1973. Social psychology as history. *Journal of Personality and Social Psychology* 26:309–320.

Goodman, N. 1968. *Languages of Art.* New York: Bobbs-Merrill.

Hallpike, C. R. 1979. *The Foundations of Primitive Thought.* Oxford: Clarendon Press.

Holland, D., and N. Quinn. 1986. *Cultural Models in Language and Thought.* New York: Cambridge University Press.

Howard, A. 1985. Ethnopsychology and the prospects for a cultural psychology. In G. M. White and J. Kirkpatrick, eds., *Person, Self, and Experience.* Los Angeles: University of California Press.

Kleinman, A. 1986. *Social Origins of Distress and Disease.* New Haven: Yale University Press.

Kuhn, T. 1962. *The Structure of Scientific Revolutions.* Chicago: University of Chicago Press.

Lakoff, G. 1987. *Women, Fire, and Dangerous Things.* Chicago: University of Chicago Press.

Lakoff, G., and M. Johnson. 1980. *Metaphors We Live By.* Chicago: University of Chicago Press.

Latour, B., and S. Woolgar. 1981. *Laboratory Life: The Social Construction of Scientific Facts.* Beverly Hills: Sage.

LeVine, R. A. n.d. Environments in child development: An anthropological perspective. Manuscript, School of Education, Harvard University.

Lévi-Strauss, C. 1963. *Structural Anthropology.* New York: Basic Books.

Lévy-Bruhl, L. 1910. *Les fonctions mentales dans les sociétés inférieures.* Paris: Alcan.

McClosky, D. 1985. *The Rhetoric of Economics.* Madison: University of Wisconsin Press.

MacIntyre, A. 1981. *After Virtue: A Study in Moral Theory.* Notre Dame: University of Notre Dame Press.

Milgram, S. 1974. *Obedience to Authority.* New York: Harper and Row.

Miller, G. 1956. The magical number seven, plus or minus two: Some limits on our capacity for processing information. *Psychological Review* 63:81–97.

Miller, P., and L. L. Sperry. 1987. The socialization of anger and aggression. *Merrill-Palmer Quarterly* 33:1–31.

Mischel, W. 1973. Towards a cognitive social learning reconceptualization of personality. *Psychological Review* 80:252–283.

Nerlove, S., and A. K. Romney. 1967. Sibling terminology and cross-sex behavior. *American Anthropologist* 69:179–187.

Obeyesekere, G. 1981. *Medusa's Hair: An Essay on Personal Symbols and Religious Experience.* London and Chicago: University of Chicago Press.

———. 1985. Depression, Buddhism, and the work of culture in Sri Lanka. In A. Kleinman and B. Good, eds., *Culture and Depression.* Berkeley: University of California Press.

Ochs, E., and Schieffelin, B. B. 1984. Language acquisition and socialization: Three developmental stories and their implications. In R. A. Shweder and R. A. LeVine, eds., *Culture Theory: Essays on Mind, Self, and Emotion.* New York: Cambridge University Press.

Peacock, J. L. 1984. Religion and life history: an exploration in cultural psychology. In E. M. Bruner, ed. *Text, Play and Story: The Construction and Reconstruction of Self and Society.* Washington, D.C.: American Ethnological Society.

Peirce, C. S. 1940. *The Philosophy of Peirce: Selected Writings.* London: Routledge and Kegan Paul.

Plomin, R. 1986. *Development, Genetics, and Psychology.* Hillsdale, N.J.: Lawrence Erlbaum Associates.

Putnam, H. 1981. *Reason, Truth and History.* Cambridge: Cambridge University Press.

———. 1987. *The Many Faces of Realism.* La Salle, Ill.: Open Court Publishing.

Richter, F. 1986. Non-linear behavior. In D. W. Fiske and R. A. Shweder, eds., *Metatheory in Social Science: Pluralisms and Subjectivities.* Chicago: University of Chicago Press.

Sahlins, M. 1976. *Culture and Practical Reason.* Chicago: University of Chicago Press.

Sapir, E. 1924. Culture: Genuine and spurious. *American Journal of Sociology* 29:401–429. Reprinted in D. Mandelbaum, ed., *Selected Writings of Edward Sapir in Language, Culture and Personality.* Berkeley: University of California Press, 1963.

———. 1929. The status of linguistics as a science. *Language* 5:207–214.

Scarr, S., and K. McCartney. 1983. How people make their own environments: A theory of genotype → environment effects. *Child Development* 54:424–435.

Schank, R., and R. Abelson. 1977. *Scripts, Plans, Goals, and Understanding.* Hillsdale, N.J.: Lawrence Erlbaum Associates.

Schelling, T. C. 1984. *Choice and Consequence.* Cambridge, Mass.: Harvard University Press.

Schneider, D. M. 1968. *American Kinship: A Cultural Account.* Englewood Cliffs, N.J.: Prentice-Hall.

———. 1984. *A Critique of the Study of Kinship.* Ann Arbor: University of Michigan Press.

Shepard, R. 1987. Toward a universal law of generalization for psychological science. *Science* 237:1317–23.

Shweder, R. A. 1982. On savages and other children. *American Anthropologist* 84:354–366.

———. 1984. Preview: A colloquy of cultural theorists. In R. A. Shweder and R. A. LeVine, eds., *Culture Theory: Essays on Mind, Self, and Emotion.* New York: Cambridge University Press.

———. 1986. Divergent rationalities. In D. W. Fiske and R. A. Shweder, eds., *Metatheory in Social Science: Pluralisms and Subjectivities.* Chicago: University of Chicago Press.

Spiro, M. E. 1955. Symposium: Projective testing in ethnography. *American Anthropologist* 57:245–270.

———. 1983. *Oedipus in the Trobriands.* Chicago: University of Chicago Press.

Stephens, W. N., ed., 1962. *The Oedipus Complex: Cross-Cultural Evidence.* New York: Free Press.

Stigler, J. W. 1984. "Mental Abacus": the effect of abacus training on Chinese children's mental calculation. *Cognitive Psychology* 16:145–176.

Stigler, J. W., and R. Baranes. 1988. Culture and mathematics learning. In E. Rothkopf, ed., *Review of Research in Education.* New York: AERA.

Stigler, J. W., L. Chalip, and K. F. Miller. 1986. Consequences of skill: The case of abacus training in Taiwan. *American Journal of Education* 94:447–479.

Toulmin, S. 1972. *Human Understanding.* Vol. 1. Princeton: Princeton University Press.

Whiting, B. B., and J. W. M. Whiting. 1975. *Children of Six Cultures.* Cambridge, Mass.: Harvard University Press.

Whiting, B. B., and C. P. Edwards. 1988. *Children of Different Worlds: The Formation of Social Behavior.* Cambridge, Mass.: Harvard University Press.

Wittgenstein, L. 1968 [1953]. *Philosophical Investigations,* trans. G. E. M. Anscombe. New York: Macmillan.

4. The Study of Culture, Ethnicity, and Race in American Psychology

Hector Betancourt and Steven Regeser López

Culture and its significant role in human behavior have been recognized for many years, as far back as Hippocrates from the classical Greek era (see Dona, 1991) as well as near the beginning of psychology as a discipline (Wundt, 1921). More recently, a number of authors have questioned the cross-cultural generalizability of psychological theories (e.g., Amir & Sharon, 1987; Bond, 1988; Pepitone & Triandis, 1987), some arguing for the inclusion of culture in psychological theories (e.g., Harkness, 1980; Rokeach, 1979; Smith, 1979; Triandis, 1989). An abundant literature demonstrates cultural variations in many areas of psychology that can guide such theoretical efforts (see handbooks edited by Triandis et al., 1980, and by Munroe, Munroe, & Whiting, 1981; see also Berman, 1990). Most recently, the need to study culture in psychology was highlighted in an American Psychological Association (APA) report on education (McGovern, Furumoto, Halpern, Kimble, & McKeachie, 1991). Because of the changing demographics in the nation as well as in the student population, McGovern et al. indicated that an "important social and ethical responsibility of faculty members is to promote their students' understanding of gender, race, ethnicity, culture, and class issues in psychological theory, research, and practice" (p. 602).

Despite the historical and contemporary awareness concerning the importance of culture among a number of scholars, the study of culture and related variables occupies at best a secondary place in American (mainstream) psychology. It appears to be the domain of cross-cultural psychology and is often associated with the replication

Reprinted by permission of the American Psychological Association from *American Psychologist* 28 (1993): 629–37. Copyright © 1993 by the American Psychological Association.

of findings in some remote or exotic part of the world. In the United States, it is often associated with the study of ethnic minorities, which is as segregated from mainstream psychology (see Graham, 1992) as is cross-cultural research. There seems to be a widespread assumption that the study of culture or ethnicity contributes little to the understanding of basic psychological processes or to the practice of psychology in the United States.

The general purpose of this article is to share some of our preoccupations and views concerning the status of the study of culture and related concepts, such as race and ethnicity, in psychology. Our main concern is that whereas mainstream investigators do not consider culture in their research and theories, cross-cultural researchers who study cultural differences frequently fail to identify the specific aspects of culture and related variables that are thought to influence behavior. Consequently, we learn that cultural group, race, or ethnicity may be related to a given psychological phenomenon, but we learn little about the specific elements of these group variables that contribute to the proposed relationship. The limited specificity of this research impedes our understanding of the behavior of a group or groups. In addition, it serves to limit the delineation of more universal processes that cut across cultural, ethnic, and racial groups. In this article, we promote the study of culture. This is not to say that culture is the single most important variable in psychology. It is one of many factors that contribute to the complexities of psychological processes, and it is obviously important to the understanding of culturally diverse populations both inside and outside of the United States. In addition, even though the higher uniformity of cultural elements makes it less obvious, cultural factors also play an important role in the behavior of mainstream individuals. Thus, our focus will be on culture, some of the problems that in our opinion preclude progress in our understanding of its role in psychology and some propositions on how to overcome them. To illustrate our points, we draw from research in the social and clinical domains; these reflect our areas of expertise.

As a general approach, we propose that both mainstream and cross-cultural investigators identify and measure directly what about the group variable (e.g., what cultural element) of interest to their research influences behavior. Then, hypothesized relationships between such variables and the psychological phenomenon of interest could be examined and such research could be incorporated within a theoretical framework. We believe that an adherence to this approach will serve to enhance our understanding of both group-specific and group-general (universal) processes as well as contribute to the integration of culture in theory development and the practice of psychology. Our focus is on the general approach rather than on specific methodological issues already treated elsewhere in the literature (see Brislin, Lonner, & Thorndike, 1973; Lonner & Berry, 1986; Triandis et al., 1980, Vol. 2).

Because culture is closely intertwined with concepts such as race, ethnicity, and social class, and because conceptual confusion has been an obstacle for progress in this area, it is important to first define culture and point out its relationship to these related concepts. Hence, we first focus on these definitions and conceptual problems. Then, we address some of the limitations of cross-cultural and mainstream psychology and suggest ways in which to infuse the study of culture in mainstream research and both experimentation and theory in cross-cultural research. Finally, we illustrate ways in which to study cultural variables and discuss the importance of infusing theory in ethnic minority research.

DEFINITIONS

Variations in psychological phenomena observed in the comparative study of groups identified in terms of nationality, race, ethnicity, or socioeconomic status (SES) are often attributed to cultural differences without defining what is meant by culture, and what about culture and to what extent is related to the differences. This is so common, even among cross-cultural psychologists, that it has led to the criticism that little research in cross-cultural psychology actually deals with culture (e.g., Rohner, 1984). Thus, an important problem is the lack of a clear definition and understanding of culture from a psychological perspective.

Culture

A number of psychologists interested in the study of culture agree that the confusion concerning its definition has been an obstacle for progress (e.g., Brislin, 1983; Jahoda, 1984; Rohner, 1984; Triandis et al., 1980). Although it would be desirable to have a definition that everyone agrees upon, as noted by Segall (1984), consensus is not absolutely necessary to advance knowledge. Even without consensus, progress is possible if, as we propose, cultural research specifies what is meant by culture in terms that are amenable to measurement.

After reviewing the elements found in the anthropological and cross-cultural psychology views of culture, Rohner (1984) proposed a conceptualization of culture in terms of "highly variable systems of meanings," which are "learned" and "shared by a people or an identifiable segment of a population." It represents "designs and ways of life" that are normally "transmitted from one generation to another." We consider this conception as equivalent to that proposed by Herkovits (1948), who conceives culture as the human-made part of the environment. Perhaps the most distinctive characteristic of Rohner's formulation is the explicit statement of aspects such as the learned, socially shared, and variable nature of culture.

Within the context of this general conception of culture, we consider Triandis et al.'s (1980) reformulation of Herkovits's (1948) definition as the most practical one for the purpose of our work. In addition to differentiating between the objective and subjective aspects of Herkovits's human-made part of the environment, Triandis's formulation is quite explicit about the psychologically relevant elements that constitute culture. According to Triandis, although physical culture refers to objects such as roads, buildings, and tools, subjective culture includes elements such as social norms, roles, beliefs, and values. These subjective cultural elements include a wide range of topics, such as familial roles, communication patterns, affective styles, and values regarding personal control, individualism, collectivism, spirituality, and religiosity.

When culture (or subjective culture) is defined in terms of psychologically relevant elements, such as roles and values, it becomes amenable to measurement. Moreover, the relationship of the cultural elements to psychological phenomena can be directly assessed. Hence, it is possible to deal with the complexity of the concept and at the same time pursue an understanding of the role of culture in psychology. By incorporating the conceptualization and measurement of specific cultural elements, the comparative study of national, ethnic, or cultural groups is more likely to contribute to the understanding of the role of culture than are the typical comparative studies (see Poortinga & Malpass, 1986).

Race

Scholars and pollsters often use the concept of culture interchangeably with race, ethnicity, or nationality. For example, in surveys or research instruments, individuals are often required to indicate their race by choosing one of a combination of categories including race, ethnicity, and national origin (such as Asian, American Indian, Black, Latino, and White). Latinos, for instance, can be White, Black, Asian, American Indian, or any combination thereof. We are particularly concerned about the loose way in which culture, race, and ethnicity are used to explain differences between groups. This not only limits our understanding of the specific factors that contribute to group differences, but it also leads to interpretations of findings that stimulate or reinforce racist conceptions of human behavior (see Zuckerman, 1990).

Jones (1991) recently argued that the concept of race is fraught with problems for psychology. For example, race is generally defined in terms of physical characteristics, such as skin color, facial features, and hair type, which are common to an inbred, geographically isolated population. However, the classification of people in groups designated as races has been criticized as arbitrary, suggesting that the search for differences between such groups is at best dubious (Zuckerman, 1990). Specifically, there are more within-group differences than between-group differences in the characteristics used to define the three so-called races (Caucasoid, Negroid, and Mongoloid). Also, studies of genetic systems (e.g., blood groups, serum proteins, and enzymes) have found that differences between individuals within the same tribe or nation account for more variance (84%) than do racial groupings (10%) (Latter, 1980; Zuckerman, 1990). This indicates that racial groups are more alike than they are different, even in physical and genetic characteristics. Still, too often in the history of psychology, race has been used to explain variations in psychological phenomena between the so-called racial groups, without examining the cultural and social variables likely to be associated with such variations (e.g., Allport, 1924; Barrett & Eysenck, 1984; Jensen, 1985). We agree with Zuckerman (1990) that the study of racial differences in psychological phenomena is of little scientific use without a clear understanding of the variables responsible for the differences observed between the groups classified as races. We consider racial group or identity inadequate as a general explanatory factor of between-group variations in psychological phenomena. We encourage researchers to give greater attention to cultural elements, as discussed earlier, as they may prove fruitful in understanding behavioral differences associated with racial groupings.

Although we focus on the cultural and social variables associated with racial grouping, we do not imply that biological factors associated with such groupings are of no scientific interest. These biological variables are important, for example, in the study of group differences in essential hypertension, for which Afro-Americans are at a higher risk than Anglo-Americans (Anderson, 1989). From our perspective, what is of scientific interest is not the race of these individuals but the relationship between the identified biological factors (e.g., plasma renin levels and sodium excretion) and hypertension. Moreover, even if a cause-effect relationship is demonstrated between these biological variables and hypertension, one cannot attribute this relationship to race because of intraracial variability and interracial overlap with regard to the biological variables (Anderson, 1989). Psychological stress or factors such as diet, life-style, and objective and subjective culture could be responsible for the racial-group differences in the biological factors. Also, this difference may not be observed in a group of the same race in another part of the world or under different living conditions.

In summary, we suggest that when behavioral variations are studied in relation to race, the so-called racial variable under study should be defined, measured, and the proposed relationships tested. The role of specific cultural and social variables could be clearly separated from that of biological and other variables. The area of research will determine the relative importance of any one of these variables. The important point is that the research be on the relevant variable and not on racial groupings alone.

Ethnicity

The concept of ethnicity is also associated with culture and is often used interchangeably with culture as well as with race. Usually, ethnicity is used in reference to groups that are characterized in terms of a common nationality, culture, or language. The concept of ethnicity is related to the Greek concept of ethnos, which refers to the people of a nation or tribe, and ethnikos, which stands for national. Hence, ethnicity refers to the ethnic quality or affiliation of a group, which is normally characterized in terms of culture. However, the distinction between these two related concepts is an important one for psychology. Although cultural background can be a determinant of ethnic identity or affiliation, being part of an ethnic group can also determine culture. As members of an ethnic group interact with each other, ethnicity becomes a means by which culture is transmitted. According to Berry (1985), because an ethnic group is likely to interact with other ethnic groups, such interactions should not be ignored as possible sources of cultural influences. Hence, it is important that comparative studies of ethnic groups identify and measure cultural variables assumed to be responsible for observed differences in psychological phenomena before such differences are attributed to culture on the basis of group membership. This issue is particularly important in the United States today because, beyond face-to-face interactions, interethnic communication takes place through the mass media.

We believe that the study of variations in psychological phenomena between ethnic groups is relevant as far as the specific variable of theoretical interest is measured and related to the relevant psychological phenomena. In addition to the specific cultural elements, there are a range of ethnic-related variables, such as ethnic identification, perceived discrimination, and bilingualism. Increased specification with regard to what about ethnicity is of interest could reduce the confusion and conceptual problems in this area (for an illustration of research in this direction, see Sue, 1988; Sue & Zane, 1987).

Social and Related Variables

The effect of variables such as the social system and socioeconomic level on behavior can also be confounded with the influence of culture, race, and ethnicity (for a discussion, see Rohner, 1984). Some authors do control for the effects of socioeconomic variables. For example, Frerichs, Aneshensel, and Clark (1981) found that the prevalence of depressive symptoms was significantly different for Latinos, Anglos, and Afro-American community residents. More Latinos reported significant levels of depressive symptoms than did the other ethnic groups. However, when controlling for SES-related variables (e.g., employment status and family income), the ethnic effect disappeared. This suggests that ethnicity, and possibly culture, are of little or no significance in the prevalence rates of depression, whereas SES, that is, economic strain, is viewed as being more significant.

Although this approach has the advantage of reducing the likelihood of misattributing to culture the influence of SES, the possibility of confusion still exists. It is possible, for instance, that cultural influences are not identified and are wrongly attributed to SES. We see at least two instances in which this can happen. First, in societies with a history of ethnic or racial discrimination, segregation may result in significant overlap between culture and SES. For example, in the United States the majority of Anglos are represented in higher social strata, whereas the majority of Latinos are represented in lower social strata. Thus, by methodologically or statistically controlling for SES, the cultures are also separated, and the variance associated with culture is removed along with the effects of SES. This may then lead one to wrongly assume that culture does not play a role.

Second, even if two social classes are represented in each of the two cultures, the economic, social, or living conditions of a segregated lower class that includes both cultural groups may generate beliefs, norms, or values specific to that social strata. These cultural elements associated with lower SES may become significantly different from that of other groups (e.g., the middle class) of the same ethnic group. Although it is possible that some cultural elements associated with ethnicity are consistent across the different SES levels of a given ethnic group, it is also possible that there are beliefs, norms, and values that are common to an SES level across cultural (ethnic) groups. Hence, even when social classes are compared within the same ethnic group, cultural elements unique to a lower strata may be wrongly attributed to SES—that is, income or educational level— when in fact they reflect cultural or subcultural elements—that is, beliefs and attitudes associated with lower class reality.

Sobal and Stunkard (1989) illustrated this point with regard to obesity and socioeconomic status. They argued that the prevalence of obesity in developing societies is a function of structural elements in society, such as the availability of food supplies, and "cultural values favoring fat body shapes" (p. 266). The former reflect SES-related variables, whereas the values associated with body shapes may be more cultural in nature, even though the cultural beliefs are associated with social strata. The work of Sobal and Stunkard is consistent with our recommendation to measure the specific proximal variables thought to underlie a given behavioral phenomenon. By doing so, the comparative study of social as well as cultural groups will be able to better identify the specific social variables (e.g., income, educational level) as well as cultural elements (e.g., values, beliefs) that are relevant to the behavioral phenomena of interest.

In summary, we encourage investigators to think carefully about the group of interest, whether it be cultural, racial, ethnical, or social, and go beyond the group category to the specific factors that underlie the group category. By doing so, studies will be able to identify what about culture, race, ethnicity, or social class is related to the psychological phenomenon of interest. We argue that cultural variables, specifically social roles, norms, beliefs, and values, are likely to contribute significantly to the effects of these demographic variables. However, culture is only one dimension. Depending on the research problem and the interests of the investigator, more biological or social variables could also be assessed. The important point is that further specification will likely lead to a greater understanding of the roles of culture, race, ethnicity, and social class in psychological phenomena.

LIMITATIONS OF MAINSTREAM AND CROSS-CULTURAL PSYCHOLOGY

The need to study and understand culture in psychology represents a major challenge to mainstream and cross-cultural psychology. A review of the literature reveals important limitations in the ways both mainstream and cross-cultural psychology have responded to this challenge. On the one hand, the study of culture has largely been ignored in mainstream psychology and is often seen as the domain of cross-cultural psychology. Usually, theories do not include cultural variables and findings or principles are thought to apply to individuals everywhere, suggesting that psychological knowledge developed in the United States by Anglo-American scholars using Anglo-American subjects is universal. Even in areas such as social psychology, in which the importance of variables such as norms and values is particularly obvious, there is little regard for the cultural nature of such variables (Bond, 1988).

On the other hand, cross-cultural psychology, normally segregated from mainstream psychology, has focused on the comparative (cross-cultural) study of behavioral phenomena, without much regard for the measurement of cultural variables and their implications for theory. Attributing to culture the differences observed between countries or groups assumed to represent different cultures ignores the complexity of culture as well as the cultural heterogeneity of nations or ethnic groups (see Berry, 1985). Moreover, it tells us little about the role of culture in human behavior. Without a theoretical focus, cross-cultural research has little connection to mainstream psychology, thus maintaining its segregation.

Although there is no simple solution to the noted limitations (see Lonner & Berry, 1986; Malpass, 1977; Reyes-Lagunes & Poortinga, 1985), we believe that the following two approaches would help psychologists to enhance the study of culture: (a) Begin with a phenomenon observed in the study of culture and apply it cross-culturally to test theories of human behavior, and (b) begin with a theory, typically one that ignores culture, and incorporate cultural elements to broaden its theoretical domain. The former might be considered a bottom-up approach; one is beginning with an observation from the study of cultures and moving toward its implications for psychological theory. The latter might be considered a top-down approach; one is beginning with theory and moving to observations within as well as between cultures, examining the role of culture and searching for universals.

Triandis and associates' research illustrates a bottom-up approach to cross-cultural research. Drawing from anthropological research that identified dimensions of cultural variations, they proposed the following steps: (a) Develop measures of such dimensions, (b) assess different cultures along the dimensions so that the cultures could be placed on a continuum of a designated dimension, and (c) test predictions relating the cultural dimension and behavioral phenomenon across cultures. These steps are evident in the work of Triandis et al. (1986) on collectivism versus individualism. They first developed a measure; second, they assessed students from Illinois and Puerto Rico along this dimension. Then, as expected, this dimension was found to be related to behaviors such as cooperation and helping (Triandis, Bontempo, Villareal, Asai, & Lucca, 1988). Not only did they find differences between U.S. mainland students and Puerto Rican students with regard to helping and cooperation, they also found that the cultural dimension of collectivism versus individualism accounted in part for these differences. Thus, in line with the bottom-up approach, the observed cultural phenomenon, in this case individualism-collectivism, has served to inform theoretical accounts of helping and cooperation.

The research of Betancourt and his associates serves to illustrate a top-down approach to the study of cultural influences. They began with a theory and took steps to incorporate cultural factors in the theory. In a first study, Betancourt and Weiner (1982) examined the cross-cultural generality of an attribution theory of motivation (see Weiner, 1986), specifically assessing whether the relationships between the dimensional properties of attributions and related psychological consequences differed for Chilean and U.S. college students. Evidence for both cultural generality and cultural specificity was found. The relationship between the perceived stability of a given causal attribution and expectancy of future success was similar for both groups, suggesting that this part of the theory has cross-cultural generality. The influence of perceived controllability of attributions for a person's achievement on interpersonal feelings and reactions was less important for Chilean students than for students from the United States; this part suggested cultural specificity. For example, although Chileans tended to like the person more when success was due to controllable than to uncontrollable causes, the effect of controllability over liking was significantly lower than for the students from the United States. Chileans tended to like the successful individual, regardless of whether the cause of his or her achievement behavior was perceived as controllable (e.g., effort) or uncontrollable (e.g., aptitude). On the other hand, U.S. students more systematically liked the person according to the degree the achievement behavior was perceived as within the person's volitional control.

In explaining these findings, Betancourt and Weiner (1982) suggested that the generality observed in the relationship between perceived stability of causes and expectancy of success was a reflection of the logic of cause—effect relationships (e.g., if A is the cause of B, and A is stable, B should also be stable). They also suggested that when such logic applies, we might expect psychological principles to be fairly universal. However, in the case of perceived controllability and its relation to interpersonal feelings and behavior, elements of the culture such as norms and values are thought to play a role.

Recall that we have criticized comparative studies of cultures as insufficient in that the aspects of culture responsible for the observed differences are not identified or measured, nor are the relationships between these and the corresponding psychological phenomena demonstrated. From this perspective, Betancourt and Weiner's (1982) study was appropriate as a first step, but limited in that cultural variables responsible for observed variations were not identified and measured. Hence, one may not conclusively attribute differences to cultural factors.

To more directly test the specific cultural element that might underlie the noted difference, Betancourt (1985) first reviewed the cross-cultural literature on attribution processes in an effort to identify possible cultural dimensions that might contribute to explaining further these findings. Key studies were identified that suggested that the perception of control and the effects of causal controllability are culturally determined. Specifically, the relationship observed in the United States between controllability for success and failure and reward and punishment (Weiner & Kukla, 1970) was replicated in Germany (Meyer, 1970) but was not fully replicated in Brazil (Rodrigues, 1981). In addition, Salili, Maehr, and Gillmore (1976) only partially replicated in Iran the findings of Weiner and Peter (1973) concerning developmental aspects of the proposed relationship between controllability of attributions and interpersonal judgment.

The findings from these key studies, in conjunction with the work of Kluckhohn and Strodtbeck (1961) on dimensions of cultural variation, suggested that the cultural dimension of "control over nature versus subjugation to nature" (control–subjugation) was potentially relevant. When the results on the control–subjugation value orientation are compared for the countries noted in the cross-cultural attributional research, Germany, a country in which results are replicated, scores high on control, as does the United States, whereas Brazil, Chile, and Iran, where variations are observed, score low on control.

A series of studies was then designed (e.g., Betancourt, Hardin, & Manzi, 1992) to investigate the control–subjugation value orientation and related cultural beliefs in relation to the attributional components of a model of helping behavior (Betancourt, 1990). Although no cross-cultural comparison took place, within-culture measures of the control-subjugation value orientation were used to examine the influence of value orientation on the attribution process, as well as the relationship between controllability of attributions and helping behavior. In addition, the manipulation (activation) of beliefs associated with this value orientation demonstrated how it relates to the other components of the helping behavior model.

The research by Betancourt and associates progresses from mainstream social psychological research and theory to the study of cultural variables relevant to the theory and search for universals. They identify a specific cultural element hypothesized to be related to the cognitive process and behavior under study and then test the relationships. Their findings indicate that value orientation influences attributional processes. Accordingly, attention to values in attribution theory may serve to broaden the scope and universality of the theory. This is an example in which attention to culture may serve to enhance theory development in mainstream research. In addition, the work of Betancourt et al. (1992) has methodological implications. Although these authors could have taken a cross-cultural or between-groups approach by selecting cultures that vary with regard to value orientation, they chose a within-culture approach. Specifically, they measured differences on the theoretically relevant cultural dimension and tested its relationship to helping. This research suggests that cultural variables can be studied within a single culture and that research with mainstream subjects can also examine culture.

The main limitation of mainstream theories is that they ignore culture and therefore lack universality. The limitation of a segregated cross-cultural psychology is that it fails to use experimentation and develop theory. Two approaches were described above (Betancourt et al., 1992; Triandis et al., 1988) to illustrate how these limitations might be overcome. We submit that progress will follow if mainstream investigators include cultural elements in their research and theory and if cross-cultural researchers incorporate the measurement of cultural variables within a theoretical network.

LIMITATIONS OF ETHNIC MINORITY RESEARCH

Ethnic minority research shares conceptual problems similar to those of cross-cultural psychology. Direct measures of cultural elements are frequently not included, yet cultural factors are assumed to underlie ethnic group differences. Furthermore, ethnic minority research often lacks sufficient attention to psychological theory. It appears that investigators of ethnicity are more inclined toward description than testing theoretically derived hypotheses. In this section, we examine ethnic minority research as it pertains to the study of psychopathology. We draw attention to the importance of directly examining the cultural basis of psychopathology and suggest ways to incorporate psychological theory.

Like cross-cultural research, a typical cross-ethnic design compares a given set of variables across samples of two ethnic groups. In the study of ethnic differences in psychopathology, such research is frequently based on community or clinic surveys of psychological distress or rates of mental disorders. Usually, methodological or statistical controls are included to rule out the effects of socioeconomic status, age, and other sociodemographic variables that could possibly be related to the given dependent variable. If group differences are found with these controls in place, then the investigator frequently argues that the differences between Asian Americans and Anglo Americans, for example, reflect cultural influences. In other words, the observed group differences are thought to be the result of differences in the groups' cultural values and beliefs.

Often, researchers will discuss the cultural differences that are thought to contribute to the observed differences. It is important to note that the "cultural differences" thought to underlie the observed group differences are frequently not directly measured or assessed. It is assumed that because the two groups are from two distinct cultural or ethnic groups, they differ from one another on key cultural dimensions. This may or may not be the case. Without directly assessing these cultural dimensions, one cannot be sure whether culture plays a role, nor can one understand the nature of the relationship between cultural variables and psychological processes.

In an attempt to more directly assess cultural influences associated with ethnicity, some investigators have been using measures of acculturation. Acculturation typically refers to the degree to which minority groups adhere to traditional cultural practices (in many cases, those practices that are associated with people from their country of origin) or to U.S. cultural practices (for a review, see Berry, 1990). These efforts represent a step forward as they serve to increase the specificity in measuring cultural influences.

The inclusion of acculturation measures are not without limitations. First of all, such measures are usually based on behavioral indices such as language usage (native language or English) and place of birth (country of origin or the United States). At best, these are indirect measures of cultural values and beliefs. It is assumed that individuals of low acculturation are more likely to adhere to traditional cultural values regarding such variables as sex role orientation and collectivism—individualism. This may not be the case for a given sample.

Another reason why acculturation is a poor measure of cultural influences is that it is confounded with acculturative stress, or the stress experienced in adjusting from one culture to another culture (Berry, 1990). Some investigators have attempted to determine whether certain levels of acculturation are related to psychological adjustment and distress, as well as rates of mental disorders (see Rogler, Cortes, & Malgady, 1991, for a recent review of Latino research). For example, some researchers find that low-acculturated Latinos, in this case Mexican Americans, report more distress than do more acculturated Latinos and Anglos (Vega, Kolody, & Warheit, 1985). It is not reasonable to interpret findings such as these as only reflecting acculturative stress. It seems possible that the results could also reflect the association between level of distress and specific cultural values, indirectly assessed.

Acculturation indices may serve then as indirect measures of adherence to cultural values, but they may also serve as indices of stress associated with adjusting to the Anglo culture. If an investigator is interested in examining cultural influences, he or she would do best to incorporate direct measures of culture-relevant variables rather than a global measure of acculturation. Furthermore, if acculturative stress is the focus of an investigation, a direct measure of this construct should be included (see Cervantes, Padilla, & Salgado de Snyder, 1991). Without directly assessing cultural values and beliefs and without directly assessing acculturative stress, it is difficult to know the meaning of finding significant relationships between acculturation and psychological variables.

In a recent study, López, Hurwicz, Karno, and Telles (1992) attempted to approximate the goal of directly measuring culture in the study of psychopathology. Drawing from the Los Angeles Epidemiologic Catchment Area database, a large epidemiologic study of the prevalence rates of several mental disorders among Mexican-origin Latinos and Anglos (Karno et al., 1987), López et al. took two significant steps to examine possible cultural influences. First, they chose symptoms as the dependent variable rather than disorders, the dependent variable used in past analyses. Influenced by the work of Draguns (1980) and Persons (1986), they argued that symptoms may be more sensitive to possible sociocultural influences.

The second step was to test hypotheses regarding ethnic differences in the report of specific symptoms and to examine whether specific sociocultural variables accounted for the hypothesized ethnic differences. To develop specific hypotheses, they turned to prior descriptive work of a clinical nature. For example, some clinical observers had noted that Latinos may have the experience of hearing voices, which is reflective of a high degree of spirituality or religiosity and not reflective of psychosis (Abad, Ramos, & Boyce, 1977; Torrey, 1972). Religiosity was also implicated in the relative absence of hypersexuality in the symptomatology of Amish with bipolar disorders (Egeland, Hostetter, & Eshleman, 1983). On the basis of these clinical observations, López et al. (1992) hypothesized that, relative to Anglo residents, Mexican-origin residents would report more evidence of auditory hallucinations, a symptom frequently associated with schizophrenia, and less evidence of hypersexuality, a symptom frequently associated with mania. Furthermore, they hypothesized that religiosity would account for these ethnic differences.

Consistent with their hypotheses, there were significant differences in the reporting of these two symptoms among Latinos of Mexican origin (U.S. born and Mexican born) and Anglos. Furthermore, the patterns of findings are consistent with the hypotheses. With regard to auditory hallucinations, more Mexican-born Latinos reported this symptom (2.3%) than U.S.-born Latinos (1.6%), who reported more such symptoms than Anglos (0.6%). The opposite pattern resulted for hypersexuality: Mexican-born Latinos (2.2%), U.S.-born Latinos (4.3%), and Anglos (6.8%). Although these findings are consistent with cultural hypotheses—that is, there is something about one or both cultures that contributes to these symptom patterns—there is no direct evidence that cultural elements are responsible for the findings.

To more closely approximate a direct cultural test, López et al. (1992) examined the role of religiosity in the report of these symptoms. Regression analyses revealed that ethnicity is an important variable in the reporting of hypersexuality; however, Catholicism accounts for a greater proportion of the variance. Thus, ethnicity appears to be a more distal variable, whereas religious affiliation is a more proximal variable. In contrast to the report of hypersexuality, religiosity was not found to be significantly related to the report of auditory hallucinations. It might be that the report of auditory hallucinations is more related to spiritual beliefs that may exist independent of religious background.

Although the past Los Angeles Epidemiologic Catchment Area research indicates that there are no ethnic differences in the prevalence rates of disorders such as schizophrenia and bipolar disorder (Karno et al., 1987), suggesting that sociocultural factors are unimportant, the López et al. (1992) study indicates that ethnic and sociocultural factors are related to psychopathology as reflected in the report of specific symptomatology. Their findings are consistent with the notion that cultural elements or the values and beliefs of individuals are likely to shape the manner in which psychological distress and disorder are manifest.

This research goes beyond the typical comparative ethnic study by examining specific sociocultural factors that are related to psychopathology; however, it falls short of the ideal study. For example, although Catholicism may represent a more proximal variable to hypersexuality than ethnicity, it is not a direct measure of values and beliefs. Measuring values and beliefs about sexual relations would have provided a more direct assessment of cultural elements. Another limitation is that the relationship between Catholicism and hypersexuality may reflect the reticence on the part of Catholics to report this symptom and not their relatively less hypersexual behavior. Also, this study lacks a specific theoretical base. To incorporate theory, the authors might have linked conceptual processes thought to underlie the given symptoms. One such theoretical framework is offered by Bentall (1990), who posited that hallucinations are the result of impaired reality discrimination. In spite of the noted limitations, this research serves to illustrate the importance of including more proximal sociocultural variables in the study of ethnic group behavior, in this case psychopathology.

CONCLUSION

We have discussed some of our concerns about the status of culture in American psychology. We have pointed out three areas of concern that in our opinion represent limitations that preclude the advancement of knowledge concerning the role of culture in human behavior and the universality of psychological theories. At the same time we have suggested possible ways in which to deal with some of the limitations in these areas. First, we addressed and tried to clarify some confusion in the understanding and use of the concepts of culture, race, ethnicity, and social variables, all of which are often used as general explanatory factors for intergroup variations in psychological phenomena. Second, addressing the limitations of mainstream psychology, we suggested ways in which to infuse the study of culture in mainstream research and theory as well as ways to enhance experimentation and the use of theory in cross-cultural research. Finally, we illustrated ways in which to study sociocultural variables and to consider theory in ethnic minority research. In general, we propose that by clearly conceptualizing and measuring cultural and related variables and by including theory, cross-cultural, ethnic, and mainstream research, we can advance the understanding of the role of culture as well as contribute to theory development and applications.

We believe that psychology as a discipline will benefit both from efforts to infuse culture in mainstream research and theory and from efforts to study culture and develop theory in cross-cultural and ethnic psychology. Specifically, we believe that the advancement of knowledge in this area is necessary for psychology to enhance its status as a scientific discipline and its standards of ethical and social responsibility as a profession. As a scientific discipline, progress in the understanding of culture and its role in psychology would result in more universal principles and theories. As a profession, it would result in instruments and interventions that are more sensitive to the reality and cultural diversity of society and the world. Our hope is that this article may stimulate attempts to overcome the limitations we have noted and advance the study of culture in psychology.

REFERENCES

Abad, V., Ramos, J., & Boyce, E. (1977). Clinical issues in the psychiatric treatment of Puerto Ricans. In E. Padilla & A. Padilla (Eds.), *Transcultural psychiatry: An Hispanic perspective* (Monograph No. 4, pp. 23–24). Los Angeles: Spanish Speaking Mental Health Research Center.

Allport, F. (1924). *Social psychology.* New York: Houghton Mifflin.

Amir, Y., & Sharon, I. (1987). Are social psychological laws cross-culturally valid? *Journal of Cross-Cultural Psychology, 8,* 383–470.

Anderson, N. B. (1989). Racial differences in stress-induced cardiovascular reactivity and hypertension: Current status and substantive issues. *Psychological Bulletin, 105,* 89–105.

Barrett, P., & Eysenck, S. (1984). The assessment of personality factors across 25 countries. *Personality and Individual Differences, 5,* 615–632.

Bentall, R. P. (1990). The illusion of reality: A review and integration of psychological research on hallucinations. *Psychological Bulletin, 107,* 82–95.

Berman, J. J. (Ed.). (1990). *Nebraska Symposium on Motivation, 1989: Cross-cultural perspectives* (Vol. 37). Lincoln: University of Nebraska Press.

Berry, J. (1985). In I. Reyes-Lagunes & Y. Poortinga (Eds.), *From a different perspective: Studies of behavior across cultures.* Lisse, The Netherlands: Swets & Zeitlinger.

Berry, J. (1990). Psychology of acculturation. In J. J. Berman (Ed.), *Nebraska Symposium on Motivation, 1989: Cross-cultural perspectives* (Vol. 37, pp. 201–234). Lincoln: University of Nebraska Press.

Betancourt, H. (1985, July). *Cultural variations in attribution processes and the universality of psychological principles.* Paper presented at the XX Congress of the Interamerican Society of Psychology, Caracas, Venezuela.

Betancourt, H. (1990). An attribution–empathy model of helping behavior: Behavioral intentions and judgements of help-giving. *Personality and Social Psychology Bulletin, 16,* 573–591.

Betancourt, H., Hardin, C., & Manzi, J. (1992). Beliefs, value orientation, and culture in attribution processes and helping behavior. *Journal of Cross-Cultural Psychology, 23,* 179–195.

Betancourt, H., & Weiner, B. (1982). Attributions for achievement-related events expectancy, and sentiments: A study of success and failure in Chile and the United States. *Journal of Cross-Cultural Psychology, 13,* 362–374.

Bond, M. (Ed.). (1988). *The cross-cultural challenge to social psychology.* Newbury Park, CA: Sage.

Brislin, R. W. (1983). Cross-cultural research in psychology. *Annual Review of Psychology, 34,* 363–400.

Brislin, R., Lonner, W., & Thorndike, R. (1973). *Cross-cultural research methods.* New York: Wiley.

Cervantes, R. C., Padilla, A. M., & Salgado de Snyder, N. (1991). The Hispanic Stress Inventory: A culturally relevant approach to psychosocial assessment. *Psychological Assessment: A Journal of Consulting and Clinical Psychology, 3,* 438–447.

Dona, G. (1991). Cross-cultural psychology as presaged by Hippocrates. *Cross-Cultural Psychology Bulletin, 25,* 2.

Draguns, J. G. (1980). Psychological disorders of clinical severity. In H. C. Triandis & J. G. Draguns (Eds.), *Handbook of cross-cultural psychology: Psychopathology* (Vol. 6, pp. 99–174). Boston: Allyn & Bacon.

Egeland, J. A., Hostetter, A. M., & Eshleman, S. K., III. (1983). Amish study: 3. The impact of cultural factors on diagnosis of bipolar illness. *American Journal of Psychiatry, 140,* 67–71.

Frerichs, R. R., Aneshensel, C. S., & Clark, V. A. (1981). Prevalence of depression in Los Angeles County. *American Journal of Epidemiology, 113,* 691–699.

Graham, S. (1992). Most of the subjects were White and middle class: Trends in published research on African Americans in selected APA journals, 1970–1989. *American Psychologist, 47,* 629–639.

Harkness, S. (1980). Child development theory in anthropological perspective. *New Directions in Child Development, 8,* 7–13.

Herkovits, M. (1948). *Man and his works.* New York: Knopf.

Jahoda, G. (1984). Do we need a concept of culture? *Journal of Cross-Cultural Psychology, 15,* 139–151.

Jensen, A. R. (1985). The nature of the Black-White difference on various psychometric tests: Spearman's hypothesis. *The Behavioral and Brain Sciences, 8,* 193–263.

Jones, J. M. (1991). Psychological models of race: What have they been and what should they be? In J. D. Goodchilds (Ed.), *Psychological perspectives on human diversity in America* (pp. 5–46). Washington, DC: American Psychological Association.

Karno, M., Hough, R. L., Burnam, M. A., Escobar, J. I., Timbers, D. M., Santana, F., & Boyd, J. H. (1987). Lifetime prevalence of specific psychiatric disorders among Mexican Americans and Non-Hispanic Whites in Los Angeles. *Archives of General Psychiatry, 44,* 695–701.

Kluckhohn, F., & Strodtbeck, F. (1961). *Variations in value orientations.* Evanston, IL: Row, Peterson.

Latter, B. (1980). Genetic differences within and between populations of the major human subgroups. *The American Naturalist, 116,* 220–237.

Lonner, W., & Berry, J. (1986). *Field methods in cross-cultural research.* Newbury Park, CA: Sage.

López, S. R., Hurwicz, M., Karno, M., & Telles, C. A. (1992). *Schizophrenic and manic symptoms in a community sample: A sociocultural analysis.* Unpublished manuscript.

Malpass, R. (1977). Theory and method in cross-cultural psychology. *American Psychologist, 32,* 1069–1079.

McGovern, T. V., Furumoto, L., Halpern, D. F., Kimble, G. A., & McKeachie, W. J. (1991). Liberal education, study in depth, and the arts and sciences major — Psychology. *American Psychologist, 46,* 598–605.

Meyer, W. U. (1970). *Selbstverantwortlichkeit und Leistungs-motivation* [Self-concept and achievement motivation]. Unpublished doctoral dissertation, Ruhr Universitat, Bochum, Federal Republic of Germany.

Munroe, R. H., Munroe, R. L., & Whiting, B. (Eds.). (1981). *Handbook of cross-cultural human development.* New York: Garland STPM.

Pepitone, A., & Triandis, H. (1987). On the universality of social psychological theories. *Journal of Cross-Cultural Psychology, 18,* 471–498.

Persons, J. B. (1986). The advantages of studying psychological phenomena rather than psychiatric diagnoses. *American Psychologist, 41,* 1252–1260.

Poortinga, Y., & Malpass, R. (1986). In W. Lonner & J. Berry (Eds.), *Fields methods in cross-cultural research* (pp. 17–46). Newbury Park, CA: Sage.

Reyes-Lagunes, I., & Poortinga, Y. (1985). *From a different perspective: Studies of behavior across cultures.* Lisse, The Netherlands: Swets & Zeitlinger.

Rodrigues, A. (1981). Causal ascription and evaluation of achievement related outcomes: A cross-cultural comparison. *International Journal of Intercultural Relations, 4,* 379–389.

Rogler, L. H., Cortes, D. E., & Malgady, R. G. (1991). Acculturation and mental health status among Hispanics: Convergence and new directions for research. *American Psychologist, 46,* 585–597.

Rohner, R. P. (1984). Toward a conception of culture for cross-cultural psychology. *Journal of Cross-Cultural Psychology, 15,* 111–138.

Rokeach, M. (1979). Some unresolved issues in theories of beliefs, attitudes, and values. In *Proceedings of the Nebraska Symposium on Motivation* (pp. 261–304). Lincoln: University of Nebraska Press.

Salili, F., Maehr, M. L., & Gillmore, F. (1976). Achievement and morality: A cross-cultural analysis of causal attribution and evaluation. *Journal of Personality and Social Psychology, 33,* 327–337.

Segall, M. H. (1984). More than we need to know about culture, but are afraid not to ask. *Journal of Cross-Cultural Psychology, 15,* 153–162.

Smith, M. B. (1979). Attitudes, values, and selfhood. In *Proceedings of the Nebraska*

Symposium on Motivation (pp. 305–350). Lincoln: University of Nebraska Press.

Sobal, J., & Stunkard, A. J. (1989). Socioeconomic status and obesity: A review of the literature. *Psychological Bulletin, 105,* 260–275.

Sue, S. (1988). Psychotherapeutic services for ethnic minorities: Two decades of research findings. *American Psychologist, 43,* 301–308.

Sue, S., & Zane, N. (1987). The role of culture and cultural technique in psychotherapy: A critique and reformulation. *American Psychologist, 42,* 37–45.

Torrey, E. F. (1972). *The mind game: Witch doctors and psychiatrists.* New York: Emerson Hall.

Triandis, H. (1989). The self and social behavior in differing cultural contexts. *Psychology Review, 96,* 506–520.

Triandis, H., Bontempo, R., Betancourt, H., Bond, M., Leung, K., Brenes, A., Georgas, J., Hui, C. H., Marin, G., Setiadi, B., Sinha, J. B. P., Verma, J., Spangenberg, J., Touzard, H., & de Montmollin, G. (1986). The measurement of the etic aspects of individualism and collectivism across cultures. *Australian Journal of Psychology, 38,* 257–267.

Triandis, H., Bontempo, R., Villareal, M. J., Asai, M., & Lucca, N. (1988). Individualism and collectivism: Cross-cultural perspectives on self-ingroup relationships. *Journal of Personality and Social Psychology, 54,* 323–338.

Triandis, H., Lambert, W., Berry, J., Lonner, W., Heron, A., Brislin, R., & Draguns, J. (Eds.). (1980). *Handbook of cross-cultural psychology: Vols. 1–6.* Boston: Allyn & Bacon.

Vega, W. A., Kolody, B., & Warheit, G. (1985). Psychoneuroses among Mexican Americans and other Whites: Prevalence and caseness. *American Journal of Public Health, 75,* 523–527.

Weiner, B. (1986). *An attribution theory of motivation and emotion.* New York: Springer-Verlag.

Weiner, B., & Kukla, A. (1970). An attributional analysis of achievement motivation. *Journal of Personality and Social Psychology, 15,* 1–20.

Weiner, B., & Peter, N. (1973). A cognitive developmental analysis of achievement and moral judgments. *Developmental Psychology, 9,* 290–309.

Wundt, W. (1921). *Völkerpsychologie: Vols. 1–10.* Leipzig, Germany: Alfred Kroner Verlag.

Zuckerman, M. (1990). Some dubious premises in research and theory on racial differences: Scientific, social, and ethical issues. *American Psychologist, 45,* 1927–1303.

5. Problems in the Study of the Interplay between Science and Culture

David Ingleby

. . . So we tried it with every adjustment of the microscope known to man. With only one of them did I see anything but blackness or the familiar lacteal opacity, and that time I saw, to my pleasure and amazement, a variegated constellation of flecks, specks and dots. These I hastily drew. The instructor, noting my activity, came back from an adjoining desk, a smile on his lips and his eyebrows high in hope. He looked at my cell drawing. "What's that?" he demanded, with a hint of a squeal in his voice. "That's what I saw," I said. "You didn't, you didn't, you didn't!" he screamed, losing control of his temper instantly, and he bent over and squinted into the microscope. His head snapped up. "That's your eye!" he shouted. "You've fixed the lens so that it reflects! You've drawn your eye!"

from James Thurber, "University Days" (1965, p. 257)

ETHNOCENTRISM AND PSYCHOLOGY

The problem I wish to discuss in this paper is: how is it possible to use psychological methods to illuminate cultural differences, when psychology itself is so heavily bound up with one particular culture? That is, how can there be a cross-cultural psychology which is not ethnocentric—which does not leave us, like the young James Thurber, staring down the microscope at a reflection of ourselves?

The problem of ethnocentrism has, of course, long been recognised—but far more acutely by anthropologists than by psychologists. The former tend to play it up; after all, if there *were* no great gulf separating our own from other cultures, anthropology would hardly be worth doing. Ever since the culture-and-personality school

Reprinted by permission of the author and Tilburg University Press from *The Investigation of Culture: Current Issues in Cultural Psychology* © 1990 Tilburg University Press.

of Kardiner (1945), anthropologists have tended to look askance at the activities of their psychologist colleagues. Psychologists, in contrast, have tended to play down the problem of ethnocentrism — perhaps because they perceive the threat it poses to their activities.

Of course, cross-cultural psychology takes as its very point of departure the notion that members of other cultures might differ psychologically in interesting ways from ourselves. To this extent, it cannot be accused of making universalist assumptions, because it is precisely such assumptions which it sets out to put to the test.

The problem, however, lies on another level. When it tries to test these assumptions, cross-cultural psychology usually applies methods of observation and measurement which have been developed within its own (industrially advanced, western) societies. The ethnocentricity of these methods *themselves* is not usually considered to be worth worrying about. After all (so the reasoning goes), they are merely tools for collecting data — tools, indeed, which have been specially designed to be more objective than the impressionistic, subjective methods which anthropologists are fond of using. Selective they may be, but that is both inevitable and desirable: the astronomer's telescope and the biologist's microscope are also selective (so the argument continues) — but only by choosing not to observe everything at once can one succeed in observing anything at all.

This view of data gathering, however, is bound up with a philosophy of science which in the natural sciences has long been abandoned. According to this view — which I shall refer to as "naïve empiricism" — the relation between science and its object is one of objective detachment: the fact that both psychology and the people it studies are cultural products is thus not a particular source of embarrassment. Even Karl Popper, however — perhaps the last and greatest of the empiricist philosophers — opened a breach in this notion of detached observation, when he conceded that all observations are necessarily "theory-laden."

After Popper, the "post-empiricist" view of science — the approach pioneered by such philosophers as Lakatos and Musgrave (1970), Kuhn (1970), and Hesse (1980) — turned this concession into the starting-point for their whole programme. On this view, scientific theories are developed within "paradigms" or "research programmes" containing fundamental presuppositions which are not themselves put to the test. This "hard core" determines the heuristic which allows a certain domain of reality to be interrogated — but it cannot, so to speak, pull itself up by its own bootstraps, i.e., seek support for itself in the data which it generates. It can, according to Lakatos, claim to be more successful than other programmes, but not in terms of how faithfully it mirrors reality. For scientific methods do not "mirror" anything—they "construct" or "produce" a particular truth. The form this truth takes may well be empirically *constrained,* but it can never be completely empirically *determined.* The aim of the naïve empiricist was to let the facts "speak for themselves"—but facts are silent: they can only speak with the voice that the scientist gives to them.

Even to the most hard-boiled experimental psychologists, this position is hardly new, but I suggest its implications have not yet been fully taken to heart. The notion of a firm separation between subject and object is still sacred to psychologists. Yet if we take seriously the notion of scientific methods as constructing truths, we have to admit that psychological procedures influence the reality they set out to observe in at least two fundamental ways. Firstly, they set up a situation in a particular way, in order to make observation possible: just like the biologist who, in fixing and staining cells on a slide, fundamentally alters the object being studied. A start was made in studying this phenomenon in the work on experimenter effects during the 1970s, but this work has had surprisingly limited influence (see, however, Elbers, 1986, for an application to Piagetian conservation experiments). Secondly, because of the widespread influence that psychological theories and practices have already had in the developed countries, psychology has to a large extent "contaminated" its own object. If the individuals it studies largely conform to its expectations, this is in part because intensive effort has been devoted to making them do so. The psychologist, therefore, is involved up to the hilt in influencing the reality he or she studies.

Yet the traffic between subject and object is, in fact, two-way: for psychologists themselves are formed by the society upon which they make their observations. There is not much point in trying to decide in which direction the influence is more important—whether we should see psychology as a cultural product, or culture as produced by psychology. The fact is—and there is no point in trying to hide the fact or being ashamed of it—psychological ways of seeing and doing stand at the very centre of our culture: perhaps no other science is so quintessentially "modern," in its stress on the individual, on the importance of constructively solving problems, on rationality, on gaining control over oneself and nature, and so forth. Psychology as a science is thus deeply entangled with its own object, the inhabitants of the modern western world. The question is, can it disentangle itself sufficiently in order to open up to us the reality of *other* cultures?

In order to deal with this question, I shall first try to outline the different ways in which psychology can be regarded as culturally embedded. I shall start by using a very simple division: a) psychology viewed as *ideas;* b) psychology viewed as *practices;* c) psychology viewed as a combination of *both.* Finally, I shall examine the consequences of these different forms of "embedding" for the possibility of a non-ethnocentric cross-cultural psychology.

HOW IS PSYCHOLOGY EMBEDDED IN ITS OWN CULTURE?

Curiously enough, it is only in the last two decades (since that fateful year 1968) that the above question has been given serious attention—and then only by critics of psychology, rather than those within the mainstream. Why should this be? The answer lies, I think, within the "professional ideology" of psychology itself. Since psychology sought to be a truly modern, authoritative source of information on how to tackle human problems, it modelled its self-image on current notions of science—predominately of the naïve empiricist sort referred to above. These implied that psychology ought to be detached, value-free, presuppositionless, and purely technical (as opposed to moral) in its concerns. The psychologist posed as a sort of visitor from outer space, unbiased by the myths of common sense, unfettered by religion, morality or politics, and unflinching in the face of emotion. That the psychologist underneath the white coat might be an ordinary human being was an admission that would have completely punctured this facade. (The availability of computers from the 1960s onwards provided psychologists with another prop to reinforce this charade: the need for human judgement in psychology appeared to have been all but eliminated—psychologists simply relayed to the public what the computer had "told" them.)

It was precisely the cultural *detachment* of psychology which was supposed to provide it with authority: therefore, any suggestion that it was embedded *within* a culture was tantamount to denying this authority. For this reason, I suggest, those who ventured this claim were almost by definition critics of the profession.

To condense these twenty years of critical work into a few paragraphs, I will divide it (oversimplifying, of course) into two phases. In the first of these, criticism of *theory* predominated; in the second, criticism of *practice.*

The analyses of the cultural significance of psychological *ideas* which were circulating around 1968 mostly took as their starting-point the Marxist notion of "ideology critique." Psychological notions were seen as a form of "false consciousness"—as myths justifying the *status quo* and thus serving the interests of those in power. Criticism of psychology amounted to an attack on its truthfulness—an exposure of errors, distortions, biases or (if you were lucky enough to find them) downright *lies.* Psychology was thus placed in its cultural context via a functionalist type of analysis, adapted from the Marxist analysis of religion. Psychologists did not necessary *invent* the myths that sustained social inequality and exploitation—but they refined and perfected them.

The easiest target for this kind of analysis were reductionistic biological theories with an obvious eugenic or fascist lineage, such as those which ascribed class, race and sex differences, or crime and deviance, to genetic causes. But this left most of psychology unscathed: in fact, it was psychologists who had invented the alternatives to these theories! Another line of criticism therefore dealt with environmentalist psychological theories, accusing them of "blaming the victim" by locating psychological dispositions in the individual, and seeking no further than the early childhood environment or face-to-face interactions for the determinants of behaviour. Feminist as well as Marxist critiques concentrated on the individualism of psychology, its disregard for the historical and political context—its reinforcement of the dominant "one-dimensional" culture. The theories were seen as self-fulfilling prophecies: attachment theory, for example, by *seeing* the mother as responsible for the child's future destiny, in fact *made* her responsible for it. Not only critical psychologists joined in this attack: the sociologist Peter Berger (1965) analysed psychoanalysis as a cultural device for making sense of life in exclusively individual terms, while the historian Christopher Lasch (1977) complained about the way psychology had undermined our traditional cultural patterns of self-understanding.

However, ideology critique was soon to find its days were numbered, and authors such as Ingleby (1970) hardly had a chance to grow comfortably middle-aged before they were attacked for being part of the problem, rather than part of the solution. The new wind of criticism came from France, under the inspiration of Foucault and the post-structuralists. According to this view, ideology critique was an inadequate way of understanding the political and cultural dimensions of psychology, because it only concentrated on the parts which were "untrue": it left the psychologists whose theories could not be shown to contain errors or biases free to cherish the illusion that their thinking somehow stood *outside* history and politics. Moreover, it failed to pay sufficient attention to the direct, practical influence which psychologists had on the day-to-day management of our lives, in schools, hospitals, factories, shops and at home.

The followers of Foucault proposed instead to analyse psychology as an apparatus of social regulation and management. Foucault, who himself had borrowed this idea from Canquilhem's analysis of biology, investigated the historical roots of the social sciences: the origin of the professionalised, scientific welfare state lay in the "bio-politics" of 18th and 19th century Europe—the measures taken to investigate and regulate health, reproduction and behaviour. Social science was born out of demographic and epidemiological studies undertaken from these managerial motives: psychology, in particular, arose as a set of interventions to deal with methods of social regulation (sorting, grading, training, resocialising) for which traditional methods were no longer effective. Increasingly, psychology came to set the agenda for its own interventions, telling the politicians, educators, judges and industrialists what the "real problems" were.

According to this view, psychology produces its object in two ways. Firstly, in the epistemological sense of providing a perceptual and conceptual grid whereby the object is rendered visible. Secondly, in the concrete sense of shaping hearts and minds through practical interventions aimed at family life, education, health care, law, industry and so on. These two senses are not easy to distinguish, because the epistemological "grids" are closely linked with practical interventions (think of the therapeutic session, the IQ test, the developmental assessment, and so on). Thus, psychology does not simply—as the ideology critics had maintained—"distort" reality: it actually *creates* it. In this vein, Donzelot's (1980) history of the family set out to show how the modern family is virtually the product of the various professions that have set out to "police" it (i.e., to manage and regulate it).

Thanks to the French influence, then, a way of analysing the cultural embeddedness of psychology came to dominate from around 1975 which was apparently quite at loggerheads with the earlier ideology critique. In the new approach, far more emphasis was laid on concrete practices than on theoretical ideas. Indeed, the latter tended to be dismissed as merely the icing on the cake. Donzelot, for example, wrote as if psychoanalysis was the undisputed paradigm for interventions in family life and child development: it is not, of course—but for Donzelot the subtle distinctions between different psychological theories were so unimportant that the mistake did not really matter.

Yet such a split between theory and practice is ultimately impossible to maintain. Indeed, ideology critique on the level of abstract ideas alone is a travesty of a Marxist approach: the Marxist analyses of medicine put forward by, say Navarro (1977) and Figlio (1982) put just as much emphasis on practice as any post-structuralist French work has done. Conversely, to study practices in isolation from the *theoretical* discourses which inform them is a travesty of Foucault's approach, in which the notion of "power/knowledge" as a *unitary* phenomenon stands central. All this suggests that the contrast between "abstract" Marxist approaches and "concrete" Foucaultian ones is erroneous; the cultural embeddedness of psychology has to be analysed on *both* a theoretical *and* a practical level.

What do we learn from such an analysis? One theme that emerges is that the role which psychology plays in regulating the lives of individuals resembles closely that which *religion* formerly played. It is a cliché to say that psychologists are the priests of today—but it is also, in several ways, literally true. Formerly, religion was an absolutely central part of European culture; it is no coincidence that Bishop and Knight are lined up next to King and Queen on the chessboard, for church and state were intimately linked. The church exercised its power on three levels: through concrete *institutions* such as schools, universities and hospitals; through *ideas*—theological and commonplace; and through *practices,* such as the confessional or the discipline of regular devotional services.

On each of these three levels, psychology has taken over from religion. (It has also won ground from medicine and law, though these pillars of society are very much still standing.) In accordance with Max Weber's notion of "secularisation," the type of reasoning psychologists use is different from that of priests: they use an instrumental rationality instead of a moral or transcendental one, and rest their claims on empirical "proof" rather than biblical or papal authority. However, the authority psychology exercises remains curiously *irrational:* the devotion it elicits, from practitioners as well as clients, is sometimes every bit as superstitious — not to say fanatical — as that formerly enjoyed by the church. This suggests that Weber's thesis needs to be modified: religion may have been replaced by science, but in the process science has been turned into a religion.

It is in this light that we must view the naïve empiricist philosophy of science discussed above. The notion that scientific theories were grounded exclusively on objective data gave the theories the kind of absolute authority formerly enjoyed by the bible or the Pope. In contrast, a genuinely "scientific" attitude would adopt a permanently sceptical attitude to knowledge, regarding scientific theories as creative conjectures which at best are *compatible* with "the data." On this view, both religious and naïve-empiricist approaches represent a wishful striving for a type of certainty which human knowledge by nature lacks.

However, it would be wrong to see psychology as simply performing old tasks in a new way. In important respects, it has changed the nature of the problems to which solutions are sought. We may list a number of obvious changes. Firstly, the range of problems catered for has been expanded. In particular, the domain of the personal, of "inner space," has been enlarged. In its regulation of family life, the church emphasised "objective" matters such as procreation and moral standards: the medical profession concentrated on physical well-being. Psychological interventions in the family, however, created the new category of *mental* hygiene and the notion of a "mentally healthy" environment. It problematised relationships and the emotional, as opposed to purely physical or moral, nurture of the child (see Van Berkel, 1990). New topics such as the improving of intelligence and the prevention of delinquency were placed on the agenda.

Secondly, the concept of a "problem" has itself been changed. Medical treatment is based on a dichotomy between sickness and health: one consults a doctor only in connection with an actual symptom. Psychologists, however, — beginning with Freud — have placed "having a problem" on a continuum with "normality." In keeping with the preventive goals of the early mental health movements, more attention is in fact devoted to *potential* problems than to actual ones. Because everyone is "at risk" for something, this means that we are *all* clients of psychology, *all the time.* And unlike the doctor, who has nothing to do when the sickness is cured, the psychologist is on duty all the time.

Thirdly, the nature of professional power has changed. Both the priest and the doctor exerted an authoritarian, hierarchical power in relation to those they dealt with. Psychologists, however, have pioneered the notion of a *partnership,* in which the active contribution of the client is vital. (Psychotherapy with an unmotivated client, or — worse still — one who has been forced to undergo it, is a nonstarter.) Psychologists are thus able to present themselves as furthering the "self-fulfilment" of the individuals they treat, or the readers they inform. Whereas the patient in traditional medicine was passive, the consumer of psychology — whether receiving therapy or studying psychology books and magazines — takes an active role. Psychological interventions in the sacred arena of family life, in fact, could take place on no other basis than a partnership. The psychologist lacked the hierarchical status of the priest, doctor or judge. In matters of child-rearing, for example, the psychologist is mostly impotent to interfere with the power of parents to do what they like: he or she has to rely on friendly, rational persuasion to encourage them to follow the advice given. The client, or reader, is addressed as an autonomous fellow-citizen and given scientific insight, not normative prescriptions (or so it seems). Furthermore, psychology encourages its consumers to identify with it, and construct their *own* relationships on such a rational, democratic basis: it encourages "child-centred" approaches to the care and education of the young, "client-centred" forms of treatment for problems, and a "human relations" approach in industry. All these approaches in fact exercise considerable power over their subjects; but it is power of a type which is extremely hard to discern and analyse (see Davis, 1988).

Fourthly, the goal of interventions has changed. Psychology aims to change individuals, rather than the circumstances in which they live: in this, it resembles church, state and the medical profession. However, it aims to bring about a particular *kind* of change — a change of mind, rather than merely of behaviour or symptoms. This was of course also a goal of the church, but there are important differences as well as similarities in the way psychology tries to achieve it. Donzelot refers to this as "the regulation of images": a change in the way a person *construes* his or her situation. Of course, this has behavioural consequences, but the way these have to be brought about is through "insight," otherwise they are not lasting. (Traditional behaviourists, who took over much of the disciplinarian ethic of the 19th century, seem to deny the importance of insight: however, in order to survive the criticisms of humanists and to make their product saleable in the liberal culture of today, they have been forced to water down their creed considerably.)

Fifthly, the type of logic or argumentation used has changed. As mentioned above, the predominately moral discourse of the church and the law has given way to a means-end or instrumental form of rationality. The priest talked about good and evil: the psychologist, or doctor, discusses what is "good for you" or "bad for you." The pros and cons of different ways of living are debated in terms of the probability that they will lead to a desired end state, not in terms of their desirability in themselves. Van Nijnatten (1986), in his study of child-protection dossiers from 1930 and 1975, illustrates this change in the dominant form of argumentation. Before "psychologi-sation," children could be described as wayward, mothers as irrespon-sible, and fathers as lazy. Today, court reports refer to socially mal-adjusted children, mothers with role conflicts, and fathers with achievement-motivation deficiency. In advice on relationships or child-rearing, increasing emphasis is laid on *skills*—again, a typi-cally instrumental concept.

This shift in justificatory logic is not confined to psychologists, but is to be found throughout the culture. According to Billig (1987), "common sense has the structure of an argument" (a statement which has intriguing parallels with Lacan's "the unconscious is structured like a language"). If this is so, then the replacement of moral by instrumental reasoning is a profound shift in the nature of common sense.

Finally, psychology has focussed particular attention on women. Many of the interventions directed at the family are channelled via the wife or mother: women seek psychological help more often (Chesler, 1974), are more willing to discuss problems (O'Brien, 1988), and are much more involved in child-rearing than men. A woman, rather than a man, is particularly likely to be on the receiv-ing end of psychological advice—at least if it concerns the personal sphere. Van Berkel (1990) points out that the church's advice to parents was directed just as much to fathers as to mothers, if not more so: psychologists, however, (as well as doctors) have formed a special "alliance" (as Donzelot puts it) with the mother. We should not, therefore, regard the cultural influence of psychology as gender-neutral.

Here, then, are six respects in which psychology represents new ways of dealing with problems and new forms of cultural self-consciousness. The list is, of course, incomplete and somewhat arbitrary: nevertheless, it has shown that psychology is intimately related, on many levels, to recent cultural developments. The word "intimately" is particularly appropriate because of all scientific professions, psychology is the one which brings itself closest to the client or consumer: if psychologists are "partners" of the laity, the latter are themselves partly involved in constructing it. For this reason I would hesitate to say that psychology has *caused* the cultural transformations described above. No doubt there are deeper historical forces at work — but I hope enough has been said to justify my contention that psychological ways of seeing and doing stand at the very centre of our culture.

IMPLICATIONS FOR
CROSS-CULTURAL PSYCHOLOGY

If the thrust of my argument is correct, then there are indeed serious problems about using ready-made psychological tools to investigate members of other cultures — because these tools have been fashioned to suit the members of our own culture. Psychologists who adhere to the strict subject-object distinction which underlies naïve empiricism do not, of course, recognise these problems. They will argue that there is no *need* for the psychologist to be attuned to the culture he or she studies. After all (they will say), a digital thermometer may be a typical western invention, but it works just as well in the Sahara as in New York City: why should not the same be true of the WISC [Wechsler Intelligence Scale for Children] or the MMPI [Minnesota Multiphasic Personality Inventory]?

This, however, is to oversimplify the nature of the operations involved in making psychological observations. These operations are typically highly elaborate ones, drawing on complex cultural resources for the interpretation of what people say and do, and making profound — if implicit — assumptions about the cultural background of the behaviour being studied. We can illustrate this with examples from two fields: mental welfare and cognitive development.

In the field of *mental welfare,* cross-cultural studies of child-rearing practices and psychological well-being tend to be carried out against a background of normative assumptions based on modern western culture. For example, well-meaning researchers attempting to assess the psychic damage inflicted on the development of children by poverty and military conflict in the Third World routinely utilise measures of developmental disturbance which presuppose western cultural patterns. Yet, as I have argued elsewhere (Ingleby, 1989), we learn very little about the psychological predicament of Brazilian street children by studying their scores on the Ainsworth Strange Situation Test—a measuring device which presupposes a strict distinction between "familiar" figures and "strange" ones. Such a distinction is central to our child-rearing practices, because in the course of industrial modernisation a widening gulf has arisen between the segregated atmosphere of "home" and the "outside world" of work and the public sphere. To say this is not to argue that Brazilian street children are happy: it simply means that one cannot measure the development of a child who lacks the modern western concept of home in terms of the anxiety they experience (or fail to experience) in the presence of strangers. The child is a "cultural invention," in the words of William Kessen (1983), and our methodology must adapt to the different ways in which childhood is invented in different cultures.

As it happens, the same objection may well apply to the use of standard developmental and clinical methods *within* modern western societies—for these societies are by no means culturally homogeneous. This applies in particular when the group being tested deviates from the white, middle-class cultural norms which these methods typically presuppose. The quality of mother-infant interaction, for example, is frequently measured in terms of the degree of maternal responsiveness to the child's demands. Yet the "child-centered" approach to child-rearing which this presupposes is essentially a recent middle-class creation: in terms of working-class culture, it is questionable whether a high degree of maternal responsiveness is desirable, necessary or even practicable.

In the field of *cognitive development,* the pitfalls of transferring tests to a situation in which they may not be "ecologically valid" are even more familiar—thanks largely to the controversy in the 1970s around IQ tests and "culture-fairness." Cole and Means (1981) have explored at length the mistaken inferences which may be drawn from comparative studies which attempt to apply the "same" test in different cultures. The chances that the test is in fact the "same" are, according to these authors, slight! A substantial research tradition, in which Michael Cole and his associates have played a central part, has shown how tests are sensitive to the way in which cognitive skills are culturally embedded in everyday practices (see Laboratory of Comparative Human Cognition, 1983).

Moreover, western tests of intelligence tend to emphasise the types of reasoning (decontextualised, "logical") which are valued in our own culture: they ignore other ways in which people can be astute or foolish. They tend to measure the achievement of other groups in terms of how far they come up to our norms: "difference" is routinely presented as "deficit." A devastating attack on this attitude was delivered by Labov (1970), with his notion of "the functional equivalence of languages" and his demonstration that Standard English can in some respects be regarded as more primitive and inefficient than ghetto talk. As long as we only measure achievement in terms of how successfully others approximate to *us,* we will never become aware of the alternative modes of development which other cultures make available to their inmates.

To sum up, standard psychological procedures provide us with a microscope, as it were, down which we gaze at the inhabitants of other cultures. The fact that what we see looks remarkably like ourselves—if somewhat less well-developed—reassures us that the methods are indeed applicable to other cultures: but what we see is, in fact, a *construction* of our own ethnocentric data-gathering procedures—and what we *do not* see, we never worry about. Like James Thurber, we stare down the microscope at a reflection of ourselves.

Can we ever fix the lens of psychology to reveal to us something other than our own cultural preconceptions? Must one, when confronted with a cultural gulf, simply throw up one's hands in despair and walk away? This would be the answer of a strict relativist such as Winch (1964), who argued that members of a given culture can only be understood in terms of the self-understanding of the culture itself. However, this approach is too dogmatic, as MacIntyre (1971) has argued: it leaves cultures hermetically sealed-off from each other and inaccessible to new perspectives. The answer would seem to lie in a method of successive approximations (something like the classic hermeneutic circle), in which one enters a *dialogue* with one's subjects and attempts to build discursive bridges from one's own culture to theirs. (For psychologists, a more familiar notion is perhaps Piaget's concept of "equilibration": when attempts to "assimilate" the distant culture to our own fail, we must "accommodate" our own cognitive structures appropriately.) However, the development of a culture sensitive methodology has until now been pioneered chiefly by anthropologists (e.g., Geertz, 1973) and sociologists (e.g., Glaser & Strauss, 1968), who have explicitly set out to deal with alien mentalities.

Nevertheless, psychological methods which are capable of being adapted to different cultures have, to a certain extent, already been developed in the context of "social-contextualist" theoretical approaches (Ingleby, 1986). In the most radical of these approaches (the Soviet cultural-historical approach of Vygotsky, post-structuralism, and social constructionism), the psychological individual is not seen as a pre-given entity, different aspects of which develop faster or slower according to the degree to which the cultural environment facilitates them. Rather, the very *form* which individuality takes is seen as culturally given. In these terms, it is not sufficient to reassure oneself that one's measures of emotional or cognitive development are ecologically valid (cf. the examples just given): the very *distinction* between emotion and cognition may be one which the culture in question does not recognise. This is likely to be the case in cultures which do not take the characteristically western dualism of mind and body as their ontological starting-point. More fundamentally still, a culture which does not embody a dualistic view of "individual" and "society" will have little use for the very category of "psychological states": anthropologists, indeed, report the existence of cultures in which such essentially "psychological" phenomena as emotions are experienced as predicates of situations rather than individuals (see Harré et al., 1985), and in which a "sense of self" may be virtually absent (Heelas & Lock, 1981).

Cultural relativity will always pose a challenge to psychological theory, but it is clear (Ingleby & Nossent, 1986) that a social-contextualist approach can more readily meet this challenge than the strongly dualistic approaches which up to now have dominated western psychology. There are signs that this domination may not be for all time. In developmental psychology, more attention is currently being paid to the culturally determined "frames" or "formats" (Bradley, 1989) which structure development from the very moment of birth. In the study of cognition—despite a simultaneous revival of neurologically-based approaches—there is increasing awareness of the way in which even the most elementary cognitive operations are embedded in a context of everyday cultural practices (Light, 1986). More attention to cross-cultural issues can only further the development of these social-contextualist approaches in psychology.

REFERENCES

Berger, P. (1965). Toward a sociological understanding of psychoanalysis. *Social Research, 32,* 26–41.

Billig, M. (1987). *Arguing and thinking: A rhetorical approach to social psychology.* Cambridge: Cambridge University Press.

Bradley, B. (1989). *Visions of infancy: A critical introduction to child psychology.* Oxford: Polity Press.

Chesler, P. (1974). *Women and madness.* London: Allen Lane.

Cole, M., & Means, B. (1981). *Comparative studies of how people think.* Cambridge, MA: Harvard University Press.

Davis, K. (1988). *Power under the microscope: Toward a grounded theory of gender relations in medical encounters.* Dordrecht: Foris Publications.

Donzelot, J. (1980). *The policing of families.* New York: Pantheon.

Elbers, E. (1986). Interaction and instruction in the conservation experiment. *European Journal of Psychology of Education, 1,* 77–89.

Figlio, K. (1982). How does illness mediate social relations? In P. Wright & A. Treacher (Eds.), *The problem of medical knowledge* (pp. 174–224). Edinburgh: Edinburgh University Press.

Geertz, C. (1973). *The interpretation of cultures: Selected essays.* New York: Basic Books.

Glaser, B. G., & Strauss, A. L. (1968). *The discovery of grounded theory.* London: Weidenfeld & Nicholson.

Harré, R., Clarke, D., & De Carlo, N. (1985). *Motives and mechanisms: An introduction to the psychology of action.* London: Methuen.

Heelas, P., & Lock, A. (1981). *Indigenous psychologies: The anthropology of the self.* London: Academic Press.

Hesse, M. B. (1980). *Revolutions and reconstruction in the philosophy of science.* Sussex: The Harvester Press.

Ingleby, D. (1970). Ideology and the human sciences. *The Human Context, 2,* 159–187.

———. (1986). Development in social context. In M. Richards & P. Light (Eds.), *Children of social worlds* (pp. 297–317). Oxford: Polity Press.

———. (1989). Critical psychology in relation to political repression and violence. *International Journal of Mental Health, 17,* 16–24.

Ingleby, D., & Nossent S. (1986). Cognitieve ontwikkeling en historische psychologie. In H. F. M. Peeters & F. J. Mönks (Eds.), *De menselijke levensloop in historisch perspectief* (pp. 122–138). Assen: Van Gorcum.

Kardiner, A. (1945). *Psychological frontiers of society*. New York: Columbia University Press.

Kessen, W. (1983). The American child and other cultural inventions. In F. Kessen & A. Siegel (Eds.), *The child and other cultural inventions* (pp. 261–270). New York: Praeger.

Kuhn, T. (1970). *The structure of scientific revolutions*. Chicago: University of Chicago Press.

Laboratory of Comparative Human Cognition (1983). Culture and cognitive development. In P. H. Mussen (Ed.), *Handbook of child psychology* (4th ed., Vol. 1, pp. 295–356). New York: Wiley.

Labov, W. (1970). *The study of non-standard English*. Champaign, IL: National Council of Teachers of English.

Lakatos, I., & Musgrave, A. (1970). *Criticism and the growth of knowledge*. Cambridge: Cambridge University Press.

Lasch, C. (1977). *Haven in a heartless world: The family besieged*. New York: Basic Books.

Light, P. (1986). Context, conservation and conversation. In M. Richards & P. Light (Eds.), *Children of social worlds* (pp. 170–190). Oxford: Polity Press.

MacIntyre, A. (1971). *Against the self-images of the age*. London: Duckworth.

Navarro, V. (1977). *Medicine under capitalism*. London: Croom Helm.

O'Brien, M. (1988). Men and fathers in therapy. *Journal of Family Therapy, 10*, 109–123.

Thurber, J. (1965). University days, from *The Thurber Carnival*. Harmondsworth: Penguin Books.

Van Berkel, D. (1990). *Moeders tussen zielzorg en psychohygiëne*. Assen: Van Gorcum.

Van Nijnatten, C. (1986). *Moeder Justitia en haar kinderen*. Lisse: Swets & Zeitlinger.

Winch, P. (1964). Understanding a primitive society. *American Philosophical Quarterly, 1*, 307–324.

B. NATURE OF INQUIRY: WHOSE QUESTIONS? WHOSE ANSWERS?

The kinds of questions that get asked and the route the researcher takes to get answers is, in most of the social sciences, at the heart of current debates over epistemology (the nature of knowledge) and methodology (approaches to inquiry). Nowhere are the debates more lively and profoundly challenging to old scientific paradigms than in the arena claimed by culture and gender theorists, that is, the arena in which the primary questions express a concern over the nature and implications of human differences. At one end of the spectrum are those who search for universals across individuals and across cultures, that is, those who expect to unearth answers about our common humanity and arrive at laws of human behavior; at the other end of the spectrum are those who are interested in human variety and search for ways of describing and understanding individual subjectivities and culture specificity. Broadly speaking, psychology (especially during the positivist era) has been associated with the search for human universals and anthropology with the effort to describe cultural differences. However, when the question becomes how do individuals living in different societies and cultural communities compare on the presumably universal yardsticks of behavior, academic discussion heats up. The recent history of this discussion over strategies of inquiry is in large part the history of the struggle over the question of difference and the problem of comparison.

Whenever psychologists or anthropologists move into cross-cultural comparative studies (whether the comparison be between different culture groups within one society or between cultures in different parts of the world), they face what has come to be known as the emic-etic distinction. In his essay (chapter 6) Gustav Jahoda addresses the common assumption that it is possible to maintain a clear distinction between the emic approach (studying behavior of only one culture from inside the culture) and the etic approach (studying behavior from the outside by examining and comparing many cultures). In the process of examining how researchers have (or have not) applied these two strategies, Jahoda also involves us in the important question of how and when it is appropriate to generalize.

The scientific criteria for "good science"—generalizability and validity—are further taken to task by the feminist psychologist Stephanie Riger in chapter 7. As she forcefully points out, scientific generalizations and scientific truth have been and always will be a matter of who holds the power to define what knowledge claims are valid. If all knowledge is "situated" (Haraway 1988) and some knowledge is "subjugated" (Foucault 1980), then all scientific efforts must be examined first in terms of power differentials. What is the intention of a study—to protect the status quo? to protect the power structure? Who will benefit or who might suffer from the study? If we accept the relativism of knowledge, reality, and truth, how can we arrive at evaluative criteria of research and theory? While juggling these issues, Riger asks whether there can be a feminist methodology that is more sensitive to historical and social context, power, and thus more gender- and culture-fair.

A pessimistic view of research generalizability and validity is presented by Wade Nobles in chapter 8 whose work in the early 1970s was among the first to address structural inequality and its dire effects on research outcomes. By examining various theoretical approaches to the study of the black self-concept, he points out how subject white theorists and researchers can be to selective (mis)perception of people different from themselves and how this in turn leads to interpretive distortion. This is such a serious limitation, Nobles feels, that "we must . . . question whether the researchers' actual presence in the black community is at all warranted."

In Pamela Trotman Reid's essay (chapter 9), we again face the question of both research validity and the validity of commonly applied and studied social categories such as gender and race. Reid asserts that even ideologically based theorists—for example, feminist theorists of the 1970s and 1980s—can be category and culture blind. Early feminists made claims about women's experience of gender as if there were some essential category "woman"; such claims, Reid argues, ignore the confounds of class, race, and culture. "What do we need to know, and what do we need to do," she asks, "to understand and explain the true diversity of women?" This question of Reid echoes the basic questions of deconstructionism: Does any category for grouping people or cultures—such as "woman" or "'American" or "black"—carry any meaning that is valid across all individual members of the group, or is understanding inevitably lodged in individual "subjectivities" and particularities.

We are including in this section a chapter (here chapter 10) from Jamake Highwater's influential book *The Primal Mind* (1980) in which he addresses "vision and reality" from the perspective of Native Americans. Highwater—himself a product of two Native American lineages, the Blackfeet and the Cherokee—rejects the notion that non-Western knowledge is inferior to or more primitive than Western knowledge. In fact, he argues, "perhaps in primal people . . . there survives a precious reservoir of humanity's visionary power." Primal mentality, in which nature is immediately experienced rather than "dubiously abstracted," may lead us further than Western reason in confronting the inevitability of "otherness" while arriving at the visionary position that "we are all related."

REFERENCES

Foucault, M. 1980. *Power/knowledge: Selected interviews and other writings, 1972–1977,* ed. and trans. C. Gordon. New York: Pantheon Books.

Haraway, D. 1988. Situated knowledges: The science question in feminism and the privilege of partial perspective. Feminist Studies 14: 575–99.

Highwater, J. 1980. The primal mind: Vision and reality in Indian America. New York: Harper & Row.

6. In Pursuit of the Emic-Etic Distinction: Can We Ever Capture It?

Gustav Jahoda

The basic dichotomy was first proposed by a linguist, Pike (1954, 1966), and seems to have been introduced into psychology by French (1963). Since then the emic-etic distinction has become part of the conventional wisdom of cross-cultural psychology. With some important exceptions, most of the books in the field mention it, though usually without much detailed discussion (Lloyd, 1972; Brislin et al., 1973; Berry and Dasen, 1974; Serpell, 1976). The general message is that one is faced with a dilemma that must be resolved; unfortunately the means for doing this are never clearly indicated.

Given this concern proclaimed for over a decade, one might expect cross-cultural psychologists to be acutely sensitive to the issue. Thus one would expect them to collect and interpret their data with the emic-etic distinction constantly in mind, and one would look in their research reports for accounts as to how they handled the problem. Yet in fact anyone scanning the research literature over the period is likely to come across at most a few scattered references to the emic-etic issue. The position appears to be this: when cross-cultural psychologists are wearing their theoretical-methodological hats they tend to make ritual emic-etic gestures; having discharged their duty in this manner they turn to getting on with research and forget all about it.

Does this mean that cross-cultural psychologists are acting in a reprehensible way, and we should try to reform ourselves? I think the answer should be a qualified 'no', and the remainder of this paper is an attempt to justify this. In order to do so, it will be necessary to make a careful scrutiny of the way in which the emic-etic distinction

Reprinted by permission of Swets and Zeitlinger B. V. from Y. H. Poortinga, ed., *Basic Problems in Cross-Cultural Psychology* © 1977 Swets and Zeitlinger B. V.

has been conceptualized, beginning with a quotation from French (1963, p. 398):

Pike identifies the emic approach as a structural one. The investigator assumes that human behaviour is patterned, even though the members of the society being studied may not be aware of many units of the structuring. In Pike's view, the goal of the emic approach is to discover and describe the behavioural system in its own terms, identifying not only the structural units but also the structural classes to which they belong.

In contrast, an etic approach can be characterized as an external one. Items of behaviour are examined not in the light of the systems in which they occur, but rather in that of criteria brought to bear on them by the observer. The observer classifies all comparable data into a system which he is creating, using criteria which were in existence before the classification began.

Like most subsequent accounts of the emic-etic contrast, this is highly abstract. What does emerge clearly is the emphasis on structure and system within a culture as distinguishing the emic approach. In fact French states quite explicitly that cross-cultural studies must be etic 'since *all of culture* [1] cannot now be handled as a system which can be studied emically' (1963, p. 398). He offers one concrete illustration relating to weaning, which would have to be studied in terms of the total pattern of mother-child relationships, plus any other relevant aspects within the given culture, in order to qualify as emic. It would seem from all this that the emic approach corresponds more to the habitual research style of anthropologists, and it is therefore useful to look at their stance on the issue.

In so far as anthropologists wish to go beyond the analysis of a particular culture and embark on comparative studies, they face the emic-etic problem. One would therefore imagine them to be more sensitive than psychologists to this issue, and to have devised more effective methods for dealing with it. While this is to some extent true, the general picture is rather different — very complex and hard to summarize. In the first place there are some anthropologists, of whom the most extreme was perhaps the late Evans-Pritchard, who reject generalization altogether. In their view the business of anthropology is to analyze patterns within particular cultures and interpret them within the systems framework of that culture; hence comparative studies aiming at generalizations across cultures are regarded as inappropriate. This might be called the 'emic only' view.

At the opposite extreme there is Murdock who long ago concluded that: 'In anthropology, the initial classificatory task has now been

sub-stantially accomplished in the field of social structures . . .'
(1955, p. 361). In other words, an adequate set of etic units has now
been isolated, and it would follow that the emic-etic dilemma has
been largely resolved. While a majority of anthropologists would
probably dissent from this, the adherents of the 'hologeistic' school
seem to take it for granted. Thus Driver discussing proceedings at a
1970 HRAF Cross-Cultural Research Conference writes as follows:
'Most participants in the conference seemed ready to use etic concepts
whether or not they existed anywhere in the emics of individual
societies. It seems quite obvious to me that the entire history of
science shows a regular and progressive substitution of etic concepts
for culture-bound and language-bound emic ones' (1973, p. 347).

This point of view that there is nothing more to worry about,
probably accounts for the absence of any reference to the emic-etic
issue among psychological writers connected with HRAF-type research (e.g. Lambert and Weisbrod, 1971; Munroe and Munroe,
1975).

In between the opposite poles described, anthropologists do struggle with the problem of comparison, although they do not seem
to conceptualize it very often in terms of the emic-etic distinction.
However, there is one area of great potential interest to psychologists
where the distinction is salient, namely what has come to be known
as 'cognitive anthropology'. In fact one critic (Harris, 1968) discussed the controversy in terms of the dichotomy of 'emicists' versus
'eticists' (cf. also Pelto, 1970). One of the main protagonists of the
new approach, Tyler, states that 'cultures then are not material
phenomena; they are cognitive organizations of material phenomena.
. . . The object of study is not the material phenomena themselves,
but the way they are organized in the minds of men' (1969, p. 3).
This is done by comparing whole systems, superimposing an 'etic
grid' on the emic material, and the units of comparison are then
reduced to certain formal features instead of substantive elements.
The reaction of critics may be typified by the comment of Leach:
'In the pursuit of elegance and formal rigour the more ingenious
practitioners of the art of componential analysis habitually move so
far away from the original ethnography that the whole exercise becomes worthless' (Leach, 1971). What I understand Leach to be
saying is that the emic aspects get lost in the process—the babies
were thrown away and only the bathwater is kept, which is not
helpful for understanding babies.

The object of presenting this excessively condensed sketch of anthropological perspectives is to make two main points. First, among those anthropologists who are aiming at comparative studies, there are those who follow Murdock in believing that the emic-etic problem has been successfully solved, or at least by-passed. Second, among the larger number who accept that there is an important emic-etic dilemma that needs to be resolved, there is no consensus about how it might be done. Is the position any more hopeful in psychology?

There are two psychologists who have not only been prominent in advocating the emic-etic distinction for cross-cultural psychological studies, but have also tried to suggest how this could be implemented in practice. They are Berry (1969) and Triandis (1972), whose views will now be considered in some detail.

Berry shows a table typifying the distinction, which is reproduced below:

Emic approach	*Etic approach*
studies behaviour from within the system.	studies behaviour from a position outside the system.
examines only one culture.	examines many cultures, comparing them.
structure discovered by the analyst.	structure created by the analyst.
criteria are relative to internal characteristics.	criteria are considered absolute or universal.

This is presented as it stands without any comment or exemplification, as though the scheme were self-explanatory. While it may look plausible at first sight, this conceals a number of difficult problems that deserve closer scrutiny. The first point to note is the assumption implicit in the statements that the object of study is a system, including behaviour to be understood in relation to the system. Now if one examines the first pair of statements, their meaning is far from self-evident or even clear. Remembering that Pike, from whose writing they are derived, is a linguist one can readily make sense of them in these terms: e.g. a speaker of English studying the structure of his own language. However, any single culture contains of course many sets of overlapping and interlocking systems at different levels, e.g. linguistic, kinship, political, category, and so on. In the light of this the phrase 'from within the system' is seen to be highly obscure and ambiguous. Moreover, does it mean that the investigator has to be a member of the culture—this is surely unlikely; what, then, does 'a position outside the system' denote? There is an important sense in which anyone who studies a system must be 'outside' it, if not literally then figuratively or he will be incapable of seeing it as a whole. If one takes in this context the anthropologist studying a particular culture by living among the people as a prototype of the 'emic' approach, the inadequacies of this simple dichotomy become apparent; for while the anthropologist tries as far as possible to immerse himself in the culture, he can never become entirely part of it. Furthermore, it is essential for him to maintain at the same time a certain detached objectivity, without which he could not do his work (cf. Middleton, 1970).

Among the other pairs, that about one versus many cultures is unexceptionable. When it comes to the 'discovery' as opposed to the 'creation' of structure, this is a highly contentious matter. The very concept of 'structure' is an exceedingly difficult one (cf. Boudon, 1971); and since the structures referred to are not physical ones like scaffolding, but have to be inferred as underlying certain overt phenomena, there is no easy way to decide that a structure is actually in existence waiting to be discovered. Perhaps more often than not its logical status is that of a construct or model serving as a guide to interpretation. In other words, in relation to social and psychological systems 'structures' are nearly always 'creations', including those put forward by Piaget. Another structuralist, Lévi-Strauss, wrote: "The term 'social structure' has nothing to do with empirical reality but with models built up after it" (1963, p. 279). Taken out of context this might sound self-contradictory, but in his fuller exposition Lévi-Strauss develops the notion that structures of rather different kinds may be found at several levels. The matter cannot be pursued here, yet enough has been said to indicate that the statement about 'discovery' of structure within cultures is perhaps somewhat misleading. The fourth pair of statements, concerning relative versus absolute criteria, is too general to serve as a useful guide.

Berry then goes on to outline an appropriate research strategy, condemning the usual procedure of applying concepts from outside the culture for which he coined the phrase 'imposed etic'. Whilst admitting the need to begin in this way, he suggests a progressive modification of culture-alien concepts until they approximate the indigenous ones. If they share some communality with the imported ones, it then becomes possible to move in the opposite direction and build up a 'derived etic' which, if it can be shown to fit the different behaviour settings, can be used for comparisons. He concluded as follows: 'When all systems which may be compared . . . have been included, then we have achieved a *universal* for that particular behaviour' (p. 124). The terminology here refers to 'systems', but no attempt is made to specify their nature. Psychologists, not excluding cross-cultural ones, tend to be primarily concerned with intra-personal systems rather than socio-cultural ones; yet much of the theoretical argument seems to assume the latter.[2]

This view is confirmed when one gets to the actual concrete examples provided, relating to intelligence and field dependence. With regard to the former Berry is hammering at an open door, and as noted by Lloyd (1972) his conclusions are much the same as those of Vernon (1969) who did not find it necessary to apply the etic-emic distinction. The example of field dependence, an etic concept if ever there was one, is even weaker. There is thus a sharp disparity between the abstract theoretical discussion and the actual examples, which are rather unconvincing.

Berry's (1969) article has been dealt with at some length because he did make strenuous efforts to retain the original meaning of the emic-etic distinction and relate it to the kinds of research cross-cultural psychologists are most concerned with. Triandis (1972) on the other hand focuses mainly on concrete research problems, and is thereby led to dilute the concepts to such an extent that they may be regarded as dispensable.

At the outset he berates the many psychologists using what he calls a pseudo-etic approach, which he characterizes as being in fact an emic one developed in a Western culture and applied without any adaptation. As the discussion proceeds, it becomes evident that Triandis is entirely concerned with psychometric, attitude and similar correlational measures; and it is very doubtful whether the emic-etic distinction is at all appropriate in such a context. Thus in commenting on the work of Irvine (1969) he refers to emic and etic factors, a terminology, it should be noted, not used by Irvine himself. Now by 'emic factors' Triandis means factors relating to emic elements, but even this is a claim that cannot be sustained. About half of the extensive test battery administered by Irvine consisted of ordinary Western tests, and even those specially constructed and standardized on African samples contained mainly Western-type material such as English or mechanical information. The so-called etic and emic factors therefore in essence boil down to factors common to the cultures versus those that were culture-specific; yet even the latter are certainly not 'emic' in any acceptable sense.

Triandis goes on to suggest what he regards as solutions to the emic-etic dilemma, giving as an example a study of his own concerned with social distance. Taking this as an etic universal from the fact that student informants in several cultures understood what it meant, he asked samples of students to produce what they regarded as suitable items; he called this the emic stage of the procedure. The resulting measure was administered in the several cultures, which yielded an assessment of the proportion of variance governed by the different characteristics of the hypothetical stimulus persons. Now is this really a solution to the emic-etic dilemma?

If one accepts the basic systems postulate of definitions of the concept of 'emic', then I think the answer must be negative. This is because the stress of findings is on the description of specific differences; it fails to throw light on either the global social category system within the cultures, or the manner in which such systems are functionally related to patterns of social behaviour. In other words, it would have been necessary to treat the social distance data merely as a first stage, proceeding thereafter to examine the systems within each of the cultures and consider whether common elements could be extracted. Something of the kind was attempted by Mitchell (1957) who used a social distance scale in the Rhodesian Copper Belt. Mitchell then went on to show how the categories elicited served to structure the social behaviour of migrant Africans in towns. A similar procedure employing more informal methods was followed by Mayer (1961) in South Africa, also leading to a specification of the emic system. It might also be mentioned that an effort was subsequently made to arrive at etic concepts useful for understanding and comparing different cultural situations (Mitchell, 1969). While the emic-etic terminology was not employed by these writers, their approach is a closer approximation on the ideal requirements than that of Triandis. It must be concluded that Triandis provides sound methodological advice for cross-cultural psychologists, but it has scant bearing on the emic-etic issue.[3]

When several outstandingly able people have struggled hard to pin down a distinction with only a moderate degree of success, perhaps it is time to ask whether there might be something wrong with it. This has been hinted in his gentle yet incisive way by Price-Williams (1975), in whose book the emic-etic distinction is one of the major themes. He suggests that the sharp dichotomy will need to be softened, and points out that within a framework of the sociology of knowledge all etic systems become emic. Price-Williams' general approach is epitomized by his comments on Berry's (1969) paper:

If we begin with an etic approach category we are *ipso facto* most probably introducing a category which has little or no functional significance to the culture at hand. An emic category has, by definition, to be very much functionally related. Further, the emic category points to a rule-system in that culture, which needs to be teased out by the investigator; this rule-system needs an extensive in-depth intra-culture analysis. At this point the emic-etic distinction becomes confusing, since the rules underlying the emic distinction may not be explicit in the culture. Our detection of it is an etic process. (Price-Williams, 1975, p. 25)

In this passage Price-Williams not only re-emphasizes the systems aspect of the emic-etic distinction, but he also points to the relativity of the distinction which seems to have escaped most other writers. Yet such is the seductiveness of the concept that Price-Williams, far from being prepared to jettison it, gives it great prominence in his book. He also proposes an experimental design involving a series of graduating steps in terms of familiarity, ranging from naturally occurring situations to the standard experiment; and he states that this 'amounts to an emic-etic continuum' (p. 46). The phrasing is cautious, indicating an awareness that the terms are being loosely employed. Moreover, they are not essential to the argument: Cole, who strongly favours this approach, is one of those who have largely ignored the emic-etic debate, not even mentioning it in the textbook of which he is the co-author (Cole and Scribner, 1974).

Cole and, it should be added, Gay are particularly important figures in this respect since they, more than most other cross-cultural psychologists, have been able to immerse themselves in Kpelle culture and stress the 'inside' perspective. Yet they do not seem to have felt the need to conceptualize their theoretical insights in terms of the emic-etic distinction. This suggests that it is even less necessary for the majority of cross-cultural psychologists who generally have neither the opportunity nor the competence to study the systems and structures underlying the behaviour in the cultures in which they work. In so far as the 'system' aspect is an essential core of the emic-etic distinction (otherwise it would merely denote something like 'culture-specific versus non-specific'), this means that it might be regarded as dispensable. For if one drops the systems requirement as unrealistic, what remains are issues that can be subsumed under other headings such as functional equivalence or translation problems.

Does it follow from this that the emic-etic distinction should just be assigned to the limbo of useless intellectual limber? As far as most of the active areas of cross-cultural psychological research are concerned, such as perception, developmental psychology and probably also studies of abilities and attitudes, no great loss would result in my view if we were to do this. On the other hand there are probably two main exceptions, one being the linguistic context within which the concepts originated, including the study of category systems. This may be illustrated by the work of Moerman (1972) on Lue (a dialect of Thai) conversation. His analysis served the dual purpose of relating the behaviour to emic rules and roles as well as extracting some etic features of conversation in general; the emic-etic terminology, incidentally, was not employed by Moerman but 'imposed' by me.

The other possible exception where the distinction might be important related to areas of social life where the interests of psychologists, sociologists and anthropologists overlap. In such areas there is a danger that psychologists might overlook the social-structural features of the problem and operate with pseudo-universals. An example would be incest, which far from being a simple universal varies widely across cultures. It is not just a matter of differing social structures and systems of descent, but psychological reactions also vary and the notorious 'grisly horror' is not universal. The attention to the nature of indigenous system entailed in the emic-etic distinction might avoid some crude errors in such a field. However, it could equally well be argued that a competent cross-cultural psychologist would not go astray in this manner, whether or not he were concerned with the emic-etic distinction.

Lastly, when it comes to the postulated sequence of moving from etic via emic to derived etic concepts, this appears to me at present as little more than a pipe-dream. As was indicated earlier, anthropologists have largely failed to put any such strategy to practical use; and no psychologist appears to me to have adequately demonstrated how it could be done in our field. The general answer to the question in the title is therefore, in my view, negative. The pursuit of the emic-etic distinction appears to me a little like the alchemists' search for the philosopher's stone. As in that case, perhaps an entirely new way of transmuting emic into etic will be found in future, which we cannot even imagine now. Meantime we should cease to exhort others to engage in a somewhat unprofitable enterprise, to which we ourselves pay mainly lip service.

NOTES

1. Italics in the original.
2. In fairness it should be mentioned that Berry (1975) is in fact one of the very few cross-cultural psychologists who has formulated and to some extent tested an eco-cultural systems model.
3. It is curious that Triandis (1972, p. 39) discusses what seems to be a truly emic concept, namely 'philotimos', in another section!

REFERENCES

Berry, J. W., On cross-cultural comparability. *International Journal of Psychology,* 1969, 4, pp. 119–128.

———, An ecological approach to cross-cultural psychology, *Nederlands Tijdschrift voor de Psychologie,* 1975, 30, pp. 51–84.

———, and Dasen, P. R., *Culture and Cognition.* London, Methuen, 1974.

Boudon, R., *The Uses of Structuralism.* London, Heinemann, 1971.

Brislin, R. W., Lonner, W. J., and Thorndike, R. M., *Cross-Cultural Research Methods.* New York, Wiley, 1973.

Cole, M., and Scribner, S., *Culture and Thought.* New York, Wiley, 1974.

Driver, H. E., Cross-cultural studies. In: Honigman, J. J. (ed.), *Handbook of Social and Cultural Anthropology.* Chicago, Rand McNally, 1973.

French, D., The relationship of anthropology to studies in perception and cognition. In: Koch, S. (ed.), *Psychology: A Study of a Science,* Vol. 6, New York, McGraw-Hill, 1963.

Harris, M., *The Rise of Anthropological Theory.* New York, Crowell, 1968.

Irvine, S. H., Factor analysis of African abilities and attainments. *Psychological Bulletin,* 1969, 71, pp. 20–32.

Lambert, W. W., and Weisbrod, R., *Comparative Perspectives in Social Psychology.* Boston, Little Brown and Co., 1971.

Leach, E., More about 'Mama' and 'Papa'. In: Needham, R. (ed.), *Rethinking Kinship and Marriage.* London, Tavistock, 1971.

Lévi-Strauss, C., *Structural Anthropology.* New York, Basic Books, 1963.

Lloyd, B., *Perception and Cognition.* Harmondsworth, Penguin, 1972.

Mayer, P., *Townsmen or Tribesmen: Conservatism and the Process of Urbanization in a South-African City.* Cape Town, Oxford University Press, 1961.

Middleton, J., *The Study of the Lugbara: Expectation and Paradox in Anthropological Research.* New York, Holt, Rinehart and Winston, 1970.

Mitchell, J. C., *The Kalela Dance.* Rhodes-Livingstone Paper No. 27. Manchester, University Press, 1957.

————. (ed.), *Social Network in Urban Situations*. Manchester, University Press, 1969.

Moerman, M., Analysis of Lue conversation. In: Sudnow, D. (ed.), *Studies in Social Interaction*. New York, Free Press, 1972.

Munroe, R. L., and Munroe, R. H., *Cross-Cultural Human Development*. Monterey, Brooks-Cole, 1975.

Murdock, G. P., Changing emphases in social structures. *South-Western Journal of Anthropology*, 1955, 11, pp. 361–370.

Pelto, P., *Anthropological Research: The Structure of Inquiry*. New York, Harper and Row, 1970.

Pike, K. L., *Language in Relation to a Unified Theory of the Structure of Human Behaviour*. Part I. Glendale California, Summer Institute of Linguistics, 1954.

————, *Language in Relation to a Unified Theory of the Structure of Human Behaviour*. The Hague, Mouton, 1966.

Price-Williams, D. R., *Explorations in Cross-Cultural Psychology*. San Francisco, Chandler and Sharp, 1975.

Serpell, R., *Culture's Influence on Behaviour*. London, Methuen, 1976.

Triandis, H. C., *The Analysis of Subjective Culture*. New York, Wiley, 1972.

Tyler, S. A., (ed.), *Cognitive Anthropology*. New York, Holt, Rinehart and Winston, 1969.

Vernon, P. E., *Intelligence and Cultural Environment*. London, Methuen, 1969.

7. Epistemological Debates, Feminist Voices: Science, Social Values, and the Study of Women

Stephanie Riger

Modern scientific methods, invented in the 16th century, were not only a stunning technical innovation, but a moral and political one as well, replacing the sacred authority of the Church with science as the ultimate arbiter of truth (Grant, 1987). Unlike medieval inquiry, modern science conceives itself as a search for knowledge free of moral, political, and social values. The application of scientific methods to the study of human behavior distinguished American psychology from philosophy and enabled it to pursue the respect accorded the natural sciences (Sherif, 1979).

The use of "scientific methods" to study human beings rested on three assumptions:

(1) Since the methodological procedures of natural science are used as a model, human values enter into the study of social phenomena and conduct only as objects; (2) the goal of social scientific investigation is to construct laws or lawlike generalizations like those of physics; (3) social science has a technical character, providing knowledge which is solely instrumental. (Stewart, 1979, p. 311)

Critics recently have challenged each of these assumptions. Some charge that social science reflects not only the values of individual scientists but also those of the political and cultural milieux in which science is done, and that there are no theory-neutral "'facts" (e.g., Cook, 1985; Prilleltensky, 1989; Rabinow & Sullivan, 1979; Sampson, 1985; Shields, 1975). Others claim that there are no universal, ahistorical laws of human behavior, but only descriptions of how

Reprinted by permission of the author and the American Psychological Association from *American Psychologist* 47 (1992): 730–40. Copyright © 1992 by the American Psychological Association.

139

people act in certain places at certain times in history (e.g., K. J. Gergen, 1973; Manicas & Secord, 1983; Sampson, 1978). Still others contend that knowledge is not neutral; rather, it serves an ideological purpose, justifying power (e.g., Foucault, 1980, 1981). According to this view, versions of reality not only reflect but also legitimate particular forms of social organization and power asymmetries. The belief that knowledge is merely technical, having no ideological function, is refuted by the ways in which science has played handmaiden to social values, providing an aura of scientific authority to prejudicial beliefs about social groups and giving credibility to certain social policies (Degler, 1991; Shields, 1975; Wittig, 1985).

Within the context of these general criticisms, feminists have argued in particular that social science neglects and distorts the study of women in a systematic bias in favor of men. Some contend that the very processes of positivist science are inherently masculine, reflected even in the sexual metaphors used by the founders of modern science (Keller, 1985; Merchant, 1980). To Francis Bacon, for example, nature was female, and the goal of science was to "bind her to your service and make her your slave" (quoted in Keller, 1985, p. 36). As Sandra Harding (1986) summarized,

Mind vs. nature and the body, reason vs. emotion and social commitment, subject vs. object and objectivity vs. subjectivity, the abstract and general vs. the concrete and particular—in each case we are told that the former must dominate the latter lest human life be overwhelmed by irrational and alien forces, forces symbolized in science as the feminine. (p. 125)

Critics see the insistence of modern science on control and distance of the knower from the known as a reflection of the desire for domination characteristic of a culture that subordinates women's interests to those of men (Hubbard, 1988; Reinharz, 1985). Some go so far as to claim that because traditional scientific methods inevitably distort women's experience, a new method based on feminist principles is needed (M. M. Gergen, 1988). Others disagree, claiming that the problem in science is not objectivity itself, but rather lack of objectivity that enables male bias to contaminate the scientific process (Epstein, 1988). The first part of this article summarizes feminist charges against standard versions of science; the second part explores three possibilities for a distinctly "feminist" response to those charges: *feminist empiricism, feminist standpoint epistemologies,* and *feminist postmodernism.* (By feminist, I refer to a system of values that challenges male dominance and advocates social, political, and economic equity of women and men in society.)

BIAS WITHIN PSYCHOLOGY IN THE STUDY OF WOMEN

Since Naomi Weisstein denounced much of psychology as the "fantasy life of the male psychologist" in 1971, numerous critics have identified the ways that gender bias permeates social science (summarized in Epstein, 1988, pp. 17–45; Frieze, Parsons, Johnson, Ruble, & Zellman, 1978, pp. 11–27; Hyde, 1991, pp. 7–15; Lips, 1988, pp. 64–75; Millman & Kanter, 1975; Wilkinson, 1986). For many years, subjects of relevance to women, such as rape or housework, have been considered either taboo topics or too trivial to study, marginal to more central and prestigious issues, such as leadership, achievement, and power (Epstein, 1988; McHugh, Koeske, & Frieze, 1986; Farberow, 1963; Smith, 1987). Women's invisibility as subjects of research extends to their role as researchers as well, with relatively few women in positions of power or prestige in science (Rix, 1990). Even today, women make up only 25% of the faculty in psychology departments and only 15% of editors of psychological journals (Walker, 1991). When women are studied, their actions often are interpreted as deficient compared with those of men. Even theories reflect a male standard (Gilligan, 1982). The classic example dates back to Freud's (1925/1961) formulation in 1925 of the theory of penis envy.

Over the last two decades, critics have compiled a long and continually growing list of threats to the validity of research on women and sex differences (see Jacklin, 1981). For example, a great many studies have included only male samples. Sometimes women are included only as the stimulus, not the subject of study—they are seen but not heard—but conclusions are generalized to everyone (Meyer, 1988). Sex-of-experimenter effects contaminate virtually every area of research (Lips, 1988), and field studies yield different findings than laboratory research on the same phenomenon (Unger, 1981). Multiple meanings of the term *sex* confound biological sex differences with factors that vary by sex (i.e., sex-*related* differences) and are more appropriately labeled *gender* (McHugh et al., 1986; Unger, 1979). Sex is treated as an independent variable in studies of gender difference, even though people cannot be randomly assigned to the "male" or "female" group (Unger, 1979). The emphasis on a "difference" model obscures gender similarities (Unger, 1979); this emphasis is built into the methods of science because experiments are formally designed to reject the null hypothesis that there is no difference between the experimental group and the control group. When a difference is found, it is usually small, but the small size is often overshadowed by the fact that a difference exists at all (Epstein, 1988). A focus on between-gender differences and a lack of attention to within-gender differences reflects a presupposition of gender polarity that frames this research (Fine & Gordon, 1989).

Findings of the magnitude of sex differences have diminished over time, perhaps because of an increasing willingness to publish results when such differences are not significant (Hyde, 1990), or perhaps because of a reduction in operative sex role stereotypes. For example, findings of differences in cognitive abilities appear to have declined precipitously over the past two decades (Feingold, 1988), and researchers have found greater influenceability among women in studies published prior to 1970 than in those published later (Eagley, 1978). Carol Jacklin (1981) pointed out that the more carefully a study is carried out, the less likely it is that gender differences will be found: "With fewer variables confounded with sex, sex will account for smaller percentages of variance. Thus, paradoxically, the better the sex-related research, the less useful sex is as an explanatory variable" (p. 271). The decline in findings of difference suggest either that increasing care in designing studies has eliminated differences that were artifacts of bias, or that historical factors, rather than ahistorical, universal laws, shape behavior, whether of subjects or experimenters. In fact, so many studies find no sex differences that this research might more appropriately be called the study of sex similarities (Connell, 1987).

Psychological research on women often contains another source of bias, the lack of attention to social context. The purpose of the laboratory experiment is to isolate the behavior under study from supposedly extraneous contaminants so that it is affected only by the experimental conditions. The experimental paradigm assumes that subjects leave their social status, history, beliefs, and values behind as they enter the laboratory, or that random assignment vitiates the effects of these factors. The result is to abstract people's action from social roles or institutions (Fine & Gordon, 1989; Parlee, 1979;

Sherif, 1979). Instead of being contaminants, however, these factors may be critical determinants of behavior. By stripping behavior of its social context, psychologists rule out the study of sociocultural and historical factors, and implicitly attribute causes to factors inside the person. Moreover, an absence of consideration of the social context of people's actions is not limited to laboratory research (Fine, 1984). In an ironic reversal of the feminist dictum of the 1960s, when social context is ignored, the political is misinterpreted as personal (Kitzinger, 1987).

Ignoring social context may produce a reliance on presumed biological causes when other explanations of sex differences are not obvious, even when the biological mechanisms that might be involved are not apparent (Lips, 1988). Social explanations become residual, although sociocultural determinants may be just as robust and important as biological causes, if not more so (Connell, 1987). Although biological differences between the sexes are obviously important, it is critical to distinguish between biological difference and the social meaning attached to that difference (Rossi, 1979).

Alice Eagley (1987) raised a different objection to experimentation. She disagreed that the psychological experiment is context-stripped, and contended instead that it constitutes a particular context. An experiment typically consists of a brief encounter among strangers in an unfamiliar setting, often under the eye of a psychologist. The question is whether this limited situation is a valid one from which to make generalizations about behavior. To Eagley, the problem is that social roles (such as mother, doctor, or corporation president) lose their salience in this setting, bringing to the foreground gender-related expectations about behavior.

Cynthia Fuchs Epstein (1988) stated that "Much of the bias in social science reporting of gender issues comes from scientists' inability to capture the social context or their tendency to regard it as unnecessary to their inquiry — in a sense, their disdain for it" (p. 44). In psychology, this disdain has at least two sources (Kahn & Yoder, 1989; Prilleltensky, 1989). First, psychology focuses on the person as he or she exists at the moment. Such a focus leads the researcher away from the person's history or social circumstances. Second, the cultural context in which psychology is practiced (at least in the United States) is dominated by an individualistic philosophy (Kitzinger, 1987; Sampson, 1985). The prevailing beliefs assume that outcomes are due to choices made by free and self-determining individuals; the implication is that people get what they deserve (Kahn & Yoder, 1989). Not only assumptions of individualism, but also those of male dominance are often so taken for granted that we are not aware of them. Recognition that supposedly scientific assertions are permeated with ideological beliefs produces, in Shulamit Reinharz's (1985) words, a condition of "feminist distrust." Perhaps one of the most difficult challenges facing social scientists is to disengage themselves sufficiently from commonly shared beliefs so that those beliefs do not predetermine research findings (McHugh et al., 1986).

FEMINIST RESPONSES TO THE CRITICISMS OF SCIENCE

Challenges to the neutrality of science have long been a concern to those who study women, and have prompted three different reactions among feminists (Harding, 1986). Some remain loyal to scientific traditions, attempting to rise above the cultural embeddedness of these traditions by adhering more closely to the norms of science (e.g., Epstein, 1988; McHugh et al., 1986). Others seek to redress the male-centered bias in science by giving voice to women's experience and by viewing society from women's perspective (e.g., Belenky, Clinchy, Goldberger, & Tarule, 1986; Gilligan, 1982; Smith, 1987). Still others abandon traditional scientific methods entirely (e.g., Hare-Mustin, 1991). Philosopher of science Sandra Harding (1986) labeled these three approaches, respectively, feminist empiricism, feminist standpoint science, and postmodernism (see also Morgan's, 1983, distinction among positivist, phenomenological, and critical/praxis-oriented research paradigms). Next, I examine the manifestations of these three positions in the study of the psychology of women.

Feminist Empiricism

The psychologists who identified the problem of experimenter effects did not reject experimentation. Instead, they recommended strategies to minimize the impact of the experimenter (Rosenthal, 1966). Likewise, feminist empiricists advocate closer adherence to the tenets of science as the solution to the problem of bias. From this perspective, bias is considered error in a basically sound system, an outbreak of irrationality in a rational process. Scrupulous attention to scientific methods will eliminate error, or at least minimize its impact on research findings (Harding, 1986). Once neutrality is restored, scientific methods, grounded in rationality, will give access to the truth.

Maureen McHugh et al. (1986) presented a set of guidelines for eliminating bias. In addition to obvious corrections of the problems described earlier, other steps can be taken to ensure that the impact of the researcher's values is minimized, such as specifying the circumstances in which gender differences are found (because contexts tend to be deemed more appropriate for one sex than the other) and assessing experimental tasks for their sex neutrality (because many tasks are perceived to be sex linked; Deaux, 1984). The sex composition of the group of participants in research also may affect behavior because individuals act differently in the presence of females or males (Maccoby, 1990). Finally, attention ought to be paid to findings of sex similarities as well as sex differences, and the magnitude of such differences reported.

These suggestions are intended to produce gender-fair research using traditional scientific methods. The assumption is that a truly neutral science will produce unbiased knowledge, which in turn will serve as a basis for a more just social policy (Morawski, 1990). Yet the continuing identification of numerous instances of androcentric bias in research has lead some to conclude that value-free research is impossible, even if it is done by those of good faith (Hare-Mustin & Maracek, 1990). Technical safeguards cannot completely rule out the influence of values; scientific rigor in testing hypotheses cannot eliminate bias in theories or in the selection of problems for inquiry (Harding, 1986, 1991). Hence critics assert that traditional methods do not reveal reality, but rather act as constraints that limit our understanding of women's experiences.

Feminist Standpoint Epistemologies

Feminist empiricism argues that the characteristics of the knower are irrelevant to the discovery process if the norms of science are followed. In contrast, feminist standpoint epistemologies claim that we should center our science on women because "what we know and how we know depend on who we are, that is, on the knower's historical locus and his or her position in the social hierarchy" (Maracek, 1989, p. 372). There are several justifications for this viewpoint (see Harding, 1986). First, some argue that women's cognitive processes and modes of research are different than men's. It has been suggested that a supposedly feminine communal style of research that emphasizes cooperation of the researcher and subjects, an appreciation of natural contexts, and the use of qualitative data contrasts with a supposedly masculine agentic orientation that places primacy on distance of the researcher from the subjects, manipulation of subjects and the environment, and the use of quantitative data (Carlson, 1972; cf. Peplau & Conrad, 1989). Evelyn Fox Keller (1985) attempted to provide grounds for this position in a psychoanalytic view of child development. She argued that the male child's need to differentiate himself from his mother leads him to equate autonomy with distance from others (see also Chodorow, 1978). The process of developing a masculine sense of self thus establishes in the male a style of thinking that both reflects and produces the emphasis in science on distance, power, and control. Keller identifies an alternative model of science based not on controlling but rather on "conversing" with nature.

Keller's (1985) argument that science need not be based on domination is salutary, but her explanation is problematic. She presumes, first, that male and female infants have quite different experiences and, second, that those early experiences shape the activities of adult scientists, but she does not substantiate these claims. The supposedly masculine emphasis on separation and autonomy may be a manifestation of Western mainstream culture rather than a universal distinction between women and men. Black men and women who returned from northern U.S. cities to live in the rural South manifest a relational as opposed to autonomous self-image (Stack, 1986), and both Eastern and African world views see individuals as interdependent and connected, in contrast to the Western emphasis on a bounded and independent self (Markus & Oyserman, 1989). Identifying a masculine cognitive style as the grounds for scientific methods seems to doom most women and perhaps non-White men to outsider status. Furthermore, an emphasis on cognitive style ignores the role played by social structure, economics, and politics in determining topics and methods of study (Harding, 1986). Experimental methods in psychology characterized by control and objectivity are accorded prestige partly because they emulate the highly valued physical sciences (Sherif, 1979). Within social science, the prestige of a study mirrors the prestige of its topic (Epstein, 1988). Sociocultural factors such as these seem more likely as determinants of the shape of science than individual psychology.

A more plausible basis for a feminist standpoint epistemology is the argument that women's life experiences are not fully captured in existing conceptual schemes. Research often equates *male* with the general, typical case, and considers *female* to be the particular — a subgroup demarcated by biology (Acker, 1978). Yet analytical categories appropriate for men may not fit women's experience. Dorothy Smith (1987) argued that women are alienated from their own experience by having to frame that experience in terms of men's conceptual schemes; in Smith's terms they have a "bifurcated consciousness" — daily life grounded in female experience but only male conceptual categories with which to interpret that experience. Starting our inquiries from a subordinate group's experience will uncover the limits of the dominant group's conceptual schemes where they do not fully fit the subordinates (see also Miller, 1986). Accordingly, a science based on women's traditional place in society not only would generate categories appropriate to women, but also would be a means of discovering the underlying organization of society as a whole (see also Code, 1981).

In contrast to traditional social science in which the researcher is the expert on assessing reality, an interpretive-phenomenological approach permits women to give their own conception of their experiences. Participants, not researchers, are considered the experts at making sense of their world (Cherryholmes, 1988). The shift in authority is striking. Yet phenomenological approaches are limited in at least two ways. First, they require that the subjects studied be verbal and reflective (Reinharz, 1992); second, they run the risk of psychological reductionism (attributing causation simply to internal, psychological factors; Morawski, 1988).

Carol Gilligan's (1982) theory of women's moral development is the most influential psychological study in this tradition. Her work asserting that women stress caring in the face of moral dilemmas in contrast to men's emphasis on justice has been criticized because other researchers have found no sex differences in moral reasoning using standardized scales (e.g., Greeno & Maccoby, 1986; Mednick, 1989). Gilligan (1986) retorted that women's responses on those scales are not relevant to her purposes:

The fact that educated women are capable of high levels of justice reasoning has no bearing on the question of whether they would spontaneously choose to frame moral problems in this way. My interest in the way people *define* moral problems is reflected in my research methods, which have centered on first-person accounts of moral conflict. (p. 328)

Although standardized scales might tell us what women have in common with men, they will not reveal the way women would define their own experiences if given the opportunity to do so. The absence (and impossibility) of a comparison group of men in Gilligan's definitive study of 29 women considering abortions raises questions about whether moral orientations are sex linked, however (Crawford, 1989; Epstein, 1988, pp. 81–83).

The feminist standpoint epistemologies aim not simply to substitute "woman centered" for "man centered" gender loyalties, but rather to provide a basis for a more accurate understanding of the entire world. Howard Becker (1967) claimed that

In any system of ranked groups, participants take it as given that members of the highest group have the right to define the way things really are. . . . Credibility and the right to be heard are differentially distributed through the ranks of the system. (p. 241)

Feminist standpoint epistemologies argue that traditional methods of science give credibility only to the dominant group's views. Listening to subordinates reveals the multifocal nature of reality (Riger, 1990). The term *subjugated knowledges* describes the perspectives of those sufficiently low on the hierarchy that their interpretations do not reflect the predominant modes of thought (Foucault, 1980, p. 81). Giving voice to women's perspective means identifying the ways in which women create meaning and experience life from their particular position in the social hierarchy.

Moreover, women (and minorities) sometimes have a better vantage point to view society than do majorities because minority status can render people socially invisible, thus permitting them access to the majority group that is not reciprocated (Merton, 1972). Accordingly, incorporating subordinates' experience will not only "add" women and minorities to existing understandings, it will add a more thorough understanding of the dominant group as well. For example, Bell Hooks (1984) described African Americans living in her small Kentucky hometown as having a double vision. They looked from the outside in at the more affluent White community across the railroad tracks, but their perspective shifted to inside out when they crossed those tracks to work for White employers. Movement across the tracks was regulated, however: Whites did not cross over to the Black community, and laws ensured that Blacks returned to it.

The arguments for feminist standpoint epistemologies have stimulated rich and valuable portrayals of women's experience. Yet there are problems with a feminist standpoint as the basis for science. First, assuming a commonality to all women's experience glosses over differences among women of various racial and ethnic groups and social classes (Spelman, 1988). The life experience of a woman wealthy enough to hire childcare and household help may have more in common with her spouse than with a poor woman trying to raise her children on a welfare budget. Standpoint epistemology can recognize multiple subjugated groups demarcated by gender, race, social class, sexual orientation, and so on. Yet carried to an extreme, this position seems to dissolve science into autobiography. A critical challenge for feminist standpoint epistemology is to identify the commonalities of subjugated experience among different groups of women without losing sight of their diversity. Moreover, those who are subjugated may still adhere to a dominant group's ideology.

Furthermore, we each have multiple status identities (Merton, 1972). The poet Audre Lorde (1984) described herself as "a forty-nine-year-old Black lesbian feminist socialist mother of two, including one boy, and a member of an interracial couple" (p. 114). Each of these identities becomes salient in a different situation; at times, they conflict within the same situation. The hyphenated identities that we all experience in different ways—Black feminist, lesbian mother, Asian American, and so on—call into question the unity of the category of woman, making it difficult to generalize about "women's experience" (Harding, 1987).

Nonetheless, feminist standpoint epistemologies do not claim that social status alone allows the viewer clarity. Reasonable judgments about whether views are empirically supported are still possible. Rather than proclaiming the one true story about the world, feminist standpoint epistemologies seek partial and less distorted views. These partial views, or situated knowledges, can be far less limited than the dominant view (Haraway, 1988).

Feminist Postmodernism

A number of perspectives, including Marxism, psychoanalysis, and postmodernism, share a challenge to the primacy of reason and the autonomy of the individual. Here I focus on postmodernism and, in particular, poststructuralism, because of its influence on an emerging stream of feminist psychology (e.g., Hare-Mustin & Maracek, 1990; Wilkinson, 1986). A traditional social scientist entering the terrain of poststructuralism at times feels a bit like Alice falling into a Wonderland of bewildering language and customs that look superficially like her own yet are not. Things that seem familiar and stable—the meaning of words, for example—become problematic. What once were nouns (e.g., privilege, valor, foreground) now are verbs. Even the landscape looks different, as words themselves are chopped up with parentheses and hyphens to make visible their multiple meanings. What is most unsettling, perhaps, is the fundamental poststructuralist assertion that science does not mirror reality, but rather creates it (i.e., making science a process of invention rather than discovery; Howard, 1991). Many scientists would agree that an unmediated perception of reality is impossible to obtain, and that research findings represent (rather than mirror) reality. However, they would maintain that some representations are better than others. The traditional scientific criteria of validity, generalizability, and so forth determine how close research findings come to actual truth. In contrast, poststructuralists reject traditional notions of truth and reality, and claim instead that power enables some to define what is or is not considered knowledge. Expressing our understanding of experience must be done through language, but language is not a neutral reflection of that experience because our linguistic categories are not neutral:

If statements and not things are true or false, then truth is necessarily linguistic: if truth is linguistic, then it is relative to language use (words, concepts, statements, discourses) at a given time and place; therefore, ideology, interests, and power arrangements at a given time and place are implicated in the production of what counts as "true." (Cherryholmes, 1988, p. 439)

Or, as Humpty Dumpty said to Alice in *Through the Looking Glass:*

"When I use a word," Humpty Dumpty said, in a rather scornful tone, "it means just what I choose it to mean—neither more or less."

"The question is," said Alice, "whether you can make words mean so many different things."
"The question is," said Humpty Dumpty, "which is to be master—that's all." (Carroll, 1872/1923, p. 246)

The central question in poststructuralism is not how well our theories fit the facts, or how well the facts produced by research fit what is real. Rather, the question is which values and social institutions are favored by each of multiple versions of reality (i.e., discourses). Of critical concern is whose interests are served by competing ways of giving meaning to the world (Weedon, 1987). Feminists of a postmodern bent claim that positivism's neutral and disinterested stance masks what is actually the male conception of reality; this conception reflects and maintains male power interests (Gavey, 1989). As legal scholar Catherine MacKinnon (1987) put it, "Objectivity—the nonsituated, universal standpoint, whether claimed or aspired to—is a denial of the existence of potency of sex inequality that tacitly participates in constructing reality from the dominant point of view" (p. 136). In MacKinnon's view, rather than being neutral, "the law sees and treats women the way men see and treat women" (p. 140). The same criticism can be made about traditional social science in its exclusion, distortion, and neglect of women.

The social constructionist stance, as poststructuralism is known within psychology (K. J. Gergen, 1985), offers a particular challenge to the psychology of women. In contrast to feminist empiricism, the central question no longer asks whether sex or gender differences exist. Knowing the truth about difference is impossible (Hare-Mustin & Maracek, 1990). Varying criteria of differentness can produce divergent findings, for example, when conclusions based on averages contradict those based on the amount of overlap of scores of men and women (Luria, 1986). When an assumed difference is not scientifically supported, the argument simply shifts to another variable (Unger, 1979), and similar findings can be interpreted in opposing ways. Given the impossibility of settling these questions, poststructuralism shifts the emphasis to the question of difference itself (Scott, 1988):

What do we make of gender differences? What do they mean? Why are there so many? Why are there so few? Perhaps we should be asking: What is the point of differences? What lies beyond difference? Difference aside, what else is gender? The overarching question is choice of question. (Hare-Mustin & Maracek, 1990, pp. 1–2)

One goal of a feminist constructionist science is "disrupting and displacing dominant (oppressive) knowledges" in part by articulating the values supported by alternate conceptions of reality (Gavey, 1989, p. 462). An analysis of contrasting perspectives on sex differences demonstrates the relationship among values, assumptive frameworks, and social consequences. According to Rachel Hare-Mustin and Jeanne Maracek (1988), the received views of men and women tend either to exaggerate or to minimize the differences between them. On the one hand, the tendency to emphasize differences fosters an appreciation of supposedly feminine qualities, but it simultaneously justifies unequal treatment of women and ignores variability within each sex group. The consequence of emphasizing difference, then, is to support the status quo. On the other hand, the tendency to minimize differences justifies women's access to educational and job opportunities, but it simultaneously overlooks the fact that equal treatment is not always equitable, because of differences in men's and women's position in a social hierarchy. Gender-neutral grievance procedures in organizations, for example, do not apply equally to men and women if men are consistently in positions of greater power (Riger, 1991).

Researchers have widely different interpretations of the implications of poststructural critiques for social science methods. Some use empirical techniques for poststructuralist ends. Social constructionists see traditional research methods as a means of providing "objectifications" or illustrations, similar to vivid photographs, that are useful in making an argument persuasive rather than in validating truth claims (K. J. Gergen, 1985). Traditional methods can also help identify varying versions of reality. For example, Celia Kitzinger (1986, 1987) used Q-sort methodology to distinguish five separate accounts of lesbians' beliefs about the origin of their sexual orientation. Techniques of attitude measurement can also be used to assess the extent to which people share certain versions of reality. Rhoda Unger and her colleagues used surveys to assess belief in an objectivist or subjectivist epistemology, finding that adherence to a particular perspective varied with social status (Unger, Draper, & Pendergrass, 1986).

Others propose that we treat both psychological theories and people's actions and beliefs as texts (i.e., discursive productions located in a specific historical and cultural context and shaped by power), rather than as accounts, distorted or otherwise, of experience (Cherryholmes, 1988; Gavey, 1989). Methods developed in other disciplines, particularly literary criticism, can be used to analyze these texts. For example, through careful reading of an interview transcript with an eye to discerning "discursive patterns of meaning, contradictions, and inconsistencies," Nicola Gavey (p. 467) identified cultural themes of "permissive sexuality" and "male sexual needs" in statements by a woman about her experiences of heterosexual coercion (see also Hare-Mustin, 1991; Walkerdine, 1986). A particular technique of discourse analysis, deconstruction, can be used to expose ideological assumptions in written or spoken language, as Joanne Martin (1990) did to identify forces that suppress women's achievement within organizations. Deconstruction highlights the revealing quality not just of what is said, but rather of what is left out, contradictory, or inconsistent in the text. Deconstruction offers a provocative technique for analyzing hidden assumptions. Yet it is a potentially endless process, capable of an infinite regress, inasmuch as any deconstruction can itself be deconstructed (Martin, 1990).

The absence of any criteria for evaluation means that the success of accounts of social construction "depend primarily on the analyst's capacity to invite, compel, stimulate, or delight the audience, and not on criteria of veracity" (K. J. Gergen, 1985, p. 272). This raises the possibility that what Grant (1987) said in another context could apply here: "Such theories risk devolving into authoritarian nontheories more akin to religions" (p. 113). The relativism of poststructuralism can be countered, however, by the identification of moral criteria for evaluation (K. J. Gergen, 1985; Unger, 1983). Theory and research can be assessed in terms of their pragmatic utility in achieving certain social and political goals, rather than the allegedly neutral rules of science (Gavey, 1989). However, because feminists disagree about whether celebrating women's difference or emphasizing the similarity of the sexes is most likely to change women's basic condition of subordination (Snitow, 1990), agreement about criteria for evaluation seems unlikely.

What poses perhaps the greatest dilemma for feminists is the view of the subject advocated by poststructuralist theory. Poststructuralists consider the attribution of agency and intentionality to the subject to be part of a deluded liberal humanism, complicit with the status quo. The multiple discourses of selfhood, intentionality, and so forth that are present in our culture compete for dominance; those that prevail constitute individual subjectivity. Social cognition on the part of the individual is channeled into certain ways of thinking that dominate society (although resistance is possible). Those discourses antedate our consciousness and give meaning to our experience, which otherwise has no essential meaning (Weedon, 1987). In contrast, feminist standpoint epistemologies consider individuals to be the active construers of their reality, albeit within a particular social and historical context; women's subjectivity is considered an important source of information about their experience. Poststructuralism's rejection of intentionality on the part of the individual seems to deny the validity of women's voices, just at a time when women are beginning to be heard (see also Hartsock, 1987).

Poststructuralism offers a provocative critique of social science and makes us critically aware of the relationship of knowledge and power. Yet the focus on "problematizing the text" of our disciplines, although admirably self-reflexive, can lead to an inward emphasis that neglects the study of women in society. In a parallel manner, poststructuralism's emphasis on language as determining consciousness can lead to the disregard of other determinants, such as women's position in a social hierarchy (Segal, 1986). Furthermore, Rhoda Unger (1988) identified a dilemma for social scientists who reject traditional empirical methods:

The attempt to infer cause-and-effect relationships about human behavior using the tools of empiricism is one of the few unique contributions that psychology as a discipline can offer to the rest of scholarship. If such tools may not be used by feminist psychologists there is little likelihood that their insights will be taken seriously by the rest of the discipline. (p. 137)

Feminist foremothers in psychology, such as Helen Thompson (Woolley) and her colleagues, at the turn of this century, used traditional scientific methods to contest social myths about women (Reinharz, 1992; Rosenberg, 1982); they may still serve that purpose today. Poststructuralists would likely retort that the fact that Thompson's insights have had to be repeatedly rediscovered (or, rather, reinvented) demonstrates that power, not truth, determines which version of reality will prevail.

IS THERE A FEMINIST METHOD?

On the basis of multiple critiques of the social sciences, some propose an alternative research method based on feminist values. The lack of consensus on what values are feminist makes this a daunting project, yet many would agree on the need for more interactive, contextualized methods in the service of emancipatory goals (cf. Peplau & Conrad, 1989). A feminist method should produce a study not just *of* women, but also *for* women, helping to change the world as well as to describe it (Acker, Barry, & Esseveld, 1983; Wittig, 1985). Mary Gergen (1988) advocated the following as central tenets of a feminist method (see also Wilkinson, 1986):

1. recognizing the interdependence of experimenter and subject;
2. avoiding the decontextualizing of the subject or experimenter from their social and historical surroundings;
3. recognizing and revealing the nature of one's values within the research context;
4. accepting that facts do not exist independently of their producers' linguistic codes;
5. demystifying the role of the scientists and establishing an egalitarian relationship between science makers and science consumers. (p. 47)

Joan Acker et al. (1983) attempted to implement some of these principles in a study of women who had primarily been wives and mothers and were starting to enter the labor market. Interviews became dialogues, a mutual attempt to clarify and expand understandings. Often friendships developed between researchers and the women in the study. Acker and her colleagues discovered that these methods are not without problems, however. The researcher's need to collect information can (perhaps inadvertently) lead to the manipulation of friendship in the service of the research. Methods that create trust between researchers and participants entail the risk of exploitation, betrayal, and abandonment by the researcher (Stacey, 1988). Acker's study took place over a number of years, and participant's interpretations of their lives were constantly changing in hindsight, raising problems of validity in the research. The desire to give participants an opportunity to comment on researchers' interpretations of the interviews became a source of tension when disagreements arose. The solution to these dilemmas reached by Acker and her colleagues — to report the women's lives in their own words as much as possible — was not satisfactory to the women in the study who wanted more analysis of their experience. Finally, it was difficult to determine if this research experience had an emancipatory effect on participants. Intending to create social change is no assurance of actually doing so.

The conflict between the researcher's perspective and that of the participants in this study raises a critical issue for those who reject positivism's belief in the scientist as expert. Because a feminist method (at least according to the principles listed) assumes that there is no neutral observer, whose interpretations should prevail when those of the researcher and the people under study conflict? Feminism places primacy on acknowledging and validating female experience (Wilkinson, 1986), yet postmodern perspectives challenge the authority of the individual (Gavey, 1989; Weedon, 1987). Consider, for example, Margaret Andersen's (1981) study of 20 corporate wives. She disbelieved their claims of contentment and attributed their lack of feminism to *false consciousness,* a Marxist term meaning that these women identified with (male) ruling class interests against their own (female) class interests. The women wrote a rebuttal rejecting Andersen's interpretation. In response, Andersen revised her position to accept the women's statements of satisfaction with their lives. Instead of treating them as deluded or insincere, she looked for sources of their contentment in their position in the social hierarchy. Lather (1986, 1988) recommended this kind of dialogic process to avoid imposing on research participants interpretations that disempower them (see also Kidder, 1982). Without it, we grant privilege to the authority of the researcher, even if on postmodern rather than positivist grounds.

CONCLUSION

Although the strategies intended as a feminist method overcome some of the objections to traditional social science, they raise as many problems as they solve (see Reinharz, 1992). No method or epistemology seems devoid of limitations or perfectly true to feminist values, which are themselves contested (e.g., Jaggar & Struhl, 1978). Feminism is most useful as a set of questions that challenge the prevailing asymmetries of power and androcentric assumptions in science and society, rather than as a basis for a unique method (Reinharz, 1992). Feminism thus identifies "patterns and interrelationships and causes and effects and implications of questions that nonfeminists have not seen and still do not see" (Lorber, 1988, p. 8).

The psychological study of women emerged from the field of individual differences. Dominated by the question of sex differences, this tradition assumes that an inner core of traits or abilities distinguishes women from men (Buss, 1976). Such a conceptualization no longer seems useful. Few gender differences in personality or abilities have been reliably demonstrated (Feingold, 1988; Hyde, 1990), and factors other than individual dispositions influence our behavior (Maccoby, 1990). A more appropriate strategy for the study of women would consider the ways in which gender is created and maintained through interpersonal processes (Deaux & Major, 1987).

From this perspective, gender does not reside within the person. Instead, it is constituted by the myriad ways in which we "do" rather than "have" gender; that is, we validate our membership in a particular gender category through interactional processes (West & Zimmerman, 1987). Gender is something we enact, not an inner core or constellation of traits that we express; it is a pattern of social organization that structures the relations, especially the power relations, between women and men (Connell, 1985, 1987; Crawford & Maracek, 1989): "In doing gender, men are also doing dominance and women are doing deference" (West & Zimmerman, 1987, p. 146). Transsexuals know well that merely altering one's sex organs does not change one's gender. Membership in the category of "male" or "female" must be affirmed continuously through social behavior (see, e.g., Morris, 1974).

Each of the epistemological positions described can contribute to this perspective, despite their contradictions. An interactional conceptualization of gender recognizes that the behavior and thoughts of men and women are channeled into certain sociocultural forms, as poststructuralism claims. As Peter Manicas and Paul Secord (1983) stated:

Social structures (e.g., language) are reproduced and transformed by action, but they preexist for individuals. They enable persons to become persons and to act (meaningfully and intentionally), yet at the same time, they are "coercive," limiting the ways we can act. (p. 408)

The dominant ideology of a society is manifested in and reproduced by the social relations of its members (Unger, 1989). Unlike poststructuralism, however, an interactional view of gender also acknowledges individual agency in the production and transformation of social forms. Such a perspective would regard the person as an initiator of action and construer of meaning within a context composed not only of varying modes of interpreting the world but also of structural constraints and opportunities (see, e.g., Buss, 1978; Riegel, 1979; Sampson, 1978; Unger, 1983), as standpoint epistemologies claim.

Diverse methods, evaluated by reasonable criteria, are needed to capture the rich array of personal and structural factors that shape women and girls, and in turn are shaped by them. What is critical is that we are aware of the epistemological commitments—and value assumptions—we make when we adopt a particular research strategy (Unger, 1983). Moreover, rather than abandoning objectivity, systematic examination of assumptions and values in the social order that shape scientific practices can strengthen objectivity (Harding, 1991).

Epistemological debates in recent years have shattered the traditional picture of science as neutral, disinterested, and value free and have replaced it with a view of knowledge as socially constructed. Feminists' contributions to this debate highlight not only the androcentric nature of social science, but also its collusion in the perpetuation of male dominance in society. To assume that the multiple voices of women are not shaped by domination is to ignore social context and legitimate the status quo. On the other hand, to assume that women have no voice other than an echo of prevailing discourses is to deny them agency and, simultaneously, to repudiate the possibility of social change. The challenge to psychology is to link a vision of women's agency with an understanding of the shaping power of social context.

NOTES

Michael S. Pallak served as action editor for this article.

The use of first names herein is intended to highlight the contributions of women to psychology. I am grateful to Dan A. Lewis for comments and discussion on numerous iterations of this article; to Marilyn Yalom, Karen Offen, and other members of the Affiliated and Visiting Scholars Seminar of the Institute for Research on Women and Gender of Stanford University; to Sandra Bartky, Cynthia Fuchs Epstein, Christopher Keys, Jane Mansbridge, and Shula Reinharz for helpful comments; and to Rondi Cartmill for outstanding research assistance. An extended version of this article will appear in *Psychology of Women: Biological, Psychological and Social Perspectives* (Riger, in preparation).

REFERENCES

Acker, J. (1978). Issues in the sociological study of women's work. In A. Stromberg & S. Harkness (Eds.), *Women working* (pp. 134–161). Palo Alto, CA: Mayfield.

Acker, J., Barry, K., & Esseveld, J. (1983). Objectivity and truth: Problems in doing feminist research. *Women's Studies International Forum, 6,* 423–435.

Andersen, M. (1981). Corporate wives: Longing for liberation or satisfied with the status quo? *Urban Life, 10,* 311–327.

Becker, H. S. (1967). Whose side are we on? *Social Problems, 14,* 239–247.

Belenky, M. F., Clinchy, B. M., Goldberger, N. R., & Tarule, J. M. (1986). *Women's ways of knowing: The development of self, voice, and mind.* New York: Basic Books.

Buss, A. R. (1976). Galton and sex differences: An historical note. *Journal of the History of the Behavioral Sciences, 12,* 283–285.

Buss, A. R. (1978). The structure of psychological revolutions. *Journal of the History of the Behavioral Sciences, 14,* 57–64.

Carlson, R. (1972). Understanding women: Implications for personality theory and research. *Journal of Social Issues, 28,* 17–32.

Carroll, L. (1923). *Alice's adventures in Wonderland; and Through the looking glass.* Philadelphia: Winston. (Original work published 1872)

Cherryholmes, C. H. (1988). Construct validity and the discourses of research. *American Journal of Education, 96,* 421–457.

Chodorow, N. (1978). *The reproduction of mothering.* Berkeley: University of California Press.

Code, L. B. (1981). Is the sex of the knower epistemologically significant? *Metaphilosophy, 12,* 267–276.

Connell, R. W. (1985). Theorizing gender. *Sociology, 19,* 260–272.

Connell, R. W. (1987). *Gender and power: Society, the person and sexual politics.* Stanford, CA: Stanford University Press.

Cook, T. D. (1985). Postpositivist critical multiplism. In L. Shotland & M. M. Mark (Eds.), *Social science and social policy* (pp. 21–62). Beverly Hills, CA. Sage.

Crawford, M. (1989). Agreeing to differ: Feminist epistemologies and women's ways of knowing. In M. Crawford & M. Gentry (Eds.), *Gender and thought: Psychological perspectives* (pp. 128–145). New York: Springer-Verlag.

Crawford, M., & Maracek, J. (1989). Psychology reconstructs the female, 1968–1988. *Psychology of Women Quarterly, 13,* 147–165.

Deaux, K. (1984). From individual differences to social categories. *American Psychologist, 39,* 105–116.

Deaux, K., & Major, B. (1987). Putting gender into context: An interactive model of gender-related behavior. *Psychological Review, 94,* 369–389.

Degler, C. (1991). *In search of human nature.* New York: Oxford University Press.

Eagley, A. H. (1978). Sex differences in influenceability. *Psychological Bulletin, 1978, 85,* 86–116.

Eagley, A. H. (1987). *Sex differences in social behavior: A social-role interpretation.* Hillsdale, NJ: Erlbaum.

Epstein, C. F. (1988). *Deceptive distinctions: Sex, gender and the social order.* New Haven, CT: Yale University Press.

Farberow, N. L. (1963). *Taboo topics.* New York: Atherton Press.

Feingold, A. (1988). Cognitive gender differences are disappearing. *American Psychologist, 43,* 95–103.

Fine, M. (1984). Coping with rape: Critical perspectives on consciousness. *Imagination, Cognition, and Personality: The Scientific Study of Consciousness, 3,* 249–67.

Fine, M., & Gordon, S. M. (1989). Feminist transformations of/despite psychology. In M. Crawford & M. Gentry (Eds.), *Gender and thought: Psychological perspectives* (pp. 146–174). New York: Springer-Verlag.

Foucault, M. (1980). *Power/knowledge: Selected interviews and other writings, 1972–1977* (C. Gordon, Ed. and Trans.). New York: Pantheon Books.

Foucault, M. (1981). *The history of sexuality: Vol. 1. An introduction.* Harmondsworth, England: Viking.

Freud, S. (1961). Some psychical consequences of the anatomical distinctions between the sexes. In J. Strachey (Ed. and Trans.), *The complete psychological works of Sigmund Freud* (Vol. 19, pp. 248–258). London: Hogarth Press. (Original work published 1925)

Frieze, I. H., Parsons, J. E., Johnson, P. B., Ruble, D. N., & Zellman, G. L. (1978). *Women and sex roles: A social psychological perspective.* New York: Norton.

Gavey, N. (1989). Feminist poststructuralism and discourse analysis: Contributions to a feminist psychology. *Psychology of Women Quarterly, 13,* 459–476.

Gergen, K. J. (1973). Social psychology as history. *Journal of Personality and Social Psychology, 26,* 309–320.

Gergen, K. J. (1985). The social constructionist movement in modern psychology. *American Psychologist, 40,* 255–265, 272.

Gergen, M. M. (1988). Building a feminist methodology. *Contemporary Social Psychology, 13,* 47–53.

Gilligan, C. (1982). *In a different voice.* Cambridge, MA: Harvard University Press.

Gilligan, C. (1986). Reply by Carol Gilligan. *Signs: Journal of Women in Culture and Society, 11,* 324–333.

Grant, J. (1987). I feel therefore I am: A critique of female experience as the basis for a feminist epistemology. In M. J. Falco (Ed.), *Feminism and epistemology: Approaches to research in women and politics* (pp. 99–114). Binghamton, NY: Haworth Press.

Greeno, C. G., & Maccoby, E. E. (1986). How different is the "different voice"? *Signs: Journal of Women in Culture and Society, 11,* 310–316.

Haraway, D. (1988). Situated knowledges: The science question in feminism and the privilege of partial perspective. *Feminist Studies, 14,* 575–599.

Harding, S. (1986). *The science question in feminism.* Ithaca, NY: Cornell University Press.

Harding, S. (1987). Introduction: Is there a feminist method? In S. Harding (Ed.), *Feminism and methodology: Social science issues* (pp. 1–14), Bloomington: Indiana University Press.

Harding, S. (1991). *Whose science? Whose knowledge?* Ithaca, NY: Cornell University Press.

Hare-Mustin, R. T. (1991). Sex, lies, and headaches: The problem is power. In T. J. Goodrich (Ed.), *Women and power: Perspectives for therapy.* New York: Norton.

Hare-Mustin, R. T., & Maracek, J. (1988). The meaning of difference: Gender theory, postmodernism, and psychology. *American Psychologist, 43,* 355–364.

Hare-Mustin, R. T., & Maracek, J. (1990). *Making a difference: Psychology and the construction of gender.* New Haven, CT: Yale University Press.

Hartsock, N. (1987). Epistemology and politics: Minority vs. majority theories. *Cultural Critique, 7,* 187–206.

Hooks, B. (1984). *Feminist theory: From margin to center.* Boston: South End Press.

Howard, G. S. (1991). Culture tales: Narrative approach to thinking, cross-cultural psychology, and psychotherapy. *American Psychologist, 46,* 187–197.

Hubbard, R. (1988). Some thoughts about the masculinity of the natural sciences. In M. M. Gergen, *Feminist thought and the structure of knowledge* (pp. 1–15). New York: New York University Press.

Hyde, J. (1990). Meta-analysis and the psychology of gender differences. *Signs: Journal of Women in Culture and Society, 16,* 55–73.

Hyde, J. (1991). *Half the human experience: The psychology of women* (4th ed.). Lexington, MA: Heath.

Jacklin, C. N. (1981). Methodological issues in the study of sex-related differences. *Developmental Review, 1,* 266–273.

Jaggar, A., & Struhl, P. R. (1978). *Feminist frameworks: Alternative theoretical accounts of the relations between women and men.* New York: McGraw-Hill.

Kahn, A. S., & Yoder, J. D. (1989). The psychology of women and conservatism: Rediscovering social change. *Psychology of Women Quarterly, 13,* 417–432.

Keller, E. F. (1985). *Reflections on gender and science.* New Haven, CT: Yale University Press.

Kidder, L. (1982). Face validity from multiple perspectives. In D. Brinberg & L. Kidder (Eds.), *Forms of validity in research* (pp. 41–58). San Francisco: Jossey-Bass.

Kitzinger, C. (1986). Introducing and developing Q as a feminist methodology: A study of accounts of lesbianism. In S. Wilkinson (Ed.), *Feminist social psychology: Developing theory and practice* (pp. 151–172). Milton Keynes, England: Open University Press.

Kitzinger, C. (1987). *The social construction of lesbianism.* London: Sage

Lather, P. (1986). Research as praxis. *Harvard Educational Review, 56,* 257–277.

Lather, P. (1988). Feminist perspectives on empowering research methodologies. *Women's Studies International Forum, 11,* 569–581.

Lips, H. (1988). *Sex and gender: An introduction.* Mountain View, CA: Mayfield.

Lorber, J. (1988). From the editor. *Gender & Society, 1,* 5–8.

Lorde, A. (1984). *Sister outsider: Essays and speeches.* New York: Crossing.

Luria, Z. (1986). A methodological critique. *Signs: Journal of Women in Culture and Society, 11,* 316–320.

Maccoby, E. E. (1990). Gender and relationships: A developmental account. *American Psychologist, 43,* 513–520.

MacKinnon, C. A. (1987). Feminism, Marxism, method and the state: Toward feminist jurisprudence. In S. Harding (Ed.), *Feminism and methodology: Social science issues* (pp. 135–156). Bloomington: Indiana University Press.

Manicas, P. T., & Secord, P. F. (1983). Implications for psychology of the new philosophy of science. *American Psychologist, 38,* 399–413.

Maracek, J. (1989). Introduction: Theory and method in feminist psychology [Special issue]. *Psychology of Women Quarterly, 13,* 367–377.

Markus, H., & Oyserman, D. (1989). Gender and thought: The role of the self-concept. In M. Crawford & M. Gentry (Eds.), *Gender and thought: Psychological perspectives* (pp. 100–127). New York: Springer-Verlag.

Martin, J. (1990). Deconstructing organizational taboos: The suppression of gender conflict in organizations. *Organizational Science, 5,* 339–359.

McHugh, M., Koeske, R., & Frieze, I. (1986). Issues to consider in conducting nonsexist psychological research: A guide for researchers *American Psychologist, 41,* 879–890.

Mednick, M. T. (1989). On the politics of psychological constructs: Stop the bandwagon, I want to get off. *American Psychologist, 44,* 1118–1123.

Merchant, C. (1980). *The death of nature: Women, ecology, and the scientific revolution.* New York: Harper & Row.

Merton, R. (1972). Insiders and outsiders: A chapter in the sociology of knowledge. *American Journal of Sociology, 78,* 9–47.

Meyer, J. (1988). Feminist thought and social psychology. In M. Gergen (Ed.), *Feminist thought and the structure of knowledge* (pp. 105–123). New York: New York University Press.

Miller, J. B. (1986). *Toward a new psychology of women* (2nd ed.). Boston: Beacon.

Millman, M., & Kanter, R. (Eds.). (1975). *Another voice: Feminist perspectives on social life and social sciences.* Garden City, NY: Anchor Books.

Morawski, J. G. (1988). Impasse in feminist thought? In M. M. Gergen (Ed.), *Femi-*

nist thought and the structure of knowledge (pp. 182–194). New York: New York University Press.

Morawski, J. G. (1990). Toward the unimagined: Feminism and epistemology in psychology. In R. L. Hare-Mustin & J. Maracek, *Making a difference: Psychology and the construction of gender* (pp. 150–183). New Haven, CT: Yale University Press.

Morgan, G. (Ed.). (1983). Toward a more reflective social science. In G. Morgan (Ed.), *Beyond method: Strategies for social research* (pp. 368–376). Beverly Hills, CA: Sage.

Morris, J. (1974). *Conundrum.* New York: Harcourt, Brace, Jovanovich.

Parlee, M. (1979). Psychology and women. *Signs: Journal of Women in Culture and Society, 5,* 121–133.

Peplau, L. A. & Conrad, E. (1989). Feminist methods in psychology. *Psychology of Women Quarterly, 13,* 379–400.

Prilleltensky, I. (1989). Psychology and the status quo. *American Psychologist, 44,* 795–802.

Rabinow, P., & Sullivan, W. M. (1979). The interpretive turn: Emergence of an approach. In P. Rabinow & W. M. Sullivan (Eds.), *Interpretive social science A reader* (pp. 1–21). Berkeley: University of California Press.

Reinharz, S. (1985). Feminist distrust: Problems of context and context in sociological work. In D. N. Berg & K. K. Smith (Eds.), *The self in social inquiry: Researching methods* (pp. 153–172). Beverly Hills, CA: Sage.

Reinharz, S. (1992). *Feminist methods in social research.* New York: Oxford University Press.

Riegel, K. F. (1979). *Foundations of dialectical psychology.* San Diego, CA: Academic Press.

Riger, S. (1990). Ways of knowing and organizational approaches to community research. In P. Tolan, C. Keys, F. Chertok, & L. Jason (Eds.), *Researching community psychology* (pp. 42–50). Washington, DC: American Psychological Association.

Riger, S. (1991). Gender dilemmas in sexual harassment policies and procedures. *American Psychologist, 46,* 497–505.

Riger, S. (in preparation). *Psychology of women: Biological, psychological and social perspectives.* New York: Oxford University Press.

Rix, S. E. (Ed.). (1990). *The American woman, 1990–1991.* New York: Norton.

Rosenberg, R. (1982). *Beyond separate spheres.* New Haven, CT: Yale University Press.

Rosenthal, R. (1966). *Experimenter effects in behavioral research.* New York: Appleton-Century-Crofts.

Rossi, A. (1979). Reply by Alice Rossi. *Signs: Journal of Women in Culture and Society, 4,* 712–717.

Sampson, E. E. (1978). Scientific paradigms and social values: Wanted—A scientific revolution. *Journal of Personality and Social Psychology, 36,* 1332–1343.

Sampson, E. E. (1985). The decentralization of identity: Toward a revised concept of personal and social order. *American Psychologist, 40,* 1203–1211.

Scott, J. W. (1988). Deconstructing equality-versus-difference: Or, the uses of post-structuralist theory for feminism. *Feminist Studies, 14,* 33–50.

Segal, L. (1986). *Is the future female? Troubled thoughts on contemporary feminism.* London: Virago.

Sewart, J. J. (1979). Critical theory and the critique of conservative method. In S. G. McNall (Ed.), *Theoretical perspectives in sociology* (pp. 310–322). New York: St. Martin's Press.

Sherif, C. W. (1979). Bias in psychology. In J. A. Sherman & E. T. Beck (Eds.), *A prism of sex: Essays in the sociology of knowledge* (pp. 93–133). Madison: University of Wisconsin Press.

Shields, S. (1975). Functionalism, Darwinism, and the psychology of women: A study in social myth. *American Psychologist, 30,* 739–754.

Smith, D. (1987). *The everyday world as problematic.* Boston: Northeastern University Press.

Snitow, A. (1990). A gender diary. In M. Hirsch & E. F. Keller (Eds.), *Conflicts in feminism* (pp. 9–43). New York: Routledge.

Spelman, E. V. (1988). *Inessential woman: Problems of exclusion in feminist thought.* Boston: Beacon Press.

Stacey, J. (1988). Can there be a feminist ethnography? *Women's Studies International Forum, 11,* 21–27.

Stack, C. (1986). The culture of gender: Women and men of color. *Signs: Journal of Women in Culture and Society, 11,* 321–324.

Unger, R. K. (1979). Toward a redefinition of sex and gender. *American Psychologist, 34,* 1085–1094.

Unger, R. K. (1981). Sex as a social reality: Field and laboratory research. *Psychology of Women Quarterly, 5,* 645–653.

Unger, R. K. (1983). Through the looking glass: No wonderland yet! (The reciprocal relationship between methodology and models of reality). *Psychology of Women Quarterly, 8,* 9–32.

Unger, R. K. (1988). Psychological, feminist, and personal epistemology. Transcending contradiction. In M. M. Gergen (Ed.), *Feminist thought and the structure of knowledge* (pp. 124–141). New York: New York University Press.

Unger, R. K. (1989). Sex, gender, and epistemology. In M. Crawford & M. Gentry (Eds.), *Gender and thought: Psychological perspectives* (pp. 17–35). New York: Springer-Verlag.

Unger, R. K., Draper, R. D., & Pendergrass, M. L. (1986). Personal epistemology and personal experience. *Journal of Social Issues, 42,* 67–79.

Walker, L. (1991). The feminization of psychology. *Psychology of Women Newsletter of Division 35, 18,* 1, 4.

Walkerdine, V. (1986). Post-structuralist theory and everyday social practices: The family and the school. In S. Wilkinson (Ed.), *Feminist social psychology: Developing theory and practice* (pp. 57–76). Milton Keynes, England: Open University Press.

Weedon, C. (1987). *Feminist practice and poststructuralist theory.* New York: Basil Blackwell.

Weisstein, N. (1971). *Psychology constructs the female: Or, the fantasy life of the male psychologist* Boston: New England Free Press.

West, C., & Zimmerman, D. H. (1987). Doing gender. *Gender & Society, 1,* 125–151.

Wilkinson, S. (1986). Sighting possibilities: Diversity and commonality in feminist research. In S. Wilkinson (Ed.), *Feminist social psychology: Developing theory and practice* (pp. 7–24). Milton Keynes, England: Open University Press.

Wittig, M. A. (1985). Metatheoretical dilemmas in the psychology of gender. *American Psychologist, 40,* 800–811.

8. Psychological Research and the Black Self-Concept: A Critical Review

Wade W. Nobles

Since one of the most widely researched areas in modern psychology concerns the concept of self, it is not surprising that researchers in black communities have generated a considerable amount of literature concerning the black or "Negro" self-concept.

The purpose of this paper is to review briefly the major theoretical approaches to the concept of self and show the strengths and weaknesses of these in relationship to the investigation of the black self-concept. In anticipation of subsequent discussion, I can note here that most of the theoretical approaches taken in the empirical investigation of the black self-concept have failed to incorporate African conceptions. My thesis is that only through a full understanding of the African concept of self can valid or reliable research be done in the area.

In beginning this task I will first examine four major theoretical approaches which have typified American research in the area. These are the phenomenological, the behavioral, the existential, and the symbolic interactional.

Phenomenological Approaches

The phenomenological approach advances the proposition that the way an individual perceives stimuli is the primary determinant of his behavior (Snygg & Combs, 1949). In such approaches to self-concept, the study of self in the phenomenal sense refers to the continuum of clarity in the phenomenal or conscious field.

Historically, phenomenology has postulated that the self-concept

Reprinted by permission of the Society for the Psychological Study of Social Issues from *Journal of Social Issues* 29 (1973): 11–31 © The Society for the Psychological Study of Social Issues.

was a preestablished entity and as such could be explored only through introspection. As psychology became more and more nomologically scientific, the suggested measurement of the phenomenologist, i.e., introspection, was seen to violate a basic requirement for scientific data—namely, that data should be available for reliable replication by independent and neutral investigators (observers). Up to this point the researcher, as Crowne and Stephens (1961) pointed out, had little choice but to accept the validity and reliability of self-report data at face value.

However, most of the empirical work in the contemporary phenomenological area has been research which reflected some aspect of self-awareness—self-regard, self-characteristics, self-esteem, etc. Typically, studies in this area have attempted to test hypotheses which concerned the development of self-concept (Ames, 1952; Smith & Lebo, 1956; Mussen & Jones, 1957; Engel, 1959) or studies in which the current characteristics of self-concept were influenced by some variable (Manis, 1958; Lazowick, 1955; Jourard & Remy, 1955; Gebel, 1954; Hill, 1957; Coates & Pellegrin, 1957).

Behavioral Approaches

The behaviorist approach assigns to the self-concept the status of a psychological construct. Its chief value is its utility in predicting or explaining an individual's behavior (e.g., Lowe, 1961; Gordon & Gergen, 1968). Thus the behavioral conception of the self-concept is that it is essentially an intervening variable which explains behavioral consistencies under varying environmental stimuli, and the behavioral approach views behavior as depending on or being influenced by the self-concept (i.e., the self-concept as the antecedent).

Contemporary studies of self-concept as related to behavior have been concerned with both the influence of self-concept on behavior and the influence of behavior on the self-concept. Some studies test the effects of self-concept on performance in learning tasks (Doris, 1959; Harvey, Kelley, & Shapiro, 1957; Cartwright, 1956; Cowen, Heilizer, & Axelrod, 1955); other studies relate self-concept to antisocial and delinquent behavior (Reckless, Dinitz, & Kay, 1957; Engel, 1959). The studies of Bills (1953), Sears (1941), Martire (1956), Lepine and Chodorkoff (1955), and Gilinsky (1949) all attempt to understand the relationship between level of aspiration behavior and self-regard.

Existential Approaches

The first two approaches are based on the assumption that the scientific method can be fruitfully used to test phenomenological theories in order to establish nomological laws.

Existentialists criticize the nomological scientific assumption which is reflected in the methods of modern behavioral science. They note that modern science, particularly social science, is concerned with finding methods and procedures for selecting, isolating, and observing factors and phenomena (allegedly from a detached perspective) which can be reduced to abstract laws. In relation to conceptions of self, the existentialists note that these abstract laws generally have very little relation to the person in his unique, changing, and concrete world of experience. The existentialists, however, as Wylie (1961) notes, do not rule out the empirical study of drives, dynamism, and patterns of behavior. What they in fact assert is that these drives and patterns of behavior and dynamism must be understood in relation to the context of the person as existing or being. The implications this has for the study of self can be seen in May's (1958) work where he writes:

Grasping of the being of the other person occurs on a quite different level from our knowledge of specific things about him [p. 38].
Being together means being together in the same world . . . cannot be understood as an external collection of objects which we view from the outside [in which case we never really understand it] [p. 55].

Existentialism is a philosophical orientation which endeavors to describe the reality of the human subject in its totality. Within this orientation there is an implicit rejection of the nomological method with its Lockean/S-R model. Explicit is the rejection of the attempt to reduce the vital whole to an operational bond between its parts.

In his essay, "Existential Self and the Person," Tiryakian (1968) suggests that in spite of radical empiricism (i.e., "what you can measure is what there is") a basic reflection in human thought is that what we find before us is not always uniform in significance. He notes that some aspects are more real than others and that this qualitative differentiation in reality corresponds in experience directly to what is considered "really me" and "not really me." Respecting this qualitative differentiation in reality, Tiryakian suggests that existential analysis in relation to the conception of the nature of the self makes clear the distinction between those two levels of existence, which he calls the "ontic" and the "ontological." The ontic refers to finite things recognizable by the senses and locatable in time and space, e.g., mass, color, weight, etc.; ontological refers to the transcendental foundation of empirical entities, that is, the ontological existence is the grounding of the self as a source of unity and identity which corresponds to the "really me." In relation to the grounding of the self, Tiryakian notes:

I am today what I am in part because of my historical past and in part because of what I anticipate to be my historical future. I am also historical in a collective or social sense; that is, I . . . take as mine the history of my people and . . . realize that I am not contained in my finite and solid appearance but that my being goes out spatially and temporally [p. 80].

Through consciousness, especially collective consciousness, the self transcends its finiteness as a physical body. According to Tiryakian, subjectivity as consciousness is much more ontological than an individual consciousness (an "I" consciousness); it is a consciousness of temporality and a collective consciousness; the self is integrally a "we," a being together. Thus self-awareness, for instance, existentially speaking is not just being cognitively aware of one's finiteness but is also awareness of one's historical transcendence which determines one's being a "we." This conception is quite important in understanding the African conception of self.

The "person" in the existential model is defined as that which provides the existential self with a concrete grounding in social space and time. The person is the social self, i.e., the self as perceiver of others, the self as perceived by others, and the self as interacting with others. It should be noted, though, that the person existentially is not only a physical referent or objective entity—it is the presence of the self in the social world just as the body is the grounding of the person in the physical world (Tiryakian, 1968).

Several empirical studies (Nunnally, 1955; Rogers, 1954; Frisch & Cranston, 1956; Edelson & Jones, 1954) have attempted to investigate the notion of self as an existential being or entity. Applying inverse factor analysis to their studies, most of these have been intensive examinations of a single subject. Wylie (1961) notes that there has been considerable difference among psychologists about the value of the single case study method and inverse factor analysis technique; the scope of this paper cannot include an analytical evaluation of existential methodology and data analysis.

The purpose in briefly reviewing the main points in existential analysis of self is to provide a reference for the awareness of self called "we." As stated above, self-awareness is also awareness of one's self being a "we." The importance of this will become clearer after the other references for awareness of self—awareness of being an "I" and awareness of being a "me"—are explicated.

Symbolic Interaction Approaches

The symbolic interaction approach to the study of self-concept was originally conceived by Cooley (1902) and Mead (1934). This approach makes the assumption that one's self-conception is a continual product of social interaction with others. Cooley (1902) developed a conceptual framework for dealing with the relationship between self and society, the central aspect of which was the assumption that a fundamental unity existed between mind and society. He considered society and mind to be aspects of the same whole and, in recognition of this, concluded that the mind was a social entity and that society was a mental entity. Thus the development of the relationship between the two entities could best be understood, so Cooley thought, by the idea of a "looking-glass self." According to this looking-glass self, what an organism internalized as his own was based on information about oneself which one received from others.

Mead's approach conflicted with that of the behaviorists who thought that all psychic phenomena could be observed and understood in the same manner as other natural processes. With this contention in mind, the behaviorists dismissed introspection or at best replaced it with laboratory controls and empirical measurements which reflected their orientation. Mead (1934) objected to this dismissal. It was his feeling that the scope of behaviorism could be extended to include the neglected (dismissed) introspective method. Mead criticized the behaviorist conception of the organism because it was based on the abstraction of the individual from the social process in which it occurs. The consequence of this artificial abstraction, which Mead felt was a fundamental error, was a conception of individuals acting and reacting in a causal mode similar to the physical "behavior" of billiard balls. Mead objected to the implication that individuals passively respond to stimuli. It was his contention that organisms determine their own environments to a great extent. He noted that before an organism makes any overt movement an inner mobilization of energy takes place which no other organism can observe. He further suggested that where attention enables the organism to organize the field in which it is going to act, in so doing we have an organism acting and determining its environment. Therefore, Mead contended that the self was not simply a set of passive senses played upon by stimuli which came from without.

Thus Mead, in agreement with Cooley's conception of the "looking-glass self," suggested that the self was essentially a social process within the individual involving two analytically distinguishable phases — or what I have referred to as references for awareness of self — the "I" and the "me." Mead felt that through symbols (shared meanings and values) men could stimulate other men. He further proposed that through the learning of a culture (an elaborate set of symbols shared by the members of society) man is able to predict other men's behavior as well as predict the predictions other men make of one's own behavior. Not only are objects, actions, and characteristics defined (given some shared meaning and value), but the individual himself is also so defined. Accordingly, Mead felt that the definition of oneself as a specific role-player in a given relationship was accomplished by recognizing and sharing the meanings and values others have of you. This Mead called the "me." That is, Mead saw the "me" as representing the incorporated "other" within the individual.

Mead's "I" was the perception of oneself as reflected by the shared meanings and values of "others." He suggested that the incorporated attitudes (meanings and values) of others constituted the organized "me"; that the way one perceived the "me" constituted the "I"; and that both combined constituted the nature of self.

"I," "me," and "we." Inasmuch as a reevaluation or expansion of Mead's analytically distinguishable phases is important for a clear understanding of black self-conceptions, it may be appropriate to discuss this expansion briefly here prior to a review of the types of studies which fall into the symbolic interaction approach. The necessity for the expansion stems from Mead's omission of a very crucial aspect or phase (to use his term) of the internal social process which defines the self. Mead omitted the reference for oneself as being a member or part of the group (society), or what is descriptively discussed as the feeling of "we-ness." Most students of Mead would suggest that the "we" is handled in Mead's analytical thinking by the "me" which is in fact the internalization or incorporation of the "other," e.g., society. Yet when one examines the analysis more

closely, it is clear that Mead meant for the "me" to stand for the incorporation of *others'* attitudes and feelings about oneself; the "I" stood for one's perception or feeling about the organized "me." Nothing represents clearly and distinctly the perception or feeling of the relationship between one's combined "I," "me," and society. The feeling of being defined as a member of the group and the subsequent interactions one has as a member of a particular group are an important and distinguishable phase or referent for self, which I am calling the "we."

In expanding Mead's analytically distinguishable phases, I would now like to suggest that the notion of self is a social process within the individual which reflects the awareness of three referents for self: the "I" —the self as perceiver of oneself in relation to others' attitudes and feelings toward you, the "me" —the self as the internalized or incorporated perceptions of others, and the "we" —the self as the feelings or perceptions one has toward the group and being (or interacting with) the group. For example, the "other" for someone could be American psychologists. Then that someone's "me" would be the internalization of the attitudes and feelings the "other" has toward him. The someone's "I" would be the feelings and attitudes the person has about the organized "me." The "we" would be the feelings the person has about American psychologists and his interaction with them.

Symbolic Interaction Studies. The studies in this area demonstrate that there are a number of ways in which social interaction and self-concept may be related. All of the studies reflect the assumption that one's self-concept is shaped in social interaction. Many researchers (Hill, 1957; Mason, 1954; Klausner, 1953; Havighurst & Taba, 1949) have translated this to mean that particular types of social interaction (experiences) were associated with particular self-concept characteristics. Other researchers (Lawson & Fagen, 1957; Coates & Pellegrin, 1957) have concerned themselves with the association between self-concept and particular roles, e.g., prison guards or executives.

Three studies by McKee and Sherriffs (1957, 1959; Sherriffs & McKee, 1957) concerned the effects of male and female stereotypes on self-concept. Some studies (Turner & Vanderliffe, 1958; Zukerman, Baer, & Monashkin, 1956; Berger, 1955) examined the differences between a man's self-concept and a woman's self-concept. The studies of Manis (1955), Davitz (1955), and Lundy (1956) defined the social interaction as peer interaction and self-concept.

This area of symbolic interaction which postulates that the self-concept is shaped in the social interaction is a good point of transition to the literature concerning the self-concept of the (so-called) Negro.

REVIEW OF THE LITERATURE ON "NEGRO" SELF-CONCEPT

It is interesting to note that Wylie's (1961) comprehensive review and evaluation of the research in the area of self-concept does not include one single study which considers race as a factor or aspect of self-concept. Clearly if sex, religious affiliation, and socioeconomic class status are important factors, race too must have some importance in relation to self-concept. Indeed, it is even more interesting to note that, five years prior to Wylie's review, Seward (1956) cautioned her fellow researchers against judging the "Negro" by white norms and emphatically stated that "color is inherent in the concept of self [p. 129]." The following discussion is an attempt to partially correct Wylie's oversight. The sample of work reviewed here is believed typical of the work published.

Negative Self-Concept: Negro Self-Hate

The phenomenon of minority group self-hatred has received considerable attention (Adelson, 1953; Radke-Yarrow & Lande, 1953; Sarnoff, 1951; Clark & Clark, 1947; Stevenson & Stewart, 1958; Radke & Trager, 1950; Goodman, 1952; Moreland, 1958; Landreth & Johnson, 1953). The original question was posed in the form: Does the Negro like being a Negro? The answer, based partially on the now classic study by Clark and Clark (1947) was no. Researchers interpreted the Clarks' findings as indicative of self-hate. The Negro child's choice of dolls or playmates was viewed not only as preference for whites but also as an emphatic rejection of one's own racial group (Proshansky & Newton, 1968). Other studies (Goodman, 1952; Stevenson & Stewart, 1958) supported this notion. In a later book, Clark (1955) notes that a child "can not learn what racial group he belongs to without being involved in the larger pattern of emotions, conflicts, and desires which are part of his growing knowledge of what society thinks about his race [p. 23]." Thus early in life the

Negro child absorbs the cultural norms, values, and judgments made about his race. Proshansky and Newton (1968) suggest that what the Negro child learns is to associate "Negro" with "dirty," "bad," and "ugly," while the white child learns to associate "white" with "clean," "nice," and "good." For the Negro child, these judgments operate to establish his own racial group as inferior to white people.

Typically, the Negro self-hate area developed as an attempt to duplicate earlier studies concerning Jewish minorities. For instance, Sarnoff (1951) reviewed and discussed the relationship between Anna Freud's (1946) theory of identification with the aggressor and Jewish anti-semitism. Believing that the position of the Negro in America was similar to that of the Jew, Maliver (1970) wanted to know if the notion of identification with the aggressor could help to explain self-hatred and self-rejection. Thus he attempted to determine whether conclusions in support of the theory of identification with the aggressor drawn from Sarnoff's study were applicable to the hypothesized similar phenomenon of anti-Negro bias amongst Negroes.

The assumption in most of these studies is that the Negro who feels disdain or hatred for his own racial group expresses, at some level, disdain and hatred for himself. This assumption led to considerations of the conditions which fostered Negro self-identity or a particular self-concept which was characteristically Negro. In particular, this Negro self-concept was assumed to be the consequence of the experiences of Negroes. It was also assumed that the self-concept of the Negro was the antecedent of his particular behavior. Research in the area reflected both of these approaches. Pettigrew (1964a), for instance, suggested that the "real tragedy" of the Negro is that, having been forced to play the servile, passive, and inferior role, he came to believe in it as a reflection of his self-image. Pettigrew noted that by judging himself the way others do, the Negro grows into the servile role, which in time becomes indistinguishable from the person himself. Deutsch (1960), on the other hand, suggested that Negro children generally had more negative self-concepts and were therefore more morose, more passive, and more fearful than their white schoolmates.

The point which much of this research attempted to establish was that the experiences of Negroes amounted mainly to an unending source of conflict, which detrimentally affected their self-conceptions. Rainwater (1966) gave even greater importance to the family experience. He focussed on the Negro family's central role in transmitting the values and attitudes of and toward society. He suggested that, for most children, growing up involves developing feelings of competence and mastery over the environment, while for the slum child the process is reversed. In growing up, the Negro child learns what he cannot do. He learns about the blocks and barriers to his mastery of his environment, and he learns most of all the futility of trying. Thus Rainwater concludes by defining the lower-class urban Negro family as the "crucible of identity."

Both Pettigrew (1964a) and Rainwater (1966) ultimately conclude by implying, and in some instances explicitly stating, that the life patterns of the lower-class urban Negro from a distinctive subculture which arose in response to, as well as in consequence of, the discriminatory system in America.

Negro Self-Hate: Fact or Fantasy?

Much of the self-hatred literature should be accepted as valid information only with considerable doubt and caution. Oftentimes researchers have demonstrated only one insignificant finding and regardless of their own results concluded their studies with assertions which were contrary to their own evidence. Brown (1967), for instance, compared the self-perceptions of four-year-old Negro lower-class and white middle-class children. The children were asked to look at pictures of themselves and to describe the child in the picture by choosing words from a list of bipolar adjectives (happy-sad, good-bad, etc.). Each child was also asked to respond as he thought his parents and teachers would respond. Brown then derived for each child a self-as-object and self-as-subject measure. In the subjects' responses to how their teachers perceived them, Brown reported that the greatest difference between Negro and white children was on the part of the self-as-object measure—particularly, black children believed their teacher saw them as "sad" rather than "happy," while the white children believed the reverse. This Brown in fact did demonstrate. However, on several other dimensions (i.e., stupid vs. smart; like vs. not like to talk; liking the way his clothes looked vs. not liking the way his clothes looked) Brown found no statistically significant difference; yet he concludes that on each of these characteristics the Negro children more often than white children tended to believe that their teacher perceived them negatively.

Pettigrew (1964b) compared the effects of "father present" and "father absent" working-class individuals on the perpetuation of what he calls the lower-class Negro family pattern, i.e., instability. While the data indicates that there were no statistically significant differences between the two groups, Pettigrew nevertheless suggested that the "father-absent" individuals (who incidentally were most often black) felt more "victimized" and "less in control of the environment." Thus he concludes that father-absence in early childhood has some influence on personality development and marital status.

In the previously mentioned study by Maliver (1970) concerning anti-Negro bias among Negroes, Maliver had to reject all his major hypotheses and conclude that the conclusions drawn from Sarnoff's (1951) study of Jewish anti-semitism were shown to be not applicable to Negroes. Yet in summary Maliver suggested that a high degree of acceptance of anti-Negro statements was associated with a negative view of one's father and a generalized fear of rejection by adult figures.

It may be noted here that this kind of experimental treatment is not atypical. However, one must be cautioned not to discard water, bathtub, and baby—all because of the filth in the water. Even though in most of these studies the conclusions and interpretations are misleading, some aspects of the findings and a few of the assumptions seem to be correct and potentially useful.

Proshansky and Newton (1968), for instance, note that contrary to Pettigrew's (1964a) assertion, many Negroes do not find satisfaction or adjustment in passively complying with the demands of white society. A report by the Group for the Advancement of Psychiatry (1957) suggested that beneath the Negro's mask of compliance lies fear, anger, and resentment; and that furthermore the Negro who conforms to the demands of white society and consequently rejects himself pays a high price. One of the important things Kardiner and Ovesey (1951) revealed in their book is that, in hiding his feelings, the Negro may suffer serious psychological consequences. This they in turn hypothesize to be the "mark of oppression." That is, the Negro has a strong identification with whites who he (the Negro) simultaneously hates. The studies of Grossack (1956), Noel (1964), and Seward (1956) indicate the importance of group identification and group belongingness to self-conception. Even though Clark (1965) implies that blacks would prefer not to be with their own people, this assertion must be tempered with caution. The studies by

Parker and Kleiner (1965) suggest in fact that the person's own group is of crucial importance for the individual's identity.

In discussing some resources for positive self-identity, the previously mentioned study by Proshansky and Newton (1968) indicates that in order to understand why some Negroes feel little or no conflict about their identity, researchers need to explore all aspects of being a Negro. In particular, researchers need to look at the Negro who accepts his group membership and who frequently gains self-support and self-enhancement from being black. The assumption implicit in the Proshansky and Newton argument is that negative self-identity is frequently rooted in negative group identity and, conversely, positive identity is dependent upon or rooted in positive group identification.

Given the apparent changes in the contemporary images of blackness—Black is Beautiful; I'm Black and I'm Proud—and without even suggesting that there is some real concern and doubt about whether historically the self-hatred research did in fact demonstrate that black people hated themselves and that this hatred was reflected in a denial or rejection of group membership, it is now very important that research be conducted to discover what is in fact the black self-concept and what, if any, is the dynamic relationship between it and the individual's conception of his group.

SELF-CONCEPT: A COGNITIVE STRUCTURE

Carl Rogers (1951) postulated that human beings had a drive to maintain the organization of their self-concept. The implications of Rogers's postulation not only came from, but in a sense helped formulate, the notion of phenomenal self being an internally differentiated Gestalt. Several researchers have attempted to test Rogers's contention empirically. Matthews, Hardyck, and Sarbin (1953) combined Rogers's notion with Sarbin's (1952) earlier theory of self-development and repostulated three developmental levels of self-organization, concluding that the self should be considered as a cognitive structure. The selves (structural parts), they suggested, operate as reference-schemata for the person's cognitive, affective, and conative behavior.

At first glance this line of research seems provocative and potentially fruitful; however, very little research has come forth. Wylie (1961) noted in this connection that the reason so little empirical work has resulted is probably due to the vagueness and ambiguousness of the theoretical propositions which refer to self as having organizational properties. Wylie further notes that none of the statements she reviewed spelled out a clearly defined criterion for operationally defining organization, configuration, differentiation, and consistency characteristics of the self-organization. Nevertheless, a few investigators have given serious attention to the consistency aspect of the cognitive-self structure.

R. D. Cartwright (1957) dealt with consistency between social self-concepts, attempting to measure the subject's idea of how three different people viewed him. Using Q-sorts she employed the mean item variance among the Q-sorts as an index of the subject's self-organizational consistency. Thus large mean variances in the data indicated disagreement among the subject's social self-concepts, or lack of consistency in "self-organization." In a similar study, D. S. Cartwright (1956) studied the consistency between experience and the self-concept structure. Specifically, he attempted to test Rogers's contention that experiences which conflict with the structure of self will either be ignored or distorted. Defining inconsistent stimuli as those experiences having a content or meaning that is either unrelated to or descriptive of the opposite of some aspect of the self-structure, Cartwright attempted to measure the consistency between experience (stimuli) and the self-concept as reflected in three different types of experiences (stimuli): nonsense syllables, adjectives, and names of possessions.

Hodges (1966), more so than other cognitive self-consistency researchers, contends that the self as conceived by Cooley (1902), Mead (1934), and Burrows (1953) can be conceptualized as a principle of balance. Hodges attempted to test explicitly the theoretical principles of balance theory as they relate to the cognitive structuring of the self. Adapting Heider's (1958) conventional notation to Cooley's emphasis on the looking-glass self and Mead's distinction between the "I" and the "me," Hodges demonstrated in his research a concise illustration of how a person enhances and/or maintains his self-image by maintaining balanced cognitive-self units.

AFRICANITY AND SELF-CONCEPTION

It is probably true that in the establishment of self one must join with some and depart from others, or at least make salient characteristics similar to some while denying qualities similar to still others. Accordingly, the self is established as a consequence of two processes—apposition and/or opposition. Even though most (Western) scholars recognize the two possibilities, most define the self as being established oppositionally, i.e., the self is "individually" unique and different from the other selves.

Some non-Western world-views, particularly the African, place a totally different emphasis on self (Mbiti, 1970; Abrahams, 1962), conceiving of the self as coming into being as a consequence of the group's being. This can be contrasted with the Western orientation which views the group as depending totally on individual ingression. The African world-view suggests that "I am because *we* are and because *we* are, therefore, I am." In so emphasizing, this view makes no real distinction between the self and others. They are in a sense one and the same: One's being is the group's being; one's self is the "self of one's people"; one's being is the "we" instead of the 'I.'" One's self-identity is therefore always a *people* identity, or what could be called an *extended identity* or *extended self* (Nobles, 1972a). Accordingly the African world-view requires that when focussing on the self, one not be bound to the examination of distinct, separate individuals, but, rather, one should examine the dynamics of the "we" or the feelings of belonging to as well as being the "group." Unlike Western conceptions which examine independent and individual selves, research involving the African world-view cannot make a critical distinction between the self (I) and one's people (we).

The task here is not to explicate in detail what the original African conception of self was. The main reason for this is because the African perspective of self has not been objectified into abstract information or knowledge. The concern here is with what kind of cognitive organization exists as a function of the African world-view jibing and/or colliding with the American (Western) world-view.

It is important to note that many, if not most, of the peoples of African descent living in America operate in everyday life from a perspective which reflects their Africanity. This fact is supported by many scholars (Billingsley, 1968; DuBois, 1908; Herskovitz, 1958). And, as experience relates to self-conception, Festinger (1961) indirectly lends support to the abovementioned contention. He notes that to change the self-concept one must be induced by some "mild pressure or reward" to do something contrary to one's present self-concept. Only if one defines slavery, imprisonment, killings, racism, and oppression as mild forms of pressure and/or reward can one suggest that, in the main, the African conception of self has radically changed.

For the purposes of this essay it is not necessary to make explicit the distinction between Western (white) and African (black) conceptions of the self. It is only necessary to note that the Western conception suggests that the self is that which makes one individually unique or different from, while the African conception suggests that the self is a "Transcendence into Extendation" or an *extended self.* That is to say, the African self is one's people or tribe; the two — oneself and one's people — are more than simply interdependent or interrelated, they are one and the same.

It was suggested earlier that the self is the consequence of either oppositionary or appositionary placement in time and space in relation to other people. It was also suggested that the work of most Western students of the self supports the fact that the oppositionary process is utilized most often. This, however, is not universal even in the West. Within the philosophical heritage of Western people of African descent, the self can not be defined individualistically, nor is it in the oppositionary mode. The notion of self for peoples of African descent is reflected as a distinct cognitive structural organization.

Differential Cognitive Structures

Earlier I suggested that Mead's two analytically distinguishable phases, the "I" and the "me," might be expanded to include the notion of the "we." The rationale for this was that people generally conceive of themselves in one of these three ways. Each in its own quality relates particular information to the person about (his) self; combined they form what is known as "the self." The importance of these distinct referents for self (and it should be noted that the importance is only in its analytical power or utility) is that they allow us to discuss in depth the dynamic character of self. Hence one would hypothesize that the organizational character of self, its Gestalt, is its combined "I," "me," and "we" referential aspects.

The dynamic character of the cognitive-self structure, therefore, is the relationship between the referential component parts. That is, the dynamic character of the cognitive-self structure is the relationship between the self as "I," the self as "me," and the self as "we." It was also discussed earlier in relation to Hodges's study that consistency between the "I" and the "me" is necessary if the person is to maintain a particular self-image. Given the importance of the group (the "we") in relation to self-identity (Grossack, 1956; Noel, 1964; Seward, 1956; Parker & Kleiner, 1965), it must also be true that consistency between the self-referents ("I," "me," and the "we") is of fundamental importance to the individual's conception of self.

One could suggest that those individuals who have some real discrepancy between their self-referents would more likely have a low or negative self-concept and, conversely, those individuals who experience no real discrepancy (consistency) between their self-referents would be more likely to have a high or positive self-concept. However, this is too simplistic and in fact doesn't reveal the true differences in cognitive structures. For one thing, one must recognize that if consistency is operationally defined as balanced units in the Heiderian sense and as represented in Hodges's (1966) study, then what may be consistent for one individual may be discrepant (in the sense of unbalanced unit relations) for another individual. For instance, it may be extremely important for some individuals to have at all times a strong positive unit relation between the "I" and "me" self-referents and the "we" self-referent; while for others having a very weak or none-at-all unit relation between the "I" and "me" self-referents and the "we" self-referent may be the necessary balanced cognitive-self organization to maintain. In both cases, consistency in the cognitive-self organization is being maintained but in entirely different ways.

The abovementioned concern for Africanity and its relation to self, suggests that peoples of African descent—based on an "African perspective"— are more inclined to adhere to the self as reflecting the principle of "I am because *we* are, and because *we* are, therefore, I am." Such people would find it extremely important to maintain a strong, positive unit relation between their "I," "me," and "we" self-referents. Consequently, cognitive-self consistency would be reflected in the positive relations between all three awareness referents for self. In the same sense, those people who adhere to the self as reflected in the principle, "I am (my) self by virtue of setting myself off and away from others, by opposing myself to others [Jasper, 1962]," are more inclined also to adhere to the self as reflected in an organization where the unit relations between the awareness referents for self are weak or nonexistent. Thus, it could be that the differential cognitive units in relation to self for African peoples are represented by a cognitive-self organization which is extended or inclusive, while that of European peoples must be described as independent or exclusive. The methodological tasks associated with the testing of this hypothesis are considerable (Nobles, 1972b).

The relationship between the orientation of most of the black self-concept research reviewed in this essay and the race of most of the researchers involved is not a statistical artifact. It is evident that the data collected by these researchers reflects not the reality of African (black) self-conception but rather the researchers' natural selective [mis]perception of it. We note that the definitional significance of Africa to black self-conception has not been considered, even though Africa has been critically important in the lives of the great majority of black people. It is possible and highly probable that these researchers are unable to take into account the "African reality" of black people living in America.

The inability of these researchers to document this aspect of black social reality casts doubt on their ability to understand and/or document other social psychological questions in the black community. Because of this, not only is the rejection of all previous research called for, but we must also question whether or not the researchers' actual presence in the black community is at all warranted.

REFERENCES

Abrahams, W. E. *The mind of Africa*. Chicago: University of Chicago Press, 1962.

Adelson, J. A. A study of minority group authoritarianism. *Journal of Abnormal and Social Psychology,* 1953, 48, 477–485.

Ames, L. B. The sense of self of nursery school children as manifested by their verbal behavior. *Journal of Genetic Psychology,* 1952, 91, 193–232.

Berger, E. M. Relationship among acceptance of self, acceptance of others and MMPI scores. *Journal of Counseling Psychology,* 1955, 2, 279–284.

Billingsley, A. *Black families in white America*. Englewood Cliffs, N.J.: Prentice-Hall, 1968.

Bills, R. E. A comparison of scores on the index of adjustment and values with behavior as measures of change in emotionality. *Journal of Counseling Psychology,* 1953, 17, 135–138.

Brown, B. *The assessment of self-concept among four-year-old Negro and white children: A comparative study using the Brown-IDS self-concept referents test*. New York: Institute for Developmental Studies, 1967. (Mimeo)

Burrows, T. *Science and man's behavior*. New York: Philosophical Library, 1953.

Cartwright, D. S. Self-consistency as a factor affecting immediate recall. *Journal of Abnormal and Social Psychology,* 1956, 52, 212–218.

Cartwright, R. D. Effects of psychotherapy on self consistency. *Journal of Counseling Psychology,* 1957, 4, 15–22.

Clark, K. B. *Prejudice and your child*. Boston: Beacon Press, 1955.

Clark, K. B. *Dark ghetto: Dilemmas of social power.* New York: Harper & Row, 1965.

Clark, K. B., & Clark, M. P. Racial identification and preference in Negro children. In T. M. Newcomb & E. L. Hartley (Eds.), *Readings in social psychology.* New York: Holt, Rinehart, & Winston, 1947.

Coates, C. H., & Pellegrin, R. J. Executives and supervisors: Contrasting self-conceptions and conceptions of each other. *American Sociological Review,* 1957, 22, 217–220.

Cooley, C. H. *Human nature and social order.* New York: Scribners, 1902.

Cowen, E. L., Heilizer, F., & Axelrod, H. S. Self-concept conflict indicators and learning. *Journal of Abnormal and Social Psychology,* 1955, 51, 242–245.

Crowne, D. P., & Stephens, M. W. Self-acceptance and self-evaluation behavior: A critique of methodology. *Psychological Bulletin,* 1961, 58, 104–119.

Davitz, J. R. Social perceptions and sociometric choice in children. *Journal of Abnormal and Social Psychology,* 1955, 50, 173–176.

Deutsch, M. Minority group and class status as related to social and personality factors in scholastic achievement. Monograph No. 2. *Society of Applied Anthropology,* 1960.

Doris, J. Test anxiety and blame assignment in grade school children. *Journal of Abnormal and Social Psychology,* 1959, 58, 181–190.

DuBois, W. E. B. *The Negro American family.* Atlanta: The Atlanta University Press, 1908.

Edelson, M., & Jones, A. E. Operational explorations of conceptual self systems and of the interaction between frames of references. *Genetic Psychology Monographs,* 1954, 50, 43–139.

Engel, M. The stability of the self-concept in adolescence. *Journal of Abnormal and Social Psychology,* 1959, 58, 211–215.

Festinger, L. The psychological effects of insufficient reward. *American Psychologist,* 1961, 16, 1–11.

Freud, A. *The ego and the mechanisms of defence.* New York: International University Press, 1946.

Frisch, P., & Cranston, R. Q-technique applied to a patient and the therapist in a child guidance setting. *Journal of Clinical Psychology,* 1956, 12, 178–182.

Gebel, A. S. Self-perception and leaderless group discussion status. *Journal of Social Psychology,* 1954, 40, 309–318.

Gilinsky, A. S. Relative self-estimate and level of aspiration. *Journal of Experimental Psychology,* 1949, 39, 256–259.

Goodman, M. E. *Race awareness in young children.* Reading, Mass.: Addison-Wesley, 1952.

Gordon, C., & Gergen, K. J. *The self in social interaction.* Vol. 1. New York: Wiley, 1968.

Grossack, M. Group belongingness among Negroes. *Journal of Social Psychology,* 1956, 43, 167–180.

Group for the Advancement of Psychiatry. *Psychiatric aspects of school desegregation.* New York, 1957.

Harvey, O. J., Kelley, H. H., & Shapiro, M. M. Reactions to unfavorable evaluations of the self made by other persons. *Journal of Personality.* 1957, 25, 398–411.

Havighurst, R. J., & Taba, H. *Adolescent character and personality.* New York: Wiley, 1949.

Heider, F. *The psychology of interpersonal relations.* New York: Wiley, 1958.

Herskovitz, M. L. *The myth of the Negro past.* Boston: Beacon Press, 1958.

Hill, T. J. Attitudes toward self: An experimental study. *Journal of Educational Sociology,* 1957, 30, 395–397.

Hodges, D. L. The self and cognitive balance: Improvements in balance theory's predictive power. *Pacific Sociological Review*, 1966, 9, (1), 22–34.

Jasper, K. Allgemeine psychopathologie, 1959. Quoted in A. Wenkart, The self in existentialism. *Annals of the New York Academy of Science*, 1962, 96.

Jourard, S. M., & Remy, R. M. Perceived parental attitudes, the self and security. *Journal of Consulting Psychology*, 1955, 19, 364–366.

Kardiner, A., & Ovesey, L. *The mark of oppression*. Cleveland, Ohio: World, 1951.

Klausner, S. Z. Social class and self-concept. *Journal of Social Psychology*, 1953, 38, 201–205.

Landreth, C., & Johnson, B. C. Young children's responses to picture and inset test design to reveal reactions to persons of different skin color. *Child Development*, 1953, 24, 63–79.

Lawson, E. D., & Fagen, E. R. Stereotypes of prison guards. *Journal of Correctional Psychology*, 1957, 2, 13–22.

Lazowick, L. M. On the nature of identification. *Journal of Abnormal and Social Psychology*, 1955, 51, 175–183.

Lepine, L. T., & Chodorkoff, B. Goal setting behavior, expressed feelings of adequacy and the correspondence between the perceived and the ideal self. *Journal of Clinical Psychology*, 1955, 11, 395–397.

Lowe, C. M. The self-concept: Fact or artifact? *Psychological Bulletin*, 1961, 58, 325–336.

Lundy, R. M. Self-perceptions and descriptions of opposite sex sociometric choices. *Sociometry*, 1956, 19, 272–278.

Maliver, B. L. Anti-Negro bias among Negro college students. In M. L. Goldschmid (Ed.), *Black Americans and white racism*. New York: Holt, Rinehart, & Winston, 1970.

Manis, M. Social interpretations of the self-concept. *Journal of Abnormal and Social Psychology*, 1955, 51, 362–370.

Manis, M. Personal adjustment, assumed similarity to parents and inferred parental evaluations of the self. *Journal of Consulting Psychology*, 1958, 22, 481–485.

Martire, J. G. Relationships between self-concepts and difference in strength and achievement motivation. *Journal of Personality*, 1956, 24, 364–375.

Mason, E. P. Some factors in self-judgments. *Journal of Clinical Psychology*, 1954, 10, 336–340.

Matthews R., Hardyck, C., & Sarbin, T. R. Self organizations as a factor in the performance of selected cognitive task. *Journal of Abnormal and Social Psychology*, 1953, 48, 500–502.

May, R. I. I. The origins and significance of the existential movement in psychology. II. Contributions of existential psychotherapy. In R. May, et al. (Eds.), *Existence: A new dimension in psychiatry and psychology*. New York: Basic Books, 1958.

Mbiti, J. S. *African religions and philosophy*. New York: Anchor, 1970.

McKee, J. R., & Sherriffs, A. C. The differential evaluation of males and females. *Journal of Personality*, 1957, 25, 356–371.

McKee, J. R. & Sherriffs, A. C. Men's and women's belief, ideals, and self-concepts. *American Journal of Sociology*, 1959, 64, 356–363.

Mead, G. H. *Mind, self and society*. Chicago: University of Chicago, 1934.

Moreland, J. K. Racial recognition by nursery school children in Lynchburg, Virginia. *Social Forces*, 1958, 37, 132–137.

Mussen, P. H., & Jones, M. C. Self-conceptions, motivations, and interpersonal attitudes of late- and early-maturing boys. *Child Development*, 1957, 28, 243–256.

Nobles, W. W. African philosophy: Foundations for black psychology. In R. L. Jones (Ed.), *Black psychology*. New York. Harper & Row, 1972. (a)

Nobles, W. The effects of African identification vs. American identification and cultural message vs. economic message exposure on group unity. Unpublished doctoral dissertation, Stanford University, 1972. (b)

Noel, D. L. Group identification among Negroes: An empirical analysis. *Journal of Social Issues*, 1964, 20(2), 71–84.

Nunnally, J. C. An investigation of some propositions of self-concept: The case of Miss Sun. *Journal of Abnormal and Social Psychology*, 1955, 50, 87–92.

Parker, S., & Kleiner, R. J. *Mental illness in the urban Negro community*. New York: Free Press, 1965.

Pettigrew, T. F. *A profile of the Negro American*. Princeton, N.J.: Van Nostrand, 1964. (a)

Pettigrew, T. F. Father-absence and Negro adult personality: A research note. Cited in Pettigrew, T. F. *A profile of the Negro American*. Princeton, N.J.: Van Nostrand, 1964. (b)

Proshansky, H., & Newton, P. The nature and meaning of Negro self-identity. In M. Deutsch, I. Katz, & A. R. Jensen (Eds.), *Social class, race and psychological development*. New York: Holt, Rinehart, & Winston, 1968.

Radke, M., & Trager, H. G. Children's perceptions of the social roles of Negroes and whites. *Journal of Psychology*, 1950, 29, 3–33.

Radke-Yarrow, M., & Lande, B. Personality correlates of minority group belonging. *Journal of Social Psychology*, 1953, 38, 253–272.

Rainwater, L. Crucible of identity: The Negro lower-class family. *Daedalus*, 1966, 95, 172–217.

Reckless, W. C., Dinitz, S., & Kay, B. The self component in potential delinquency and potential non-delinquency. *American Sociological Review*, 1957, 22, 566–570.

Rogers, C. R. *Client-centered therapy*. Boston: Houghton Mifflin, 1951.

Rogers, C. R. The case of Mrs. Oaks: A research analysis. In C. R. Rogers & R. T. Dymond (Eds.), *Psychiatry and personality change*. Chicago: University of Chicago Press, 1954.

Sarbin, T. R. A preface to a psychological analysis of the self. *Psychological Review*, 1952, 59, 11–22.

Sarnoff, I. Identification with the aggressor: Some personality correlates of anti-semitism among Jews. *Journal of Personality*, 1951, 20, 199–218.

Sears, P. Level of aspiration in relation to some variables of personality: Clinical studies. *Journal of Social Psychology*, 1941, 14, 311–336.

Seward, G. *Psychotherapy and culture conflict*. New York: Ronald Press, 1956.

Sherriffs, A. C., & McKee, J. P. Qualitative aspects of beliefs about men and women. *Journal of Personality*, 1957, 25, 251–264.

Smith, W. D., & Lebo, D. Some changing aspects of the self-concept of pubescent males. *Journal of Genetic Psychology*, 1956, 88, 61–75.

Snygg, P. A., & Combs, A. W. *Individual behavior: A new frame of reference for psychology*. New York: Harper, 1949.

Stevenson, H. W., & Stewart, E. C. A developmental study of racial awareness in young children. *Child Development*, 1958, 29, 399–410.

Tiryakian, E. A. Existential self and the person. In C. Gordon & K. Gergen (Eds.), *The self and social interaction*. Vol. 1. New York: Wiley, 1968.

Turner, R. H., & Vanderliffe, R. H. Self ideal congruence as an index of adjustment. *Journal of Abnormal and Social Psychology*, 1958, 57, 202–206.

Wylie, R. C. *The self-concept*. Lincoln, Nebraska: University of Nebraska, 1961.

Zukerman, M., Baer, M., & Monashkin, I. Acceptance of self, parents and people in patients and normals. *Journal of Clinical Psychology*, 1956, 12, 327–332.

9. Poor Women in Psychological Research: Shut Up and Shut Out

Pamela Trotman Reid

The inspiration for my title came from a quote of Simone de Beauvoir in which she described the difficulty women have dealing with the simultaneous limitations and variety of our roles. She said that women were "shut up in our world" (cited in Bernard, 1981, p. 20). She referred to social limitations and exclusions based on gender. I want to extend de Beauvoir's words to women who experience the world of poverty and low economic status. I plan to consider how women with few resources have been poorly served by psychological researchers, including researchers who focus on the psychology of women. My title is intended to convey that low-income women have been silenced through a lack of attention and have been excluded from participation in the process of defining their life experiences by our methodological strategies and our theoretical formulations.

In the psychology of women, we often claim to study women *qua* women. As Elizabeth Spelman (1988) and others have suggested, this claim appears false, or at least misleading. For the most part, theory and empirical study in the psychology of women have failed to recognize many distinctions among women. Indeed, the focus of feminist theory and research has been directed to the explication of women's essential experience of gender, as if this could be separated from the confounds of class and race. The traditional and simplistic notions of our discipline continue to lead us to search for the atoms of experience, although human behavior would be better represented by a more complex model. The persistent belief has been advanced that we can distill segments of personal experience and then add these segments together for an accurate characterization and understand-

Reprinted by permission of the author and Cambridge University Press from *Psychology of Women Quarterly* 17 (1993) : 133–50. © 1993 *Cambridge University Press.*

ing of reality. The strategy of "add social class and mix" or "add race and mix" has not worked. Thus, we should feel compelled to ask, "What do we need to know, and what should we do, to understand and explain the true diversity of women?"

Purpose of Study

I have chosen to focus on poor women because the work and attitudes toward them may best represent how psychology remains both ego-centric and introspective. Too often we have taken the easy road, examining our own middle-class educated thoughts and our own middle-class educated experiences and using them as criteria against which we measure others. Feminist psychology does not differ greatly in this respect from traditional psychology. Indeed, poor women are virtually unnamed in feminist work. In research and practice, poor women are underrepresented as participants for observation and clients for intervention. Even though some of us may have originated in low-income families, these past experiences are now filtered through our current perspectives. I am reminded of how my own experiences and views differ from those of my grandmother, who emigrated as a teenager from Trinidad to work in a New York garment factory shortly before the 1920s.

Just as the perspectives of women of color have been ignored by White American women in the psychological literature (Reid, 1988), so too have the perspectives of poor women been ignored by the middle class. I want to underscore that the omission of these perspectives is not exclusively an oversight of one race or another. I believe that the reduction of poor women's perspectives to a coinciding version of the middle-class view occurs repeatedly, both implicitly and explicitly, in our thinking and writing.

To examine this phenomenon, we should recognize that the majority of professional women, psychologists among them, come from well-educated middle-class homes, from families that, if not exactly middle class in income, are middle class in values, that is, who have placed a high value on education and who subscribe to middle-class beliefs. There was support for this contention in a survey of African-American women and men with doctorates. The African-American women with doctorates came from families that could be described as middle class more frequently than did African-American men with doctorates (Reid & Robinson, 1985).

Certainly not all middle-class female psychologists are removed from close associations with poor women and working-class women; however, many have few daily connections with economically deprived people. Whether or not we have these connections, we can recognize that there have been few discussions within our discipline that offer insight or understanding of lives different from our own. There appears instead an implicit assumption that only quantitative differences separate women's experiences, that is, there is a belief that all women undergo, more or less, the same socialization and oppression. It seems easier for us to accept that poor White women may experience more oppression than do middle-class White women but not that they experience different forms of oppression. Similarly, poor women of color are seen as enduring more racism and sexism but not anything fundamentally different from what middle-class women of color endure. The egocentricity of this belief has allowed us to accept a psychology of women that treats the middle-class experience as totally representative, if not the totality, of women's worlds.

Diversity among "Poor" Women

If we are to challenge this basic notion, perhaps we need first to examine who are the poor women. Of course, the largest numbers of poor women, men, and children do not live in the United States, but considering the limitations of space and expertise, I will focus on low-income populations in this country. According to the U.S. Bureau of the Census (1991b), in 1990 over 33 million people in the U.S. (more than 15% of the total population) lived below the poverty level. This group included more women and girls than men and boys overall, and at every specific age group.

Smith (1984) explained that the growth of women's poverty in the U.S. was largely because more women than ever before must support themselves through income or welfare, more women are working, fewer women are marrying, and most new jobs offer little opportunity for self-sufficiency or escape from poverty. D'Ercole (1988) concurred in this analysis. Her review of factors that impact the lives of poor women indicated that increased education and labor force participation have not really changed the economic status of women. The earnings of women still fall far below that of men, and the number of women who are considered below the poverty line is increasing. Smith credited (or blamed) the growth of the low-paid service sector, which includes retail work, as the major factor in poverty in the U.S. Also contributing to poverty is the assumption that women are in a position to accept less than full-time work or temporary positions that do not carry health and retirement benefits.

The U.S. Bureau of the Census (1991a) also noted that the strongest predictor of poverty is being a female householder with no spouse. Single-parent female householders constituted almost half of all poor households in the U.S. Although poor families with children were only about 20% of all families with children, female-headed families represented more than 50% of this group. In addition to being poor in their own households, women are also poor in male-headed households as wives and daughters. Other poor women live alone.

Poor women are elderly with inadequate medical care and emotional support. Poor women are teenage mothers and high-school dropouts. They are welfare recipients and underpaid employees. They are clerical workers, receptionists, sales clerks, waitresses, babysitters, hotel maintenance staff, and domestic workers. Thus, even when women are in the labor market, they earn less than men (Taeuber & Valdisera, 1986).

Increasingly, poor women are among the homeless. They are disproportionately, but not exclusively, ethnic minorities, African Americans, and Latinas. They live in the crowded urban areas of our country such as Baltimore, Chicago, Newark, San Francisco, Seattle, and the nation's capital. They also live in the rural areas of our country such as Hope, AK; Polk County, TN; rural New Mexico and Oklahoma; in the villages of Puerto Rico; and in the remote towns of Alaska. Poor women are immigrants from China, Ecuador, Guiana, Ghana, Mexico, and Vietnam.

In short, poor women, just as any other group of people, may not be represented in simple terms. They have a diversity of backgrounds. They live different daily existences that depend on their particular family responsibilities, their local region, and the composition and expectations of their communities. Their languages, religious practices, personal beliefs, educational experiences, and aspirations may also vary greatly. From our research, we know little about such women. They do appear to share the distinction of being largely ignored in psychological research. (This exclusion may be somewhat greater in psychology than in any other of the social sciences because our discipline demands that we seek universal explanations for individual behavior.)

Although we may look at the government thresholds[1] to provide some indication of who is seriously financially deprived, economic status cannot be accepted as the sole criterion for the classification of working class or poor. Although I refer in part to the economic conditions that limit and define the lives of many women, I am also inferring the state of mind that this condition engenders. Being poor, like being middle class or Black or Jewish and maybe even like being too fat or too short, is more than a quantitative difference. It is a condition that affects how we look at ourselves and how others look at us.

Being poor carries a set of expectations, a way of living, a way of thinking about the world. Instead of merely another variable to be added to or subtracted from our investigations, being poor may set the context for many other dimensions of daily existence. Although little psychological data exist, there are indications that class differences influence aspirations, parenting styles, language, social perception, and many other behaviors.

POOR WOMEN SHUT OUT

The exclusion of poor women is not limited to the psychology of women or any one subarea of psychology. Mulvey (1988) decried the paucity of diverse populations in community psychology, Spencer (1990) and McLoyd (1990a, 1990b) pointed to the lack of diversity in developmental psychology, and Graham (1992) documented the limited attention to ethnic populations in mainstream psychology journals. Most relevant for us, however, is Laura Brown's (1990) argument that White populations and eurocentric attitudes are the sole basis of the development of feminist theories and therapies. I must agree that in spite of the prodding of many scholars, empirical and theoretical psychology has remained as insensitive to the complexities of race and social class as any other institution in this society.

Riger (1992) suggested that the bias demonstrated in research on psychology of women results from the lack of attention to social context. Like Brown (1990), she pointed out that although feminists maintain the importance of context, the research and theory demonstrate an ignorance of the variety of contexts that are possible. I find it rather difficult to believe that there really is an ignorance of social context among scholars who so often and so elegantly articulate the perspective of social construction. Indeed, recognition of the importance of context has been a legacy of feminist research dating back to the work of Carolyn Sherif (cited in Frieze, Sales, & Smith, 1991). Yet, Frieze et al. (1991) pointed out that the contexts that have typically been investigated are limited by the convenience of our participant populations. They asserted that we have been particularly constrained when using traditional White college students. Their analysis suggests caution when interpreting results from samples controlled for age, race, class status, and so on. In practice, few investigators appear circumspect in discussing the results of their efforts. Instead, studies project conclusions that encompass all women and men, while the severe limitations of the sample are forgotten.

Is it really "forgetting," as Brown (1990) suggested, that leads us to equate the socialization of a 20-year-old White middle-class Jewish woman with that of a 35-year-old middle-class African-American Southern Baptist woman or that of a 16-year-old Latina who is middle class and Catholic? I cannot easily discard the notion that the framing of questions from the perspective of the dominant group and the perpetual oversight of ethnic and class issues represent anything other than elements of racism and incipient class bias. The suggestion that racism, classism, and ethnic stratification are inherent in the traditional research enterprise has been strongly intimated by Landrine, Klonoff, and Brown-Collins (1992). They described the difficulty of disembedding the culture of the investigator from the entire process of investigating. Furthermore, through an empirical example, they attempted to demonstrate that equivalent behavior does not convey similar meanings when cultural contexts are understood and appropriately considered.

The difficulty of contextual and cultural variability was made most dramatically at the American Psychological Association (APA) convention of 1991 in the speech given by an American Indian woman (the designation she gave herself). Robbie Ferron (1991) stunned our pro-choice feminist sensibilities when she presented a perspective on reproductive problems from a culture that was focused on group survival rather than on individual rights. We were prepared to hear a different version of our same story, not a different story. Her message about the fear of cultural extinction raised issues that members of a majority group need never seriously consider. At the same time, she inadvertently challenged the willingness of feminists to accept legitimate, but contradictory, views. As many have indicated, race and class bias play an important role in the inability to accept divergence from a set world view. However, bias alone is too simplistic to serve as a complete explanation for the apparent unwillingness to change from a unidimensional view in research on women. Other factors must play a role in this process.

If the exclusion or shutting out of poor people in general and poor women in particular in psychological research has resulted from factors other than racism and class bias, central among them must be the widespread acceptance of the White middle class as the norm group for every behavior. Feminists have worked insistently to overturn the use of the male norm. Unfortunately, the acceptance of both race and class standards has remained virtually untouched. As White middle-class men were treated as the standard for people, White middle-class women are now treated as the standard of appropriate female behavior (Brown, 1990; Denny, 1986; Espin, 1991; Lorde, 1984). Women in low socioeconomic groups are often held to middle-class White standards, and feminist research offers little or no recognition of the realities and disparities of their lives.

A library computer search provided a gross assessment of the degree of attention given to women in lower socioeconomic groups. Using the data base for the years 1984–1991, I found that the word "woman" accessed 14,517 abstracts; "poverty" produced 556. The combination of "woman" and "poverty" provided only 86 abstracts. "Woman" and "working class" resulted in 82 citations; "woman" and "low income," 99. This represented little more than 0.5% of the abstracts that contained the word "woman." Considering that a sizable proportion of the abstracts were not empirical and that others offered only demographic information and not psychological analysis, the findings were fairly disappointing. Even more devastating was the combination of "feminist" and "poverty," which produced only seven abstracts, or "feminist" and "working class," which resulted in five.

As a discipline, psychology seems to cast ethnic minorities of both genders and working-class people of all colors into marginal roles. If recent histories of the discipline are used to indicate the place of social status and ethnicity, these issues are low in importance. Two special journal issues are illustrative: the *American Psychologist*'s Special Issue on the History of Psychology (Benjamin, 1992) and the 50th anniversary issue of the *Journal of Social Issues* (Levinger, 1986). Neither issue dealt directly with social class, ethnicity, or race.

The Need to Disentangle Ethnicity and Class

The issue of how to deal with ethnicity and class has in recent years had a somewhat superficial solution. Now, more than in the past, researchers are likely to be meticulous in providing demographic information about populations they have studied. However, this effort is not sufficient. Although the race and social class of participants are included as descriptors, they are typically not evaluated as factors that affect the experience of the participants. For example, in research on college students, we see little or no recognition that there is privilege associated with being White, middle class, and well educated. Questions about the impact of race remain reserved for people of color, and queries on social class are saved for working-class and poor people.

There appears to be a type of segregation in the topics selected for feminist research. Brown (1990, p. 7) called it "word ghettos." The manifestation of this grouping is seen in many forums. For example, only middle-class White women are studied when there are issues of body image, eating disorders, professional work issues, and sexual harassment. Middle-class White women are sought for illustrations of theoretical assumptions and for scale or measurement development. And middle-class White women are used for basic studies of developmental, social, and personal functioning. Low-income and working-class women, when investigated, have been isolated from mainstream academic psychology. Research on such real-world groups is typically considered applied, so that there is a stratification or dichotomy of populations, with the higher ones being theoretical research on middle-class populations.

This separation of theoretical middle-class populations from applied lower-income populations is not admitted but is regularly accepted. As feminists, we regularly discuss issues of violence, intimacy, and deprivation, yet apparently we still feel uncomfortable in discussing the stigmatization of racism or the impact of class bias. In the literature on homelessness, for example, there has been obvious resistance to considering racism as a component of the experience of economic deprivation among minority groups (Milburn & D'Ercole, 1991). Study after study has failed to make explicit the recognition that much of the hostility and anger against the homeless and poor in our society is the result of their depiction as ethnic minorities and foreign born (e.g., Bassuk, 1990; Belle, 1990; Masten, 1992). In-

deed, few empirical investigations examine these complex phenomena.

Reviews of studies of poor women of color suggest that research
may have produced commonly held views that are distortions of
reality. For example, many investigations of women of color have
focused on their childbearing behavior, often to the exclusion of other
life experiences. Amaro (1988) found this to be the case for Mexican-
American women. In her interviews with these women, she found
greater heterogeneity than previous studies suggested, even among
those who were low income and relatively unacculturated. Similarly,
Wyatt and Lyons-Rowe's (1990) interviews with low-income African-American women revealed complexities in their sexual attitudes
and sexual behavior not suggested in earlier investigations of similar
populations.

The insistence that "women" are not only White but middle class
has undoubtedly assisted in the creation of a counterimage of poor
women. This stereotype, which is depicted nightly by the media,
holds that poor women are best represented as African American and
Latina. The acceptance of these characterizations are also obvious in
the review of studies of teenage and single mothers (Goodman, 1987;
Panzarine, 1989; Pillary, 1987), homeless women (Bassuk, 1990),
and welfare recipients (Glassman, 1970). In these studies, where
women are presented as aberrant, disturbed, abnormal, and needy,
minority women are treated as the appropriate norm group.

This skewed image of ethnic minority women is, as most distortions, only a partial misrepresentation. Ethnic minority women are
overrepresented among the poor. Almost 80% of all U.S. women are
White, 12% Black, and 8% Hispanic (as designated by the government). However, the U.S. Bureau of the Census (1991b) reported
that 35% of all Black women are poor (6 million) and 30% of Hispanic women live in poverty (3 million). Only 12% of all White
women are poor. However, this 12% represents two thirds of all poor
women, that is 13 million poor women are White (U.S. Bureau of the
Census, 1991b). Thus, the images created serve to facilitate the
distancing that occurs from women in poverty and to limit the sampling of their experiences to those society has already defined as aberrant.

Feminist psychologists apparently have accepted and reified these
media and social stereotypes in our research populations. In feminist
books and journal articles, "women" typically refers to middle-class

White women, unless otherwise indicated (Reid, 1988). Measure of attitudes toward women and other feminist scales have already been created using middle-class White women as the norm group. Brown (1990), myself (Reid, 1988), and others have cited feminist authors from de Beauvoir to Gilligan who have developed entire arguments without mention of women of color, differences in economic conditions, or the relevance of sexual orientation. Thus, we are left, as Diane Harriford (1991, p. 3) suggested, "to refute the reality created by others."

Causes of Exclusion

Although acceptance of the White middle-class norm is of paramount significance, there are several other factors that also contribute to the exclusion of poor women in psychological research. Some of these factors are strongly influenced by practicality and professional expectations. These factors include personal affiliation, effort maximization, and investigator training.

I have defined *personal affiliation* as a combination of access and interest. Psychologists tend to study people who are close at hand, that is, our children, our friends, our clients, and, most of all, our students. Data indicate that much of the research in psychology of women has been conducted on populations of convenience, that is, those to whom easy access is possible. For many academic researchers, this has meant an unusually strong reliance on students. Confirmation of our dependence on student participants was revealed by the number of *PsycLIT* data base citations that included both "woman" and "students." There were close to 2,500 citations, that is, 17% of all abstracts. The Division 35 journal, *Psychology of Women Quarterly,* has recently responded to this challenge of bias by changing its editorial policy. It will no longer accept college students as representative of all women but will limit articles on students to research about students.

Personal affiliation also leads psychologists to investigate populations that are like them. Male psychologists have been more likely to study men, female psychologists to study women, and ethnic minorities to study ethnic minorities. Contributing to the likelihood that we study people like us may be what Bem and Bem (1970) called a nonconscious ideology. They suggested that it never occurred to men to study women because at some level they already "knew" about women's behavior. There may well be an analogous nonconscious ideology for middle-class feminists who appear to believe that low-income and working-class women are like them or not like them in ways that need not be articulated. Indeed, many White feminists feel that all female experience can be subsumed under a single feminist perspective. Similarly, there are some feminists of color who believe that regardless of social status, the ethnic experience is a unified one. Diane Harriford, an African-American woman who conducted a study of 600 working-class female labor union members, challenged the belief that women's experiences may be reduced to a single dimension (1991). Although she shared "skin color and the experience of racial oppression," "familiarity with the lives of Black women, ability to see and value their standpoint," and "willingness to rearticulate their reality" (p. 10), as a university-educated woman she was not defined by the union women as a member of their group. She did not find an African-American style of knowledge; instead she found that women, regardless of race, who shared the routine of a dreary work-a-day world defined their own group based on a similarity of economic and political realities.

A second factor identified as leading to the exclusion of poor women from research is *effort maximization.* Effort maximization may be defined as a concern for getting the most benefit for your work. Dealing with working-class and poor populations in either research or practice typically means greater effort. Working-class and poor populations may live in different communities, speak a different language, and hold attitudes that make them less willing to cooperate in research. Research may be delayed as investigators attempt to establish rapport and obtain consent. In work with poor and working-class women, not only may different research strategies be necessary, but often new research measures must be developed. Many of the existing measures and assessment techniques have not been normed or used with poor populations of any ethnicity or for any ethnic groups. More time and effort to obtain access makes the research more expensive to conduct and more time consuming to complete. Many psychologists are led to conclude that the cost—benefit ratio for working with poor populations is low.

An additional disincentive is the fact that it is not easy to publish nontraditional research in the traditional psychology journals. Publications in less traditional journals lack the prestige or the benefit to the researcher. Therefore, it appears that the lack of incentives in environments that stress the need to produce inhibits the desire to examine certain populations. This inability to maximize one's benefit for one's effort is both perceived and real and may well be viewed as an impediment to research that addresses issues of diversity.

A third factor that I have identified as a barrier to research on diverse populations is *investigator training.* Along with the overall higher level of difficulty of conducting research among nontraditional populations, most psychologists are not trained to work with diverse populations. The lack of strong data or a well-developed theoretical base makes it difficult for an investigator to prepare herself. The lack of training with and exposure to low-income populations, particularly ethnic populations, also raises legitimate concerns about the researcher's ability to assess behavior and interpret results. As are many of my colleagues, I am concerned about healthcare providers and professors who hold stereotyped, and at times pernicious, view of the clients and students they allegedly serve. Herein lies the circularity and the dilemma: there are few data, curricula, or sources of information with which to prepare psychologists, yet we need majority as well as minority faculty, researchers, and practitioners to concern themselves with poor and ethnically diverse populations.

Although the causes of exclusions are not trivial, none of them are insurmountable barriers to research with low-income women. Yet, barriers do exist, together with what Graham (1992) and Scarr (1988) have referred to as a fear associated with conducting socially sensitive research. The factors of exclusion do impede the progress of our science, the development of theory, and the delivery of appropriate services. Additionally, the impact of the exclusion of a wider variety of women in our research serves to solidify the narrowness of the discipline and to maintain its gatekeeping functions.

POOR WOMEN SHUT UP

If a woman cries out in the forest and no one listens, does she make a sound? Women who have had the experience of their words being literally ignored in meetings understand the fleeting bewilderment and remember thinking, "Didn't I just say something?" The experience of being silenced is more than a symbolic gagging; it is also a literal restraint of the ability to voice one's perspective. Lois Gould (1974) presented this dialogue between two women in her book *Final Analysis* (p. 52):

"Why the hell don't women ever make a scene? Men are always making scenes, yelling in the halls. Why can't you yell in the halls?" "Because," she sighed, "women don't get away with yelling in the halls. They call you a hysterical bitch if you yell in the halls." "Also," Sophy noted wryly, "they fire you. It's their halls."

Being silenced means having no access to dialogue and decision making. It means that others will set policies and define rules. In psychological research, poor women have been shut out and also shut up, that is, effectively silenced. When we accept middle-class standards without evaluating what the implications are, we ignore the experiences of large numbers of women whom we purport to represent. The result is that we begin to believe that poor women need us (psychologists) to define their problems and articulate their needs. Indeed, there is ample evidence that low-income women are aware of the issues and problems they face. They have voices, but if no one listens. . . .

Causes of Silencing

The silencing of poor women in psychological research has resulted in large part from psychology's reliance on *expert testimony,* that is, a reliance on our own interpretations of the experiences of others. We have not provided sufficient mechanisms to allow diverse groups of women to tell their own stories; instead, we have felt comfortable in making assumptions and drawing parallels, which may be inappropriate and incorrect. Even when researchers purport to study working-class women, middle-class values are frequently imposed into the investigation. For example, Luttrell (1989) interviewed 30 African-American and White American working-class women to describe their "ways of knowing." She argued that the knowledge base held by these women was "embedded in community, family, and work relationships and could not be judged by dominant academic standards" (p. 33). Ironically, the women she interviewed were all enrolled in adult basic education classes and sought (in her words) "to change their lives through education" (p. 34). Implicit in her selection of participants, and undoubtedly transparent at some level to them, was the author's agreement and approval of their attempts to further their education. In effect, she selected participants who had adopted her values. In fairness to Luttrell, she acknowledged the danger of interpreting the experiences of those who have different backgrounds, and in her analysis she included selected quotes from the women themselves. Nevertheless, the unavoidable impact of the status differential between her and her participants (she was formerly a teacher in the program) was never addressed.

In addition to the silencing that occurs due to the gatekeeping of expert witnesses, Mulvey (1988) observed an aloofness, which she described as "professionalism." She suggested that the sense of aloofness allows psychologists to maintain a distance from the general population of women. She further contended that the use of global theories (macro level) rather than specific models has encouraged this distancing on the part of both academics and healthcare providers. Gardner, Dean, and McKaig (1989) also identified distancing as a problem. They suggested that the glorification of objective knowledge has led to discounting experiential knowledge. The current movement to increase the acceptability of qualitative data and innovative research is a direct response to this charge. However, the distancing that feminist psychology appears to practice may be more than an attempt to maintain an appropriate stance or the reaction developed through traditional techniques; instead, the distancing may be a form of denial on the part of middle-class women of their elevated and privileged status. Such elevation and privilege is, on the other hand, antithetical to the principals of feminism and is, on the other hand, consistent with being middle class. Middle-class feminists may not want to be reminded of the distinctions that appear to exist among groups of women.

Reviews of research reveal that although a number of investigators have confirmed that distinctions exist between working-class and middle-class women (Ferree, 1984; Luttrell, 1989; Nelson, 1983; Unger, Draper, & Pendergrass, 1986), there are often contradictory findings. Some studies indicate that members of the middle class are less stereotyped; others indicate that it is the lower class who hold more egalitarian views. For example, Romer and Cherry (1980) demonstrated that middle-class children's self-descriptions were more blended across genders than were those of working-class children. However, it has also been suggested that women with lower incomes hold strongly feminist views. For example, Faludi (1991) cited a 1986 Gallup poll that found that significantly more upper-income women than lower-income women disavowed the label "feminist." Anyon (1984) also found that lower-income girls held stronger feminist aspirations. The unexpected direction of some studies reinforces the suggestion that distancing may signal a desire to deny the impact of class and other differences among women.

A second factor contributing to the silencing of low-income women is the establishment of a feminist hierarchy. Silencing of women in society was originally achieved by men. However, so-called "high status" women now appear to participate in the silencing of poor women through the control of what is accepted as feminist knowledge. In an analysis of a psychology of women class, Gardner et al. (1989) found that when differences in knowledge, class, or sexuality arose, a hierarchical mode of conceptualizing and responding to differences typically resulted. They observed that the women who held the identity of feminist for the longest time and those who were most familiar with feminist concepts and assumptions appropriated positions of dominance over those women who were newly considering feminism. Similar contests involving who is more feminist have occurred among psychologists. In part, this competition results because feminists have posed questions of hierarchy almost exclusively in terms of gender. As long as we accept the arrogation that gender is more important than any other status characteristic, we appear to diminish unrealistically the potency of those other characteristics.

Much of the psychological research on women reifies positions of privilege by neglecting to address other life situations or by implicitly suggesting that middle-class values, behavior, and ethics are the standards by which all women should be evaluated. However, analysis of Black and White working-class women strongly challenges claims for a single or universal mode of knowing among women (Luttrell, 1989). When we listen to working-class women, we learn about the complex gender, race, and class relations of power that shape how women think and the paradoxical situations to which they must respond. The privilege of middle-class women appears to render them unaware of this complexity. In Espin's words (1991), they have an "impairment"; she suggested that they cannot see what they cannot see, or to maintain my metaphor, they cannot hear what they cannot hear. For the advancement of our theory and practice, we cannot afford to let an "impairment" force us into a defensive attitude with respect to women from low-income groups. Neither can we abrogate our individual responsibility by failing to correct the existing discrepancy between "what is" and "what should be" in feminist research.

Need to Include Social Class and Ethnicity

Although I often assume that the need for including class and ethnic issues is obvious, on occasion I have encountered colleagues who question this assumption. For some researchers, the training they received represents the way to truth, and that truth does not include references to groups considered outside the traditional spheres of attention. Indeed, one social psychologist explained to me that his attraction was to psychology as a science devoted to seeking and identifying general principles and universal laws. He implied that I was subverting this goal by insisting on addressing specific populations. He did not seem disturbed by a sense of inconsistency. For example, it was acceptable that studies of White middle-class people could represent universals and studies of Asian working-class populations could not. Perhaps the explanation lies in what McPherson (1992) referred to as "the subordination of subject matter to method" (p. 334). He suggested that psychologists appear more concerned with data than with real life.

When we consider real life demographic data, the pressing need for feminist psychology to concern itself with poor and working-class women, men, and children is apparent. Our theories must become more representative of the world around us. Many believe that psychology is in a state of turmoil and transition (Spence, 1987), that we face not only a breakup of discipline loyalty but also an erosion of credibility with the public we purport to serve. Our need to address the diversity of real life comes at a time when people are more aware of what science and healthcare services are supposed to accomplish. People are not afraid to be critical of professionals. The science of psychology has been demystified; the practice of psychology is grist for television comedies.

In these times of reformation, the call for increased diversity is not a new alert for the psychological community. Almost every year, voices are raised to express dismay about the lack of attention to these issues. For example in 1986, Denny warned that we must be aware of the dysfunctional areas in feminist therapy, particularly those that have served to create new biases and stereotypes that continue to exclude some groups. She advised that if "feminist therapy is to serve the lower classes, it must be cognizant of the peculiarities of sex role socializations as they relate to socialization into a socioeconomic class within a stratified social system" (p. 62). Mulvey (1988) claimed that although diversity is valued by the women's movement, we have failed to achieve our goals by focusing too narrowly and maintaining nonrepresentative perspectives. Russo (1990) identified poverty as one of the major areas in need of more research for women. Herek, Kimmel, Amaro, and Melton (1991) discussed bias in research on gay and lesbian populations and called into question the representativeness of samples with respect to age, ethnicity, and social class. It is now time to move beyond the rhetoric to an action agenda.

STRATEGIES TO REACH FEMINIST GOALS

I offer suggestions for concrete commitments that we must make for psychology in general and feminist psychology in particular to progress according to our publicly espoused goals and principles. Although there are many needs and many strategies, I propose only two.

The first is directed primarily at the research community. As we recognize that women's economic status is interwoven with factors such as political clout, educational achievement, and occupational roles, we must seek to analyze women in multiple contexts. The contexts that are particularly in need of study include those of poor and working-class women. We must attempt to move our science beyond the realms of convenience. As feminists, we have demanded that investigators eschew studies of males only, except when it is theoretically reasonable; we should similarly refrain from conducting studies that unnecessarily focus on a single social class or on a single race. It is no longer acceptable to offer a weak disclaimer. To tell the consumers of our research that the participants were 95% White or that they were largely from middle-class backgrounds tells them nothing useful.

Our goal must be to conduct research that provides a meaningful analysis of gender as it is experienced in many different contexts. We can no longer pretend that we can ignore context and still understand gender. Given the inattention and dearth of psychological research on working-class women, on poor women, and on ethnic women, we must accept the call to develop a sound data base that can lead us to meaningful theory about the many spheres inhabited by women. The accomplishment of this goal will necessitate collaborative efforts of middle-class psychologists with women from different communities. To gain access, we must share our expertise while learning from those who already are skilled in those communities. (Those skilled may include our students, colleagues, and people outside the psychological community.)

The second goal applies to everyone: researchers, practitioners, professors, consultants. As we recognize the limitations inherent in our own training, in the classes we teach, and in the services we offer, we must make the commitment to expand our own knowledge and then to assist in extending the knowledge of our students and colleagues. At universities, at mental health centers, and in private practices across the country, psychologists should be leading the efforts to address issues of social class and ethnicity. There is an increasing number of workshops, books, and articles that attempt to meet this objective. However, these attempts are inadequate. The need is so great that each one of us must make the commitment to include these issues in every forum, to reach out for assistance to community resources, and to develop a sense of respect for the values of communities and their various perspectives. We should also consider seriously the consequences if we maintain a collective unwillingness to do so.

The poet, Audre Lorde (1984), who described herself as a Black lesbian warrior, noted that we cannot create bonds of sisterhood among women by pretending that everyone is alike. Her message is well taken. As feminists, we must admit our differences if we are to respect each other's perspectives. As psychologists, we must create forums to discuss and examine these differences and the relationship they have to the way we construct our world.

I would like to see the celebration of the APA Centennial as the occasion for a new beginning. We can take the initiative to institute revolutionary changes in the way we do our business of research, practice, and teaching. If we wish to make the pledge to forge a new era of psychology, we might be wise to keep in mind the words of civil rights activist, Frances M. Beal (1969). She said, "to die for the revolution is a one-shot deal; to live for the revolution means taking on the more difficult commitment of changing our day-to-day life patterns" (p. 352). I propose that we accept the challenge of living for a new feminist psychology, that is, living by the resolution to understand real diversity and to explore multiple perspectives. I think that 1993 is not too early for us to begin.

NOTES

A brief version of this manuscript was presented as the Presidential Address for the Division of Psychology of Women at the Centennial Convention of the American Psychological Association in Washington, DC, on August 16, 1992.

1. The official economic threshold for poverty is set by the Office of Management and Budget (OMB) and is updated annually based on the Consumer Price Index. Thus, in 1990 the average poverty threshold for a family of four was $13,359, for a person living alone it was $6,352, and for a family of nine or more members it was $26,848. Basically OMB suggests that a household with one person has a basic need of $6,600 and that any number of additional persons may be supported with an allotment of less than $2,500 each.

REFERENCES

Amaro, H. (1988). Women in the Mexican-American community: Religion, culture, and reproductive attitudes and experiences. *Journal of Community Psychology, 16,* 6–20.

Anyon, J. (1984). Intersections of gender and class: Accommodation and resistance by working-class and affluent females to contradictory sex role ideologies. *Journal of Education, 166,* 25–48.

Bassuk, E. L. (1990). Who are the homeless families? Characteristics of sheltered mothers and children. *Community Health Journal, 26,* 425–434.

Beal, F. M. (1969). Double jeopardy: To be Black and female. In R. Morgan (Ed.), *Sisterhood is powerful* (pp. 340–353). New York: Random House.

Belle, D. (1990). Poverty and women's mental health. *American Psychologist, 45,* 385–389.

Bem, S. L., & Bem, D. J. (1970). Training the woman to know her place: The power of nonconscious ideology. In D. J. Bem (Ed.), *Beliefs, attitudes, and human affairs.* Belmont, CA: Brooks/Cole.

Benjamin, L. T. (1992). Special issue: The history of American psychology. *American Psychologist, 47,* 109–335.

Bernard, J. (1981). *The female world.* New York: Free Press.

Brown, L. S. (1990). The meaning of a multicultural perspective for theory-building in feminist therapy. *Women and Therapy, 9,* 1–21.

Denny, P. A. (1986). Women and poverty: A challenge to the intellectual and therapeutic integrity of feminist therapy. *Women and Therapy, 5,* 51–63.

D'Ercole, A. (1988). Single mothers: Stress, coping and social support. *Journal of Community Psychology, 16,* 41–54.

Espin, O. M. (1991, August). *Ethnicity, race and class and the future of feminist psychology.* Invited address presented at the ninety-ninth annual convention of the American Psychological Association, San Francisco, CA.

Faludi, S. (1991). *Backlash: The undeclared war against American women.* New York: Crown.

Ferree, M. M. (1984). Class, housework, and happiness: Women's work and life satisfaction. *Sex Roles, 11,* 1057–1074.

Ferron, R. (1991). *Current issues in the lives of American Indian women.* Unpublished manuscript, University of Washington, Seattle.

Frieze, I. H., Sales, E., & Smith, C. (1991). Considering the social context in gender research: The impact of college students' life stage. *Psychology of Women Quarterly, 15,* 371–392.

Gardner, S., Dean, C., & McKaig, D. (1989). Responding to differences in the classroom: The politics of knowledge, class, and sexuality. *Sociology of Education, 62,* 64–74.

Glassman, C. (1970). Women and the welfare system. In R. Morgan (Ed.), *Sisterhood is powerful* (pp. 102–115). New York: Random House.

Goodman, S. H. (1987). Emory University project on children of disturbed parents. *Schizophrenia Bulletin, 13,* 411–423.

Gould, L. (1974). *Final analysis.* New York: Random House.

Graham, S. (1992). "Most of the subjects were White and middle class": Trends in published research on African Americans in selected APA journals, 1970–1989. *American Psychologist, 47,* 629–639.

Harriford, D. (1991). *The occlusion of class in and by Black feminist thought.* Unpublished manuscript, Vassar College, Poughkeepsie, NY.

Herek, G. M., Kimmel, D. C., Amaro, H., & Melton, G. B. (1991). Avoiding heterosexist bias in psychological research. *American Psychologist, 46,* 957–963.

Landrine, H., Klonoff, E. A., & Brown-Collins, A. (1992). Cultural diversity and methodology in feminist psychology: Critique, proposal, empirical example. *Psychology of Women Quarterly, 16,* 145–164.

Levinger, G. (Ed.). (1986). SPSSI at 50: Historical accounts and selected appraisals [Special issue]. *Journal of Social Issues, 42*(4).

Lorde, A. (1984). *Sister outsider.* Trumansburg, NY: Crossing Press.

Luttrell, W. (1989). Working-class women's ways of knowing: Effects of gender, race, and class. *Sociology of Education, 62,* 33–46.

Masten, A. S. (1992). Homeless children in the United States: Mark of a nation at risk. *Current Directions in Psychological Science, 1,* 41–44.

McLoyd, V. C. (1990a). Minority children: Introduction to the special issue. *Child Development, 61,* 267–269.

McLoyd, V. C. (1990b). The impact of economic hardship on Black families and children: Psychosocial distress, parenting and socioemotional development. *Child Development, 61,* 311–346.

McPherson, M. W. (1992). Is psychology the science of behavior? *American Psychologist, 47,* 329–335.

Milburn, N., & D'Ercole, A. (1991). Homeless women: Moving toward a comprehensive model. *American Psychologist, 46,* 1161–1169.

Mulvey, A. (1988). Community psychology and feminism: Tensions and commonalities. *Journal of Community Psychology, 16,* 70–84.

Nelson, M. K. (1983). Working class women, middle class women, and models of childbirth. *Social Problems, 30,* 284–297.

Panzarine, S. (1989). Interpersonal problem solving and its relation to adolescent mothering behaviors. *Journal of Adolescent Research, 4,* 63–74.

Pillary, A. L. (1987). Psychological disturbances in children of single parents. *Psychological Reports, 61,* 803–806.

Reid, P. T. (1988). Racism and sexism: Comparisons and conflicts. In P. A. Katz & D. A. Taylor (Eds.), *Eliminating racism* (pp. 203–221). New York: Plenum.

Reid, P. T., & Robinson, W. L. (1985). Professional Black men and women: Attainment of terminal degrees. *Psychological Reports, 56*, 547–555.

Riger, S. (1992). Epistemological debates, feminist voices: Science, social values, and the study of women. *American Psychologist, 47*, 730–740.

Romer, N., & Cherry, D. (1980). Ethnic and social class differences in children's sex-role concepts. *Sex Roles, 6*, 245–263.

Russo, N. F. (1990). Overview: Forging research priorities for women's mental health. *American Psychologist, 45*, 366–373.

Scarr, S. (1988). Race and gender as psychological variables: Social and ethical issues. *American Psychologist, 43*, 56–59.

Smith, J. (1984). The paradox of women's poverty: Wage-earning women and economic transformation. *Signs, 10*, 291–310.

Spelman, E. V. (1988). *Inessential woman: Problems of exclusion in feminist thought.* Boston, MA: Beacon Press.

Spence, J. T. (1987). Centrifugal versus centripetal tendencies in psychology: Will the center hold? *American Psychologist, 42*, 1052–1054.

Spencer, M. B. (1990). Development of minority children: An introduction. *Child Development, 61*, 267–269.

Taeuber, C. M., & Valdisera, V. (1986). *Women in the American economy* (U.S. Bureau of the Census, Current Population Reports, Series P-23, No. 146). Washington, DC: U.S. Government Printing Office.

Unger, R. K., Draper, R. D., & Pendergrass, M. L. (1986). Personal epistemology and personal experience. *Journal of Social Issues, 42*, 67–79.

U.S. Bureau of the Census. (1991a). *Population profile of the United States: 1991* (Current Population Reports, Series P-23, No. 173). Washington, DC: U.S. Government Printing Office.

U.S. Bureau of the Census. (1991b). *Poverty in the United States: 1990* (Current Population Reports, Series P-60, No. 175). Washington, DC: U.S. Government Printing Office.

Wyatt, G., & Lyons-Rowe, S. (1990). African American women's sexual satisfaction as a dimension of their sex roles. *Sex Roles, 22*, 509–524.

10. The Intellectual Savage

Jamake Highwater

Our most stubborn and pertinacious assumptions are precisely those whi :h remain unconscious and therefore uncritical, concepts like creative imagination or expressive communication, and others which we take for granted without realizing that we do so, their pristine novelty and vigor eroded by the platitudinous complacency of middle age. The best and perhaps the only sure way of bringing to light and revivifying these fossilized assumptions, and of destroying their power to cramp and confine, is by subjecting ourselves to the shock of contact with a very alien tradition.

—Harold Osborne

The greatest distance between people is not space but culture.

When I was a child I began the arduous tasks of exploring the infinite distance between peoples and building bridges that might provide me with a grasp of the mentality of Native Americans as it relates to the worldview of other civilizations. I had to undertake this task in order to save my life; for had I simply accepted the conventions by which white people look at themselves and their world I would have lost the interior visions that make me an Indian, an artist, and an individual.

This perilous exploration of reality began for me in southern Alberta and in the Rockies of Montana when I was about five years old. One day I discovered a wonderful creature. It looked like a bird, but it was able to do things that many other birds cannot do. For instance, in addition to flying in the enormous sky, it swam and dove in the lakes and, sometimes, it just floated majestically on the water's silver surface. It would also waddle rather gracelessly in the tall grasses that grew along the shores. That bird was called *méksikatsi,* which, in the Blackfeet language, means "pink-colored feet." Méksi-

"The Intellectual Savage" from *The Primal Mind: Vision and Reality in Indian America* by Jamake Highwater. Copyright © 1981 by Jamake Highwater. Reprinted by permission of HarperCollins Publishers, Inc.

katsi seemed an ideal name for the versatile fly-swim bird, since it really did have bright pink feet.

When I was about ten years old my life changed abruptly and drastically. I was placed in an orphanage because my parents were destitute, and eventually I was adopted by a non-Indian foster father when my own parent was killed in an automobile accident. I found myself wrenched out of the world that was familiar to me and plunged without guidance into an entirely alien existence. I was told to forget my origins and try to become somebody I was not.

One day a teacher of English told me that méksikatsi was not really méksikatsi. It didn't matter that the word described the bird exactly for me or that the Blackfeet people had called it méksikatsi for thousands of years. The bird, I was told, was called duck.

"DUCK?"

Well, I was extremely disappointed with the English language. The word "duck" didn't make any sense, for indeed méksikatsi doesn't look like the word "duck." It doesn't even sound like the word "duck." And what made the situation all the more troublesome was the realization that the English verb "to duck" was derived from the actions of the bird and not vice versa. So why do people call méksikatsi *duck?*

This lesson was the first of many from which I slowly learned, to my amazement, that the people of white America don't *see* the same things that Indians see.

As my education in the ways of non-Indian people progressed, I finally came to understand what duck means to them—but I could never forget that méksikatsi also has meaning, even though it means something fundamentally different from what duck means.

This lesson in words and the ideas they convey is very difficult to understand, especially if we grow up insulated by a single culture and its single language. In fact, it has been the most complicated lesson of my life. As I have gained experience and education in both the dominant culture and that of Indians, I have found it progressively more difficult to pass from one world to the other. I had to discover a place somewhere between two worlds. It is not simply a matter of language, for, as everyone knows, it is possible to translate with fair accuracy from one language to another without losing too much of the original meaning. But there are no methods by which we can translate a mentality and its alien ideas.

I am very much alienated by the way some ideas find their way into English words. For instance, when an English word is descriptive—like the word "wilderness"—I am often appalled by what is implied by the description. After all, the forest is not "wild" in the sense that it is something needing to be tamed or controlled and harnessed. For Blackfeet Indians, the forest is the natural state of the world. It is the cities that are wild and seem to need "taming." For most primal peoples the earth is so marvelous that their connotation of it requires it to be spelled in English with a capital "E." How perplexing it is to discover two English synonyms for Earth—"soil" and "dirt"—used to describe uncleanliness, *soiled* and *dirty.* And how upsetting it is to discover that the word "dirty" in English is also used to depict obscenities! Or take the English word "universe," in which I find even more complicated problems, for Indians do not believe in a "*uni*-verse," but in a "*multi*-verse." Indians don't believe that there is *one* fixed and eternal truth; they think there are many different and equally valid truths.

The late Hannah Arendt has given a vivid depiction of this concept of Indian reality, though she did not intend to clarify anything but the multifaceted nature of reality itself. She said in her last book, *The Life of the Mind,* that the impulse behind the use of reason is not the discovery of truth but the discovery of meaning—and that truth and meaning are not the same things.

If we can accept the paradox that the real humanity of people is understood through cultural differences rather than cultural similarities, then we can make profound sense of our differences. It is possible that there is not one truth, but many; not one real experience, but many realities; not one history, but many different and valid ways of looking at events.

At the core of each person's life is a package of beliefs that he or she learns and that has been culturally determined long in advance of the person's birth. That is equally true for Indians and for white people. The world is made coherent by our description of it. Language permits us to express ourselves, but it also places limits on what we are able to say. What we call things largely determines how we evaluate them. What we see when we speak of "reality" is simply that preconception—that cultural package we inherited at birth. For me it was méksikatsi; for an English-speaking child it was duck.

Indian children have long been urged by educators to see things and to name them in terms of the cultural package of white people, though such training essentially divests Indians of their unique grasp of reality, of their own dissimilar cultural package. Children of the dominant society are rarely given the opportunity to know the world as others know it. Therefore they come to believe that there is only one world, one reality, one truth—the one they personally know; and they are inclined to dismiss all other worlds as illusions.

Evidence that Indians have a different manner of looking at the world can be found in the contrast between the ways in which Indian and non-Indian artists depict the same events. That difference is not necessarily a matter of "error" or simply a variation in imagery. It represents an entirely individual way of seeing the world. For instance, in a sixteenth-century anonymous engraving of a famous scene from the white man's history an artist depicted a sailing vessel anchored offshore with a landing party of elegantly dressed gentlemen disembarking while regal, Europeanized Indians look on—one carrying a "peace pipe" expressly for this festive occasion.

The drawing by an Indian, on the other hand, records a totally different scene: Indians gasping in amazement as a floating island, covered with tall defoliated trees and odd creatures with hairy faces, approaches.

When I showed the two pictures to white people they said in effect: "Well, of course you realize that what those Indians thought they saw was not really there. They were unfamiliar with what was happening to them and so they misunderstood their experience." In other words, there were no defoliated trees, no floating island, but a ship with a party of explorers.

Indians, looking at the same pictures, pause with perplexity and then say, "Well, after all, a ship is a floating island, and what really are the masts of a ship but the trunks of tall trees?" In other words, what the Indians saw was real in terms of their own experience.

The Indians saw a floating island while white people saw a ship. Isn't it also possible—if we use the bounds of twentieth-century imagination—that another, more alien people with an utterly different way of seeing and thinking might see neither an island nor a ship? They might for example see the complex networks of molecules that physics tells us produce the outward shapes, colors, and textures that we simply *see* as objects. Albert Einstein showed us that objects, as well as scientific observation of them, are not experienced directly, and that common-sense thinking is a kind of shorthand that attempts to convert the fluid, sensuous animation and immediacy of the world into illusory constructs such as stones, trees, ships, and stars.

We see the world in terms of our cultural heritage and the capacity of our perceptual organs to deliver culturally predetermined messages to us. We possess no closer, no less fallible hold on reality. Yet among politically concerned people there is a good-natured insistence that all peoples are fundamentally the same. Some libertarians seem to believe that even biology is democratic, but what they see when they refer to the homogeneous attributes of all human physiology is not blood or nerve cells, but things much more cultural. They do not like to notice that races and national groups tend to evolve distinctive stereotypes emotionally and physically. They believe that all people are fundamentally the same because all people—they insist—need and want the same things. They do not take into consideration, for example, the reason a Navajo family may rip the toilet out of its newly built government house. Traditional Navajos believe it is disgusting to put a toilet under the roof of their living quarters rather than at a distance from the dwelling place. People come away from the Navajo Reservation expressing their sorrow in finding that "the poor Indians do not have indoor plumbing and live in terrible, primitive conditions unfit for human beings." But their concern is misplaced, as they would realize if they knew a bit more about Navajo tribal attitudes. What they have done is to confuse tradition with squalor. They come away feeling sorry for people simply because those people don't possess the things they themselves need and want out of life.

Liberal people have been polarized by the atrocities and inequities of history—especially the incredible cruelties of our own times. They want to do away with human misery even if it means the destruction of the realities of other cultures. What they fail to take into account is the great variety of ways in which the members of a single culture respond to the same things, let alone the vaster differences that exist between cultures. There is no question that all people feel sorrow and happiness, but the things that evoke these responses and the manner in which such feelings may be expressed socially and privately can be highly dissimilar from culture to culture. The Mexican poet and scholar Octavio Paz (1967) has stated: "The ideal of a single civilization for everyone, implicit in the cult of progress and technique, impoverishes and mutilates us."

Political idealists have overemphasized the uniformity of people in their efforts to destroy intolerance. It is exceedingly dangerous to take democratic idealism out of politics and attempt to apply it to psychology, science, and art. The uniformity that biologists and physicists discover at the core of the material world is tenuous at best and is easily distorted into conformity when applied to less fundamental issues, and gradually we find that the very democratic process that is supposed to set us free has deprived cultures and individuals of the right to be dissimilar.

For many decades it was unfashionable to suggest that all people are not the same. It was equally unpopular to insist that we can learn more about a culture from its differences than from its similarities to other cultures, and that the basis of human nature is probably more visible in human diversity than through the relatively few ways in which we are really and fundamentally the same. Liberals have striven for admirable but somewhat naive political goals: one nation, one world, one equation by which everything and everybody can be understood. In the process of trying to unify the world we must be exceedingly careful not to destroy the diversity of the many cultures of humankind that give our lives meaning, focus, vision, and vitality.

For a long time the viewpoints of primal peoples, such as the Indians of the Americas, were considered naive and primitive, especially if the peoples kept their history alive through oral and pictorial traditions rather than by writing history books. Today we are learning that people are not the same, and that we cannot evaluate all experience in the same way. We are also learning that everybody doesn't have to be the same in order to be equal. It is no longer realistic for dominant cultures to send out missionaries to convert everyone to their singular ideas of the "truth." Today we are beginning to look into the ideas of groups outside the dominant culture; we are finding different kinds of "truth" that make the world we live in far bigger than we dreamed it could be.

"Psychological differences exist between all nations and races," Carl Jung insisted—though his concepts of human archetypes have been repeatedly used to claim the contrary. "There are in fact differences between families and individuals. That is why I attack every leveling psychology when it raises a claim to *universal* validity. All leveling produces hatred and venom in the suppressed and it prevents any broad human understanding. All branches of mankind unite in one trunk, yes! . . . but what is a tree without its many separate branches?"

. . .

The conception of the one, the absolute, has dominated the mentality of a long succession of technological civilizations. The monopolistic, monotheistic mandate has largely deprived all but primal peoples of a grasp of "the other." Perhaps this capacity for vision was lost in the West long ago when the makers of great sagas and the painters of sacred images in caves passed out of existence. Perhaps in primal people like American Indians there survives a precious reservoir of humanity's visionary power. Antonio Machado-Ruiz, the Spanish poet and scholar, came to the same conclusions, though his perspective was Western and he therefore saw our diversity as an incurable but marvelous affliction. "The *other* does not exist: this is the conclusion of rational faith, the incurable belief of human reason. Identity equals Reality . . . as if, in the end, everything must necessarily and absolutely be *one and the same.* But the *other* refuses to disappear; it subsists, it persists; it is the hard bone on which reason breaks its teeth." With a poetic faith as human as rational faith, Machado-Ruiz believed in the other, in "the essential Heterogeneity of being," in what might be called "the inscrutable *otherness* from which oneness must always suffer."

The exploration of this otherness began for me in northern Montana when I was a child. I was born in the twilight of Western monopolism. Like many young, nearly assimilated primal people all over the world, I became for the first time conscious of the "intelligence" at work in my own culture. I ceased being ashamed of it and I ceased trying to justify it. I became aware of the potential of vivifying my heritage rather than sacrificing it. Of course there were many isolated and brave Indian spokespersons in the past,[1] but mine was the first generation for whom the use of the Western type of intelligence became a pervasive tool rather than a vehicle for assimilation and ethnic suicide. During the early decades of this century, private and parochial organizations and the federal government sponsored massive Indian educational efforts, often involving boarding schools. As the Oglala Sioux writer Michael Taylor has pointed out: "Disruptive of ordinary tribal life and sometimes brutal and insensitive to human needs, the schools notably failed in their initial purpose of eradicating native languages, religions, and customs. What the schools did accomplish, accidentally, was to provide Indian people from divergent backgrounds with a means of communication —the English language."

With our skills in the language of the dominant culture came significant insights about who "we" are and who "they" are. Social changes greatly facilitated our efforts to become educated fully in the cultures of two different worlds without giving up any important aspect of our own cultural and individual identities. My generation was the first to attend in great numbers both the ritual "schools" of our own cultures and the higher institutions of the white world. We grew up in two Americas—the ancient one that had existed for our ancestors for tens of thousands of years and the new one that is written about in history books. The tales of those two Americas are rarely compatible—and we quickly came to grasp our perilous situation. We had to make convincing use of our newly acquired intellectual skills in order to sustain our primal culture. We had to release a tide of communication between two worlds, and to do this we had to be a kind of people who had never before existed. We had to abandon both Andrew Jackson's *Wild Indians* and Jean-Jacques Rousseau's *Noble Savage* and emerge as a new cultural mutant—the *Intellectual Savage*—who was capable of surviving equally in two worlds by tenaciously retaining the ritual apparatus of primal people at the same time that we were attaining the intellectual and communications paraphernalia of the dominant societies.

It is through the visionary apprehension of "the other" that we attain each other. Without a grasp of the *essential heterogeneity of being* we commit ourselves to solitary confinement. All the education and refinement in the world cannot supplant a capacity for otherness. There can be nothing more horrifying for the victors of the Western world than to discover that they have won everything and in the process lost themselves. By methodically divesting their children of the capacity for vision they have forfeited the ability to see anybody but themselves.

Among the languages of American Indians there is no word for "art." For Indians everything is art . . . therefore it needs no name. My efforts, however, to find communicative accesses between the Native American world and the world of the dominant society convinced me that the metaphoric form of expression called "art" in the West is the best means of transcending the isolation of vastly dissimilar cultures. Curiously, this very important artistic connection can never be factual—for ultimately facts do not inform us. No matter how well informed a spectator may be on the techniques of the arts or the many aspects of an alien culture, if someone does not experience an aesthetic relationship to what is before him or her, all the information and education will not permit that person to cross the distance that exists between different peoples and, for that matter, between different individuals of the same technological society.

Art puts us in touch with "the other." Without art we are alone.

For me, art gradually became the essential bridge between my cultural, my individual alienation and the great world community, but the viability of that bridge depends upon what philosopher F. S. C. Northrop has called an aesthetic component, an attribute that is curiously lost among nonprimal peoples of both the West and the East.

Wherever the world is understood exclusively in terms of discursive facts there can be no access to other worlds. The poet René Char has said: "For those who are walled up everything is a wall . . . even an open door." The vistas of all the great windows of walled-up cultures are simply mirrors. We see the world in terms of ourselves. Therefore when discussing the cosmos of the Indians of the Americas I inevitably find myself trying to open windows. To do this I must talk about art.

Artists all over the world have always known that art is fundamentally a way of *seeing.* Art, like matter-of-fact reality, has a real existence within all of us even though it seems to exist in the imaginal world. Artists are among the very few people in Western civilizations who have been permitted to deal with this visionary reality as something tangible and significant. The techniques and styles created by artists are not invented in order to be "original," but contrarily, they are the means by which they achieve something almost impossible: to provide for others the personal visions they have as artists.

In the dominant society people are asked to rely as little as possible on individual vision. In fact, if we rely too heavily upon it and depart too much from our acceptable cultural framework we are likely to be regarded as peculiar or dangerous. We may be considered dangerous because our experiences do not parallel those of our peers. Only the contemporary artist is allowed to look at the world in terms of an individual vision rather than in terms of his or her "cultural eye."

Though I would prefer to speak of primal mentality strictly in terms of the attitudes and cultures of American Indians, the primal mind has too recently become aware of itself and cannot yet, and perhaps by nature never will be able to, vivify itself in terms that are both its own and intelligible to non-Indians. Therefore I have attempted, during the years since I first learned that méksikatsi is "really" duck, to evolve a set of metaphors out of Western mentality that conveys something of the fundamental otherness of Indians. Of course this is exactly what Carlos Castaneda achieved in his cycle of Don Juan parables—a literature strikingly similar to the parables of Jesus and equally subject to the harsh Pauline "realism" of interpreters. Castaneda's work may not be truthful but it is meaningful, and that is ultimately what counts about any work of art or any philosophy.

Since I must employ metaphors evolved out of Western mentality, it is inevitable that my discussions of the primal mind will invoke contrasts and comparisons between discursive Western mentality and the aesthetic component that is at the core of the primal mind. Such contrasts and comparisons tend to polarize people, making them feel either attacked or excluded, because all of us tend to think of comparisons as judgmental. It remains, however, that I would not have grasped what Anglo-Americans mean by the words "duck" and "universe" if I had not attained a fundamental understanding of how these terms compare and contrast with Blackfeet words. Comparisons are inevitable and so too is the important cultural bias that all of us foster as part of our heritage.

In the broadest sense, the primal mind is a point of departure for a much larger idea. It is a metaphor for a type of otherness that parallels the experience of many people born into the dominant society who feel intensely uncomfortable and alien. It is this condition of alienation during the last decades of the twentieth century that has motivated this book. There is "an alien" in all of us. There is an artist in all of us. Of this there is simply no question. The existence of a visionary aspect in every person is the basis for the supreme impact and pervasiveness of art. Art is a staple of humanity. It can serve as a class distinction but it does so unwittingly. In fact, art has fundamentally the opposite relation to society insofar as it can function for any economic, intellectual, or social group. Art is so urgent, so utterly linked with the pulse of feeling in people, that it becomes the singular sign of life when every other aspect of civilization fails: in concentration camps, among the brutalized and the dispossessed, the mad and the too mighty. The people of the caves of Altamira built scaffolds in the dark interiors of their rock caverns, and with pigments made from ground roots and bark and minerals they painted an amazing world upon their ceilings by the meager light of oil lamps. They were spending their time drawing pictures when some would say that they should have been out finding food and facing the tremendous improbabilities of their survival. American Indian life perpetuates the primary idealism of those uncommonly common people who scaled scaffolds to invest the rocks with their story: their myths, their histories, their totems. That peculiar act of expression (which has only recently become known to us as art) makes visible much of the unique sensibility of primal people.

By associating the primal mind with an innate art impulse in humanity, I am talking not simply about American Indians, for whom this impulse is the entire life force, but about everyone in whom the marvelously ordinary capacity for vision survives.

"The point to be noted here," the American philosopher F. S. C. Northrop (1966) has written, "is not that art of this traditional Western type and theoretical knowledge of this Western kind are not the most excellent of art and knowledge of their kind, but merely that they are but one type of art and but one type of knowledge." There is an equally important and significant kind of experience that Northrop champions. It is the visionary, the aesthetic vantage point, which provides genuine knowledge in its own right. And it is specifically this illusive and alternative kind of knowledge that finds its creative source in the primal mind.

NOTES

1. Among the important Indian spokespersons in the past were such leaders and writers as Thayendanegea (Joseph Bran, 1742–1809); Tecumtha (Tecumseh, 1768–1813); Pontiac (1720–69); Keokuk (1780–1848); Aleek-chea-ahoosh (Plenty Coups, 1848–1932); Highn'moot Tooyalakekt (Chief Joseph, 1840–1904); Ohiyesa (Charles Eastman, 1848–1939); and many other outstanding Native people.

REFERENCES

Northrop, F. S. C. 1966. *The Meeting of East and West.* New York: Collier Books.
Paz, Octavio. 1967. *The Labyrinth of Solitude.* London: Allen Lane, Penguin Press.

PART II

Development, Adaptation, and the Acquisition of Culture

The notion that a child growing up "acquires a culture" is fairly new to psychology. Although most models of human development acknowledge that environmental influences—especially the primary socializing institutions of family and school—help shape the growing child, psychological researchers have tended to steer clear of complex models of human growth which draw in such elusive (to them) and unmanageable constructs as "culture." In fact, as the cognitive psychologist Howard Gardner points out, psychology has studied how people have developed as "single persons rather than . . . how they develop as productive and interacting members of their respective cultures." The essays we have included in this part all address the related topics of how people grow up and into a culture, how they acquire the rules for living successfully in their culture, and how individuals who grow up in bicultural or multicultural communities negotiate what may be conflicting rules, belief systems, and adaptive strategies for living. Thus, in this group of essays, we begin to hear more about "cultures in collision" and the effects this has on the development of human competence.

Howard Gardner, best known perhaps for his theory of multiple intelligences, brings to bear the agenda of culture to our understanding of cognitive development in chapter 11. We must go further, he argues, in our theorizing and study of how individuals develop the special skills that allow them to acquire culture. Although Gardner identifies seven basic forms of intellectual intelligence, he observes that cultures may highlight certain ones and minimize or negate others; thus, Gardner argues for "universality without uniformity," a notion introduced in this volume by Shweder. Gardner suggests that developmental psychologists and anthropologists should bring their special skills to the collaborative study of "what forms of knowledge are in fact valued [in a particular culture], how they are codified within the culture, and what systems have been developed for these forms of transmissions."

One of the leading exponents of the cultural-ecological model of development, John Ogbu, forcefully identifies the ethnocentrism of leading developmental models which search for generalizable patterns in child rearing and development by studying white middle-class children. We must consider "the imperatives of culture" (Cohen 1971), Ogbu claims in chapter 12, when studying minority groups which maintain a symbiotic relationship with a dominant group, as is true in the United States. Ghettoized people develop alternative instrumental competencies and strategies that allow them to live and survive in two worlds.

Jualynne Dodson, in an essay on black families (chapter 13), echoes Ogbu's concern about the ethnocentrism of our developmental models. After contrasting the cultural ethnocentric school, which operates on the assumption of American cultural homogeneity and norms for behavior, with the cultural relativity school, which assumes that America is a multicultural society with a variety of standards for behavior, she sharpens the debate by introducing the issue of class. Class distinctions, Dodson asserts, are too often left out of the empirical arguments of culture theorists; when they are included, they are operationalized with measures developed by whites, for whites. To ignore the fundamentally different realities of black families and classify them according to white social class distinctions is "to commit serious historical, methodological, and theoretical errors."

In chapter 14, Algea Harrison, Melvin Wilson, and their colleagues concretize the issues raised by the other essays concerning the interconnectedness of the place of an ethnic minority in the larger cultural context (the ecological niche), their adaptive strategies and socialization goals, and child development. Of particular importance in this study is the introduction of "ancestral world views" as a major factor in understanding how individuals in bicultural communities integrate, reject, or assimilate new cultural experience. By examining the belief systems and adaptive strategies that distinguish African American, American Indian/Alaskan Native, Asian Pacific Americans, and Hispanic Americans, the authors draw attention to what they call "discontinuity" problems, that is, for some culture groups, the abrupt transitions in mode of being and behaving as individuals move back and forth between the minority and the dominant culture.

REFERENCES

Cohen, Y. A. 1971. The shaping of men's minds: Adaptations to the imperatives of culture. In *Anthropological perspectives on education,* ed. M. L. Wax, S. Diamond, and F. O. Gearing. New York: Basic Books.

11. The Development of Competence in Culturally Defined Domains: A Preliminary Framework

Howard Gardner

Whether it be the niches assumed by individual members of a royal family or the more democratic choice among "butcher, baker and candlestick maker," every culture features a set of roles that must be filled by individuals in each generation and then passed on from one generation to the next. Some roles, such as those of a tribal chief or a singer of tales, are so specific that they are filled by only a single person or a handful of individuals: Others, such as a mother or a friend, are widely held positions, which can be assumed by a large proportion of the population. In addition to individually prescribed roles, each culture values certain competences that must be mastered by at least some members of each generation: One could cite the American preoccupation with technological expertise, the Japanese valuation of social finesse, the Balinese concern with artistic achievement. Some of the skills required for fulfilling these roles or mastering these competences contribute to survival in a direct sense, whereas others provide the less tangible, but equally important, sinew that allows a culture to function smoothly. Failure to acquire the relevant roles or skills severely limits the realization of the potential of an individual, a group, or the overall culture.

In this essay I propose a framework for conceptualizing how various cultural competences might be transmitted from one generation to the next. In a manner of speaking, I attempt to bring to bear upon the agenda of culture (as formulated by Tylor and his successors) certain assumptions and tools of developmental psychology (as propounded by Piaget and his collaborators).

Reprinted by permission of the author and Cambridge University Press from *Culture Theory: Essays on Mind, Self, and Emotion* © 1984 Cambridge University Press.

Given the centrality in social science of concepts of human development, the desirability of a theory of the acquisition of culture may seem self-evident; and, indeed, many scholars have perceived the relevance of this set of issues. Yet the amount of progress made on such issues as how an individual learns to be (or becomes) a king or a singer of tales, a mother or a friend, a skilled engineer, diplomat, or painter is distressingly scanty. Why we know so little about these issues is perhaps worth a moment's consideration.

Certainly, there has been considerable progress within the area of developmental psychology in explicating how individuals attain various cognitive and communicative skills. We have learned much about the acquisition of certain key facets of logical-rational thought, of language, and of other symbolic systems. But given the empirical, task-oriented nature of most developmental psychology, it has proved difficult for workers in this tradition to tackle the more pervasive, but more elusive, themes, topics, styles, and values that come to the fore in formulations of culture. Developmental psychologists lack a sense (and a method) of how to investigate the attainment of a competence (as in the political sphere) or a role (like that of a friend). At an extreme, there may be skepticism about whether such broad, vague, and inherently elusive aspects of culture are really a fit topic for scientific work.

From their perspective, anthropologists have no difficulty in affirming the reality of culture: In fact, the "super-organic" constitutes the keystone of their discipline. However, so pervasive is culture that there is resistance to the notion that it can ever have been absent from the life of the individual. Accordingly, there is a paradox in the notion of acquiring culture; for culture is as much (and as inviolate) a part of the child's surroundings as the air that he breathes or the talk that he hears. If one adds to this a suspicion of task-oriented investigations (with their risks of ethnocentrism) and a parallel resistance to the fragmentation, atomism, and reductionism all too often associated with empirical psychology, it becomes less mysterious why a program that investigates the acquisition of culture is considered risky by many in the anthropological camp.

To be sure, there have been many studies relevant to the acquisition of culture, from the camps of both developmental psychology and cultural anthropology: Much of the work done in the psychoanalytic and personality-and-culture schools may be thought of as contributions to a model of the acquisition of culture (Erikson 1963; Gorer

1948; Kardiner 1945; Kluckhohn & Murray 1953). It is worth noting, however, that most of this work is focused on the domains of personality and affect, that is, on the question of how individuals develop as single persons rather than on how they develop as productive and interacting members of their respective cultures. What has received much less attention are the processes by which individuals develop cognitive competences—those skills and modes of thinking requisite for assuming various roles in the technological and economic spheres of their society. In a way, this lack is not surprising, for, after all, an explicit concern with cognition has been only a recent trend in psychology and an even later arrival on the anthropological scene. Yet it is my own view (and hence, a burden of this essay) that many of the deepest insights about the acquisition of culture can only be attained if one examines the various cognitive skills that individuals accrue over a lifetime.

DEVISING A FRAMEWORK

To lay out a full-blown theory of the acquisition of culture is clearly beyond the ken of any contemporary researcher. Not only do we lack the empirical information about how these processes develop in various corners of the world, but we do not even possess an appropriate categorical scheme for confronting and analyzing the issues. Hence, the more modest, but still formidable, goal of the current exercise is to lay out a framework for thinking about the ingredients involved in acquiring competence in various cultural domains. Given the current state of knowledge in psychology and my own predilections this exercise will have an unmistakably cognitive bias. A second purpose of the chapter is to invoke certain findings, concepts, and insights from the field of developmental psychology that might eventually guide efforts to develop a field of study devoted to the acquisition of culture.

To make this project viable, it is necessary to make certain basic assumptions. The initial, if controversial, assumption is that culture need not be approached as a single, inviolate, and undifferentiable whole. Instead, it makes sense, at least for heuristic purposes, to divide culture into a number of discrete domains, each of which can be separately analyzed while still avoiding the fate of Humpty-Dumpty.

Delineation of domains involves judgments and flexibility. Domains can be relatively broad, for example, the cognitive versus the social domain, or far more specific, the domain of the algebraist, the nuclear physicist, or the flutist. The crucial point being urged is this: One may legitimately ferret out a particular area of accomplishment within a culture, describe the desired end state of a competent adult member of a culture, and then commence the exercise of defining various steps or stages en route to the attainment of an end state of competence. Such a "domain approach" assumes that, initially, the young organism within the society has but a nascent or imperfect competence within the domain, but that, given exposure to examples of cultural competence and perhaps explicit training as well, the young child has the potential of acquiring successively higher degrees of skills. I might note that this assumption now guides much work in the social sciences, including investigations by individuals who believe that the acquisition of various competences is largely a genetically determined process, such as Chomsky; those who believe that competence is basically a learned process, such as the behaviorists; and those who favor an intrinsically interactive approach, such as Piaget and most developmental psychologists (see Piatelli-Palmarini 1980). And indeed, one may adhere to these other quite divergent points of view and still join in an effort to describe the acquisition of cultural competences.

In addition to these assumptions about the existence and autonomy of different domains of competence, our effort to lay out a theory of cultural acquisition will require a consideration from four different perspectives or vantage points, which I'll reify for present purposes. The first two vantage points may be considered diametrically opposed to one another. At one extreme, there is the *culture* as a whole, with its domains, beliefs, and values, which have evolved over many years. This historical and geographical unit provides the agenda of what needs to be acquired by individuals within the culture. At the other extreme is the *individual,* equipped with his or her genetic inheritance, including various neurological and psychological mechanisms, which will ultimately permit the individual to achieve the competences that are essential or desirable within his or her culture.

A third vantage point explores the *symbol* systems within the culture, the inventions that have evolved over thousands of years — organized systems of meaning, such as forms of dance, dress, or address. The individual generally encounters symbol systems as they are captured in various organized productions (e.g., stories and rituals): The individual must become facile with such meaningful structures if he or she is to become a competent member of the culture. A final essential vantage point encompasses the various *loci* and *modes of transmission* of cultural competence: These are institutions devised and presided over by the culture wherein younger individuals are exposed to various models of cultural competence and given the opportunity, usually with some guidance, to attain such competence.

Of course, these various assumptions and vantage points entail simplifications, but not, I hope, of such magnitude as to render the entire analytic effort futile. Having introduced them, we can now proceed to consider in somewhat more detail the four principal aspects involved in the acquisition of culture.

FOUR ASPECTS OF THE ACQUISITION OF CULTURE

Culture

As a means of delineating the aspects of culture that need to be mastered by its members, I find it useful to consider three different realms that must necessarily be confronted in every corner of the world. It may be the case that these realms are not divided identically across the range of cultures and that domains are conceptualized differently within (and across) these realms, yet each culture must somehow come to terms with the existence and importance of each. The three realms are: (1) *the physical world,* the world of material natural objects and the elements as well as various forms of living matter; (2) *the world of man-made artifacts,* such as tools, works of art, and the less tangible world of words and ideas; (3) *the social world,* which includes other persons, those in the family, in one's community, and, increasingly, in the rest of the world as well.[1]

Every individual in every culture must acquire the skills needed to deal effectively with these three realms (Lockhart, Abrahams, & Osherson 1977; Nucci & Turiel 1978). Moreover, the individual must develop some ability to work in these worlds, both on an intuitive and practical level and at the level of explicit propositional knowledge. To invoke a distinction that has become widespread, the individual must acquire "know-how" as well as "know that" in each of these domains. Thus, early in life, individuals develop skills in dealing with the physical world so that they will not be harmed by natural causes and so that they can attain desired goals. These skills are later joined by propositional knowledge, which may be formalized in the area of physics or biology but also can exist, of course, in ritual, law, stories, and other less formal modes of discourse. Included in the latter area would be "folk knowledge" about the genesis, nature, and ultimate fate of the physical world. By the same token in the world of man-made objects and in the social world, the individual must also acquire practical skills as well as the more formal codes that prescribe how one is to behave and what one is to believe.

Of course, the differences across cultures in the way in which this cultural knowledge is encoded and negotiated constitutes a major issue for philosophers, anthropologists, and other social scientists. It scarcely needs saying that cultures differ vastly from one another in the way in which they define these three realms (and their constituent domains), in the gamut of more or less explicit forms of knowledge that have evolved, in the kind of knowledge that is captured in each realm, and, perhaps most important, in the values that they place upon each. For example, in Western culture we place a great deal of importance on explicit knowledge about the physical world, and indeed this knowledge is central to much of the educational system with its focus on the physical and natural sciences. More recently, of course, we have also emphasized explicit knowledge about the social world, and this has given rise, for good or ill, to the social sciences.

In many other corners of the world, explicit knowledge, particularly as it is captured in scientific form, is of much less importance; though, of course, there may be innumerable adages that capture less formal aspects of knowledge about the physical and social world. However, at the same time, in such cultures as Japan or India, knowledge about the social world and how one negotiates one's way within it is valued much more and harnesses far more energy than does knowledge about the physical world. Thus, it must be emphasized once again that the ways in which cultures divide the universe of cultural knowledge differ vastly. The constant is that every culture must have some way of dealing with these different domains and must attach some value, though it may be a shifting one, to implicit and explicit knowledge within each. An understanding of how one's culture divides the universe of knowledge and of the values placed on each of the individual domains represents an end state of cultural knowledge, which must ultimately be acquired by individuals growing up in any corner of the globe.

The Individual

Situated at the opposite pole of our equation of cultural acquisition is the single biological organism, the human being, who, starting from a state of total ignorance about his or her particular culture, must within a decade or two acquire sufficient competence so that he or she can carry out productive work and interact effectively with other individuals to achieve valued ends. In one sense, the individual *is* his or her genetic inheritance: He or she can achieve nothing that lies beyond the potential of the species. In practice, however, this limitation need not be a major concern, for cultures have evolved in such a way as to reflect the capabilities and the limitations of the species. Ultimately, however, a fullblown theory of cultural acquisition must take into account what is known about human genetic heritage: the structure of the nervous system, the principles of brain development; the effects of early and later experiences on neurological and psychological maturing; and how these exercise a constraining (or, viewed differently, a liberating) role in the processes whereby the acquisition of culture takes place.

For present purposes, I propose to focus on the intellectual competences that human beings as a species seem to have the potential to acquire. The particular competences that I propose are controversial, and the full case for their existence and centrality has yet to be made.[2] For now, however, the precise identity of these cognitive potentials is less crucial than the claims that there exists a finite number of them and that a student of cultural acquisition needs to take each of them into account.

I contend that there exist at least seven separate computational or information-processing systems that human beings, as a species, have evolved over the millennia. Aspects of these computational systems can be located in other animals, though probably never in the precise forms or with the interconnections realized in human beings. These computational systems are best thought of as raw information-processing devices, neural mechanisms that are predisposed to take in certain forms of sensory information, either from the external world or from the viscera, to analyze and eventually to transform these "raw" forms of information in various ways. In most normal human beings, each of these computational devices operates with some fluency and fluidity, and by exploiting these individual computational systems, individuals can go on to acquire quite elaborate forms of knowledge. But computational mechanisms cannot work in a vacuum: They have evolved to expect organized sets of information from a culture, which they in turn analyze, organize, and synthesize (Geertz 1962). Individuals also differ from one another in the potential they have for elaborating each of these intelligences: It is a task of differential psychology to identify these differences and a task of education to deal with, exploit, or compensate for the differences.

It proves difficult to demonstrate the existence, and to unravel the operation, of each of these computational mechanisms in the normal functioning human being. One aspect of smooth and productive human functioning is the perpetual interaction of these competences. Therefore, a chief source of insight about their autonomous existence and their modes of processing comes from atypical populations: brain-damaged individuals in whom one or more forms of intelligence can be spared or destroyed in isolation; prodigies—individuals who show a precocious development in one or more competences; freaks or idiot savants—individuals with limited development in most intellectual competences but with an extreme or precocious development in one of these. Studies of specific mechanisms in animals, such as birdsong in sparrows or interpersonal rituals in chimpanzees, can also illuminate aspects of human intellectual competences (see Gardner, 1975, 1982).

With this sketchy introduction, let me list seven forms of information processing that appear to exist in human beings. It is necessary to furnish rough-and-ready labels in order to permit communication about their nature, but it should be stressed that we are actually dealing here with organismic *potentials:* They might well be marshaled in ways other than the current labels intimate.

1. *Linguistic competence.* Building upon the phonological and syntactic-analytic abilities subserved by certain regions of the left hemisphere of the brain, human beings have the potential to develop communication systems like the natural languages. In those cases where natural languages are not available in the environment, individuals may well develop *ersatz* communication systems, for

example, the gestural systems contrived by deaf children, which nonetheless exhibit some of the syntactic, semantic, and distinctive-feature properties of natural language.

2. *Spatial competence.* Building upon the capacity of the nervous system to discern visual patterns, to transform them in various ways, and to calculate the depth element of visual displays, spatial intelligence forms the basis of such mature roles as architect, artist, engineer, and physicist. Spatial intelligence may develop to some extent in the absence of visual information, but achievement of full-blown competence in this sphere may well presuppose a functioning visual system.

3. *Logical-mathematical competence.* Built upon the human capacity to enumerate elements and to appreciate cause-and-effect relationships, the logical-mathematical capacity culminates in our society in the ability to carry out high-level mathematical and scientific work. Most of Piaget's descriptions pertain particularly to the development of logical-mathematical intelligence.

4. *Bodily kinesthetic competence.* Under discussion here is the capacity of human beings to carry out complex motor patterns and to harness these to the service of various utilitarian or aesthetic-expressive ends. Bodily kinesthetic intelligence is reflected in all manner of crafts, as well as in such roles as the athlete, the actor, the hunter, and the dancer.

5. *Musical competence.* Analogous in some respects to linguistic or numerical intelligence, the core of the musical faculty involves sensitivity to pitch and tonal relations as well as rhythmic structures. Whereas spatial intelligence may depend on visual processing, musical competence presupposes a functioning auditory system.

6. *Interpersonal competence.* Based initially on the child's interaction with his parents and various "significant others," social or interpersonal intelligence culminates in a sensitivity to the needs, desires, and fears of other individuals and capacity to collaborate with them and thus achieve one's goals in communal situations. This form of competence has been especially valued in certain non-Western societies, where cooperation, and even merging with others, are at a premium.

7. *Intrapersonal, or self, competence.* A form of knowledge especially valued in the West, knowledge of self consists of an individual's sensitivity to, and understanding of, his own needs, desires, anxi-

eties, and the like. Quite possibly, it derives in the first instance from sensitivity to, and monitoring of, one's reactions to events and culminates in a mature "sense of self," "identity," or "executive function." Distinct from interpersonal intelligence, it is this form of knowledge that Rousseau sought so unsparingly and that Freud has so acutely described in his own writings. In a different garb, intrapersonal knowledge may also be the end state sought in certain Oriental religions.

Making the detailed case for the existence of these intelligences is, of course, a task for another occasion (see Gardner, 1983). At present a few clarifying remarks will have to suffice. First, although superficially similar to previous factor-analytic views of intelligence, this scheme purports to be quite different: Rather than deriving entirely from empirical correlations among test scores, it is based in the first instance on the putative existence of quasi-autonomous biological systems, which have their separate evolutionary course and which can be specified—and possibly localized—in the nervous system.

Indeed, this view of intelligence may serve as a critique of "general intelligence" approaches of the unitary (Spearman 1904) and the pluralistic sort, whether empirically derived (Thurstone & Thurstone 1941) or based in part on an a priori analysis (Guilford 1959). At the same time, this view doubles as a challenge to the Piagetian view of intelligence, where general operations are assumed to underlie work across disparate domains. In contradistinction to each of these approaches, it is claimed here that each intelligence has its own genesis and can evolve according to its own rules of processing. And, as part of this claim, I wish to call into question the notion that there exist general principles of psychology, such as learning, perception, attention, and memory, and generalized kinds of operations, such as transformations, which operate in identical fashion across different domains. Instead, a clear implication of this view is that there may be separate forms of perception, memory, and so on in each domain; whereas there may well be certain similarities across domains, there is no necessary link. For instance, musical memory may operate in a different fashion from, and have no intrinsic link to, a keen memory in the spatial, logical-mathematical, or interpersonal realms.[3]

Even if this view of intellectual competences has some validity and is supported by subsequent researches, it clearly neglects evidently important aspects of cognition and raises many enigmas. To mention just a few: It is by no means apparent how a belief in separate computational mechanisms could account for common sense, wisdom, metaphoric insights, synthesizing powers, or the g that customarily emerges in factor-analytic studies of tests of intellectual performance. The processes by which individuals recognize and deal with recurrent situations in daily life (how they devise, store, access, transform, and utilize "scripts" or "frames") have not been specified. Finally, it remains to be determined whether some general organizing "self" or "executive function" coordinates the intelligences and decides which should be selected or whether the implementation of particular intellectual competences or combinations of competences is better viewed as an automatic, unsupervised process.

Although I have chosen to describe seven forms of intellectual competence here, no magic inheres in the number or in the names. Clearly, each intelligence has subcomponents, and these may well be represented separately in neuroanatomical zones: We know, for example, that in the single sphere of linguistic intelligence phonological, syntactic, and semantic capacities can be affected in distinctive and nonoverlapping ways as a consequence of brain damage. By the same token, there are no doubt certain processes characteristic of one intelligence that can also be seen at work in other intelligences: Thus certain aspects of temporal processing are marshaled by both linguistic and musical intelligence, even as certain kinds of spatial intuition can be utilized by the spatial, the bodily kinesthetic, and the logical-mathematical forms of reasoning. The decision to nominate seven, rather than three or three hundred, intellectual competences is dictated by a trio of diverse considerations: (1) the belief that there exist discrete neurological systems subserving each, (2) the desire to describe competences of sufficient scope and flexibility that they correspond with broad skills that can be readily identified and deliberately exploited by a functioning community (language rather than phonological competence), and (3) the need for a set of categories sufficiently small to allow the analysis of particular ongoing activities and tasks but sufficiently comprehensive to cover most of the skills needed in a functioning culture.

It should be stressed that these intellectual proclivities do not ordinarily exist in pure form or function in isolation. Except in the case of certain "freaks," they are always absorbed and utilized with reference to meaning systems within the culture. Moreover, any role within a society will call upon a combination of intelligences, just as any intelligence can itself be put to a number of disparate purposes. As we have already seen, the spatial intelligence is exploited by individuals as diverse as an architect, a pilot, or an artist. By the same token, an individual (like a lawyer) may achieve competence through combinations of linguistic, logical-mathematical, and/or interpersonal skills, with a particular lawyer differing significantly from her or his brethren in terms of the particular intelligences that happen to be highlighted. Similarly, given cultures or subcultures may choose to highlight certain intelligences while minimizing or even negating certain other ones. (Both the labeling and the examples offered here necessarily exhibit a Western bias.) For example, logical-mathematical intelligence may be of crucial importance in our culture but of relatively little importance elsewhere, whereas musical or interpersonal intelligences may be valued much more in cultural settings other than our own.

Symbol Systems

The creations (or instrumentalities) whereby the culture's bodies of knowledge (Factor A) are transmitted to the individual with his intellectual competences (Factor B) are here termed *symbol systems.* These are sets of elements, sometimes physical (like pictures or texts), sometimes nonmaterial (like spoken words or unspoken thoughts), in which knowledge can be captured and transmitted from one individual to another. They are meaningful: That is, individual symbols, finished symbolic productions, and organized symbol systems can communicate particular referential and/or expressive meanings from one individual to another. And, indeed, because human beings are meaning-seeking and meaning-creating individuals, symbol systems are the *preferred* mechanisms for the development and cultivation of intelligences. Only in unusual or freakish individuals, such as autistic children, can one see an intelligence in its raw form, unmediated by systems of meaning (Rimland 1964; Selfe 1977).

How meanings are attached to behaviors and experiences is, of course, a pivotal and, as yet, poorly understood aspect of human psychology, one neglected by most information-processing approaches to cognition, which seem to pride themselves on their indifference to content. As a start, we can assume that the human infant is predisposed to be sensitive to, and to search for, meanings and that, as a result, meanings become attached to experiences from the earliest moments of life. Thus, individuals, objects, locations, and the like, no matter how arbitrary or inchoate they may seem to an alien observer, soon acquire significance for the young organism. These entities, accompanied by strong feelings of well-being, irritation, or terror, become consistently attached to rewards and punishments, predictable outcomes, specific products, and events and situations. Initially, such significances attach directly to the physical and social beings in the world. However, after the first year or two of life, the individual enters into negotiations not merely with physical or social objects but also, and increasingly, with sets of symbols and discourses of meaning with words, pictures, gestures, numbers, ritualistic activities, and other "mediators of significance"; and it is here that the differences across cultures become most manifest, increasingly profound, and sometimes irremediable.

With respect to each of the intelligences sketched here, one may nominate symbol systems and products that exist within our culture. For example, in the area of language, one has, of course, natural language, formal languages, and also various informal languages, which can be invented or transformed by individuals. The systems are realized and encountered in such products as stories, reports, formal messages, and daily conversations. In the area of spatial intelligence, one has the symbol systems of drawing and architecture; in number, various arithmetics; in kinesthetic and bodily intelligence, gestural communication and dance; in logic, the various symbol systems of the sciences. There are less particulate but equally pervasive symbol systems in the realm of personal (dream) and interpersonal (ritual) intelligence. It is the task of the culture to ensure that the beliefs, values, knowledge, and so on of greatest import can be suitably captured and expressed in the available symbol systems. It is the task of the individual, exploiting his intellectual competences, to master and then utilize these various symbol systems. It is the task of the analyst to examine cultural competences, including those as broad as successful friendship or skilled parenting, and to determine how these are captured, transmitted, and apprehended in symbol systems.

The question arises as to how these symbol systems map onto the two forms of knowledge that we distinguished in our discussion of cultural competence: the intuitive or direct "know-how" involved in dealing with the world of physical and social objects as opposed to explicit propositional knowledge, the "know that" which eventually emerges in various cultural domains. Tracing the connections between these forms of knowledge and the various symbol systems in the culture is a vexed issue, which cannot be dealt with here. As a preliminary suggestion, I propose that initial use of a symbol system is relatively intuitive and nonreflective, a species (at a higher level) of "know-how"; only with the codification of the symbol system and its use in a more reflective or "meta" way does one invade the realm of explicit propositional symbolic knowledge, the "know that," about a domain. For example, in the area of language or numbers the individual (like Molière's Monsieur Jourdain) first learns to use words or numbers as tools in an intuitive or nonreflective way. Later, the individual becomes capable of making statements about language or numbers that are much more explicit in form and involve "knowledge about" a domain. These statements may be in formats ranging from folk adages to mathematical proofs. Needless to add, cultures differ greatly in the extent to which they tolerate, or promote, such propositional knowledge about various intellectual domains; and individuals, too, differ in the extent to which they indulge in, and benefit from, such "metaknowledge."

Modes and Loci of Transmission

Symbol systems represent the crystallized content or knowledge of a culture that the competent individual must master. However, the modes and the loci of transmission themselves constitute an area that requires separate attention. Our own review suggests the existence of several loci and modes of transmission, which cultures may variously exploit in order to transmit knowledge across generations. Although the following description focuses primarily on teaching, an analysis can be carried out equally well with respect to learning.

Turning first to loci of transmission, the processes whereby knowledge is passed on can take place at the home, around the home, within the community at large, or in specific institutions, ranging from schools to churches. The individuals involved may include parents, siblings, peers, other family members, and individuals designated specially by the community, including itinerant teachers, gurus, or master craftsmen. A final locus of transmission, which assumes special importance in the modern world, is a *medium of communication,* such as radio or television. In the latter case, vast amounts of information can be conveyed wherever a receiver exists without the intervention of any individual who is known personally to the student.

There is an equally wide range of methods whereby the learner acquires knowledge. Perhaps the simplest form is *sheer imitation* or *observation learning,* where the mature organism performs and the novice, either immediately or eventually, reproduces salient (though not always apt) features of that performance. This mode of transmission is basic: It exists as well in infrahuman primates and seems to be adopted spontaneously by young children the world over. In fact, for many types of learning, observation learning alone seems sufficient to produce a competent performance.

But simple observation is often supplemented by more focused forms of instruction. The instructor may issue verbal instructions, or where they are unlikely to be effective, paralinguistic cues, such as gestures or pantomime, may be preferred. Powerful positive or negative incentives may be provided. Considerable learning can also take place if proper materials are simply provided to the learner. There may be rules to follow or procedures to memorize. Should the individual learn how to read, he also has the option of instructing himself by studying works in which the acquisition of a skill or competence is described.

When information achieves a level of complexity where sheer demonstration, or learning a list of rules, is unlikely to lead to mastery, two new forms of information processing appear to evolve across cultures. One mode, here called the *master–apprentice relationship,* is used primarily to teach complex techniques, such as arts and crafts or meditation, to younger members of the culture. In a typical pattern, the young individual goes to live in the house of the master and initially serves simply as a helping hand with diverse aspects of the work, not least the drudgery. The formation of strong interpersonal and dependent bonds may be an intrinsic aspect of the first stages of this mode of mastery. Eventually, the novice is allowed to pass through a series of higher level steps, often called journeyman and master, and sometimes entailing a series of gradations that occupy a lifetime. How these steps are negotiated and what milestones must be passed is generally determined by the master.

Another form of transmission also suited to knowledge of greater complexity, and particularly associated with the invention of a literacy system, may be termed the *traditional* or *premodern school.* Frequently, the purpose of this school is to allow the individual to master a form of literacy, usually a written language, which preserves and transmits doctrine. Examples would include medieval church schools, the Hebrew cheder, the *gurukula* in India, and analogous schools in other parts of the world in which a scripture must be mastered.

In a system that shares certain features with the master–apprentice relationship, the young pupil initially forges a close tie with the master and also passes through a set of stages: These may begin with sheer memorization but eventually include the abilities to decode the language phonemically, to understand its meaning, to engage in critical discussion and interpretation of the text, to read secular writings as well, and perhaps even to contribute to the corpus of writings.

A final variety of transmission of knowledge is the *modern technological* or *secular school.* In contrast to the traditional school, there is no emphasis on religion here; the school is often age-graded, rather than ability-graded, and the individual studies an assortment of disciplines during abutting periods. Given textbooks and tests and a meritocratic mode of evaluation, there is little need for a close tie to the teacher: In fact, teachers can be replaced, and individuals can advance when they meet objective criteria. Emphasis is placed on critical analysis, on the abilities to summarize and to revise, rather than on sheer memorization (Cole & Scribner 1974; Greenfield & Bruner 1969). The context in which the knowledge will eventually be used is underplayed, and, indeed, there is a heightened emphasis on presenting materials that are abstract and far removed from the usual locus of practice. One assumption central to the secular school is that such "decontextualization" will ensure greater generalization and "transfer of learning" than can be expected from traditional modes of learning: At present, this assumption is a hope rather than an established fact.

The focus in developed societies on more sophisticated modes of transmission, such as modern technological schools, should not be interpreted as an effort to dismiss or undervalue more traditional modes. Observation learning continues to be effective for some purposes at every level and in every area of society. Also, even within the most modern forms of schooling—for example, graduate training in physics—such apparently elementary modes of transmission as imitation and the master–apprentice relationship are often important, though they are not frequently remarked upon (Polanyi 1958).

SUMMARY

I have touched briefly upon four separate elements involved in the equation of cultural acquisition. To recapitulate, we begin with those forms of knowledge valued by the culture. These can exist in three realms—those of physical objects, social objects, and man-made objects. Cultures will differ in their emphasis upon intuitive knowledge within these realms (as opposed to explicit propositional knowledge about these realms). Arrayed at the opposite end of the equation is the individual, with his general biological proclivities toward learning, as well as the potential for intellectual competence in at least seven different realms, each of which may have a specific neurological underpinning.

The points of contact between the culture, with its valued forms of knowledge, and the individual, with his intellectual proclivities, are various symbol systems: the forms of crystallized knowledge within the culture to which the individual is exposed from his earliest years, which may be said to constitute the systems of meaning within that culture. Finally, one may also isolate several modes for the transmission of knowledge, ranging from simple observation to the most complex forms of technological and secularized schooling. The loci for these modes of transmission may also vary, running the gamut from direct interaction within the nuclear family to transmission over long distances by modern electronic equipment.

IMPLICATIONS AND APPLICATIONS

Even if the present framework seems plausible, it provides at most a starting point for the investigation of the acquisition of culture. As already suggested, very little is known about these various components and about their interactions: A first and very important task is to examine specific cultures to determine whether, and to what extent, this particular framework has utility. Such work virtually demands close collaboration between anthropologists and developmental psychologists, who would have complementary gifts for such an inquiry.

As already noted, the present formulation is very heavily skewed toward the cognitive aspects of culture and toward those cultural skills important for the transmission of knowledge. Future work must take into much fuller account the roles of motivation, emotions, personality factors, and underlying values, all of which undoubtedly play an important role, if they do not entirely transmute the processes whereby culture is acquired. It may well also be necessary to develop instruments, such as new projective techniques, which will allow a nonobtrusive securing of information about what forms of knowledge are in fact valued, how they are codified within the culture, and what systems have been developed for these forms of transmission.

Whatever its theoretical utility, the practical usefulness of such a framework also merits brief comment. My own hope is that it may prove useful in analyzing the various educational interventions that have been introduced into disparate cultural settings. Typically, these programs, no matter how well motivated, are based on implicit assumptions about *what* knowledge is and *how* it should be transmitted. These assumptions may differ greatly in the minds of the planners of the program, the practitioners who are entrusted with implementing it, and those who are supposedly the beneficiaries.

Let me take as an example the recent efforts by the Ministry of Intelligence in Venezuela to raise the intelligence of the entire population of that country (Machado 1980; Skryzniarz 1981). This is not the place for a full-fledged critique of this ambitious program, which in any case is still in progress at the time of this writing. However, it seems evident that the planners of the program have adopted a monolithic view of intelligence, which is quite far removed from the perspective of this chapter and which also may be outmoded as far as contemporary cognitive science is concerned. Little attention has been paid to the indigenous knowledge systems that exist within the Venezuelan context, through which any new version of knowledge would presumably have to be transmitted. Perhaps more important, the project assumes a certain mode of transmission, that of technological secularized schooling, which may be at variance with forms that have been traditionally favored in Venezuela. None of these disparities necessarily predicts the failure of the Venezuelan project; nor, if it does fail, can we necessarily assume that the present analysis is telling. Nonetheless, it would seem that future efforts at intervention in knowledge transmission might well benefit from an analysis in terms of the four components introduced in this essay.

A related use for this framework is its application in those cases where a program has been judged ineffective. It may well be that recognition of a plurality of intelligences, symbol systems, and modes of transmission will allow a more precise determination of where problems may lie and suggest the use of prosthetics to circumvent them. This framework can serve a critical function, warning individuals away from various kinds of interventions that may turn out to be at odds with the most deeply held assumptions of a culture. And, finally, it may help to explain why certain interventions have proved successful in given settings.

In addition to its possible practical utility, this conceptualization of issues in the acquisition of culture may also be of scientific value. Nearly all of what is known about the development of human beings has been obtained from research carried out by Western investigators, almost always in Western settings. In truth, the developmental psychology of today *is* the story of the development of Western children. Only by studying human development in vastly different cultural contexts, where there are different value systems, alternative modes of transmission, and the like, do we have any hope of gaining a more universal and more valid human science. Indeed, if human sciences can validly exist at all, they can only do so when a relatively large and representative sample of the human population has been included.

To be sure, contemporary developmental psychology may help us as we undertake the search for a more universal discipline. To begin with, we can obtain some "working notions" of how children acquire specific skills and general competences. Even those at odds with the influential Piagetian position would likely agree that children should be thought of as hypothesis-generators, active problem-solvers, who are continually attempting to make sense of the objects, events, and symbol systems around them. Children will attempt to find or *make* order in any system or domain they encounter: They are able to overlook a fair amount of noise and, in any case, are much less likely to be crippled by it. In LeVine's terms (1981), children will assume that there is organization—not chaos—in their culture and will attempt to discern that organization. This assumption ought certainly to be embraced—and tested—by workers in disparate cultural settings.

From studies conducted in the West, we can also introduce useful distinctions among domains of competence, in terms of the extent to which they are readily mastered by some or all normal youngsters and to the extent to which they are eventually available to normal adults within a culture. At one extreme we have the realm of natural language, which seems to be acquired without the need for explicit external interventions throughout the human world. Certain other competences are acquired with equal facility but only by a far smaller percentage of individuals within a culture. In our own culture, we can point to areas like music or mathematics where prodigies are not that rare (Feldman 1980; Gardner 1982). Conversely, there are other areas that are acquired without undue difficulty by most individuals, like reading or visual-spatial competence, but pose surprisingly severe problems for a small proportion of the population. It is crucial to determine whether such domains, which engender "learning disabilities" within the American context, give rise to an analogous bimodal distribution in cultures that have different reading systems or place a different value on visual-spatial intelligence.

Not all domains of knowledge are readily available to youngsters. Some, such as logical reasoning involving abstract propositions, may prove relatively difficult to master and relatively easy to forget, once the supporting contexts are no longer present (Wason & Johnson-Laird 1972). Other forms of knowledge, such as the ability to adjudicate among different value systems or sensitivity to the motivations behind individual utterances, are readily accessible to most adults but prove surprisingly opaque to preadolescents. Finally, moving away from the notion of cognition *sensu strictu,* there are predictable progressions in the area of moral development (Kohlberg 1969), social development (Selman 1980), and ego development (Loevinger 1976) that cry out for validation, or alteration, in the light of work in cultures with different end states of competence in these person-oriented domains. Attending to developmental psychology can provide plausible predictions or frameworks that can be critically examined in other cultural settings: Indeed, the very definition or delineation of domains may be altered in the light of such inquiry.

From developmental psychology, one can also obtain models of how different aspects of the cultural equation may work. For example, the investigations of my collaborators at Harvard Project Zero suggest the existence of four principal stages in the mastery of symbol systems: (1) an initial mastery at two years of age of narrative or role-structuring formats, which permits the understanding of stories and play sequences; (2) the emerging ability around three years to capture in a visual-spatial form the topological similarities between a two- and three-dimensional object, as occurs in representational drawing; (3) the capacity at age four to appreciate simple numbers and numerical relations, which allows the capturing of precise correspondences rather than simple topological relationships; (4) the facility, around the age of five or six, to attain a new "second-order" level of symbolization, where one can invent various notations that themselves refer to earlier forms of symbolization; this final step smoothes the road to "knowledge about" as well as "knowledge that" (Shotwell, Wolf, & Gardner 1979; Wolf & Gardner 1982). Once again, the point of such a scheme is not to insist on its correctness but rather to invite examination, in the light of cross-cultural knowledge about symbol acquisition, and revision, consequent upon insights obtained from such an inquiry.

Having a theory of the acquisition of cultural competence seems a worthwhile scientific goal, and it is hoped that this chapter has provided some useful, if tentative, suggestions about how such a goal might be pursued. Paradoxically, however, it is only by a serious embarking on this research course that we can determine whether, in fact, the overall goal is tenable. That is, only by studying the acquisition of culture in a variety of settings will it ever become clear whether the parallels in approach and method across cultures lend themselves to systematization and simplification; or whether, on the contrary, the differences in construing the problem and in the actual transmission of knowledge are so profound as to render this an area more suited for humanistic speculation or literary re-creation rather than for the dogged collection of data. And only through such work can we determine whether a study of individual domains of knowledge, as I have proposed, can flow together and lead to increased understanding of the most pervasive motifs of a culture or whether such an inquiry instead proceeds like a group of radiating streams, each receding farther and farther from the central source.

NOTES

Preparation of this essay was made possible by a grant to the Harvard Graduate School of Education from the Bernard Van Leer Foundation of the Hague. I am grateful to all my colleagues on that project for many discussions on these topics; no longer can I determine where their ideas end and my own begin. The empirical research described in this essay was supported by grants from the Spencer Foundation, the Carnegie Corporation, the National Institute of Neurological Diseases, Communication Disorders and Stroke (NS 11408), and the Veterans Administration.
1. This scheme has some parallels to, but is by no means identical with, the theory of "three worlds" put forth by the British philosopher Karl Popper (1972).
2. Such an inquiry, which includes an examination of the neurobiological bases of intellectual competence, is being pursued at the Harvard Van Leer Project on Human Potential. See Gardner (1983).
3. This point of view has certain parallels with the "modularity hypothesis" about cognition, which is currently being developed by Jerry Fodor (1983) and others at MIT. An analysis of the distinctions between the two approaches should eventually be undertaken.

REFERENCES

Cole, M., & Scribner, S. 1974. *Culture and Thought: A Psychological Introduction.* New York: Wiley.

Erikson, E. 1963. *Childhood and Society,* 2nd ed. New York: Norton.

Feldman, D. 1980. *Beyond Universals in Cognitive Development.* Norwood, N.J.: Ablex.

Fodor, J. 1983. *The Modularity of Mind.* Cambridge, Mass.: Bradford Books, 1983.

Gardner, H. 1975. *The Shattered Mind.* New York: Knopf.

———. 1982. *Art, Mind, and Brain.* New York: Basic Books.

———. 1983. *Frames of Mind: The Theory of Multiple Intelligences.* New York: Basic Books.

Geertz, C. 1962. The growth of culture and the evolution of mind. In J. M. Scher, ed., *Theories of the Mind.* New York: Free Press.

Gorer, Geoffrey. 1948. *The American People, a Study in National Character.* New York: Norton.

Greenfield, P. M., & Bruner, J. S. 1969. Culture and cognitive growth (revised version). In D. A. Goslin, ed., *Handbook of Socialization Theory and Research.* Chicago: Rand McNally.

Guilford, J. P. 1959. Three faces of intellect. *American Psychologist* 14: 469–79.

Kardiner, Abram. 1945. *The Psychological Frontiers of Society.* New York: Columbia University Press.

Kluckhohn, Clyde, & Murray, Henry A. 1953. *Personality in Nature, Society, and Culture,* 2nd ed. New York: Knopf.

Kohlberg, L. 1969. Stage and sequence: The cognitive-developmental approach to socialization. In D. A. Goslin, ed., *Handbook of Socialization Theory and Research.* Chicago: Rand McNally.

LeVine, R. 1981. Remarks at the SSRC conference on Concepts of Culture and Its Acquisition, New York.

Lockhart, K. L., Abrahams, B., & Osherson, D. N. 1977. Children's understanding of uniformity in the environment. *Child Development* 48: 1521–31.

Loevinger, Jane. 1976. *Ego Development: Conceptions and Theories.* San Francisco: Jossey-Bass.

Machado, L. A. 1980. *The Right to Be Intelligent.* New York: Pergamon Press.

Nucci, L. P., & Turiel, E. 1978. Social interactions and the development of social concepts in preschool children. *Child Development* 49: 400–7.

Piatelli-Palmarini, M., ed. 1980. *Language and Learning: The Debate Between Jean Piaget and Noam Chomsky.* Cambridge, Mass.: Harvard University Press.

Polanyi, Michael. 1958. *Personal Knowledge: Towards a Post-critical Philosophy.* Chicago: University of Chicago Press.

Popper, K. 1972. *Objective Knowledge: An Evolutionary Approach.* Oxford: Clarendon Press.

Rimland, B. 1964. *Infantile Autism.* New York: Appleton-Century-Crofts.

Selfe, L. 1977. *Nadia.* London: Academic Press.

Selman, R. 1980. *The Growth of Interpersonal Understanding.* New York: Academic Press.

Shotwell, J., Wolf, D., & Gardner, H. 1979. Styles of achievement in early symbolization. In M. Foster & S. Brandes, eds., *Symbols as Sense.* New York: Academic Press.

Skryzniarz, W. S. 1981. *A review of projects to develop intelligence in Venezuela: Developmental, philosphical, policy, and cultural perspectives on intellectual potential.* Unpublished manuscript.

Spearman, C. 1904. General intelligence objectively determined and measured. *American Journal of Psychology* 15: 840–8.

Thurstone, L. L., & Thurstone, T. G. 1941. *Factorial Studies of Intelligence,* Psychometric Monographs, no. 2. Chicago: University of Chicago Press.

Wason, Peter C., & Johnson-Laird, P. N. 1972. *Psychology of Reasoning: Structure and Content.* Cambridge Mass.: Harvard University Press.

Wolf, D. P., & Gardner, H. 1982. On the structure of early symbolization. In R. Schiefelbusch & D. Bricker, eds., *Early Language: Acquisition and Intervention.* Baltimore: University Park Press.

12. Origins of Human Competence: A Cultural-Ecological Perspective

John U. Ogbu

In this essay I am concerned with the problem of developing an appropriate model for cross-cultural research in child rearing and development, particularly for studying minority children in the United States. The essay is divided into five parts. The first deals with definition of competence and majority-group developmentalists' approach to child rearing and development in a plural society. In the second section I present alternative models, one currently used by some minority researchers, the other — a cultural-ecological model — being the model I am proposing as appropriate for cross-cultural research. I speculate in the third section on some implications of the cultural-ecological model for research on minority children. This is followed with some further observations in the fourth section on the relationship between child rearing and schooling among urban ghetto blacks. Here I try to point out an almost unrecognized feature of ghetto culture, namely, that it is not merely different from white middle-class culture shared by the public schools, but in some important respects it appears to be an alternative to mainstream culture. The concluding part of the paper briefly considers the practical implications of the cultural-ecological model.

Let me make it clear from the outset that I do not rule out cross-cultural research on minority children or on any other group of children; nor do I rule out cross-cultural comparisons. But I reject the absurdity of searching for a pattern of child rearing and development derived from studying one group (e.g., white middle-class children) in another group (e.g., urban ghetto black children). The first step toward majority-minority or cross-cultural comparison is to

Reprinted by permission of The Society for Research in Child Development from *Child Development* 52 (1981) 413–29. © The Society for Research in Child Development, Inc.

study majority child rearing and development qua majority child rearing and development, and to study minority child rearing and development qua minority child rearing and development. A general theory of child rearing and development should emerge from data derived from mapping out patterns of child rearing and development of different groups (e.g., minorities, majority, social classes, etc.) or societies (Gearing 1976, p. 188) in their respective contexts.

A MODEL OF COMPETENCE IN A PLURAL SOCIETY

What Is Human Competence?

"Competence" is increasingly being used to distinguish people who possess certain attributes associated with a white middle-class type of success in school and society, but there is not as yet an accepted definition of the term. Common to most definitions, however, is the notion that competence is the ability to perform a culturally specified task. For example, Ainsworth and Bell (1974, p. 98) define competence in part as the ability to influence environment, and for Inkeles (1968) it is the ability to perform socially valued roles as defined in a given society. Upon a close inspection, "ability" as used in various definitions of competence refers to a set of skills which makes it possible to perform the given task. This is at least the impression one gains from Connolly and Bruner's introduction to *The Growth of Competence* (1974). They state that "in any given society there are sets of skills which are essential for coping with existing realities," and that how individuals function depends on their acquisition of the competencies (i.e., skills) required by these realities. Connolly and Bruner distinguish between specific skills and general skills, with emphasis on the importance of the latter. They give as an example of general skills "middle-class education," or the set of skills associated with technological management. This general skill includes "the capacity for combining information in a fashion that permits one to use flexibility; to go beyond the information given; to draw inferences about things yet to be encountered; and to connect and probe for connection" (p. 4). They call this "operative intelligence —*knowing how* rather than simply *knowing that*" (p. 3). Competence is, then, a set of functional or instrumental skills. While Connolly and Bruner are primarily concerned with cognitive or intellectual competencies, others focus on linguistic, social-emotional, and practical competencies (White 1973; Williams 1970).

A Universal Model of Human Development

The dominant research approach, which may be designated as the universal model of human development, makes three fundamental assumptions. The first is that the origins of human competence lie in intrafamilial relationships and parent (or surrogate parent)-child interaction or in early childhood experiences. As Connolly and Bruner (1974) put it, "The general skills, cognitive and emotional, appear to depend on what has properly been called a 'hidden curriculum in the home' " (p. 5). The second assumption is that the nature of human competencies can be adequately studied by focusing on micro-level analyses of the child's early experiences, such as an analysis of the child's experiences within the family and similar settings. The third assumption is that a child's later school success and perhaps success in adult life depend on the acquisition of white middle-class competencies through white middle-class child-rearing practices.

The work of Burton White and his associates at Harvard illustrates well this approach to the origins of human competence. For about 2 years White and his associates visited the homes of each of 40 children for about 1 hour a week and observed and recorded how the child interacted with its mother and, occasionally, with other people such as the father, older siblings, housekeeper, and peers. From these observations they concluded that "a close social relationship, particularly during the first few months following their first birthday, was a conspicuous feature in the lives of the children who developed best" (White 1979, p. 7). They went on to say that within this parent-child interaction it was important for the adult to provide the child with a reasonable amount of safe space and materials to explore, to act as the child's consultant when he needed help and comforting, and to be firm and consistent in discipline. These are some of the maternal behaviors constituting "the core of effective child-rearing" (p. 13). On the child's part it was determined important that he carry out certain social and nonsocial tasks. For example, he should be able to use adults as a resource, learn how to gain people's attention, gain information through vision and steady staring, and listen to people speaking to him directly. Effective child rearing combined with appropriate child tasks appeared to correlate with the development of appropriate cognitive, language, and social competencies by the age of 3, a development which is hypothesized to ensure their future success in school and probably in society at large.

Using findings from this "naturalistic" study, White (1979) designed an experiment in which a group of mothers were taught to rear their children according to the core of effective child-rearing practices, and their children were taught to perform the core of effective child tasks. The results were not entirely as expected. For example, although the child's total social experience correlated with his language development, it did not correlate with his cognitive competence as measured by the Binet test scores. Nevertheless, the researchers concluded that their experiment had established the importance of early childhood experiences not only for cognitive development in general but also for formal schooling. Citing Bronfenbrenner (1974), they stated that "while excellent early development does not guarantee lifelong excellent development, poor progress during the early years seems to be remarkably difficult to overcome" (p. 181). These researchers made three concluding points which are relevant to the present essay. First, they claimed that the origins of competence lie indeed in the hidden curriculum of the home. "After 20 years of research," they said, "we are convinced that much that shapes the final human product takes place [in the home] during the first years of life" (pp. 182, 183). Second, the most important or most essential ingredient in the hidden curriculum of the home is the mother's skills as a teacher. Some children do not develop appropriate competencies for later success in school and society because their parents (i.e., mothers) fail in their child-rearing tasks. Third, the failure of some mothers in this vital task calls for society to intervene in order to train such parents to become good teachers. "We are convinced," they concluded, "that the traditional failure to offer training and assistance to new parents has several harmful consequences. Put simply, people could grow up to become more able and more secure if their first teachers did not have to be 'self-taught' and unsupported" (p. 183).

Inadequacy of the Universal Model for Cross-cultural Research

The White (1979) studies do not directly address the issue of cross-cultural research. But they started out with the assumption that there are universal "laws" of optimal development. If these laws could be discovered, as they appear to claim to have done with their recent experimental study, then such findings can be used to help groups who do not do as well in school and who are, therefore, in need of compensatory education (White 1979, p. 8). Others are more explicit in pointing out that children from black ghettos and similar "disadvantaged" minorities do not succeed in school and society because they do not have the kind of early childhood experiences described by White et al. (see Powledge 1967; Stanley 1972, 1973). Connolly and Bruner (1974), for example, believe that ghetto blacks do not have the operative intelligence essential for managing modern technology because of inadequate early childhood experiences. "Research over the last several years has taught us much," they declare. "The slum child, the ghetto, the subculture of defeat do not equip their children with the easy abstract skills of the doctor's, lawyer's, or professor's children" (Connolly & Bruner 1974, p. 5). They point out that the official ideology of despair in these subcultures is produced by generations of unemployment, job discrimination, and the like. Ghetto parents subtly transmit this despair to their children, thus stunting their mental development. The way out of this developmental dilemma is not necessarily to eliminate unemployment and job discrimination (points at which the authors are silent), but to intervene in child-rearing practices, to make "supplementary child-rearing practices available to the parents" (p. 6).

Thus, proponents of the universal model attribute minority children's failure in school to developmental "deficits," and they propose a rehabilitation to correct the deficits and to enhance school success. This deficit perspective is nowhere more fully articulated than in various preschool programs for "disadvantaged children" begun in the 1960s. These programs are based on assumptions that an early acquisition of competencies is critical for later functioning in school and society, that children's experiences with certain types of "curriculum" during the preschool years promote optimal development, and that it is possible to correct the developmental deficits through intervention programs for preschoolers and/or preventive programs directed at parents. The emphasis of a particular program tells us what instrumental competencies are presumed "missing" in minority child rearing and development. For example, we know what competencies are thought to be "missing" when programs are designed to increase parents' knowledge of the core of effective child rearing through lectures, counseling, group discussion, and the like; when programs attempt to train mothers in techniques of cognitive stimulation and social training by showing them how and how much to talk to and play with children; or when programs aim to develop children's cognitive, social-emotional, preacademic skills or a combination of these competencies (Ogbu 1974, pp. 208–211; Rees 1968; White 1973).

It is now generally acknowledged that most of these programs have not been successful in permanently inculcating the competencies assumed to facilitate a white middle-class type of school success (Goldberg 1971; Ogbu 1978). Explanations for their failure have merely encouraged the proponents to stress the need for earlier and earlier intervention, including more emphasis on parent education and parent training. But parent education—increasing parents' knowledge of the core of effective child rearing—has not been particularly successful or effective either. And although parent training seems more effective, its results cannot be generalized because of the selective nature of the participants and because of unresolved methodological problems (White 1973, pp. 245, 257).

I have discussed the inadequacies of the deficit explanations and their attendant remedies elsewhere (Ogbu 1978; Ogbu, Note 1). The point to emphasize here is that the universal model upon which they are derived is not a useful model for cross-cultural study of either the development of human competence or school success. Contrary to the assumptions of the model, there are some nonwhite immigrant groups in the United States who have done relatively well in school even though they were not raised in the way the model suggests or in the manner described to some extent by White (1979) and in various remedial programs (see DeVos 1973; Ogbu 1978; Ogbu, Note 2). Moreover, in the Third World countries some groups do relatively well in Western-type schools even though they do not follow the child-rearing practices advocated in the model. Of particular interest is the fact that "impoverished children" in such societies also tend to do well in school and are not characterized by the same "problems" said to exist among "disadvantaged children" in America (Heyneman 1979; van den Berghe 1980).

The case for the current pattern of intervention rests largely on the belief in the determinism of early childhood events—"that much that shapes the final human product takes place during the first years of life" (White 1979, p. 193). But as far as schooling is concerned, the cross-cultural examples cited above cast serious doubts on the necessity of particular socialization experiences. Not only can children from different child-rearing backgrounds learn well in the same school, but people with different childhood backgrounds can at varying points in their lives acquire the general skills or competencies which, according to Connolly and Bruner (1974), are essential for technological management. Given the opportunity, one does not have to be born and raised in a white middle-class home or receive "supplementary childhood care" to become a doctor, lawyer, or professor in the Western social and economic system.

Furthermore, it will be obvious in my later discussion that the ghetto child's later experiences in the street are probably just as important in shaping his adult instrumental cognitive, linguistic, motivational, socioemotional, and practical competencies as his early childhood experiences in the home. For example, no one who has observed or studied hustlers and pimps in the ghetto will deny that they possess the general skills or operative intelligence — "*knowing how* rather than simply *knowing that*" — which Connolly and Bruner attribute to the white middle class (see Foster 1974, p. 38; Perkins 1975; Milner, Note 3). But hustlers and pimps appear to have acquired their operative intelligence primarily in postchildhood in the street (Perkins 1975; Milner, Note 3). Then, of course, we note that racial barriers have traditionally forced such "intelligent" ghetto people to apply their competencies to the management of activities in a "street economy" rather than in the conventional, corporate economy.

ALTERNATIVE MODELS: RELATIVISTIC AND CULTURAL ECOLOGICAL

All three assumptions underlying the universal model are inappropriate for cross-cultural research, especially for research in black urban life. I propose an alternative model more suitable for cross-cultural studies, a model that does not set up the white middle-class child-rearing practices and competencies as the standard upon which all others are measured. Before doing so, I will briefly indicate other efforts to develop an alternative model for cross-cultural research, which may be designated as a relativistic model.

The Relativistic Model

By the late 1960s many blacks and other minority-group members rejecting the deficit explanations of school failure began to argue that their people have different cultures whose child-rearing practices promote competencies different from those of the white middle class. If their children failed in school it was probably because the schools' methods of teaching and testing failed to recognize the unique skills of these children (Boykin 1978; Gibson 1976; Ramirez & Castenada 1974; Wright 1970).

Some researchers have made serious efforts to demonstrate that America's minorities have their own cultures. For example, a strong case has been made for the existence of a distinct black culture, with roots in African culture and black experience in the United States (Hannerz 1969; Keil 1977; Lewis 1976; Nobles & Traver 1976; Valentine 1979; Young 1970, 1974; Shack, Note 4). However, there has been very little effort to specify the instrumental competencies unique to black culture except in areas of "expressive life-styles" (e.g., adaptability, social interactional skills, and "styles" in dress, walking, etc.) and language and communication (Abrahams 1972; Hannerz 1969; Keil 1977; Kochman 1972; Labov 1972; Mitchell-Kernan 1972; Rainwater 1974; Simons, Note 5). It is largely in the area of language and communication that researchers have gone further to understand unique instrumental competencies of blacks in relation to problems of formal schooling. In general it can be said that researchers have not yet reached the point of clearly delineating the unique competencies of minority groups and how such competencies are acquired.

More germane to the task of this essay is the growing number of studies of competencies outside Western societies (see Cole, Gay, Glick, & Sharp 1971; Dasen 1977; Greenfield 1966). Of particular importance is the suggestion by anthropologists (e.g., LeVine 1967), sociologists (Inkeles 1966, 1968), and cross-cultural psychologists (Berry 1977) that the child-rearing patterns of a population may be influenced by the nature of its instrumental competencies which, in turn, depends on its role repertoire. These researchers agree that competence is defined differently in different populations, and that in each case it is the main task of child rearing to train "infants, children, adolescents (and sometimes adults) so that they can ultimately fulfill the social obligations that their society and culture will place on them" (Inkeles 1966, p. 64). Competencies—cognitive, linguistic, social-emotional, and practical—are cultural requirements which parents and other child-rearing agents are obligated to inculcate in children. Such insights suggest another model—a cultural-ecological model—which studies competencies in the context of real-life situations, thereby avoiding ethnocentrism.

Cultural-Ecological Perspective

The underlying assumptions of the model we propose are that origins of human competencies—general and specific skills—lie in the nature of culturally defined adult tasks, such as the subsistence tasks of a given population; that insofar as most adults in the population perform their sex-appropriate tasks competently as defined in the culture, it follows that most children in the population grow up as competent men and women; that child-rearing techniques serve only as a mechanism for inculcating and acquiring certain culturally defined instrumental competencies and are, in fact, shaped largely by the nature of those particular instrumental competencies; that child categories and instrumental competencies resulting from child-rearing techniques eventually develop into adaptive adult categories and instrumental competencies in the population; and that minority groups maintaining a kind of symbiotic relationship with a dominant group in a specific environment like the United States tend to evolve alternative rather than merely different instrumental competencies which are characteristic of a spatially distant and nonsymbiotic culture. The last assumption has important educational implications which will be explored in the concluding part of the essay.

Cultural Tasks and Competence. Certain populations possess unique instrumental competencies that meet their societal needs, and they adapt their child-rearing techniques to inculcate these needs. These societal needs may be defined as the cultural tasks which are appropriate for age, sex, and other criteria of distinction. For adults in any population, these culturally defined tasks are to be found in all areas of life, including those pertaining to subsistence, social organization and relations, political organization, and so on. Differences in such cultural tasks are not as readily acknowledged for populations within the United States as they may be for geographically distant ones. But, as we shall argue later, these tasks, particularly subsistence tasks, are in important ways different for the white middle class than for black ghetto residents and similar minorities.

Child Rearing as Culturally Organized Formulas for Inculcating Competencies. An adequate framework for studying child rearing must begin with the acknowledgment that in every relatively stable population or its segment most children grow up to be competent adult men and women. And there appear to be three reasons why this is the case: children are taught more or less the same set of instrumental competencies, they are taught with the same culturally standardized techniques, and the members of the population share the same incentives for teaching the same competencies by the same techniques and to acquire the same competencies. Within this general pattern there are, of course, individual differences due to differences in constitution, "accidents of birth," and, to some extent, individual preferences.

In every relatively stable human population, instrumental competencies have prior existence before individual families which teach these competencies to their offspring through the process of child rearing. Child rearing is thus the process by which parent and other child-rearing agents transmit and by which children acquire the prior existing competencies required by their social, economic, political, and other future adult cultural tasks. The study of the child-rearing process informs us of how the prior existing cognitive, linguistic, social-emotional, and practical competencies are transmitted and acquired; but the study of the range and nature of the cultural tasks requiring these competencies provides us with the knowledge of why a given range and form of such competencies exist at all within the population.

The causal relationship between competencies and child-rearing practices appears to be the reverse of our conventional thinking. Contrary to our usual interpretation of differences in competencies between members of two populations (e.g., white middle class and urban ghetto blacks) as resulting from differences in child-rearing practices, cross-cultural studies would suggest that the nature of the instrumental competencies in a population may determine the techniques parents and parent surrogates employ to raise children and how these children seek to acquire the attributes as they get older (see Aberle 1961; Barry, Child, & Bacon 1959; Inkeles 1966, 1968; Kohn 1969; LeVine 1967; Maquet 1971; Mead 1939; Miller & Swanson 1958).

Barry et al. (1959) provide a good example of both how subsistence tasks determine personal attributes and how the latter appear to influence child-rearing practices. They first describe the personal attributes valued and rewarded in two types of societies distinguished by levels of subsistence economy, namely, low-food-accumulation societies of hunters and gatherers and high-food-accumulation societies of pastoralists and farmers. The first type of societies rewarded individualism, independence, assertiveness, and risk taking, whereas the second type of societies rewarded conscientious, compliant, responsible, and conservative adult behaviors. Instrumental competencies characteristic of each type of society were congruent with adult subsistence tasks. For example, the authors note that the high-food-accumulation societies of farmers and pastoralists need "responsible adults who can best ensure the continuing welfare of a society with high-accumulation economy whose food supply must be protected and developed gradually throughout the year" (p. 62). In such societies people must adhere to a routine designed to maintain high accumulation of food. In contrast, societies with low food accumulation encouraged individual initiative to wrest food daily from nature in order to survive (pp. 62–63). Equally important is the authors' suggestion that these attributes tended to be generalized to the rest of behavior in everyday life (p. 63).

What is the relationship between the instrumental competencies and child-rearing practices of these two types of societies? The authors hypothesized that differences in instrumental competencies would cause the two types of societies to employ different techniques of child rearing: "The kind of adult behavior useful to the society is likely to be taught to some extent to the children, in order to assure the appearance of this behavior at the time it is needed. Hence we predict that the emphasis in childrearing will be toward the development of kinds of behaviors useful for adult economy" (p. 53). When they rated 104 societies on several aspects of child-rearing practices, the results generally supported this hypothesis, especially with respect to training in compliance and assertiveness (p. 59).

Another example is Cohen's study (1965) among the Kanuri of Nigeria which shows how the society's rule of behavior for achievement defines social competence and how the latter shapes child-rearing practices. In order to attain higher economic, political, or social status, a Kanuri must show those who have the power to bestow these resources that he is loyal, obedient, and servile. Loyalty, obedience, and servility are therefore not only highly prized in superior-inferior relationships but also generalized to other forms of relationships such as that between parent and child, teacher and student, religious leader and followers. Kanuri parents consciously employ particular techniques to ensure that their children learn to behave properly like clients, that is, that they acquire the instrumental competencies which formed the most important social capital for achieving high status (p. 363).

Some studies in the United States further contribute to our understanding of the linkage between subsistence/cultural tasks and instrumental competencies, and between the latter and child-rearing practices. One such study, by Miller and Swanson (1958), indicates that earlier middle-class Americans involved in entrepreneurial subsistence tasks tended to value and stress self-control and self-denial, whereas later generations of the middle class involved in bureaucratic economic tasks tend to value other personal attributes, like the ability to get along with other people and self-confidence. The study shows that there also has been a concomitant change in the child-rearing practices of the middle class because, in contrast to earlier generations, the contemporary middle class trains its children to be accommodating, to express their impulses more spontaneously, and so on (p. 58). Finally, Kohn's study (1969) shows that middle-class bureaucratic and professional jobs are associated with personal attributes of self-direction and the ability to manipulate interpersonal relations, ideas, and symbols. Working-class jobs, on the other hand, are associated with respect for authority and conformity to externally imposed rules. In this study, subjects in the sample from each class employed child-rearing techniques which encouraged their children to develop an adaptive constellation of instrumental competencies. For example, middle-class subjects used reasoning, isolation, appeals to guilt, and the like to elicit appropriate behavior in their children, whereas working-class subjects relied more on physical punishment and other means that enhanced compliance to external rules.

These studies deal mainly with social-emotional competence. In general they show that the cultural tasks—subsistence tasks in our examples—generate, adaptive, functional personal attributes or instrumental social-emotional competencies. These qualities are perceived as useful by parents and other child-rearing agents and are taught by appropriate techniques. Berry (1971) suggests why we should more or less expect the nature of instrumental competencies to influence choice of child-rearing practices when he states that "one would not expect to discover a society in which independence and self-reliance are conveyed as goals by a harsh, restrictive method of socialization. Nor, conversely, would one expect to discover a society in which conformity is taught by a method characterized by a stimulation of a child's own interest and of his curiosity" (p. 328). To reiterate, the first reason most children in a given group or society grow up as competent adults is that they are taught more or less the same set of instrumental competencies.

The second reason that most children in a relatively stable population grow up as competent adult men and women is that their sex-appropriate instrumental competencies are taught and acquired through culturally standardized techniques. A given population develops its child-rearing practices over a period of time as a set of standardized techniques designed to ensure both that its children survive into adulthood and that they acquire the competencies essential for their adult cultural tasks. This development is based on the people's experiences as a group in dealing with the demands of their physical, social, political, economic, and supernatural environments, that is, the demands of their cultural tasks.

As members of a population learn which strategies are effective and appropriate in exploiting their subsistence resources and which competencies facilitate the use of the strategies, they also learn how best to inculcate these instrumental competencies in their children. The discovery of child-rearing techniques would initially be characterized by trial and error. But as more effective techniques are found, they become standardized and encoded in the people's customs and are transmitted like other aspects of their culture to subsequent generations. The transmission of standardized knowledge and skills of child rearing and their rationale ensures that parents and other adults in the population will share more or less the same ideas of what children must learn and be —what instrumental competencies they must possess —in order to become competent adults. It also ensures that adults share similar ideas of the techniques and skills with which to help children acquire these functional competencies.

From the perspective of cultural ecology, the child-rearing practices of a population are not an irrational or random set of activities; they form a part of a culturally organized system which evolves through generations of collective experiences in tasks designed to meet environmental demands. The child-rearing practices are a part of a people's cultural knowledge of their adult tasks, of essential competencies, and of the methods of transmitting these competencies to succeeding generations.

Parents and other child-rearing agents are not really independent actors in child-rearing tasks, for two reasons. First, they treat children in the manner constrained by their awareness that their children must develop particular instrumental competencies essential for more or less foreordained social, economic, political, and other culturally standardized knowledge, techniques, and skills of rearing competent children as defined by their society or social group. Individual parents do not invent new ways to raise their children, nor do they invent new competencies to transmit to their children. Except under conditions of rapid social change, both the competencies and the method are culturally sanctioned and more or less preordained.

The third reason most children grow up as competent adults is that people in a given population are motivated to inculcate and to acquire the competencies essential for adult cultural tasks by societal rewards for competence and penalties for incompetence. This phenomenon can be described with the concept of the status-mobility system (LeVine 1967) or "native theory of success." In every population there usually exists a folk theory of how one performs cultural tasks in order to succeed in the status system. That is, how one "makes it," however "making it" is defined, is a shared cultural knowledge. In a population in which status positions or cultural tasks are ranked, "making it" includes both the ability to attain higher status positions or more desirable adult tasks and the ability to perform these tasks successfully. A native theory of success thus includes knowledge of the range of available cultural tasks or status positions, their relative importance or value, the competencies essential for attainment or performance, the strategies for attaining the positions or obtaining the cultural tasks, and the expected penalties and rewards for failures and successes.

A people's theory of success develops out of past experiences with cultural tasks, social rewards, and relative costs. The theory is either reinforced or altered by contemporary experiences, that is, by perceptions and interpretations of available opportunity structures.

As noted earlier, cultural tasks require appropriate instrumental competencies. It follows that those who are successful in performing cultural tasks are likely to be characterized to some degree by appropriate instrumental competencies, qualities, or attributes. Such people become models whose attributes child-rearing agents admire and want to inculcate in children. As children get older and become more aware of the status-mobility system of their society or social group and especially of the competencies for success, they, too, actively seek to acquire the instrumental competencies of the successful members of their population. The images of successful people, living or dead, are culturally buttressed and form a substantial portion of the values guiding parents and other child-rearing agents in their child-rearing tasks and guiding older children in their responses to these efforts (LeVine 1967).

Members of a population do not conceptualize the instrumental competencies which facilitate success in their status-mobility system and do not necessarily explain the relationship between their cultural tasks and instrumental competencies or between the latter and their child-rearing techniques the way social scientists do. Nevertheless, to suggest that natives (be they white middle-class Americans, black ghetto residents, or African tribesmen) usually have a good knowledge of their status system and of what it takes to make it as behavioral guides is not too far removed from reality.

The Scope of "Environment" in Human-development Research. If the way parents and parent surrogates relate to children and the way children respond are influenced by the more or less foreordained social, economic, political, and other cultural tasks by culturally patterned techniques of child rearing and by shared theories of status mobility and child rearing, then concentration of conventional studies on parent-child relationship in the laboratory, home, or other settings has serious limitations. Some of these limitations have been noted by others from different perspectives (see Bronfenbrenner 1974, 1977, 1979; Inkeles 1966, 1968). Bronfenbrenner (1977, p. 515), for instance, points out that emphasis on rigor by developmental psychologists leads them to design elegant experiments of limited scope and use. "This limitation," he explains, "derives from the fact that many of these experiments involve situations that are unfamiliar, artificial, and short-lived and that call for unusual behaviors that are difficult to generalize to other settings." As an alternative he proposes to study the child in *"the enduring environment in which he lives* or might live if social policies and practices were altered" (1974, p. 2).

From a different perspective, Inkeles (1968, p. 123) points out the shortcoming of researchers' preoccupation with events in the micro setting (e.g., the family) and their inability or unwillingness to examine the impact of social, economic, and political systems—"the imperatives of culture" (Cohen 1971)—under which the child will live and perform as an adult. He notes that those studying child rearing are mostly concerned with personality developmental problems and that this dominant concern leads them to concentrate "on purely intrafamilial and interpersonal aspects of parent-child relations." Even when some researchers introduce social class, occupational differences, ethnicity, and the like as control variables, their investigation still focuses "on the individual parent as the socialization agent." Inkeles then suggests that the study of child rearing should be broadened to include the interests of society and its influences on the child-rearing process. He also suggests that we include how the child learns the content of the significant role he will play as an adult (pp. 123–24).

Cultural ecology provides a framework for broadening our conception of environmental influences on competencies and their acquisition. This framework is derived from the work of anthropologist Julian Steward and his followers. They define cultural ecology as the study of institutionalized and socially transmitted patterns of behavior interdependent with features of the environment (Netting 1968, p. 11; see also Geertz 1962; Goldschmidt 1971). A variant definition more germane to my interest is by Bennett (1969), for whom cultural ecology is the study of how the way a population uses its natural environmental influences and is influenced by its social organization and cultural values and how the relationship between the personal attributes and behaviors of its members and their environment is to be found in the strategies or tasks they have devised for coping with their environmental demands, in the ways of exploiting available resources to attain their subsistence goals and solve recurrent and new problems, as well as in ways of dealing with one another. In this population-environment relationship via cultural tasks, the adaptive, instrumental competencies and behaviors are properties of the total group, not of isolated individuals.

One environmental demand which has a powerful influence on human competence and is faced by all human groups is subsistence, or making a living. For this reason the model I propose deals primarily with the role of subsistence tasks and strategies in the origins of human competence. There are additional reasons for focusing on subsistence demands. First, this is an area where significant cross-cultural studies like those discussed earlier exist, showing its influence on child-rearing practices and outcomes. Furthermore, subsistence quest has dominated man's evolutionary history and has acquired a symbolic significance far beyond the need to satisfy biological drives of hunger; it has become intimately tied to man's quest for status enhancement or self-esteem, especially in modern industrial societies.

While all human populations respond to subsistence demands, they do not all respond alike or with the same set of strategies because they do not occupy the same environment, because their environments do not contain the same resources, and because they have different histories of resource exploitation and of quest for protection. Different populations, therefore, seem to have evolved different strategies more or less appropriate for their given circumstances. And each constellation of subsistence strategies has selected, as it were, from a vast array of practical skills and cognitive, language (communicative), and social-emotional competencies most compatible with it. A given population has usually invested such instrumental competencies with cultural values and stressed them for the upbringing of its children.

Still another reason for focusing on subsistence demands is that the influence of subsistence strategies on personal attributes is just as powerful, even if not direct, in modern industrial societies like the United States as it is in societies of hunter-gatherers and subsistence farmers. In modern industrial societies subsistence strategies largely determine how children are prepared for adult life in the home, community, and school. The linkage between subsistence strategies (i.e., work, job), on the one hand, and instrumental competencies on the other, in the United States is widely recognized by researchers in education and child development (White 1973; Baumrind, Note 6). The direction of causal linkage between participation in American economy and instrumental competencies conventionally stressed is important but quite different from that suggested here. It is often asserted, for instance, that the nature of one's participation in this economy determines not only one's subsistence status but also his or her general status enhancement or self-esteem. As one observer has written (Miller 1971, p. 18), a person's job in the United States is about the most important symbol of his social standing. It is also said that the level of economy at which one participates (e.g., as an unskilled, skilled, or professional worker) is determined primarily by one's instrumental competencies acquired during child rearing or genetically inherited, which subsequently enabled one to acquire formal education appropriate for the attainment of that level of job (Hunt 1969; Jensen 1969; Schultz 1961; Weisbrod 1975). What has not been widely recognized and much less adequately studied is the influence of the nature of one's participation in that economy on his personal attributes. This is the special concern of the cultural-ecological perspective.

The Cultural-Ecological Model

The cultural-ecological model I propose is represented in Figure 1; showing a range of factors that should be considered in order to obtain a more complete and accurate view of the instrumental competencies prevalent in a given population, of their origins, and of their relationship to child rearing.

Basic Concepts. The model begins with the concept of effective environment *(A),* because cultural ecology does not deal with the total physical environment. It deals only with those aspects of it which directly affect subsistence quest and protection from threats to physical survival. Major elements of the effective environment include the population's level of technology and knowledge and nature of available resources. Technology refers to both tools and their uses in subsistence exploitation and protection; knowledge includes people's understanding of the nature of their environment and the necessary techniques for exploiting its resources (Netting 1968, p. 16). The model posits that a people's effective environment largely shapes their

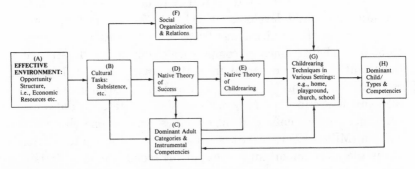

FIGURE 1
A Cultural-Ecological Model of Child Rearing

subsistence strategies *(B)* or modes of resource exploitation. The latter constitute the main cultural tasks in the model and include the range of economic activities available to members of the population.

Available adaptive adult categories *(C)*, or what are usually called adult role models, in the population depend partly on the nature of the subsistence strategies an partly on the native theory of success *(D)*. The adult categories are types of people who in the native view are successful; usually there are native labels for the categories. Each category is not necessarily tied to a particular subsistence strategy. The categories are often distinguished, but not too rigidly, by their constellation of instrumental competencies *(C)*. Some instrumental competencies are likely to be shared by many people in the population.

Native theory of success *(D)* is an important element influencing child-rearing values and practices. As discussed earlier, it is the people's idea of how members of their society or social group get ahead. Its study provides an important clue about what instrumental competencies people consciously inculcate in children and how they do it, what kinds of adults they want their children to be, and perhaps what kinds of adults older children strive to be.

Child rearing is a future-oriented activity to a large degree because it prepares children to perform cultural tasks competently as adults (Ogbu 1978, p. 16; see also Aberle & Naegele 1952; Inkeles 1968). To facilitate this there usually is a kind of native theory of child rearing *(E)*. People's beliefs about proper ways to raise children are partly based on their notion of how to succeed, their image of successful people in their community, and their organization of child-rearing tasks. The native theory of child rearing does not necessarily correspond to the researcher's or "scientific" model of the same, but it exists to guide adults in their relationship to children and to rationalize what happens between them and children. From the cultural-ecological perspective an adequate study of child rearing in a given population must probe into the people's conscious model of how children should be raised and the sources of this model (Mayer 1970).

The way people organize their subsistence activities influences how they organize the upbringing of their children. Thus social organization and relations of child rearing *(F)* depends on the organization of and participation in subsistence activities because the latter may affect family or household structure, the type of settings in which children are raised, as well as the personnel or child-rearing agents. Furthermore, the social organization of child rearing is affected by and affects the native theory of child rearing and the actual techniques of child rearing.

Child-rearing techniques *(G)*—the actual process by which adults inculcate and children acquire instrumental competencies for their adult cultural tasks—exist as a part of the culturally organized formulas for upbringing: children are trained by more or less the same standardized techniques which have evolved for transmission of adaptive instrumental competencies functional in adult life. The model posits that actual child-rearing techniques are influenced by the need to produce functional adult categories and to inculcate their competencies; they are also influenced by the native theory of child rearing and by the social organization of child rearing. Particular forms of techniques may be employed in particular settings, such as home and playground, at particular times and by particular child-rearing agents. These are matters for empirical study. Furthermore, particular child-rearing techniques may depend on the nature of instrumental competencies the child-rearing agents are obligated to inculcate or reinforce.

Ultimately we want to understand the outcomes of child rearing in a given culture. This can be assessed by examining characteristic or dominant attributes of children. The outcomes are labeled in the model as dominant child types and competencies *(H)* and are assumed to be those most likely to develop into dominant adult types and competencies.

CROSS-CULTURAL RESEARCH IMPLICATIONS: GHETTO EXAMPLE

The universal model reviewed earlier focuses on the relationship between child-rearing techniques and child outcomes (boxes *G* and *H* in the ecological model). It interprets developmental outcomes (e.g., dominant child types and competencies) as products of parental teaching skills and knowledge and specific child outcomes. When the universal model is applied comparatively to white middle-class and a minority population, differences in child competencies are not only interpreted narrowly as consequences of parental teaching skills, but also minority parents' teaching skills are termed deficient. The cultural-ecological model requires that we study the transmission and acquisition of competencies in a given population in the context of the demands of the population's cultural tasks, especially its subsistence tasks. Furthermore, it requires that we make no evaluative judgment in terms of good or bad, adequate or inadequate, deficient or not deficient, before we have established that the two populations studied share the same or similar effective environment, employ the same or similar subsistence strategies and/or other cultural tasks, and share the same theories of success and child rearing (Ogbu, in press). Prevailing invidious comparison is not excusable on the ground that researchers are studying the so-called high-risk children or high-risk families (Remy, Note 7) because the results of such studies eventually come to be interpreted by some as typical of minority populations. The challenge is to study first minority child rearing and development qua minority child rearing and development, Navajo child rearing and development qua Navajo child rearing and development, etc. If the researcher lacks the competence, the resources, or the time to study the various forces suggested in the model as shaping child rearing and development in a population, he or she should at least become familiar with the literature describing these forces as a background to the interpretation of his or her research findings.

The Ghetto Case

The cultural-ecological model has not been applied to the study of child rearing in the ghetto or in any other population. What I do here is indicate some possible features of the variables and linkages in the model if such a study were carried out in a black urban ghetto. The brief outline presented here is based on my reading of ethnographic and other studies in the ghetto.

Urban ghetto blacks maintain a kind of symbiotic relationship with the dominant white population and occupy an effective environment marked by marginal conventional economic resources and a substantial amount of nonconventional resources or "street economy" (Bullock 1973; Ferman, Kornbluh, & Miller 1968; Harrison 1972). Conventional employment is the major subsistence strategy, but for many the job is menial and employment is irregular and in some cases nonexistent. Equally important are "survival strategies" like collective struggle, clientship, hustling, pimping, preaching-hustling, entertainment, sports, and the like. All these subsistence strategies are "normal" in the ghetto and form the basis of judging adult competence (Ellis and Newman 1971; Hudson 1972; Newman

1978; Scott 1976; Valentine 1979; Milner, Note 3). Thus the adult categories of success not only include conventional jobs but also include hustlers, pimps, preacher-hustlers, entertainers, and the like. Each is marked by a constellation of instrumental competencies which are not exclusive.

The ghetto theory of success is influenced by these success models. Moreover, it differs significantly from the success theory of the white middle class, but not in terms of goals which appear to be essentially the same—money, power, social credit, and self-esteem. Rather, the difference lies largely in how these things can be attained, such as the extent to which each group believes that appropriate school credentials will result in the desired goal. Having experienced a long history of racial barriers, ghetto blacks believe less in the sufficiency of schooling and tend to approve the use of other alternatives by themselves or in combination with school credentials (Foster 1974; Nobles & Traver 1976; Wolfe 1970; Milner, Note 3). Ghetto theory of success is undoubtedly a part of the value system guiding the preparation of children for competent adult life as defined by ghetto people, that is, a ghetto theory of child rearing. We have very little information on the latter.

The marginal participation of ghetto residents in the conventional economy and their participation in the street economy affect the way they organize their child rearing. The marginal economic status of the black male makes it difficult for many to participate in raising their children as husband-fathers in the family; marginal economic status also forces many ghetto parents to rely on relatives and friends for child care; parents who depend on public assistance for subsistence often experience pressures to accept supplementary child care sponsored by government and private agencies even when the theories and practices of these supplementary child-care programs are perceived as alien and in conflict with those of parents; finally, parents who are actively involved in the street economy appear to have difficulty maintaining stable and intimate family relations, with the result that their children may be inducted early into street culture (Ogbu 1974, 1978, pp. 200–201; Stack 1974; White 1973).

Actual child-rearing techniques which facilitate the development of ghetto instrumental competencies are not limited to those employed in the home and in parent-child interaction. The ghetto child's early experiences in the home constitute but one in a series leading to the development of competent adulthood. Later experiences in the street, church, school, and other settings may reinforce or change the course of development. Some techniques used by ghetto parents may not receive white middle-class approval, but seem to be adapted to produce ghetto functional competencies.

Among such techniques are the contrasting treatment of the infant with abundant nurturance, warmth, and affection and their scarcity in postinfancy; establishment of a child-adult contest relationship in the postinfancy period; inconsistent demands for obedience in sanctions and in other ways of relating to the child; and the use of verbal rebuffs and physical punishment. These techniques probably promote functional competencies like self-reliance, resourcefulness, ability to manipulate people and situations, mistrust of people in authority, ability to "fight back" or to ward off attacks, etc. (Ladner 1978, p. 214; Nobles & Traver 1976, pp. 25–34; Schulz 1968, 1977, pp. 9–13; Webster 1974, pp. 86–98; Young 1974). Early induction into street culture ensures a prolonged interaction with peers and street adults, which enhances the child's development into adaptive adult categories (Perkins 1975; Silverstein & Krate 1975; Young 1970). School adds to this development by providing a setting for peer-group formation and participation as well as through its classification of children into educables and noneducables and subsequent treatment whereby the latter are driven into early encapsulation in peer and street cultures (Mercer 1973; Rist 1970; Silverstein & Krate 1975).

So far we have no labels for child categories and their competencies in literature on the ghetto, except for those of elementary school children based on school expectations (Silverstein & Krate 1975). However, several researchers provide a list of clearly labeled categories in studies of adolescence. These include regulars, ivy-leaguers, squares, cool cats, jesters, gowsters, and the like (Ellis & Newman 1971; Foster 1974; Perkins 1975). Each category is marked by a constellation of competencies, although most ghetto adolescents, especially males, seem to share the following: adaptability, verbal skills and manipulation, role-playing, interactional skills, and resourcefulness. A close inspection suggests that the adolescent categories and their competencies resemble the adult categories and their competencies mentioned earlier. We may speculate that many regulars, ivy-leaguers, and squares develop eventually into conventional employees or conventional successful adults, some cool cats become hustlers and pimps, and some gowsters turn gangsters. But the development into adult categories does not follow a rigid course; in a

recent study in Oakland, California, one of the young men interviewed was found to have been at different points of life "a submis-
sive, an ambivalent, a precocious independent, a cool cat, a stoic, a
working man, a hustler, and an intellectual in the broader sense of
one who engages in the creative exploration of culture" (Hickerson,
Note 8).

SURVIVAL STRATEGIES AND SCHOOLING:
THE PROBLEM OF ALTERNATIVE CULTURE

I suggest that the research model of dominant-group developmentalists reviewed earlier is ethnocentric. Rather than being truly universal, it is merely a pseudouniversal rooted in the beliefs of an ethnocentric population. It is false because it looks at the origins of
competence from the wrong end of the relationship between childhood experiences and the competencies essential for functioning in
adult life. It decontextualizes competencies from realities of life. As a
result, it confuses the process of acquiring and transmitting adaptive,
functional, or instrumental competencies with their causes, or origins, which are the reasons for their very presence or absence in a
given population.

The consensus among dominant-group developmentalists is that a
disproportionate number of ghetto children fail in school because
they lack white middle-class types of competencies, including rules of
behavior for achievement. And they lack these competencies because
ghetto parents lack the capability to raise their children as white
middle-class parents raise their own children. In this essay I have
argued that ghetto blacks indeed acquire different rules of behavior
for achievement and related competencies because such is the requirement for their competence in adult cultural/subsistence tasks and not
merely because ghetto parents lack white middle-class capability in
child rearing.

I now add that differences in rules of behavior for achievement and
related competencies do not always result in more or less permanent
learning handicaps or disproportionate school failure, and that where
the latter occurs there are probably additional reasons. For example,
differences in rules of behavior for achievement and related competencies may cause initial difficulties in school learning among immigrants to the United States and among Third World peoples adopting
Western education. But these people eventually learn successfully

either by abandoning or modifying substantially their native competencies and rules of behavior for achievement in favor of those which
facilitate school success. They do so for two reasons: first, they tend
to perceive school success as providing opportunities to achieve new
desirable adult cultural/subsistence tasks; and second, they realize
that their native rules of behavior for achievement and related competencies may not provide access to the new desirable adult cultural
tasks (Heyneman 1979; van den Berghe 1980; Ogbu, Note 9).

In contrast, ghetto rules of behavior for achievement and related
competencies have been developed historically as alternatives to those
of the school insofar as the latter represents white middle-class cultural ways whose racial policies and practices prevented generations
of blacks from using the same rules of behavior and the same competencies to attain desirable adult tasks open to whites. Under this
circumstance ghetto blacks are not oriented toward abandoning or
substantially modifying their rules of behavior for achievement and
their related instrumental competencies in favor of adopting those
of the white middle class. The overall impression one gains from
interviewing ghetto blacks, especially males, is that many consider
acting white in school and community as unacceptable. People should
learn how to deal with white people — how to manipulate white people — and retain their own safety and identity, but not how to behave
like white people. This type of "bicultural learning" dates back to a
period in black American history when acting white often led to
beatings, prison, or death. It is this historical and structural situation which transforms differences in rules of behavior for achievement and in competencies into alternatives that are not easily given
up in the school setting.

CONCLUSION

In this essay I have attempted to make the following points. First,
the origins of human competence — specific and general skills — prevalent in a given population lie in the nature of adult cultural tasks.
Second, the nature of the instrumental competencies influences child-
rearing techniques and outcomes by sharing people's success models,
their theories of success and child rearing, and their social organization for child rearing. Third, child-rearing ideas and techniques in a
given culture are shared by the home/family and other institutions
or settings containing the child in such a way as to make child

rearing a kind of culturally organized formula to ensure competence and survival. Fourth, the outcomes of child rearing — the child types and their competencies — appear to be those that eventually develop into adaptive adult types and their competencies. Fifth, minority groups experience a continuing disproportion of school failure mainly when their historical and structural relationship with the dominant groups has led to evolution of alternative competencies. Finally, I have proposed the cultural-ecological model as a framework for studying child rearing and developmental issues in a way that is not ethnocentric and as a framework broad enough to encompass many important forces often excluded in conventional research.

I have been concerned in this essay primarily with *what is.* But there are policy implications of our analysis with regard to minority children, such as those of the ghetto. First, we think that because instrumental competencies of ghetto children are adaptive alternatives, for example, they are not easily eliminated or modified permanently so long as the originating and supporting conditions (e.g., marginal conventional subsistence resources coupled with availability of attractive street economy) exist or are perceived to exist. That is, efforts to improve ghetto school success which focus primarily on the family and early childhood experiences cannot result in fundamental and enduring changes in ghetto children's characteristic rules of behavior for achievement and related competencies as long as such attributes are functional in a ghetto effective environment and can be acquired during the postinfancy period in the street and other settings.

Second, it follows that the most effective way to improve ghetto or minority school success is to increase and improve their conventional economic resources (e.g., provide more and better conventional jobs for youths and adults) to the point where *(a)* significant changes occur in perceptions of opportunity structures in the conventional economy, and *(b)* the street economy and associated survival strategies become less attractive. Finally, until the attractiveness of these alternatives is sufficiently reduced or altogether eliminated, ghetto or minority rules of behavior for achievement and related competencies should be studied systematically and harnessed for teaching and learning in school settings. This cannot be achieved by research focusing on atypical ghetto children and their families — those "at risk." We advocate studying ghetto people and minority people as viable cultural groups. But this should be a transitional strategy and not a permanent approach to social change which is to eliminate all structural barriers.

REFERENCE NOTES

1. Ogbu, J. U. An ecological approach to minority education. Special invited lecture, International Year of the Child, presented at the biennial meeting of the Society for Research in Child Development, San Francisco, 1979.
2. Ogbu, J. U. Education, clientage, and social mobility: caste and social change in the United States and Nigeria. Paper presented at Burg Wartenstein Symposium No. 80: Social inequality: comparative and developmental approaches, Vienna, August 25–September 3, 1978.
3. Milner, C. A. Black pimps and their prostitutes. Unpublished doctoral dissertation, University of California, Berkeley, 1970.
4. Shack, W. A. On black American values in white America: some perspectives on the cultural aspects of learning behavior and compensatory education. Paper prepared for the Social Science Research Council: Subcommittee on Values and Compensatory Education, 1970–1971.
5. Simons, H. D. Black dialect, reading interference and classroom interaction. Unpublished manuscript, Department of Education, University of California, Berkeley, 1976.
6. Baumrind, D. Subcultural variations in values defining social competence: An outsider's perspective on the black subculture. Unpublished manuscript, Institute of Human Development, University of California, Berkeley, 1976.
7. Remy, C. T. The abecedarian approach to social competence: Cognitive and linguistic intervention for disadvantaged preschoolers. Paper presented at a workshop on Socialization of Children in a Changing Society, College of Education and Home Economics, University of Cincinnati, April 1979.
8. Hickerson, R. Survival strategies and role models in the ghetto. Unpublished manuscript, Department of Anthropology, University of California, Berkeley, 1980.
9. Ogbu, J. U. Minority school performance as an adaptation. Unpublished manuscript, Department of Anthropology, University of California, Berkeley, 1978.

REFERENCES

Aberle, D. F. Culture and socialization. In F. L. K. Hsu (Ed.), *Psychological anthropology.* Evanston, Ill.: Dorsey, 1961.

Aberle, D. F., & Naegele, K. D. Middle-class father's occupational role and attitudes toward children. *American Journal of Orthopsychiatry,* 1952, 22, 366–378.

Abrahams, R. D. Joking: the training of the man of words in talking broad. In Kochman (Ed.), 1972.

Ainsworth, M. D. S., & Bell, S. M. Mother-infant interaction and the development of competence. In K. Connolly and J. S. Bruner (Eds.), *The growth of competence.* New York: Academic Press, 1974.

Barry, H.; Child, I. L.; & Bacon, M. K. Relation of childtraining to subsistence economy. *American Anthropologist,* 1959, 61, 51–63.

Bennett, J. W. *Northern plainsmen: adaptive strategy and agricultural life.* Arlington Heights, Ill.: AHM, 1969.

Berry, J. W. Ecological and cultural factors in spatial perceptual development. *Canadian journal of behavioral science review,* 1971, 3(4), 324–337.

Berry, J. W. *Human ecology and cognitive style: comparative studies in cultural and psychological adaptations.* New York: Halsted, 1977.

Boykin, A. W. Psychological/behavioral verve in academic/task performance: A pretheoretical consideration. *Journal of Negro Education,* 1978, 47, 343–354.

Bronfenbrenner, U. Developmental research and public policy and the ecology of childhood. *Child Development,* 1974, 45, 1–5.

Bronfenbrenner, U. Toward an experimental ecology of human development. *American Psychologist,* 1977, 32, 513–531.

Bronfenbrenner, U. *The ecology of human development: experiments by nature and design.* Cambridge, Mass.: Harvard University Press, 1979.

Bullock, P. *Aspirations vs. opportunity: "careers" in the inner city.* Ann Arbor: University of Michigan Press, 1973.

Cohen, R. Some aspects of institutionalized exchange: a Kanuri example. *Cahiers d'études africaines,* 1965, 5(3), 353–369.

Cohen, Y. A. The shaping of men's minds: Adaptations to the imperatives of culture. In M. L. Wax, S. Diamond, and F. O. Gearing (Eds.), *Anthropological perspectives on education.* New York: Basic, 1971.

Cole, M.; Gay, J.; Glick, J. A.; & Sharp, D. W. *The cultural context of learning and thinking: An exploration in experimental anthropology.* New York: Basic, 1971.

Connolly, K. J., and Bruner, J. S. Introduction, competence: Its nature and nurture. In K. J. Connolly and J. S. Bruner (Eds.), *The growth of competence.* London: Academic Press, 1974.

Dasen, P. (Ed.). *Piagetian psychology: Cross-cultural contributions.* New York: Garden, 1977.

DeVos, G. *Socialization for achievement: Essays on the cultural psychology of the Japanese.* Berkeley: University of California Press, 1973.

Ellis, H., & Newman, S. N. "Gowster," "ivy-leaguer," "hustler," "conservative," "mackman," and "continental": A functional analysis of six ghetto roles. In E. B. Leacock (Ed.), *The culture of poverty: a critique.* New York: Simon & Schuster, 1971.

Ferman, L. A.; Kornbluh, J. L.; & Miller, J. A. (Eds.), *Negroes and jobs: A book of readings.* Ann Arbor: University of Michigan Press, 1968.

Foster, H. L. *Ribbin', jivin', and playin' the dozens: The unrecognized dilemma of inner city schools.* Cambridge, Mass.: Ballinger, 1974.

Gearing, F. O. Where we are and where we might go: steps toward a general theory of cultural transmission. In Joan I. Roberts and S. K. Akinsanya (Eds.), *Educational patterns and cultural configurations: The anthropology of education.* New York: McKay, 1976.

Geertz, C. *Agricultural involution: the process of ecological change in Indonesia.* Berkeley: University of California Press, 1962.

Gibson, M. A. (Ed.). Approaches to multicultural education in the United States: Some concepts and assumptions. *Anthropology and Education Quarterly,* 1976, 7, Special Issue.

Goldberg, M. L. Socio-psychological issues in the education of the disadvantaged. In A. Harry Passow (Ed.), *Urban education in the 1970s.* New York: Teachers College, 1971.

Goldschmidt, W. Introduction: the theory of cultural adaptation. In R. B. Edgerton, *The individual in cultural adaptation: A study of four East African peoples.* Berkeley: University of California Press, 1971.

Greenfield, P. M. On culture and conservation. In J. S. Bruner et al. (Eds.), *Studies in cognitive growth.* New York: Wiley, 1966.

Hannerz, U. *Soulside: inquiries into ghetto culture and community.* New York: Columbia University Press, 1969.

Harrison, B. *Education, training and the urban ghetto.* Baltimore: Johns Hopkins University Press, 1972.

Heyneman, S. P. Why impoverished children do well in Ugandan schools. *Comparative Education,* 1979, 15(2), 175–185.

Hudson, J. The hustling ethic. In Kochman (Ed.), 1972.

Hunt, N. McV. *The challenge of incompetence and poverty.* Urbana: University of Illinois Press, 1969.

Inkeles, A. Social structure and the socialization of competence. In the Editors, Harvard Educational Review, *Socialization and Schools.* Cambridge, Mass.: Harvard University Press, 1966.

Inkeles, A. Society, social structure and child socialization. In John A. Clausen (Ed.), *Socialization and society.* Boston: Little, Brown, 1968.

Jensen, A. R. How much can we boost I.Q. and scholastic achievement? In the Editors, Harvard Educational Review, *Environment, heredity, and intelligence.* Cambridge, Mass.: Harvard University Press, 1969.

Keil, C. The expressive black male role: the bluesman. In D. Y. Wilkinson and R. L. Taylor, (Eds.), *The black male in America today: Perspectives on his status in contemporary society.* Chicago: Nelson-Hall, 1977.

Kochman, T. (Ed.). *Rappin' and stylin' out: Communication in urban black America.* Chicago: University of Illinois Press, 1972.

Kohn, M. L. Social class and parent-child relationships: An interpretation. In R. L. Coser (Ed.), *Life cycle and achievement in America.* New York: Harper & Row, 1969.

Labov, W. *Language in the inner city.* Philadelphia: University of Pennsylvania Press, 1972.

Ladner, J. A. Growing up black. In J. H. Williams (Ed.), *Psychology of women: Selected writings.* New York: Norton, 1978.

LeVine, R. W. *Dreams and deeds: Achievement motivation in Nigeria.* Chicago: University of Chicago Press, 1967.

Lewis, D. K. The black family: Socialization and sex roles. *Phylon,* 1976, 36, 221–237.

Maquet, J. *Power and society in Africa.* New York: World University Library, 1971.

Mayer, P. (Ed.). *Socialization: The approach from social anthropology.* London: Tavistock, 1970.

Mead, M. *From the south seas: Studies of adolescence and sex in primitive societies.* New York: Morrow, 1939.

Mercer, J. R. *Labeling the mentally retarded.* Berkeley: University of California Press, 1973.

Miller, D., & Swanson, G. *The changing American parent.* New York: Wiley, 1958.

Miller, H. P. *Rich man, poor man.* New York: Crowell, 1971.

Mitchell-Kernan, C. Signifying, loud-talking, and marking. In Kochman (Ed.), 1972.

Netting, R. McC. *Hill farmers of Nigeria: Cultural ecology of the Jos Plateau.* Seattle: University of Washington Press, 1968.

Newman, D. K. *Protest, politics, and prosperity: Black Americans and white institutions, 1940–1975.* New York: Pantheon, 1978.

Nobles, W. W., & Traver, S. Black parental involvement in education: The African connection. In *Child Welfare and Child Development: Alton M. Childs Series.* Atlanta, Ga.: Atlanta University School of Social Work, 1976.

Ogbu, J. U. *The next generation: An ethnography of education in an urban neighborhood.* New York: Academic Press, 1974.

Ogbu, J. U. *Minority education and caste: The American system in cross-cultural perspective.* New York: Academic Press, 1978.

Ogbu, J. U. Childrearing: a cultural-ecological perspective. In K. Borman (Ed.), *Socialization of children in a changing society,* in press.

Perkins, E. *Home is a dirty street.* Chicago: Third World, 1975.

Powledge, F. *To change a child.* Chicago: Quadrangle, 1967.

Rainwater, L. *Behind ghetto walls: Black families in federal slums.* Chicago: Aldine, 1974.

Ramirez, M., & Castenada, A. *Cultural democracy, bicognitive development and education.* New York: Academic Press, 1974.

Rees, H. E. *Deprivation and compensatory education: A reconsideration.* Boston: Houghton Mifflin, 1968.

Rist, R. C. Student social class and teacher expectations: The self-fulfilling prophecy in ghetto schools. *Harvard Educational Review,* 1970, 40, 411–450.

Schultz, T. W. Investment in human capital. *American Economic Review,* 1961, 5(1), 1–17.

Schulz, D. A. Variations in the father role in complete families of the Negro lower class. *Social Science Quarterly,* 1968, 49, 651–659.

Schulz, D. A. Coming up as a boy in the ghetto. In D. Y. Wilkinson and R. L. Taylor (Eds.), *The black male in America.* Chicago: Nelson-Hall, 1977.

Scott, J. W. *The black revolts: Racial stratification in the U.S.A.* Cambridge, Mass.: Schenkman, 1976.

Silverstein, B., & Krate, R. *Children of the dark ghetto: A developmental psychology.* New York: Praeger, 1975.

Stack, C. B. *All our kin: Strategies for survival in black urban community.* New York: Harper & Row, 1974.

Stanley, J. C. (Ed.). *Preschool programs for the disadvantaged: Five experimental approaches to early childhood education.* Baltimore: Johns Hopkins University Press, 1972.

Stanley, J. C. (Ed.). *Compensatory education for children ages 2 to 8: Recent studies of educational intervention.* Baltimore: Johns Hopkins University Press, 1973.

Valentine, B. *Hustling and other hardwork: Lifestyles in the ghetto.* New York: Free Press, 1979.

van den Berghe, P. Review: Minority education and caste, by John U. Ogbu. *Comparative Education Review,* 1980, 24, 126–130.

Webster, S. W. *The education of black Americans.* New York: Day, 1974.

Weisbrod, B. A. Education and investment in human capital. In D. M. Levine and M. J. Bane (Eds.), *The "inequality" controversy.* New York: Basic, 1975.

White, B. L. *The origins of human competence: The final report of the Harvard preschool project.* Lexington, Mass.: Heath, 1979.

White, S. H. *Federal programs for young children: Review and recommendations.* Vol. 1. *Goals and standards of public programs for children.* Washington, D.C.: Government Printing Office, 1973.

Williams, F. (Ed.). *Language and poverty: Perspectives on a theme.* Chicago: Markham, 1970.

Wolfe, T. *Radical chic and mau-mauing the flack catchers.* New York: Straus & Giroux, 1970.

Wright, N., Jr. (Ed.). *What black educators are saying.* New York: Hawthorn, 1970.

Young, V. H. Family and childhood in a southern negro community. *American Anthropologist,* 1970, 72, 269–288.

Young, V. H. A black American socialization pattern. *American Ethnologist,* 1974, 1(2), 415–431.

13. Conceptualizations
of Black Families

Jualynne Dodson

CONTRASTING APPROACHES TO THE STUDY
OF BLACK FAMILIES

The pathological and dysfunctional view of black families has been primarily related to the cultural ethnocentric approach and associated with the work of E. Franklin Frazier (1939) and Daniel P. Moynihan (1965). The works of these scholars have culminated in the adaptation of social policies predicated on the assumption that the black family is unstable, disorganized, and unable to provide its members with the social and psychological support and development needed to assimilate fully into American society.

The cultural relativity school, on the other hand, begins with the assumption that black American culture and family patterns possess a degree of cultural integrity that is neither related to nor modeled on white American norms. Most members of this school trace the origins of these cultural differences back to black American's African cultural heritage, and all tend to focus on the "strengths" of black families rather than their weaknesses.

The cultural relativistic view, developed primarily as a reaction to the deficit view, maintains that the black family is a functional entity. This conceptualization is designed to challenge the theories and social policies emanating from the ethnocentric approach.

Underlying the theoretical and empirical arguments of the two schools is the common assumption that black families and white families are qualitatively different culturally. The schools diverge from each other, however, in their interpretation and explanation of the causes of these differences. The cultural ethnocentric school,

Reprinted by permission of Sage Publications, Inc. from H. McAdoo, ed., *Black Families* © 1981 Sage Publications, Inc.

operating on the assumption that America is culturally homogeneous and that there are universal norms for American cultural behavior to which all groups must conform, points to certain presumed inadequacies in black people to account for the differences. Similarly, it places a negative value judgment on the fact that black families deviate from the American norm. The cultural relativity school, on the other hand, assumes that America is a multicultural society and concludes that differences are largely accounted for by the variation in the cultural backgrounds and experiences of black and white Americans.

The assumption that black and white families are qualitatively different culturally is not shared by all students of black family life, however. A third set of studies that can be said to fall outside the two schools noted above emphasizes the role of social class in determining family patterns and characteristics. The scholars of this perspective maintain that when you control for social class, no appreciable differences exist between black and white families. In-depth discussions of each of the two contrasting major approaches to the study of black family life follow. I will then consider some of the limitations of using social class as a variable in analyzing black family structure and functioning.

THE CULTURAL ETHNOCENTRIC SCHOOL

E. Franklin Frazier (1894–1962) was the leading twentieth-century exponent of the cultural ethnocentric school. He and W. E. B. DuBois pioneered in the study of the black family as a social phenomenon, but, unlike DuBois, one of Frazier's major concerns was understanding the process through which the black family became culturally assimilated into American life. It is important to note that Frazier's works, according to Lyman (1972), were influenced by his determination to (a) refute the argument advanced by Melville Herskovits (and DuBois) that much of black life is a continuation of African cultural forms and (b) empirically demonstrate Robert E. Park's race relations cycle. Frazier believed that black American marriage and family patterns, customs, and structures were the consequence of slavery and American culture, not African cultural transfers. He did not accept Herskovits's conclusion that black family structure, marital customs, and sexual practices were derived from African cultures. Rather, for example, Frazier (1939) interpreted "indiscriminate" and extramarital sexual behavior among blacks as being a product of slavery and unrelated to customs and practices in traditional polygamous African cultures.

Researchers attempting to discover possible African cultural trans-ferences to the New World focused on the slavery period. At the time Frazier began his work, leading authorities on the history of American Negro slavery shared Frazier's rather than Herskovits's position. Frazier's assertion that as "a result of the manner in which the Negro was enslaved, the Negro's African cultural heritage has had practically no effect on the evolution of his family in the United States" (1939: 66) reflected the views of both U. B. Phillips (1929), and, subsequently, Stanley Elkins (1959). Both concluded that while significant African cultural traits, such as names and folklore, did survive initially, they were eventually lost or distorted. Accordingly, Uncle Remus stories were altered to reflect the new animals and surroundings of the storytellers (Phillips, 1929: 195). If the culture of the African slaves was destroyed, then it is hopeless to expect that the evolution of the black family was influenced by that culture. So begins the logic of the cultural ethnocentric school.

The stability of the black family during slavery was controlled, they maintain, by the plantation owners. If a family arrangement failed to produce offspring, some slaveowners matched the couple, usually the woman, with other mates. Additionally, slave families were frequently broken up, its members sold individually. In spite of the slaves' unstable formal or legal marital and familial life, these authorities believed that blacks accepted and attempted to conform to the social norms of the majority society.

Frazier viewed blacks as an assimilation-oriented minority follow-ing the race-relations cycle as predicted and outlined by Ezra Parks (1926–1950). Indeed, Frazier saw the black family's assimilation toward the dominant American norms as part of the process by which it evolved from slavery and servitude toward freedom. In his study of blacks living in Chicago, Frazier found that as they moved outward from the inner city, black families appeared more culturally and physically assimilated, based on the proportion of interracial mar-riages (1939). It was his faithfulness to Park's race relations cycle which seemingly motivated Frazier to interpret black masses as as-similative and to ignore evidence to the contrary.[1] Although the race relations cycle has yet to be empirically validated, Frazier earnestly attempted to do so. It is, in a sense, a tragic conclusion to his intellec-tual career that he was forced to observe on the last page of one of his last books, *Black Bourgeoisie: The Rise of a New Middle Class in the United States,* that when blacks achieve "middle-class status their lives generally lose both content and significance" (1957: 238).

The line of research as pursued by Frazier was followed by a number of investigators and culminated in proposals for social policy. In 1965, the Office of Policy Planning and Research of the United States Department of Labor issued a 78-page document prepared by the assistant secretary, Daniel P. Moynihan, under the title, *The Negro Family—The Case for National Action.* This report repeatedly cited Frazier as support for its conclusions that the black community was characterized by broken families, illegitimacy, matriarchy, economic dependency, failure to pass armed forces entrance tests, delinquency, and crime. Moynihan placed the cause of these problems on a supposedly broken and unstable black family. Following his trend-making step, other investigators began to concentrate on the pathologies of black families.

In 1966, Elliot Liebow conducted a participant-observation study of 24 streetcorner black men. He concluded that the men had internalized the American norms for family roles, but that the oppressive conditions of their societal environment prevented their fulfilling these expectations. Lee Rainwater (1968), examining the matrifocal character of black American and Caribbean families, concluded that matriarchal families were pathological and detrimental to the personality development of black children. He also suggested that such families interfered with the ability of black males to develop normal heterosexual roles.

Jessie Bernard (1966) traced the evolution of the black family's stability from 1880 to 1963 and reported that the decrease in the proportion of black infants born out of wedlock was related to two distinct lifestyles independent of social class. One lifestyle was oriented toward the pursuit of pleasure and material consumption, while the other adhered to a firm belief in and acceptance of the Protestant ethic. This hedonistic orientation accounts for the decline in legitimate births among blacks. Having failed to internalize the marital norms of the American society, it is suggested that this subgroup ignores their responsibility when adherence becomes too difficult. The matrifocal family is seen as an outgrowth of the failure of black men to fulfill their paternal roles.

Parker and Kleiner (1966) contrasted the adjustment and attitudes of mothers in broken and intact families and examined the possible impact of these characteristics of their children. They found that mothers in broken family situations had poorer psychological adjustment and were less concerned about goals for their children. It was suggested that children raised in female-headed households would not have the psychological support of their mothers. Such research advances the argument that matriarchy and female-headed households are pathological and undermine any male-female relationship in the family (Blood and Wolfe, 1969; Duncan and Duncan, 1969; Bracey et al., 1971; Parker and Kleiner, 1966).

Other investigators have reported that the data supporting Moynihan's matriarchal concept are conclusive (Hyman and Reed, 1969). Investigators who focused on the validity of the female role in the black family have generally concluded that matrifocal families are not produced by values of the black community but by structural factors in the society which necessitate that males frequently abandon their roles (Yancey, 1972; Staples, 1974). Tenhouten (1970) was unable to substantiate the dominant role attributed to black mothers as implied in the Moynihan Report. Further, King (1967, 1969) found that black fathers were not perceived by their children as passive in decision making, and black mothers were perceived as less dominant than as reported in earlier studies. Delores Mack (1971) examined social class and racial differences in the distribution of power attributable to race. And Heiss (1972) found that instability in the black family does not necessarily lead to instability in future generations.

Studies which concentrated on the dysfunctional and disorganized aspects of black family life have deduced that the typical black family is fatherless, on welfare, thriftless, and overpopulated with illegitimate children. Inevitably, they have recommended economic reforms for "saving" black families from their own pathology (see, for example, Moynihan, 1965; Rainwater, 1965; Rodman, 1968). However, Andrew Billingsley (1968) challenged these stereotypes, pointing out that two-thirds of black families living in metropolitan areas are headed by husbands with their wives: Half have managed to pull themselves into the middle-class and nine-tenths are self-supporting.

There remains, then, considerable controversy among researchers concerning the ability of nonwhite Americans to establish and maintain viable marital and familial relations. Particularly, there are a large number of studies that underscore the dysfunctionality of black families. Implicit in the dichotomous conceptualization of functional versus dysfunctional capacities of black families is an assumption regarding normative model families. The belief that a statistical model of the American family can be identified and used to ascertain the character of the families of all American cultural groups is mythical at best. Further, such an assumption contradicts the ideals of a democratic society and the realities of a culturally plural one.

THE CULTURAL RELATIVITY SCHOOL

The cultural relativity view, primarily in reaction to the cultural ethnocentric view, advocates that the black family is a functional entity. This conceptualization is largely advanced and supported by Andrew Billingsley (1968), Virginia Young (1970), Robert Hill (1972), Wade Nobles (1974), and others. The perspective has been buttressed with old and new investigations which see black Americans' culture as different from that of whites (Valentine, 1968; Young, 1974) and possibly related to their African heritage (Herskovits, 1941; Nobles, 1974; Dodson, 1975, 1977). Although not all proponents of the cultural relativistic school agree on the degree to which African culture influenced the culture of black Americans, they do concur that black Americans' cultural orientation encourages family patterns that are instrumental in combating the oppressive racial conditions of American society.

American studies of the black family, and of blacks in general, have long ignored the works of Melville Herskovits (1885–1963), one of the first scholars to recognize similarities in African cultural patterns and those of African descendants living in the United States, the West Indies, and Brazil. Herskovits (1966) found what he considered to be authentic African cultural patterns reflected in language, music, art, house structure, dance, traditional religion, and healing practices. To many students of the black family, Herskovits's research raises the possibility that other aspects of "Africana" could have influenced the nature of the black family in the United States. Herskovits's works deal only limitedly with such possible relations. However, one of his major contributions was a truer conceptualization of family life in traditional African societies, which are characterized by unity, stability, and security (Herskovits, 1938).

Other writers have since reexamined the unity and stability of

African families to refute any assertion that chaos and problems of African families paralleled the problems of contemporary black American families. From such studies, Billingsley concluded:

Thus the men and women who were taken as slaves to the New World came from societies every bit as civilized and "respectable" as those of the Old World settlers who mastered them. But the two were very different types of society [sic] for the African family was much more closely integrated with the wider levels of kinship and society [1968: 48].

In examining the American black family, proponents of cultural relativism in North America point out that slavery did not totally destroy the traditional African base of black family functioning (Blassingame, 1972; Nobles, 1974; Turnbull, 1976). To these scholars, the black family represents a continuing fountain of strength and endurance built on, and issuing from, its African cultural heritage.

The field research of Young reflects that blacks are not merely versions of white Americans impoverished by lack of access to many of the rewards of American culture. She found that southern rural black families were culturally distinct from white families and demonstrated retention of African forms. This closely paralleled Herskovits's (1941) contentions. Her findings were especially supportive in the areas of interpersonal behavior and deep-level communication.

Similar to Charles Johnson (1934) and Hortense Powdermaker (1939), but contrary to Frazier (1939) and Moynihan (1965), Young did not find black families disorganized or dysfunctional. Young (1970) observed patterns of high illegitimacy rates and frequent marital dissolutions, which are usually associated with disorganization; however, she interpreted these patterns as natural to the emotional underpinnings of the family system and, thus, functional.

Nobles (1974, 1975) has indicated that the black community is oriented primarily toward extended families, in that most black family structures involve a system of kinship ties. This idea has been supported by Hayes and Mendel (1973), Billingsley (1968), Hill (1972), Stack (1974), and others. The extended family system is assumed to provide support for family members, either as assistance for protection or for mobility. It is argued that the extended family in the black community consists not only of conjugal and blood relatives, but of nonrelatives as well. Additionally, the prevalence of extended families, as compared with nuclear families, is held as another cultural pattern which distinguishes whites and blacks. However, the extent to which such families are characteristic of the black community has not been adequately substantiated.

Hayes and Mendel (1973) demonstrated that the extended family is a more prominent structure for black families and that blacks differ from whites in intensity and extent of family interaction. Their study of midwestern urban families, however, included a sample of only 25 complete and incomplete black and white families. The findings show that, with the exception of parents, blacks interact with more of their kin than do whites. Black families also receive more help from kin and have a greater number and more diversified types of relatives living with them than do white families. It is suggested by Hayes and Mendel that minority status in a hostile society strengthens kinship ties.

In a related study, Dubey (1971) examined the relationship between self-alienation and extended family using black, white, and Puerto Rican subjects. His data supported the hypothesis that subjects with a high degree of powerlessness were significantly more oriented toward the extended family. Dubey's study raises the question of whether the extended family is used as a buffer between oppression of the dominant society and the unmet needs of the family. Stack (1974) proposed that the extended family is, in part, a strategy for meeting physical, emotional, and economic needs of black families, and involves a reciprocal network of sharing to counter the lack of economic resources. McAdoo (1978) found that the reciprocal extended family-help patterns transcended economic groups and continued to be practiced even when families had moved from poverty to the middle-income level.

Nobles (1974) believes that the black kinship pattern was derived from African cultures not destroyed in the "Middle Passage" or in slavery; this suggests that perhaps the survival of "Africana" among black American families is not as remote as Elkins (1959) and Frazier (1939) have argued. Blassingame (1972) stated that not only did African cultural patterns survive American slavery, but new cultural patterns unique to black Americans were created. Even Frazier (1963) has noted indisputable non-Western religious practices in the black church. A more recent advocate of this view, Colin Turnbull, sums it succinctly: "(T)he slaves who were exported to the Americas were Africans before they were slaves and Africans afterwards, and *their descendants are still Africans today*" (1976: 242; emphasis added).

According to Turnbull, it is interesting to note that in some cases African cultural patterns were developed and preserved in the western hemisphere while they were lost in Africa. A case in point is Surinam (South America), where slaves escaped and recovered their independence. Although some of the ethnic cultures resemble original African cultures, Turnbull cautions that the Surinam cultures (comprising six "tribal" groups) could not have remained totally in isolation. With the exception of clearly identifiable African cultural patterns in islands along the Georgia coast, Turnbull stated that the splintering of ethnic clans during slavery, along with enforced acceptance of language and Western values, did much to repress African cultures in the United States.

A model that may prove useful for a further understanding of the New World "Africana" culture and black American families has been developed by Smith (1962). Equally important to the clarification of these issues is Nobles's work currently being conducted on African orientations in American families. However, we must await further research findings from the cultural relativistic perspective before determining the cultural origin of black family life.

AN ISSUE FROM BOTH SCHOOLS: SOCIAL CLASS

Research on racial differences in black family structure and function has been contaminated by methodological problems that make it difficult to conceptualize clear differences within and between groups. Social class has been widely employed as a variable in social science research. It is primarily used for classifying individuals into categories above or below one another on some scale of inferiority and superiority. The scale is intended to denote one's position in terms of social and economic prestige and/or power.

The most popular measure of social class in the United States is an occupation-scaled measure that is commonly used to reflect prestige. Other types of class measurement consist of single variables, such as education, income, and possessions. A number of multiple indices also exist. It has been questioned whether such measures can be applied equitably to all groups in an oppressive, pluralistic, and fluid society such as the United States. This is especially critical, since most measures of social class were developed by and for whites, and there is little convincing evidence that they accurately measure social class for black Americans.

A number of investigators, among them Drake (1965) and Jencks (1972), have demonstrated that education and income are less related for blacks compared to whites than may be expected. It has been shown that blacks are more frequently underemployed, in that they often have more education, training, or skills than their jobs require. Consequently, they receive salaries and wages disproportionate to their preparation. Since an underemployed black person has a lower income than a white with equivalent years of education, the former cannot afford the same standard of living as the latter. This lower standard of living requires the black person to adopt a different lifestyle than his or her status, as measured by education, would indicate.

Neither does occupation tend to indicate the same social classification for blacks as for whites. The owner of a small business in a black shopping area, for example, might not have nearly the same income as the owner of a similar business located in a white shopping area. However, according to the occupation categories of the Hollingshead-Redlich scale (1968), both persons would be designated in a middle-income social classification. Another problem with occupational ranking is that disparities exist within occupations as well as between them.

Jencks (1972) contends that one limitation to the definition of occupation as the indicator of social class is that it refers only to occupations, not to specific jobs within them. Accordingly, some jobs are more attractive and rewarding than others, even though they are classified together as a single occupation.

Billingsley's assertion that current indicators of social class are relatively more reliable when used for white ethnic groups than when used unmodified with black groups has never been adequately refuted. He believes that such indicators have resulted in an overestimation of the number of lower-class blacks and that this obscures rather than clarifies the variety of social class and behavior among black Americans (1968: 123). Although Billingsley accepts the utility of social class, he claims that current measures are mostly indicators of economic and social positions in the wider white community, not accurate descriptions of which blacks associate with whom and why.

It should be pointed out that social classification depends primarily on the degree to which an individual or individuals are held in esteem by their fellow group members. Social class, therefore, depends on the cultural values of the group. Deference is awarded according to what the group cherishes as being noble or worthy. Hence, social class could be based on such characteristics as age, wisdom, heredity, or economic power, and it could vary from one cultural group to another. Since the cultural distinctiveness of black Americans still warrants investigation, measures of social class also await clearer determination. The extent to which blacks possess different values regarding what is worthy in an individual determines their different orientation to family, to their community, and to the wider white community.

Cultural relativity becomes an important, yet complicated, factor when attempting to make social class comparisons of heterogenous groups within a single society. It appears logical to assume that different ethnic groups within the same society can be compared using the same social class criterion. However, this is not the empirical reality for the United States. The logical but incorrect assumption that because both peoples live within the same societal geography (nation), social class is perceived the same way in white and black communities is misleading.

I concur with Billingsley that the importance of social class is that the higher the social class of an individual, the greater will be his or her ability to survive with integrity in a hostile society. For a historically subjugated group such as black America, survival and dignity may be invaluable social qualities. Furthermore, given the nature of the historical and material experiences of, and relationship between, blacks and whites in North America, the extent to which they can be compared using similar social indicators is dubious. To ignore these fundamentally different realities and classify them into common social classes is to commit serious historical, methodological, and theoretical errors.

TOWARD REFLECTIVE ANALYSIS

This examination of major schools of thought in studies of the black family in the United States has been done to help direct thinking regarding prerequisite components of a "reflective analysis." Admittedly, this has been a limited review. For example, individual roles of family members have not been addressed. These are seen primarily as intertwined with the sociocultural patterns of marriage and family in contemporary black communities. For those who desire a more thorough and complete review of literature on black American families, there are at least three substantive sources: Allen (1976), Staples (1974, 1978), and Peters (1978). The particular approach I have taken has emphasized the ideological assumptions undergirding researchers' definitions of and approaches to research of black family life. This perspective was used because it is assumed that the ideological debate has indeed created the current impasse in black family research. Given the review of the debate, Walter Allen's conclusions about the status of studies on black family life is accurate:

The literature on black families is characterized by inconsistent findings, poor problem conceptualization, overly simplistic research designs, questionable inferences from data and general disagreement over the relative appropriateness of competing perspectives of black family life. The question to be addressed now is: How might researchers go about the business of reconciling some of these problems and in the process strengthening the literature? To begin, theory construction/codification activities should be intensified. . . .

The area of black family studies would also benefit from a change in focus of empirical research.

Any attempt to bring theoretical clarity to human phenomena must be informed by an understanding of the sociocultural, economic, and political contexts in which the phenomena occur. This axiom applies especially when exploring questions related to contemporary black family life in the United States.

In recommending the following components for a "reflective analysis" of black family life, my conceptualizations have been developed in concert with Ruth Dennis, Harriette McAdoo, Art Mathis, and Howard Dodson. This group of black scholars and researchers met and worked together from 1974 through 1977 to develop "Toward a Reflective Analysis" of black family life.

Drawing from the strengths and weaknesses of previous studies, a "reflective analysis" would minimally include the following:

(a) focus on socialization of black families as the process which brings together individual, cultural group(s), and society in a dynamic interactive process;

(b) account for the impact—positive and/or negative—of the relative unavailability of maximum social, economic, and political societal resources to black families and;

(c) account for the environmental reality that black families are forced to use relatively minimal resources to effect a socialization process and product which allows individuals to function in two social realities of the United States—a nonblack world of consistent, sufficient social support and a black world of fluctuating scarcity of resources.

Using these minimal components as a guide, a schema for evaluating black family socialization can be suggested. Positive evaluations can be placed on socialized behavior which allows the individual to interact with any segment of the society and maintain a sense of self-worth. However, because the realities of black family life are often contradictory, socialized behavior that may be evaluated as positive within one level of social functioning may be evaluated as negative within another. Black families must be able to socialize individuals who are able to participate in and yet protect self from the negative social attitudes and actions impinging on self-esteem, feelings of self-worth, and human evolutionary development.

NOTES

1. For example, the widespread support among black Americans for Marcus Garvey's Universal Negro Improvement Association (Cronon, 1955).

REFERENCES

Allen, W. R. (1976) Private correspondence in response to "Reflective Analysis" manuscript. Atlanta, Georgia.
——— (1978) "Search for applicable theories of Black family life." Journal of Marriage and the Family 40: 117–129.
Ausubel, D. P. and P. Ausubel (1963) "Ego development among segregated Negro children," in A. H. Passow (ed.) Education in Depressed Areas. New York: Bureau of Publications, Teachers College, Columbia University.
Bernard, J. (1966) Marriage and Family Among Negroes. Englewood Cliffs, NJ: Prentice-Hall.
Bettelheim, B. (1964) Review of B. S. Bloom's Stability and Change in Human Characteristics. New York Review of Books 3: 1–4.
Billingsley, A. (1968) Black Families in White America. Englewood Cliffs, NJ: Prentice-Hall.
Blassingame, J. W. (1972) The Slave Community: Plantation Life in Antebellum South. New York: Oxford.
Blauner, R. (1970) "Internal colonialism and ghetto revolt," in M. Westheimer (ed.) Confrontation. Glenview, IL: Scott, Foresman.
——— (1972) Racial Oppression in America. New York: Harper & Row.

Blood, R. and D. Wolfe (1969) "Negro-white differences in blue collar marriages in a northern metropolis." Social Forces 48: 59–63.

Bracey, J. H., A. Meier and E. Rudwick [eds.] (1971) Black Matriarchy: Myth or Reality. Belmont, CA: Wadsworth.

Bronfenbrenner, U. (1967) Paper read at Conference on Poverty, University of Wisconsin, Madison.

Cloward, R. A. and J. A. Jones (1962) "Social class: Education attitudes and participation," in A. H. Passows (ed.) Education in Depressed Areas. New York: Bureau of Publications, Teachers College, Columbia University.

Cronon, E. D. (1955) Black Moses: The Story of Marcus Garvey and the Universal Negro Improvement Association. The University of Wisconsin Press.

Davis, A. and J. Dollard (1940) Children of Bondage. New York: Harper & Row.

Davis, A. and R. J.Havighurst (1946) "Social class and color differences in childrearing." American Sociological Review 11: 698–710.

Dodson, J. (1975) Black Stylization and Implications for Child Welfare. Final Report (OCD-CB-422-C2). Washington, DC: Office of Child Development.

——— (1977) Afro American Culture: Expressive Behaviors. Atlanta: Atlanta University.

Drake, S. C. (1965) "The social and economic status of the Negro in the United States," in T. Parsons and K. B. Clark (eds.) The Negro American. Boston: Beacon.

Dubey, S. N. (1971) "Powerlessness and orientation toward family and children: a study in deviance." Indian Journal of Social Work 32: 35–43.

Duncan, B., and O. D. Duncan (1969) "Family stability and occupational success." Social Problems 16: 273–285.

Elkins, S. W. (1959) Slavery. Chicago: University of Chicago Press.

Fogel, R. W. and S. L. Engerman (1975) Time on the Cross, Volumes I and II. Boston: Little, Brown.

Frazier, E. F. (1932) The Negro Family in Chicago. Chicago: University of Chicago Press.

——— (1939) The Negro Family in the United States. Chicago: University of Chicago Press.

——— (1949a) "The Negro family in America," in R. W. Anshen (ed.) The Family: Its Function and Destiny. New York: Harper & Row.

——— (1949b) The Negro in the United States. New York: Macmillan.

——— (1957) Black Bourgeoisie: The Rise of a New Middle Class in the United States. New York: Free Press.

——— (1963) The Negro Church in America. New York: Schocken.

Hayes, W. and Mendel, C. H. (1973) "Extended kinship in black and white families." Journal of Marriage and the Family 35: 51–57.

Heiss, J. (1972) "On the transmission of marital instability in black families." American Social Review 37: 82–92.

Herskovits, M. J. (1938) Dahomey: An Ancient African Kingdom. New York: J. J. Augustin

——— (1941) The Myth of the Negro Past. New York: Harper & Row.

——— (1966) The New World Negro. Bloomington, IN: Indiana University Press.

Hill, R. (1972) The Strengths of Black Families. New York: Emerson-Hall.

Hollingshead, A. B. and F. C. Redlich (1968) Social Class and Mental Illness. New York: John Wiley.

Hyman, H. H. and J. S. Reed (1969) "Black matriarchy reconsidered: evidence from secondary analysis of sample survey." Public Opinion Quarterly 33: 346–354.

Inkles, A. (1966) "A note on social structure and the socialization of competence." Educational Review 36: 265–283.

Jencks, C. (1972) Inequality. New York: Basic Books.

Johnson, C. S. (1934) Shadow of the Plantation. Chicago: University of Chicago Press.

Kardiner, A. and L. Ovesey (1951) The Mark of Oppression. New York: World.

Katz, I. (1969) "A critique of personality approaches to Negro performance, with suggestions." Journal of Social Issues 25: 12–27.

King, K. (1967) "A comparison of the Negro and white family power structure in low-income families." Child and Family 6: 65–74.

——— (1969) "Adolescent perception of power structure in the Negro family." Journal of Marriage and the Family 31: 751–755.

Liebow, E. (1967) Tally's Corner: A Study of Negro Streetcorner Men. Boston: Little, Brown.

Lyman, S. M. (1972) The Black American in Sociological Thought. New York: Capricorn Books.

Mack, D. E. (1971) "Where the black-matriarchy theorists went wrong." Psychology Today 4: 24, 86–87.

McAdoo, H. P. (1974) The Socialization of Black Children: Priorities for Research in Social Research and the Black Community: Selected Issues and Priorities.

——— (1978) "Factors related to stability in upward mobile black families." Journal of Marriage and the Family 40: 761–766.

McClelland, D. C. (1961) The Achieving Society. New York: Van Nostrand.

Moynihan, D. P. (1965) The Negro Family—The Case for National Action. Washington: Office of Policy Planning and Research, U.S. Department of Labor.

Nobles, W. W. (1974) "Africanity: its role in black families." The Black Scholar 5: 10.

——— (1975) A Formulative and Empirical Study of Black Families. Publication No. 00–255. San Francisco: Westside Community Mental Health Center.

Park, R. E. (1939) "The nature of race relations," in E. T. Thompson (ed.) Race Relations and the Race Problem. Durham, NC: Duke University Press.

Parker, S. and Kleiner, R. (1966) "Characteristics of Negro mothers in single-headed holds." Journal of Marriage and the Family 28: 507–513.

Peters, M. F. [ed.] (1978) Special issue of Journal of Marriage and the Family, Vol. 4 November.

Pettigrew, T. F. (1964) A Profile of the Negro American. Princeton, NJ: D. Van Nostrand.

Phillips, U. B. (1929) Life and Labor in the Old South. Boston: Little, Brown.

Powdermaker, H. (1939) After Freedom: The Portrait of a Negro Community in South. New York: Viking.

Rainwater, L. (1965) Family Design. Chicago: AVC.

——— (1968) "Crucible of identity: the Negro lower-class family." Daedalus 95: 258–264.

Riessman, F. (1962) The Culturally Deprived Child. New York: Harper & Row.

Rodman, H. (1968) "Family and social pathology in the ghetto." Science 161: 756–762.

Smith, M. G. (1962) West Indian Family Structure. Seattle: University of Washington Press.

Stack, C. B. (1974) All Our Kin. New York: Harper & Row.

Staples, R. E. (1974) "The black family revisited: a review and a preview." Journal of Social and Behavior Sciences Spring: 65–77.

——— (1978) The Black Family: Essays and Studies. Belmont, CA: Wadsworth.

Tenhouten, W. (1970) "The black family: myth and reality." Psychiatry 33: 145–173.

Turnbull, C. M. (1976) Man in Africa. Garden City, NY: Doubleday.

Valentine, C. A. (1968) Culture and Poverty. Chicago: University of Chicago Press.

Warner, W. L., M. Meeker, and K. Eells (1949) Social Class in America. Chicago: Science Research Associates.

Willie, C. V. [ed.] (1970) The Family Life of Black People. Columbus, OH: Charles E. Merrill.

Yancey, W. (1972) "Going down home: family structure and the urban trap." Social Science Quarterly 52: 893–906.

Young, V. H. (1970) "Family and childhood in a southern Negro community." American Anthropologist 72: 269–288.

Young, V. H. (1974) "A black American socialization pattern." in American Ethnologist 1: 405–413.

14. Family Ecologies of Ethnic Minority Children

Algea O. Harrison, Melvin N. Wilson,
Charles J. Pine, Samuel Q. Chan, and Raymond Buriel

U sing an ecological framework, this article explores the relation between ecologies of ethnic minority families, adaptive strategies, socialization goals, and developmental outcomes for ethnic minority children. The article is divided into four sections: (a) demographic information on ethnic minority families, (b) a discussion of the strategies groups have used to adapt to their social status, (c) a presentation of socialization goals that have emerged from the adaptive strategies, and (d) a discussion of child outcomes. The theoretical conceptions of the ecological orientation extend beyond the behavior of individuals to encompass functional systems both within and between settings, nested structures, and a complex interaction between the developing person and the environment (Bronfenbrenner, 1979). In short, an ecological perspective considers how the individual develops in interaction with the immediate social environment and how aspects of the larger social context affect what goes on in the individuals' immediate settings (Garbarino, 1982). Ethnic minority families in America have faced similar ecological challenges from larger social systems and have developed similar adaptive strategies.

Adaptive strategies refer to observable social behavioral cultural patterns that are interpreted as socially adaptive or maladaptive within the social nexus (DeVos, 1982). Importantly, when a strategy is effective in facilitating adaptation for a minority group, it involves some aspect of the dominant culture's mores and the knowledge that one is a minority at some specified level in a social hierarchy (DeVos, 1982). As members of groups learn which strategies are effective and

Reprinted by permission of The Society for Research in Child Development from *Child Development* 61 (1990) 347–62. © The Society for Research in Child Development, Inc.

appropriate, they also learn how best to inculcate these competencies in their children (Ogbu, 1981). The socialization goals of a people are partially derived from their cultural knowledge of their adult tasks, of essential competencies for adequate functioning, and of the methods of transmitting these competencies to succeeding generations (Ogbu, 1981). These cultural patterns are a part of the family ecologies of ethnic minority groups. Family ecology refers to important family functionings that are a reflection of the interactions between the family as a social system and other societal institutions and systems. The family ecologies of ethnic minority children will differ somewhat from those of majority children, where compromising with minority group status is not needed. Consequently, the family ecologies of ethnic minority, when compared to majority, families have the potential of differential outcomes in the development of children. This is especially true if development is viewed as a person's evolving conception of the ecological environment, one's relation to it, as well as one's growing capacity to discover, sustain, or alter its properties (Bronfenbrenner, 1979).

The aim of this article is to explore the interconnectedness between the status of ethnic minority families, adaptive strategies, socialization goals, and child outcomes. Historically, ethnic minority children were not included in samples of subjects studied for establishing normative trends or investigating theoretical questions. Most often data on ethnic minority children came from comparative studies with a controversial deficit explanation (Harrison, Serafica, & McAdoo, 1984; McLoyd & Randolph, 1985). Currently, social scientists are aware of the methodological and conceptual shortcomings of those studies. This essay offers a different conceptual perspective for considering ethnic minority families and their children.

Issues in the Study of Family Ecologies of Ethnic Minority Children

The discussion is organized around four general questions, the first of which addresses which groups of people we refer to as ethnic minorities. Minority groups are subordinate segments of their respective societies. However, "Once people perceive ethnic differences and ethnic groups compete against each other, the crucial variables in majority-minority relations is the differential power of one group relative to another" (Yetman, 1985, p. 2). Ethnocentrism, competition, and differential power are the salient ingredients for the emergence and initial stabilization of ethnic stratification. Ethnic stratification refers to a system of arrangements where some relatively fixed group membership (e.g., race, religion, or nationality) is used as one of the standards of judgment for assigning social position with its attendant differential rewards (Noel, 1985). This article focuses on groups of people in the position of minorities in America's ethnic stratification system: African Americans, American Indians/Alaskan Natives, Asian Pacific Americans, and Hispanic Americans. Some of these groups are referred to as castelike minorities by Ogbu (1987, p. 258); "minorities incorporated into a society more or less involuntarily and permanently through slavery, conquest, and colonization." Each group's story is different but includes a common element of exploitable resources: (a) the enslavement of Africans and, after emancipation, their segregation and perceived inferior status based on race; (b) military conflicts over land and territory between American Indians and European Americans, and the forced removal and transfer of Indians to reservations; and (c) Asian Americans whose recent immigrants from Indochina sometimes suffer from the same subordination and exploitation endured by earlier immigrants from China, the Philippines, and Japan (the latter were incarcerated during World War II); (d) Hispanics who were incorporated through conquest and displacement. In this article, we present a brief demographic summary of the current status of each of these groups.

The second question concerns the strategies these minority families use to adapt to their social environments. Historically, the selected ethnic minority groups have suffered from discrimination and racism. Yet they have formed communities, social institutions, and other organizations for adapting and adjusting to these ecological challenges. What are some of the adaptive strategies of these ethnic minority families? These adaptive strategies form the basis of the family ecologies of ethnic minorities.

The third question concerns the relation between families' adaptive strategies and socialization goals. Adults in families have formed beliefs about what it means to be a member of that ethnic group and what behaviors and attitudes are reflective of adaptations to that status (DeVos, 1982; Ogbu, 1981). These beliefs shape the socialization goals and techniques of ethnic minority families. What socialization goals of ethnic minority families derive from their adaptive strategies?

The final question concerns whether there are developmental patterns among ethnic minority children as a function of their family ecologies. In other words, are there any empirically based trends or patterns among ethnic minority children that can be attributed directly or indirectly to distinct cultural behavioral patterns found among their families? The review will be limited to literature in the cognitive area, where research on ethnic minority children is concentrated. However, there are other developmental domains where empirical studies have been completed but are not as expansive or focused on the relation between family ecologies and child outcomes (e.g., Gibbs, Huang, & Associates, 1989; Irvine & Berry, 1986; McShane, 1988; Powell, Morales, Romero, & Yamamoto, 1983; Rogoff, Gauvain, & Ellis, 1984; Spindler & Spindler, 1987). Shortcomings and the lack of relevant information are highlighted and directions for future research are discussed.

ETHNIC MINORITIES

The ecological challenges facing ethnic minorities are not sudden temporary economic calamities, but derive from a long history of oppression and discrimination. Currently it is reported that one-third of the nation, constituting mainly ethnic minorities, are afflicted by the ills of poverty and discrimination (Report on Minorities in Higher Education, 1988). On all of the major social indicators (e.g., employment, housing, health, etc.) of individual and social well-being, gaps persist — and in some instances are widening — between members of minority groups and the majority population (U.S. Department of Commerce Series, 1988). Nevertheless, when confronted with these challenges, ethnic minority families and communities still strive toward goals and accomplishments as they have done historically. Educational achievement, economic development in the community, political power, affordable housing, and maintaining cultural and religious traditions are some of the goals of these groups (U.S. Department of Commerce Series, 1988).

Demographic Status

African Americans, 96% of whom are descendants of slaves, are currently the largest ethnic minority group in the United States (Reed, 1982). Only recently has the term "African American" been preferred by some persons in the group rather than the term "black." American Indians are the smallest ethnic minority group, although there are more than 500 tribes or nations in the United States (La-Fromboise, 1988). Typically, American Indians prefer their tribal designation to the term American Indian (Burgess, 1980). Asian Pacific Americans comprise the fastest-growing population group in the United States (Gardner, Robey, & Smith, 1985). This dramatically accelerated growth is attributable to the continuing influx of immigrants and refugees (for a more detailed discussion of Asian American demographics, see Bouvier & Agresta, in press; Gardner et al., 1985; National Indochinese Clearinghouse, 1980; Pan Asian Parent Education Project, 1982; Peterson & Yamamoto, 1980; Powell et al., 1983). Persons in this group prefer ethnic terms that identify their country of origin. Hispanics are projected to become the largest minority group by the turn of the century. The Hispanic population consists primarily of *mestizo* peoples born of the Spanish conquest of the Americas who intermixed with populations indige-

TABLE 1

Total Number, Composition of Subgroups, and Geographic Location of Ethnic Minority Groups

Ethnic Group	Total Number	Composition of Subgroups	Geographic Concentration
African American	28.2 million	African-Caribbean, recent immigrants from Africa	South, Northeast
American Indian/ Alaskan Native	1.5 million/ 64,103	Largest tribes: Cherokee, Navajo, Sioux, Chippewa/ Aleuts, Eskimos	Northwest, West
Asian Pacific Americans	10.0 million	Chinese, Japanese, Korean, Vietnamese, Cambodian, Thai, Filipino, Laotian, Lao-Hmong, Burmese, Samoan, Guamanian	West, Northeast
Hispanic	18.8 million	Mexican, Puerto Rican, Cuban, Central and South Americans	Southwest, Midwest, Northeast, Florida, and California

nous to the geographic areas. Persons in this group also prefer ethnic terms that identify their country of origin, and when it is necessary to refer to themselves collectively, they prefer the terms Latino or *la Raza* (Buriel, 1987). More detailed demographics of the groups are presented in Table 1.

Currently, a majority of ethnic minority families live in urban areas. American Indians were the exception for urban residence patterns, residing mainly in rural areas and on reservations. Demographic trends, however, suggest an increase in the number of American Indians migrating to large metropolitan areas (Snipp & Sandefur, 1988). In 1980, 55% of American Indians resided in urban locations. Also, these ethnic minority families are younger and have higher birthrates in comparison to majority families.

ADAPTIVE STRATEGIES

Ethnic minority status has potent meaning for persons in the group because of the difficulties these groups have experienced in attempting to coexist with the European American culture. Examples are prevalent in history, literature, and psychology of persons with political and social power and members of the intelligentsia creating negative stereotypes for members of other groups (Padilla & O'Grady, 1987). The groups usually targeted for negative attributions and stereotypes are those in economically subservient positions within the society, as well as groups outside the society that are perceived as political, military, and economic threats. These experiences have influenced the individual and group beliefs about what it means to be a member of an ethnic minority group. There is agreement among psychologists that beliefs form an important psychological guide to action (Sigel, 1985); therefore, it is assumed that these beliefs have been a factor in shaping the strategies that members of low-status groups develop.

Adaptive strategies are proposed cultural patterns that promote the survival and well-being of the community, families, and individual members of the group. The term "adaptive strategies" as used refers to observable social behavior, not to personality dynamics (DeVos, 1982). A review of the literature describing the values, attitudes, and behaviors of ethnic minority families high lights the adaptive strategies these groups have in common. Although there are differences in the salience of a strategy, the similarities across family ecologies are striking. Family extendedness and role flexibility, bicul-turalism, and ancestral worldviews are all part of the life-styles of these groups. Although ethnic minority groups share a commonality in minority status and ethnic stratification, there have been differences in the impact of ecological challenges from the majority population on these groups. Some of the factors that have mediated the experiences of these different groups are motives for coming to America (Suzuki, 1980), time of immigration (Serafica, in press), educational opportunities (Olmedo, 1981), attitude toward educational establishment (Ogbu, 1981), voluntarily or involuntarily coming to America (Harding, 1980), and the American caste system (Ogbu, 1985). Nevertheless, limited access to societal resources has forged a similarity among ethnic minority families. All have had to develop ways of gaining access to European American cultural and social institutions (e.g., educational, medical, political, legal) for services, employment, power, etc.

Family Extendedness and Role Flexibility

The pattern of establishing extended families is an adaptive strategy common to ethnic minority peoples. Although there are traditional and nontraditional types of families in ethnic minority communities, the extended family form is frequently mentioned by social scientists as a typical family structure in ethnic minority communities (Mindel & Habenstein, 1988). For example, Langston (1980) reported that 85% of her African American elderly sample shared their residence with someone who was either a spouse, an adult child, or a grandchild. Nationally, panel and census data analyses (Beck & Beck, 1989; Sweet, 1977) have indicated that 53% of the African American elderly population shared a residence with a relative, as compared to 40% of the white elderly population. In fact, about 10 percent of African American children below the age of 18 lived with their grandparents and 25 percent of young African American adults between the ages of 18–26 lived with their parents (Beck & Beck, 1984, 1989; Sweet, 1977). Three times as many African American children under age 18 lived with their grandparents than white children, whereas the proportion of African American and white young adults living with parents was about equal (Soldo & Lauriat, 1976; U.S. Bureau of the Census, 1989).

The extended family is a problem-solving and stress-coping system that addresses, adapts, and commits available family resources to normal and nonnormal transitional and crisis situations (Wilson, 1989). Family resources involve family members' ability to contribute tangible help, such as material support, income, childcare, and household maintenance assistance, and nontangible help, such as expressive interaction, emotional support, counseling, instruction, and social regulation (Wilson, 1986, 1989). Through patterns of kin contact and interactions that are proximal, available, frequent, and functional (Gibson, 1972), a family provides its members with a sense of group and personal identities, behavioral rules, roles and responsibilities, and emotional affiliations and attachments (Goode, 1964; Schneider, 1968, 1980). Indeed, extended family refers to family composition, structure, and interaction that go beyond the nuclear family unit to include consanguine, affinal, and fictive relationships (Foster, 1984; Wilson, 1986). Wilson (1986, 1989) asserts that in the African American family, experiencing nonnormal changes and events is a primary reason for the formation of extended family support networks. A common stressful situation in the African American community is the lack of adequate adult resources in single-parent family units. The formation occurs when one family unit absorbs another one. Once formed, the extended family occupies most of the family life span. Martin and Martin (1978) describe the characteristics of extended families as found among African Americans as interdependent, bilateral, and multigenerational; headed by a dominant family figure; having a family-based household; reaching across geographical boundaries; and processing a built-in mutual aid system providing material aid and moral support. Historically, the African American extended family system supports a familial tradition that existed throughout the periods of slavery, emancipation, and mass rural southern exodus (Agesti, 1978; Aoyagi, 1978; Flanagan, 1978; Fogel & Engelman, 1974; Genovese, 1976; Gutman, 1976; Martin & Martin, 1978; Meacham, 1983; Nobles, 1978).

Similarly, American Indian families may be characterized as a collective, cooperative social network that extends from the mother and father union to the extended family and ultimately to the community and tribe (Burgess, 1980). Although such a family structure is not as prevalent as it once was (Ryan, 1981), it has not disappeared (Burgess, 1980; LaFromboise, 1988; Medicine, 1981), and it has endured many changes brought about by influences of the European-American culture. The typical family has several forms, but the basic social unit consisted of the man, woman, and their children and is embedded in the community, multigenerational, collateral, and comprised sibling groupings of different types. Generally, a strong extended family system characterizes many urban and rural contemporary American Indian families (Goodluck & Eckstein, 1978; Medicine, 1981; Red Horse, 1983). American Indian patterns of extended family include several households representing significant relatives along both vertical and horizontal lines, therefore assuming village-type characteristics (Light & Martin, 1986; Red Horse, 1983).

In the same manner, among Asian Pacific American families, selected practices have persisted throughout the process of increasing acculturation in successive generations and are further maintained by recent immigrants (Chan, 1986). The traditional Asian Pacific family is characterized by well-defined, unilaterally organized, and highly interdependent roles within a cohesive patriarchal vertical structure (Serafica, in press). Prescribed roles and relationships emphasize subordination and interdependence. Familial and social behaviors are thus governed by esteem for hierarchical roles and relationships and the virtue of filial piety (Tseng, 1973).

Likewise, familism among Hispanics involves strong feelings of identification, loyalty, and solidarity with the parents and the extended family, and behaviors associated with these feelings, such as frequent contact and reciprocity among members of the same family (Marin, 1986; Ramirez & Castaneda, 1974; Sabogal, Marin, Otero-Sabogal, Marin, & Perez-Stable, 1987). Much like the Asian Pacific family, the Hispanic family is characterized by strong familism. In addition, the Hispanic extended family is similar to the African American family in that it is bilaterally organized and includes nonrelative members (e.g., compadres).

It is clear from empirical writings and discussions that the extended family system is a value and ideal among ethnic minorities. Do demographic changes within ethnic minority groups alter the structure and importance of family extendedness to family members? McAdoo's (1978) investigations found that the extended family structure was still prevalent among upwardly mobile African American families, while community activists from the same community noted that its effectiveness was declining among low socioeconomic status families because of the tremendous burdens of contemporary social problems (Height, 1985). Further empirical studies are needed to delineate when, how, and under what conditions extended families are adaptive or serve as a source of conflict. For example, involvement in extended families increases economic resources among low-income families but reduces consumable income among middle- and working-class families. Stack (1981) found that extended family relationships often produced conflictual feelings among young African American females. Young African American females were often torn between their commitment and loyalties to the extended family and their feelings and commitments to their boyfriends. Similar findings were noted by Dressler (1985) in his study of families in a southern community. Extended kin support appeared to be less effective in reducing the risk of depression among young women compared to young men. Opposite-sex differences were found by Brown and Gary (1987) in their sample of urban northern African American families. Young females were provided more benefits from the extended family in comparison to young males. Clearly more systematic studies are needed on how this adaptive strategy functions in modern life for all ethnic minority groups.

In addition, ethnic minority families have used social role flexibility as a coping mechanism out of historic necessity (Munoz & Endo, 1982). Familial social roles can be regarded as flexible in definition, responsibility, and performance. Parenting of young siblings by older siblings, sharing of the breadwinner role among adults, and alternative family arrangements have been found to be more prevalent in ethnic minority communities than in majority communities (Allen, 1978; Allen & Stukes, 1982).

Biculturalism

A bicultural orientation is not new or unique to ethnic minority groups. Historically, America's formal and informal policies toward non-English-speaking immigrants were to Americanize people as fast as possible (Wagner, 1981). Most immigrant groups go through the process of acculturation, a cultural change that is initiated by the conjunction of two or more autonomous cultural systems (Bing, 1980). For ethnic minorities in America this has presented a problem because of the devaluing of their ethnic culture by the majority culture. Further, the cultures of African Americans and American Indians have been presented frequently from the European perspective rather than from the writings of persons from the respective ethnic group dominating the prevailing perspectives. One of the ways some ethnic minorities have adapted to the conflictual situation is a bicultural orientation to the acculturation process. (See McShane [1983] or McShane & Berry [1986] for an expanded discussion of alternative pathways [e.g., integration, assimilation, rejection, or marginality].)

Szopocznik and Kurtines (1980) proposed that if the cultural context within which acculturation takes place is bicultural, then acculturation will tend to take place along two dimensions. A linear process of accommodating to the host culture is the first dimension, and the second dimension is a complex process of relinquishing or retaining characteristics of the culture of origin. The person learns to function optimally in more than one cultural context and to switch repertoires of behavior appropriately and adaptively as called for by the situation (Laosa, 1977). Although all ethnic groups have expressed biculturalism as an important adaptive strategy (Harrison et al., 1984), a majority of the empirical investigations of the process have studied Hispanic Americans.

Nonetheless, African Americans and American Indians have a set of beliefs and behaviors that have their origins in their ancestral cultures (Nobles, 1978, 1988; Red Horse, 1983). These cultures are distinct from European American culture (Myers, 1982) as a result of the desire to continue the values and traditions of previous generations, and the limited access to the larger society and its social institutions. Yet there are no extensive systematic investigations of biculturalism among these two groups.

Shon and Ja (1983) describe two interrelated levels of adaptive cultural transaction as part of Asian Pacific immigrants' experiences. At the first level of physical or material transition, immigrants must consistently struggle to overcome language barriers and to achieve economic security and educational and occupational success. The second level of cultural transition involves cognitive and affective changes in which the family attempts psychologically to incorporate various features of their new environment. One of several empirical questions from this process is whether these families continue to maintain a bicultural orientation or select other pathways of adaptation.

Sabogal et al. (1987) examined the effects of acculturation on three attitudinal components of Hispanic familism: (1) familiar obligations, (2) perceived support from family, and (3) family as referents. They found that attitudes concerning familial obligations and family as referents diminished with increasing levels of acculturation (as measured by language preference and usage), but that perception of family support remained constant. The selective effect of acculturation on familism is further supported by the research of Reuschenberg and Buriel (1988), who used the Family Environment Scale (FES) (Moos, Insel, & Humphrey, 1974) to study Mexican American families who were either short- or long-term arrivals from Mexico or U.S. born. The FES is primarily a behavioral rather than attitudinal scale and can be scored to distinguish between interactions involving only family members and those involving family members and outside social systems. Reuschenberg and Buriel (1988) found that acculturation was related to differences in families' interaction patterns with outside social agencies, but not to internal family system variables. In other words, acculturation may change the way individual family members interact and present themselves to outside agents, but internal family dynamics remain mostly intact. This finding suggests the dual existence of public and private domains of family life among Hispanic Americans. Hispanics often achieve a bicultural adaptation that uniquely combines aspects of European American and Hispanic cultures, leading to behaviors that are not entirely characteristic of either culture (Buriel, 1987). According to Ramirez (1983), the diversity inherent in Hispanics' heritage has provided this group with a worldview that values integration and synthesis of new cultural experiences rather than complete assimilation.

Biculturalism has been the topic of edited books and reviews of empirical studies. The effects of biculturalism have been investigated from the conceptual frameworks of bilingualism and the need for changes in the delivery of mental health services to ethnic minority groups (e.g., Hakuta & Garcia, 1989; Penalosa, 1980; Powell et al., 1983; Ramirez, 1986; Spindler & Spindler, 1987; Serafica, in press; Willig, 1985; Wolfson & Manes, 1985). What is needed for more in-depth understanding of biculturalism is more information on the psychological mechanisms involved and the resulting positive or negative effects for individuals as well as the group.

Ancestral Worldviews

American culture is dominated by the belief in individualism, that is, the notion that "each of us is an entity separate from every other and from the group and as such is endowed with natural rights" (Spence, 1985, p. 1288). One of the ways the concept of individualism is incorporated into American cultural heritage is through the lauding of the Protestant work ethic as the pathway to success for individuals (Sampson, 1985). The social order of the majority culture is guided by an acceptance of individualism, which is reflected in encouragement and recognition of individual achievements and accomplishments, especially the attainment of material property (Spence, 1985). Given the status of ethnic minorities, generally individualism has not been their pathway to the American Dream. Further, individualism is incompatible with the ancestral worldviews of ethnic minorities.

The indigenous psychology of ethnic minority cultures differs from the majority culture in how interwoven the interest and well-being of the self is with the ethnic group to which one belongs. Self-contained individualism is an indigenous psychology of the majority culture (Heelas & Lock, 1981; Nobles, 1978; Ramirez, 1983; Sampson, 1988). In contrast, the degree of fluidity of boundaries between self- and non-self-interests among ethnic minorities is based on a more inclusive conception of the person or self, that is, persons are attached to families, households, communities, and the group (Heela & Lock, 1981; Sampson, 1988). Thus, when confronted in American society with racism, discrimination, occupational barriers, and negative portrayals of the ethnic group, ethnic minorities have used their ancestral worldviews as an adaptive strategy for pathways to achievement and sense of personal worth.

The salience of ancestral worldviews as reflected in spirituality/religiosity and philosophical orientations in contemporary ethnic minority communities is well documented (Garbarino, 1976; Gill, 1982a; Medicine, 1980; Ramirez & Castaneda, 1974; Shon & Ja, 1983; Taylor, 1988; Taylor, Thornton, & Chatters, 1988; Thornton & Taylor, 1988). The term "religiosity" is used in the scholarly orientation to refer to images, actions, and symbols that define the extent and character of the world for the people and provide the cosmic framework for which their lives find meaning, purpose, and fulfillment (Gill, 1982b).

Sudarkasa (1988) and Nobles (1988) have noted that African Americans possess a worldview that is akin to an African belief in collectivism rather than a European belief in individualism. However, research has not been conducted on these concepts among African Americans, and it is not known whether such orientations affect family functioning. On the other hand, research has documented the persistence of some African cultural patterns among contemporary African American families for both rural and urban areas (Sudarkasa, 1988). For example, emphasis on consanguinity, kinship that is biologically based, is a salient feature of African and African American family organization. Researchers have noted the role of religion in enhancing life satisfaction among a national sample of African Americans (e.g., Taylor, 1988).

In American Indian traditions, all aspects of life take on religious significance, and religion and culture are intimately connected (Medicine, 1981; Michaelsen, 1983). American Indians do not share a single dominant religion (Gill, 1982b; Hultkrantz, 1981; Hurdy, 1970), yet a common practice across a variety of American Indian tribal cultures is the quest for a guardian spirit (Garbarino, 1976; Hamer, 1980; Lewis, 1981). The attaining of a guardian spirit is seen as a confidence builder, which at the very least would result in the capability to manage most of life's stresses and demands.

Traditional cultural orientations and values among many Asian Pacific American subgroups are deeply rooted in the doctrines and philosophies of Buddhism, Confucianism, and Taoism; each offers a worldview and prescription for living that emphasizes selected virtues and adherence to codes of behavior. Confucian thought, important to Asian/Pacific families, is guided by a philosophical orientation wherein *harmony* is the core of existence, and persons' obligation is to sustain harmony within the social order (Chan, 1986; Sampson, 1988; Sue & Sue, 1987). The Hispanic value system of familism is supported and reinforced by the pervasive religious practices in the community. For example, the image of the Virge de Guadalupe (the *Mestizo* equivalent of the Virgin Mary) is both a religious and an unofficial national symbol of *la Raza* (Ramirez & Castaneda, 1974).

In short, the worldviews of ethnic minorities have emphasized collectivism or loyalty to the group in some form. One of the interesting empirical questions needing investigation is how prevalent is the regard for collectivism as compared to individualism among ethnic minorities groups. Do attitudes about collectivism predict behavior? What are the contributing factors to intra- and intergroup differences on these dimensions?

SOCIALIZATION GOALS

Adaptive responses to ecological challenges have shaped the family ecologies of ethnic minorities and affected the socialization of children. Socialization refers to the processes by which individuals become distinctive and actively functioning members of the society in which they live (Elkin & Handel, 1984; Zigler, Lamb, & Child, 1982). The family ecologies of ethnic minority children differ from majority children's and partially provide the basis for variations in the context of socialization. The mechanisms for transmittal of the culture are the same for both ethnic minority and majority children (e.g., reinforcement, modeling, identification, etc.). Yet ethnicity is potent in the socialization process of families since it includes group patterns of values, social customs, perceptions, behavioral roles, language usage, and rules of social interactions that group members share in both obvious and subtle ways (Phinney & Rotheram, 1987).

Attribution theory (Dix & Grusec, 1985), distancing theory (which reflects the theories of Piaget, Kelley, & Weiner [Johnson & Martin, 1985; McGillicuddy-DeLisi, 1985]), and social learning theories have provided the conceptual underpinning for the assumption that parental beliefs are important determinants in the socialization process. In addition, other theoretical orientations have expanded beyond the consideration of parental beliefs and behaviors to include the cultural context in which those processes occur (Bronfenbrenner, 1979; Rogoff, 1982). Ogbu's cultural-ecological model of child rearing is a part of this trend and offers a viable conceptual framework for understanding the relation between the strategies ethnic minorities have adopted to meet the group's ecological challenges and the selection of certain socialization goals.

Ogbu (1981) proposes that child rearing in the family and similar micro settings during the periods of infancy, childhood, and adolescence is geared toward the development of instrumental competence. Instrumental competence refers to the ability to perform culturally specific tasks that are required for adult economic, political, and social roles. Indeed, Ogbu (1981, p. 417) notes, "child categories and instrumental competencies resulting from child-rearing techniques eventually develop into adaptive adult categories and instrumental competencies in the population." In the sections that follow, we identify some of the socialization goals espoused by ethnic minority families. We argue that these goals emerge from the adaptive strategies of ethnic minority families identified earlier. The child-rearing goals so identified and described are positive orientation toward ethnic group and socialization for interdependence.

Positive Orientation toward Ethnic Groups

One goal of the socialization practices among ethnic minority families is to foster a positive orientation among children toward their ethnic group as a means of promoting biculturalism and acceptance of the orientations of the ancestral worldview. Children are taught to view their role within the family and society in terms of relationships and obligations to the family (Chan, 1986; Tseng, 1973). In one of the few empirical studies investigating family socialization of ethnic attitudes, Bowman and Howard (1985) offer insightful information regarding the effect on children of parents actively socializing them regarding the consequences of their ethnicity in the larger society. This study of a national sample of African American three-generational families indicated that the manner in which parents oriented their children toward racial barriers was a significant element in children's motivation, achievement, and prospects for upward mobility. Parents of successful children emphasized ethnic pride, self-development, awareness of racial barriers, and egalitarianism in their socialization practices.

A large percentage of ethnic minority children are growing up in homes where English is not the dominant language and where American culture does not govern most aspects of family life, especially child rearing (Gutierrez, Sameroff, & Karrer, 1988). These children are oriented toward the family group as a source of information regarding their ethnic identity and culture. There is a body of literature on socialization of ethnic identification and the social-behavioral correlates of ethnic identity (e.g., Phinney & Rotheram, 1987).

Socialization for Interdependence

Ethnic minority families typically stress interdependence as a socialization goal for children as a logical accompaniment to emphasis on extended families and the ancestral worldview of collectivism. Parents tend to reinforce personality traits that are consistent with this goal. Given ecological challenges for achievement and accomplishment in American society, the pathway for individual and group members of ethnic minorities has been generally through collective actions that open opportunities for individual achievement. Thus socializing children toward interdependence with the group fosters the continuation of that pathway.

Generally, ethnic minority children are taught to think, feel, and act in ways that involve the development of a cooperative view of life, rather than one of a singularly competitive nature (Chan, 1986; Green, Sack, & Pambrum, 1981). Individuals are instructed to view themselves as an integral part of the totality of their family and the larger social structure and experience a social/psychological dependence on others. Cooperation, obligation, sharing, and reciprocity are essential elements of social interaction (Delgado-Gaitan, 1987; Serafica, in press). These values sharply contrast with Western ideals of competition, autonomy, and self-reliance (Sampson, 1988).

Sims (1978, 1979), in an empirical study concerned with sharing among African American children, found that children were more willing to share their toys and possessions when the request was made in the context of group reference. Establishing an ethnic minority reference facilitated more personal concern on the part of children and thus heightened children's motivation to share. Also, sharing was identified as an appropriate behavior of an ethnic group member. Children were probably affected by the expected group norm that sharing and cooperation were to be done with other group members. Although the number of studies on the topic is limited, there is evidence that American Indian and Hispanic American children are more cooperative and conciliatory in resolving potential interpersonal conflicts than are majority children (Delgado-Gaitan, 1987; Kagan & Madsen, 1971; Knight & Kagan, 1977; Osborne, 1985). There are no comparable studies for Asian American children.

COGNITIVE DEVELOPMENTAL OUTCOMES

How do socialization goals stemming from adaptive strategies of ethnic minority families influence children's cognitive development? The socialization process is complex, and it is difficult to ascribe developmental outcomes to specific factors. The research evidence for these and similar questions is diffuse, sparse, uneven across ethnic minority groups, and lacking for some (McShane, 1988), yet some insights can be obtained from the general literature on ethnic minority children and families. Caution should be exercised in generalizing from group data to individuals within any single ethnic minority group (Laosa, 1977). Further, within-group differences are an important source of variance when studying developmental outcomes on child behavioral measures. Investigators have examined the variables of social class (Carter, 1983; DeVos, 1973; Hakuta, 1987; Shon & Ja, 1983), identification with ethnic culture (Buriel, 1984; McShane, 1983), generation status, geographic origin (Shon & Ja, 1983), father absence (Powell et al., 1983; Scott-Jones, 1987), gender (Hare & Castenell, 1985), home environment (Slaughter & Epps, 1987), and geographical habitats (McShane & Berry, 1986) as examples of important determinants of intragroup heterogeneity.

Theories abound explaining the determinants, course, and trends of cognitive development. Currently, the concepts of Vygotsky (1978) are receiving increased attention as a framework for investigating the importance of culture to cognitive development. Vygotsky viewed children as active participants who attempted to master and competently function in the world around them. One of the ways they mastered their world was through the use of auxiliary stimuli. Auxiliary stimuli are introduced as a means of active adaptation and include the tools of the culture into which the child is born, the language of those who relate to the child, and other means produced by the child himself. Thus, Vygotsky concluded that in order to study development in children one must begin with an understanding of two principally different entities, the biological and the cultural.

The ideas of Vygotsky (1978) have been expanded and serve as a source of fresh insights in the area of developmental psychology (e.g., Irvine & Berry, 1986). Bronfenbrenner (1989) summarized the essence of this trend as proposing that the attributes of the person most likely to shape the beginning of the course of one's cognitive development are those that induce or inhibit dynamic dispositions toward the immediate environment, referred to as developmentally instigative characteristics. For an elaborate discussion of these complex ideas, see Bronfenbrenner (1989). In the section that follows, we examine cognitive flexibility and sensitivity to discontinuity as aspects of cognitive development shaped by the socialization goals of ethnic minority families.

Cognitive Flexibility

Researchers have consistently found that ethnic minority families are concerned with biculturalism —or preparing children to function in both the ethnic and nonethnic communities (Harrison et al., 1984; Peters, 1988). Theoretical and empirical evidence (Ramirez, 1983) indicates that biculturalism often involves more than using two cultural modalities in a simple additive manner (Gutierrez et al., 1988). The process of integrating two cultural systems involves greater cognitive and social flexibility that eventuates in a unique synthesis of both ethnic and nonethnic cultures as well as separateness of both cultures. Achieving the new synthesis is a complex process fraught with many obstacles and conflicts.

Biculturalism can be expressed in values, identity, and customs. Nonetheless, bilingualism is perhaps the most investigated indicator (Hakuta & Garcia, 1989). Balanced bilingual children show more cognitive flexibility than monolingual children (McShane & Berry, 1986; McShane & Cook, 1985; Osborne, 1985; Ramirez & Castaneda, 1974) that is, the ability to detect multiple meanings of words and alternative orientations of objects. Studies also indicate that bilingualism fosters metalinguistic awareness, the cognitive ability to attend to language as an object of thought rather than just for the content or idea (Diaz, 1983). In the same manner, Boykin (1979) investigated cognitive flexibility by exploring whether differences in the format variability of a set of problem-solving tasks affected the problem-solving performance of ethnic and majority school children. He found that African American children as compared to majority children performed better on tasks that were presented in a varied, as opposed to an unvaried, format. The majority children performed equally well with both formats. The differences between the performance of African American and majority children are explained by Boykin with the concept of psychological/behavioral verve. Psychological/behavioral verve is a unique adaptation to the high-energy pace of home experiences that is manifested in one's attitude, orientation, and responsiveness to varied, constantly changing stimulation.

Sensitivity to Discontinuity

Discontinuity has been defined as an abrupt transition from one mode of being and behaving to another accompanied by noticeable differences in social role assignments and expectations (Marcias, 1987). The problems generated by discontinuity between the home environments of ethnic minority children and the school environment are of concern. Discontinuity has the possibility of negative consequences on cognitive functioning because it affects academic achievement and social adjustment (Osborne, 1985; Spindler & Spindler, 1987). Ethnic minority children are more likely to be exposed to discontinuities between their family ecologies and school environment than majority children, whose family ecologies are more likely to be similar to the academic setting. In her studies of the social ecologies of African American children, Holliday (1985) observed that the discontinuity between home, neighborhood, and school facilitated the development of situational problem solving among young persons. In the home and neighborhood, children's roles most frequently demanded problem-solving skills, that is, the ability to recognize, adapt to, circumvent, or change an encountered predicament. In the school environment, however, children's interpersonal skills—the ability to become a participant, to gain leadership, and to cooperate and collaborate—as well as academic excellence were in greatest demand. Continuity between learning environments of home and school is an important element in the performance of children on problem-solving tasks (Delgado-Gaitan, 1987; Laosa & Sigel, 1982; Marcias, 1987). Research studies have found that ethnic minority children show improvements in their achievement levels, memory, and problem-solving abilities when the context of the learning environment is consistent with their background (Boykin, 1979; Hare, 1985; Holliday, 1985; Spindler & Spindler, 1987). This phenomenon is highlighted in the teaching strategies parents use in interactions with children. The teaching/learning strategies used in the home influence how children perform on problem-solving situations in school (Laosa, 1980; Laosa & DeAvila, 1979; Steward & Steward, 1973).

SUMMARY AND DISCUSSION

Recent population projections of the increase in the proportion of Americans who are members of an ethnic minority group have heightened the need for social scientists to understand these populations. The purpose of this essay was to consider the interconnectedness of ecologies of ethnic minority families, adaptive strategies, socialization goals, and child behavioral outcomes. Ethnic minority groups have adaptive strategies that developed as responses to ecological challenges. The adaptive strategies discussed were family extendedness and role flexibility, biculturalism, and ancestral worldview. Adult members of the group have as their socialization goals fostering a positive orientation to the ethnic group and interdependence for children. Cognitive flexibility and sensitivity to discontinuities in children were viewed as developmental outcomes. We hope that this essay will stimulate research that can be utilized by those who educate, parent, socialize, and support ethnic minority children.

Although progress has been made in initiating writings and empirical investigations of ethnic minority families and children, a majority of the publications focus on mental health rather than on developmental issues. There is also unevenness in the quality of the research efforts on ethnic minorities, and the social sciences have serious shortcomings in this area.

In the future, researchers need to attend to the extreme heterogeneity among various ethnic groups. It is important to identify the specific ethnic/demographic characteristics of the group studied in empirical investigations. It is important to note that although the cognitive domain was selected for review because there were more empirical investigations in that area, other aspects of development should be studied using this conceptual framework. Earlier literature on ethnic minority children concentrated on cognitive issues and subsequently has been criticized for narrowness of focus and shortcomings in methodology.

Researchers need to consider level of acculturation, period of immigration, social class, and appropriateness of comparison group in research designs. Failure to do so are principal pitfalls in the study of development among ethnic minorities. Also, social scientists need to take stock of the ethnocentrism biases in the formulation of research questions and interpretations of data from studies of ethnic minority children. Sampson (1988) and Spence (1985) offer insightful comments on the percursors for this tendency. With increased interest in the cultural context of development, there is hope that more culturally sensitive research will yield more insightful information regarding development among ethnic minority children.

Two examples of research designs that may be fruitful are offered. One is to study the socialization practices of different ethnic minority families that are rearing successful children. What are the similarities and differences in their parenting techniques, and what factors account for them? Second, in every culture there are critical social pathways to success. What were the procedures or pathways taken by adult members of the ethnic groups that led to success? What environmental factors and psychological processes can best explain how ethnic group members have managed to succeed? Finally, more effort needs to be directed to the formulation of conceptual models that can best explain the development of ethnic minority children. The models should not only be explanatory, but also suggestive of empirical investigations. These efforts are worthwhile as we continue our attempts to understand human development in a cultural context.

NOTES

Except for the first two, authors are listed in the order of joining the project. Special thanks to Charles Nakamura, hector Myers, Barbara Rogoff, Teresa LaFromboise, Kenyon Chan, Sue Gottschalk, and unknown reviewers for their helpful comments in the preparation of this manuscript.

REFERENCES

Agesti, B. F. (1978). The first decades of freedom: Black families in a southern county, 1870–1885. *Journal of Marriage and the Family, 46,* 697–706.

Allen, W. R. (1978). Black family research in the United States: A review, assessment, and extension. *Journal of Comparative Family Studies, 2,* 167–189.

Allen, W. R., & Stukes, S. (1982). Black family life-styles and the mental health of black Americans. In F. U. Munoz & R. Endo (Eds.), *Perspectives on minority group mental health* (pp. 43–52). Washington, DC: University Press of America.

Aoyagi, K. (1978). Kinship and friendship in black Los Angeles: A study of migrants from Texas. In D. Shimkin, E. Shimkin, & D. Frate (Eds.), *The extended family in black societies* (pp. 277–355). Chicago: Aldine.

Beck, R. W., & Beck, S. H. (1984). Formation of extended households during middle age. *Journal of Marriage and the Family, 46,* 277–287.

Beck, R. W., & Beck, S. H. (1989). The incidence of extended households among middle-aged black and white women. *Journal of Family Issues, 10,* 147–168.

Bing, J. (1980). Acculturation as varieties of adaptations. In A. M. Padilla (Ed.), *Acculturation Theory, models and some new findings* (pp. 9–23). Boulder, CO: Westview.

Bouvier, L. F., & Agresta, A. (in press). Projections of the Asian American population. In J. T. Fawcett & B. Carino (Eds.), *Asian and Pacific immigration to the United States.*

Bowman, P. J., & Howard, C. (1985). Race-related socialization, motivation, and academic achievement: A study of black youth in three-generation families. *Journal of the American Academy of Child Psychiatry, 24,* 134–141.

Boykin, A. W. (1979). Psychological behavioral verve: Some theoretical explorations and empirical manifestations. In A. W. Boykin, A. J. Franklin, & J. F. Yates (Eds.), *Research directions of black psychologists* (pp. 351–367). New York: Russell Sage.

Bronfenbrenner, U. (1979). *The ecology of human development.* Cambridge, MA: Harvard University Press.

Bronfenbrenner, U. (1989, June). *The ecology of cognitive development: Research models and fugitive findings.* Paper prepared for presentation as the keynote address for the Nineteenth Annual Symposium of the Jean Piaget Society. Philadelphia.

Brown, D. R., & Gary, L. (1987). Stressful life events, social support networks, and the physical and mental health of urban black adults. *Journal of Human Stress, 13,* 165–174.

Burgess, B. J. (1980). Parenting in the Native American community. In M. D. Fantini & R. Cardenas (Eds.), *Parenting in a multicultural society* (pp. 63–73). New York: Lougman.

Buriel, R. (1984). Integration with traditional Mexican-American culture an sociocultural adjustment. In *Chicano psychology* (2d ed, pp. 95–130). New York: Academic Press.

Buriel, R. (1987). Ethnic labeling and identity among Mexican Americans. In J. S. Phinney & M. J. Rotheram (Eds.), *Children's ethnic socialization* (pp. 134–152). Beverly Hills, CA: Sage.

Carter, J. (1983). *Vision or sight: Health concerns for Afro-American children.* In G. J. Powell (Ed.), *The psychological development of minority children* (pp. 13–25). New York: Brunner/Mazel.

Chan, S. (1986). Parents of exceptional Asian children. In M. K. Kitano & P. C. Chinn (Eds.), *Exceptional Asian children and youth* (pp. 36–53). Reston, VA: Council for Exceptional Children.

Delgado-Gaitan, C. (1987). Tradition and transitions in the learning process of Mexican children: An ethnographic view. In G. Spindler & L. Spindler (Eds.), *Interpretive ethnography of education: At home and abroad* (pp. 333–359). Hillsdale, NJ: Erlbaum.

DeVos, G. A. (Ed.). (1973). *Socialization for achievement.* Berkeley: University of California Press.

DeVos, G. A. (1982). Adaptive strategies in U.S. minorities. In E. E. Jones & S. J. Korchin (Eds.), *Minority mental health* (pp. 74–117). New York: Praeger.

Diaz, R. (1983). Thought and two languages: The impact of bilingualism on cognitive development. In E. Gordon (Ed.), *Review of research in education, Vol. 10.* Washington, DC: American Educational Research Association.

Dix, J. H., & Grusec, J. E. (1985). Parent attribution processes in the socialization of children. In I. E. Sigel (Ed.), *Parental belief systems* (pp. 201–233). Hillsdale, NJ: Erlbaum.

Dressler, W. W. (1985). Extended family relationships, social support, and mental health in a southern black community. *Journal of Health and Social Behavior, 26,* 39–48.

Elkin, F., & Handel, G. (1984). *The child and society: The process of socialization.* New York: Random House.

Flanagan, W. G. (1978, August). *The extended family as an agent of social change.* Paper presented at the Ninth World Congress of the International Sociological Association, Uppsala University, Uppsala, Sweden.

Fogel, R., & Engelman, S. (1974). *Time on the cross* (Vols. 1 and 2). Boston: Little, Brown.

Foster, H. J. (1984). African patterns in Afro-American families. *Journal of Black Studies, 14,* 201–232.

Garbarino, J. (1982). Sociocultural risk: Dangers to competence. In C. B. Kopp & J. B. Krakow (Eds.), *The child: Development in a social context.* Reading, MA: Addison-Wesley.

Garbarino, M. S. (1976). *Native heritage.* Boston: Little, Brown.

Gardner, R. W., Robey, B., & Smith, P. C. (1985). Asian Americans: Growth, changes and diversity. *Population Bulletin, 40,* 4.

Genovese, E. D. (1976). *Roll, Jordan, roll.* New York: Random House.

Gibbs, J. T., Huang, L. N., & Associates (1989). *Children of color.* San Francisco: Jossey-Bass.

Gibson, G. (1972). Kin family network: Overheralded structure in past conceptualizations of family functioning. *Journal of Marriage and the Family, 34,* 13–23.

Gill, S. D. (1982a). *Beyond "the primitive": The religions of non-literate peoples.* Englewood Cliffs, NJ: Prentice-Hall.

Gill, S. D. (1982b). *Native American religions.* Belmont, CA: Wadsworth.

Goode, W. J. (1964). *The family.* Englewood Cliffs, NJ: Prentice-Hall.

Goodluck, C. T., & Eckstein, F. (1978). American Indian adoption program: An ethnic approach to child welfare. *White Cloud Journal, 1,* 3–7.

Green, B. E., Sack, W. H., & Pambrum, A. (1981). A review of child psychiatric epidemiology with special reference to American Indian and Alaska Native children. *White Cloud Journal, 2,* 22–36.

Gutierrez, J., Sameroff, A. J., & Karrer, B. M. (1988). Acculturation and SES effects on Mexican American parents' concepts of development. *Child Development, 59,* 250–255.

Gutman, H. G. (1976). *The black family in slavery and freedom, 1750–1925.* New York: Vintage.

Hakuta, K. (1987). Degree of bilingualism and cognitive ability in mainland Puerto Rican children. *Child Development, 58,* 1372–1388.

Hakuta, K., & Garcia, E. E. (1989). Bilingualism and education. *American Psychologist, 44,* 374–379.

Hamer, J. H. (1980). Acculturation stress and the functions of alcohol among the forest Potowatomi. In J. Hamer & J. Steinwings (Eds.), *Alcohol and native peoples of the north* (pp. 107–153). Washington, DC: University Press of America.

Harding, V. (1980). *The other American revolution.* Los Angeles: Center for Afro-American Studies, University of California, Los Angeles.

Hare, B. R. (1985). Reexamining the achievement central tendency: Sex differences within race and race differences within sex. In H. P. McAdoo & J. L. McAdoo (Eds.), *Black children* (pp. 139–151). Beverly Hills, CA: Sage.

Hare, B. R., & Castenell, L. A. (1985). No place to run, no place to hide: Comparative status and future prospects of black boys. In M. B. Spencer, G. Brookins, & W. Allen (Eds.), *Beginnings: The social and affective development of black children* (pp. 201–214). Hillsdale, NJ: Erlbaum.

Harrison, A. O., Serafica, F., & McAdoo, H. (1984). Ethnic families of color. In R. D. Parke (Ed.), *The family: Review of child development research* (Vol. 7, pp. 329–371). Chicago: University of Chicago Press.

Heelas, P., & Lock, A. C. (Eds.). (1981). *Indigenous psychologies: The anthropology of the self.* London: Academic Press.

Height, D. (1985, March). What must be done about children having children. *Ebony,* p. 76.

Holliday, B. G. (1985). Developmental imperative of social ecologies: Lessons learned from black children. In H. P. McAdoo & J. L. McAdoo (Eds.), *Black children* (pp. 53–71). Beverly Hills, CA: Sage.

Hultkrantz, A. (1981). *Belief and worship in Native North America.* Syracuse, NY: Syracuse University Press.

Hurdy, J. M. (1970). *American Indian religions.* Los Angeles: Sherbourne.

Irvine, S. H., & Berry, J. W. (Eds.). (1986). *Human abilities in cultural context.* Cambridge: Cambridge University Press.

Johnson, J. E., & Martin, C. (1985). Parents' beliefs and home learning environments: Effects on cognitive development. In I. E. Sigel (Ed.), *Parental belief systems* (pp. 25–50). Hillsdale, NJ: Erlbaum.

Kagan, S., & Madsen, M. C. (1971). Cooperation and competition of Mexican, Mexican-American, and Anglo-American children of two ages under four instructional sets. *Developmental Psychology, 5,* 32–39.

Knight, G. P., & Kagan, S. (1977). Development of prosocial and competitive behaviors in Anglo-American and Mexican-American children. *Child Development, 48,* 1385–1394.

LaFromboise, T. D. (1988). American Indian mental health policy. *American Psychologist, 43,* 388–397.

Langston, E. J. (1980). Kith and kin; natural support systems: Their implications for policies and programs for the black aged. In E. P. Stanford (Ed.), *Minority aging policy issues for the '80s* (pp. 125–145). San Diego: University Center on Aging, College of Human Services, San Diego State University.

Laosa, L. M. (1977). Cognitive styles and learning strategies research. *Journal of Teacher Education, 28,* 26–30.

Laosa, L. M. (1980). Maternal teaching strategies in Chicano and Anglo American families: The influence of culture and education on maternal behavior. *Child Development, 51,* 759–765.

Laosa, L. M., & DeAvila, E. A. (1979). Development of cognitive styles among Chicanos in traditional and dualistic communities. *International Journal of Psychology, 14,* 91–98.

Laosa, L. M., & Sigel, I. E. (1982). *Families as learning environments for children.* New York: Plenum.

Lewis, R. (1981). Patterns of strengths of American Indian families. In F. Hoffman (Ed.), *The American Indian family strengths and stresses* (pp. 101–107). American Indian Social Research and Development Associates, Inc., P.O. Box 381, Iskta, NM 87022.

Light, H. K., & Martin, R. E. (1986). American Indian families. *Journal of American Indian Education, 26,* 1–5.

Marcias, J. (1987). The hidden curriculum of Papago teachers: American Indian strategies for mitigating cultural discontinuity in early schooling. In G. Spindler

& L. Spindler (Eds.), *Interpretive ethnography of education: At home and abroad* (pp. 363–380). Hillsdale, NJ: Erlbaum.

Marin, G. (1986, October). *The process of acculturatism of Latinos in the U.S.* Paper presented at the Second Puerto Rican Convention of Psychology and Mental Health, Rio Piedras, Puerto Rico.

Martin, E., & Martin, J. (1978). *The black extended family.* Chicago: University of Chicago Press.

McAdoo, H. (1978). Factors related to stability in upwardly mobile black families. *Journal of Marriage and the Family, 40,* 761–776.

McGillicuddy-DeLisi, A. V. (1985). The relationship between parental beliefs and children's cognitive level. In I. E. Sigel (Ed.), *Parental belief systems* (pp. 7–24). Hillsdale, NJ: Erlbaum.

McLoyd, V., & Randolph, S. (1985). Secular trends in the study of Afro-American children: A review of child development, 1936–1980. *Monographs of the Society for Research in Child Development,* 50(4–5, Serial No. 211).

McShane, D. (1983). Explaining achievement patterns of American Indian children: A transcultural and developmental model. *Peabody Journal of Education, 61,* 34–48.

McShane, D. (1988). An analysis of mental health research with American Indian youth. *Journal of Adolescence, 11,* 87–116.

McShane, D., & Berry, J. W. (1986). Native North Americans: Indian and Inuit abilities. In J. H. Irvine & J. W. Berry (Eds.), *Human abilities in cultural context* (pp. 385–426). Cambridge: Cambridge University Press.

McShane, D., & Cook, V. (1985). Transcultural intellectual assessment: Hispanic performance on the Wechslers. In B. Wolman (Ed.), *Handbook of intelligence: Theories, measurements, and applications.* New York: Wiley.

Meacham, M. (1983). The myth of the black matriarchy under slavery. *Mid-American Review of Sociology, 8,* 23–41.

Medicine, B. (1980). American Indian women: Spirituality and status. *Bread and Roses, 2,* 14–18.

Medicine, B. (1981). American Indian family: Cultural change and adaptive strategies. *Journal of Ethnic Studies, 8,* 13–23.

Michaelsen, R. S. (1983). "We also have a religion": The free exercise of religion among Native Americans. *American Indian Quarterly, 7,* 111–142.

Mindel, C. H., & Habenstein, R. W. (Eds.). (1988). *Ethnic families in America: Patterns and variations.* 3d ed. New York: Elsevier.

Moos, R. H., Insel, P. M., & Humphrey, B. (1974). *Manual for the Family Environment Scale.* Palo Alto, CA: Consulting Psychologists Press.

Munoz, F. U., & Endo, R. (Eds.). (1982). *Perspectives on minority group mental health.* Washington, DC: University Press of America.

Myers, H. F. (1982). Research on the Afro-American family: A critical review. In B. Bass, G. Wyatt, & G. Powell (Eds.), *The Afro-American family: Assessment treatment and research issues* (pp. 35–69). New York: Grune & Stratton.

National Indochinese Clearinghouse (1980). *Indochinese refugee education guides, general information series.* Washington, DC: National Indochinese Clearinghouse.

Nobles, W. W. (1978). African root and American fruit: The black family. *Journal of Social and Behavioral Sciences, 20,* 1–18.

Nobles, W. W. (1988). African-American family life: An instrument of culture. In H. P. McAdoo (Ed.), *Black families* (2d ed., pp. 44–53). Beverly Hills, CA: Sage.

Noel, D. L. (1985). A theory of the origin of ethnic stratification. In N. R. Yetman (Ed.), *Majority and minority* (pp. 109–120). Boston: Allyn & Bacon.

Ogbu, J. V. (1981). Origins of human competence: A cultural-ecological perspective. *Child Development,* 52, 413–429.

Ogbu, J. V. (1985). The consequences of the American caste system. In V. Neisser (Ed.), *The school achievement of minority children: New perspectives* (pp. 19–56). Hillsdale, NJ: Erlbaum.

Ogbu, J. V. (1987). Variability in minority responses to schooling: Nonimmigrants vs. immigrants. In G. Spindler & L. Spindler (Eds.), *Interpretive ethnography of education: At home and abroad* (pp. 255–280). Hillsdale, NJ: Erlbaum.

Olmedo, E. L. (1981). Testing linguistic minorities. *American Psychologist,* 36, 1018–1085.

Osborne, B. (1985). Research into Native North Americans' cognition: 1973–1982. *Journal of American Indian Education,* 24, 9–25.

Padilla, E. R., & O'Grady, K. E. (1987). Sexuality among Mexican-Americans: A case of sexual stereotyping. *Journal of Personality and Social Psychology,* 52, 5–10.

Pan Asian Parent Education Project (1982). *Pan Asian child-rearing practices: Philipino, Japanese, Korean, Samoan, Vietnamese.* San Diego: Union of Pan Asian Communities.

Penalosa, F. (1980). *Chicano sociolinguistics.* Rowley, MA: Newbury House.

Peters, M. F. (1988). Parenting in black families with young children: A historical perspective. In H. P. McAdoo (Ed.), *Black families* (2d ed., pp. 228–241). Beverly Hills, CA: Sage.

Peterson, R. O., & Yamamoto, B. Y. (Eds.). (1980). *Understanding the Pan Asian client: Book II.* San Diego: Union of Pan Asian Communities.

Phinney, J. S., & Rotheram, M. J. (Eds.). (1987). *Children's ethnic socialization: Pluralism and development.* Beverly Hills, CA: Sage.

Powell, G. J., Morales, A., Romero, A., & Yamamoto, J. (Eds.). (1983). *The psychosocial development of minority group children.* New York: Brunner/Mazel.

Ramirez, J. D. (1986). Comparing structural English immersion and bilingual education: First year results of a national study. American Journal of Education, 95, 122–148.

Ramirez, M. (1983). *Psychology of the Americas.* Elmsford, NY: Pergamon.

Ramirez, M., & Castaneda, A. (1974). *Cultural democracy, bicognitive development, and education.* New York: Academic Press.

Red Horse, J. (1983). Indian family values and experiences. In G. J. Powell, A. Morales, A. Romero, & J. Yamamoto (Eds.), *The psychosocial development of minority group children* (pp. 258–272). New York: Brunner/Mazel.

Reed, J. (1982). Black Americans in the 1980s. *Population Bulletin,* 37, 1–37.

Report on minorities in higher education (1988). Hearing before the Committee on Education and Labor, House of Representatives, One-Hundredth Congress, Serial No. 100-192. Washington, DC: Government Printing Office.

Reuschenberg, E. J., & Buriel, R. (1988). *The effects of acculturation on relationship patterns and system variables within families of Mexican descent.* Unpublished manuscript, the Claremont Graduate School, Claremont, CA.

Rogoff, B. (1982). Integrating context and cognitive development. In M. E. Lamb & A. L. Brown (Eds.), *Advances in developmental psychology* (Vol. 2, pp. 125–170). Hillsdale, NJ: Erlbaum.

Rogoff, B., Gauvain, M., & Ellis, S. (1984). Development viewed in its context. In M. H. Bornstein & M. E. Lamb (Eds.), *Developmental psychology: An advanced textbook.* Hillsdale, NJ: Erlbaum.

Ryan, R. A. (1981). Strengths of the American Indian family: State of the art. In F. Hoffman (Ed.), *The American Indian family: Strengths and stresses.* American Indian Social Research and Development Associates, Inc., P. O. Box 381, Isleta, NM 87022.

Sabogal, F., Marin, G., Otero-Sabogal, R., Marin, B., & Perez-Stable, E. J. (1987). Hispanic familism and acculturation: What changes and what doesn't? *Hispanic Journal of Behavioral Sciences, 9*, 397–412.

Sampson, E. E. (1985). The decentralization of identity. *American Psychologist, 40*, 1203–1211.

Sampson, E. E. (1988). The debate on individualism. *American Psychologists, 43*, 15–22.

Schneider, D. M. (1968). *American kinship: A cultural account.* Englewood Cliffs, NJ: Prentice-Hall.

Schneider, D.M. (1980). *American kinship: A cultural account* (2d ed.). Englewood Cliffs, NJ: Prentice-Hall.

Scott-Jones, D. (1987). Mother-as-teacher in the families of high- and low-achieving, low-income black first graders. *Journal of Negro Education, 56*, 21–34.

Serafica, F. C. (in press). Counseling Asian-American parents: A cultural-developmental framework. In F. C. Serafica et al. (Eds.), *Mental health of ethnic minorities.* New York: Praeger.

Shon, S. P., & Ja, D. Y. (1983). Asian families. In M. McGoldrick, J. K. Pearce, & J. Giordano (Eds.), *Ethnicity and family therapy.* New York: Guilford.

Sigel, M. (1985). A study of maternal beliefs and values within the context of an intervention program. In I. E. Sigel (Ed.), *Parental belief systems* (pp. 271–286). Hillsdale, NJ: Erlbaum.

Sims, S. A. (1978). Effects of modeling processes and resources on sharing among black children. *Psychological Reports, 43*, 463–473.

Sims, S. A. (1979). Sharing in black children: The impact of reference group appeals and other environmental factors. In A. W. Boykin, A. J. Franklin, & J. F. Yates (Eds.), *Research direction of black psychologists* (pp. 146–162). New York: Russell Sage.

Slaughter, D. T., & Epps, E. G. (1987). Home environment and academic achievement of black American children and youth: An overview. *Journal of Negro Education, 56*, 3–20.

Snipp, C. M., & Sandefur, G. O. (1988). Earnings of American Indians and Alaskan Natives: The effects of residence and migration. *Social Forces, 66*, 994–1008.

Soldo, B., & Lauriat, P. (1976). Living arrangements among the elderly in the United States: A log-linear approach. *Journal of Comparative Family Studies, 7*, 351–366.

Spence, J. T. (1985). Achievement American style: The rewards and costs of individualism. *American Psychologist, 40*, 1285–1295.

Spindler, G., & Spindler, L. (1987). *Interpretive ethnography of education.* Hillsdale, NJ: Erlbaum.

Stack, C. (1981). Sex roles and survival strategies in an urban black community. In F. C. Steady (Ed.), *The black woman cross-culturally* (pp. 349–367). Cambridge, MA: Schinkman.

Steward, M., & Steward, D. (1973). The observation of Anglo-Mexican and Chinese-American mothers teaching their young sons. *Child Development, 44*, 329–337.

Sudarkasa, N. (1988). Interpreting the African heritage in Afro-American family organization. In H. P. McAdoo (Ed.), *Black families* (2d ed., pp. 27–43). Beverly Hills, CA: Sage.

Sue, D., & Sue, S. (1987). Cultural factors in the clinical assessment of Asian Americans. *Journal of Consulting and Clinical Psychology, 55*, 479–487.

320 **ALGEA O. HARRISON ET AL.**

Suzuki, B. H. (1980). The Asian American family. In M. D. Fanti & R. Cardenas (Eds.), *Parenting in a multicultural society* (pp. 76–101). New York: Longman.

Sweet, J. A. (1977, October). *Further indicators of family structure and process for racial and ethnic minorities.* Paper presented at the Conference on the Demography of Racial and Ethnic Groups, Austin, TX.

Szopocznik, J., & Kurtines, W. (1980). Acculturation, biculturalism, and adjustment among Cuban Americans. In A. M. Padilla (Ed.), *Acculturation: Theory, models and some new findings* (pp. 139–161). Boulder, CO: Westview.

Taylor, R. J. (1988). Structural determinants of religious participation among black Americans. *Review of Religious Research, 2,* 114–125.

Taylor, R. J., Thornton, M. C., & Chatters, L. M. (1988). Black Americans' perceptions of the sociohistorical role of the church. *Journal of Black Studies, 18,* 123–138.

Thornton, M. C., & Taylor, R. J. (1988). Black Americans' perceptions of black Africans. *Ethnic and Racial Studies, 11,* 140–150.

Tseng, W. (1973). The concept of personality in Confucian thought. *Psychiatry, 50,* 76–86.

U.S. Bureau of the Census (1989). *Household and family characteristics: March, 1988* (Current Population Report, Series P-20, No. 437). Washington, DC: Government Printing Office.

U.S. Department of Commerce Series, Bureau of the Census (1988). *We, the Asian and Pacific Islander: We, the Black Americans; We, the first American; and We, Nosotros.* Washington, DC: Government Printing Office.

Vygotsky, L. S. (1978). *Mind in society.* Cambridge, MA: Harvard University Press.

Wagner, S. T. (1981). The historical background of bilingualism and biculturalism in the United States. In M. Ridge (Ed.), *The new bilingualism* (pp. 29–52). New Brunswick, NJ: Transaction Books.

Willig, A. (1985). A meta-analysis of selected studies on the effectiveness of bilingual education. *Review of Educational Research, 55,* 269–317.

Wilson, M. N. (1986). The black extended family: An analytical review. *Developmental Psychology, 22,* 246–258.

Wilson, M. N. (1989). Child development in the context of the black extended family. *American Psychologist, 44,* 380–385.

Wolfson, N., & Manes, J. (Eds.). (1985). *Language of inequality.* New York: Mouton.

Yetman, N. R. (Ed.). (1985). *Majority and minority.* Boston: Allyn & Bacon.

Zigler, E. F., Lamb, M. E., & Child, I. L. (1982). *Socialization and personality development.* New York: Oxford University Press.

PART III

Self and Other in Cultural Context

A. CONSTRUALS OF THE SELF

A central part of how people understand their worlds and structure their behavior has to do with how they experience the self. That the values, beliefs, and practices of different cultures result in identifiable differences in construals of self is one of the most challenging insights that derives from the study of psychology and culture. Historically, Western psychology has ignored evidence that the conceptualization of the self implicit in most psychological and developmental theory may actually be a very local view not shared by most of the world. The recent critical contributions to this topic from social constructionists and psychologists from other than Western societies has released a veritable tidal wave of literature concerning "the self in cultural context." The challenges this literature presents to deeply embedded assumptions, both personal and "scientific," promise to influence intercultural understandings in profound ways and may indeed precipitate a Kuhnian-like paradigm shift in psychological theory.

We begin this section with an essay by Harry Triandis, who has been devoted to the study of cross-cultural phenomena. In this recent study (chapter 15), Triandis reports research that suggests relationships between three factors that can be used to categorize cultures (individualism/collectivism, "tightness/looseness," and cultural complexity) and the way individuals within different cultures sort and process information with reference to three aspects of the self (the private self, the public self, and the collective self). His analysis illustrates an essentially etic approach to understanding cultural differences in construal of the self. While his analysis does not directly address differences in values, beliefs, or ways of making meaning that may differentiate cultures, his evidence could be a basis for speculation about these cultural elements as well.

Although they also base their analysis on empirical comparisons of cultures, Shinobu Kitayama and Hazel Rose Markus in chapter 16 take a somewhat different tack from Triandis. Their essay challenges the hegemony of the Western model of the self that they contend is "virtually the only model of the individual, of the person, or of the

323

self in psychology." In the Western model, the self is the rational, self-interested, self-contained actor who has a unique configuration of internal attributes and whose actions are primarily determined by those attributes. Kitayama and Markus argue that the majority of the world's people entertains a markedly different self, an interdependent self embedded in a social context and defined by social roles and relationships. They argue further that "core cultural ideas," such as independence and interdependence, are represented in structural aspects of a culture or society and thereby in the customs, institutions, beliefs, and practices that prevail. On the basis of their research Kitayama and Markus call for "multiregional, multinational, and multidisciplinary collaboration" in order to create a responsive social science required not only to address problems and challenges of life in the global community, but also to develop more comprehensive and valid theories of human social behavior.

In chapter 17, Philip Cushman critiques Daniel Stern's popular and well-respected theory of infant development from a social-constructionist perspective in order to support the view that decontextualized psychology serves to maintain and support the political status quo. Cushman argues that the very process of decontextualizing tends to obscure the ideological assumptions that inevitably arise from embeddedness in a culture. Although he emphasizes his admiration for Stern's careful observations of infants and caretakers that substantiate his theory and recognizes the creative insights that grace his work, Cushman's examination of unacknowledged assumptions of Stern's theory support his contention that "seemingly neutral, apolitical theories on such subjects as infant development have important political consequences." Cushman claims that, by locating the origin of pervasive societal problems in individual experience, attention is deflected from external socio-economic-political factors that also influence the development of the self.

The author of the final essay, Edward Sampson, has been one of the most vocal and prolific contributors to the literature on "the self in cultural context." His urgent recommendations in chapter 18 for the inclusion of indigenous psychologies in the knowledge base of all psychology are inspired both by his political analysis and his views about the requirements for a full and valid understanding of human behavior. In his essay, Sampson envisions the future world that will emerge from the major social transformations that are already taking place. He describes the postmodern era, characterized by a "postindustrial, information-based and globally linked social environment" in which current Western conceptualizations of the self—as free, independent, and self-contained—will become inadequate in providing a basis for understanding life in which the interdependence of events and people is ever more prominently demonstrated. He anticipates that it will become essential for individuals to view themselves as parts of a global world system in which "actions in one segment have consequences for all" and people's identities are inextricably linked with where they are socially located in that system. Sampson joins others in naming the postmodern self the "constitutive" self and reinforces the central importance of culture in shaping the way people construe the self. However, it is his vision of a rapidly approaching future world that may require new construals of the self that makes his essay a particularly provocative and fitting end piece for this section.

15. The Self and Social Behavior in Differing Cultural Contexts

Harry C. Triandis

The study of the self has a long tradition in psychology (e.g., Allport, 1943, 1955; Baumeister, 1987; Gordon & Gergen, 1968; James, 1890/1950; Murphy, 1947; Schlenker, 1985; Smith, 1980; Ziller, 1973), anthropology (e.g., Shweder & LeVine, 1984), and sociology (e.g., Cooley, 1902; Mead, 1934; Rosenberg, 1979). There is a recognition in most of these discussions that the self is shaped, in part, through interaction with groups. However, although there is evidence about variations of the self across cultures (Marsella, DeVos, & Hsu, 1985; Shweder & LeVine, 1984), the specification of the way the self determines aspects of social behavior in different cultures is undeveloped.

This article will examine first, aspects of the self; second, dimensions of variation of cultural contexts that have direct relevance to the way the self is defined; and third, the link between culture and self.

DEFINITIONS

The Self

For purposes of this essay, the self consists of all statements made by a person, overtly or covertly, that include the words "I," "me," "mine," and "myself" (Cooley, 1902). This broad definition indicates that all aspects of social motivation are linked to the self. Attitudes (e.g., *I* like X), beliefs (e.g., *I* think that X results in Y), intentions (e.g., *I* plan to do X), norms (e.g., in *my* group, people should act this

Reprinted by permission of the author and the American Psychological Association from *Psychological Review* 98 (1989): 506–20. Copyright © 1989 by the American Psychological Association.

way), roles (e.g., in *my* family, fathers act this way), and values (e.g., *I* think equality is very important) are aspects of the self.

The statements that people make, that constitute the self, have implications for the way people sample information (sampling information that is self-relevant more frequently than information that is not self-relevant), the way they process information (sampling more quickly information that is self-relevant than information that is not self-relevant), and the way they assess information (assessing more positively information that supports their current self-structure than information that challenges their self-structure). Thus, for instance, a self-instruction such as "I must do X" is more likely to be evaluated positively, and therefore accepted, if it maintains the current self-structure than if it changes this structure. This has implications for behavior because such self-instructions are among the several processes that lead to behavior (Triandis, 1977, 1980).

In other words, the self is an active agent that promotes differential sampling, processing, and evaluation of information from the environment, and thus leads to differences in social behavior. Empirical evidence about the link of measures of the self to behavior is too abundant to review here. A sample will suffice: People whose self-concept was manipulated so that they thought of themselves (a) as "charitable" gave more to charity (Kraut, 1973), (b) as "neat and tidy" threw less garbage on the floor (Miller, Brickman, & Bolen, 1975), and (c) as "honest" were more likely to return a pencil (Shotland & Berger, 1970). Self-definition results in behaviors consistent with that definition (Wicklund & Gollwitzer, 1982). People who defined themselves as doers of a particular behavior were more likely to do that behavior (Greenwald, Carnot, Beach, & Young, 1987). Identity salience leads to behaviors consistent with that identity (Stryker & Serpe, 1982). Self-monitoring (Snyder, 1974) has been linked to numerous behaviors (e.g., Snyder, 1987; Snyder, Simpson, & Gangestad, 1986). The more an attitude (an aspect of the self) is accessible to memory, the more likely it is to determine behavior (Fazio & Williams, 1986). Those with high self-esteem were found to be more likely to behave independently of group norms (Ziller, 1973).

As Snyder (1987) has shown, the differences between those who do more sampling of social situations (high self-monitors) and those who do more sampling of the self (low self-monitors) have implications about the way people feel, what they believe, and how their attitudes are linked to behavior. The pattern of differences described by Snyder has implications for every aspect of social motivation.

To the extent such aspects are *shared* by people who speak a common language and who are able to interact because they live in adjacent locations during the same historical period, we can refer to all of these elements as a cultural group's *subjective culture* (Triandis, 1972). This implies that people who speak different languages (e.g., English and Chinese) or live in nonadjacent locations (e.g., England and Australia) or who have lived in different time periods (e.g., 19th and 20th centuries) may have different subjective cultures.

Some aspects of the self may be universal. "I am hungry" may well be an element with much the same meaning worldwide, and across time. Other elements are extremely culture-specific. For instance, they depend on the particular mythology—religion—world-view and language of a culture. "My soul will be reincarnated" is culture-specific. Some elements of the self imply action. For example, "I should be a high achiever" implies specific actions under conditions in which standards of excellence are present. Other elements do not imply action (e.g., I am tall).

Contradictions among elements of the self are apparently more tolerated in some cultures than in others. Bharati (1985) argued that in India the self contains many contradictory elements, because all elements are seen as aspects of unitary universal forces.

The self may be coterminous with the body (e.g., a Western view) or with a group such as the family or the tribe (an African and Asian view, at least in some cases), and may be conceived as independent of groups or as a satellite of groups (Centre National de la Recherche Scientifique, 1973; Shweder & Bourne, 1982). Corresponding to a body-bounded self may be a name (as in the West), or a person's name may be a nonsense syllable (Geertz, 1963) that is rarely used, and instead, people are referred to by teknonyms (e.g., mother of X).

One major distinction among aspects of the self is between the private, public, and collective self (Baumeister, 1986b; Greenwald & Pratkanis, 1984). Thus, we have the following: *the private self*— cognitions that involve traits, states, or behaviors of the person (e.g., "I am introverted," "I am honest," "I will buy X"); *the public self*— cognitions concerning the *generalized other*'s view of the self, such as "People think I am introverted" or "People think I will buy X"; and *the collective self*—cognitions concerning a view of the self that is found in some collective (e.g., family, coworkers, tribe, scientific society); for instance, "My family thinks I am introverted" or "My coworkers believe I travel too much."

The argument of this essay is that people sample these three kinds of selves with different probabilities, in different cultures, and that has specific consequences for social behavior.

The private self is an assessment of the self by the self. The public self corresponds to an assessment of the self by the generalized other. The collective self corresponds to an assessment of the self by a specific reference group. Tajfel's (1978) notion of a *social identity,* "that part of the individual's self-concept which derives from his (or her) knowledge of his (her) membership in a social group (or groups) together with the values and emotional significance attached to that membership," (p. 63) is part of the collective self. Tajfel's theory is that people choose ingroups that maximize their positive social identity. However, that notion reflects an individualistic emphasis, because in many collectivist cultures people do not have a choice of ingroups. For instance, even though the Indian constitution has banned castes, caste is still an important aspect of social identity in that culture. Historical factors shape different identities (Baumeister, 1986a).

The notion of sampling has two elements: a *universe* of units to be sampled and a *probability* of choice of a unit from that universe. The universe can be more or less complex. By complexity is meant that the number of distinguishable elements might be few versus many, the differentiation within the elements may be small or large, and the integration of the elements may be small or large. The number of nonoverlapping elements (e.g., I am bold; I am sensitive) is clearly relevant to complexity. The differentiation of the elements refer to the number of distinctions made within the element. For example, in the case of the social class element, a person may have a simple conception with little differentiation (e.g., people who are unemployed vs. working vs. leading the society) or a complex conception with much differentiation (e.g., rich, with new money, well educated vs. rich with new money, poorly educated). *Integration* refers to the extent a change in one element changes few versus many elements. Self-structures in which changes in one element result in changes in many elements are more complex than self-structures in which such changes result in changes of only a few elements (Rokeach, 1960).

In families in which children are urged to be themselves, in which "finding yourself" is valued, or in which self-actualization is emphasized, the private self is likely to be complex. In cultures in which families emphasize "what other people will think about you," the public self is likely to be complex. In cultures in which specific groups are emphasized during socialization (e.g., "remember you are a member of this family," ". . . you are a Christian"), the collective self is likely to be complex, and the norms, roles, and values of that group acquire especially great emotional significance.

The probability of sampling refers to whether the element that will be sampled is more likely to be an element of the private, public, or collective self. Thus, if the private self is complex, there are more "private-self units" that can be sampled, and thus the probability that the private self will be sampled will be high; correspondingly with the other selves, if they are complex they have a higher probability of being sampled.

In addition to differences in the complexity of the private, public, and collective self, the salience of the units that constitute these selves is likely to be different. Units of a particular self are likely to interact among themselves. Each time a unit is activated, adjacent and similar units will increase in salience, as the well-known phenomena of stimulus and response generalization suggest. Thus, the fact that a unit of the private self (e.g., I am bold) is activated increases the chances that other units of the private self (e.g., "I am fearless;" even "I am confident") will become more salient than they were. Salience of a unit increases its probability of being sampled.

One of many methods that are available to study the self requires writing 20 sentence completions that begin with "I am . . ." (Kuhn & McPartland, 1954). The answers can be content-analyzed to determine whether they correspond to the private, public, or collective self. If a social group is part of the answer (e.g., I am a son = family; I am a student = educational institution; I am Roman Catholic = religion), one can classify the response as part of the collective self. If the generalized other is mentioned (e.g., I am liked by most people), it is part of the public self. If there is no reference to an entity outside the person (e.g., I am bold), it can be considered a part of the private self. Experience with this scoring method shows that coders can reach interrater reliabilities in the .9+ range. The percentage of the collective responses varies from 0 to 100, with sample means in Asian cultures in the 20 to 52% range and in European and North American samples between 15 and 19%. Public-self responses are relatively rare, so sample means of private-self responses (with student samples) are commonly in the 81 to 85% range. In addition to such content analyses, one can examine the availability (how frequently a particular group, e.g., the family, is mentioned) and the accessibility (when is a particular group mentioned for the first time in the rank-order) of responses (Higgins & King, 1981).

This method is useful because it provides an operational definition of the three kinds of selves under discussion. Also, salience is reflected directly in the measure of accessibility, and the complexity of particular self is suggested by the availability measure.

Although this method has many advantages, a multimethod strategy for the study of the self is highly recommended, because every method has some limitations and convergence across methods increases the validity of our measurements. Furthermore, when methods are used in different cultures in which people have different expectations about what can be observed, asked, or analyzed, there is an interaction between culture and method. But when methods converge similarly in different cultures and when the antecedents and consequences of the self-construct in each culture are similar, one can have greater confidence that the construct has similar or equivalent meanings across cultures.

Other methods that can tap aspects of the self have included interviews (e.g., Lobel, 1984), Q-sorts of potentially self-descriptive attributes (e.g., Block, 1986), the Multistage Social Identity Inquirer (Zavalloni, 1975; Zavalloni & Louis-Guerin, 1984), and reaction times when responding to whether a specific attribute is self-descriptive (Rogers, 1981).

The utility of the distinction among the various selves can be seen in Hogan and Cheek (1983) and Breckler and Greenwald (1986). The latter integrates many social psychological phenomena using these distinctions. However, other distinctions seem to be useful as well, such as the ideal versus actual self, the desired versus undesired self (Ogilvie, 1987), and discrepancies among various selves that correspond to distinct emotional states (Higgins, 1987).

The self is dynamic (Markus & Wurf, 1987), so that different elements of the self will be sampled in different situations, across time, moods (e.g., Szalay & Deese, 1978), and depending on negotiations the person has had with others about the way the situation is to be defined. Depending on which elements are sampled and if the elements have action components, social behavior will be influenced by the particular self. Sampling of both public and collective elements suggests an allocentric self; sampling of exclusively private elements suggests an idiocentric self. Of course, in most cases the elements that are sampled are of all three (private, public, collective) kinds.

A number of social psychological literatures, such as those dealing with self-monitoring (e.g., Snyder, 1974; Snyder & Gangestad, 1986), self-consciousness (e.g., Carver & Scheier, 1985), and the complexity of the self (e.g., Linville, 1985), can be related to the distinctions made earlier. High self-monitors sample the situation and sample the public self more than do low self-monitors, who have a more stable (situation independent) self and sample mostly the private self; the distinction between private and public self-consciousness is obviously related to such differential sampling; highly complex selves should include more elements in all three domains of the self, although no research on this seems to have been reported in the literature, as yet.

I have defined the self as one element of subjective culture (when it is shared by members of a culture) and distinguished the private, public, and collective selves, and indicated that the complexity of these selves will depend on cultural variables. The more complex a particular self, the more probable it is that it will be sampled. Sampling of a particular self will increase the probability that behaviors implicated in this aspect of the self will occur, when situations favor such occurrence. For example, data suggest that people from East Asia sample their collective self more frequently than do Europeans or North Americans. This means that elements of their reference groups, such as group norms or group goals, will be more salient among Asians than among Europeans or North Americans. In the next section I will describe cultural variation along certain theoretical dimensions that are useful for organizing the information about the sampling of different selves, and hence can account for differences in social behavior across cultures.

Cultural Patterns

There is evidence of different selves across cultures (Marsella et al., 1985). However, the evidence has not been linked systematically to particular dimensions of cultural variation. This section will define three of these dimensions.

Cultural complexity. A major difference across cultures is in cultural complexity. Consider the contrast between the human bands that existed on earth up to about 15,000 years ago and the life of a major metropolitan city today. According to archaeological evidence, the bands rarely included more than 30 individuals. The number of relationships among 30 individuals is relatively small; the number of relationships in a major metropolitan area is potentially almost infinite. The number of potential relationships is one measure of cultural complexity. Students of this construct have used many others. One can get reliable rank orders by using information about whether cultures have writing and records, fixity of residence, agriculture, urban settlements, technical specialization, land transport other than walking, money, high population densities, many levels of political integration, and many levels of social stratification. Cultures that have all of these attributes (e.g., the Romans, the Chinese of the 5th century B.C., modern industrial cultures) are quite complex. As one or more of the aforementioned attributes are missing, the cultures are more simple, the simplest including the contemporary food gathering cultures (e.g., the nomads of the Kalahari desert).

Additional measures of complexity can be obtained by examining various domains of culture. Culture includes language, technology, economic, political, and educational systems, religious and aesthetic patterns, social structures, and so on. One can analyze each of these domains by considering the number of distinct elements that can be identified in it. For example, (a) language can be examined by noting the number of terms that are available (e.g., 600 camel-related terms in Arabic; many terms about automobiles in English), (b) economics by noting the number of occupations (the U.S. Employment and Training Administration's *Dictionary of Occupational Titles* contains more than 250,000), and (c) religion by noting the number of different functions (e.g., 6,000 priests in one temple in Orissa, India, each having a different function). The subject is left to the specialists such as Carneiro (1970), Lomax and Berkowitz (1972), and Murdock and Provost (1973), who do have reliable ways of measuring the construct.

One of the consequences of increased complexity is that individuals have more and more potential ingroups toward whom they may or may not be loyal. As the number of potential ingroups increases, the loyalty of individuals to any one ingroup decreases. Individuals have the option of giving priority to their personal goals rather than to the goals of an ingroup. Also, the greater the affluence of a society, the more financial independence can be turned into social and emotional independence, with the individual giving priority to personal rather than ingroup goals. Thus, as societies become more complex and affluent, they also can become more individualistic. However, there are some moderator variables that modify this simple picture, that will be discussed later, after I examine more closely the dimension of individualism—collectivism.

Individualism—Collectivism. Individualists give priority to personal goals over the goals of collectives; collectivists either make no distinctions between personal and collective goals, or if they do make such distinctions, they subordinate their personal goals to the collective goals (Triandis, Bontempo, Villareal, Asai, & Lucca, 1988). Closely related to this dimension, in the work of Hofstede (1980), is *power distance* (the tendency to see a large difference between those with power and those without power). Collectivists tend to be high in power distance.

Although the terms *individualism* and *collectivism* should be used to characterize cultures and societies, the terms *idiocentric* and *allocentric* should be used to characterize individuals. Triandis, Leung, Villareal, and Clack (1985) have shown that within culture (Illinois) there are individuals who differ on this dimension, and the idiocentrics report that they are concerned with achievement, but are lonely, whereas the allocentrics report low alienation and receiving much social support. These findings were replicated in Puerto Rico (Triandis et al., 1988). The distinction of terms at the cultural and individual levels of analysis is useful because it is convenient when discussing the behavior of allocentrics in individualist cultures and idiocentrics in collectivist cultures (e.g., Bontempo, Lobel, & Triandis, 1989).

In addition to subordinating personal to collective goals, collectivists tend to be concerned about the results of their actions on members of their ingroups, tend to share resources with ingroup members, feel interdependent with ingroup members, and feel involved in the lives of ingroup members (Hui & Triandis, 1986). They emphasize the integrity of ingroups over time and de-emphasize their independence from ingroups (Triandis et al., 1986).

Shweder's data (see Shweder & LeVine, 1984) suggest that collectivists perceive ingroup norms as universally valid (a form of ethnocentrism). A considerable literature suggests that collectivists automatically obey ingroup authorities and are willing to fight and die to maintain the integrity of the ingroup, whereas they distrust and are unwilling to cooperate with members of outgroups (Triandis, 1972). However, the definition of the ingroup keeps shifting with the situation. Common fate, common outside threat, and proximity (which is often linked to common fate) appear to be important determinants of the ingroup/outgroup boundary. Although the family is usually the most important ingroup, tribe, coworkers, co-religionists, and members of the same political or social collective or the same aesthetic or scientific persuasion can also function as important ingroups. When the state is under threat, it becomes the ingroup.

Ingroups can also be defined on the basis of similarity (in demographic attributes, activities, preferences, or institutions) and do influence social behavior to a greater extent when they are stable and impermeable (difficult to gain membership or difficult to leave). Social behavior is a function of ingroup norms to a greater extent in collectivist than individualist cultures. (Davidson, Jaccard, Triandis, Morales, and Diaz-Guerrero, 1976).

In collectivist cultures, ingroups influence a wide range of social situations (e.g., during the cultural revolution in China, the state had what was perceived as "legitimate influence" on every collective). In some cases, the influence is extreme (e.g., the Rev. Jones's People's Temple influenced 911 members of that collective to commit suicide in 1978).

In collectivist cultures, role relationships that include ingroup members are perceived as more nurturant, respectful, and intimate than they are in individualistic cultures; those that include outgroup members are perceived to be more manipulative and exploitative in collectivist than in individualist cultures (Sinha, 1982; Triandis, Vassiliou, & Nassiakou, 1968). In other words, more ingroup social relationships are communal in the collectivist and more exchange relationships can be found in the individualist cultures. Outgroup relationships follow exchange patterns everywhere.

The distinction between communal and exchange relations (Mills & Clark, 1982) is useful. The attributes of communal and exchange relationships involve a number of contrasts, such as (a) lack of clarity versus clarity about what is to be exchanged, and when and where,

(b) concern for the other person's needs versus concern for equity, (c) importance of maintaining equality of affect (if one is sad, the other is sad) as opposed to emotional detachment, (d) inequality of the benefits exchanged versus equality or equity bases of the benefits exchanged, and (e) benefits are not comparable versus benefits are comparable. Mills and Clark (1982) gave many examples in which exchange theory (e.g., Thibaut & Kelley, 1959) does not seem to provide adequate accounts of social behavior, makes predictions about the conditions under which exchange theory will be adequate, and tests experimentally some of these predictions. We expect that in collectivistic cultures the applicability of exchange theories will be more limited than in individualistic cultures.

As discussed earlier, over the course of cultural evolution there has been a shift toward individualism (i.e., exchange relationships). Content analyses of social behaviors recorded in written texts (Adamopoulos & Bontempo, 1986) across historical periods show a shift from communal to exchange relationships. Behaviors related to trading are characteristic of individualistic cultures, and contracts emancipated individuals from the bonds of tribalism (Pearson, 1977).

The distribution of collectivism–individualism, according to Hofstede's (1980) data, contrasts most of the Latin American, Asian, and African cultures with most of the North American and Northern and Western European cultures. However, many cultures are close to the middle of the dimension, and other variables are also relevant. Urban samples tend to be individualistic, and traditional–rural samples tend toward collectivism within the same culture (e.g., Greece in the work of Doumanis, 1983; Georgas, 1989; and Katakis, 1984). Within the United States one can find a good deal of range on this variable, with Hispanic samples much more collectivist than samples of Northern and Western European backgrounds (G. Marin & Triandis, 1985).

The major antecedents of individualism appear to be cultural complexity and affluence. The more complex the culture, the greater the number of ingroups that one may have, so that a person has the option of joining ingroups or even forming new ingroups. Affluence means that the individual can be independent of ingroups. If the ingroup makes excessive demands, the individual can leave it. Mobility is also important. As individuals move (migration, changes in social class) they join new ingroups, and they have the opportunity to join ingroups whose goals they find compatible with their own.

Furthermore, the more costly it is in a particular ecology for an ingroup to reject ingroup members who behave according to their own goals rather than according to ingroup goals, the more likely are people to act in accordance with their personal goals, and thus the more individualistic is the culture. Such costs are high when the ecology is thinly populated. One can scarcely afford to reject a neighbor if one has only one neighbor. Conversely, densely populated ecologies are characterized by collectivism, not only because those who behave inappropriately can be excluded, but also because it is necessary to regulate behavior more strictly to overcome problems of crowding.

As rewards from ingroup membership increase, the more likely it is that a person will use ingroup goals as guides for behavior. Thus, when ingroups provide many rewards (e.g., emotional security, status, income, information, services, willingness to spend time with the person) they tend to increase the person's commitment to the ingroup and to the culture's collectivism.

The size of ingroups tends to be different in the two kinds of cultures. In collectivist cultures, ingroups tend to be small (e.g., family), whereas in individualist cultures they can be large (e.g., people who agree with me on important attitudes).

Child-rearing patterns are different in collectivist and individualist cultures. The primary concern of parents in collectivist cultures is obedience, reliability, and proper behavior. The primary concern of parents in individualistic cultures is self-reliance, independence, and creativity. Thus, we find that in simple, agricultural societies, socialization is severe and conformity is demanded and obtained (Berry, 1967, 1979). Similarly, in working-class families in industrial societies, the socialization pattern leads to conformity (Kohn, 1969, 1987). In more individualist cultures such as food gatherers (Berry, 1979) and very individualistic cultures such as the United States, the child-rearing pattern emphasizes self-reliance and independence; children are allowed a good deal of autonomy and are encouraged to explore their environment. Similarly, creativity and self-actualization are more important traits and are emphasized in child-rearing in the professional social classes (Kohn, 1987).

It is clear that conformity is functional in simple, agricultural cultures (if one is to make an irrigation system, each person should do part of the job in a well-coordinated plan) and in working-class jobs (the boss does not want subordinates who do their own thing).

Conversely, it is disfunctional in hunting cultures, in which one must be ingenious, and in professional jobs, in which one must be creative. The greater the cultural complexity, the more is conformity to one ingroup disfunctional, inasmuch as one cannot take advantage of new opportunities available in other parts of the society.

The smaller the family size, the more the child is allowed to do his or her own thing. In large families, rules must be imposed, otherwise chaos will occur. As societies become more affluent (individualistic), they also reduce the size of the family, which increases the opportunity to raise children to be individualists. Autonomy in child-rearing also leads to individualism. Exposure to other cultures (e.g., through travel or because of societal heterogeneity) also increases individualism, inasmuch as the child becomes aware of different norms and has to choose his or her own standards of behavior.

Although both collectivism and individualism have elements that are characteristic of all collectivist and all individualist cultures (Triandis, 1978), there are also culture-specific collectivist and culture-specific individualist elements. There is a large literature that described cultural patterns, that cannot be reviewed here. Interested readers can find details about the culture-specific forms of these cultural patterns in the following publications: for collectivism in Africa (Holzberg, 1981), Bali (Geertz, 1963), China (Deem & Salaman, 1985; Feather, 1986; Hsu, 1981; Hui, 1984; Wu, 1985; Yang, 1986), Egypt (Rugh, 1985), Greece (Doumanis, 1983; Katakis, 1984; Triandis, 1972), India (Sinha, 1982), Italy (Banfield, 1958; Strodtbeck, 1958), Japan (Caudill & Scarr, 1962; Lebra, 1976; Mendenhall & Oddou, 1986), among U.S. Jews (Strodtbeck, 1958), Latin America (Diaz-Guerrero, 1979; Holtzman, Diaz-Guerrero, & Swartz, 1975; Marin & Triandis, 1985; Tallman, Marotz-Baden, & Pindas, 1983; Triandis, Marin, Hui, Lisansky, & Ottati, 1984; · Triandis, Marin, Lisansky, & Betancourt, 1984), Navaho tribes (Northrop, 1949), Philippines (Church, 1987; Guthrie, 1961), Turkey (Basaran, 1986), the USSR (Kaiser, 1984), and in U.S. corporations (Whyte, 1956). The contrasting pattern of individualism is best described for the case of the United States in such publications as Bellah, Madsen, Sullivan, Swindler, and Tipton (1985), Kerlinger (1984), Wallach and Wallach (1983), and Waterman (1984). Decision making differs in collectivist and individualist cultures (Gaenslen, 1986). A summary of the common elements that characterize the two cultural patterns can be found in Triandis et al. (1988).

Tight versus loose cultures. In collectivist cultures, ingroups demand that individuals conform to ingroup norms, role definitions, and values. When a society is relatively homogeneous, the norms and values of ingroups are similar. But heterogeneous societies have groups with dissimilar norms. If an ingroup member deviates from ingroup norms, ingroup members may have to make the painful decision of excluding that individual from the ingroup. Because rejection of ingroup members is emotionally draining, cultures develop tolerance for deviation from group norms. As a result, homogeneous cultures are often rigid in requiring that ingroup members behave according to the ingroup norms. Such cultures are *tight.* Heterogeneous cultures and cultures in marginal positions between two major cultural patterns are flexible in dealing with ingroup members who deviate from ingroup norms. For example, Japan is considered tight, and it is relatively homogeneous. Thailand is considered loose, and it is in a marginal position between the major cultures of India and China; people are pulled in different directions by sometimes contrasting norms, and hence they must be more flexible in imposing their norms. In short, tight cultures (Pelto, 1968) have clear norms that are reliably imposed. Little deviation from normative behavior is tolerated, and severe sanctions are administered to those who deviate. *Loose* cultures either have unclear norms about most social situations or tolerate deviance from the norms. For example, it is widely reported in the press that Japanese children who return to Japan after a period of residence in the West, are criticized most severely by teachers because their behavior is not "proper." Japan is a tight culture in which deviations that would be considered trivial in the West (such as bringing Western food rather than Japanese food for lunch) are noted and criticized. In loose cultures, deviations from "proper" behavior are tolerated, and in many cases there are no standards of "proper" behavior. Theocracies are prototypical of tight cultures, but some contemporary relatively homogeneous cultures (e.g., the Greeks, the Japanese) are also relatively tight. In a heterogeneous culture, such as the United States, it is more difficult for people to agree on specific norms, and even more difficult to impose severe sanctions. Geographic mobility allows people to leave the offended communities in ways that are not available in more stable cultures. Urban environments are more loose than rural environments, in which norms are clearer and sanctions can be imposed more easily. Prototypical of loose cultures are the Lapps and the Thais. In very tight cultures, according to Pelto, one finds corporate control of property, corporate ownership of stored food and production power, religious figures as leaders, hereditary recruitment into priesthood, and high levels of taxation.

The latter list of attributes suggests that collectivism and tightness are related, but the two cultural patterns can be kept distinct for analytical purposes. It is theoretically possible for a group to be collectivist (give priority to ingroup goals) yet allow considerable deviation from group norms before imposing sanctions. For example, a group may have the norm that group goals should be given priority over personal goals, but may do nothing when individuals deviate substantially from that norm. A case reported in the Chinese press (*Peking Daily,* May 1987) is interesting: A student, whose behavior was bizarre, was assumed to be an "individualist" and was not diagnosed as mentally ill until he killed a fellow student, at which point the authorities took action. China is a collectivist, but "relatively" loose culture.

The intolerance of inappropriate behavior characteristic of tight cultures does not extend to all situations. In fact, tight cultures are quite tolerant of foreigners (they do not know better), and of drunk, and mentally ill persons. They may even have rituals in which inappropriate behavior is expected. For example, in a tight culture such as Japan one finds the office beer party as a ritual institution, where one is expected to get drunk and to tell the boss what one "really" thinks of him (it is rarely her). Similarly, in loose cultures, there are specific situations in which deviance is not tolerated. For example, in Orissa (India), a son who cuts his hair the day after his father dies is bound to be severely criticized, although the culture is generally loose.

Relationships Among Dimensions of Cultural Variation. Individualism is related to complexity according to a curvilinear function, because protoindividualism is found in nomadic groups of food gatherers. Such groups, although characterized by intensive involvement with a family or band, allow individuals to have considerable freedom of action outside the collective because it is more effective to gather food in a dispersed rather than in a collective manner. In agricultural societies one finds high levels of collectivism, and most theocracies have an agricultural basis. In modern industrial settings one finds neoindividualism, in which, again, a small group, the family or the work group, plays an important role in determining behavior, but the individual has considerable freedom of action outside the group. Because complexity increases from food gathering, to agricultural, to industrial societies, the relationship of individualism and complexity is curvilinear.

Child-rearing patterns also follow a curvilinear pattern with complexity. Simple food gathering and hunting cultures tend to socialize their children with emphasis on independence and self-reliance; agricultural, more complex cultures, tend to emphasize obedience; very complex industrial cultures, particularly among cognitive complex (professionals, upper class) subsamples, emphasize, again, independence and self reliance (Berry, 1967, 1979; Kohn, 1969, 1987).

Cultural complexity and tightness are not related; it is possible to identify types of cultures in the four quadrants defined by these two variables: Boldt (1978) has described the loose/complex quadrant as characteristic of the industrial democracies, the tight/complex quadrant as characteristic of the totalitarian industrial states, the loose/simple quadrant as characteristic of hunters and gatherers, and the tight/simple quadrant as characteristic of the agricultural simple cultures.

Finally, the relationship between collectivism and tightness is likely to be linear, but probably not very strong. Because the two constructs have different antecedents (collectivism = common fate, limited resources that must be divided in order to survive; tightness = cultural homogeneity, isolation from external cultural influences), we can expect many exceptions from the pattern of tightness and collectivism versus looseness and individualism.

I have defined the dimensions of cultural complexity, individualism, and tightness. In the next section I examine how these dimensions influence the probability that the private, public, or collective self will be sampled, and hence the patterns of social behavior that are most likely in different cultures.

CULTURE AND SELF

Culture is to society what memory is to the person. It specifies designs for living that have proven effective in the past, ways of dealing with social situations, and ways to think about the self and social behavior that have been reinforced in the past. It includes systems of symbols that facilitate interaction (Geertz, 1973), rules of the game of life that have been shown to "work" in the past. When a person is socialized in a given culture, the person can use custom as a substitute for thought, and save time.

The three dimensions of cultural variation just described reflect variations in culture that have emerged because of different ecologies, such as ways of surviving. Specifically, in cultures that survive through hunting or food gathering, in which people are more likely to survive if they work alone or in small groups because game is dispersed, individualism emerges as a good design for living. In agricultural cultures, in which cooperation in the building of irrigation systems and food storage and distribution facilities is reinforced, collectivists designs for living emerge. In complex, industrial cultures, in which loosely linked ingroups produce the thousands of parts of modern machines (e.g., a 747 airplane), individuals often find themselves in situations in which they have to choose ingroups or even form their own ingroups (e.g., new corporation). Again, individualistic designs for living become more functional. In homogeneous cultures, one can insist on tight norm enforcement; in heterogeneous, or fast changing, or marginal (e.g., confluence of two major cultural traditions) cultures, the imposition of tight norms is difficult because it is unclear whose norms are to be used. A loose culture is more likely in such ecologies.

Over time, cultures become more complex, as new differentiations prove effective. However, once complexity reaches very high levels, moves toward simplification emerge as reactions to too much complexity. For example, in art styles, the pendulum has been swinging between the "less is more" view of Oriental art and the "more is better" view of the Roccoco period in Europe. Similarly, excessive individualism may create a reaction toward collectivism, and excessive collectivism, a reaction toward individualism; or tightness may result from too much looseness, and looseness from too much tightness. Thus, culture is dynamic, ever changing.

Similarly the self is dynamic, ever changing. It changes in different environments (e.g., school vs. home, see McGuire, McGuire, & Cheever, 1986), when the group climates are different (e.g., Aronson, 1986), or when drugs are used (e.g., Hull, 1986).

The three dimensions of cultural variation described earlier are systematically linked to different kinds of self. In this section I provide hypotheses linking culture and self.

Individualism—Collectivism

Child-rearing patterns in individualistic cultures tend to emphasize self-reliance, independence, finding yourself, and self-actualization. As discussed earlier, such child-rearing increases the complexity of the private self, and because there are more elements of the private self to be sampled, more are sampled. Thus, the probability that the private rather than the other selves will be sampled increases with individualism. Conversely, in collectivist cultures, child-rearing emphasizes the importance of the collective; the collective self is more complex and more likely to be sampled.

The expected lower rates of sampling of the collective self in individualistic cultures was obtained by Triandis in research to be reported. University of Hawaii students of Northern European backgrounds were compared with University of Hawaii students of Japanese, Chinese, or Filipino backgrounds. The mean percentages of their responses that referred to a "social category" (family, ethnicity, occupation, institution, religious group, or gender), after completing 20 sentences that started with "I am. . . ." were 17 to 21 for students of different European backgrounds and 19 to 29 for students of Asian and Pacific backgrounds. When a sample of students from the University of Illinois (n = 159) was compared with another sample from Hawaii (n = 64), the mean social category responses from Illinois were 19% and from Hawaii 29%. Social psychology students (n = 118) from the University of Athens, Greece, who were found to be quite individualistic by other measurements, had a mean of 15%; social psychology students from the University of Hong Kong (n = 112), who are fast becoming individualistic but still have collectivist tendencies, had a mean of 20%;[1] university graduates from the Peoples' Republic of China (PRC; n = 34) attending a course taught by Triandis had a mean of 52%.

One can ask what social categories constituted these percentages. An Illinois sample of 188 men and 202 women indicated that family and educational institution were the most important categories. Family was more important for the women (2.0 average availability vs. 1.4 for men, $p < .001$; average accessibility of 12 for women vs. 9 for men, $p < .000$), but athletic club was more important for men than for women (1.2 in availability vs. 0.5, $p < .000$; 8 in accessibility vs. 4, $p < .000$, respectively). Gender was more accessible to the women than to the men (11 vs. 8, $p < .002$, respectively). Similarly, family was most important for the PRC sample. Athletic club, religion, age, and race were categories used by Americans but not by the PRC, whereas work unit, Communist Party, and "mass clubs" (e.g., chess club) were used by the PRC but not by the American samples. The Greek samples were like the U.S. sample; specifically, the Greek women were much like the U.S. women (e.g., gender was more important for them than it was for the Greek men).

Of course, samples of students are unusual (Sears, 1986), and from our theoretical perspective, they should be highly individualistic. It seems likely that nonliterate populations, with few ingroups, will give a larger percentage of their responses as social categories. Furthermore, keeping literacy levels constant, one would expect a curvilinear relationship between the hunting/gathering-agricultural-industrial continuum and percentage social category, with a maximum to be obtained in agricultural samples.

Social class should also moderate the sampling of the collective self. One expects upper-middle- and upper-class individuals to sample the collective self less frequently than lower class individuals, although lower lower-class individuals may again sample more the private self. This expectation derives from reliable differences in child-rearing patterns (Kohn, 1969, 1987), which indicate that in many societies (Italy, Japan, Poland, the U.S.) child-rearing emphasizes conformity to family norms in the lower classes and self-direction, creativity, and independence from the ingroup in the upper social classes. The lower lower class might be an exception, because the evidence (see Triandis, 1976) is that, in that case, the social environment often appears to them to be chaotic. It seems difficult to sample chaos.

The less people sample the collective self, the more confusing should be their social identity. This is consistent with Tajfel's (1978) definition of identity, Baumeister's (1986a) discussion of the trivialization of ascribed attributes between the 16th and the 20th centuries, and Dragonas's (1983) studies of the self-concepts of 11- and 12-year-olds in small villages, transitional cities, and a large city.

Factors that increase ethnocentrism (LeVine & Campbell, 1972), such as external threat, competition with outgroups, and common fate, should also increase the probability that the collective self will be sampled.

Homogeneous relatively isolated cultures tend to be tight, and they will sample the collective self more than heterogeneous, centrally located cultures. This follows from perceptual mechanisms that are well-known. Quattrone (1986) reviewed perceptual studies that indicate that people who have few exposures to stimuli that have both common and distinct features tend to notice and remember the common elements first and the diverse elements only after many exposures to the stimulus set. Homogeneous, isolated cultures are primarily exposed to their particular ingroups, and so are likely to sample the collective self.

As indicated earlier, collectivism is associated with child-rearing patterns that emphasize conformity, obedience, and reliability. Such patterns are usually associated with rewards for conformity to ingroup goals, which leads to internalization of the ingroup goals. Thus, people do what is expected of them, even if that is not enjoyable. Bontempo et al. (1989) randomly assigned subjects from a collectivist (Brazil) and an individualist (U.S.) culture to two conditions of questionnaire administration: public and private. The questionnaire contained questions about how the subject was likely to act when the ingroup expected a behavior that was costly to the individual (e.g., visit a friend in the hospital, when this was time consuming). Both of the questions How should the person act? and How enjoyable would it be to act? were measured. It was found that Brazilians gave the same answers under both the anonymous and public conditions. Under both conditions they indicated that they would do what was expected of them. The U.S. sample indicated they would do what was expected of them in the public but not in the private condition. The U.S. group's private answers indicated that the subjects thought that doing the costly behaviors was unlikely, and certainly not enjoyable. Under the very same conditions the Brazilians indicated that they thought the costly prosocial behaviors were likely and enjoyable. In short, the Brazilians had internalized the ingroup norms so that conformity to the ingroup appeared enjoyable to them.

When ingroups have resources that allow them to reward those who conform with ingroup norms and provide sanctions to those who do not conform, one expects individuals to sample the collective self more than when ingroups do not have such resources. This is derived directly from behavior theory. Anthropological observations are also consistent with it. For example, in the case of extreme lack of resources, such as was observed among the Ik (Turnbull, 1972), basic family structures and norms became irrelevant and did not regulate behavior.

The size of ingroups has some relevance to the question of sampling of the collective self. Very large ingroups (e.g., mankind) have very few (e.g., survival) and unclear goals and norms. The very definition of norm implies agreement. When the ingroup is large it is unlikely that monolithic conceptions of correct behavior will be found. Also, small ingroups, such as the nuclear family, can notice deviations from norms more readily and provide sanctions. Thus, we expect that the larger the size of the ingroup, the lower the probability that the collective self will be sampled. The data from Hawaii and Illinois, mentioned earlier, agree with this derivation. For example, the religious group (e.g., I am Roman Catholic) is clearly larger than the family and was mentioned less frequently than an educational institution (e.g., I am a student at the University of Hawaii), occupation (e.g., I am a computer programmer), ethnic group (e.g., I am a Japanese American), or the family. Very large ingroups (I am a citizen of the world) were mentioned by only 2 individuals out of a sample of 183.

Observations indicate that the extent to which an ingroup makes demands on individuals in few or in many areas shows considerable variance. For example, in the United States, states make very few demands (e.g., pay your income tax), whereas in China during the cultural revolution, the Communist Party made demands in many areas (artistic expression, family life, political behavior, civic action, education, athletics, work groups, even location, such as where to live). It seems plausible that the more areas of one's life that are affected by an ingroup, the more likely the individual is to sample the collective self. We do not yet have such data, but plan to collect them.

When individuals have *few* ingroups, they are more dependent on them. It follows that they are more likely to sample the collective self when they have fewer than when they have many ingroups. When *many* ingroups are salient, conflicting norms lead individuals to turn inward to decide what to do. Thus, they are more likely to sample the private self. But the resources available to the ingroups will moderate this tendency. An ingroup with large resources (e.g., a rich family) can "control" the individual even when other ingroups make conflicting demands. As conflict among ingroups increases, the individual will be more aware of the ingroups in conflict and hence will be more likely to sample the collective self.

Ingroups clearly vary in stability. A friendship group formed at a Saturday night party will have an impact during the period it is in existence, but will have little influence later. If an individual has stable ingroups there is a greater probability that the collective self will be sampled. Also, stable ingroups can reward and punish over long time periods, and thus will have to be considered by individuals more often than unstable ingroups.

We expect people in the more complex, individualistic, and loose cultures to sample the private self more than the public self, because complexity, individualism, and looseness lead to a more complex private self. Complexity means that if a person is not accepted by an ingroup, there will be other ingroups to which to turn; individualism means that the individual is not so attached to the ingroup that conformity to the ingroup is always essential; looseness means that if the person acts consistently with the private self, the ingroup will tolerate the behavior. Conversely, in collectivism, the opposite conditions are important; hence, there is more sampling of the public self. This is particularly the case if the culture is both collectivist and tight. I discuss the sampling of the private and public selves more extensively under cultural tightness.

Tight—Loose Cultures

Homogeneous, relatively isolated cultures tend to be tight, and they will sample the collective self more than will heterogeneous, centrally located cultures. The more homogeneous the culture, the more the norms will be clear and deviation from normative behavior can be punished. Cultural heterogeneity increases the confusion regarding what is correct and proper behavior. Also, cultural marginality tends to result in norm and role conflict and pressures individuals toward adopting different norms. Because rejection of the ingroup members who have adopted norms of a different culture can be costly, individuals moderate their need to make their ingroup members conform to their ideas of proper behavior. So, the culture becomes loose (i.e., tolerant of deviations from norms).

The looser the culture, the more the individual can choose what self to sample. If several kinds of collective self are available, one may choose to avoid norm and role conflict by rejecting all of them and developing individual conceptions of proper behavior. Thus, sampling of the private self is more likely in loose cultures and sampling of the collective self is more likely in tight cultures. Also, tight cultures tend to socialize their children by emphasizing the expectations of the generalized other. Hence, the public self will be complex and will be more likely to be sampled. In other words, tight cultures tend to sample the public and collective self, whereas loose cultures tend to sample the private self.

When the culture is both collectivist and tight, then the public self is extremely likely to be sampled. That means people act "properly," as that is defined by society, and are extremely anxious in case they do not act correctly. Their private self does not matter. As a result, the private and public selves are often different. Doi (1986) discussed this point extensively, comparing the Japanese public self *(tatemae)* with the private self *(honne)*. He suggested that in the United States there is virtue in keeping public and private consistent (not being a hypocrite). In Japan, proper action matters. What you feel about such action is irrelevant. Thus, the Japanese do not like to state their personal opinions, but rather seek consensus.

Consistently with Doi's (1986) arguments is Iwao's (1988) research. She presented scenarios to Japanese and Americans and asked them to judge various actions that could be appropriate responses to these situations. For example, one scenario (daughter brings home person from another race) included as a possible response "thought that he would never allow them to marry but told them he was in favor of their marriage." This response was endorsed as the *best* by 44% of the Japanese sample but by only 2% of the Americans; it was the *worst* in the opinion of 48% of the Americans and 7% of the Japanese.

Although the private self may be complex, this does not mean that it will be communicated to others if one can avoid such communication. In fact, in tight cultures people avoid disclosing much of the self, because by disclosing they may reveal some aspect of the self that others might criticize. In other words, they may be aware of the demands of the generalized other and avoid being vulnerable to criticism by presenting little of this complex self to others. Barlund (1975) reported studies of the self-disclosure to same-sex friend, opposite-sex friend, mother, father, stranger, and untrusted acquaintance in Japan and in the United States. The pattern of self-disclosure was the same—that is, more to same-sex friend, and progressively less to opposite-sex friend, mother, father, stranger, and least to the untrusted acquaintance. However, the amount disclosed in each relationship was about 50% more in the United States than in Japan.

Cultural Complexity

The more complex the culture, the more confused is likely to be the individual's identity. Dragonas (1983) sampled the self-concepts of 11- and 12-year-olds in Greek small villages (simple), traditional cities (medium), and large cities (complex) cultures. She found that the more complex the culture, the more confusing was the identity. Similarly, Katakis (1976, 1978, 1984) found that the children of farmers and fisherman, when asked what they would be when they are old, unhesitatingly said *farmer* or *fisherman,* whereas in the large cities the responses frequently were of the "I will find myself" variety. Given the large number of ingroups that are available in a complex environment and following the logic presented here, individuals may well opt for sampling their private self and neglect the public or collective selves.

Content of Self in Different Cultures

The specific content of the self in particular cultures will reflect the language and availability of mythological constructs of that culture. Myths often provide ideal types that are incorporated in the self forged in a given culture (Roland, 1984a). For example, peace of mind and being free of worries have been emphasized as aspects of the self in India (Roland, 1984b) and reflect Indian values that are early recognizable in Hinduism and Buddhism (which emerged in India). Mythological, culture-specific constructs become incorporated in the self (Sinha, 1982, 1987b). Roland (1984b) claimed that the private self is more "organized around 'we', 'our' and 'us' . . ." in India than in the West. But particular life events may be linked to more than one kind of self. For example, Sinha (1987b) found that the important goals of Indian managers are their own good health and the good health of their family (i.e., have both private and collective self-elements).

Sinha (personal communication, November 1985) believes the public self is different in collectivist and individualist cultures. In individualistic cultures it is assumed that the generalized other will value autonomy, independence, and self-reliance, and thus individuals will attempt to act in ways that will impress others (i.e., indicate that they have these attributes). To be distinct and different are highly valued, and people find innumerable ways to show themselves to others as different (in dress, possessions, speech patterns). By contrast, in collectivist cultures, conformity to the other in public settings is valued. Thus, in a restaurant, everyone orders the same food (in traditional restaurants, only the visible leader gets a menu and orders for all). The small inconvenience of eating nonoptimal food is more than compensated by the sense of solidarity that such actions generate. In collectivist cultures, being "nice" to ingroup others is a high value, so that one expects in most situations extreme politeness and a display of harmony (Triandis, Marin, Lisansky, & Betancourt, 1984). Thus, in collectivist cultures, the public self is an extension of the collective self. One must make a good impression by means of prosocial behaviors toward ingroup members, acquaintances, and others who may become ingroup members. At the same time, one can be quite rude to outgroup members, and there is no concern about displaying hostility, exploitation, or avoidance of outgroup members.

The collective self, in collectivist cultures, may be structured in concentric circles (Hsu, 1985). Hsu distinguishes eight layers, from the unconscious self to the self facing the "outer world" of strangers. However, this much refinement of concepts seems difficult to test empirically.

The collective self in collectivist cultures includes elements such as "I am philotimos" (traditional Greece, meaning "I must act as is expected of me by my family and friends"; see Triandis, 1972), "I must sacrifice myself for my ingroup," "I feel good when I display affection toward my ingroup," and "I must maintain harmony with my ingroup even when that is very disagreeable." The person is less self-contained in collectivist than in individualistic cultures (Roland, 1984).

Identity is defined on the basis of different elements in individualistic and collectivist cultures. Individualistic cultures tend to emphasize elements of identity that reflect possessions—what do I own, what experiences have I had, what are my accomplishments (for scientists, what is my list of publications). In collectivist cultures, identity is defined more in terms of relationships—I am the mother of X, I am a member of family Y, and I am a resident of Z. Furthermore, the qualities that are most important in forming an identity can be quite different. In Europe and North America, being logical, rational, balanced, and fair are important attributes; in Africa, personal style, ways of moving, the unique spontaneous self, sincere self-expression, unpredictability, and emotional expression are most valued. The contrast between classical music (e.g., Bach or Mozart) and jazz reflects this difference musically.

Consequences of Sampling the Private and Collective Self

In the previous section I examined the relationship between the three dimensions of cultural variation and the probabilities of differential sampling of the private, public, and collective selves. In this section I review some of the empirical literature that is relevant to the theoretical ideas just presented.

An important consequence of sampling the collective self is that many of the elements of the collective become salient. Norms, roles, and values (i.e., proper ways of acting as defined by the collective) become the "obviously" correct ways to act. Behavioral intentions reflect such processes. Thus, the status of the other person in the social interaction—for example, is the other an ingroup or an outgroup member—becomes quite salient. Consequently, in collectivist cultures, individuals pay more attention to ingroups and outgroups and moderate their behavior accordingly, than is the case in individualistic cultures (Triandis, 1972).

Evidence in support of this point has been provided by a study of Gudykunst, Yoon, and Nishida (1987), who had subjects from Korea (very collectivist), Japan (somewhat collectivist), and the United States (very individualistic culture) interact with ingroup members (classmates) and outgroup members (strangers). After the interaction, the subjects rated several attributes of the interaction, such as the degree of intimacy, depth, breadth, coordination, and the difficulty they experienced during the interaction. A LISREL analysis showed the same structures of the rated attributes in the three cultures. The factors were called *personalization* (intimate, deep, broad, flexible, spontaneous, smooth, and satisfying interactions), *synchronization* (effortless, well coordinated), and *difficulty*. As expected, in collectivist cultures, interacting with ingroup members was more personalized and synchronized and less difficult than in individualistic cultures. The difference when interacting with the ingroup and the outgroup was larger in the collectivist than in the individualist cultures. The size of t tests for the ingroup versus the outgroup ratings of the interaction is suggestive. Although all of them were significant at $p < .001$, their sizes were as follows: for personalization, United States, 5.9, Japan, 9.9, and Korea, 12.2; for synchronization, United States, 7.1, Japan, 8.9, and Korea, 9.2; and for difficulty, United States, 4.9, Japan, 7.7, and Korea, 10.9. Thus, the more collectivist the culture, the more of a difference there is in the ingroup and outgroup interactions.

Who is placed in the ingroup is culture specific. For example, ratings of the "intimacy" of relationships on a 9-point scale suggest that in Japan there is more intimacy with acquaintances, coworkers, colleagues, best friends, and close friends than in the United States (Gudykunst & Nishida, 1986).

Atsumi (1980) argued that understanding Japanese social behavior requires distinguishing relationships with benefactors, true friends, coworkers, acquaintances, and outsiders (strangers). The determinants of social behavior shift depending on this classification. Behavior toward benefactors requires that the person go out of his way to benefit them. Behavior toward true friends is largely determined by the extent the behavior is enjoyable in itself, and the presence of these friends makes it enjoyable. Behavior toward coworkers is determined by both norms and cost/benefit considerations. Finally, behavior toward outsiders is totally determined by cost/benefit ratios.

Because individualistic cultures tend to be more complex (industrial, affluent), individuals can potentially be members of more ingroups (Verma, 1985). If required behavior toward each ingroup is somewhat distinct, individuals should be higher in self-monitoring in individualistic than in collectivist cultures. Support for this prediction was obtained by Gudykunst, Yang, and Nishida (1987). They developed Korean and Japanese versions of the self-monitoring scale and found that the U.S. mean was higher than the Korean or Japanese means.

Forgas and Bond (1985) asked collectivist (Hong Kong) and individualist (Australian) subjects to make multidimensional scaling judgments involving 27 episodes (e.g., arrive very late for a tutorial). They also used semantic differential scales to interpret the dimensions that did underlie these judgments. They found rather similar dimensions discriminating among the 27 episodes in the two cultures. However, the most important dimension (on the basis of variance accounted for) for the Hong Kong sample was not found in Australia, and the most important Australian dimension was not found in Hong Kong. The Hong Kong culture-specific dimension reflected inequalities of power, communal versus isolated episodes, and commonplace versus rare incidents. The semantic differential scales related to it were pleasant—unpleasant, communal—individualistic, and unequal—equal. Another Chinese dimension, only weakly present in Australia, included the intimate—nonintimate, involving—superficial, and pleasant—unpleasant scales. These ideas are clearly linked to collectivism, where pleasant, unequal, intimate, involving interactions are typical of relationships within the ingroup.

The Australian culture-specific dimension that discriminated the episodes reflected competitiveness: the scales, cooperation versus competition, pleasant versus unpleasant, relaxed versus anxious, and self-confident versus apprehensive. In a collectivist culture, then, the episodes were discriminated in terms of whether they had qualities found in ingroup or outgroup relationships, whereas in an individualistic culture they were discriminated in terms of cooperation versus competition.

Although the concepts ingroup—outgroup and cooperation—competition are parallel, there is a difference. There is a rigidity, inflexibility, difficulty of moving from group to group in the ingroup—outgroup distinction that is not present in the cooperation—competition contrast. One can think of athletic games in which a player moves from team to team, switching from cooperation to competition as a characteristic of individualism, whereas in collectivist cultures, mobility is less common.

The behavioral intentions of persons in collectivist cultures appear to be determined by cognitions that are related to the survival and benefit of their collective. In individualist cultures, the concerns are personal. An example comes from a study of smoking. A collectivist sample (Hispanics in the U.S.) showed significantly more concern than an individualist sample (non-Hispanics) about smoking affecting the health of others, giving a bad example to children, harming children, and bothering others with the bad smell of cigarettes, bad breath, and bad smell on clothes and belongings, whereas the individualist sample was more concerned about the physiological symptoms they might experience during withdrawal from cigarette smoking (Marin, Marin, Otero-Sabogal, Sabogal, & Perez-Stable, 1987).

The emphasis on harmony within the ingroup, found more strongly in collectivist than in individualist cultures, results in the more positive evaluation of group-serving partners (Bond, Chiu, & Wan, 1984), the choice of conflict resolution techniques that minimize animosity (Leung, 1985, 1987), the greater giving of social support (Triandis et al., 1985), and the greater support of ingroup goals (Nadler, 1986). The emphasis on harmony may be, in part, the explanation of the lower heart-attack rates among unacculturated than among acculturated Japanese-Americans (Marmot & Syme, 1976). Clearly, a society in which confrontation is common is more likely to increase the blood pressure of those in such situations, and hence the probability of heart attacks; avoiding conflict and saving face must be linked to lower probabilities that blood pressure will become elevated. The probability of receiving social support in collectivist cultures may be another factor reducing the levels of stress produced by unpleasant life events and hence the probabilities of heart attacks (Triandis et al., 1988).

Although ideal ingroup relationships are expected to be smoother, more intimate, and easier in collectivist cultures, outgroup relationships can be quite difficult. Because the ideal social behaviors often cannot be attained, one finds many splits of the ingroup in collectivist cultures. Avoidance relationships are frequent and, in some cases, required by norms (e.g., mother-in-law avoidance in some cultures). Fights over property are common and result in redefinitions of the ingroup. However, once the ingroup is defined, relationships tend to be very supportive and intimate within the ingroup, whereas there is little trust and often hostility toward outgroup members. Gabrenya and Barba (1987) found that collectivists are not as effective in meeting strangers as are individualists. Triandis (1967) found unusually poor communication among members of the same corporation who were not ingroup members (close friends) in a collectivist culture. Bureaucracies in collectivist cultures function especially badly because people hoard information (Kaiser, 1984). Manipulation and exploitation of outgroups is common (Pandey, 1986) in collectivist cultures. When competing with outgroups, collectivists are more competitive than individualists (Espinoza & Garza, 1985) even under conditions when competitiveness is counterproductive.

In individualistic cultures, people exchange compliments more frequently than in collectivist cultures (Barlund & Araki, 1985). They meet people easily and are able to cooperate with them even if they do not know them well (Gabrenya & Barba, 1987). Because individualists have more of a choice concerning ingroup member-ships, they stay in those groups with whom they can have relatively good relationships and leave groups with whom they disagree too frequently (Verma, 1985).

Competition tends to be interpersonal in individualistic and in-tergroup in collectivist cultures (Hsu, 1983; Triandis et al., 1988). Conflict is frequently found in family relationships in individualistic cultures and between families in collectivist cultures (Katakis, 1978).

There is a substantial literature (e.g., Berman, Murphy-Berman, & Singh, 1985; Berman, Murphy-Berman, Singh, & Kumar, 1984; Hui, 1984; Marin, 1985; Triandis et al., 1985) indicating that individualists are more likely to use equity, and collectivists to use equality or need, as the norms for the distribution of resources (Yang, 1981). This is consistent with the emphasis on trading discussed earlier. By contrast, the emphasis on communal relationships (Mills & Clark, 1982) found in collectivist cultures leads to emphases on equality and need. The parallel with gender differences, where men emphasize exchange and women emphasize communal relationships (i.e., equity and need; Major & Adams, 1983; Brockner & Adsit, 1986), respectively, is quite striking. Private self-consciousness, also, tends to result in the use of equity, whereas public self-consciousness increases the probability that the equality norm will be used (Carver & Scheier, 1985).

Situational Determinants of Emphases on Different Selves

In addition to culture, the situation determines how the self is sam-pled. Sampling of the collective self is more likely and more detailed (Lobel, 1986) when the ingroup is distinctive in the particular situa-tion (McGuire, McGuire, Child, and Fujioka, 1978). In public situa-tions, such as when the person is identified by name or has to "per-form" in public, the public self is more likely to be sampled. In private situations, as when the individual is anonymous or deindivi-duated (e.g., Zimbardo, 1969), the public self may not be sampled at all. In situations in which future interaction between the person and others is expected, the public self is more likely to be sampled. Although a camera is likely to engage the public self, a mirror is likely to emphasize the private self (Scheier & Carver, 1980). In situations in which no future interaction with another is expected, the private self will be emphasized.

There is evidence that insecure (Bettelheim & Janowitz, 1950; Triandis & Triandis, 1960) and cognitively simple (Rokeach, 1960) individuals are more likely to conform to ingroup norms. It seems plausible that the same conditions will result in greater sampling of the collective self.

To the extent that ingroup membership is rewarding (e.g., confers high status), that there is competition with outgroups, that the ingroup is frequently mentioned in childhood socialization (e.g., patriotic songs are frequently used in schools), and that the ingroup has distinct norms and values from other salient groups, we also expect that the collective self will be sampled.

The greater an individual's dependence on a collective, the more likely it is that the individual will sample the collective self.

In many nonliterate cultures, survival depends on resources that are scarce and unpredictable. Social patterns are often found that increase the probability of survival by sharing resources. For example (see Triandis et al. 1988, for a review), in many such cultures, after hunting, one is expected to divide the food among ingroup members, or there is a strong preference for food grown by another rather than oneself. Such patterns increase interdependence. It seems plausible that they will be associated with greater sampling of the collective and public self.

In simple, noncomplex cultures there are, by definition, fewer potential ingroups. When there are few ingroups, an ingroup has a greater probability of influencing its members; hence, we expect greater sampling of the collective self. Also, in simple cultures, both groups and individuals have fewer goals (often just the goal of survival), and thus the probability of overlap of group/individual goals is higher. As cultural complexity increases, so does the number of goals and so does the probability that the goals will not overlap, and hence the greater the sampling of the private self.

Nail's (1986) useful analysis of social responses when the individual is under the influence of others emphasizes eight types of responses to pressures from others. The analysis is focused on the public and private self, but the very same analysis can also be done with the collective and private selves.

CONCLUSIONS

Aspects of the self (private, public, and collective) are differentially sampled in different cultures, depending on the complexity, level of individualism, and looseness of the culture. The more complex, individualistic, and loose the culture, the more likely it is that people will sample the private self and the less likely it is that they will sample the collective self. When people sample the collective self, they are more likely to be influenced by the norms, role definitions, and values of the particular collective, than when they do not sample the collective self. When they are so influenced by a collective, they are likely to behave in ways considered appropriate by members of that collective. The more they sample the private self, the more their behavior can be accounted for by exchange theory and can be described as an exchange relationship. The more they sample the collective self, the less their behavior can be accounted for by exchange theory; it can be described as a communal relationship. However, social behavior is more likely to be communal when the target of that behavior is an ingroup member than when the target is an outgroup member. Ingroups are defined by common goals, common fate, the presence of an external threat, and/or the need to distribute resources to all ingroup members for the optimal survival of the ingroup. Outgroups consist of people with whom one is in competition or whom one does not trust. The ingroup—outgroup distinction determines social behavior more strongly in collectivist than in individualist cultures. When the culture is both collectivist and tight, the public self is particularly likely to be sampled. In short, a major determinant of social behavior is the kind of self that operates in the particular culture.

NOTES

C. Harry Hui and J. B. P. Sinha made important suggestions that helped in the development of the theoretical argument presented here. Helpful comments on an earlier version of the article were made by R. Bontempo, R. Brislin, J. Georgas, S. Lobel, G. Marin, and C. Scott.
1. I thank James Georgas of the University of Athens, and Harry Hui of the University of Hong Kong, who collected this data from their social psychology classes.

REFERENCES

Adamopoulos, J., & Bontempo, R. N. (1986). Diachronic universals in interpersonal structures. *Journal of Cross-Cultural Psychology, 17,* 169–189.

Allport, G. W. (1943). The ego in contemporary psychology. *Psychological Review, 50,* 451–478.

Allport, G. W. (1955). *Becoming.* New Haven, CT: Yale University Press.

Aronson, E. (1986, April). *Increasing and decreasing self-esteem in educational settings.* Paper presented at the meeting of Polish and American social psychologists at the Educational Testing Service, Princeton, New Jersey.

Atsumi, R. (1980). Patterns of personal relationships: A key to understanding Japanese thought and behavior. *Social Analysis, 6,* 63–78.

Banfield, E. (1958). *The moral basis of a backward society.* Glencoe, IL: Free Press.

Barlund, D. C. (1975). *Public and private self in Japan and the United States.* Tokyo: Simul Press.

Barlund, D. C., & Araki, S. (1985). Intercultural encounters: The management of compliments by Japanese and Americans. *Journal of Cross-Cultural Psychology, 16,* 9–26.

Basaran, F. (1986, July). *University students' values in Turkey.* Paper presented at the International Congress of the International Association of Cross-Cultural Psychology, Istanbul, Turkey.

Baumeister, R. F. (1986a). *Identity: Cultural change and the struggle for self.* New York: Oxford University Press.

Baumeister, R. F. (1986b). *Public self and private self.* New York: Springer.

Baumeister, R. F. (1987). How the self became a problem: A psychological review of historical research. *Journal of Personality and Social Psychology, 52,* 163–176.

Bellah, R. N., Madsen, R., Sullivan, W. M., Swindler, A., & Tipton, S. M. (1985). *Habits of the heart: Individualism and commitment in American life.* Berkeley: University of California Press.

Berman, J. J., Murphy-Berman, V., & Singh, P. (1985). Cross-cultural similarities and differences in perceptions of fairness. *Journal of Cross Cultural Psychology, 16,* 55–67.

Berman, J. J., Murphy-Berman, V., Singh, P., & Kumar, P. (1984, September). *Cross-cultural similarities and differences in perceptions of fairness.* Paper presented at the International Congress of Psychology, in Acapulco, Mexico.

Berry, J. W. (1967). Independence and conformity in subsistence level societies. *Journal of Personality and Social Psychology, 7,* 415–418.

Berry, J. W. (1979). A cultural ecology of social behavior. In L. Berkowitz (Ed.), *Advances in experimental social psychology* (Vol. 12, pp. 177–207). New York: Academic Press.

Bettelheim, B., & Janowitz, J. (1950). *Dynamics of prejudice.* New York: Harper.

Bharati, A. (1985). The self in Hindu thought and action. In A. J. Marsella, G. DeVos, & F. L. K. Hsu, *Culture and self* (pp. 185–230). New York: Tavistock Publications.

Block, J. (1986, March). *Longitudinal studies of personality.* Colloquium given at the University of Illinois, Psychology Department.

Boldt, E. D. (1978). Structural tightness and cross-cultural research. *Journal of Cross-Cultural Psychology, 9,* 151–165.

Bond, M. H., Chiu, C., & Wan, K. (1984). When modesty fails: The social impact of group effacing attributions following success or failure. *European Journal of Social Psychology, 16,* 111–127.

Bontempo, R., Lobel, S. A., & Triandis, H. C. (1989). *Compliance and value internalization among Brazilian and U.S. students.* Manuscript submitted for publication.

Breckler, S. J., & Greenwald, A. G. (1986). Motivational facets of the self. In R. M. Sorrentino & E. T. Higgins (Eds.), *Handbook of motivation and cognition* (pp. 145–164). New York: Guilford.

Brockner, J., & Adsit, L. (1986). The moderating impact of sex on the equity satisfaction relationship: A field study. *Journal of Applied Psychology, 71,* 585–590.

Carneiro, R. L. (1970). Scale analysis, evolutionary sequences, and the ratings of cultures. In R. Naroll & R. Cohen (Eds.), *A handbook of method in cultural anthropology* (pp. 834–871). New York: Columbia University Press.

Carver, C. S., & Scheier, M. F. (1985). Aspects of self and the control of behavior. In B. Schlenker (Ed.), *The self and social life* (pp. 146–174). New York: McGraw-Hill.

Caudill, W., & Scarr, H. (1962). Japanese value orientations and cultural change. *Ethnology, 1,* 53–91.

Centre National de la Recherche Scientifique (1973). *La notion de personne en Afrique noire* [The idea of the person in black Africa]. Paris: Éditions du Centre Nationale de la Recherche Scientifique (No. 544).

Church, A. T. (1987). Personality research in a non-Western culture: The Philippines. *Psychological Bulletin, 102,* 272–292.

Cooley, C. H. (1902). *Human nature and the social order.* New York: Scribner.

Davidson, A. R., Jaccard, J. J., Triandis, H. C., Morales, M. L., & Diaz-Guerrero, R. (1976). Cross-cultural model testing: Toward a solution of the etic-emic dilemma. *International Journal of Psychology, 11,* 1–13.

Deem, R., & Salaman, G. (Eds.). (1985). *Work, culture and society.* Milton Keynes, England: Open University Library.

Diaz-Guerrero, R. (1979). The development of coping style. *Human Development, 22,* 320–331.

Doi, T. (1986). *The anatomy of conformity: The individual versus society.* Tokyo: Kodansha.

Doumanis, M. (1983). *Mothering in Greece: From collectivism to individualism.* New York: Academic Press.

Dragonas, T. (1983). *The self-concept of preadolescents in the Hellenic context.* Unpublished doctoral dissertation, University of Ashton, Birmingham, England.

Espinoza, J. A., & Garza, R. T. (1985). Social group salience and interethnic cooperation. *Journal of Experimental Social Psychology, 231,* 380–392.

Fazio, R. H., & Williams, C. J. (1986). Attitude accessibility as a moderator of the attitude-perception and attitude-behavior relations: An investigation of the 1984 presidential election. *Journal of Personality and Social Psychology, 51,* 505–514.

Feather, N. T. (1986). Value systems across cultures: Australia and China. *International Journal of Psychology, 21,* 697–715.

Forgas, J. P., & Bond, M. H. (1985). Cultural influences on the perception of interaction episodes. *Personality and Social Psychology Bulletin, 11,* 75–88.

Gabrenya, W. K., & Barba, L. (1987, March). *Cultural differences in social interaction during group problem solving.* Paper presented at the meetings of the Southeastern Psychological Association, Atlanta.

Gaenslen, F. (1986). Culture and decision making in China, Japan, Russia and the United States. *World Politics, 39,* 78–103.

Geertz, C. (1963). *Peddlers and princes: Social change and economic modernization in two Indonesian towns.* Chicago: Chicago University Press.

Geertz, C. (1973). *The interpretation of cultures.* New York: Basic Books.

Georgas, J. (1989). Changing family values in Greece: From collectivist to individual-ist. *Journal of Cross-Cultural Psychology, 20,* 80–91.

Gordon, C., & Gergen, K. J. (1968). (Eds.), *The self in social interaction.* New York: Wiley.

Greenwald, A. G., Carnot, C. G., Beach, R., & Young, B. (1987). Increasing voting behavior by asking people if they expect to vote. *Journal of Applied Psychology, 71,* 315–318.

Greenwald, A. G., & Pratkanis, A. R. (1984). The self. In R. S. Wyer & T. K. Srull (Eds.), *Handbook of social cognition* (Vol. 3, pp. 129–178). Hillsdale, NJ: Erlbaum.

Gudykunst, W. B., & Nishida, T. (1986). The influence of cultural variability on perceptions of communication behavior associated with relationship terms. *Human Communication Research, 13,* 147–166.

Gudykunst, W. B., Yang, S., & Nishida, T. (1987). Cultural differences in self-consciousness and self-monitoring. *Communication Research, 14,* 7–36.

Gudykunst, W., Yoon, Y. C., & Nishida, T. (1987). The influence of individualism–collectivism on perceptions of communication in ingroup and outgroup relation-ships. *Communication Monographs, 54,* 295–306.

Guthrie, G. M. (1961). *The Filipino child and Philippine society.* Manila: Philippine Normal College Press.

Higgins, E. T. (1987). Self-discrepancy: A theory relating self to effect. *Psychological Review, 94,* 319–340.

Higgins, E. T., & King, G. (1981). Accessibility of social constructs: Information-processing consequences of individual and contextual variability. In N. Cantor & J. F. Kihlstrom (Eds.), *Personality, cognition and social interaction* (pp. 69–121). Hillsdale, NJ: Erlbaum.

Hofstede, G. (1980). *Culture's consequences.* Beverly Hills, CA: Sage.

Hogan, R. T., & Cheek, J. M. (1983). Identity, authenticity and maturity. In T. R. Sarbin & K. E. Scheibe (Eds.), *Studies in social identity* (pp. 339–357). New York: Praeger.

Holtzman, W. H., Diaz-Guerrero, R., & Swartz, J. D. (1975). *Personality development in two cultures.* Austin: University of Texas Press.

Holzberg, C. S. (1981). Anthropology and industry: Reappraisal and new directions. *Annual Review of Anthropology, 10,* 317–360.

Hsu, F. L. K. (1981). *American and Chinese: Passage to differences.* Honolulu: Univer-sity of Hawaii Press.

Hsu, F. L. K. (1983). *Rugged individualism reconsidered.* Knoxville: University of Tennessee Press.

Hsu, F. L. K. (1985). The self in cross-cultural perspective. In A. J. Marsella, G. DeVos & F. L. K. Hsu (Eds.), *Cultural and self* (pp. 24–55). New York: Tavistock Publications.

Hui, C. H. (1984). *Individualism–collectivism: Theory, measurement and its relationship to reward allocation.* Unpublished doctoral dissertation, Department of Psychology, University of Illinois at Champaign-Urbana.

Hui, C. H., & Triandis, H. C. (1986). Individualism–collectivism: A study of cross-cultural researchers. *Journal of Cross Cultural Psychology, 17,* 225–248.

Hull, J. G. (1986, April). *Self-awareness and alcohol use: An update.* Paper presented at a meeting of Polish and American social psychologists at the Educational Test-ing Service, Princeton, New Jersey.

Iwao, S. (1988, August). *Social psychology's models of man: Isn't it time for East to meet West?* Invited address to the International Congress of Scientific Psychology, Sydney, Australia.

James, W. (1950). *The principles of psychology.* New York: Dover. (Original work published 1890).

Kaiser, R. G. (1984). *Russia: The people and the power.* New York: Washington Square Press.

Katakis, C. D. (1976). An exploratory multilevel attempt to investigate interpersonal and intrapersonal patterns of 20 Athenian families. *Mental Health and Society, 3,* 1–9.

Katakis, C. D. (1978). On the transaction of social change processes and the perception of self in relation to others. *Mental Health and Society, 5,* 275–283.

Katakis, C. D. (1984). *Oi tris tautotites tis Ellinikis oikogenoias* [The three identities of the Greek family]. Athens, Greece: Kedros.

Kerlinger, F. (1984). *Liberalism and conservatism: The nature and structure of social attitudes.* Hillsdale, NJ: Erlbaum.

Kohn, M. L. (1969). *Class and conformity.* Homewood, IL: Dorsey.

Kohn, M. L. (1987). Cross-national research as an analytic strategy. *American Sociological Review, 52,* 713–731.

Kraut, R. E. (1973). Effects of social labeling on giving to charity. *Journal of Experimental Social Psychology, 9,* 551–562.

Kuhn, M. H., & McPartland, T. (1954). An empirical investigation of self-attitudes. *American Sociological Review, 19,* 68–76.

Lebra, T. S. (1976). *Japanese patterns of behavior.* Honolulu, Hawaii: East-West Center.

Leung, K. (1985). *Cross-cultural study of procedural fairness and disputing behavior.* Unpublished doctoral dissertation, Department of Psychology, University of Illinois, Champaign-Urbana.

Leung, K. (1987). Some determinants of reactions to procedural models for conflict resolution: A cross-national study. *Journal of Personality and Social Psychology, 53,* 898–908.

LeVine, R., & Campbell, D. T. (1972). *Ethnocentrism.* New York: Wiley.

Linville, P. W. (1985). Self-complexity and affective extremity: Don't put all your eggs in one cognitive basket. *Social Cognition, 3,* 94–120.

Lobel, S. A. (1984). *Effects of sojourn to the United States. A SYMLOG content analysis of in-depth interviews.* Unpublished doctoral dissertation, Harvard University.

Lobel, S. A. (1986). *Effects of intercultural contact on variance of stereotypes.* Manuscript submitted for publication.

Lomax, A., & Berkowitz, N. (1972). The evolutionary taxonomy of cultures. *Science, 177,* 228–239.

Major, B., & Adams, J. B. (1983). Role of gender, interpersonal orientation, and self-presentation in distributive justice behavior. *Journal of Personality and Social Psychology, 45,* 598–608.

Marin, G. (1985). Validez transcultural del principio de equidad: El colectivismo-individualismo como una variable moderatora [Transcultural validity of the principle of equity: Collectivism–individualism as a moderating variable]. *Revista Interamericana de Psicologia Occupational, 4,* 7–20.

Marin, G., & Triandis, H. C. (1985). Allocentrism as an important characteristic of the behavior of Latin Americans and Hispanics. In R. Diaz-Guerrero (Ed.), *Cross-cultural and national studies in social psychology* (69–80). Amsterdam. The Netherlands: North Holland.

Marin, G. V., Marin, G., Otero-Sabogal, R., Sabogal, F., & Perez-Stable, E. (1987). *Cultural differences in attitudes toward smoking: Developing messages using the theory of reasoned action* (Tech. Rep.). (Available from Box 0320, 400 Parnassus Ave., San Francisco, CA 94117).

Markus, H., & Wurf, E. (1987). The dynamic self-concept. A social psychological perspective. *Annual Review of Psychology, 38,* 299–337.

Marmot, M. G., & Syme, S. L. (1976). Acculturation and coronary heart disease in Japanese Americans. *American Journal of Epidemiology, 104,* 225–247.

Marsella, A. J., DeVos, G., & Hsu, F. L. K. (1985). *Culture and self.* New York: Tavistock.

McGuire, W. J., McGuire, C. V., & Cheever, J. (1986). The self in society: Effects of social contexts on the sense of self. *British Journal of Social Psychology, 25,* 259–270.

McGuire, W. J., McGuire, C. V., Child, P., & Fujioka, T. (1978). Salience of ethnicity in the spontaneous self-concept as a function of one's distinctiveness in the social environment. *Journal of Personality and Social Psychology, 36,* 511–520.

Mead, G. H. (1934). *Mind, self, and society.* Chicago: University of Chicago Press.

Mendenhall, M. E., & Oddou, G. (1986). The cognitive, psychological and social context of Japanese management. *Asia-Pacific Journal of Management, 4,* 24–37.

Miller, R. L., Brickman, P., & Bolen, D. (1975). Attribution versus persuasion as a means of modifying behavior. *Journal of Personality and Social Psychology, 31,* 430–441.

Mills, J., & Clark, E. S. (1982). Exchange and communal relationships. In L. Wheeler (Ed.), *Review of personality and social psychology* (Vol. 3, pp. 121–144). Beverly Hills, CA: Sage.

Murdock, G. P., & Provost, C. (1973). Measurement of cultural complexity. *Ethnology, 12,* 379–392.

Murphy, G. (1947). *Personality.* New York: Harper.

Nadler, A. (1986). Help seeking as a cultural phenomenon: Differences between city and kibbutz dwellers. *Journal of Personality and Social Psychology, 51,* 976–982.

Nail, P. R. (1986). Toward an integration of some models and theories of social response. *Psychological Bulletin, 100,* 190–206.

Northrop, F. S. C. (1949). *Ideological differences and world order.* New Haven, CT: Yale University Press.

Ogilvie, D. M. (1987). The undesired self: A neglected variable in personality research. *Journal of Personality and Social Psychology, 52,* 379–385.

Pandey, J. (1986). Sociocultural perspectives on ingratiation. *Progress in Experimental Personality Research, 14,* 205–229.

Pearson, H. W. (Ed.). (1977). *The livelihood of man: Karl Polanyi.* New York: Academic Press.

Pelto, P. J. (1968, April). The difference between "tight" and "loose" societies. *Transaction,* 37–40.

Quattrone, G. A. (1986). On the perception of a group's variability. In S. Worchelz & W. G. Austin (Eds.), *Psychology of intergroup relations* (pp. 25–48). Chicago: Nelson-Hall.

Rogers, T. B. (1981). A model of the self as an aspect of the human information processing system. In N. Cantor & J. F. Kihlstrom (Eds.), *Personality, cognition and social interaction* (pp. 193–214). Hillsdale, NJ: Erlbaum.

Rokeach, M. (1960). *The open and closed mind.* New York: Basic Books.

Roland, A. (1984a). Psychoanalysis in civilization perspective. *Psychoanalytic Review, 7,* 569–590.

Roland, A. (1984b). The self in India and America: Toward a psychoanalysis of social and cultural contexts. In V. Kovolis (Ed.), *Designs of selfhood* (pp. 123–130). New Jersey: Associated University Press.

Rosenberg, M. (1979). *Conceiving the self.* New York: Basic Books.

Rugh, A. (1985). *Family in contemporary Egypt.* Cairo, Egypt: American University Press.

Scheier, M. F., & Carver, C. S. (1980). Private and public self-attention, resistance to change, and dissonance reduction. *Journal of Personality and Social Psychology, 39,* 514–521.

Schlenker, B. R. (1985). Introduction. In B. R. Schlenker (Ed.), *Foundations of the self in social life* (pp. 1–28). New York: McGraw-Hill.

Sears, D. O. (1986). College sophomores in the laboratory: Influence of a narrow data base on social psychology's view of human nature. *Journal of Personality and Social Psychology, 51,* 515–530.

Shotland, R. L., & Berger, W. G. (1970). Behavioral validation of several values from the Rokeach value scale as an index of honesty. *Journal of Applied Psychology, 54,* 433–435.

Shweder, R. A., & Bourne, E. J. (1982). Does the concept of person vary cross-culturally? In A. J. Marsella & G. M. White (Eds.), *Cultural conceptions of mental health and therapy* (pp. 97–137). London: Reidel.

Shweder, R. A., & LeVine, R. A. (1984). *Cultural theory: Essays on mind, self and emotion.* New York: Cambridge University Press.

Sinha, J. B. P. (1982). The Hindu (Indian) identity. *Dynamische Psychiatrie, 15,* 148–160.

Sinha, J. B. P. (1987a). The structure of collectivism. In C. Kagitcibagi (Ed.), *Growth and progress in cross-cultural psychology* (pp. 123–130). Lisse, The Netherlands: Swets & Zeitlinger.

Sinha, J. B. P. (1987b). *Work cultures in Indian Organizations* (ICSSR Report). New Delhi, India: Concept Publications House.

Smith, M. B. (1980). Attitudes, values and selfhood. In H. E. Howe & M. M. Page (Eds.), *Nebraska Symposium on Motivation,* 1979 (pp. 305–358). Lincoln: University of Nebraska Press.

Snyder, M. (1974). Self-monitoring and expressive behavior. *Journal of Personality and Social Psychology, 30,* 526–537.

Snyder, M. (1987). *Public ap; 'arances as private realities: The psychology of self-monitoring.* New York: Freeman.

Snyder, M., & Gangestad, S. (1986). On the nature of self-monitoring: Matters of assessment, matters of validity. *Journal of Personality and Social Psychology, 51,* 125–139.

Snyder, M., Simpson, J. A., & Gangestad, S. (1986). Personality and sexual relations. *Journal of Personality and Social Psychology, 51,* 181–190.

Strodtbeck, F. L. (1958). Family interaction, values, and achievement. In D. McClelland (Ed.), *Talent and society* (pp. 135–195). New York: Van Nostrand.

Stryker, S., & Serpe, R. T. (1982). Commitment, identity salience, and role behavior: Theory and research example. In W. Ickes & E. S. Knowles (Eds.), *Personality, roles and social behavior* (pp. 199–218). New York: Springer.

Szalay, L. B., & Deese, J. (1978). *Subjective meaning and culture: An assessment through word association.* Hillsdale, NJ: Erlbaum.

Tajfel, H. (1978). *Differentiation between social groups.* London: Academic Press.

Tallman, I., Marotz-Baden, R., & Pindas, P. (1983). *Adolescent socialization in cross-cultural Perspective.* New York: Academic Press.

Thibaut, J., & Kelley, H. (1959). *The social psychology of groups.* New York: Wiley.

Triandis, H. C. (1967). Interpersonal relations in international organizations. *Journal of Organizational Behavior and Human Performance, 2,* 26–55.

Triandis, H. C. (1972). *The analysis of subjective culture.* New York: Wiley.

Triandis, H. C. (1976). *Variations in black and white perceptions of the social environment.* Urbana: University of Illinois Press.

Triandis, H. C. (1977). *Interpersonal behavior.* Monterey, CA: Brooks/ Cole.

Triandis, H. C. (1978). Some universals of social behavior. *Personality and Social Psychology Bulletin, 4,* 1–16.

Triandis, H. C. (1980). Values, attitudes, and interpersonal behavior. In H. Howe & M. Page (Eds.), *Nebraska Symposium on Motivation,* 1979 (pp. 195–260). Lincoln: University of Nebraska Press.

Triandis, H. C., Bontempo, R., Betancourt, H., Bond, M., Leung, K., Brenes, A., Georgas, J., Hui, C. H., Marin, G., Setiadi, B., Sinha, J. B. P., Verma, J., Spangenberg, J., Touzard, H., & de Montmollin, G. (1986). The measurement of etic aspects of individualism and collectivism across cultures. *Australian Journal of Psychology* (Special issue on cross-cultural psychology), *38,* 257–267.

Triandis, H. C., Bontempo, R., Villareal, M. J., Asai, M., & Lucca, N. (1988). Individualism and collectivism: Cross-cultural perspectives on self–ingroup relationships. *Journal of Personality and Social Psychology, 54,* 323–338.

Triandis, H. C., Leung, K., Villareal, M. J., & Clack, F. L. (1985). Allocentric versus idiocentric tendencies: Convergent and discriminant validation. *Journal of Research in Personality, 19,* 395–415.

Triandis, H. C., Marin, G., Hui, C. H., Lisansky, J., & Ottati, V. (1984). Role perceptions of Hispanic young adults. *Journal of Cross-Cultural Psychology, 15,* 297–320.

Triandis, H. C., Marin, G., Lisansky, J., & Betancourt, H. (1984). *Simpatia* as a cultural script of Hispanics. *Journal of Personality and Social Psychology, 47,* 1363–1375.

Triandis, H. C., & Triandis, L. M. (1960). Race, social class, religion and nationality as determinants of social distance. *Journal of Abnormal and Social Psychology, 61,* 110–118.

Triandis, H. C., Vassiliou, V., & Nassiakou, M. (1968). Three cross-cultural studies of subjective culture. *Journal of Personality and Social Psychology* [Monograph suppl.], *8* (4, pp. 1–42).

Turnbull, C. M. (1972). *The mountain people.* New York: Simon & Schuster.

United States Employment and Training Administration. *Dictionary of occupational titles.* Washington, DC: Government Printing Office.

Verma, J. (1985). The ingroup and its relevance to individual behaviour: A study of collectivism and individualism. *Psychologia, 28,* 173–181.

Wallach, M. A., & Wallach, L. (1983). *Psychology's sanction of selfishness: The error of egoism in theory and therapy.* San Francisco, CA: Freeman.

Waterman, A. S. (1984). *The psychology of individualism.* New York: Praeger.

Whyte, W. H., Jr. (1956). *The organization man.* New York: Simon & Schuster.

Wicklund, R. A., & Gollwitzer, P. M. (1982). *Symbolic self-completion.* Hillsdale, NJ: Erlbaum.

Wu, D. Y. H. (1985). Child rearing in Chinese culture. In D. Y. H. Wu & W-S. Tseng (Eds.), *Chinese culture and mental health* (pp. 113–134). New York: Academic Press.

Yang, K. S. (1981). Social orientation and individual modernity among Chinese students in Taiwan. *Journal of Social Psychology, 113,* 159–170.

Yang, K. S. (1986). Chinese personality and its change. In M. H. Bond (Ed.), *The psychology of the Chinese people* (pp. 106–170). Hong Kong: Oxford University Press.

Zavalloni, M. (1975). Social identity and the recoding of reality. *International Journal of Psychology, 10,* 197–217.

Zavalloni, M., & Louis-Guerin, C. (1984). *Identité sociale et conscience: Introduction à l'égo-écologie* [Social identity and conscience: Introduction to the ego ecology]. Montréal, Canada: Les presses de l'université de Montreal.

Ziller, R. C. (1973). *The social self.* New York: Pergamon.

Zimbardo, P. (1969). The human choice: Individuation, reason and order versus deindividuation, impulse and chaos. In W. J. Arnold & D. Levine (Eds.), *Nebraska Symposium on Motivation* (Vol. 16, pp. 237–307). Lincoln: University of Nebraska Press.

16. Culture and Self: Implications for Internationalizing Psychology

Shinobu Kitayama and Hazel Rose Markus

Why is a multicultural perspective useful in education and research in social sciences? The immediate, practical reason to internationalize and globalize the social sciences stems from the changing nature of the nation and the world. American diplomats, business people, and scientists can no longer expect their international colleagues to behave like Americans. They must be aware of how cultural differences and institutional patterns affect people's thoughts, feelings, and actions. Many of the problems to be faced by American students today, and it is increasingly true with each new cohort, are multicultural in nature. The prevention of AIDS or solving the ozone depletion problem will be impossible without extensive international, intercultural cooperation. In business, of course, it is important to know one's market, and the market for many modern products can be nearly anywhere on the globe.

We will argue, however, that beyond the important goal of equipping our students to more fully understand their future colleagues is another compelling, but not yet fully appreciated or developed, rationale. The internationalization and globalization of research and education is essential for developing valid theories of human social behavior. We have gradually realized this perspective through our own research on cultural variation in the self. In pursuing our studies we have found that virtually the only model of the individual, of the person, or of the self in psychology, or indeed, in any of the social sciences is that of the rational, self-interested actor. The unexamined assumption in social science research is that the individual is a self-contained entity who (a) comprises a unique configuration of internal attributes (e.g., preferences, traits, abilities, values, right, etc., and (b) who behaves primarily as a consequence of these internal attri-

Reprinted by permission of H. R. Markus.

butes. The problem is that this model of the self is quite simply not the one that is held by the majority of the people in the world. And the model or theory of the individual characterizing a given group or society matters because all other theories of social behavior are directly rooted in this model.

This chapter will illustrate why a group's view of the self matters and why it is necessary to expand the scope of the social sciences as currently formulated so we can begin to understand the range and variation in the world's approach to individuality, subjectivity, and selfhood. The illustration takes the form of a story about "what if?". What if a group (lay people or social scientists) had very different assumptions or beliefs about what the person is or what the self is supposed to be? What if a very different set of assumptions about the self were used to organize social practices and institutions? What if persons were not viewed as autonomous and separate, but rather as connected and relational? Would it make any difference? We will show that the answer is "yes" because collective ideas about what a self is and how to be a self shape individual-level psychological processes of thinking, feeling, and acting. It is in this sense that the self is a cultural frame.[1]

There are many anecdotes suggesting that construals of the self can be dramatically different across cultures. For example, in America standing out and asserting one's self is a virtue. It is the squeaky wheel that gets the grease. But in many other parts of the world, certainly in Japan, China, or Korea, standing out often leads to being punished. The proverbial message in these places is quite different. The nail that sticks up shall get pounded down. Or consider the arena of politics. American politicians routinely credit success to trusting their instincts, self-confidence, and the ability to make decisions and stick by them. A headline after Clinton's successful presidential bid credited "leadership, will, and discipline" for his victory. Sounding a very different note, a former vice-prime minister of Japan, Shin Kanamaru, claimed that in his thirty-year career in public life it was interpersonal relations that had been most important to him, while Zenko Suziki, a former Japanese prime minister, explained his career in terms of the practice of the "politics of harmony." The American anecdote emphasizes expressing one's own inner attributes and not being unduly influenced by others. In contrast, the Japanese anecdotes highlight relations —fitting-in and harmonious interdependence with others.

CULTURAL PSYCHOLOGY

The perspective we will develop here is that of a growing interdisciplinary field called *cultural psychology*. This is an area that is reviving time-honored claims about the social nature of the mind or psyche. It holds that what people think, feel, what holds their attention, how they know and understand, and what counts as knowledge is shaped importantly by the theories, values, and commitments of their various sociocultural contexts. In broad strokes, cultural psychology is an attempt to probe, equipped with many of the empirical methods and theoretical models of the current psychological inquiry, the ways in which culture and the psyche give rise to each other. It takes seriously the idea that many so-called basic psychological phenomena or processes—self, emotion, motivation, cognition, time, morality, health, development—are given form and are governed by various sociocultural contexts. Culture is defined very broadly to include gender, ethnicity, religion, cohort or generation, historical period, profession, social class, and country of origin. Cultural psychology is being built on the ideas and theories of anthropologists such as Shweder and LeVine (1984), D'Andrade (1984), Hsu (1983), Shweder (1991), Geertz (1973, 1975), and psychologists such as Sampson (1985), Gergen (1990), Vygotsky (1962), Bruner (1990), and Triandis (1989). From the perspective of cultural psychology, we suggest that people everywhere need to have some idea of who they are and to attach some sort of value or dignity to this self. Every human group must solve the who am I problem, and the particular solution functions as a core cultural idea. It simultaneously influences individual psychological mechanisms and social practices and institutions. Each sociocultural context is associated with a set of behavioral norms, lay theories, beliefs, and/or images of how to live a life, how to be a good or moral being, or more generally, how to be. The self develops as amalgamation of these messages and images which, depending on one's context, are sometimes quite coherent with one another or, in fact, quite disparate. From this point of view, it should not come as any surprise that there is considerable variation across cultures in what people understand about who they are and their relations to others in society.

   In this essay we will take a systematic look at two divergent construals of the self. We will contrast the Euro-American construal of self as an independent, separate entity with another construal of self that is more common in many non-Western, particularly Asian cultures. According to this latter construal, the person is viewed as inherently connected or interdependent with others and deeply embedded within a social context. We will illustrate how these divergent cultural schemas of self function as mediating and interpretive frameworks that will systemically bias what people notice and think about, how they feel, what motivates them, and how they act.

The existence of alternative views of the self and the importance of the self in organizing individual experience has only become evident as anthropologists and social psychologists have attempted to assess their theories and methods on non-Western populations. The findings to be presented indicate that the internationalization of psychology is an essential step in charting the social nature and functioning of the mind. Each cultural group can be viewed as expert in some domain of experience and by using their understanding and construction of experience, we can extend and illuminate our own.

TWO CONSTRUALS OF SELF: INDEPENDENT AND INTERDEPENDENT

Virtually all Euro-American research on the self, which is to say 99 percent of all research on the self and identity, has been done on one particular population—contemporary, secularized, Western, urban, white middle-class people—and it has been assumed in this research that the self takes on a particular form. The self is conceived of as an autonomous bounded entity, and there is an assumption of the inherent separateness of individuals. The normative task of these cultures is to maintain the autonomy of the individual as a self-contained entity. Accordingly, it is extremely important to be unique, to express the self, to realize and actualize the inner self, to promote one's own goals, and so on. Under this *independent* construal of self, individuals tend to focus on their own internal attributes—their own preferences, traits, and abilities. There is a concern with expressing and verbalizing these attributes in both public and private. Other people are crucial in maintaining the independent construal of self, but they are crucial primarily for their role in evaluating and appraising the self.

By contrast, many Asian cultures neither assume nor value such an overt separateness among people. Instead, these cultures emphasize what may be called the fundamental connectedness of human beings. The primary normative task is to adjust oneself so as to fit in and maintain the interdependence among individuals. From this *interdependent* construal of self, individuals tend to focus on their interdependent status with other people and strive to meet duties, obligations, and social responsibilities. Their thoughts, feelings, and social actions are organized and made meaningful in reference to the thoughts, feelings, and actions of others in the relationship. The relationship is granted primacy and the self is defined in reference to the relationship. It is extremely important, therefore, to fit into the relationship, and to occupy one's proper place, to engage in appropriate actions, and even to promote others' goals.

Americans are socialized to believe that they are independent, autonomous, and free from social influence. Further, they come to believe that they have preferences and distinctive attributes and that they must express them. As a consequence, Americans are motivated to feel unique and special, and to experience positive self-feelings, and when this happens, they feel satisfied with their lives. In contrast, Japanese, rather than trying as Americans to "feel good about themselves," are socialized to be interdependent, connected and concerned with others, and to be constantly aware of relationships. Positive feelings attributed to the inner self are not the primary source of satisfaction in life. Japanese are motivated to feel connected, to rely on and be relied on by others, and to share a common, intersubjective understanding of themselves and the social situation. It is when this happens that they are most likely to feel satisfied with their lives. Independence and interdependence thus can be seen as cultural schemas, which is to say they are culturally mediated frames of reference that organize all aspects of social life — *both* customs, practices, or socially instituted behavioral scripts, *and* psychological skills, processes, or mechanisms.

SELF-ENHANCEMENT AND SELF-EFFACEMENT

These cultural schemas can have a variety of consequences on psychological processes and experience (for a review, see Markus and Kitayama 1991). These cultural schemas have particular types of effects on individual functioning. The cultural schema of independence fosters the elaboration of internal attributes, and the sense that one is different from and better than others. The schema of interdependence fosters the sense of one's similarity and connection to others. These divergent tendencies are likely to be revealed in any judgment task that requires an implicit or explicit comparison of self and others. For example, American subjects demonstrate a powerful self-serving bias—a tendency to see themselves in a positive light—in all types of social judgment. They readily take credit for their successes, explain away their failures, and in various ways aggrandize themselves (e.g., Gilovich 1983; Lau 1984; Miller 1986; Whitley & Frieze 1985; Zuckerman 1979).

Similarly, Wylie (1979) reported that American adults consider themselves to be more intelligent and more attractive than average, and Myers (1989), in a national survey of American students, found that 70 percent believe that they are above average in leadership ability and, with respect to the ability to get along with others, 60 percent thought that they are in the top 10 percent. Further, a recent study by Harter (1990) demonstrated that American children show a clear self-favorability bias at as early as four years of age. These well-documented biases can be understood as a result of one's motivation or tendency to discover, affirm, and express positive internal features of the self, and have been assumed to be universal. Robust and powerful as they are, however, these biases may be highly local, limited largely to those with a Euro-American cultural background. In fact, they typically completely vanish or, in some cases, even reverse themselves (to show self-effacement) in many Asian cultures.

Markus and Kitayama (1991) found on average that American college students reported that only 30 percent of their peers are better than themselves across a wide variety of domains. But this American tendency to overestimate the positive uniqueness of the self virtually disappeared among a Japanese college student sample. The absence of the American tendency has also been documented in Korea, Taiwan, and Thailand (Shinohara, personal communication, 1991). Similarly, Shikanai (1978, 1983, 1984) examined causal attribution of success and failure in Japanese college students. In the United States, it is typically found that successes are attributed to factors, such as ability and effort, that are internal to the self, whereas failures are attributed to factors, such as task difficulty or absence of good luck, that are relatively unstable over time and external to the self. This attributional pattern works to protect or enhance self-esteem.

By contrast, the Japanese tend to attribute their successes to factors that were either unstable over time, external of the self, or both (such as the ease of task, luck, and the mental or physical shape of the self on that particular day and time). Moreover, they tend to explain their failures primarily by a lack of their own effort — a factor that was internal to the self. The absence in Japan of the typical American tendency of blaming others or the situation when explaining failure is not limited to the experimental laboratory. In a study by Hess, Azuma, Kashiwagi, Dickson, Nagano, Holloway, Miyake, Price, Hatano, and McDevitt (1986), Japanese mothers explained poor performance of their children by claiming a lack of effort. In contrast, American mothers emphasized much more strongly in their explanations the ability of teachers and the quality of school instruction along with a lack of effort.

An analogous contrast can be drawn even more dramatically in social comparison. A series of studies done in Japan by Takata (1987) and another set of studies done in the United States by Schwartz and Smith (1976) use entirely comparable procedures, yet show diametrically opposite patterns of results. In these studies subjects performed several anagram tasks (alleged to indicate some important aspect of intelligence). Upon completion of the task, subjects were given feedback about their own performance and the performance of another subject. The direction of the self-other difference and its magnitude were systematically varied. In the United States (Schwartz and Smith 1976), as might be predicted, subjects showed much greater confidence in feedback when the comparison was favorable to the self and expressed considerable suspicion to it when the comparison was unfavorable. In Japan (Takata 1987), there was an equally strong bias, but in an opposite, what Takata terms a "self-harmonizing" direction. The respondents immediately accepted the feedback if it was unfavorable to the self, but requested more information if it was favorable to the self. It appears that in both countries the ease of assimilating self-relevant information depends on its valence (i.e., whether it is favorable or unfavorable to the self). But the exact nature of this effect diverges in entirely different directions. Americans seem to more readily and easily accept favorable information as a credit to the self, but Japanese appear more inclined to "swallow" unfavorable information as a liability of the self.

A CULTURAL PERSPECTIVE
ON JUDGMENT BIASES

Efforts to explain these divergent tendencies have allowed us to see these various biases in judgment and attribution as a reflection of underlying core cultural ideas. Without an internationalized psychology that explored these judgment tendencies outside of American laboratories, we may have continued to conclude, as the initial studies did, that such biases were universal and the product of the human central processing machinery. Overall, self-enhancement seems highly pervasive and robust in American culture; but hardly so in Japanese culture. Even within American culture, the phenomenon is not completely general; men, especially those with high self-esteem, show a much stronger bias of this kind than women (Josephs, Markus, and Tafarodi, 1992). All in all, it seems likely that the bias is rooted in some characteristics of Western, predominantly male, culture that are not completely shared by women in the Western culture nor by people in non-Western cultures, particularly in Japan.

There are at least three culturally rooted bases of the self-enhancement bias among Americans, and the self-effacement bias among the Japanese. Self-effacement may be seen, from a perspective of an independent construal of the self, as a result of tactical self-presentation designed to convince others that one is modest — a desirable trait in many Asian cultures. There is no question that such deliberate, self-presentational tactics operate. At the same time, however, there are some reasons to believe that these effects reflect, in many cases, an "authentic" inner experience of the self's inferiority, and the attendant awareness and acceptance of one's own faults or shortcomings. Within the relevant cultural frame, self-effacement may be central to maintaining the sense of the self as a fully interdependent and thus respectable agent, just as self-enhancement is indispensable for self-esteem and the mental health of those with independent construals of the self. Within an interdependent cultural frame, therefore, self-effacement can lead to the sense of fitting-in, the recognition of fully participating in a relationship, and to the ultimate sense of satisfaction as a worthy member of the community, all of which is related to contentment or satisfaction in one's own life.

Among American undergraduates the cognitive structures for encoding, interpreting, and organizing self-relevant information tend to be especially rich and differentiated in domains of success. With such structures, one can easily interpret a variety of social information that is extremely ambiguous in a way that is quite favorable to the self. Indeed, from very early in life, children in Western culture are encouraged to identify their own desirable features. One often hears a caretaker say to the child, "Mary you did such a nice job painting, story, song, etc. —I am so proud of you!" This socialization practice is based on an often implicit belief in the value of standing out, and of discovering one's positive unique attributes. Children may eventually internalize this habit of identifying positive features in their own behaviors, leading to self-enhancing perceptions on their part, and the authentic belief that they are better than others.

By contrast, in Japan a more typical comment from a caretaker to a child might be "Masaru, you are acting very strange —your friends may laugh at you if they see it." This socialization practice is based on a belief in the value of fitting in, and in maintaining interdependence with others within a given relationship. As a consequence, children may internalize a practice of identifying negative features in their behaviors so as to correct them to fit in with the expectations of others. Such a practice may lead to the "authentic" self-fitting or self-harmonizing perceptions on their part and the sense that one is like others.

Another explanation for cultural divergence in self/other judgment concerns the role of feeling good about one's internal features. With an independent construal of the self, experiencing positive feelings within the self can be highly self-definitional. Thus, feeling good about one's self may be the primary source of satisfaction in life, and may function as a barometer of the adequacy and integrity of the self. This may be one important reason for the strong motivation of those with independent selves to try to see their own internal attributes as superior. Such a motivational tendency, however, may not be nearly so prominent among those with interdependent selves. Among these individuals, it is the nature of one's relationship with other people that matters. The recognition that one is fully participating in the relationship is the primary source of satisfaction in life. If so, good feelings resulting from one's inner attributes may be relatively detached from one's general sense of satisfaction in life.

In fact, the very meaning of happiness or general satisfaction in life may also differ depending on the over-arching, yet implicit assumptions about the self as independent or interdependent. Happiness or satisfaction may derive primarily from one's recognition that one has adequately performed the culturally sanctioned task of independence or interdependence. To explore this issue, we asked a number of American undergraduates in the United States and Japanese undergraduates in Japan to report how frequently they experience each of three different kinds of good feelings. Some good feelings were of a very general type, such as "feeling calm," "feeling relaxed," and "feeling elated." Some other good feelings were those derived from personal, individual achievement, such as "feeling proud," "feeling good about oneself," "feeling superior to someone else," and the like. Finally, still some other good feelings were those deriving from close interpersonal relationships, such as "feeling connected," "friendly feelings," or "communal feelings." As may be expected, general happiness seems to have very different meanings across cultures. In the United States, general happiness was more highly correlated with good feelings based on individual or personal achievement than those based on close interpersonal relationships. In Japan, however, this pattern was completely reversed. In fact, there was no correlation between general happiness and good feelings derived from individual or personal achievement. Thus, individual achievements or accomplishments in Japan, if taken by themselves, may be relatively detached and separated from a general sense of happiness.

COLLECTIVE REPRESENTATIONS OF CORE CULTURAL IDEAS

So far we have described the powerful influence that construals of self as independent or interdependent can have on a variety of psychological processes including cognition, motivation, and emotion, and illustrated our point by specifically focusing on biases in self-relevant judgments. We have demonstrated that several processes in cognition, motivation, and emotion that are rooted in the construals of self work in concert with each other to generate those powerful effects. These theoretical and empirical considerations lead us to ask: By what means or processes are these construals of self represented or carried within a given cultural group, and how can these culturally shared *ideas* be transformed into divergent psychological *processes* and *experience?*

In psychology today, cultural values such as independence and interdependence are commonly regarded as cognitive representations — that is, beliefs stored in each individual's memory (Schwartz and Bilsky 1990). It may be important, however, to take a broader view of the ways in which these cultural values interact with larger societal processes and practices. Specifically, we propose that the core cultural ideas of a given society, such as independence in the United States and interdependence in Japan, give rise to a variety of customs, practices, institutions, rules, or norms of the society. Perhaps, those "culturally constructed things" (D'Andrade 1984) that are consistent with or that even promote the core cultural idea are selected and instituted into the society over time, while those that are inconsistent with it or that counter it are neglected or simply forgotten over time. As a result of the constructive, selective function of a core cultural idea, many of the artifacts, practices, and institutions of a society may tend to reflect and promote this very idea.

For example, one important aspect of endorsing the construal of self as an independent entity is an effort to appreciate, whenever possible, the "natural rights" of each individual (Shweder, Mahapatra, and Miller 1990). The Declaration of Independence, for example, guarantees the protection of certain inalienable rights. These include life, liberty, and the pursuit of happiness. The idea of human rights as inherent and "God-given" is reflected in the independent construal and is also embodied in an array of legal statutes protecting individual rights. Another related quality assigned to an independent entity is its capacity to make one's own choice. In Western culture, especially in North America, there are numerous everyday scripts that presuppose the actor's right to make a choice. For example, it is a commonplace at a party that a host will instruct her guests, "Help yourself!" Similarly, a question about one's choice, preference, or taste is one of the most frequent questions that caregivers ask of their children ("Which sport would you like, basketball or swimming?"). Finally, the merit pay system, which is common and pervasive in Western culture, works to maintain a strong emphasis on one's inner attributes.

In many non-Western cultures, such as Japan, there exists an equally large number of practices in each of these corresponding domains, but these practices tend to be rooted in a schema of the self as an interdependent entity. For example, in place of (or, to a certain extent, in addition to) the emphasis on human rights, there exist rules or norms that highlight duties of each individual to the pertinent collectivity whether it is the company, school, or even the nation. There are decidedly fewer statutes protecting individual rights. Instead of soliciting the choices of the partner of the interaction, a typical Japanese may do her best trying to read the partner's mind and then to satisfy what she sees as the partner's expectations or desires. Thus, a Japanese mother might tell her child, "I think basketball will be best for you—why don't you choose this sport rather than swimming." Or instead of asking the guest to make their choices at a lunch, the Japanese host would do his best preparing and offering what he sees the best possible treat for the guest, saying for example, "Here's a turkey sandwich for you. I thought you said that you liked turkey better than beef last time we met." Finally, wages in a large number of Japanese companies and institutions are determined within a seniority system, that is, in terms of one's position within an age-based hierarchy, and thus one relatively uninfluenced by each person's merit.

CULTURAL FRAME AND CONSCIOUS EXPERIENCE

We hypothesize then, that the construals of the self as independent or as interdependent tend to shape the nature of everyday practices or customs, and even the social structure of the respective society. And the construals are, in turn, reinforced and bolstered by their attendant social practices and the social structure. There are several intriguing consequences of this constructive function of culturally shared ideas. Most importantly, the core ideas of a society may become *both* powerful *and* tacit. To illustrate, in an independent culture like that of the United States, each individual does not have to strongly endorse the values associated with the independent construal of self. These values are, in fact, implicit in everyday practices (e.g., emphasis of personal choice) and in the social structure (e.g., merit pay system), and as a consequence, one can behave in accordance with these independence-related values by merely living in this society. These notions do not have to be focal in individual consciousness. Similarly, in an interdependent culture like that of Japan, each individual does not have to strongly endorse the values associated with the interdependent construal of self. These values are socially enforced and institutionalized in everyday practices and customs (e.g., customs that emphasize the duties that one has to a group to which he or she belongs) as well as in the social structure (e.g., seniority system). Thus, to behave in accordance with these values means no more than to become a citizen in the society — no conscious effort or intention to be interdependent may be required.

IMPLICATIONS FOR INTERNATIONALIZING EDUCATION AND RESEARCH IN PSYCHOLOGY

We have presented two views of the nature of the person and suggested that they are extremely powerful in shaping individual's psychological processes and experience. We have also suggested that because these core cultural ideas are institutionalized in the society's practices and structure, they do not have to be present in each individual's consciousness to influence and control behavior. This work offers an initial rationale for a concerted effort to internationalize research and education in the social sciences. Currently, the social sciences are linked with only one model or theory of the individual. The model is implicit and seldom specified. But what social scientists believe about the nature and functioning of the self influences every aspect of their theorizing about people and the relations among them, at both the individual and the group level. The prevailing model is that of the rational, self-interested actor. A reliance on this single model may restrict our understanding of human agency and social behavior, even within North America and Europe.

For example, research in both psychology and economics repeatedly finds that individuals do not behave as neo-classical models of the rational, autonomous, self-interested actor suggest that they should. Their judgments and decisions are apparently fraught with a whole variety of biases, errors, and fallacies. It is possible, however, that it is the underlying model of the self that is in need of some correction. From the brief overview presented in this chapter, it is evident that there are other viable models of how to be a person or a self. Social psychological studies reveal that people are exquisitely sensitive to others and to social pressure. They conform, obey, allow themselves to be easily persuaded about all manner of things and become powerfully committed to others on the basis of minimal action. Even within this highly individualist Western culture, most people are still much less self-reliant, self-contained, or self-sufficient than the prevailing model suggests. Here again, the prevailing model of the self appears to be somewhat at odds with actual social behavior and might be reformulated to reflect the substantial interpersonal

sensitivity and concerns that characterize even Western individualists. Thus, the need to internationalize social science research arises
not just because it would be just or equitable to have the ideas of
other groups represented within social science, although within a
science rooted in a democratic system such a case could be easily
made. The need for internationalization also stems from a need to
expand the ways in which social scientists conceive of human behavior and its potential.

The work of those pursuing cultural psychology and multicultural
efforts of various kinds allow social scientists to see what would
otherwise be quite invisible, that is, the ways in which our psychological functioning, as well as our theories about this psychological
functioning, are in many ways culture-specific and conditioned by
particular meaning systems. This is a reclaiming theory of many of
social science's earliest ideas about the social nature of the individual
and taking them much more seriously than has been done previously.
In the process of linking contrasting cultural assumptions to differences in lived experience, we can begin to see how social behavior is
thoroughly culturalized. In many domains, even within "social" science there is a readiness to assume that the processes revealed in our
studies are universal and the product of relatively invariant com-
puter-like human processors. The goal then of an internationalized
social science is for a more comprehensive social science, one that can
fulfill the promise of understanding the nature and extent of the
interdependency between individuals and their various social environments.

Efforts toward an enriched and more fully comprehensive social
science will require a cross-disciplinary integration of techniques,
methods, and theories. For example, traditionally in psychology,
relatively little attention is given to the surrounding social environment. The world is important because it is assumed to be the source
of stimuli, but rarely is it characterized in detail. In contrast, elaborate attention is given to the structure and functioning of the mind
which responds to or processes these stimuli. In sociology, anthropology, and political science this state of affairs is reversed. It is the
social world—the patterns of social behavior, customs, practices, and
institutions—that are carefully detailed, and the nature of the human mind or human agency that is left unelaborated. Neither approach is satisfactory by itself. Many psychological processes and
phenomena can only be understood in the context of the social reali-

ties the actor encounters. And these very social realities are importantly shaped by core cultural ideas like those which prescribe the nature of the self. A comprehensive social science then will require multiregional, multinational, and, perhaps the most challenging of all, multidisciplinary collaboration.

As the chapters of this volume reveal, becoming more international and global is a difficult challenge because it requires moving forward while simultaneously reexamining many of the assumptions, frameworks, and theories that have been the basis of previous work. This complex process can be facilitated by a number of practical steps. The development of alternative models of the individual, or the group, or of the interdependence of the two will require the development and elaboration of indigenous psychologies. This may be accomplished best by the establishment of exchange programs for young scholars. Arranging for large numbers of foreign scholars to complete doctoral or postdoctoral degrees in the United States is an important component of such an exchange, but many more Americans should also complete some of their training abroad. Bringing the theories and research of international scholars to the attention of American scholars and their social science journals could be facilitated by the development of a network of scholars that would encourage collaborative, multiregional research, disseminate research in progress, and commission working papers on alternative models or underresearched problems. Such a network might also create new journals focused on cultural or international social science or arrange for existing journals to commit pages to such concerns.

Dramatic changes in curricula await the research that will result from the various cross-disciplinary networks and research programs now being developed. There are, however, some initial changes that might be put in place immediately. Most obvious perhaps, psychologists could frame their lectures and discussions with the idea that our current mainstream psychology is in many senses a "local" psychology that is rooted in Euro-American culture, and as a consequence, it is not yet a fully comprehensive psychology. Such an approach would make it evident that a full knowledge of Euro-American culture is essential, thus perhaps encouraging more cross-disciplinary study — history, philosophy, literature. Second, it would facilitate the realization that it is all too easy to claim that any given phenomenon, such as self-esteem, or well-being or achievement motivation that is identified in the researcher's own, typically North American culture, is a universally shared building block of the mind. Along with this notion should go the appreciation that any given process that is adaptive, good, desirable, and thus typical or normal with one cultural frame may not be so from the perspective of an alternate cultural frame. So with reference to the discussion of this chapter, in many Asian cultures, self-effacement lends itself to psychological adaptation and is highly regarded as a cultural ideal. In contrast, self-enhancement, American style, is seen as a manifestation of one's childishness or immaturity. In the United States, however, where self-enhancement leads to psychological adjustment and is seen as a sign of self-esteem, a person who engages in self-effacement will be regarded as wishy-washy and indecisive, or perhaps even as untrustworthy or abnormal. Discussions of this type throughout various relevant courses should serve to underscore the need for extensive cross-national, cross-cultural studies before making conclusions about human universals, and emphasize the importance of psychology, and more generally, social science in understanding the diversity of human behavior.

NOTES

This chapter will appear in J. D'Arms, R. G. Hastie, S. E. Hoelscher, and H. K. Jacobson, *Becoming More International and Global: Challenges for American Higher Education.*

1. The self is conceptualized here as one important aspect of the person, individual, or personality. It is the insider's grasp of the person; in Sullivan's (1940) terms, the self is what one "takes oneself to be." The self is viewed as the larger concept that includes within it various identities. Identities are constructions of the person behaving in particular roles. Thus, one's ethnic identity, for example, is a subset of one's self.

REFERENCES

Bruner, J. 1990. *Acts of meaning.* Cambridge, Mass.: Harvard University Press.

D'Andrade, R. 1984. Cultural meaning systems. In *Cultural theories: Essays on mind, self, and emotion,* ed. R. A. Shweder and R. A. LeVine, 88–119. New York: Cambridge University Press.

Geertz, C. 1973. *Interpretation of cultures.* New York: Basic Books.

———. (1975). On the nature of anthropological understanding. *American Scientist* 63: 47–53.

Gergen, K. J. 1990. Social understanding and inscription of self. In *Cultural psychology,* ed. J. W. Stigler, R. A. Shweder, and G. Herdt 569–606. Cambridge: Cambridge University Press.

Gilovich, T. 1983. Biased evaluation and persistence in gambling. *Journal of Personality and Social Psychology* 40: 797–808.

Harter, S. 1990. Causes, correlates, and the functional role of global self worth: A life span perspective. In *Competence considered,* ed. R. J. Sternberg and J. Kolligian, Jr., 67–97. New Haven, Conn.: Yale University Press.

Hess, R., H. Azuma, K. Kashiwagi, W. P. Dickson, S. Nagano, S. Holloway, K. Miyake, G. Price, G. Hatano, and T. McDevitt 1986. Family influences on school readiness and achievement in Japan and the United States: An overview of a longitudinal study. In *Child development and education in Japan,* ed. H. Stevenson, H. Azuma, and K. Hakuta, pp. 147–66. New York: Freeman.

Hsu, F. L. K. 1983. *Rugged individualism reconsidered.* Knoxville, Tenn.: University of Tennessee Press.

Josephs, R. A., H. Markus, and R. W. Tafarodi 1992. Gender differences in the source of self-esteem. *Journal of Personality and Social Psychology* 63: 391–402.

Lau, R. R. 1984. Dynamics of the attribution process. *Journal of Personality and Social Psychology* 46: 1017–28.

Markus, H., and S. Kitayama 1991. Culture and the self: Implications for cognition, emotion, and motivation. *Psychological Review* 98: 224–53.

Miller, J. B. 1986. *Toward a new psychology of women,* 2nd ed. Boston: Beacon Press.

Myers, D. 1989. *Social psychology,* 3rd ed. New York: McGraw-Hill.

Sampson, E. E. 1985. The decentralization of identity: Toward a revised concept of personal and social order. *American Psychologist* 40: 1203–11.

Schwartz, J. M., and W. P. Smith 1976. Social comparison and the inference of ability difference. *Journal of Personality and Social Psychology* 34: 1268–75.

Schwartz, S. H., and W. Bilsky 1990. Toward a theory of the universal content and structure of values: Extensions between cross-cultural replications. *Journal of Personality and Social Psychology* 58: 878–91.

Shikanai, K. 1978. Effects of self-esteem on attribution of success-failure. *Japanese Journal of Experimental Social Psychology* 18: 47–55.

———. 1983. Effects of self-esteem on attributions of others' success or failure. *Japanese Journal of Experimental Social Psychology* 23: 27–37.

———. 1984. Effects of self-esteem and one's own performance on attribution of others' success and failure. *Japanese Journal of Experimental Social Psychology* 24: 37–46.

Shinohara, T. 1991. Personal communication.

Shweder, R. A. 1991. *Cultural psychology: Thinking through cultures.* Cambridge, Mass.: Harvard University Press.

Shweder, R. A. and R. A. LeVine 1984. *Cultural theory: Essays on mind, self and emotion.* New York: Cambridge University Press.

Shweder, R. A., M. Mahapatra, and J. G. Miller 1990. Cultural and moral development. In *Cultural psychology,* ed. J. W. Stigler, R. A. Shweder, and G. Herdt, 130–204. Cambridge: Cambridge University Press.

Sullivan, H. S. 1940. *Conceptions of modern psychiatry.* New York: Norton.

Takata, T. 1987. Self-deprecative tendencies in self-evaluation through social comparison. *Japanese Journal of Experimental Social Psychology* 27: 27–36.

Triandis, H. C. 1989. The self and social behavior in differing cultural contexts. *Psychological Review* 96: 506–20.

Vygotsky, L. 1962. *Thought and language.* Cambridge, Mass.: MIT Press.

Whitley, B. E., Jr., and I. H. Frieze 1985. Children's causal attributions for success and failure in achievement settings: A meta-analysis. *Journal of Educational Psychology* 77: 608–16.

Wylie, R. C. 1979. *The self-concept: Vol. 2. Theory and research on selected topics.* Lincoln, Nebr.: University of Nebraska Press.

Zuckerman, M. 1979. Attribution of success and failure revisted; or, The motivational bias is alive and well in attribution theory. *Journal of Personality* 47: 245–87.

17. Ideology Obscured: Political Uses of the Self in Daniel Stern's Infant

Philip Cushman

From its early years the major research program of the dominant branch of modern psychology has been the search for the foundational laws of a universal, transhistorical human nature. However, several historians and social theorists have developed an argument that casts doubt on psychology's agenda (Foucault, 1979; Gergen, 1985; Hales, 1986; Harre, 1984; Levin, 1987; Sampson, 1983; Smedslund, 1985). They argue that from a social-constructionist, hermeneutic perspective, psychology's program is both philosophically impossible and politically dangerous. Psychology's program is impossible because a human being is constructed by the social practices of local communities. Any attempt to remove individuals from the history and culture in which they are embedded and to study them as isolated, decontextualized monads is, from a constructionist point of view, a neo-Enlightenment fantasy — it is simply not doable. Constructionists consider psychology's decontextualized program to be politically dangerous because psychologists claim to present truth that emanates from a privileged source (i.e., the psychological laboratory) that is putatively exempt from challenge and removed from the vicissitudes of history and politics.

Constructionists dispute psychology's claim to be an apolitical science (Gergen, 1973; Kessen, 1979; Prilleltensky, 1989; Sampson, 1977) because psychologists' findings are embedded in a particular sociopolitical matrix and, like any social artifact, are naturally prescriptive as well as descriptive (Fowers, 1990; Sass, 1988a). Because they reify the current sociopolitical moment, psychological experimentation has a built-in circularity (Smedslund, 1985); it assumes

Reprinted by permission of the author and the American Psychological Association from *American Psychologist* 46 (1991): 206–19. Copyright © 1991 by the American Psychological Association.

the universality of current configurations of self and society and unavoidably "proves" the validity of current social forms and conventions (Sampson, 1983). Psychologists have thereby put forth an agenda that is relative and political without appearing to do so, and thus have obscured the ideologies embedded in their theories.

To illustrate this argument and carry it forward, I offer an interpretation of Daniel Stern's (1985) book *The Interpersonal World of the Infant*. I will argue that Stern holds innate, "predesigned" qualities of the self and the universal process of language acquisition responsible for the isolation, dividedness, and alienation that are characteristic of the modern Western self. By doing so, he has dismissed the possibility that these ills, which he portrayed as natural, unavoidable aspects of universal human experience, could be caused by the predominant political and economic structures of their time. By ruling out the sociohistorical causes of psychiatric ills, Stern and other decontextualized psychology theorists discount sociopolitical change as a viable solution. Their focus is riveted on intrapsychic or dyadic explanations for emotional suffering. As a consequence they often valorize and then prescribe apolitical, intrapsychic healing techniques to the exclusion of more contextual, structural solutions.

This article is not meant to be a thorough critique of Stern's (1985) theory because Stern is not the central issue. Only certain aspects of his theory will be discussed because the goal of the article is to articulate the social-constructionist criticism of all decontextualized psychology theories. Many psychologists remove their research problems, subjects, and conclusions from their sociohistorical contexts. The basic epistemological framework of psychology is the focus of this argument.

Stern (1985) has produced a warm, insightful, creative, and deeply moving argument that places the Western configuration of self at the core of a hypothesized universal experience of infancy. The work is a brilliant effort that elucidates the masterful, bounded, feeling self. Psychotherapists in general and Kohutians in particular responded to his ideas with an enthusiasm rarely seen in the field. However, I believe Stern's popularity is not due to his discovery of universal elements of human development. Rather, his theory is popular because his formulation is such a clear statement of the present indigenous psychology. In other words, Stern has captured the heart of psychotherapists because he has reproduced it in the guise of a universal scientific theory.

SOCIAL CONSTRUCTIONISM

Stern's circularity is not surprising. Ontological hermeneuticists, sociologists of knowledge, and cultural historians have for years been beseeching psychologists to examine their assumptions and practices, especially their insistence on an empiricist, scientistic model. The social-constructionist argument, summarized, is simply this: Humans cannot be studied outside of their lived context. Any attempt to do that, and thereby to develop a set of universal laws of human nature, is bound to fail. It is not possible to develop universal, transhistorical laws because humans are not separable from their culture and history: they are fundamentally and inextricably intertwined. The distinction between the individual and the society is seen by some theorists as an ethnocentric, post hoc reification of what could be better described as a field interaction process (N. Adler, personal communication, October 27, 1990).

Constructionists argue that human nature is not universal, it is local (Geertz, 1973; Heelas & Lock, 1981). The indigenous psychologies of particular cultures are not evolving from primitive and incorrect to civilized and correct. There is no one cultural paradigm that is universally accurate about human nature. In fact, the single-minded pursuit of the universal laws of a transhistorical human nature is itself an artifact of a particular indigenous psychology (Toulmin & Leary, 1985).

Many writers (e.g., Smedslund, 1985; Toulmin, 1986) have demonstrated that a culture delineates which topics are important to study, which in turn influence the overall strategy of the study, which in turn influences what is proper data, which in turn influences how the data are collected and analyzed. Smedslund argued that social science reaffirms the indigenous psychology of the culture because its hypotheses and findings are reflexive—that is, they are "necessary" and "true" from the outset. Knowledge production is, therefore, a child of its era. It is an artifact of its time and is related to and in various ways unknowingly serves the particular constellation of power and privilege of that era.

Thus, the very act of claiming the high ground of an objective, positivist social science is a political act that obscures the cultural context (and the political uses) of its truth claims. The force with which a theory is claimed to be the product of an objective gathering of uncontaminated "facts" is the degree to which its political roots and potential uses are obscured. As Foucault (1988) taught, discourse is power, and with the advent of the modern Western state, the social sciences have become indispensable to the exercise of power (Rose, 1990).

Social constructionists call on researchers to think of human beings in a fundamentally different manner than Westerners in general and psychologists in particular are accustomed. This sometimes leads to confusion and fear because constructionists appear to call into question the foundations of the current cultural frame of reference. Such fears are often expressed in two criticisms. First, constructionists are thought to advocate a radical relativism in which there is no objective reality or transcendent moral code; therefore, they are accused of being amoral. Second, because constructionists are thought to claim that there are no universal human characteristics, it is feared that there is nothing for psychology as a discipline to study.

The first criticism is an expression of the Western, objectivist correspondence theory of truth that has been prominent in the West for almost 2,500 years. This combined with post-18th-century empiricism and 20th-century positivism to produce the epistemology of the modern physical sciences. The objectivist claim provided a scientific justification for the development and positioning of psychology within the modern state and especially in the American university (Ash, 1983; Danziger, 1979; Foucault, 1979; Poster, 1984). In response to the first criticism, theorists (e.g., Faulconer & Williams, 1985; Flax, 1989; Fowers, 1990; Gadamer, 1988; Taylor, 1989) have contributed to a constructionist argument that describes cultural frameworks that are grounded in moral discourses.[1] All cultural enterprises are considered to be constituted by shared understandings, the values and mores of everyday life, and the everyday practices that express and construct those values. Far from being a radically relativist or amoral philosophy, social constructionism is rooted in the moral. But it is not a moral code that receives its authority because it is removed from, transcends, and is superior to the particulars of everyday living. The everyday is real and moral, it is just not transcendently real and moral.

Similarly, Gergen and Gergen (1984), Gadlin and Rubin (1979), Harre (1984), Morawski (1984), and Sampson (1983) have argued that, although discovering significant universals is highly unlikely, not possible, or not relevant, it is most certainly not the only activity psychology can undertake. Local, historical, and particular phenomena cannot be removed from either the data psychological subjects produce or the findings that researchers produce. Constructionists, therefore, suggest that psychologists should embrace the inevitable and study local, historical, and particular phenomena and the indigenous psychologies of the multitude of cultures on earth. Psychologists have usually framed the search for universals through the language of the person–situation/nature–nurture debate. However, by reframing the relationship between the self and its habitat, constructionists have argued that the debate is based on a folk belief. Humans (i.e., the person or "nature") and their local habitat (i.e., the situation or "nurture"), once conceptualized by positivistically influenced psychologists as discrete forces, can be thought of in constructionism as a fluid, interpenetrating unity (Gadlin & Rubin, 1979; Sampson, 1981). Person–situation distinctions, rather than eternal verities, could simply be interpreted as versions or reflections of Cartesianism. Psychologists try to separate and factor out the particular moral discourse and everyday practices of local communities in order to find a universalizing sanction for our particular practices. Instead, we could do the possible, and, valuing them, study them. One implication of constructionists' vision is that we should undertake historically situated research about the history of contemporary Western psychology and the political impact of psychological theories. Several writers (e.g., Buss, 1979; Danziger, 1979; Gergen, 1985; Harre, 1984; Sampson, 1985; Smedslund, 1984, 1985; Taylor, 1989) have been laboring with that task. My recent work (Cushman, 1986, 1987, 1990) on the history of the self has been informed by their work. I have briefly traced the history of the Western self over the course of the last 2,500 years and explored how it developed a bounded, masterful, inner shape. The shelf changes over time not because of some essential inner nature or metaphysical evolution, but because it is simply part of what Heidegger (1977) called the *clearing* of a particular era, and must continually adapt to shifting cultural horizons (Sass, 1988a). The self is a social artifact; it is part of the clearing and therefore is influenced by and in turn influences the political structures and the economic forces of its era.

If one sets out to study the self, one must necessarily study the historical context in which it exists. That means one must study the political and economic requirements of the era and the way the self functions in order to accommodate and comply with those requirements. For instance, I have argued (Cushman, 1990) that in the post-World War II era in the United States, the predominant form of the masterful, bounded Western self is the communally isolated, empty, consumer self, hungry for food, consumer items, and charismatic leaders. To consider this self to be the single, universal self is to overlook its particular, local nature and thus to excuse its characteristic illnesses, mystify its political and economic constituents, and obscure its ideological functions.

Stern's (1985) interpersonal theory of human development, I will argue, is a good example of the subtle uses to which a decontextualized psychology theory can be put. He did not discover a transhistorical law, as he implied; his theory is a restatement of a local theory of a particular culture. This type of unintentional misrepresentation necessarily contributes to the mystification of power and the reproduction of wealth and privilege in our time.

STERN'S RESEARCH

In brief, Stern's (1985) infant research used laboratory experiments and naturalistic observations to develop a theoretical schema that challenged the normative psychodynamic separation—individuation model (Mahler, Pine, & Bergman, 1975). Stern argued that developmental theorists must guard against pathomorphic and retrospective assumptions: Theory must grow out of the data, and not vice versa. In his theory developmental phases are layered rather than mutually exclusive critical stages. The issues dealt with in one stage are not mastered and then mechanistically disappeared, or not mastered and then forever fixated upon. Phases build on one another and are interdependent. True to current social trends in the West, a crucial aspect of Stern's theory is his emphasis on the self of the infant. His entire theory is structured around the emergent, core, subjective, and verbal selves as they arise and evolve. Also in step with current trends, each phase of the evolving infant self carries with it a particular domain of interpersonal relatedness that corresponds to the particular sense of self in each phase. It is immediately obvious that, as developmental theories go, this is not a mechanistic, rigid, one-dimensional schema. It is a sophisticated and complex vision.

For the purposes of this essay only three aspects of Stern's (1985) theory will be summarized and discussed. Stern's discussion of the core self will be analyzed first. Second, the concept of a parental behavior that Stern called *attunement responses* will be discussed from a social-constructionist perspective. Third, Stern's view of the acquisition and effect of language will be explored.

Stern's Circularity

Smedslund (1984, 1985) argued that failure to place the subject of psychological study in its historical and cultural context creates a certain circularity that makes a hypothesis "necessarily true," the data predictable, and the conclusions inevitable. I believe that this circular process has resulted in the description of Stern's (1985) marvelous infant: masterful, bounded, interior, full of feelings, eager to share its subjectivity—relentlessly relational. Stern pictured the infant as a bounded, cohesive, independent, continuous Western self who is preoccupied with relating to others. Even heretofore strictly physiological activities such as eating, sleeping, and defecating were depicted by Stern as being performed within and to some extent in order to facilitate the holding container. This image is extremely appealing to modern Western readers. Why? Because it *is* them. It describes so well who they are, what they are interested in, what is most vital to them. One might well say that this concept of infancy is irresistible to them.

The question one should ask is not, "*Is* this an accurate picture?" but rather, "*Why* is the picture accurate?" If language, culture, and the historical moment have conspired to construct modern Westerners into this very singular shape, how have they done so, and for what purposes?

Stern should be acknowledged for his intellectual dedication, creativity, and expressiveness. But one must also keep Smedslund's (1984, 1985) argument about circularity in mind. The degree to which Stern's (1985) description appears accurate is the degree to which his interests, methods, and ideas fit with the dominant social construction of the time. Instead of universal laws, Stern articulated the shape of the cultural horizon at this historical moment. He did that by using methods that are valued by his professional colleagues, and in doing so collected information that is meaningful to us, in order to aid us in efficiently performing professional roles that are indispensible to our current Western way of life.

Stern's Research Goals

The evidence of circularity in Stern's (1985) book is evident from the beginning, in his explanation of the goals of his research. These goals, Smedslund would argue, determined Stern's strategies, subjects, data collection techniques, and ultimately, his conclusions. Stern explained,

I am most concerned with those senses of the self that are essential to daily social interactions. . . . I will therefore focus on those senses of the self that if severely impaired would disrupt normal social functioning and likely lead to madness or great social deficit. (Stern, 1985, p. 7)

On one hand that seems like a reasonable place to start, especially if one's readers are primarily psychotherapists whose job it is to work within the everyday social world. But Stern's (1985) basic stance also established a certain ontological frame of reference that, because it is unacknowledged, obscured his ideology and limited his theory from the outset. With that statement Stern revealed his fundamental mistake. He articulated the particular self of White, middle- and upper-class, late 20th-century Westerners, and the traits that allow that self to adequately function within its era, and yet he implied his theory is universal and transhistorical. In fact, most cultures of the world construct vastly different kinds of selves that would, to refer to Stern's original concerns, "disrupt normal social functioning" in 20th-century Western society and "likely lead to [a diagnosis of] madness or great social deficit" if displayed in that society. The anthropological studies featured in Heelas and Lock (1981), Shweder and Bourne (1984), Stigler, Shweder, and Herdt (1990), Tuan (1982), and White and Kirkpatrick (1985) describe many varieties of self configurations. For instance, the Chewong of Malaysia (Howell, 1981) believe the location of the self is in the liver; according to Heelas and Lock (1981, p. 35), the ancient Greeks believed it was in the lungs, and the ancient Egyptians placed it in the heart. The Tallensi of West Africa, Heelas and Lock (1981, p. 34) summarized, conceive of the self as "under the control of an external force located in the past," whereas Hindus believe the self is "under the control of an internal force located in the past". But Stern consistently disregarded cross-cultural reports, preferring instead to use the terms *society* and *daily social interactions* without qualifying or particularizing them whatsoever.

Similarly, Stern (1985) mentioned in passing why he considered certain senses of the self to be present at birth, if not before: because "then we are freed from the partially semantic task of choosing criteria to decide, a priori, when a sense of self *really* begins" (p. 6). This is not adequate. It is precisely this dilemma of how and when the sense of self is formed that developmental theories are supposed to study. It is not a "semantic" task, it is *the* task of a developmental theory about the self. By brushing the task aside Stern opened the way for a much easier kind of study — one that accepts as a given that a universal self, or its potential, is present at birth and, given the proper conditions, will simply unfold according to a predesigned blueprint. But an easier study does not mean a better study, it just means a less disturbing one. It forecloses the possibility that Stern will grapple with the social construction of the self and the political purposes it serves.

The result of this ontological flaw is that although Stern (1985) set the horizontal limits of his vision, he did not realize that he had done so, and so he proceeded as though his vision had no limits. Because of his unexamined metapsychology he took as a given precisely what he should have accounted for. This blind spot caused him to commit many small mistakes that, taken together, make his vast theoretical claims questionable.

Stern as Romantic

Aspects of Stern's (1985) theory appear to come out of a specific tradition in the West — the humanist-romantic tradition. Sass (1988a, 1988b) has identified and described three characteristics of the expressivist branch of humanism; all three are apparent in Stern's theory. Stern presented a theory that has universal applicability across time and cultures, and features an organicistic developmental process. That is, he portrayed the infant as containing a transhistorical self that will naturally unfold out of an inner, organic logic — a predesigned pattern. The third characteristic, which Stern also exhibited, is to extol the ultimate goodness of emotional expressiveness: "[F]ulfillment," Sass explained, is thought to result "from the actualization or expression of a potential that is inner and individual" (Sass, 1988b, p. 585). In other words, "The 'good' . . . is this inner essence itself, and anything that fosters its natural unfolding; the 'bad' (or the 'unnatural') is anything that halts or inhibits this spontaneous process" (Sass, 1988b, p. 582). Sass traced the intellectual history of these values and ideas back to the Counter Enlightenment and the romantics.

In earlier articles I have speculated about *which* social forces have significantly contributed to the construction of the configuration of the modern Western self. In this essay I will try to uncover *how* certain social processes, in this case parent–infant interactions, and intellectual discourse (e.g., Stern's [1985] developmental theory that interprets those interactions) actively construct the self.

Stern's (1985) observational data provide a rich and detailed look into the very process of social construction itself. Stern's complicated electronic equipment did not reveal the unfolding of an invariant, predesigned, universal human. Instead, Stern described the enactments of millions of behavioral microprocesses that lead, teach, and demonstrate to infants that they are little bounded, masterful, feeling selves. Furthermore, I suggest that Stern's psychological theory may itself be an important constructor of the self, because its popularity may influence many parents and psychotherapists. This ontological perspective may help in the exploration of one of the great puzzles of human history—how the peculiar current Western self, which is so remarkably different from other selves throughout history and across cultures (Geertz, 1973), is made.

Issue 1: Predesigned Mastery?

The first aspect of Stern's (1985) theory that I will examine is the development of the *core self*. As always, Stern's observations were acute and his experimental structures creative. The data were fascinating and engaging. However, I do not think that one can infer from the data the larger interpretations that Stern made. Stern argued that the core self of the infant forms from three to nine months of age, as infants develop "an integrated sense of themselves as distinct and coherent bodies, with control over their own actions, ownership of their own affectivity, and a sense of continuity" (Stern, 1985, p. 69). In the core self phase a sense of the fundamental qualities of self begins to take a clearer and more recognizable shape. The infant begins to organize a sense of self around "the palpable experiential realities of substance, action, sensation, affectivity, and time" (p. 71). These qualities are referred to as a sense of agency, coherence, affectivity, and history. Stern considered them to be the "basic self-experiences . . . necessary for adult psychological health" (p. 71). The task of the early months of life is to find, identify, and integrate the four self-experiences that Stern referred to as "islands of consistency" (p. 72) or "self-invariants." That is, senses of self that do "not change in the face of all the things that do change" (p. 71).

The identification and the interpretation of these invariants are the first problem that I will discuss. Although at first reading the four invariants appear to make sense, on closer scrutiny they become more problematic. They sound suspiciously correspondent to the characteristics of the current configuration of self predominant in the United States today. What is agency if not mastery, cohesion if not boundedness, affectivity if not emotions, and history if not continuity? Stern's (1985) description of a young infant is too close to the current American self to escape close inspection. Is it just a coincidence that the invariant aspects of self in an infant correspond so directly with the current Western concept of self?

There seems little reason to question Stern's (1985) data. The tasks performed by the infants, such as recognizing the smell of their mothers' milk or realizing that the fingers they are sucking belong to another infant's body, do appear to demonstrate a certain very physical sense of agency and physical coherence. But I do not think that one can infer from the most basic of physiological perceptions the more complex aspects of self-definition that Stern suggested.

I am sure the infants did perform the tasks that Stern (1985) described. It is in his interpretations of the tasks that the influence of his indigenous psychology is revealed. It seems problematic to interpret basic orienting and perceiving tasks in terms equivalent to full-blown adult identity issues. This part of Stern's theory is unconsciously influenced by the West's 20th-century indigenous psychology. For instance, because the attached Siamese twins pull with their arms in order to keep their respective fingers in their respective mouths they appear to have a rudimentary kinesthetic sense of what muscles work what parts of their bodies, and which fingers belong to which twin (Stern, 1985, pp. 78–79). But to call that *self-agency* and *self-coherence,* terms that usually connote complex concepts, is either an unwarranted interpretive leap or an incorrect use of words. The terms self-agency and self-coherence imply complexities and advanced capacities far too sophisticated to be applied to these behaviors.

I understand that Stern (1985) gave his schema more thematic unity by organizing it according to the qualities of the self that he believed to be present in each developmental phase. But structuring the phases in this way imputed qualities to the infant self that were not sufficiently demonstrated. Stern did this, I believe, because his ontological frame of reference causes him to see the masterful, bounded self wherever he looks. He is accustomed to seeing it because it is in the cultural clearing. He sees it even before it is constructed.

For example, when discussing the "smile of recognition" (Stern, 1985, pp. 92–93), Stern attributed complex traits to the infant self that are not present until later in the child's life. Stern wrote that infants remember the smell of the mothers' milk. When a baby's head turned toward the pad soaked in his or her mother's milk, a smile appeared. Stern attributed to the infant the thought, "My mental representation works—that is, it applies to the real world—and that is pleasurable" (p. 93). This is a gigantic leap, an attribution of adult capacity and thought far in excess of the actual behavior of the infant. The infants probably were pleased—but why? What did this mean to them? It seems more reasonable to interpret the infant's smile as an indication that a pleasurable experience was being remembered or, at most, anticipated, rather than as a confirmation that certain hypothetical mental representations have been proved to be accurate. To use this as evidence of a mind that thinks conceptually in this self-reflective manner is unwarranted.

The same mistake of overestimating the infant's behavior to prove the presence of the current configuration of self occurred throughout Stern's (1985) discussion of the core self phase. Stern defined *self-agency* as a "sense of authorship of one's own actions . . . having volition . . . having control over self-generated action . . . and expecting consequences of one's actions" (p. 71). Can these characteristics of self really be ascribed to a three- to nine-month-old infant? Given the kind of infant behavior Stern described, I see no reason to impute these characteristics to the behavior he observed. For example, Stern also described the infants as dependent on others, with a predesigned need for guidance and instruction. If they have a sense of self at this age, why did Stern not describe it as a sense of being dependent on and determined by others? Why did he emphasize the characteristic of individual agency when it seems that cooperation with and dependence on others is at least as prominent? An alternative interpretation of this quality might be the sense of *social dependence.* Stern might say that this concept is too complicated for the infant to grasp at this early age. And yet there is nothing uncomplicated about his concepts of "a sense of authorship of one's own actions," or "having control over self-generated action."

Stern (1985) defined the second self-invariant of the core self phase, *self-coherence,* as "a sense of being a non-fragmented, physical whole with boundaries and a locus of integrated action" (p. 71). But what moved Stern to characterize infants as developing a sense of self-coherence just because they seem to sense that things that move coherently in time and space belong together (pp. 82–89)? Equally compelling is Stern's description of infant experience as predominantly one of being part of a social grouping, a familial interaction that also includes friends, neighbors, and others. Why did he emphasize the characteristic of self-coherence when a sense of communality seems at least as prominent? An alternative interpretation of this quality might be the sense of *group or field coherence.*

Stern (1985) defined *self-affectivity* as a sense of "experiencing patterned inner qualities of feeling" (p. 71). But why did he characterize the infants as having a sense of inner feelings? What did they do behaviorally that suggested to Stern that they had definitively located their kinesthetic feeling states within themselves? I found nothing in Stern's data that demonstrated that. He often stressed that the parent–child dyad is composed of the interactional nature of emotions. Why, then, did he refer to "inner" qualities? If one takes Stern's argument seriously, it is more plausible to characterize infants as developing a sense of the mutuality and interdependence of affect. It is more accurate to emphasize the interactive nature of infant affect by interpreting this quality as a sense of *social affectivity.* Stern's interpretation is a good example of how difficult it is for 20th-century Westerners to conceive of feeling states that are not located interiorly.

Stern (1985) defined the last of the invariants of the core self phase, *self-history,* as "the sense of enduring, of a continuity with one's own past" (p. 71). A powerful sentiment indeed, and no doubt an important one for human development. But why must one turn to this individualistic characterization, when what seems at least equally germane, given Stern's descriptions, is a sense of sustained and continuing patterns of interaction with particular others? If interrelatedness is so crucial and prominent in infant behavior, why would they not remember and embody a sense of continuity related at least as much to the social as to the individual? In fact, because social interaction is, according to some of Stern's statements, the most important aspect of experience and survival for the infant, it would seem to be the more prominent and compelling memory. An alternative interpretation of this quality is the sense of a *social history.*

It is likely that Stern (1985) found a masterful, bounded, feeling, continuous infant in his data because that is the self that can be seen in his culture. His interpretations of the data were unintentionally and necessarily affected by what constitutes the self of his time and place. He could not see the circularity of his interpretations because they are so culturally in tune with his social terrain.

Stern's (1985) circularity becomes even more obvious when cross-cultural data are contrasted with his theory. Stern stated that the development of the four self-invariants are necessary for "adult psychological health" (Stern, 1985, p. 71). But if this is true, then how does he understand the members of cultures (such as the Tiwi, the Maori, the Chewong, the Dinka, or the Lohorung Rai; see Heelas & Lock, 1981; Shweder & LeVine, 1984) that do not believe that they have developed these qualities? Does Stern believe that they are incorrect about themselves, and that he actually knows more about their experience of life than they do? Or does he suggest that somehow the qualities of self that were predesigned in them and emerged at 3 to 9 months disappeared as they got older? If, as Stern maintained, these characteristics of self are invariants, and yet some peoples do not exhibit them, does this mean that they are genetically different from current Westerners?

Issue 2: Attunement Behaviors

The data that Stern collected as he studied what he called parental attunement behavior (Stern, 1985, pp. 138–161) illuminate an important aspect of the construction process of the Western self. The interpretation of affect attunement processes might be the most insightful and creative of Stern's contributions. Attunement behavior is a remarkable concept that he has amply demonstrated with a wide variety of colorful and vivid examples from observational data. In brief, Stern thinks that during the initial development of the sense of the *subjective self,* a phase between 9 and 18 months, parents respond to their infants with a specific type of specialized behaviors. These behaviors, which Stern believes are predesigned, intuitive parental responses elicited by certain predesigned behaviors from the infant (Stern, 1985, p. 140), have the effect of producing in infants a preverbal understanding of subjectivity. Stern also believes that parental attunements communicate to the infant that the parent can understand the infant's interior sensations of intensity and rhythm. He called this *intersubjectivity*. He believes that attunement responses demonstrate to the infants that not only can the parent understand the infant's interior realm, but that the infant can actively communicate or share feelings with the parent. This is possible, Stern said, because behavioral expressions "are to some extent interchangeable as manifestations of a single, recognizable internal state" (Stern, 1985, p. 142) in the child.

Stern (1985) argued that the intensity and frequency of parental interventions in the play of the child are unconsciously calibrated to match with or attune to the intensity and frequency of the infant's behavior. This is most striking to the observer and most effective for the infant when the matching is done cross-modally, that is, when the parent's behavior is in a different sensory mode from that of the infant. For instance, if the baby is rocking in a certain kinesthetic pattern, the parent might match intensity and rhythm in a verbal mode. Stern gave the following example:

A nine month old boy bangs his hand on a soft toy, at first in some anger but gradually with pleasure, exuberance, and humor. He sets up a steady rhythm. Mother falls into his rhythm and says, "kaaaaa-*bam*, kaaaaa-*bam*," the *"bam"* falling on the stroke and the "kaaaaa" riding with the preparatory upswing and the suspenseful holding of his arm aloft before it falls. (Stern, 1985, p. 140)

Stern explained that

What is being matched is not the other person's behavior, *per se*, but rather some aspect of the behavior that reflects the person's feeling state. The ultimate reference for the match appears to be the feeling state . . . not the external behavioral event. (p. 142)

Stern's creative interpretation of this phenomenon was that by matching the infants behavior cross-modally, the parent unconsciously and nonverbally communicates the most important lessons of the subjective self phase of development. The lessons are that the baby has an interior self that contains subjective feelings that can be brought into conscious awareness and can be communicated to another person, and that another person can match these and thus somehow share the subjectivity. Stern explained, "What is at stake here is nothing less than the shape of and extent of the sharable inner universe" (Stern, 1985, p. 152). With intersubjectivity achieved, Stern argued that the infant is then ready to move to the next phase of development, the *verbal* stage. Without an awareness of subjectivity and an ability to share subjective sensations, the child will be psychologically deficient all his or her life (Stern, 1985, p. 126).

Although Stern's (1985) methodological assumption (i.e., that behaviors contain or mask more complex meanings that are located within or underneath behavior and must be properly discovered) is highly questionable, this is a most powerful interpretation of parent–child behavior. Unfortunately I also think there is something not quite right about it. What is wrong is what is wrong with Stern's whole approach. He said that parental attunement behaviors are intuitive, predesigned responses to the infant's predesigned behavior: If the parent emits the proper response, then the infant's predesigned developmental pattern—the unfolding of the inner, subjective, bounded, masterful self—will proceed naturally.

Stern's (1985) perspective seems like common sense. But, as Smedslund (1984, 1985) explained, one should beware of scientific theories that seem like common sense; when they seem like it they usually are. That is, they are so much in tune with the dominant indigenous psychology of the era that they are circular arguments, not scientific discoveries of universal truths. Why should one believe that any of this mutual interactive pattern, which Stern observed primarily in White, middle-class mothers and children, is predesigned and universal? What moved Stern to present this phenomenon as independent of the sociohistorical context in which these infants and their parents lived? Why did he emphasize so strenuously that the infant self does not learn from the parents, but simply unfolds, and that the parents do not shape the infant's self (Stern, 1985, p. 148)? In fact, Stern emphasized that the parents' major role in all this is *not* to interfere; they are simply to let the independent, predesigned process flow along unimpeded. Stern continually presumed the mechanistic, organicistic, universal aspects of this process, yet he offered no evidence to support that assumption.

I see no reason to discount Stern's (1985) data. What I dispute is the interpretation that this marvelous process is predesigned. I believe that he offered no evidence for this because there is no evidence for it. Stern did not explain how human parents could be predesigned to facilitate the development of a masterful, bounded, interior, subjective self when only a small portion of the world's population conceives of the self in that way. In fact, as researchers such as Geertz (1973) and Shweder and Bourne (1984) have pointed out, most people in the world think middle-class Westerners are very strange to conceive of the self in the way they do. If this self is predesigned why did so many people get confused and wander so far off the predesigned path?

The varieties of the self in the world and over time cannot be explained away by saying that only one view of the self—the current, Western self—is predesigned and that all the rest are aberrations, primitive misunderstandings, or poor copies. Instead, one should question the notion that cultural artifacts (in this case a particular configuration of self) could possibly be predesigned. Ontologically, this way of thinking has been roundly discredited; the vast weight of cross-cultural and historical evidence argues persuasively against it.

For instance, LeVine (1990) reported that the Gusii, a tribe in Africa, have radically different child-rearing practices from those described by Stern (1985). Gusii mothers are prohibited from looking directly into their children's eyes or encouraging their children to look into the parents' eyes. They hold their infants much more than Western mothers do, leave them alone much less, and yet pay them far less direct, intense, sustained personal attention. Around the age of 18 months, when Stern dated attunement behaviors, the infants are placed almost exclusively in the care of their slightly older siblings, cousins, and neighbors. It is difficult to imagine how attunement behaviors could be enacted in such a setting, or how a masterful, bounded self could be constructed. Indeed, LeVine observed no such attunement behavior, nor did he uncover any evidence of a Western configuration of self before the influx of Western culture.

Critics of social constructionism often claim that the theory is unbelievable because the totality of social life, especially aspects as complex as the configuration of the self, could not possibly be created, taught, and transmitted from one generation to another. I believe that Stern's (1985) attunement theory is a brilliant description of the way that such a construction is accomplished. Attunement is not a predesigned instinct, it is a historically situated tool of this era. Historians of childhood (e.g., Aries, 1962; Demos, 1970; Kessen, 1979; Van den Berg, 1961) have demonstrated how unusual this type of child-rearing practice has been in the West. For instance, Kessen quoted from a 1914 advice manual published by the government regarding parent–child interaction: "The rule that parents should not play with their children may seem hard but it is without doubt a safe one" (Kessen, 1979, p. 815).

When attunement behavior is viewed from a social-constructionist perspective, Stern's (1985) description of the process takes on new meaning:

A ten month old girl finally gets a piece in a jig saw puzzle. She looks toward her mother, throws her head up in the air, and with a forceful arm flap raises herself partly off the ground in a flurry of exuberance. The mother says "YES, thatta girl." The "YES" is intoned with much stress. It has an explosive rise that echoes the girl's fling of gesture and posture. (p. 141)

Stern wrote, "Attunement behaviors recast the event and shift the focus of attention to what is behind the behavior, to the quality of feeling that is being shared" (p. 142).

Again we see Stern's (1985) operative assumption was that the important meaning is what is behind the behavior. Even so, I find this interpretation to be powerful and compelling. There is, however, no reason to assume that attunement interactions or interior subjectivity are predesigned. Rather, through Stern's imaginative interpretation one can get an idea of how interiority is constructed. Affect attunement could very well be one way in which the more subtle and psychologically complex horizons of the current cultural clearing are formed. The construction of interiority might get its start in these amazing exchanges between the parent, who is well versed in the language of inner feelings, and the infant, who is so actively seeking instruction in how to live in the parent's world. Attunement activities can thus be interpreted as an illustration of how language and movement function as a symbolic habitat into which the infant is inducted (N. Adler, personal communication, October 27, 1990).

I suggest that the innovative ways in which parents relentlessly demonstrate the cross-modal nature of interior sensations really instruct the child in the most basic characteristics of the Western Cartesian self—the split between subject and object, emotion and reason, feeling and thought, nature and society. According to Stern (1985), attunement behaviors communicate several ideas to the infant. The primary message delivered by parent to infant is that sensations are a primary, pure kind of spiritual energy that transcends the categories of language and society and even the five senses.

These primary sensations, the parent demonstrates, come before any limitations or objective categories inherent in language. They are pure subjectivity, and they dwell in a realm beyond mere words or characterization—a realm originally safe from the mundanity and limitation of words. Before language intrudes, parent and infant enjoy a kind of pure communion (Stern, 1985, p. 148), a sort of Robinson Crusoe-like existence, that cannot be possible once language intrudes. The innerness message thus helps construct the boundedness that is characteristic of the Western self. The cross-modal communication message that there is a realm of pure experience helps teach the subject—object split. And, using Stern's emphasis on the fullness and purity of inner sensations that antedate and are destroyed by the acquisition of language, attunement processes subtly teach the fundamental, adversarial relationship between the individual and society.

Issue 3: Acquisition and Function of Language

This leads me to a discussion of the third issue under examination: Stern's (1985) concept of the acquisition and function of language and culture. A careful reading of Stern's book uncovers a series of intellectual moves that constitute a crucial element in his ideological argument. It is an argument that ultimately obscures the constructed, historically situated nature of the masterful, bounded Western self and its political uses.

In brief, Stern's portrayal and discussion of language acquisition is as follows.

1. In the second year of life language becomes a new medium of interpersonal exchange (Stern, 1985, p. 162).

2. The acquisition of language is dependent on the development of emergent, core, and subjective senses of self and their capacities of boundedness, mastery, emotionality, interiority, and self-objectification.

During the period from two to six months, infants consolidate the sense of a core self as a separate, cohesive, bounded, physical unit, with a sense of their own agency, affectivity, and a continuity in time. . . . The period of life from roughly nine to eighteen months. . . . involves learning that one's subjective life . . . can be shared with another. (Stern, 1985, p. 10)

[The] period of the formation of the sense of a subjective self provides the experience with analogue . . . an essential step toward the use of symbols. (Stern, 1985, p. 161)

Toward the middle of the second year . . . children begin to imagine or represent things in their minds in such a way that signs and symbols are now in use. Symbolic play and language now become possible. Children can conceive of and then refer to themselves as external or objective entities. (Stern, 1985, p. 163)

3. In the early months of life, infants are guided by a mysterious and somewhat mystical process that Stern (1985) described as predesigned. For instance, he wrote that,

Infants are predesigned to be able to perform a cross-modal transfer of information . . . [which] is brought about by way of the innate design of the perceptual system not by way of repeated world experience. (p. 48)

Stern implied that infant behavior is governed initially by a set of biochemical patterns that were somehow determined before they were designed, and that infant behavior is broadly determined by these inherited and universal characteristics. According to Stern (1985), this predesigned capacity can be seen most graphically in the infant's relationship to sensation and experience. The infant has the capacity to experience the world in an unmediated, pure way. "Prior to . . . linguistic ability, infants are confined to [directly] reflect the impress of reality" (p. 182). In other words, Stern argued that the infant can experience reality without the contaminating effects of linguistic–cultural interpretations (p. 176).

4. Language is the first major skill that is learned through interpersonal interactions that are not primarily predesigned. It is only with the acquisition of language that the first influences of culture affect the previously uncontaminated infant. After language acquisition,

objectifiable selves and others can be translated into words. . . . [Then] mutually shared meaning becomes possible. (pp. 167–168)

The advent of language is a very mixed blessing to the child. . . . The infant gains entrance into a wider cultural membership, but at the risk of losing the force and wholeness of original experience. (p. 177)

5. Language is used primarily by the parent–child dyad to create new shared meanings between them.

The . . . process of learning to speak is [one] . . . of forming shared experiences, of re-establishing the "personal order," of creating a new type of "being with" between adult and child . . . a sharing of mutually created meanings about personal experience. (p. 172)

6. These shared meanings, developed through language, are symbolic, impersonal, mediated, generalized, abstract, superficial, and alienated from subjective, lived experience.

[Language] moves relatedness onto the impersonal, abstract level intrinsic to language and away from the personal, immediate level. (p. 163)

By binding it to words, they isolate the experience from the amodal flux in which it was originally experienced. Language can thus fracture amodal global experience. A discontinuity in experience is introduced. (p. 176)

Language is inadequate to the task of communicating about specific lived experience. . . . [There are] forms of slippage between personal world knowledge and official or socialized world knowledge as encoded in language. . . . The very nature of language, as a specifier of the sensory modality in use . . . and as a specifier of the generalized episode . . . ensures that there will be points of slippage. (p. 178)

7. Language progressively separates lived experiences from verbally represented experiences. It also alienates earlier senses of self from the verbal sense of self.

[Language] makes some parts of our experience less sharable with ourselves and with others. It drives a wedge between two simultaneous forms of interpersonal experience: as it is lived and as it is verbally represented. (p. 162)

8. Language requires infants to have the capacity to represent the self as an objective and instrumental entity that is seen from the outside. In other words, the self has become an objective category as well as a subjective experience. The capacity for acquiring language is the natural, unavoidable cause of this development.

Infants' initial interpersonal knowledge is mainly unshareable, amodal, instance specific. . . . Language changes all of that. With its emergence, infants become estranged from direct contact with their own personal experience. Language forces a space between interpersonal experience as lived and as represented. And it is exactly across this space that the connections and associations that constitute neurotic behavior may form. (p. 182)

9. Language is significant to the degree that it is a union experience for infant and parent, and because it provides a way to move to the next developmental level, in which infants begin to express themselves in more social ways and begin to build a narrative of their lives (Stern, 1985, p. 162).

10. Language, by attempting to translate amodal experience into words, drives amodal experiences underground. It is inevitable that

the unconscious is created; consequently the infant becomes unavoidably fragmented and divided.

To the extent that events in the domain of verbal relatedness are held to be what has really happened, experiences in these other domains suffer an alienation. (They can become the nether domains of experience.) (Stern, 1985, p. 163)

[Sometimes] the language version [of experience] and the globally experienced version do not coexist well. The global experience may be fractured or simply poorly represented, in which case it wanders off to lead a misnamed and poorly understood existence. . . . Some global experiences. . . . simply continue underground, nonverbalized, to lead an unnamed . . . but nonetheless very real existence. (p. 175)

11. Forms of "slippage" between personal and social knowledge become inevitable. These slippages cause a divergence between reality and fantasy, and between the existential self and the verbal self. Therefore, the infant's growing self is unavoidably divided by language. The self becomes divided, fragmented, alienated from itself, less intense, less emotional, less connected to its own feelings and sensory experiences, less connected to reality (especially personal reality), and less able to be in the moment.

With the advent of language and symbolic thinking, children now have the tools to distort and transcend reality. They can create expectations contrary to past experience. They can elaborate a wish contrary to present fact. They can represent someone or something in terms of symbolically associated attributes . . . that can be pulled together from isolated episodes into a symbolic representation ("the bad mother" or "incompetent me"). These symbolic condensations finally make possible the distortion of reality and provide the soil for neurotic constructs. (Stern, 1985, p. 182)

Stern (1985) depicted humans as individual, separate atoms that relate. Therefore language, like the traits of emerging consciousness and subjectivity before it, was relegated by Stern to the category of processes by which separate atoms interact. He conceived of language as something external to the individual—intrusive, creative, even revolutionizing, but a dangerous imposition nonetheless.

I will examine each of Stern's (1985) points in turn. His first point was that in the verbal self phase, language becomes a new medium of exchange for the parent–child dyad. I suppose this depends on how one defines language. The parent, of course, has been speaking to the infant from the moment of birth (and probably before). It does not seem correct to consider language new just because the infant becomes more skilled with it. What, after all, is language? Is it only words? And is it only through words and verbal language that culture is transmitted? It makes far more sense to argue that the language and frame of reference of a culture, which Heiddeger (1977) called the clearing and Geertz (1973) called the "web of meaning," is enacted, taught, and discussed as soon as the parents begin interacting with the fetus through movements, touch, and sound. The millions of clues, nuances, and indicators that delineate the shared horizons of the clearing and the microexpressions of approval or proscription that pass across the face or through the body of the parent are all aspects of language. This all begins to happen long before infants can articulate their culture's indigenous language and string sentences together. Culture comes to the infant in this way: It arrives, literally and figuratively, with mother's milk. Thus, Stern's contention that culture arrives with language acquisition misses the point. The infant is immediately and profoundly surrounded, held by, and embedded in the practices of a culture.

Stern's (1985) second point was that language acquisition depends on earlier phases of self and their growing qualities of mastery, boundedness, and subjectivity. Two things are interesting in this. First, Stern framed his entire developmental theory around the self and its vicissitudes. This was directly in keeping with the social construction of his era (Baumeister, 1987; Sass, 1988a). Second, if language acquisition is dependent on the rudimentary capacities of the Western self, then how do other peoples whose configurations of self do not include boundedness, mastery, and inner psychological feelings (Geertz, 1973; Hardman, 1981; Highwater, 1981; Howell, 1981; Shweder & Bourne, 1984) learn to talk?

In Stern's (1985) third and fourth points, he implied that with language and its prerequisite, the capacity to make symbols and to objectify the self come the impositions, limitations, and distortions of culture. Predesigned characteristics that unfolded naturally in earlier phases are replaced by the mediations of cultural concepts. Behavior ceases to be the enactments and elicitations of innate psychology and becomes instead the effects of linguistic forms and social rules. I believe that Stern had to propose this in order to protect his entire methodological structure. He needed to maintain that there is a time in life immune from the influence of culture, in which scientists can study the infant in vivo and maintain that the resultant data are uncontaminated by sociohistorical forces such as philosophical ideas and economic modes of production. But Stern's distinction is an artificial one: Infants are born into a social world that immediately speaks, gestures, and holds them. Language is not an external imposition, it is a habitat. From the more general influences of architecture, body language, and clothing to the more intimate interactions of voice, gaze, and touch within the parent–infant dyad, the cultural frame of reference is omnipresent. It is a convenient fiction for decontextualized theorists to maintain that the preverbal infant is free of culture, and it is certainly in keeping with popular notions of language and culture prevalent in the West since the Enlightenment (Geertz, 1973; Shweder, 1984). It allows researchers to interpret the behavior of the infant without having to take culture and politics into consideration.

Stern's (1985) fifth point was that the function of language is the creation of shared meaning within the parent–infant dyad. But are these shared meanings not fundamentally cultural in origin? The implication that the parent and infant create from scratch meanings that are exclusive to the dyad alone seems impossible from an ontological perspective. The activities that parents and infants participate in, the language they use, and the meanings imputed to them, consist of everyday habits, songs, games, and stories that are embedded in a culturally transmitted heritage. It was also incomplete for Stern to imply that language's primary function is something other than cultural transmission. Again Stern revealed a tendency that is characteristic of him—to see only the present dyadic relationship. He rarely acknowledged or discussed issues and relationships beyond the dyad or temporal concerns that extend beyond the immediate moment.

Stern's (1985) sixth and seventh points characterized language's shared meanings as alienated from subjective, lived experience and as driving a wedge between lived and verbally represented experience and between earlier senses of self and the verbal self. This argument attacks language as the cause of a "fall from grace." With language, Stern argued, comes the splits between nature and society and between emotion and rationality. Because Stern did not acknowledge these splits as historical artifacts, he was required to explain them in another way, through the universal nature of language.

This argument contains a type of "noble savage" view of infant development: When infants are without language or the capacity for language they experience the world in an immediate, unmediated way, directly through the sensorium. As a result the infant is pure and whole. But with the advent of language the infant self becomes divided and fragmented; its experience of the world becomes mediated, superficial, and abstract. The infant loses the pristine communion with nature into which it was born. This view of human nature has been roundly discredited by numerous authors. If this view is correct, then what is the "I" by which the infant self views and interprets the world? From what vantage point or with which tools can the infant categorize, discriminate, and make choices?

Stern's (1985) stance regarding language is simply untenable. I believe he was forced to take this position in order to introduce the influence of culture, which he did not wish to acknowledge in earlier stages of development. When he did introduce it, he depicted it as an evil (or at best a two-sided) force that disrupts the natural purity and beauty of the predesigned self and causes irreparable damage to a previously natural wholeness. He placed the full weight of the cultural enterprise on language, and held it responsible for the particular illnesses of Western culture, such as alienation, fragmentation, and emotional isolation. Stern's decontextualized schema required a way to hold universal aspects of development responsible for the influences and consequences of cultural factors such as political and economic systems. Otherwise, he would have been forced to analyze the minute influences of the particular Western systems on the particular Western self. This he chose not to do.

Stern's (1985) eighth point explained the way that language requires infants to objectify and instrumentalize the self. Stern portrayed the split between subject and object, which is so characteristic of and exclusive to the modern Western self, as a universal occurrence. If he had not done this, Stern would have had to study and explain how and to what purposes sociohistorical forces constructed the modern self.

Stern's (1985) ninth point was to claim that language is important because it helps achieve union between parent and infant, and because its achievement is necessary for the next stage of development. Again, Stern's cultural frame of reference emerged in his conclusions. Language assists the self in its two greatest tasks: the dual achievement of relatedness and continual personal growth. Stern ignored language as a tool of cultural transmission and communal well-being. He valued it primarily to the degree to which it promotes the counter-Enlightenment values of the primacy of dyadic relationships and individual expressiveness.

In Stern's (1985) 10th point responsibility for the loss of amodal perception and the origin of the unconscious was placed squarely on the acquisition of language. The result of these occurrences, he suggested, is an increasingly fragmented and divided self. Universalizing the cause and the interiorized location of the unconscious allows Stern to disregard its historical causes and the part it played in the development of the capitalist, industrial state. Also, by using language as the scapegoat, he explained away a potentially embarrassing gap in his theory: Because amodal perception has been discovered, its disappearance from adult experience had somehow to be explained. He accomplished this by blaming language for its absence or undergroundness. The historical constituents and political functions of cultural artifacts such as the unconscious have been discussed by such authors as Jacoby (1975), Lowe (1982), Sass (1987), and Taylor (1989). To ignore the historical roots of an artifact such as the interior unconscious mystifies its historical origins and thus obscures its sociopolitical functions.

Stern's (1985) 11th point was to posit the unavoidability of slippage between personal and social knowledge. This slippage, he argued, causes a divergence between reality and fantasy, and finally, between the natural and the social self. Most of the ills of the 20th century Western self—its divided, fragmented, alienated qualities, and its loss of immediate feeling capacities—are laid at the feet of language acquisition. This argument again reflected Stern's steadfastness in imputing the causes of particular social and historical products to universal, predesigned features of human development.

Thus Stern (1985) unintentionally supported the current political constellations of power and privilege by defining psychological problems as originating in universal, normative human development. To Stern, psychological problems occur between individuals who are members of dyads, between an individual and his or her own senses of self, and between various internal objects within the self. Stern implied that psychological problems are exclusively cured by personal, intrapsychic changes such as getting more in touch with and expressing more directly one's subjective feelings, living more in the existential moment, and developing more intimate moments with loved ones. Stern's formulation ignored sociohistorical causes of personal alienation and thus potential political solutions. It is a vision that is inner directed, ahistorical, and anticultural. Critiques of this type of person-centered, cognitivist approach have been developed by Gadlin and Rubin (1979) and Sampson (1981), among others.

I have concluded that Stern executed these moves because his argument depended on them. He had to posit a time of life essentially free from cultural influence in order to collect the ahistorical, decontextualized data that he values and believes exist. Therefore he also had to stipulate a time when that type of pure data and the organicistic, developmental unfolding that generated them can no longer be found in their uncontaminated state (i.e., when culture first begins to influence the infant). He chose as that developmental moment the phase in which language is acquired. Language then became the inevitable purveyor of much that is bad (i.e., not predesigned) in the world, including alienation, isolation, and self-objectivication — the basic problems of the 20th century Western self.

CONCLUSION

Of course Stern (1985) did not make these mistakes intentionally. His ahistorical, anticultural paradigm is currently favored by a majority of psychologists, both clinicians and academics. That is part of the reason his work has been received with such acclaim: He "proves" in humane and well-turned prose that the themes of the culture and world view that dominate psychology are scientifically correct. His ideas feel right to many psychologists because they seem to capture the essence of their human experience.

But, for good or ill, the ways that modern Western culture moves one to experience life and to conceive of the self are not the only ways to do so. If scientific investigators acknowledge this, they may be able to generate explanations and develop solutions to our problems that are not quite so limited by the necessity of protecting current scientific theories, the inviolability of the current configuration of self, or the political and economic status quo.

Discourse is especially powerful when theories are claimed to emanate from an unquestionable source that transcends human authority, or when data are purported to be entirely removed from history and politics. For example, the Book of Deuteronomy, which the Jewish priestly class "found" in a cave in 621 B.C.E., coincidentally granted that class vast new powers through God's holy word (Rivkin, 1971, pp. 42–63). In a second example, the avant-garde, modernist myth embedded in the landmark 1913 ballet "Rites of Spring" was claimed to draw its authority from a transcendent, prerational realm beyond good and evil. It was an essential element of the cultural clearing in which Hitler eventually came to power (Eksteins, 1989; Stigliano, 1990). Similarly, a scientific theory that explains current psychological ills through universalist, intrapsychic explanations exempts the current socioeconomic system from responsibility. Regardless of its form, any discourse that is said to be free of political influence or to have authority from the gods is dangerous.

Stern's (1985) theory of infant development is an example of this kind of subtle political discourse. Stern reinforced the current configuration of self and contributed to its ongoing construction. He did this by claiming to prove that the problematic qualities of the current Western self are universal and invariant, and by maintaining that his data were collected through a scientific process that ruled out historical and political influences. Therefore the vicissitudes of the current self, such as its alienated, divided, fragmented state, were presented as ahistorical, unavoidable, predesigned psychological phenomena and not as artifacts of the 20th century Western world in which Stern lives.

By claiming to have found scientific proof that the human infant automatically emerges as a Western infant, Stern (1985) made a profoundly political statement. He implicitly argued that the empty, divided, narcissistic, confused, isolated individual of the modern West, who has such difficulty maintaining intimate relationships and cooperating in communal endeavors, is the natural, inevitable shape of human being. He believes that socioeconomic forms have had no effect on the essential shape of this self, and therefore they can have no significant effect on changing it. In Stern's view, political forces will come and go, but they are primarily inconsequential; what matters is what has been predesigned, and nothing that can be done in the social realm can change that.

That is a political statement with profound consequences. The political problems of the present time are immense, and it is dangerous to believe that they are simply the inevitable consequences of a predesigned human nature. If that were true, there would be no hope that human intellectual activity could change them.

Although the constructionist critique challenges the foundational beliefs of most mainstream approaches to experimental psychology, constructionists do not consider all psychological research to be ill conceived. Several writers, (e.g., Danziger, 1979; Faulconer & Williams, 1985; Gadamer, 1988; Gergen, Hepburn, & Comer-Fisher, 1986; Habermas, 1987; Hare-Mustin & Marecek, 1988; Harre, 1984; Mednick, 1989; Morawski, 1984; Packer, 1985; Prilleltensky, 1989; Sampson, 1978, 1983; Smedslund, 1984; Stigliano, 1989) have advocated contextual approaches to psychological research that feature an ontological hermeneutic perspective. These writers are developing the way to a new, more historically situated psychology. New approaches would recognize a new psychological subject, and in response develop new data-collection processes, new means of analyses, and thereby more historically situated conclusions—in short, a new body of psychological literature.

I believe there is an unequivocal need for such a new body of literature. The variety of configurations of the self over time and across cultures indicates that selves are constructed socially and thus can be shaped to some degree according to what researchers value. Uncomfortable as it is to think in these terms, psychologists are in the business of doing just that. If psychologists are going to do more than support the status quo and reproduce the current forms of power and privilege in the world, we must situate our work historically, situate the current concept of self, and study how that self is constructed and how it fits with and reproduces the current sociopolitical forms and structures of our world. We will have to decide whether we approve of that fit and whether we want to contribute to it.

Those who "own" the self control our world. That is, those who are accorded the right to define, describe, understand, and heal the self are in a powerful, prescriptive position. They can determine what constitutes health and pathology, proper and improper behavior, and the appropriate objects and practices of love and hate. The self specialists have expertise in the realm of interpersonal behavior— which, in our world, means nearly all aspects of life. All social activity is thus defined, described, and controlled by those who are experts on the self.

Therefore, the battle over the self—who knows it, who is responsible for it, who can heal it—is a central aspect of this era's struggle for power and hegemony. The "mythologizing of the monadic self" (N. Adler, personal communication, October 27, 1990) is the linchpin of a particular ideological agenda. For this reason seemingly neutral, apolitical theories on such subjects as infant development have important political consequences. It is not the kind of battle that psychologists can opt out of; we are integral to the struggle. Let us be careful not to unknowingly lend our support to forces that perpetuate a kind of world that, ultimately, we would abhor.

Decontextualized psychology theorists have obscured their ideologies, denied their historical situatedness, and mystified the impact of political forces on individual lives. Decontextualized theories, creative, soothing, and eloquent though they may be, in the end prevent people from facing the political consequences of this era and developing structural solutions that might lessen the suffering that is all around us. Recently, social constructionists in psychology have offered the field an alternative direction. Let us explore the possibilities.

NOTES

I wish to thank Louis Sass, Stanley Messer, Edward Sampson, Hilde Burton, Anthony Stigliano, Nathan Adler, Jules Burstein, Margaret Guertin, Larry Wornian, and Karen Cushman, for their help in shaping this article.
1. Constructionists take seriously the differences between cultures. These differences may mean that certain actions are difficult or even impossible to interpret from the point of view of another cultural understanding. However, there are features of various cultures, especially moral and ethical concerns, that may appear to be similar. Culture appears to face questions pertaining to how a worthy life is defined and lived, and how obligations and commitments such as promises and agreements are carried out. It is not the content of a particular behavior or belief, but its contextual meaning, that is the crucial issue. Constructionists recognize and respect cultural differences without imposing an a priori unity on these differences. When resemblances between cultures emerge, they are not explainable by an underlying, common human nature (Stigliano, 1990). It is not impossible to appreciate or comprehend the meanings of other cultures, but it is difficult.

REFERENCES

Aries, P. (1962). *Centuries of childhood: A social history of family life.* New York: Vintage.

Ash, M. (1983). The self-presentation of a discipline: History of psychology in the United States between pedagogy and scholarship. In L. Graham, W. Lepinies, & P. Weingart (Eds.), *Functions and uses of disciplinary histories* (pp. 143–189). Boston: MA: Reidel.

Baumeister, R. (1987). How the self became a problem: A psychological review of historical research. *Journal of Personality and Social Psychology, 52,* 163–176.

Buss, A. (Ed.). (1979). *Psychology in social context.* New York: Irvington.

Cushman, P. (1986). The self besieged: Recruitment-indoctrination processes in restrictive groups. *Journal for the Theory of Social Behavior, 16,* 1–32.

Cushman, P. (1987). History, psychology, and the abyss: A constructionist-Kohutian proposal. *Psychohistory Review, 15,* 29–45.

Cushman, P. (1990). Why the self is empty: Toward a historically situated psychology. *American Psychologist, 45,* 599–611.

Danziger, K. (1979). The social origins of modern psychology. In A. Buss (Ed.), *Psychology in social context* (pp. 27–44). New York: Irvington.

Demos, J. (1970). *A little commonwealth: Family life in Plymouth Colony.* New York: Basic Books.

Eksteins, M. (1989). *Rites of spring: The great war and the birth of the modern age.* Boston: Houghton Mifflin.

Faulconer, J., & Williams, R. (1985). Temporality in human action: An alternative to positivism and historicism. *American Psychologist, 40,* 1179–1188.

Flax, J. (1989). *Thinking fragments: Psychoanalysis, feminism, and postmodernism in the contemporary West.* Berkeley: University of California Press.

Foucault, M. (1979). *Discipline and punishment: The birth of the prison.* New York: Vintage/Random House.

Foucault, M. (1988). The political technologies of individuals. In L. Martin, H. Gutman, & P. Hutton (Eds.), *Technologies of the self: A seminar with Michel Foucault* (pp. 145–161). Amherst: University of Massachusetts Press.

Fowers, B. (1990, August). Beyond objectivism and relativism: Overcoming psychology's legitimation crisis. Paper presented at the 98th Annual Convention of the American Psychological Association, Boston.

Gadamer, H. (1988). *Truth and method.* New York: Crossroad.

Gadlin, H., & Rubin, S. (1979). Interactionism: A nonresolution of the person-situation controversy. In A. Buss (Ed.), *Psychology in social context* (pp. 213–238). New York: Irvington.

Geertz, C. (1973). *The interpretation of cultures.* New York: Basic Books.

Gergen, K. (1973). Social psychology as history. *Journal of Personality and Social Psychology, 26,* 309–320.

Gergen, K. (1985). The social constructionist movement in modern psychology. *American Psychologist, 40,* 266–275.

Gergen, K., & Gergen, M. (Eds.). (1984). *Historical social psychology.* Hillsdale, NJ: Erlbaum.

Gergen, K., Hepburn, A., & Comer-Fisher, D. (1986). Hermeneutics of personality description. *Journal of Personality and Social Psychology, 50,* 1261–1270.

Habermas, J. (1987). Modernity—An incomplete project. In P. Rabinow & W. Sullivan (Eds.), *The interpretive turn: A second look* (pp. 141–156). Berkeley: University of California Press.

Hales, S. (1986). Epilogue: Rethinking the business of psychology. *Journal for the Theory of Social Behavior, 16,* 57–76.

Hardman, C. (1981). The psychology of conformity and self-expression among the Lohorung Rai of E. Nepal. In P. Heelas & A. Lock (Eds.), *Indigenous psychologies: The anthropology of the self* (pp. 161–180). San Diego, CA: Academic Press.

Hare-Mustin, R., & Marecek, J. (1988). The meaning of difference: Gender theory, postmodernism, and psychology. *American Psychologist, 43,* 455–464.

Harre, R. (1984). *Personal being: A theory for individual psychology.* Cambridge, MA: Harvard University Press.

Heelas, P., & Lock, A. (Eds.). (1981). *Indigenous psychologies: The anthropology of the self.* San Diego, CA: Academic Press.

Heidegger, M. (1977). *The question concerning technology and other essays.* New York: Harper & Row.

Highwater, J. (1981). *The primal mind: Vision and reality in Indian America.* New York: Meridian.

Howell, S. (1981). Rules not words. In P. Heelas & A. Lock (Eds.), *Indigenous psychologies: The anthropology of the self* (pp. 133–143). San Diego, CA: Academic Press.

Jacoby, R. (1975). *Social amnesia: A critique of conformist psychology from Adler to Laing.* Boston: Beacon Press.

Kessen, W. (1979). The American child and other cultural inventions. *American Psychologist, 34,* 815–820.

Levin, D. (1987). Psychopathology in the epoch of nihilism. In D. Levin (Ed.), *Pathologies of the modern self: Postmodern studies on narcissism, schizophrenia, and depression* (pp. 21–83). New York: New York University Press.

Levin, D. (1988). *The opening of vision: Nihilism and the postmodern situation.* New York: Routledge.

LeVine, R. (1990). Infant environments in psychoanalysis: A cross-cultural view. In J. Stigler, R. Shweder, & G. Herdt (Eds.), *Cultural psychology: Essays on comparative human development* (pp. 454–474). Cambridge, England: Cambridge University Press.

Lowe, D. (1982). *History of bourgeois perception.* Chicago: University of Chicago Press.

Mahler, M., Pine, F., & Bergman, A. (1975). *Psychological birth of the infant.* New York: Knopf.

Mednick, M. (1989). On the politics of psychological constructs: Stop the bandwagon, I want to get off. *American Psychologist, 44,* 1118–1123.

Morawski, J. (1984). Historiography as a metatheoretical text for social psychology. In K. Gergen & M. Gergen (Eds.), *Historical social psychology* (pp. 37–60). Hillsdale, NJ: Erlbaum.

Packer, M. (1985). Hermeneutic inquiry in the study of human conduct. *American Psychologist, 40,* 1081–1093.

Poster, M. (1984). *Foucault, Marxism, and history: Mode of production versus mode of information.* Cambridge, England: Polity Press.

Prilleltensky, I. (1989). Psychology and the status quo. *American Psychologist, 44,* 795–802.

Rivkin, E. (1971). *The shaping of Jewish history.* New York: Scribner.

Rose, N. (1990). *Governing the soul: The shaping of the private self.* New York: Routledge.

Sampson, E. E. (1977). Psychology and the American ideal. *Journal of Personality and Social Psychology, 32,* 309–320.

Sampson, E. E. (1978). Scientific paradigms and social values: Wanted—A scientific revolution. *Journal of Personality and Social Psychology, 36,* 1332–1343.

Sampson, E. E. (1981). Cognitive psychology as ideology. *American Psychologist, 36,* 730–743.

Sampson, E. E. (1983). *Justice and the critique of pure psychology.* New York: Plenum.

Sampson, E. E. (1985). The decentralization of identity: Toward a revised concept of personal and social order. *American Psychologist, 40,* 1203–1211.

Sass, L. (1987). Schreber's panopticism: Psychosis and the modern soul. *Social Research, 54,* 101–145.

Sass, L. (1988a). Humanism, hermeneutics, and the concept of the human subject. In S. Messer, L. Sass, & R. Woolfolk (Eds.), *Hermeneutics and psychological theory: Interpretive perspectives on personality, psychotherapy, and psychopathology* (pp. 222–271). New Brunswick, NJ: Rutgers University Press.

Sass, L. (1988b). The self and its vicissitudes: An "archeological" study of the psychoanalytic avant-garde. *Social Research, 55,* 551–607.

Shweder, R. (1984). Anthropology's romantic rebellion against the Enlightenment, or there's more to thinking than reason or evidence. In R. Shweder & R. LeVine (Eds.), *Culture theory: Mind, self, and emotion* (pp. 27–66). New York: Cambridge University Press.

Shweder, R. (1990). Cultural psychology—What is it? In J. Stigler, R. Shweder, & G. Herdt (Eds.), *Cultural psychology: Essays on comparative human development* (pp. 1–43). Cambridge, England: Cambridge University Press.

Shweder, R., & Bourne, E. (1984). Does the concept of the person vary cross-culturally? In R. Shweder & R. LeVine (Eds.), *Culture theory: Mind, self, and emotion* (pp. 158–199). New York: Cambridge University Press.

Shweder, R., & LeVine, R. (Eds.). (1984). *Culture theory: Mind, self, and emotion.* New York: Cambridge University Press.

Smedslund, J. (1984). The invisible obvious: Culture in psychology. In K. Lagerspetz & P. Niemi (Eds.), *Psychology in the 1990s* (pp. 443–452). Amsterdam: North-Holland.

Smedslund, J. (1985). Necessarily true cultural psychologies. In K. Gergen & K. Davis (Eds.), *The social construction of the person* (pp. 73–87). New York: Springer-Verlag.

Stern, D. (1985). *The interpersonal world of the infant: A view from psychoanalysis and developmental psychology.* New York: Basic Books.

Stigler, J., Shweder, R., & Herdt, G. (Eds.). (1990). *Cultural psychology: Essays on comparative human development.* Cambridge, England: Cambridge University Press.

Stigliano, A. (1989). Hermeneutical practice. *Saybrook Review, 7,* 47–69.

Stigliano, T. (1990). Moral human action as the basis for human science. *Saybrook Review, 8,* 73–104.

Taylor, C. (1989). *Sources of the self.* Cambridge, MA: Harvard University Press.

Toulmin, S. (1986). The ambiguities of self-understanding. *Journal for the Theory of Social Behavior, 16,* 41–55.

Toulmin, S., & Leary, D. (1985). The cult of empiricism in psychology, and beyond. In S. Koch & D. Leary (Eds.), *A century of psychology as science* (pp. 549–617). New York: McGraw Hill.

Tuan, U. (1982). *Segmented worlds and self.* Minneapolis: University of Minnesota Press.

Van den Berg, J. (1961). *The changing nature of man: Introduction to a historical psychology.* New York: Norton.

White, G., & Kirkpatrick, J. (Eds.). (1985). *Person, self, and experience: Exploring Pacific ethnopsychologies.* Berkeley: University of California Press.

18. The Challenge of Social Change for Psychology: Globalization and Psychology's Theory of the Person

Edward E. Sampson

A commonplace assumption maintained by those scientists who study the world of plants and animals suggests that our knowledge would not advance very far were our theories of a particular species to ignore the ecological niche the life form inhabited. We know, for example, that such environmental conditions as the composition of the soil and amount of rainfall have a significant effect on the characteristics of a plant's root system and its leaf structure (from Wicker, 1979). In the world of persons, it is likewise reasonable to suggest that our knowledge would be inadequate were our theories of the person insensitive to the social world into which persons are born and within which they carry out their lives.

Fortunately, this perspective is generally well known to many psychologists (e.g., Bronfenbrenner, 1977; Erikson, 1950; Gergen & Davis, 1985; Harré, 1984; Luria, 1976; Tajfel, 1984; Vygotsky, 1978) and has also formed a central feature in the emergence of several important interpersonally and culturally oriented theories of psychopathology (e.g., see Greenberg & Mitchell, 1983, for a useful review). Although this sensitivity to the social world is admirable, I believe that we have not gone far enough in connecting our theories of the person with social change, in particular, with major historic transformations in the social world (but see Luria, 1976, for a partial exception). What effect on our theory of the person would occur, for example, if the current social world were to undergo a major transformation of the same order as the historic change from the

Reprinted by permission of the author and the American Psychological Association from *American Psychologist* 44 (1989): 914–21. Copyright © 1989 by the American Psychological Association.

premodern to the modern era? Surely this magnitude of change would have a dramatic impact on our understanding of the person.

It is my contention that we are currently undergoing just such a major transformation (e.g., see Block, 1987; Bowles & Gintis, 1987; Mumford, 1956; Poster, 1984; Reich, 1987). The modern, industrialized world of the last several centuries is gradually but perceptably yielding to a postmodern, postindustrial (i.e., information-rich and service-oriented), globally linked world system. For the most part, psychology's current theories of the person were developed during the era of modernism and were apt descriptions of that era's framework of understanding. These theories were well suited to a world dominated by industrialization, technology, secularism, individualism, and democracy (e.g., Nisbet, 1969): a world in which the self-contained individual (Sampson, 1977, 1985) emerged from embeddedness in various collectivities to become the free-standing, central unit of the new social order.

The transformation from the modern era's industrialized and individualized settings into the postmodern era's postindustrial, information-based, and globally linked social environments will call for a dramatic transformation in psychology's theories of the person. Over 30 years ago, Mumford (1956) noted that we are on the verge of "another great historic transformation" (p. 138). He suggested that the major task humanity confronts is to create a new self, better suited than the current form, to deal with the issues that this historic change will introduce, in particular, issues that derive from the emergence of a globally linked world system. This transformation, I believe, sets the challenging task and future agenda for psychology.

THE CHANGING FUNCTIONAL UNIT OF THE SOCIAL ORDER

One of the clearest changes that characterizes the transition from traditional to modern Western society involves the change of the functional unit of the social order from the community and household to the individual (e.g., Aries & Duby, 1988). Where once households dotted the landscape and were the unit of central relevance for understanding human life, the breakdown of the traditional social order and the emergence of the individual modified this picture.

Premodern Western society understood persons as defined by their particular social contexts. Persons were fundamentally citizens of the *polis,* members of their religious communities, spouses, soldiers and so forth, not merely individuals as such. Unlike our current understanding, which distinguishes between real persons and the roles they must play, in premodern society, roles were the elements that constituted the person as such. Roles were not appended to the "real" person who somehow continued to dwell authentically somewhere behind them. There was no stepping outside one's community and one's roles within it in order to act differently; one always acted within the community and in its behalf. To be outside was in effect to be nonexistent, a stranger, or dead.

In MacIntyre's (1984, 1988) view, shared with several other commentators whose writings form the basis of my own analysis (e.g., Cahoone, 1988; Sandel, 1982), life itself had a clearly defined purpose or *telos* that provided the context of meaning and relevance for all human existence. Every person's life was carried out in the service of this larger purpose. Intrinsic value resided in the community, its objects, events, and practices.

MODERNISM: THE EMERGENCE OF THE SELF-CONTAINED INDIVIDUAL

The modern era began approximately around the 15th and 16th centuries. For a variety of complex sociopolitical and economic reasons well beyond the scope of this present essay, individuals *qua* individuals increasingly came to populate the social world. Anyone wishing to understand human life now had to contend with fathoming the dynamics of the individual. This is not to suggest that conceptions of the individual were absent in the premodern era, but rather to note that a differently formulated theory of the person was required once individuals replaced the community and household as the functional unit and organizing principle of society.

A liberal individualist framework emerged at this time, both to oppose the premodern understanding and to establish the familiar terms of modern life. Individuals were to be set free from all the ties and attachments that formerly defined them. Individuals, understood as self-determining, autonomous sovereigns, authors in charge of their own life's work, became the central actors on the social stage. Sandel (1982) referred to these newly minted individuals as disembodied, unencumbered subjects; MacIntyre (1988) described them as characters possessing "their identity and their essential human capacities apart from and prior to their membership in any particular social and political order" (p. 210). I have referred to these newly emerged subjects of modern life as self-contained individuals (Sampson, 1977, 1985, 1988).

Modernism's liberating vision called for a rather complete detachment of individuals from the ties that formerly bound them into the *telos* of their community and that defined who or what they were or could be in terms of that *telos*. This detachment set people free to determine their own self-definitions. The particular forms that communities would take were henceforth to be understood as derivative of the desires and preferences of the individuals who comprised them.

Thus, both the meaning of individual and of community dramatically changed. Individuals were constituted as entities apart from any particular community; they had priority over it and so could freely choose the forms of association to which they would subject themselves. In turn, the community became an *instrumentality* for individuals, a necessity required so that individuals could pursue their personally chosen purposes in life, or at times, a *sentimentality,* involving ties of affection freely given by one person to others (see Sandel, 1982, pp. 147–154). The premodern sense of a community that creates individuals was lost; communal associations were established by persons who fundamentally existed independently of those associations and who could as freely withdraw their consent to belong as they freely gave it in the first place (e.g., see Bowles & Gintis's, 1987 discussion of "exit" rather than "voice" to describe this form of individual power under the conditions of modern life).

The hallmark of modernism's theory of the person was the priority it established for the individual. Whatever formerly held intrinsic meaning and provided the framework within which individual's actions were undertaken (e.g., the community) lost that meaning to the meaning-endowing capacities of the individual subject. Prioritizing the individual assured that the stranglehold of tradition over the person would be undone. Persons were free to establish their own framework of belief and value, to choose the goals and purposes that they desired.

Under this theory of the person, a "well-ordered society is . . . one in which people are free to pursue their various aims" (Sandel, 1982, p. 116), and the task of government is to assure the conditions needed to allow individuals to choose their own aims and purposes in life, not to set these aims for the individual (also see MacIntyre, 1984). It was assumed that society was made up of a plurality of individuals possessing different interests and that the function of the government was to see that fairness reigned in working out the melding of this plurality of divergent interests and talents into some workable plan.

As Weber (see Gerth & Mills, 1946) noted, administration and management became central features of the modern period, and efficiency of operation emerged as the one shared standard for judging the worth of any enterprise. The state was to remain indifferent and neutral, neither taking sides nor espousing any one purpose over any other beyond ensuring that no single purpose would dominate. The individual was simply "to propose and to live by whatever conception of the good life he or she pleases" (MacIntyre, 1988, p. 336).

In effect, by giving priority to the individual, the liberal individualist's theory of the person required viewing individuals as being, at least in part, *antecedent* to the society in which they lived. Only in this way did it make sense to speak of persons as subjects capable of choosing the ends or purposes they would pursue. When ends and purposes are given the priority they held in the premodern tradition, then persons are more subjected than they are subjects. For persons to be freely capable of choosing, they must be understood to be external to and separate from society: "The subject, however heavily conditioned by his surroundings, is always, irreducibly, prior to his values and ends, and never fully constituted by them" (Sandel, 1982, p. 22).

This modern, liberal individualist theory of the person does not deny the importance of values and purposes for human life. Rather, given the priority it establishes for the individual, it emphasizes the point "that the values and relations we have are the products of choice, the possessions of a self given prior to its ends" (Sandel, 1982, p. 176). In other words, a voluntarist notion of personhood is at the center of the liberal individualist tradition. Needless to say, given this kind of theory of the person, anyone who wishes to understand human life must necessarily focus intently on the dynamics of the individuals whose activities create the features of human life that we encounter.

PSYCHOLOGY EMERGES

I have just described the larger social world within which modern psychology was born and in which its ongoing growth was assured.

With the emergence of the individual as the functional unit of the social order, a discipline such as psychology made sense as the appropriate vehicle for understanding human life by studying the dynamics of this self-contained individual.

Although psychology has taken many different forms and has developed a variety of seemingly opposing perspectives on the nature of persons, the overriding concern with understanding the individual marks the commonality across this diversity. That concern with the individual, in turn, was required by the emergence of the individual as the central unit and organizing principle of the modern era of Western social life. Studying individuals during the time in which the household was the functional unit of the social order would have made little or no sense. Once the individual emerged as central, however, seeking to understand the individual became a highly cherished cultural project (see Foucault, 1979, 1980, on a similar theme).

None of what I have said is intended to criticize either psychology or the tradition of liberal individualism within which it was born and nurtured. My point is to remind us of the profound connections among the shape of a social order, the kinds of functional units it constitutes as central, and in this case, the emergence both of the individual unit and of psychology as the discipline designed to study that unit.

TOWARD A GLOBALIZED FUNCTIONAL UNIT FOR THE SOCIAL ORDER

The point of this brief review of the historic transformation of the premodern into the modern era is to lay the foundation for what I contend is the next major societal transformation, from modernism to postmodernism. If this latter transformation introduces a functional unit for the social order other than the individual, then what sense will there be to continue to study the dynamics of the individual as currently conceived? In effect, studying the individual makes sense under the historical conditions of modernism, in which the individual became the central unit and organizing principle of society. Once modernism moves into the wings and a new organizing principle emerges as central to the social order, then another object of study, founded on a different theory of the person and a different conception of the discipline of psychology, will be required.

In my view, we are already witnessing a significant transformation in the central organizing principle of society away from the individual and toward some more globally conceptualized entity. Although space limitations do not permit my doing more than mentioning them and providing references for additional reading, we can already see signs of this change in a wide variety of cultural endeavors that have challenged the primacy of the individual as currently understood, that is, as the familiar self-contained form (Sampson, 1977, 1985, 1988). Examples are deconstructionism (e.g., Derrida, 1974, 1978, 1981), feminism (e.g., Gilligan, 1982; Lykes, 1985; Miller, 1976), cross-cultural work on concepts of the person (e.g., Geertz, 1979; Heelas & Lock, 1981; Miller, 1984; Shweder & Bourne, 1982), and the challenge to liberal individualism (e.g., Cahoone, 1988; MacIntyre, 1984, 1988; Sandel, 1982; also see Shweder's 1982 review of the "liberalism as destiny" theme reflected in Kohlberg's 1981 work on moral reasoning).

It is my contention that the age of individualism has already moved off center stage for Western, industrialized societies and is rapidly being replaced by a more globalized functional unit (see Block, 1987; Bowles & Gintis, 1987; Poster, 1984). Quite simply, understanding the individual *qua* individual is no longer relevant to understanding human life. Even today, that understanding demands theories and methods oriented toward a more global type of entity. In the years ahead, the dominance of this global functional unit will be even greater, demanding that we revise our work accordingly.

One arena in which this transformation is clearly apparent involves the functioning of the economic system (e.g., Bowles & Gintis, 1987; Reich, 1987). Even a casual observer of the economic system in the United States, for example, will be impressed with how much its operation can no longer be understood simply by examining the internal or local market system. Economic analysis must become increasingly sensitive to the linked world market system as a key unit of analysis in its own right. Those whose futures were tied up in the U.S. stock market, for example, saw how precarious those futures were when in October 1987 the U.S. market plunged; most became painfully aware of the way in which their personal economic benefits were determined by events occurring in stock exchanges in Asia and Europe and not simply by local events (see Sewell, 1988, on a similar point).

It is not only the economic sphere, however, that reveals the emergence of an essentially global functional unit. Technological innovations have made it possible to communicate with and to experience lives far removed from our own territory. Our knowledge and informational boundaries cannot be contained as they once were; our consciousness and even our rationality can no longer be assumed to be securely housed within our self-contained individuality. As technology expands our range of contacts, the sources for socializing our identities will be further enlarged.

Many other areas of current life also reveal the force of globalization. Pollution does not respect national boundaries. Policies and behaviors of states and persons far removed from our own habitats have profound implications for our longevity, economic status, and the very quality of our lives. The threat of nuclear annihilation casts a shadow that extends around the world, placing each of us in the darkness and doubt of events occurring on a truly global basis.

In these and in numerous other ways, we have become members of a large, linked world system. Our lives are elements in several dramas that can no longer be understood simply by focusing narrowly on our inner experiences or personal preferences. Whether the narrowed focus on the self-contained individual is seen to be an ideological obfuscation for the operation of sinister social forces taking place behind our backs (as Marxian analysis would suggest) or simply a survival into the late 20th century of the state of 19th century society, the point remains much the same. The functional unit whose understanding we must seek is no longer the individual as currently understood, but something more globalized in its form. In effect, the theory of the person that was suited to the era of individualization is ill suited to the era of globalization. A new theory of the person is needed, thus posing a new, different, and indeed difficult challenge to psychology, the field whose origins lay in developing and exploring the current theory of the person.

Although no one has yet come forth with a satisfactory description of the new functional unit or the revised theory of the person it entails, it is clear that the critics of the liberal individualist tradition have at least recognized the already visible winds of change (e.g., Bowles & Gintis, 1987; Cahoone, 1988; MacIntyre, 1984, 1988; Sandel, 1982). I have found their interpretations to be some of the most insightful. I hasten to note that for the most part these critiques were not written in order to establish a globalized alternative, but I believe that the direction of their analyses suggests the very kind of transformation in the theory of the person that is well suited to the postmodern, globalized era.

TOWARD A GLOBALIST THEORY OF THE PERSON

As we have seen, the liberal individualist perspective is understandable once we locate it in opposition to the premodern tradition, which it replaced. However, as persuasive as its perspective might sound to those of us reared under its auspices, Cahoone (1988), MacIntyre (1984, 1988) and Sandel (1982) have concurred in arguing that it is incoherent on its own terms, whereas Bowles and Gintis (1987) and Block (1987) have viewed it as rife with internal contradictions. In effect, the liberal individualist tradition cannot realize what it purports to achieve and continue to sustain its theory of the person.

The arguments here are complex and can only be briefly summarized. MacIntyre (1988) has suggested that the disembodied selves characteristic of the liberal individualist tradition are supposed to act rationally in choosing the ends they will seek. Yet, insofar as rationality is not a transcendent possession of individuals, but exists only as defined within a particular tradition, and insofar as liberal individualism has eschewed all tradition, it leaves persons without any grounds for acting rationally. Cahoone's (1988) argument is similar to MacIntyre's although he spoke of rationality as lodged within culture rather than using MacIntyre's term, *tradition.* Sandel's analysis of Rawls's (1971) theory of justice provides a further development of this point. He persuasively demonstrated the incoherence of Rawls's liberal individualist theory of the person by revealing the nonindividualistic understandings that are required if Rawls's claims are to be upheld.

Although I do not take issue with this strategy of undoing liberalism on its own terms, my own point involves the failure of the liberal individualist theory of the person in the context of an emerging new tradition, postmodern globalization. In agreement with MacIntyre's (1988) argument, I suggest that as world history changes, traditions that formerly presented suitable ways of conceptualizing reality may provide visions that are out of touch with newly emerging issues. In great measure, this occurred when the premodern theory of persons was no longer suited to the spirit of industrialization, capitalism, the rising dominance of the nation-state, and liberal democracy. An alternative tradition, liberal individualism, emerged and provided a more appropriate formulation of the nature of persons and their association and so replaced the premodern understanding.

The globalization of the postmodern world has created severe strains for the liberal individualist theory of the person. These strains are not simply a function of the incoherence of liberal individualist theory on its own terms, but are also due to its failure to offer a framework for an understanding of the nature of persons that is better suited to a global, linked world system. It is against this background that I see the necessary emergence of a new kind of functional unit for the social order and a theory of the person based on a postmodern tradition of human understanding.

A CONSTITUTIVE VIEW OF THE PERSON

If my analysis of historical change is correct, our present task is to unfold the essential characteristics of a globalized theory of the person. I have found Sandel's (1982) ideas most helpful. In developing his critique of liberal individualism, Sandel distinguished between *its* concept of possession (to which, following my own previous terminology [Sampson, 1977], I will refer as self-contained) and an alternative, constitutive view.

In breaking individuals free from all those attachments that formerly set the terms of their very existence, and thereby granting them priority, the liberal individualist theory of the person compels us to dissociate persons from any particularly contingent circumstances of their lives. As Sandel (1982), among others, has reminded us, persons cannot be both sovereign agents free to determine the ends they will seek and at the same time essentially *be* what they have chosen. Sovereignty means that persons must stand outside this network of their choosing; otherwise they lose their priority as subjects who choose, select, and decide. Sandel has argued that this formulation of an unencumbered subject is essential to the liberal individualist theory of the person and is found in nearly every representative of this tradition.

Although we should not invariably expect to find so direct a statement of the unencumbered view as is made here, any other possibility would be incoherent given the entire fabric of liberal individualist social, economic, political, psychological and even, for the most part, religious institutions and practices. For example, there would be little sense in viewing people as giving their voluntary consent to be governed if we simultaneously fail to view persons as the kinds of creatures who are able to give such voluntary consent. For persons to be such creatures, we logically require a theory of the person that grants priority to persons over anything to which they may choose to subject themselves.

As I previously commented, psychology has grown up within the liberal individualist tradition and should thereby reveal this central feature of the tradition in its own theories of the person. One can readily discern this emphasis on the self-contained view within most psychological understanding (e.g., Sampson, 1977, 1985, 1988). I will shortly turn to some noteworthy exceptions (e.g., Gergen & Gergen, 1988; Harré, 1984; Tajfel, 1984). Although some psychological theories try to operate interactively, I can see no reason to alter the conclusion I previously reached: These accounts emphasize two self-contained entities interacting, rather than adopting the constitutive tradition to which I will now turn (also see Lykes, 1985).

Sandel contrasted the liberal individualist (i.e., self-contained) conception with an alternative, constitutive view in which persons are seen as creatures whose very identities are constituted by their social locations. There are no subjects who can be defined apart from the world; persons are constituted in and through their attachments, connections, and relationships. Unlike the liberal individualist view in which persons choose the lives they will lead and construct the kinds of community they will inhabit, in this alternative view, persons' "more or less enduring attachments and commitments" (Sandel, 1982, p. 179) help define who the persons are. In Sandel's view, persons do not choose the ends or purposes they will select to follow, but rather they engage in a shared, common process of discovery in which their goals and purposes are revealed in a never-ending process of living with others.

Both Cahoone (1988) and MacIntyre (1984, 1988) have echoed this constitutive formulation of the person. Cahoone emphasized the internal rather than external relationship between culture and person. Culture is not something that stands in the way of persons or something that persons must overcome in order to realize their real self, but rather it is the only vehicle available for persons to know and to understand who they are.

Although MacIntyre (1984, 1988) did not use the same terminology as Cahoone or Sandel, it is clear that in his examination of the classical and the Aristotelean conceptions of the person he has adopted much this same point of view. He captured this understanding in observing that for Aristotle, "it is the individual *qua* citizen who reasons . . . [but] in the practical reasoning of liberal modernity it is the individual *qua* individual who reasons" (1988, p. 339). In other words, reasoning in the modern tradition is a kind of transcendent capacity of individuals who are reasoning personages regardless of their particular social setting. In the classical and Aristotelean tradition, by contrast, reasoning can occur only by virtue of the context within which it emerges, guided by the *telos* of that context.

In effect, for the constitutive view, there is no meaningful way to speak about persons abstracted from the particular community that is an essential ingredient of their identities as persons. The liberal individualist tradition sought to accomplish just this abstraction in the name of providing freedom and dignity for the individual. Yet, by so thoroughly detaching persons from the social and historical locus that constitutes their very being, the modern liberal individualist tradition has had the ironic effect of denying persons any kind of dignity, autonomy, or power (e.g., Bowles & Gintis, 1987). The detachment and prioritization of the individual creates an empty, functionally meaningless abstraction incapable of doing much of anything. The constitutive perspective contrasts markedly with this modern tradition. In its view, attachments within a community do not describe mere attributes of a person's identity but are in effect constituents of their identities: "The community of which they are a part . . . describes not just what they *have* . . . but also what they *are*" (Sandel, 1982, p. 150).

PERSONAL VERSUS COMMON OWNERSHIP

None of the critics of the liberal individualist tradition have set forth the complete terms of a new tradition to replace the waning liberal individualist formulations that they have criticized. As I have suggested, however, the constitutive framework they have introduced is more compatible with the emerging era of globalization than with the era of individualization, for which the self-contained view was more suitable. Let me now build on these ideas and focus on one of the most central implications of the constitutive theory of the person for understanding the person–other or person–society relationship. The key is the notion of ownership.

Within the liberal individualist tradition, individuals are assumed to have personal ownership of the identities they possess, including all of their attributes (e.g., talents and abilities) as well as the outcomes of whatever achievements their particular abilities and motivations bring to them. Macpherson (1962) referred to this understanding as possessive individualism: a "conception of the individual as essentially the proprietor of his own person or capacities, owing nothing to society for them" (p. 3). In Macpherson's view, consonant with Sandel's (1982) perspective, individual freedom is founded on this concept of the individual as fundamentally "an owner of himself" (p. 3).

Because individuals retain personal ownership, they have personal responsibility for determining how to dispose of what they own. The particular ways in which we enter into contracts or exchange relationships with others or the ways in which we negotiate an agreement would have little meaning if persons did not rightfully claim personal ownership over their possessions and achievements. Personal ownership lets persons enter into agreements in which they decide to give up a part of what they own in exchange for benefits they will receive from others who are similarly situated.

Indeed, the essence of liberal individualist society is this notion of personal ownership and the theory of the person it requires: That is, persons are understood to be antecedent to any kind of constitutive community. However, once we have reformulated our conception of the person from the self-contained to the constitutive view, we see that the attributes (e.g., possessions, abilities, and achievements) that we currently believe are private items to be disposed of as persons wish are common goods for community consideration. Sandel (1982) captured this transformed meaning as follows:

What at first glance appear as "my assets" are more properly described as common assets . . . since others made me, and in various ways continue to make me the person I am, it seems appropriate to regard them . . . as participants in "my" achievements and common beneficiaries of the rewards they bring. (p. 143)

In other words, if a person's attributes are held to be at least partly determined by the community that has constituted the person, attributes we currently consider to be private possessions are recast into attributes for use on behalf of the common good. Persons become the guardians of particular assets, not their owners. Needless to say, this is a very different way of understanding achievements, possessions, talents, and so forth. Each individual is the guardian of these assets on behalf of something larger than personal benefit; the disposition of such assets is not an individual's choice as much as a matter for community evaluation and decision in terms of its interests and purposes.

Reich (1987) has offered a similar perspective in his analysis of health and retirement benefits, urging a transformation from their current conception as individual entitlements to entitlements common to a community of persons constituted by that community. Reich expressed a concern about the current way that certain benefits are allocated within U.S. society, observing, for example, that providing medical benefits to individuals may actually encourage poor preventive health habits: Persons receive medical care whether or not their own behavior has been guided by principles of healthful living. Reich noted how in a thoroughly individuated situation, devoid of what we would term constitutive attachments, no one bears any responsibility for anyone's behavior and so we all pay for each individual's irresponsibility.

The flavor of this can be gleaned from considering efforts to legislate the wearing of helmets by motorcyclists. The battle lines involve pitting the rights of individuals to do with their lives whatever they please and the rights of the community members who eventually pay the medical bills for long-term care of the profoundly brain-injured riders. Under the liberal individualist ethic, persons own their own lives, and so long as one life does not intrude on another, persons can choose to live any way they wish, even foolishly. Riding without a helmet is a right all individuals have; the community has no stake in controlling this kind of private behavior. However, insofar as persons' relationships to their communities are more constitutive than self-contained, the community does have a stake in what occurs.

The constitutive view transforms the entire person—community relationship. The point is not simply that the community has a stake in what happens to its individual members and thus must intervene in their lives, but equally, because individuals are constituted by their communities (i.e., they are not self-contained individuals with lives apart from others) community involvement is not experienced as an improper intrusion into their personal affairs. Because persons' attributes are not privately owned apart from their community, they do not have the same sense of being violated by infringements on their freedom of self-determination that we currently have.

As I have noted, the constitutive formulation of the person better suits the global world into which we are rapidly heading than the self-contained liberal individualist conception that has dominated our self-understandings during the modern period. We have gone well beyond that modern period and have entered a new world with new issues and demands. The liberal individualist theory of the person is not simply incoherent in its own terms, promising what it cannot logically provide, but it also fails to offer a blueprint for the era of globalization in which persons will increasingly be parts of a thoroughly linked, interdependent global world system. Actions in one segment of this system have consequences for all, and therefore a more constitutive vision is required.

PSYCHOLOGY'S ROLE

By now it should be clear that the discipline of psychology emerged within the era of modernism and has participated in the liberal individualist perspective that is the hallmark of that tradition. Psychology is not to be faulted for its embeddedness in the liberal individualist tradition, but its future task will be to deal with the challenge of the era of globalization that is now looming on the horizon. A psychology for tomorrow is a psychology that begins actively to chart out a theory of the person that is no longer rooted in the liberal individualist assumptions, but is reframed in terms more suitable to resolving the issues of a global era.

I previously commented that there already exist several harbingers of this new era, including much of the feminist scholarship within psychology. In my view, however, the feminist perspective should no longer be understood as developing a psychology of women but, I believe, is better seen as developing a psychology of humanity tomorrow. The real issue, therefore, does not involve gender differences per se, as much as it speaks to an emerging theory of the person that is appropriate to the newly emerging shape of a globally linked world system.

Other recent contributions to psychology also have sought to redirect the focus of the field toward the constitutive conception of the person I have presented in this article. Harré (1984), for example, has introduced a meaning for "personal being" that is clearly constituted within the social world. In defining the fundamental human reality to be a conversation, Harré has compelled us to become aware of the manner by which personhood is socially constituted. Harré cited the works of Shotter (cited in Harré, 1984) and some of his associates on the concept of *psychological symbiosis* to describe the way in which a socially constituted personhood is learned: "In psychological symbiosis mothers do not talk *about* the child's wishes and emotions; they *supply* the child with wishes, needs, intentions, wants and the like, and interact with the child as if it had them" (p. 105).

Likewise, the recent contributions of Gergen and his associates (e.g., Gergen & Davis, 1985; Gergen & Gergen, 1988) provide a further attempt to contextualize our theory of the person (e.g., also see Sarbin, 1977). Gergen and Gergen (1988), for example, outlined a theory of the self as a narrative in which, although the object is the single individual, "it would be a mistake to view such constructions as the product or possession of single selves" (p. 37). There is a clear correspondence between this manner of understanding personal identity as narrative and the constitutive view of the person and of possession I previously outlined.

The recent two-volume compilation outlining the European approach to social psychology edited by Tajfel (1984) offers still further evidence of active efforts within the field of psychology to bring the social dimension to topics such as attribution, emotion, and cognition, which are usually considered in a more strictly individually self-contained manner.

By now it should be apparent that my point has not been to bemoan any lack either of sensitivity or of activity on the part of at least certain segments of the field to develop a differently framed theory of the person. Although these and related efforts mark significant strides in turning the field around, to my knowledge there have been few, if any, efforts (with Luria's, 1976, pioneering efforts standing as a possible exception) systematically to link changes in the theory of the person, which these authors have sought to describe, with the dramatic transformation in the social order now taking place.

For the most part, psychology has not been as reflective about its own subject matter as it needs to be, at least not in the sociohistorical sense that I have sought to describe. Psychology has not seen its role to be that of discovering what theory of the person it currently espouses, how that theory conforms to a particular kind of social and historical order, how changes in that social and historical order will require a new theory of the person, and especially how a central role for psychology is to take the lead in generating this new theory.

I have introduced not only a challenge for psychology, but also a new and somewhat different role: to begin to explore, systematically and as a central feature of its disciplinary agenda, the contours of a new theory of the person suitable for the global era into which we are rapidly heading.

REFERENCES

Aries, P., & Duby, G. (1988). *A history of private life, II: Revelations of the medieval world*. Cambridge, MA: Belknap Press of Harvard University Press.

Block, F. (1987). *Revising state theory*. Philadelphia, PA: Temple University Press.

Bowles, S., & Gintis, H. (1987). *Democracy and capitalism*. New York: Basic Books.

Bronfenbrenner, U. (1977). Lewinian space and ecological substance. *Journal of Social Issues, 33,* 199–212.

Cahoone, L. E. (1988). *The dilemma of modernity: Philosophy, culture and anti-culture*. Albany, NY: State University of New York Press.

Derrida, J. (1974). *Of grammatology*. Baltimore, MD: Johns Hopkins University Press.

Derrida, J. (1978). *Writing and difference*. Chicago: University of Chicago Press.

Derrida, J. (1981). *Dissemination*. Chicago: University of Chicago Press.

Erikson, E. (1950). *Childhood and society*. New York: Norton.

Foucault, M. (1979). *Discipline and punish: The birth of the prison*. New York: Random House.

Foucault, M. (1980). *The history of sexuality: Vol. 1. An introduction*. New York: Random House.

Geertz, C. (1979). From the native's point of view. On the nature of anthropological understanding. In P. Rabinow & W. M. Sullivan (Eds.), *Interpretive social science* (pp. 225–241). Berkeley: University of California Press.

Gergen, K. J., & Davis, K. E. (1985). *The social construction of the person*. New York: Springer-Verlag.

Gergen, K. J., & Gergen, M. M. (1988). Narrative and the self as relationship. In L. Berkowitz (Ed.), *Advances in experimental social psychology* (Vol. 21, pp. 17–56). New York: Academic Press.

Gerth, H. H., & Mills, C. W. (1946). *From Max Weber: Essays in sociology*. New York: Oxford University Press.

Gilligan, C. (1982). *In a different voice: Psychological theory and women's development*. Cambridge, MA: Harvard University Press.

Greenberg, J. R., & Mitchell, S. A. (1983). *Object relations in psychoanalytic theory*. Cambridge, MA: Harvard University Press.

Harré, R. (1984). *Personal being*. Cambridge, MA: Harvard University Press.

Heelas, P., & Lock, A. (Eds.). (1981). *Indigenous psychologies: The anthropology of the self*. London: Academic Press.

Kohlberg, L. (1981). *The philosophy of moral development: Moral stages and the idea of justice, Volume 1. Essays on moral development*. San Francisco: Harper & Row.

Luria, A. R. (1976). *Cognitive development: Its cultural and social foundations.* Cambridge, MA: Harvard University Press.

Lykes, M. B. (1985). Gender and individualistic vs. collectivist bases for notions about the self. *Journal of Personality, 53,* 356–383.

MacIntyre, A. (1984). *After virtue* (2nd ed.). Notre Dame, IN: University of Notre Dame Press.

MacIntyre, A. (1988). *Whose justice? Which rationality?* Notre Dame, IN: University of Notre Dame Press.

Macpherson, C. B. (1962). *The political theory of possessive individualism.* London: Oxford University Press.

Miller, J. B. (1976). *Toward a new psychology of women.* Boston: Beacon Press.

Miller, J. G. (1984). Culture and the development of everyday social explanation. *Journal of Personality and Social Psychology, 46,* 961–978.

Mumford, L. (1956). *The transformation of man.* New York: Harper & Row.

Nisbet, R. A. (1969). *Social change and history.* London: Oxford University Press.

Poster, M. (1984). *Foucault, Marxism and history.* Cambridge, England: Polity Press.

Rawls, J. (1971). *A theory of justice.* Cambridge, MA: Belknap Press of Harvard University Press.

Reich, R. B. (1987). *Tales of a new America.* New York: Vintage Books.

Sampson, E. E. (1977). Psychology and the American ideal. *Journal of Personality and Social Psychology, 35,* 767–782.

Sampson, E. E. (1985). The decentralization of identity: Toward a revised concept of personal and social order. *American Psychologist, 40,* 1203–1211.

Sampson, E. E. (1988). The debate on individualism: Indigenous psychologies of the individual and their role in personal and societal functioning. *American Psychologist, 43,* 15–22.

Sandel, M. J. (1982). *Liberalism and the limits of justice.* Cambridge, England: Cambridge University Press.

Sarbin, T. R. (1977). Contextualism: A world view for modern psychology. In A. W. Landfield (Ed.), *Nebraska symposium on motivation* (pp. 1–41). Lincoln: University of Nebraska Press.

Sewell, J. W. (1988, May 22). Help the third world catch up. *New York Times,* p. 7.

Shweder, R. A. (1982). Liberalism as destiny. *Contemporary Psychology, 27,* 421–424.

Shweder, R. A., & Bourne, E. (1982). Does the concept of the person vary cross-culturally? In A. J. Marsella & G. White (Eds.), *Cultural concepts of mental health and therapy* (pp. 97–137). Boston: Reidel.

Tajfel, H. (Ed.). (1984). *The social dimension: European developments in social psychology* (Vols. 1 & 2). Cambridge, England: Cambridge University Press.

Vygotsky, L. S. (1978). *Mind in society.* Cambridge, MA: Harvard University Press.

Wicker, A. W. (1979). *An introduction to ecological psychology.* Monterey, CA: Brooks/Cole.

B. IDENTITY, POWER, AND THE COLLISION OF CULTURES

In the United States today, there are increasing numbers of people who are dealing with the collision of cultures, either because they grow up in biracial or mixed ethnic families, or because they are immigrants or refugees with different cultural mores from the U.S. cultural norms, or because they are members of a marginalized or marked culture group living within the dominant culture (for example, African Americans and Native Americans, gays and lesbians, disabled people). How such individuals negotiate the multiple cultural realities, develop an identity, and come to terms with cultural power differentials and stigmatization is the thread that binds the essays in this section together.

We begin in chapter 19 with an essay by Susan Fiske because she directs our attention immediately to the relationship between power, stereotyping, and social control. No topic is more central to an understanding of cultural differences than that of stereotyping which Fiske identifies as the cognitions and beliefs that people have of an individual based on group membership. By examining how people at different rungs in a dominance hierarchy attend (or do not attend) to each other, she shows that stereotyping and power are mutually reinforcing.

The researcher J. W. Berry develops a complex model of psychological acculturation of people moving between cultures in chapter 20. Importantly, he emphasizes the process of change over time as both individuals and cultures interact and shape each other. In an extensive review of research strategies for the study of acculturation, he argues for a research model that can operationalize generational differences, flux in acculturation attitudes and acculturation stress, distinctions between different types of acculturation groups, voluntariness of contact, and marginalization/integration.

Teresa LaFromboise, known for her studies and work with Native Americans, and her colleagues Hardin Coleman and Jennifer Gerton review the literature on the psychological impact of being bicultural in chapter 21. Of particular importance, especially because of La-Fromboise's deep knowledge of Native American communities, is arriving at a model of individual development that posits that an individual can gain competence in more than one culture without having to lose one's cultural identity or chose between cultures. Most of the literature on bicultural individuals assumes that a person living in two cultures will necessarily suffer some kind of psychological distress and disadvantage.

As we have argued in the Introduction, there are some individuals within our society who are categorized and marginalized largely because outsiders label and treat them as "different." Such minority groups, for example, the physically disabled or gays and lesbians, may in fact be constituted by individuals with diverse views of themselves, their practices, and beliefs. Their "culture" may develop in part as a reaction to outsiders' definitions and stereotypes of them, in part as a function of their unity in social activism. There is good reason, however, as the authors of the next two essays point out, to consider such groups as minority groups since they meet Dworkin and Dworkin's criteria for minority group status (1976): identifiability, differential power, differential and pejorative treatment, and group awareness.

Not much research has been done, as Michelle Fine and Adrienne Asch point out in chapter 22, on the lived experience of handicapped people who as a group must live in a world built on the assumption of physical health and mobility. There are a host of stereotypes people hold about the vulnerability and neediness of disabled people —stereotypes that reveal more, perhaps, about people's fear of physical handicap and loss of control than about how disabled people view themselves. Contrary to what outsiders assume, disability may not be salient in an individual's self-definition. Fine and Asch challenge us to think about "how these assumptions get made, why they persist, and what functions they serve for researchers and society."

A central question of Laura Brown in her exploration of gay and lesbian reality in chapter 23 is: "What happens if what has previously been a conceptual ghetto, even within feminist psychology, is redefined as the center of the universe of understanding?" Are gay and lesbian issues to remain "special topics" in American psychology or can gay and lesbian experience expand our comprehension of the intrapsychic and interpersonal? Brown argues that, in spite of the diversity within these "minority" groups, there are common elements that form lesbian and gay reality: biculturalism, marginality, and normative creativity.

Maria Root also addresses the topic of biculturalism in chapter 24, but focuses on the phenomenological experience of "otherness." Root, a bicultural person herself (half-Asian, half-white), is a clinician interested in the identity development of bicultural individuals and the sociopolitical and family influences that shape a child's experience of biculturalism. She is eloquent when writing about the tensions between racial components within oneself, the dynamics in families in which parents are of different racial or ethnic heritage, and the pain of trying to live by irrational racial classification rules.

REFERENCES

Dworkin, A. and R. Dworkin, eds. 1976. *The minority report.* New York: Praeger.

19. Controlling Other People: The Impact of Power on Stereotyping

Susan T. Fiske

Issues of power and stereotyping haunt our history and our present as human beings. Without stereotypes, there would be less need to hate, exclude, exterminate. For good reasons, people object to being stereotyped, categorized, and attributed certain characteristics in common. People do not want to be stereotyped because it limits their freedom and constrains their outcomes, even their lives. In short, stereotypes exert control. Obviously, stereotypes exert control through prejudice and discrimination. Victims of stereotyping know this and rightly resist stereotypes for those reasons. I want to go beyond these fundamental truths and argue that stereotypes are controlling by their very nature and all too easily result from power, from asymmetries in control.

My argument focuses on some relationships between stereotyping and controlling others. It begins by discussing how stereotypes result from and maintain one person's control over another; it claims that stereotypes are intrinsically controlling of other people. The focus here is on how power encourages stereotyping, as well as how stereotyping maintains power. The argument also describes how powerful people can be discouraged from stereotyping by getting them to pay attention. Essentially this account rests on the motivating impetus of social structure on the individual. I suggest that social control operates through the direction and nature of attention. People in power stereotype in part because they do not need to pay attention, they cannot easily pay attention, and they may not be personally motivated to pay attention.

Reprinted by permission of the author and the American Psychological Association from *American Psychologist* 48 (1993): 621–28. Copyright © 1993 by the American Psychological Association.

To illustrate these relationships between stereotyping and control, consider two real-life examples that both pertain to gender stereotyping, although the principles apply to other forms of stereotyping as well. Both examples came from legal cases in which I served as an expert witness.[1] These cases presented superficially different but fundamentally similar cases of stereotyping; both revealed the impact of power, controlling others. Afterward, I will define terms more closely, note relevant literature, and describe some of our relevant research.

TALES OF TWO WOMEN

Lois Robinson worked as a welder in a certain Jacksonville, Florida, shipyard. Jacksonville Shipyards Inc. (JSI) repaired Navy and commercial ships in dry dock—tough, sometimes dangerous work. Women made up less than 5% of the JSI workforce and less than half of 1% of the skilled craftworkers. Typically there were no or few women on any given shift, so a woman was likely to be the only woman in the crowd getting on the shipyard buses or punching out at the time clock.

The JSI shipyard has been described as a boys' club, a man's world, with "Men Only" painted on one of the work trailers. (When someone complained, the sign was painted over, but in a cursory way.) It is perhaps best summarized as a locker-room atmosphere, with a lot of practical joking and teasing. For example, one worker put a flashlight in his pants to show how well-endowed horses are; another carved the handle of a tool to resemble a penis, waving it in the face of the women. There was open hostility to women on the part of a few men: "There's nothing worse than having to work around women; women are only fit company for something that howls." More often, there was simply a great deal of off-color joking (including one often-repeated joke about death by rape). Obscenity and profanity were routine.

Prominent in the visual environment ("every craft, every shop") were many calendars showing women in various states of undress and various sexually explicit poses. Comparable magazines were widely shared, and pinups were torn out and posted spontaneously. Decorating various public walls were graffiti, both words and cartoons, with explicit sexual content depicting women. There were no pictures or graffiti of naked men. The workers were not allowed to bring other magazines on the job, and they were not allowed to post other material that was not work-related.

The few women workers were typically called by demeaning or sexually explicit names (honey, dear, baby, sugar, momma, pussy, cunt, etc.). They were constantly teased, touched, humiliated, sexually evaluated, and propositioned; the incidents occurred "every day all day" involving "all crafts," according to depositions.

Lois Robinson, the welder, complained about the magazines and calendars, but she was brushed off, all the way up to the top. And even at the highest levels, one manager pointed out that he had his own pinups. Another manager reminded her patriotically that pinups had brought us through World War II. Robinson eventually filed a lawsuit alleging sex discrimination due to sexual harassment in a hostile work environment; she won her case at the trial court level. JSI has appealed, and that is pending.

What does this case have to do with stereotyping, control, and power? Why was it so important to the men at JSI to keep their magazines and calendars, and why were some men so openly hostile to the women? One answer lies in the social structure, specifically the dramatic power asymmetries between the men and women at JSI. It was a man's world where men controlled the distinctly male atmosphere, the coin of social acceptance, and the tangible rewards. Women as a group were radically powerless: outnumbered, out of place, and on trial. Men thus controlled the work environment and shaped it to their own needs. Essentially, one cause of stereotyping at JSI was the men's impunity; they did not need the women for any workplace rewards. The power structure at JSI contributed to the generally aversive and stereotypic work environment. I will describe the mechanisms in more detail shortly.

Moving from the male workers in general to the specific upper-level managers who heard and rejected Robinson's complaints, one can see the effects of managerial overload. Not only were these men part of the traditionally dominant group but they were also given specific institutional power, that is, control over many people's outcomes in the workplace. As managers, by definition each was attending to many underlings. Under such conditions of attentional overload, it was easier to form a superficial, stereotyped-based judgment and dismiss the complaint of one underling, especially an outsider.

Another source of stereotyping at JSI was the small number of men who not only harassed the women but also were openly hostile. In effect, some men were really "bad apples," such as the one who claimed that women were unfit company at work. Not knowing anything more about these particular men, one can only speculate, but an individual problem seems likely. I speculate that one possible problem was an overriding personal dominance orientation.

The second case was set against the boardrooms of a Big Eight accounting firm, Price Waterhouse (PW). One of the top managers brought in millions of dollars in accounts, worked more billable hours than anyone in that cohort, was well liked by clients, and was described as aggressive, hard-driving, and ambitious. But this exemplary manager was denied partnership because she was not feminine enough. Ann Hopkins was not accepted as a partner because of "interpersonal skills problems" that would be corrected, a supporter informed her, by walking, talking, and dressing more femininely.

Although the setting was not exactly Jacksonville Shipyards, it did encourage stereotyping of women in several comparable ways (see Fiske, Bersoff, Borgida, Deaux, & Heilman, 1991). First, Hopkins was in a firm that had approximately 1% female partners (7 of 662), and she was the only woman out of 88 individuals proposed for partner that year; the few women managers stood out. Second, being a manager in a Big Eight firm is a stereotypically masculine job, calling for tough, aggressive behavior; consequently people think there is a lack of fit between being a woman and being a manager (Glick, Zion, & Nelson, 1988; Heilman, 1983). Third, stereotypes operate more freely on ambiguous criteria, such as judgments of interpersonal skills, than on unambiguous counting criteria, such as number of billable hours. PW failed to guard against bias in these subjective judgments, and there were considerable differences of opinion about how to interpret Hopkins's hard-driving managerial behavior. Fourth, the partnership evaluations were based on ambiguous and scant information in many cases; hearsay and casual opinions were given substantial weight. Finally, the firm had no explicit policy against gender discrimination, although it did prohibit discrimination on the basis of age or health in partnership decisions. Ann Hopkins also filed a lawsuit alleging sex discrimination, which she won, even though PW appealed it up to the Supreme Court. The American Psychological Association filed an amicus brief that apparently was helpful to the Supreme Court in deciding this case (Fiske et al., 1991; but see Barrett & Morris, 1993a, 1993b; Fiske,

Bersoff, Borgida, Deaux, & Heilman, 1993a, 1993b; Goodman, 1993; Saks, 1993).

How does an analysis in terms of control fit here? Just as in the shipyard, the men were in power at PW, and the women were outnumbered, out of place, and on trial. The men controlled an atmosphere that might best be characterized as an exclusive gentlemen's club, in which women were guests who were expected to defer to the men's customs. The men as a group did not particularly need the few women in order to obtain workplace rewards, so again, there was a fundamental issue of resource control. In addition, these busy partners were evaluating up to 88 partner candidates, added to a grueling workload in one of the world's premier accounting firms, and perhaps overloaded conditions contributed to their lack of attention to their own decision processes. In addition to these features of social structure, there were a few bad apples who seemed to have personal problems, such as the partner who each year complained that women should not even be senior managers, let alone partners. Again, we see power asymmetries in the social structure, attentional overload, plus a few individuals with special problems.

At this point, it is important to note that this analysis is not engaging in what our graduate students call "male bashing." I am not saying that men in general are the specific culprits in stereotyping. In fact, the whole burden of this essay is that it is a matter of social structure and a matter of individual personality dynamics that are likely to encourage stereotyping. *Any* group in the kind of social structure described here would be likely to stereotype other people. *Any* individual with the kind of personality dynamics described here would be likely to stereotype other people. So, I argue for a more general theoretical basis underlying these two specific examples, even though both of them happen to include gender.

STEREOTYPING AND CONTROL

Stereotyping operates in the service of control. Stereotyping is a category-based cognitive response to another person. Apart from prejudice (affect) and discrimination (behavior), stereotyping describes people's beliefs (cognitions) about an individual based on group membership. Category-based or stereotypic responses contrast with fully individuated, attribute-by-attribute consideration of another person (Fiske & Neuberg, 1990).

It is useful to discuss two aspects of stereotyping in the context of stereotyping and control: descriptive and prescriptive beliefs (e.g., Terborg, 1977). If the stereotype is descriptive, it tells how most people in the group supposedly behave, what they allegedly prefer, and where their competence supposedly lies. People may believe that women in general are good secretaries and teachers, but poor welders, managers, or scientists (e.g., Heilman, 1983; Ruble & Ruble, 1982). Descriptive stereotypes also claim that African Americans are good athletes but poor scholars, that Asian Americans and Jews are good scholars but poor athletes, and so on (Miller, 1982). In these assumptions, there lurks an implicit pressure to fit a certain image; other people's expectations create the starting point for one's commerce with them. The easiest course for a stereotyped person is· to stay within the bounds of those expectations. But the person who is stereotyped may try to contradict the expectations. In either case, the descriptive stereotype constrains a person because it anchors the interaction, weighing it down and holding it back. Either way, the stereotype must be dealt with. A friend in college once said that she was tired of being everybody's "Black experience." Not that she wanted to change who she was, but she was tired of having that limited dimension dominate her interactions, for better or worse. In short, a descriptive stereotype is controlling simply because it exists as an anchor or starting point in the mind of one person dealing with another. Anyone in the culture, whether actively biased or not, potentially knows the contents of the stereotype (Steele, 1992), so it becomes an implicit anchor for everyone.

Another form of stereotype, the prescriptive aspect, is even more explicitly controlling. It purportedly tells how certain groups *should* think, feel, and behave. So, for example, women should be nice, African Americans should be spontaneous, Asian Americans should be good at math, and Jews should be good with money. In one sense, these are flattering stereotypes, but they also demand that the individual either conform or disappoint the holder of the stereotype. The penalties can be swift and severe if one disappoints someone else's prescriptive stereotype (e.g., Eagly, Makhijani, & Klonsky, 1992). Think of the male adolescent in an all-male group who fails to conform to stereotypically masculine prescriptions. Prescriptive stereotypes are limiting and constitute a form of social control.

The descriptive aspect of stereotypes acts as an anchor, and the prescriptive aspect of stereotypes acts as a fence. In short, stereotypes control people, which is one reason they are so aversive. No one wants to be stereotyped. Stereotypes reinforce one group's or individual's power over another by limiting the options of the stereotyped group, so in this way stereotypes maintain power. People with power do not have to put up with them, but people without power are victims. Power is control, and stereotypes are one way to exert control, both social and personal. One might argue that subordinates also stereotype those in power, which the next section will counter-argue. But even if underlings do stereotype, their beliefs simply exert less control than do those of people in power. Copeland (1992), for example, found that powerful people were more able to create self-fulfilling prophecies than were powerless people.

The controlling impact of stereotypes also explains why power maintains stereotypes. Elsewhere, Eric Dépret and I (Dépret & Fiske, in press) have defined power as asymmetrical control over another person's outcomes (for another review of definitions, see Ng, 1980). Power has traditionally been defined as the ability to influence at will (e.g., Dahl, 1957; Huston, 1983; Pruitt, 1976). However, one may have power without influence if the subordinates refuse to be influenced, despite the control of the powerful over their outcomes. Power has also been defined as status (e.g., Hogg & Abrams, 1988). However, one may have power with or without status, as when low-status groups control resources important to high-status groups. Dépret and Fiske's (in press) definition of power in terms of the intrinsic characteristics of human interdependence, that is, as asymmetrical outcome control, follows some theoretical perspectives of Thibaut and Kelley (1959).

Because power is essentially control, people pay attention to those who have power. It is a simple principle: People pay attention to those who control their outcomes. In an effort to predict and possibly influence what is going to happen to them, people gather information about those with power. Consider the direction of attention in a large organization. Attention follows power. Attention is directed *up* the hierarchy. Secretaries know more about their bosses than vice versa; graduate students know more about their advisors than vice versa. Similar dynamics operate at convention social hours, as people cluster around those perceived to be powerful. Thus, the powerless are attentive to the powerful. By the same token, the powerful need not attend very much to those with less power, because less is at stake for the powerful with regard to their subordinates.

Besides outcome control and its attendant motivations, the powerful have more demands on their attention than do the powerless. By nature of the hierarchy, the powerful have more people competing for their attention than do the powerless. If stereotypes are shortcuts, overburdened people are more likely to use them. The literature indeed indicates that stereotyping is more likely when people are distracted, when their cognitive capacity is limited (for a review, see Fiske, 1993). For example, when people are busy, they do not modify initial categories, all else being equal (Gilbert, 1989). External factors decrease people's mental capacity for thinking carefully about others, and the attentional overload of power predictably decreases people's capacity.

Finally, particular individuals, objectively powerful or not, seek power and dominance over other people, which should influence how they perceive those others (e.g., Battistich, Assor, Messé, & Aronoff, 1985). Individuals who seek to control the fates of other people may or may not more frequently end up in positions of power. Regardless, their motivation to control other people may result in the use of stereotyping as one form of control. Elsewhere, Emery and I (Fiske & Emery, 1993) have argued that such attempts at social control may come from a precarious sense of mental control. Whatever the mechanism, there may be personality analogs of the hypothesized social power processes, with lack of individuated attention as the cause.

Attention may be determined by asymmetrical outcome control, capacity overload, and personal motivation, all in ways linked to one person's actual or desired power over another. Attention then determines who has detailed knowledge of whom and who stereotypes whom. The power*less* are stereotyped because no one needs to, can, or wants to be detailed and accurate about them. The power*ful* are not so likely to be stereotyped because subordinates need to, can, and want to form detailed impressions of them. The powerless need to try to predict and possibly alter their own fates. They may have fewer competing demands on their attentional capacity. And to the extent that a low personal need for power happens to coincide with a low-power position, they may be less motivated to stereotype. The next section presents data bearing on each of these points.

Before turning to the data, one still might argue that the powerful are victims of stereotypes too. But, first, as noted, if the powerless stereotype the powerful, it simply does not matter as much; it demonstrably does not limit their behavior as much (Copeland, 1992) nor, by definition, control their outcomes as much. It is more an irritation than a fundamental threat, except when subordinates are given the power to evaluate, vote on, or otherwise judge those in power. Then the powerless have been given some outcome control, and they are by definition slightly more powerful. The other instance of the powerful being stereotyped might be argued to operate when the powerful stereotype themselves or each other. One might argue that the JSI workers stereotyped each other as all liking pornography or that the PW partners stereotyped themselves as necessarily male, but it is arguable whether more harm was done to themselves or to the women they excluded on that basis. Finally, stereotypes of one's ingroup are more flexible and variable than stereotypes of the outgroup (for a review, see Fiske & Taylor, 1991, chap. 4); hence they are less controlling.

DATA ON POWER AND STEREOTYPING FROM THE BOTTOM UP

A body of previous work from my laboratory supports half of the power—attention equation. When people were interdependent, when they needed each other to achieve their goals, they paid attention. In this work, my colleagues and I have typically manipulated expectancies, which are positive or negative. Sometimes the expectancies were simple expectancies about competence, and sometimes they were stereotypes, such as ethnic stereotypes. We also then manipulated the degree of interdependence (the degree to which the two people depended on each other for some valued outcome), and the interdependence was either high or low. Then we presented subjects with mixed information about the target person on whom their outcomes depended. Some of the information fitted the stereotype or expectancy, and some of the information did not fit it and disputed it. This simulated real life, where one gets mixed information about another person.

We have shown in a variety of contexts three consistent and replicable results: First, people pay attention to others who control their outcomes (Erber & Fiske, 1984; Neuberg & Fiske, 1987; Ruscher & Fiske, 1990; Ruscher, Fiske, Miki, & Van Manen, 1991). Interdependence increases attention in particular to stereotype-inconsistent information. This is the information that potentially undermines the stereotype; it is the most useful and informative. This means that outcome-dependent people attend to the most informative clues they can find, as if they are trying to be as accurate as possible, given the high stakes. Second, we find that people then draw inferences from the information they gather. They make dispositional comments about the inconsistency. They in effect construct personality profiles of the person on whom they depend, perhaps in an attempt to see the other person (and therefore their own fate) as predictable. If they know the other person's individual personality, they think they know what the other person will do and can infer how it will affect themselves. Finally, interdependence increases the variability of impressions across people, so they end up with more idiosyncratic impressions, often less reflective of stereotypes and expectations. This pattern occurs regardless of whether the interdependence is positive, as in cooperating pairs, or negative, as in competing pairs of people. So we have some evidence that attention follows power, at least when people are equally dependent on each other.

Recently, we extended these findings to situations of asymmetrical power (Dépret & Fiske, 1993). In these studies, undergraduates expected to complete a task under the control of others who could judge, reward, punish, or interfere with their performance. That is, the other people had power over the subjects. When those others were individuals from various outgroups (in this case, from college majors far outside of psychology), the subjects paid more attention to them as their power increased. In particular, the increase was in attention to the inconsistent information, which is the most informative because it potentially challenges the stereotype. Again, as the stakes increased, people were more careful. As in our previous work, we also found that dispositional inferences increased with the target's power, as if people were trying to make the other person as predictable as possible. The powerful people became intriguing individuals.[2]

Another lesson we are learning from our research is that the power dynamics have to be experientially real and significant to the perceiver. We have found that when power captures attention, the power is not just a matter of expecting to meet the other person, not just expecting to be evaluated by the other, and not just expecting to discuss a joint project (Stevens & Fiske, 1993). People have to expect actually to work together on some project. Demonstrable outcomes have to be present; something like effort or money has to depend on the interaction. In this case, the powerless attend to the powerful person, inconsistency and all, and they discount the inconsistencies less than do people not dependent. When no concrete outcomes depend on the other person, but the person is instead simply to evaluate the subject, then subjects concentrate on the downside, focusing on negative information and trying to discount it. In summary, then, we have evidence that powerful people, defined as those who control concrete outcomes, capture attention and that subordinates form more detailed and idiosyncratic impressions of them. In that sense, then, the powerful are not stereotyped.

DATA ON POWER AND STEREOTYPING FROM THE TOP DOWN

But what of the other half of the equation? Do the powerful *not* pay attention to the powerless? Our theory argues that the powerful do not need to pay attention because nothing is riding on the other person; their fates do not depend on the other, so their attention should be more superficial. Moreover, according to one of the other mechanisms, the powerful oversee many subordinates, and this too should interfere with careful attention. Goodwin and Fiske (1993) have recently found that power does indeed decrease attention to others, in a setting designed to mimic personnel decision making; that is, undergraduates were given the power to evaluate high school students' summer job applications. As the percentage of their power in the decision increased, their attention to the applicants actually decreased in a baseline condition. I will come back to this study shortly, but the point is that it provides initial evidence that the powerful may not pay enough attention to the powerless. This then mimics what went on at Price Waterhouse and Jacksonville Shipyards; the powerful managers simply had no need to attend to the relatively powerless women as unique individual subordinates.

At this point, one might well object that this analysis simply does not apply to the male workers at Jacksonville Shipyards. After all, the women there were receiving quite a lot of attention, although of a certain kind. And one might even argue that the men had very specific needs that depended on the women. So, one might argue, the women were indeed powerful because the men were sexually interested in them. This argument is as old as Aristophanes and *Lysistrata,* but examine the situation a bit more carefully. The men were powerful in several respects related both to the work and social environment. The women had only a modicum of social power, to the extent they were in a position to resist or to cooperate enthusiastically with the men's sexual advances. Moreover, the attention they received was of a stereotypical sort. Thus, the motivations behind the attention determine the kind of attention, and only certain kinds of increased attention will undercut stereotypes.

In a series of studies, we have examined what happens when a powerful person has social or sexual goals that depend on the subordinate. For example, what happens if a male manager wants to date a woman employee? What happens if a female boss wants to be close friends with her female assistant? If the subordinate's goals are work-related, namely recognition for work well done, then the supervisor's social interest is often experienced as interfering and irrelevant. Rather than focusing on the quality of one's work, the supervisor is focusing on whether one is appealing and available. It follows from the specifically social goals that the supervisor will not be attending as carefully to the subordinate's task performance. In effect, the supervisor is paying attention but not the right kind of attention. In our laboratory, we have investigated whether such social goals help or hinder the subordinate's work-related goals.

Fiske, Goodwin, Rosen, and Rosenthal (1993) recruited undergraduate men for a dating study that consisted of two parts: a task-oriented interaction and the actual series of dates. In the task-oriented part, the men were in a position to supervise and evaluate their female subordinate. For half the men, the subordinate was the same woman they expected to date, and half the men expected to date somebody else. Hence, for half the men, their romantic fates depended on this woman, and for the other half they did not. The woman was a confederate whose videotaped task performance was either competent or incompetent, according to pretesting. Consistent with this, the men who expected only a task-oriented interaction were able to distinguish competent from incompetent performance. But the men who expected to date her did not. This kind of bias is not limited to men in power; we have recently replicated this finding with women supervising men they expected to date. In both cases, a romantic goal clouds one's judgment, presumably because people are not paying the right kind of attention.

So far, I have focused on social structure as a cause and cure for stereotyping. But individuals are also directly involved here. Both in Jacksonville Shipyard and at Price Waterhouse, some people were worse than others; some people made particularly egregious comments. What about these bad apples? Maybe the bad apples stereotype other people because of personal problems that parallel the social structural ones. Goodwin and Fiske (1993) hypothesized that a personal need for power and dominance would have similar stereotype-confirming effects on attention. And indeed, people with highly dominant personalities pay less attention to the very information that could undermine their stereotypes. Like people who are powerful because of the social structure, people with dominant personalities ignore stereotype-discrepant information, preferring the information that confirms their stereotypes. Dominant people attend to consistent, stereotype-confirming information and attend very little to the information that could undermine their stereotypes. Nondominant people attend equally to both kinds of information. Perhaps, then, there are some similarities between those with power thrust upon them and those who take it for themselves. Control again is central here, in that dominance-oriented people are distinguished by their chronic attempts to control other people for their own ends.

HOW INTENTIONAL AND RESPONSIBLE ARE PEOPLE?

So far, the portrait of the powerful seems discouraging. These are, after all, the people who control what happens to the rest of us. It would appear that the powerful do not pay a lot of appropriate attention as they manipulate our fates. And yet, they can be held responsible for their inattention. Each of us, when we have power over someone else, can be held responsible for our attention or inattention to the other person. What kind of evidence would be relevant here? Responsibility, according to a legal analysis, depends on intent. People are responsible if the act is intentional. So, for example, discrimination is not illegal if it can be proved to be totally unintentional. Penalties for killing another person vary with the degree of intent involved, and so on. Responsibility depends on state of mind and intent in particular.

As psychologists, we know something about intent. As far back as William James, intent was defined by two factors: choice and attention (Fiske, 1989). If people have alternatives, if there is more than one way to behave, according to a reasonable person, then one condition is met for recognizing intent. For example, in many circumstances, doing something at gunpoint does not count as intentional.

Doing the only thing one knows how to do is not strictly intentional. The second feature of intent that emerges, over the decades, among psychologists and lay people, is attention. If people keep the chosen alternative in mind, they can be said to intend the one they follow. So, for example, if one is dieting and thinks about the box of Belgian chocolates on the table, one finds them harder to resist than if one's thoughts are focused elsewhere.

This analysis of intent applies to stereotyping: People's tendency to stereotype is intentional in that, first, they demonstrably have alternative ways of thinking about people, as members of a category or as unique individuals; everyone can do this (Fiske & Neuberg, 1990). Second, people can implement their alternative ways of thinking about other people according to how much attention they pay to those other people. Hence, we find again that attention is central in whether or not people stereotype. In particular, this suggests that people with power can overcome the tendency to stereotype the powerless by the very processes of attention that have been discussed so far.

WHAT CAN BE DONE?

The powerful can be influenced to be more careful by strategies consistent with the theory proposed here. The powerful are by definition not motivated by outcomes that depend directly on their subordinates. Hence, the powerful are more likely to be influenced by their own higher-ups, by their own peers, or by their self-concept. In that sense, the motivations of the powerful are independent of their relationship with the person being judged; the motivations of the powerful are more autonomous in that sense. In this view, then, the powerful are motivated by what they perceive to be acceptable, according to the norms, and by their own self-concepts. There is some evidence for this.

In the Goodwin–Fiske (1993) study in which undergraduates made job decisions about high school students, power decreased decision makers' attention to the applicants, as hypothesized, in a baseline condition. But we also predicted that shared norms concerning humanitarian and egalitarian values might remind people of their better selves, in effect. That is, if we could make accessible the decision makers' sense of responsibility, we might be able to get them to pay attention. So, some people completed a scale of shared humanitarian–egalitarian values; when we primed a sense of responsibility, their attention increased dramatically. Notice that we were not telling them what to do but only reminding them of their own values.

The powerful can also be motivated by their own self-concepts as fair-minded and careful people. Fiske and Von Hendy (1992) predicted and found that people had the capacity to think about other people in either categorical or individuating ways and that they could use either strategy depending on which aspect of their self-concept was salient to them at the time. In effect, we were bringing out different sides of people by the feedback we gave them. We found that people could be influenced by bogus feedback about their supposed special abilities to treat other people categorically or individually, if they were the kind of people who strictly followed their own proclivities. Similarly, people can be influenced by bogus information about the appropriate norms in the situation, if they are the kind of people who strictly use other people's standards as a guide.

This last set of studies focuses on values, self-concepts, and norms as motivators for powerful people. People, including those with power, can also be influenced by their own compunctions (Devine, Monteith, Zuwerink, & Elliot, 1991), public accountability (e.g., Tetlock, Skitka, & Boettger, 1989), fear of invalidity (e.g., Kruglanski, 1990), instructions to be accurate (Neuberg, 1989), and the like (see Fiske, 1993, for a review). In my opinion, they relate to the shipyard and the accounting firm in that an organization can make certain values salient, can encourage the constructive sides of people's self-concepts, can promote norms of fairness, and so on. Conversely, an organization can ignore these issues and let the powerful take the easy way out, not bothering to pay much attention to the powerless.

Our main program of research, then, has been showing that social structure affects attention, and if people pay more attention, at least some of them are less likely to stereotype. Moreover, organizations can encourage individuating attention by the structures they create.

CONCLUSION

The type of illustrative data presented here deserves some comment. These are laboratory experiments, and one might wonder about the laboratory as a way to study power, stereotyping, sexual harassment, and so forth. Does the laboratory trivialize such real world issues? These laboratory studies were designed as simulations, as microcosms. Our strategy is to create a miniature world in which we can analyze and isolate the features of the social setting that we think are important. We transport these isolated features to the lab, and we show that these are sufficient conditions to produce a phenomenon in which we are interested. It allows us to see the fine-grained mechanisms that link power, control, and stereotyping. And it allows us to demonstrate the sufficient conditions for stereotypic processes (such as lack of attention to stereotype-disconfirming information). Obviously, we depend heavily on feedback from field studies as well, and we also draw a lot of our ideas from the world outside the lab.

Similarly, one might wonder about our focus on cognitive mechanisms and attention in particular. First, attention here specifically means time looking at written materials. Attention also is an indicator of weight in a judgment (Fiske, 1980). Second, we do have other dependent variables, but attention has been the focus in this article for simplicity's sake. But also it is a strategic choice in our research to focus so much on attention as a main dependent variable, because it is the beginning of the process, without which nothing else can occur. It has a central role in whether people stereotype or not, although there are no guarantees that getting somebody to pay attention to somebody else will undercut stereotypes. But at any rate, it is a first step, and with some people it is effective some of the time. If we can begin to find ways to capture people's attention, perhaps we can undermine the control of stereotypes.

Jacksonville Shipyards, Price Waterhouse, and our laboratory data have all linked power to stereotyping as mediated through the amount and nature of attention. People in power stereotype subordinates because they do not need to pay attention to them and because it may not be easy to do so. Moreover, sometimes their own personal dispositions may be oriented toward power, and this may compound the lack of individuating attention. Power affects stereotyping through attention (or a lack of the right kind of attention), and stereotyping controls those who are stereotyped. Our organizational structures and incentives can ameliorate this problem or make it worse.

NOTES

Editors' note. This article was originally presented as a Distinguished Contribution to Psychology in the Public Interest, Early Career, award address at the 100th Annual

Convention of the American Psychological Association in Washington, DC, in August 1992.
Author's note. The research reported here was supported by National Institutes of Health Grant MH41801.

Thanks are due to four anonymous reviewers and to Jennifer Canfield, John Darley, and Stephanie Goodwin for their suggestions.

1. The descriptions of the cases (but not their relevance to stereotypes, power, and control) also appear in Fiske and Stevens (1993). A more detailed description of the second case appeared in Fiske, Bersoff, Borgida, Deaux, and Heilman (1991).

2. This process is entirely altered when the interaction is intergroup rather than interpersonal. When the powerful others are perceived to be a homogeneous outgroup, power creates a sense of threat—in effect, an outgroup conspiracy. The powerful outgroup is instead viewed more stereotypically, as people expect the ingroup to be treated in an unfair and discriminatory fashion. Similarly, Ruscher, Fiske, Miki, and Van Manen (1991) found that intergroup competition increased stereotyping processes relative to interpersonal competition. Some of these group level phenomena explain the threatened reactions of some of the JSI workers and PW partners, to the extent that they viewed the women as a group threatening the men as a group.

REFERENCES

Barrett, G. V., & Morris, S. B. (1993a). The American Psychological Association's amicus curiae brief in *Price Waterhouse v. Hopkins:* The value of science versus the values of the law. *Law and Human Behavior, 17,* 201–216.

Barrett, G. V., & Morris, S. B. (1993b). Sex stereotyping in *Price Waterhouse v. Hopkins. American Psychologist, 48,* 54–55.

Battistich, V., Assor, A., Messé, L. A., & Aronoff, J. (1985). Personality and person perception. In P. Shaver (Ed.), *Review of personality and social psychology* (Vol. 6, pp. 185–208). Beverly Hills, CA: Sage.

Copeland, J. T. (1992, August). *Motivational implications of social power for behavioral confirmation.* Paper presented at the 100th Annual Convention of the American Psychological Association, Washington, DC.

Dahl, R. A. (1957). The concept of power. *Behavioural Science, 2,* 201–215.

Dépret, E. F., & Fiske, S. T. (1993). *Perceiving the powerful: Intriguing individuals versus threatening groups.* Unpublished manuscript, University of Massachusetts at Amherst.

Dépret, E. F., & Fiske, S. T. (in press). Social cognition and power: Some cognitive consequences of social structure as a source of control deprivation. In G. Weary, F. Gleicher, & K. Marsh (Eds.), *Control motivation and social cognition.* New York: Springer-Verlag.

Devine, P. G., Monteith, M. J., Zuwerink, J. R., & Elliot, A. (1991). Prejudice with and without compunction. *Journal of Personality and Social Psychology, 60,* 817–830.

Eagly, A. H., Makhijani, M. G., & Klonsky, B. G. (1992). Gender and the evaluation of leaders: A meta-analysis. *Psychological Bulletin, 111,* 3–22.

Erber, R., & Fiske, S. T. (1984). Outcome dependency and attention to inconsistent information. *Journal of Personality and Social Psychology, 47,* 709–726.

Fiske, S. T. (1980). Attention and weight in person perception: The impact of negative and extreme behavior. *Journal of Personality and Social Psychology, 38,* 889–906.

Fiske, S. T. (1989). Examining the role of intent: Toward understanding its role in stereotyping and prejudice. In J. S. Uleman & J. A. Bargh (Eds.), *Unintended thought: The limits of awareness, intention, and control* (pp. 253–283). New York: Guilford Press.

Fiske, S. T. (1993). Social cognition and social perception. In M. R. Rosenzweig & L. W. Porter (Eds.), *Annual review of psychology.* Palo Alto, CA: Annual Reviews.

Fiske, S. T., Bersoff, D. N., Borgida, E., Deaux, K., & Heilman, M. E. (1991). Social science research on trial: The use of sex stereotyping research in *Price Waterhouse v. Hopkins. American Psychologist, 46,* 1049–1060.

Fiske, S. T., Bersoff, D. N., Borgida, E., Deaux, K., & Heilman, M. E. (1993a). A brief rejoinder: Accuracy and objectivity on behalf of the APA. *American Psychologist, 48,* 55–56.

Fiske, S. T., Bersoff, D. N., Borgida, E., Deaux, K., & Heilman, M. E. (1993b). What constitutes a scientific review? A majority retort to Barrett and Morris on gender stereotyping. *Law and Human Behavior, 17,* 217–233.

Fiske, S. T., & Emery, E. J. (1993). Lost mental control and exaggerated social control: Social-cognitive and psychoanalytic speculations. In D. M. Wegner & J. W. Pennebaker (Eds.), *Control motivation and social cognition* (pp. 171–199). New York: Springer-Verlag.

Fiske, S. T., Goodwin, S. A., Rosen, L., & Rosenthal, A. (1993). *Romantic outcome dependency and the (in)accuracy of impression formation: A case of clouded judgment.* Unpublished manuscript, University of Massachusetts at Amherst.

Fiske, S. T., & Neuberg, S. L. (1990). A continuum model of impression formation, from category-based to individuating processes: Influence of information and motivation on attention and interpretation. In M. P. Zanna (Ed.), *Advances in experimental social psychology* (Vol. 23, pp. 1–74). San Diego, CA: Academic Press.

Fiske, S. T., & Stevens, L. E. (1993). What's so special about sex? Gender stereotyping and discrimination. In S. Oskamp & M. Costanzo (Eds.), *Gender issues in contemporary society: Applied social psychology annual* (Vol. 6, pp. 173–196). Newbury Park, CA: Sage.

Fiske, S. T., & Taylor, S. E. (1991). *Social cognition* (2nd ed.). New York: McGraw-Hill.

Fiske, S. T., & Von Hendy, H. M. (1992). Personality feedback and situational norms can control stereotyping processes. *Journal of Personality and Social Psychology, 62,* 577–596.

Gilbert, D. T. (1989). Thinking lightly about others: Automatic components of the social inference process. In J. S. Uleman & J. A. Bargh (Eds.), *Unintended thought: The limits of awareness, intention, and control* (pp. 189–211). New York: Guilford Press.

Glick, P., Zion, C., & Nelson, C. (1988). What mediates sex discrimination in hiring decisions? *Journal of Personality and Social Psychology, 55,* 178–186.

Goodman, J. (1993). Evaluating psychological expertise on questions of social fact: The case of *Price Waterhouse v. Hopkins. Law and Human Behavior, 17,* 249–256.

Goodwin, S. A., & Fiske, S. T. (1993). *Impression formation in asymmetrical power relationships: Does power corrupt absolutely?* Unpublished manuscript, University of Massachusetts at Amherst.

Heilman, M. E. (1983). Sex bias in work settings: The lack-of-fit model. *Research in Organizational Behavior, 5,* 269–298.

Hogg, M. A., & Abrams, D. (1988). *Social identifications: A social psychology of intergroup relations and group processes.* New York: Routledge, Chapman & Hall.

Huston, T. L. (1983). Power. In H. H. Kelley, E. Berscheid, A. Christensen, J. H.

Harvey, T. L. Huston, G. Levinger, E. McClintock, L. A. Peplau, & D. R. Peterson (Eds.), *Close relationships* (pp. 169–219). New York: Freeman.

Kruglanski, A. W. (1990). Motivations for judging and knowing: Implications for causal attribution. In E. T. Higgins & R. M. Sorrentino (Eds.), *Handbook of motivation and cognition: Foundations of social behavior* (Vol. 2, pp. 333–368). New York: Guilford Press.

Miller, A. G. (Ed.). (1982). *In the eye of the beholder: Contemporary issues in stereotyping.* New York: Praeger.

Neuberg, S. L. (1989). The goal of forming accurate impressions during social interactions: Attenuating the impact of negative expectancies. *Journal of Personality and Social Psychology, 56,* 374–386.

Neuberg, S. L., & Fiske, S. T. (1987). Motivational influences on impression formation: Outcome dependency, accuracy-driven attention, and individuating processes. *Journal of Personality and Social Psychology, 53,* 431–444.

Ng, S. H. (1980). *The social psychology of power.* San Diego, CA: Academic Press.

Pruitt, D. G. (1976). Power and bargaining. In B. Seidenberg & A. Snadowsky (Eds.), *Social psychology: An introduction.* New York: Free Press.

Ruble, D. N., & Ruble, T. L. (1982). Sex stereotypes. In A. G. Miller (Ed.), *In the eye of the beholder: Contemporary issues in stereotyping* (pp. 188–252). New York: Praeger.

Ruscher, J. B., & Fiske, S. T. (1990). Interpersonal competition can cause individuating processes. *Journal of Personality and Social Psychology, 58,* 832–843.

Ruscher, J. B., Fiske, S. T., Miki, H., & Van Manen, S. (1991). Individuating processes in competition: Interpersonal versus intergroup. *Personality and Social Psychology Bulletin, 17,* 595–605.

Saks, M. J. (1993). Improving APA's science translation amicus brief. *Law and Human Behavior, 17,* 235–248.

Steele, C. (1992, October). *The collective nature of prejudice: Implications for the schooling of women and Black Americans.* Paper presented at a meeting of the Society of Experimental Social Psychology, San Antonio, TX.

Stevens, L. E., & Fiske, S. T. (1993). *Impression formation processes of asymmetrically dependent individuals.* Amherst: University of Massachusetts.

Terborg, J. R. (1977). Women in management: A research review. *Journal of Applied Psychology, 62,* 647–664.

Tetlock, P. E., Skitka, L., & Boettger, R. (1989). Social and cognitive strategies for coping with accountability: Conformity, complexity, and bolstering. *Journal of Personality and Social Psychology, 57,* 632–640.

Thibaut, J. W., & Kelley, H. H. (1959). *The social psychology of groups.* New York: Wiley.

20. Psychology of Acculturation

J. W. Berry

INTRODUCTION

Within cross-cultural psychology there is an interest in two broad domains: the comparative examination of psychological similarities and differences across broad ranges of cultures, and the psychological adaptations individuals make when they move between cultures. The former is the preeminent line of enquiry in cross-cultural psychology and attempts to link variations in individual behavior to cultural and ecological contexts by way of general enculturation and specific socialization; the latter is a relatively new area and seeks to understand continuities and changes in individual behavior that are related to the experience of two cultures through the process of acculturation. It is with this latter domain that this essay is concerned.

Psychological studies of acculturation are particularly relevant at present, in a variety of cultures. International migration, major refugee upheavals, and the painful process of decolonization have all increased intercultural contact, as have tourism and telecommunications. Previously culturally isolated and homogeneous peoples now rub shoulders daily with persons, ideas, and products from scattered parts of the globe, setting afoot a process of cultural and psychological adaptation to their new circumstances. How individuals negotiate their course through this process of acculturation is the focus here. I begin by outlining the process at both the cultural and the psychological levels, then consider variations in acculturating groups and strategies, and finally review a number of specific acculturation phenomena, including acculturation attitudes, behavioral changes during acculturation, and the stresses associated with the process.

Reprinted by permission of University of Nebraska Press from J. J. Berman, ed., *Nebraska Symposium on Motivation: Cross-Cultural Perspectives* © 1989 The University of Nebraska Press.

Within anthropology the first major studies of *acculturation* were done in the 1930s. The two classic definitions of acculturation are contained in related publications:

Acculturation comprehends those phenomena which result when groups of individuals having different cultures come into continuous first-hand contact, with subsequent changes in the original culture patterns of either or both groups . . . under this definition acculturation is to be distinguished from culture change, of which it is but one aspect, and assimilation, which is at times a phase of acculturation. It is also to be differentiated from diffusion, which while occurring in all instances of acculturation, is not only a phenomenon which frequently takes place without the occurrence of the types of contact between peoples specified in the definition above, but also constitutes only one aspect of the process of acculturation. (Redfield, Linton, & Herskovits, 1936)

In another formulation, acculturation was defined as

culture change that is initiated by the conjunction of two or more autonomous cultural systems. Acculturative change may be the consequence of direct cultural transmission; it may be derived from noncultural causes, such as ecological or demographic modification induced by an impinging culture; it may be delayed, as with internal adjustments following upon the acceptance of alien traits or patterns; or it may be a reactive adaptation of traditional modes of life. Its dynamics can be seen as the selective adaptation of value systems, the processes of integration and differentiation, the generation of developmental sequences, and the operation of role determinants and personality factors. (Social Science Research Council, 1954, p. 974)

The implications of these definitions for research on acculturation will be examined later, in the section dealing with acculturation research.

ACCULTURATION FRAMEWORK

The framework presented in Figure 1 draws our attention to some of the key issues to be discussed in this chapter. The framework makes a distinction, first of all, between two levels: the *population* (ecological, cultural, social, and institutional, at the left) and the *individual* (the behaviors and traits of persons, at the right). Although this distinction has not usually been made by workers in anthropology, it has become of major importance for studies of individual acculturation. Graves (1967) coined the term *psychological acculturation* to refer to the changes an individual experiences as a result of being in contact with other cultures and participating in the process of acculturation

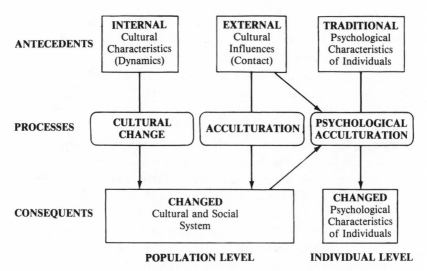

FIGURE 1
Model of Key Variables and Relationships in the Study of Culture
Change and Acculturation (modified from Berry, 1980).

that one's cultural or ethnic group is undergoing. The distinction
between acculturation and psychological acculturation is important
for two reasons. The phenomena are different at the two levels, as we
shall see later in the chapter: for example, at the population level
changes in social structure, economic base, and political organization
frequently occur, whereas at the individual level the changes are in
such areas as behavior, identity, values, and attitudes. Also, not
every acculturating individual participates in the collective changes
that are under way in the group to the same extent or in the same
way. Thus, if we want to eventually understand the relationships
between culture contact and psychological outcomes for individuals,
we will need to assess (using separate measures) changes at the population level and individuals' participation in these changes, then
relate both of these measures to the psychological consequences for
the individual.

This discussion of the need for two levels brings us to the second
major distinction, between the antecedents to change and the consequents of change. In Figure 1 antecedents are placed at the top, while
consequents are placed below. Generally speaking, the flow of events
is from antecedents to consequents, and the goal is to understand
the population- and individual-level consequents in relation to the

antecedents. Reverse influences do occur, but return arrows are not illustrated in the figure, since our focus in this chapter is on the eventual psychological outcomes, at the lower right.

The third distinction in Figure 1 is between external and internal sources of change. As noted in the definitions I quoted at the outset, change can come about by events that impinge on a group or an individual from outside the culture: both diffusion and acculturation are examples of this source of change and include the introduction both of single innovations such as the plow, writing, and firearms (all examples of diffusion) and of whole institutions such as education, colonial government, and industrialization (all examples of acculturation). Internal sources of change are those that do not come from outside contact; they include forces such as invention, discovery, and innovation (ongoing dynamics at the population level) and insight, creativity, and drive (at the individual level).

A fourth feature of Figure 1 is that of the *processes* involved in change. The term *culture change* refers to the process that results in population-level changes that are due to dynamic internal events. The term *acculturation* refers to the process that results in population-level changes that are due to contact with other cultures. Finally, the term *psychological acculturation* refers to the process by which individuals change, both by being influenced by contact with another culture and by being participants in the general acculturative changes under way in their own culture. This process necessarily involves some degree of input from, and continuity with, an individual's traditional psychological characteristics.

Although many disciplines have been working for a long time at the population level of Figure 1 (including anthropology, international development studies, rural sociology, economics, and political science), the task has fallen mainly to cross-cultural psychology to study the individual level and its relationships with the population level.

To illustrate Figure 1, we may consider two concrete cases of individuals experiencing psychological change as a result of their membership in a changing cultural group. Although there are many categories of such individuals, we may take first an immigrant moving to set up a new life in another country; this would be an example of acculturation, since external culture contact is involved, followed by both cultural and individual changes. First, the decision to emigrate is often based upon some prior contact, knowledge, and influence. Perhaps other individuals, even members of one's own family, have already settled in the new country, and this has led to some changes in one's home culture. Perhaps the foreign language is being taught in the schools, new industries are being established, and the mass media are showing the way of life in the new country. On immigration to the new country, there can be some dramatic and sometimes overwhelming contact experiences followed by psychological reactions: differences in climate, language, work habits, religi‚n and dress, for example, can all challenge the immigrant, and some response is required. These cultural differences may be accepted, interpreted, or denied, and the individual may ride with them or be run over by them.

For a second example, we may take a person whose country and culture have been colonized. In this case there is no choice made to enter into culture contact, since dominant cultures have a history of entering, uninvited, into many parts of the world, especially in Africa, Asia, and the Americas. Precontact experiences and positive motivation to acculturate are therefore lacking; however, once the process has started, individuals and communities may vary greatly in how they deal with the acculturative influences. Some may turn their backs, others may embrace them, while yet others may selectively engage the new while merging it with the old. Many options are possible (as we shall see later in this chapter), but in all cases the intercultural contact and the individual psychological response will be related to each other. It is the task of cross-cultural psychology to examine these relationships, to understand them, and finally to attempt to find systematic features in order to produce some generalizations about the processes involved in psychological responses to culture contact and change.

THE ACCULTURATION PROCESS

From the definitions of acculturation presented earlier we may identify some key elements that are usually studied in cross-cultural psychology. First there needs to be *contact* or interaction between cultures that is continuous and firsthand; this rules out short-term, accidental contact, as well as diffusion of single cultural practices over long distances. Second, the result is some *change* in the cultural or psychological phenomena among the people in contact, usually continuing for generations down the line. Third, taking these first

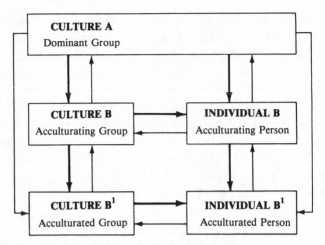

FIGURE 2

Framework for Identifying Variables and Relationships in Acculturation Research (fig. 10.1 from Berry, Trimble, & Olmeda, 1986). Reprinted by permission of Sage Publications, Inc.

two aspects together, we can distinguish between a *process* and a *state:* there is activity during and after contact that is dynamic, and there is a result of the process that may be relatively stable; this outcome may include not only changes to existing phenomena, but also some novel effects generated by the process of cultural interaction.

Considering these distinctions as part of a general system of acculturation, the framework in Figure 2 can be proposed (cf. Berry, Trimble, & Olmeda, 1986). It depicts two cultures (A and B) in contact. In principle each could influence the other equally (in a form of symbiosis), but in practice one tends to dominate the other; in this framework the "dominant group" (or "donor") is Culture A and the "acculturating group" (or "receptor") is Culture B. For completeness, mutual influence is depicted by the two arrows between Cultures A and B, as is the influence of Culture A directly on individuals in Culture B. However, the consequences for culture group A are not represented, and for the balance of this chapter I will focus on a single culture (B), the one receiving the greater influence. This is not to say that changes in the dominant culture are uninteresting or unimportant: acculturation often brings about population expansion, greater cultural diversification, attitudinal reaction (prejudice and discrimination), and policy development (for example, in the areas of immigration, cultural pluralism, bilingualism, and schooling). But these changes, however significant, have generally fallen outside the competence of cross-cultural psychology.

One result of the contact and influence is that aspects of group B become transformed so that cultural features of the acculturated group (B^1) are not identical to those in the original group at the time of first contact. Of course, if contact is still maintained, further influence from Culture A is experienced. A parallel effect is that individuals in group B undergo psychological changes (as a result of influences both from their own group and from group A), and again, if there is continuing contact further psychological changes may take place.

What characteristics of the dominant group is it important to examine? The essential ones are as follows. *Purpose:* Why is the contact taking place? What are its goals? Clearly acculturation effects will vary according to whether the purpose is colonization, enslavement, trade, military control, evangelization, education, and so on. *Length:* How long has the contact been taking place? Does it occur daily, seasonally, or annually? *Permanence:* Is the dominant group here to stay? Have they settled in, or is it a passing venture? *Population size:* How many are there? Do they form a majority, or are there only a few? *Policy:* What policies are being exercised toward acculturating groups—assimilation, eventual extermination, indirect rule, ghettoization, dispersion? *Cultural qualities:* Does the dominant group possess cultural qualities that can meet specific needs or improve the quality of life of the acculturating group? Potentially desirable cultural artifacts such as medicines, guns, and traps (for hunter populations), seeds, plows, and irrigation techniques (for agricultural populations) will obviously lead to acculturative changes more than will unwanted or nonfunctional cultural contributions. Without some indication of the nature of these variables, no account of acculturation would be complete.

A parallel account is needed of the characteristics of Culture B. *Purpose:* Is the group in contact voluntarily (e.g., immigrants) or under duress (e.g., native peoples)? *Location:* Is the group in its traditional location, with its land and other resources available, or displaced to some new environment (e.g., reservation, refugee camp)? *Length and permanence:* these variables are much the same as for the description of Culture A. In particular, the phase of acculturation needs to be specified: Has contact only begun? Have acculturative pressures been building up? Has a conflict or crisis appeared? *Popula-

tion size: How many are there? Are they a majority or a minority? Is the population vital (sustaining or increasing in number) or declining? *Policy:* To what extent does the group have an organized response to acculturation? If there is a policy orientation, is it one of resistance or exclusion (get rid of acculturative influence), of inclusion (accepting the influence), or of control (selective inclusion according to some scale of acceptability)? *Cultural qualities:* Do certain aspects of the traditional culture affect the acculturation process? For example hunter-gatherers are susceptible to habitat destruction due to war, forest reduction, or mineral exploration, and agricultural peoples may be dispossessed of their land by permanent settlers from Culture A. More complex societies may be better able to organize politically and militarily than less complex societies in order to alter the course of acculturation, while nomads may be in a position to disperse to avoid major acculturative influences.

In addition to these specific characteristics that may be discerned in particular groups, it is also important to consider how the cultural-level effects listed above for Culture B are distributed across individuals in the group: Do they vary according to age, sex, family position, and personal abilities? As I noted earlier, the crucial point is that not every person in the acculturating group will necessarily enter into the acculturation process in the same way or to the same degree. Hence, assessment of individual experience is an important aspect of the study of psychological acculturation.

At this point let us turn to the changes that have actually taken place (Culture B^1) as a result of the acculturation process (recognizing, of course, that in many cases the acculturative influences continue to affect the group). These general consequences of acculturation have received considerable attention in the literature (see Berry, 1980, for a review of some general trends) and include such global descriptors as westernization, modernization, industrialization, and Americanization. Some specific consequences follow. *Political:* Have there been changes in political characteristics as a result of acculturation? For example, has independence been lost, have previously unrelated (even warring) groups been placed within a common framework, have new authority systems (e.g., chiefs, mayors, governors) been added, have people with regional similarities been categorized as "tribes" or "provinces"? *Economic:* Has the subsistence base been changed or the distribution of wealth been altered? For example, have hunter-gatherers been converted into herders or farmers, others into industrial or wage workers? Have previous concentrations of wealth in certain families or regions been eliminated or, conversely, has a new wealthy class emerged from a previously uniform system? Have new economic activities been introduced such as mining, forestry, game management, tourism, manufacturing? *Demographic:* Has there been a change in population size, its urban/rural distribution, its age or sex profile, or its regional dispersion? *Cultural:* To what extent are there new languages, religions, modes of dress, schooling, transportation, housing, and forms of social organization and social relations in the acculturated group? How do these relate to the previous norms? Do they conflict with them, partially displace them, or merge (as in some forms of Creole, or of African Christian churches)? All of these, and possibly many more depending on one's particular field site, are important markers of the extent to which acculturation has taken place in the group.

As I noted previously, there are very likely to be individual differences in the psychological characteristics people bring to the acculturation process, and not every person will necessarily participate in the process to the same extent. Taken together, this means that we need to shift our focus away from general characterizations of acculturation phenomena to a concern for variation among individuals in the group undergoing acculturation.

We also need to be aware that individual acculturation (as well as group-level effects) do not cohere as a neat package. Not only will groups and individuals vary in their participation and in their response to acculturative influences, but some domains of culture and behavior may become altered without comparable changes in other domains. For example, attitudes toward the value of traditional technology may change without a parallel change in beliefs and behaviors associated with it. That is, the process of acculturation is an uneven one and does not affect all cultural and psychological characteristics in a uniform manner.

ACCULTURATION RESEARCH DESIGNS

Turning to some actual research designs, we have noted that acculturation is a process that takes place over time and changes both the culture and the individual. The measurement of change between two or more points in time has a considerable literature in developmental and educational psychology, but not much in anthropology or in cross-cultural psychology. This lack has recently been highlighted for anthropology by a volume devoted to conducting long-term, even continuous, fieldwork (Foster, Scudder, Colson, & Kemper, 1978), but no similar treatment exists for cross-cultural psychology.

Culture change per se can be noted and assessed only when sets of data collected at different points in time (from Cultures B and B¹) are compared. Although this is ideal, in practice such longitudinal research is difficult and time-consuming. A more usual practice is that many of the features of Culture B are identified from other sources (e.g., earlier ethnographic accounts) or are partially reconstructed from reports of the older or less acculturated members of the community. Similarly, longitudinal research is often plagued with problems of loss through death or out-migration, and by problems of the changing relevance of theoretical conceptions and the associated research instruments.

A common alternative to longitudinal research is cross-sectional research employing a time-related variable such as length of residence or generational status. For example, among immigrants, those who have resided longer in Culture A may experience more acculturation than those residing for a shorter period (usually controlling for present age and age of arrival). Similarly, it is common to classify group members by their generation (the first generation comprises the immigrants themselves, the second generation their immediate offspring, etc.). An assumption here is that acculturation is a linear process over time, an assumption we will consider later.

One longitudinal study (Berry, Wintrob, Sindell, & Mawhinney, 1982), which employed both a longitudinal and a cross-sectional design, was concerned with how the Cree Indian communities and individuals of James Bay (northern Canada) would respond to a large-scale hydroelectric project constructed in their midst. Initial fieldwork with adults and teenagers was carried out before construction began. Eight years later (after construction), about half the original sample was studied again; this sample was supplemented by an equal number of new individuals who were the same ages as the original sample had been eight years earlier. This provided a longitudinal analysis for one group (who were compared at two points in time) and a cross-sectional analysis to maintain an age control.

In this study we found evidence of both continuity and change in cultural and psychological characteristics. Although there was major upheaval in the political and economic life of the Crees, there was clear evidence that, collectively, they remained (and wanted to remain) a Cree nation. In the midst of such large-scale community and regional change, moreover, there was broad-ranging evidence for psychological continuity in abilities, attitudes, and behaviors. And though the *mean* scores on these variables changed little, there was evidence for *individual flux,* with both acculturation attitudes and acculturative stress (to be discussed later) showing a rise or a fall over time, depending on the individuals and their personal acculturation experiences. This latter finding, of course, could be uncovered only with a longitudinal design.

Other designs may be needed in other acculturation arenas. For example, where longitudinal work is not done, a respondent's age may be a suitable surrogate, since the younger are usually more exposed to acculturative influences from Culture A, while the older have a longer history of enculturation in Culture B and hence may be more resistive. The essential issue, though, is to ensure that both the design and the measures match as well as possible the local acculturation conditions.

CONTACT AND PARTICIPATION

The central issue here is the extent to which a particular individual has engaged in the acculturation process. Numerous indicators may be sought, from a variety of sources (the individual, an informant, or direct observation).

I approach the topic in two ways: first I list (and briefly comment on) many of the variables that appear in the literature; second, I present illustrative measures to show how the variables have actually been employed in fieldwork. The list includes the following. *Education:* How far has an individual gone in the formal schooling that has been introduced from outside? If one single indicator of individual contact and participation is to be taken in the field, previous research suggests that this is likely to be the most fruitful. *Wage employment:* To what extent has an individual entered the work force for wages, as opposed to remaining with traditional economic activity? *Urbanization:* In predominantly rural societies, to what extent has the individual migrated to, and lived in, a new urban agglomeration? To what extent has he traveled to or visited these urban areas? *Media:* To what extent does the individual listen to radio, watch television, and read newspapers and magazines that introduce him to Culture A? *Political participation:* To what extent does the individual involve himself in the new political structures, including voting, running for office, or volunteering for boards? *Religion:* Has the individual changed his religion to one introduced by Culture A, and to what extent does he practice it? *Language:* What is the extent of knowledge and use of the language(s) introduced by Culture A? *Daily practices:* To what extent is there a change in personal dress, housing and furniture styles, food habits, and so on? *Social relations:* To what extent does the individual relate to (marry, play with, work with, reside with) those of Culture A as opposed to those of his own group?

These numerous variables are likely to be interrelated; thus we find in the literature attempts to develop scales or indexes of contact and participation that sum across these various experiences. Two examples of these follow.

An index of contact (de Lacey, 1970) was developed as a general contact index for Australian Aboriginal children with white Australian society. It contains two sections: *exposure variables* (which include some cultural-level as well as individual-level variables) and *adaptation variables.* Exposure was assessed by the proportion of the schoolgoing population—and of the whole community—that is Euro-Australian, visits to Euro-Australian houses, shopping experiences of children, travel to Euro-Australian centers, use of English, and access to mass media and to Euro-Australian artifacts. Adaptation was assessed by ratings of persistence of Aboriginal culture, use of Euro-Australian games and hobbies, consumption of Euro-Australian food, home physical environment (Euro-Australian vs. Aboriginal), and community organization (primarily tribal vs. virtually Euro-Australian). Total scores were then calculated for each child. This index illustrates how acculturation may be assessed at the individual level, but of course the actual items will vary depending on population and research goals.

Another contact scale (Berry et al., 1986) was developed for use in central Africa with Biaka Pygmy and Bangandu villagers. It consists of eight variables: number of local languages spoken; knowledge of French; knowledge of Sango (the national lingua franca); ownership (cf. below, with items for knives, pottery, ornaments, outside goods);

employment and technology (scaled from traditional hunter or farmer through to wage earner); religion (animism through to Islam); adoption of clothing (in European style), and travel (to towns and cities). All these variables were positively and (in most cases) significantly correlated and were used to create a single standardized index for each person.

An ownership index was developed (Berry & Annis, 1974a) for use among the James Bay Crees. The scale was such that participation at the "high end" of the scale usually included activities at the "low end," but not vice versa. The items in the scale (low to high) were ownership of radio, outboard motor, snowmobile, washing machine, freezer, bank account, and life insurance. The intention was to obtain objective evidence of the extent to which an individual had "bought into" Euro-Canadian society. Once again, this illustrates how to assess one aspect of acculturation rather than suggesting a standard instrument that can be used in all field settings.

It should be emphasized that these scales and indexes are not universally valid, ready made, or standard instruments that can be taken "as is" for use in any field setting. Some variables are clearly more relevant to Pygmies than to a community of Italian-Americans (e.g., adoption of clothing), while others may be more relevant to an ethnic group undergoing acculturation (such as the language spoken in the family) than to a linguistically homogeneous community in central Africa.

ACCULTURATING GROUPS

Although many of the generalities found in the literature about the effects of acculturation have been based on a single type of group, it is clear that there are numerous types, and adaptations may vary depending upon this factor.

In the review by Berry and Kim (1988), five different groups were identified, including immigrants, refugees, native peoples, ethnic groups, and sojourners (see Figure 3). This classification into five groups represents a view from Canada, where in principle all people are thought to be attached in some way to a particular cultural heritage. The generic term "ethnic group" is most frequently used to refer to people who identify with, and exhibit, a common heritage in the second or subsequent generations after immigration. By conven-

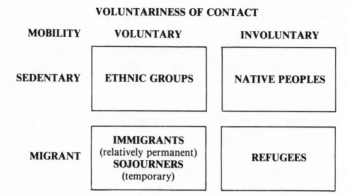

FIGURE 3

Five Types of Acculturating Groups (fig. II from Berry, Kim, Minde, & Mok, 1987). Reprinted by permission of the Center for Migration Studies of New York, Inc.

tion and by political ideology, the term "native peoples" is used to refer to those indigenous or aboriginal groups that were resident before European colonization and who remain as nations (in the cultural sense) within the larger society. "Immigrants" and "refugees" are both first-generation arrivals into the population by way of migration from some other part of the world, while "sojourners" are temporary immigrants who reside for a specific purpose and time period and intend to return eventually to their country of origin.

In other countries, the classification of groups may take different forms, based upon different histories and ideologies; however, this classification derives also from three distinctions that have import for psychological acculturation. There are variations in the degree of voluntariness, movement, and permanence of contact, all factors that might affect the health of members of the group. Those who are voluntarily involved in the acculturation process (e.g., immigrants) may experience less difficulty than those with little choice in the matter (e.g., refugees and native peoples), since their initial attitudes toward contact and change may be more positive. Further, those only temporarily in contact and who are without permanent social supports (e.g., sojourners) may experience more health problems than those who are more permanently settled and established (e.g., ethnic groups). These distinctions suggest some important variations in outcomes that are subject to empirical verifications during the course of research.

ACCULTURATION ATTITUDES

The valued goals of acculturation are not necessarily modernity or any other single alternative. Moreover, the goal as articulated by Culture A in its policy statements may not be the preferred course among the leaders or individuals of Culture B. In Australia (Sommerlad & Berry, 1970) an attempt was made to discover the attitudes of Aborigines toward their future in Australia; the Commonwealth government proposed assimilation, but others were not so sure. Since then the argument has been made (Berry, 1980) that acculturation can be viewed as multilinear—as a set of alternatives rather than a single dimension ending in assimilation or absorption into a "modern" society.

The ways an individual (or a group) of Culture B wishes to relate to Culture A have been termed "acculturation attitudes" (see Berry, Kim, Power, Young, & Bujaki, 1989, for a review of the reliability, validity, and correlates of these attitudes). In a sense they are conceptually the result of an interaction between ideas deriving from the modernity literature and the intergroup relations literature. In the former, the central issue is the degree to which one wishes to remain culturally as one has been (e.g., in terms of identity, language, way of life) as opposed to giving it all up to become part of a larger society; in the latter, the central issue is the extent to which one wishes to have day-to-day interactions with members of other groups in society, as opposed to turning away from them and relating only one's own group.

When these two central issues are posed simultaneously, a conceptual framework (Figure 4) is generated that posits four varieties of acculturation. It is, of course, recognized that each issue can be responded to on an attitudinal dimension, but for purposes of conceptual presentation, a dichotomous response (yes or no) is shown. When an individual in Culture B does not wish to maintain his identity (etc.) and seeks daily interaction with Culture A, then the assimilation path or mode is defined. In contrast, when one values holding onto one's original culture and at the same time wishes to avoid interaction with others, then the separation alternative is defined. When there is interest both in maintaining one's original culture and in daily interactions with others, integration is the option; here some degree of cultural integrity is maintained while one moves to participate as an integral part of the larger social network. Finally,

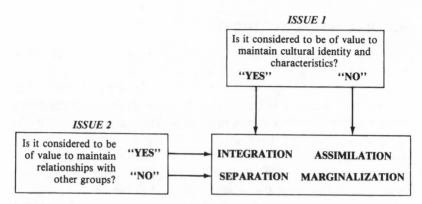

FIGURE 4

Four Varieties of Acculturation, Based upon Orientations to Two
Basic Issues (fig. 3 from Berry, Kim, Minde, & Mok, 1987).
Reprinted by permission of the Center for Migration Studies of New
York, Inc.

when there is little possibility or interest in cultural maintenance
(often for reasons of enforced cultural loss) and little interest in
relations with others (often for reasons of exclusion or discrimination), then marginalization is defined. Note that the term *integration*
as used here is clearly distinct from the term *assimilation* (although
the two sometimes appear in the literature as synonyms); cultural
maintenance is sought in the former case, whereas in the latter there
is little or no interest in such continuity. Note also that acculturation
may be "uneven" across domains of behavior and social life; for example, one may seek economic assimilation (in work), linguistic integration (by way of bilingualism), and marital separation (by endogamy).

To exemplify these four acculturation strategies, we may consider
a hypothetical family that has migrated from Italy to Canada. The
father may lean toward integration, wanting to get involved in the
economics and politics of his new society, and learning English and
French, in order to obtain the benefits that motivated his migration
in the first place; at the same time he may be a leader in the Italian-
Canadian community association, spending much of his leisure and
recreation time in social interaction with other Italian-Canadians. In
contrast, the mother may hold completely to Italian language use
and social interactions, feeling that she cannot get involved in the
work or cultural activities of the host society; she employs the separation strategy, having virtually all her personal, social, and cultural

life within the Italian world. In further contrast, the teenage daughter is annoyed by hearing the Italian language in the home, by her mother's serving only Italian food, and by being required to spend most of her leisure time with her extended Italian family. She much prefers the assimilation option: to speak English, participate in her school activities, and generally be with her Canadian age-mates. Finally, the son doesn't particularly want to recognize or accept his Italian heritage ("What use is it here in my new country?") but is rejected by his schoolmates because he speaks with an Italian accent and often smells of garlic; he feels trapped between his two possible identity groups, neither accepting nor being accepted by them. As a result he retreats into the social and behavioral sink of marginalization, experiencing social and academic difficulties and eventually coming into conflict with his parents and the police.

Each of these four conceptual alternatives has been assessed with individuals in a variety of groups that are experiencing acculturation. The original study (Sommerlad & Berry, 1970) primarily sought to measure attitudes to assimilation and integration; other studies (e.g., Berry et al., 1982) assessed all four attitudes among James Bay Cree Indians, while work with other groups (such as French-, Portuguese-, Korean- and Hungarian-Canadians, see Berry et al., 1989) has demonstrated the usefulness of the approach not only with native peoples, but also with acculturating ethnic groups.

The four scales are developed by selecting a number of topics (e.g., endogamy, ethnic media) that are relevant to acculturation in the particular group (see Table 1 for some examples of these scales). Then four statements (one for each alternative) are generated with the help of informants. Usually it is possible to establish face validity for the statements by asking judges who are familiar with the model (as depicted in Figure 4) to sort them into the four alternatives; those statements with good interrater agreement are then kept. Administration involves either a Likert scale response to each statement or a statement of preference for one of the four statements within a topic. Four scores are then calculated for each person by summing across topics within each alternative. Reliability (internal consistency) is enhanced by item selection, and validity is checked against behavioral measures (e.g., high separation scorers read only ethnic newspapers, high assimilation scorers read only newspapers in the language of Culture A, high integration scorers read both).

Further work will be necessary to bring the various measures

TABLE 1
Sample Items from Acculturation Attitudes Scale

	Friendship
S	Most of my friends are Koreans because I feel very comfortable around them, but I don't feel as comfortable around Canadians.
I	The kind of relationships that I have with Koreans are valuable while the kind of relationships with Canadians are also worthwhile.
M	These days it's hard to find someone you can really relate to and share your inner feelings and thoughts.
A	Most of my friends are Canadians because they are enjoyable and I feel comfortable around them, but I don't feel the same way with Koreans.

	Canadian Society
A	We're living in Canada, and that means giving up our traditional way of life and adopting a Canadian life-style, thinking and acting like Canadians.
I	While living in Canada we can retain our Korean cultural heritage and life-style and yet participate fully in various aspects of Canadian society.
S	Because we live in Canada, we are always pressured to assimilate to Canadian life-style. Thus we must emphasize our distinct Korean identity and restrict our association with Canadian society.
M	Politicians use national pride to exploit and to deceive the public.

Note: A = assimilation; I = integration; S = separation; M = marginalization. From Berry, et al., 1989.

together conceptually and empirically. In particular, the political and cultural context in which acculturation is taking place (usually determined by the power of Culture A) will almost certainly affect the topics chosen and the options or alternatives that are conceivable. However, in any specific setting, the most important issue is whether the scales developed are modeled in the appropriate way so that they match the actual situation in which the research is being conducted.

BEHAVIOR CHANGES

In this section I want to focus on what happens to individuals as a result of acculturation. As we saw in the last section, it is not always possible to maintain a clear separation between contact measures and attitude measures when we examine a particular acculturation study. Similarly, we will see here that not all observed changes can be linked directly to acculturation; some effects may be delayed in time, and some may even bring about acculturation in a continuing ante-cedent-consequent chain. For example, more contact often results in a more positive attitude to assimilation; thus the attitude could be classified as a "consequence of acculturation." Conversely, an initially positive attitude toward assimilation may result in a person's seeking out more contact; here the contact could just as well be classified as a consequence. Despite these qualifications, a number of studies have attempted to comprehend the results of acculturation and have devel-oped instruments specifically designed to measure them.

Another distinction can be found in the literature between two kinds of consequences (Berry, 1976). One refers to the relatively conflict-free changes in behavior, such as an individual's gradually taking on wage employment and giving up another economic role; these have been termed *behavioral shifts* and are characterized by a continuity in quality but a change in quantity (e.g., from a pattern of 20% wage employment/80% farming at Time 1 to 90% wage employment/10% farming at Time 2). The other refers to new cir-cumstances that often accompany acculturation, which appear to result from psychological conflict and social disintegration, such as an increase in homicide, spouse abuse, or a decline in mental health status; this type of consequence has been termed *acculturative stress,* and is characterized by a qualitative change in the life of an individ-ual or community. Once again it is possible to challenge the distinc-tion; after all, homicide, aggression, and neglect are present in most societies before acculturation, but we frequently encounter new forms as well as new rates, so that rather than being regarded as deviant and sanctioned (in Culture B) they become common in Culture B[1] and people learn to live with them.

As the definitions of acculturation presented earlier suggested, there can also be novel conditions stimulated or even created by the process of acculturation. These are not just shifts in previous behav-iors or problematic stress effects; they are new cultural behaviors that arise by way of social and political movements, themselves stimulated by acculturative contact.

Virtually any behavior studied by psychology is a candidate for a shift during acculturation. Of course this challenges the basic notions of the personality trait and behavioral stability, which posit continu-ity over time and across situations. However, the field of cross-cul-tural psychology has established fairly solid linkages between how an individual acts (including thoughts, feelings, and motives) and the

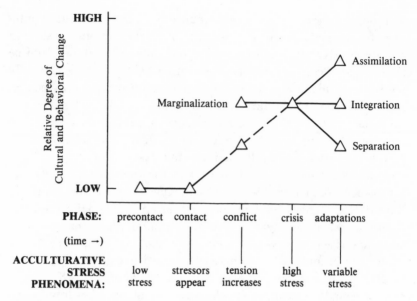

FIGURE 5

Degree of Cultural and Psychological Change as a Function of Phases and Varieties of Acculturation (fig. 9.2 from Berry & Kim, 1988). Reprinted by permission of Sage Publications, Inc.

culture that nurtured him; it should not be difficult to accept, then, that when the culture changes the individual may change as well. What may be stable over time is the culture-behavior linkage rather than the behavior itself.

The amount of behavior change with acculturation, and the way it relates to the two cultures, can vary a great deal. Figure 5 presents a general framework for examining behavior change (vertical axis) as a function of the phase or time period of acculturation (horizontal axis) and as a function of the variety or mode of acculturation (as defined in the previous section on attitudes) an individual engages in.

On the vertical axis, greater change is higher on the dimension, while little or no change is lower. Along the horizontal axis, the phase moves from precontact, through initial contact, often through a period of rising conflict (both psychological and cultural) between the two groups, sometimes resulting in a crisis, followed by three possible acculturation outcomes or forms of adaptation. In the *assimilation* outcome, behavioral change is maximal, whereas in the *separation* mode there is a return to more traditional (similar to minimally changed) behaviors; *integration* represents an outcome on which there is a relatively stable balance between behavioral continuity with one's traditional culture and change toward the new culture. In *marginalization* the individual is suspended between the two cultures, often in a state of personal and social conflict. It is in this last situation that greatest levels of acculturative stress are to be found; it will be considered in detail in the next section.

Among the many behaviors that could be considered in this examination of change, only a few can be presented. I will begin with identity, move to aspects of cognition, then to personality, and finally (to come full circle) consider attitudes and contact as psychological characteristics that themselves shift as a result of acculturation.

Identity (how one usually thinks of oneself) can be seen in terms of cultural (including ethnic and racial) or other factors (e.g., age, sex, location; Aboud, 1981). Here we are primarily interested in ethnic identity and how it may change over the course of acculturation. There is widespread evidence (e.g., De Vos, 1980) that cultural identities do change. At the beginning of contact there is usually little question: one thinks of oneself as a member of the group into which one was enculturated, be it small in scale (a village or a band) or large (a state or country). As contact continues, identity changes may be monitored by a variety of techniques that can provide evidence for simple shifts and for identity conflict and confusion (at the crisis stage, related to acculturative stress).

Cognitive shifts are also frequently observed in studies of acculturation. Indeed, cognitive shifts are often the goal of acculturation, as in the case of educational or religious missions in many parts of the world. Here we are primarily interested in the intellectual changes that may occur with acculturation. A major focus (e.g., Rogoff, 1981; Scribner & Cole, 1973) has been on the cognitive consequences of formal education, with an associated interest in the consequences of literacy (Scribner & Cole, 1981). Cognitive qualities that have been assessed are general intelligence (e.g., Vernon, 1969), cognitive style (e.g., Berry, 1976), memory (e.g., Wagner, 1981), and classification (e.g., Scribner & Cole, 1981), as well as some of the more overt consequences such as success at school.

Perhaps the most common (and ambiguous) finding is that performance on cognitive tests becomes "better" (more like the expectations of the test maker or test administrator) as the test taker becomes more acculturated to the society of origin of the tests. Phrased in this way, the finding is obvious and perhaps meaningless. The use of such tests among cultural groups in various parts of the world and among ethnic groups in plural societies continues, and continues to be criticized (e.g., Samuda, 1983), and the results continue to be open to numerous interpretations. One point of view about such results is that there is no substantive shift in cognitive functioning, only a superficial change in performance due to learning some "test taking tricks" (e.g., familiarity with the language of the test and with testlike situations). Another point of view is that new cognitive qualities or operations may indeed develop with acculturative influences such as literacy or industrialization. Although this view is held by many who carry on modernization research (e.g., Inkeles & Smith, 1974), and in literacy (e.g., Goody, 1968), the evidence for such fundamental changes is rather sparse. For example, the study by Scribner and Cole (1981) revealed very little in the way of general cognitive consequences of literacy —only a few changes that are more specific to skills directly related to the practice of literacy.

The evident conclusion to be drawn is that the search for cognitive consequences of acculturation is methodologically very difficult if one wants unambiguous results. If the point is to demonstrate that over time or over generations beliefs, abilities, or even general intelligence (as defined and measured by the larger society culture) change in the acculturating group in the direction of the norms in the larger society, then the task is rather easy. But the meaning (or "depth") of these changes is much more difficult to specify.

Personality shifts have also been observed during acculturation (which may appear to be a contradiction in terms). In one classical study by Hallowell (1955), three groups of Ojibwa Indians were administered the Rorschach test. One sample was close to Euro-Canadian influence, one was in the remote hinterland, and the third was geographically in between, with an intermediate degree of contact. Hallowell interpreted his results as showing a continuity of a modal Ojibwa personality, but with differences from one sample to another such that the most remote was most intact, the higher-contact sample had shifted more toward Euro-Canadian personality, and the middle community was in between. However, such a "linear gradient" may not always be evident. Peck et al. (1976) found that some individuals may show this pattern but others may not change at all or indeed may reverse the process. One way of interpreting these variations is to argue that those who are in the "assimilation mode" may show a linear gradient, whereas those who are separating or integrating may not exhibit the pattern.

Acculturation attitudes, as we have seen, may predispose contact and hence lead to acculturative change. To come full circle, then, we should remind ourselves that the consequences of acculturation can be changes in acculturation attitudes and changes in contact participation. Evidence does indeed show that there is a complex interrelationship among many variables; for example, a preference for assimilation has often been observed to increase as a result of acculturation experience, and it leads in turn to even more contact and participation by individuals of Culture B in the life of Culture A (Berry et al., 1989). However, lest I leave the impression that there is a continuous linear skid toward assimilation and cultural and psychological homogeneity, we may remind ourselves that conflict, reaction, and other resistive strategies also frequently occur during acculturation; these are important factors in acculturative stress phenomena, to which I now turn.

ACCULTURATIVE STRESS

One of the most obvious and frequently reported consequences of acculturation is societal disintegration accompanied by personal crisis. The old social order and cultural norms often disappear, and individuals may be lost in the change. At the group level, previous patterns of authority, civility, and welfare no longer operate; and at the individual level, hostility, uncertainty, identity confusion, and depression may set in. Taken together these changes constitute the negative side of acculturation, changes that are frequently, but not inevitably, present. The opposite, successful *adaptation,* may also take place; as we shall see, the outcome appears to vary as a function of a number of variables.

The concept of *acculturative stress* (Berry & Annis, 1974b) refers to one kind of stress, in which the stressors are identified as having their source in the process of acculturation; in addition, there is often a particular set of stress behaviors that occur during acculturation, such as lowered mental health status (especially confusion, anxiety, depression), feelings of marginality and alienation, heightened psychosomatic symptoms, and identity confusion. Acculturative stress thus may underlie a reduction in the health status of individuals (including physical, psychological, and social aspects). To qualify as *acculturative* stress, these changes should be related in a systematic way to known features of the acculturation process as experienced by the individual.

In a recent review and integration of the literature, Berry and Kim (1988) attempted to identify the cultural and psychological factors that govern the relationship between acculturation and mental health. We concluded that mental health problems clearly often do arise during acculturation; however, these problems are not inevitable and seem to depend on a variety of group and individual characteristics that enter into the acculturation process. That is, acculturation sometimes enhances one's life chances and mental health and sometimes virtually destroys one's ability to carry on; the eventual outcome for any particular individual is affected by other variables that govern the relationship between acculturation and stress.

This conception is illustrated in Figure 6. On the left of the figure, *acculturation* occurs in a particular situation (e.g., migrant community or native settlement), and individuals participate in and experience these changes to varying degrees; thus individual acculturation experience may vary from a great deal to rather little. In the middle, *stressors* may result from this varying experience of acculturation; for some people acculturative changes may all be in the form of stressors, while for others they may be benign or even be seen as opportunities. On the right, varying levels of *acculturative stress* may become manifest as a result of acculturation experience and stressors.

The first crucial point to note is that relationships among these three concepts (indicated by the solid horizontal arrows) are probabilistic rather than deterministic; the relationships all depend upon a number of moderating factors (indicated in the lower box), including the nature of the larger society, the type of acculturating group, the mode of acculturation being experienced, and a number of demographic, social, and psychological characteristics (including coping abilities) of the group and individual members. That is, each of these factors can influence the degree and direction of the relationships between the three variables at the top of Figure 6. This influence is indicated by the broken vertical arrows drawn between this set of moderating factors and the horizontal arrows.

Archival, observational, and interview methods have been employed to assess acculturative stress. Archival approaches can provide collective data for the society or community as a whole: rates of

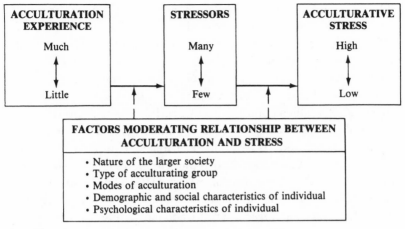

FIGURE 6
Relationships between Acculturation and Stress, as Modified by
Other Factors (fig. 1 from Berry, Kim, Minde, & Mok, 1987).
Reprinted by permission of the Center for Migration Studies of New
York, Inc.

suicide, homicide, family and substance abuse, and so on, can provide
important information about the acculturation context in which an
individual is operating. In particular, rates of psychiatric attention
have often been employed in the literature. However, all these archival records require an organized social system with equal access to
all members of society. The system may itself be suffering from
disintegration; thus such macroindicators may not always be available or reliable.

Survey studies have typically employed third-party sources of information about, or direct observations of, more specific research
subjects. For example, number of court appearances, alcohol consumption, or work and school absenteeism for specific individuals or
target communities can provide, over time, a reasonable indicator of
problem behaviors during acculturation.

Interviewing samples of individuals in acculturating communities
has been a particularly important source of evidence about stress both
in Western urban groups undergoing change (e.g., Srole, Langer, &
Michael, 1962) and in specific cultural groups experiencing acculturation (e.g., Wintrob & Sindell, 1972). Because of the popularity of
this approach, some fairly concise self-report measures have been
developed, of which we will consider two.

One scale has been developed in a number of versions from the Cornell Medical Index (Brodman et al., 1952). The full scale consists of 195 items concerned with somatic functioning and 51 items concerned with psychological life, arranged into six subscales (Inadequacy, Depression, Anxiety, Sensitivity, Anger, and Tension). Work in Alaska by Chance (1965) revealed somewhat heightened levels of psychological problems among acculturating Inuit. A 20-item version was developed by Cawte, Bianchi, and Kiloh (1968) containing 10 somatic items and 10 psychological items. This version was employed with an Australian Aborigine group that had experienced both relocation and acculturation. Berry (1976) later used the scale with various acculturating Canadian Indian groups, and Blue and Blue (1983) have employed it with Canadian Indian university students. The full 51-item psychological scales have also been used with various groups, including Vietnamese refugees (Masuda, Lin, & Tazuma, 1979–1980; Berry & Blondel, 1982), and foreign students (Berry et al., (1987).

A second scale was devised by Mann (1958) to assess the concept of marginality. The essence of being marginal is being "poised in psychological uncertainty between two worlds" (Stonequist, 1935), unable to participate fully in either culture. The scale consists of 14 items, such as "I feel that I don't belong anywhere" and "I feel that nobody really understands me." Respondents indicate which statements they agree with, and the total score is the number of items agreed with.

A major problem with these scales is that all the items are phrased in a positive direction; thus those with a tendency to agree will score higher than others. Another problem is that self-reports of these disorders may not bear any relationship to their actual presence. However, cross-validation with other tests, and with observational data, tends to support their continued use in studies of acculturation as indicators of the stresses and strains individuals experience.

Results of studies of acculturative stress have varied widely in the level of difficulties found in acculturating groups. Early views were that culture contact and change inevitably led to stress; however, current views are that stress is linked to acculturation in a probabilistic way, and the level of stress experienced will depend on a number of factors.

There is evidence (Berry & Kim, 1988) that mode of acculturation is one important factor: those who feel marginal tend to be highly stressed, and those who maintain a separation goal are also stressed; in contrast, those who pursue integration are minimally stressed, with assimilation leading to intermediate levels.

Similarly, the phase of acculturation (see Figure 5) is also important: those in first contact and those who have achieved some long-term adaptation tend to be less stressed than those caught in the conflict or crisis phase, especially, as I have noted, if they also feel marginal.

Another factor is the way the host society exerts its acculturative influences. One important distinction is the degree of pluralism extant (Murphy, 1965). Culturally plural societies, in contrast to culturally monistic ones, are likely to be characterized by two important factors: one is the availability of a network of social and cultural groups that may provide support for those entering into the experience of acculturation (i.e., provide a protective cocoon); the other is a greater tolerance for or acceptance of cultural diversity (termed "multicultural ideology" by Berry, Kalin, & Taylor, 1977). Related to this general tolerance for ethnic diversity (which is usually found in plural societies) is the pattern of specific ethnic and racial attitudes in the larger society: some acculturating groups may be more accepted and placed higher in the prestige hierarchy, while others may occupy the lower ranks in the societies' prejudice system. Taken together, one might reasonably expect the stress of persons experiencing acculturation in plural societies to be less than in monistic societies that pursue a forced inclusion or assimilationist ideology.

A related factor, paradoxically, is the existence of policies designed to *exclude* acculturating groups from full participation in the larger society; to the extent that acculturating people wish to participate in the desirable features of the larger society (such as adequate housing, medical care, and political rights), the denial of these may increase acculturative stress.

There are also many social and cultural qualities of the acculturating group that may affect the degree to which its members experience acculturative stress. The list of possible factors identified in the literature is extremely long; thus I attempt only a selective overview. It is useful to distinguish between original (precontact) cultural characteristics and those that evolve during the process of acculturation; however, some factors involve the interaction of variables from these two sets (pre- and postcontact).

One basic cultural factor that appears in the literature is the traditional settlement pattern of the group: nomadic peoples, who are usually hunters, gatherers, or pastoralists, may suffer more negative consequences of acculturation than peoples who were sedentary before contact. A complex of factors has been suggested to account for this proposal: nomadic peoples are used to relatively large territories, small population densities, and unstructured sociopolitical systems; acculturation, typically requires sedentarization into relatively dense communities with new authority systems, and this induces relatively greater tension among nomadic peoples than among others.

Status is also a factor even when one's origin is in a relatively stratified society. For example, one's "entry status" into the larger society is often lower than one's "departure status" from the home society; this relative loss of status may result in stress and poor mental health. One's status mobility in the larger society, whether to regain one's original status or just to keep up with other groups, may also be a factor. In addition, some specific features of status (such as education and employment) provide one with resources for dealing with the larger society, and these are likely to affect one's ability to function effectively in the new circumstances.

Some standard indicators, such as age and gender, may also play a role: relatively older persons, and often females, have frequently been noted to experience more stress, as have those who are unmarried, either because of loss or because no partner is available.

Perhaps the most comprehensive variable in the literature is social support — the presence of social and cultural institutions that support the acculturating individual. Included here are such factors as ethnic associations (national or local), residential enclaves ("ghetto"), extended families (including endogamy), availability of one's original group (visits to, vitality of, alienation from the culture), and more formal institutions such as agencies and clinics devoted to providing support.

A final set of social variables refers to the acceptance or prestige of one's group in the acculturation setting. Some groups are more acceptable than others on grounds of ethnicity, race, or religion; those less acceptable run into barriers (prejudice, discrimination, exclusion) that may lead to marginalization of the group and are likely to induce greater stress. The point here is that even in plural societies (those societies that may be generally more tolerant of differences) there are still relative degrees of social acceptability of the various acculturating groups.

Beyond these social factors numerous psychological variables may play a role in the mental health of persons experiencing acculturation. Here again a distinction is useful between those characteristics that were present before contact and those that developed during acculturation. The precontact set of variables includes certain experiences that may predispose one to function more effectively under acculturative pressures. These are prior knowledge of the new language and culture, prior intercultural encounters of any kind, motives for the contact (voluntary vs. involuntary contact), and attitudes toward acculturation (positive or negative). Other prior attributes that have been suggested in the literature are level of education and employment, values, self-esteem, identity confusion, rigidity/flexibility, and cognitive style.

Contact experiences may also account for variations in acculturative stress. Whether one has a lot of contacts with the larger society (or few), whether they are pleasant (or unpleasant), whether they meet current needs (or not), and in particular whether the first encounters are viewed positively (or not) may set the stage for all subsequent ones and may affect mental health.

Among factors that appear during acculturation are the attitudes toward the various modes of acculturation: as I noted in the previous section, individuals within a group do vary in their preference for assimilating, integrating, or rejecting. These variations, along with experiences of marginalization, are known to affect mental health (Berry, Kim, Minde, & Mok, 1987). Another variable, an individual's sense of cognitive control over the acculturation process, also seems to play a role; those who percieve that the changes are opportunities they can manage may have better mental health than those who feel overwhelmed. In essence, then, the attitudinal and cognitive perspectives propose that it is not the acculturative changes themselves that are important, but how one sees them and what one makes of them.

Finally, a recurring idea is that the congruity between expectations and actualities will affect mental health; individuals for whom there is a discrepancy—who aspire to or expect more than they actually obtain during acculturation—may have greater acculturative stress than those who achieve some reasonable match between them. That is, expectations and goals (and whether they can be met) appear to be major predictors of how individuals and groups will fare during the course of acculturation. Recent work (reviewed in Beiser,

Barwick, Berry, et al., 1988) indicates that a desire to participate in the larger society, or a desire for cultural maintenance, if thwarted, can lead to a serious decline in the mental health of acculturating individuals. Policies or attitudes in the larger society that are discriminatory (not permitting participation, and leading to marginalization or segregation) or assimilationist (leading to enforced cultural loss) are all predictors of psychological problems. In my view, acculturative stress is always a possible concomitant of acculturation, but the probability can be much reduced if both participation in the larger society and maintenance of one's heritage culture are welcomed by policy and practice in the larger acculturative arena.

CONCLUSION

Applications of findings reported in this chapter, especially if done with continuing evaluation and validation, should go a long way to helping the millions who find themselves in a situation of culture contact and change. Refugees, immigrants, and guest workers can all be provided with information, counseling, and other forms of psychological assistance based on these data. Receiving countries can also develop policies and programs based on these findings, and public education of the host population may also be attempted. Enough information is now available about the process of acculturation, and about factors affecting various psychological outcomes, that there could, with better programs, be a significant reduction in the problems acculturating peoples experience. However, with the possibility that there will be increasing numbers of refugees in the world, and perhaps increasing numbers of temporary migrants (out-migration followed by return migration), the potential for problems is not likely to diminish. Hence the findings reported in this chapter, and the basic principles they point to, urgently require interpretation and transfer to those responsible for managing acculturation, in both the donor and receiving countries.

REFERENCES

Aboud, F. (1981). Ethnic self identity. In R. C. Gardner & R. Kalin (Eds.), *A Canadian social psychology of ethnic relations.* Toronto: Methuen.

Beiser, M., Barwick, C., Berry, J. W., et al. (1988). *After the door has been opened: Mental health issues affecting immigrants and refugees in Canada.* Ottawa: Ministries of Multiculturalism and Health and Welfare.

Berry, J. W. (1976). *Human ecology and cognitive style: Comparative studies in cultural and psychological adaptation.* London: Sage.

Berry, J. W. (1980). Social and cultural change. In H. C. Triandis & R. Brislin (Eds.), *Handbook of cross-cultural psychology: Vol. 5. Social Psychology.* Boston: Allyn and Bacon.

Berry, J. W., & Annis, R. C. (1974a). Acculturative stress: The role of ecology, culture and differentiation. *Journal of Cross Cultural Psychology, 5,* 382–406.

Berry, J. W., & Annis, R. C. (1974b). Ecology, cultural and psychological differentiation. *International Journal of Psychology, 9,* 173–193.

Berry, J. W., & Blondel, T. (1982). Psychological adaptation of Vietnamese refugees in Canada. *Canadian Journal of Community Mental Health, 1,* 81–88.

Berry, J. W., Kalin, R., & Taylor, D. M. (1977). *Multiculturalism and ethnic attitudes in Canada.* Ottawa: Supply and Services.

Berry, J. W., & Kim, U. (1988). Acculturation and mental health. In P. Dasen, J. W. Berry, & N. Sartorius (Eds.), *Health and cross-cultural psychology* (pp. 207–236). London: Sage.

Berry, J. W., Kim, U., Minde, T., & Mok, D. (1987). Comparative studies of acculturative stress. *International Migration Review, 21,* 491–511.

Berry, J. W., Kim, U., Power, S., Young, M., & Bujaki, M. (1989). Acculturation attitudes in plural societies. *Applied Psychology, 38,* 185–206.

Berry, J. W., Trimble, J., & Olmeda, E. (1986). The assessment of acculturation. In W. J. Lonner & J. W. Berry (Eds.), *Field methods in cross-cultural research.* London: Sage.

Berry, J. W., van de Koppel, J. M. H., Sénéchal, C., Annis, R. C., Bahuchet, S., Cavalli-Sforza, L. L., & Witkin, H. A. (1986). *On the edge of the forest: Cultural adaptation and cognitive development in Central Africa.* Lisse: Swets and Zeitlinger.

Berry, J. W., Wintrob, R. M., Sindell, P. S., & Mawhinney, T. A. (1982). Psychological adaptation to culture change among the James Bay Cree. *Naturaliste Canadien, 109,* 965–975.

Blue, A., & Blue, M. (1983). The trail of stress. In R. Samuda, J. W. Berry, & M. Laferriere (Eds.), *Multiculturalism in Canada: Social and educational perspectives.* Toronto: Allyn and Bacon.

Brodman, K., et al. (1952). The Cornell Medical Index health questionnaire: 3. The evaluation of emotional disturbances. *Journal of Clinical Psychology, 8,* 119–124.

Cawte, J., Bianchi, G. N., & Kiloh, L. G. (1968). Personal discomfort in Australian Aborigines. *Australian and New Zealand Journal of Psychiatry, 2,* 69–79.

Chance, N. A. (1965). Acculturation, self-identification, and personality adjustment. *American Anthropologist, 67,* 372–393.

de Lacey, P. R. (1970). An index of contact. *Australian Journal of Social Issues, 5,* 219–223.

De Vos, G. (1980). Ethnic adaptation and minority status. *Journal of Cross-Cultural Psychology, 11,* 101–124.

Foster, G. M., Scudder, T., Colson, E., & Kemper, R. V. (Eds.). (1978). *Longterm field research in social anthropology.* Orlando, FL: Academic Press.

Goody, J. (1968). *Literacy in traditional societies.* New York: Cambridge University Press.

Graves, T. D. (1967). Psychological acculturation in a tri-ethnic community. *Southwestern Journal of Anthropology, 23,* 337–350.

Hallowell, A. I. (1955). Sociopsychological aspects of acculturation. In A. I. Hallowell, *Culture and experience.* Philadelphia: University of Pennsylvania Press.

Inkeles, A., & Smith, D. (1974). *Becoming modern.* Cambridge: Harvard University Press.

Mann, J. (1958). Group relations and the marginal man. *Human Relations, 11,* 77–92.

Masuda, M., Lin, K., & Tazuma, L. (1979–1980). Adaptation problems of Vietnamese refugees. *Archives of General Psychiatry, 36–37,* 955–961, 447–450.

Murphy, H. B. M. (1965). Migration and the major mental disorders. In M. B. Kantor (Ed)., *Mobility and mental health.* Springfield, IL: Thomas.

Peck, R., et al. (1976). A test of the universality of an acculturation gradient in three-culture triads. In K. Riegel & J. Meacham (Eds.), *The developing individual in a changing world.* The Hague: Mouton.

Redfield, R., Linton, R., & Herskovits, M. J. (1936). Memorandum on the study of acculturation. *American Anthropologist, 38,* 149–152.

Rogoff, B. (1981). Schooling and the development of cognitive skills. In H. C. Triandis & A. Heron (Eds.), *Handbook of cross-cultural psychology: Vol. 4. Development.* Boston: Allyn and Bacon.

Samuda, R. (1983). Cross-cultural testing within a multicultural society. In S. H. Irvine & J. W. Berry (Eds.), *Human assessment and cultural factors.* New York: Plenum.

Scribner, S., & Cole, M. (1973). Cognitive consequences of formal and informal education. *Science, 182,* 553–559.

Scribner, S., & Cole, M. (1981). *The psychology of literacy.* Cambridge: Harvard University Press.

Social Science Research Council. (1954). Acculturation: An exploratory formulation. *American Anthropologist, 56,* 973–1002.

Sommerlad, E. A., & Berry, J. W. (1970). The role of ethnic identification in distinguishing between attitudes towards assimilation and integration of a minority racial group. *Human Relations, 23,* 23–29.

Srole, L., Langer, T. S., & Michael, S. T. (1962). *Mental health in the metropolis.* New York: McGraw-Hill.

Stonequist, E. V. (1935). The problem of the marginal man. *American Journal of Sociology, 41,* 1–12.

Vernon, P. E. (1969). *Intelligence and cultural environment.* London: Methuen.

Wagner, D. A. (1981). Culture and memory development. In H. C. Triandis & A. Heron (Eds.), *Handbook of cross-cultural psychology: Vol. 4. Development.* Boston: Allyn and Bacon.

Wintrob, R. M., & Sindell, P. S. (1972). Culture change and psychopathology: The case of Cree adolescent students in Quebec. In J. W. Berry & G. J. S. Wilde (Eds.), *Social psychology: The Canadian context.* Toronto: McClelland and Stewart.

21. Psychological Impact of Biculturalism: Evidence and Theory

Teresa LaFromboise, Hardin L. K. Coleman, and Jennifer Gerton

Park (1928) and Stonequist (1935) developed the argument that individuals who live at the juncture between two cultures and can lay a claim to belonging to both cultures, either by being of mixed racial heritage or born in one culture and raised in a second, should be considered marginal people. Park suggested that marginality leads to psychological conflict, a divided self, and disjointed person. Stonequist contended that marginality has certain social and psychological properties. The social properties include factors of migration and racial (biological) difference and situations in which two or more cultures share the same geographical area, with one culture maintaining a higher status than another. The psychological properties involve a state of what DuBois (1961) labeled *double-consciousness,* or the simultaneous awareness of oneself as being a member and an alien of two or more cultures. This includes a "dual pattern of identification and a divided loyalty . . . [leading to] an ambivalent attitude" (Stonequist, 1935).

Words derisively used to describe the marginal person, such as "apple," "banana," or "oreo," reflect the negative stereotype often applied to people who have intimate relationships with two or more cultures. The common assumption, exemplified by the positions of Park (1928) and Stonequist (1935), is that living in two cultures is psychologically undesirable because managing the complexity of dual reference points generates ambiguity, identity confusion, and normlessness. Park also suggested, however, that the history and progress of humankind, starting with the Greeks, has depended on the inter-

Reprinted by permission of the author and the American Psychological Association from *Psychological Bulletin* 114 (1993): 395–412. Copyright © 1993 by the American Psychological Association.

face of cultures. He claimed that migration and human movement inevitably lead to intermingling. Park described the individual who is the product of this interaction as the "cosmopile," the independent and wiser person. In other words, even though marginality is psychologically uncomfortable for the individual, it has long-term benefits for society.

Goldberg (1941) and Green (1947), in their responses to the marginal human theory, suggested that people who live within two cultures do not inevitably suffer. Both authors suggested that being a "marginal person" is disconcerting only if the individual internalizes the conflict between the two cultures in which he or she is living. In fact, Goldberg perceived advantages to living at the border between two cultures. According to him, a marginal person may (a) share his or her condition with others of the same original culture; (b) engage in institutional practices that are shared by other "marginal" people; (c) experience no major blockage or frustrations associated with personal, economic, or social expectations; and (d) perceive himself or herself to be a member of a group. Goldberg argued that a person who is part of a subculture that provides norms and a definition of the individual's situation will not suffer from the negative psychological effects of being a marginal person.

The purpose of this essay is to review the literature on the psychological impact of being bicultural. We present a definition of cultural competence and discuss models that have been used to describe the psychological processes, social experiences, and individual challenges associated with being bicultural. We identify the various skills we believe are needed to successfully negotiate bicultural challenges and obstacles. Finally, we present a hypothetical model of bicultural competence.

We examined journal articles, books, technical reports, and dissertations from a two-dimensional, level-of-analysis perspective and a subject-matter perspective. Four levels of analysis from the disciplines of psychology, education, sociology, and ethnology were selected for review to support our position that the psychological impact of biculturalism is influenced by an individual's emotional and behavioral characteristics (psychology), relationship with human social structures (education), groups and diverse socioeconomic systems (sociology), and cultural heritage (ethnology). The subject areas reviewed were ones thought to be associated with second-culture acquisition. This included (a) synonyms associated with cultural interactions (e.g., biculturalism, dualism, pluralism, transactionalism, acculturation), (b) descriptors for ethnic group membership, and (c) psychological symptoms (e.g., depression, anxiety, stress) and outcomes (e.g., competence, achievement, health) associated with the process of bicultural adaptation. The time span of this review was unrestricted and yielded theoretical articles dating back to 1929 and empirical articles from around the mid-1960s. Articles not considered for inclusion were ones that were found to be atheoretical, not associated with the major models of dual cultural adaptation, or of questionable quality in terms of research design.

Unfortunately, little empirical research exists in this area and what there is is spread throughout the social sciences. We found that some aspects of the psychological impact of being bicultural have received a great deal of well-designed and controlled study, whereas others have been addressed only along theoretical lines. The result of these inconsistencies is that some of the ideas presented are speculative, whereas others have significant empirical support. We have used this liberal approach because our goal was not merely to report the findings of current empirical research but to provide a model for examining the psychology of biculturalism. At the least, we hope that this essay can be used as a springboard for more controlled research on this topic.

CULTURAL COMPETENCE

There is no single definition of culture on which all scholars can agree (Segall, 1986). Attempts to create a satisfactory definition of culture tend to either omit a salient aspect of it or to generalize beyond any real meaning. Despite these problems, there is an abundance of theories available regarding the meaning of the word *culture*. For the purpose of this essay, we use a behaviorally focused definition. Like LeVine (1982), we believe that human behavior is not just the product of cultural structure, individual cognitive and affective processes, biology, and social environment. Instead, we believe that behavior is a result of the continuous interaction among all of these components. We also ascribe to Bandura's (1978, 1986) concept of reciprocal determinism, which suggests that behavior is influenced by and influences a person's cognition and social environment.

This behavioral model of culture suggests that in order to be culturally competent, an individual would have to (a) possess a strong personal identity, (b) have knowledge of and facility with the beliefs and values of the culture, (c) display sensitivity to the affective processes of the culture, (d) communicate clearly in the language of the given cultural group, (e) perform socially sanctioned behavior, (f) maintain active social relations within the cultural group, and (g) negotiate the institutional structures of that culture.

It is important to note that the length of this list reflects the difficulty involved in developing cultural competence, particularly if one is not raised within a given culture. We do not, however, perceive cultural competence to be a dichotomous construct whereby one is either fully competent or not at all competent. We view cultural competence within a multilevel continuum of social skill and personality development. For example, an individual may be able to perform socially sanctioned behavior in two cultures with great ease but have difficulty negotiating diverse institutional structures. We also recognize that members of groups within different social strata may have differential access to social, occupational, and political roles associated with cultural competence (Ogbu, 1979). We do assume, however, that the more levels in which one is competent, the fewer problems an individual will have functioning effectively within two cultures.

MODELS OF SECOND-CULTURE ACQUISITION

Five models that have been used to understand the process of change that occurs in transitions within, between, and among cultures are assimilation, acculturation, alternation, multiculturalism, and fusion. Although each was created to address group phenomena, they can be used to describe the processes by which an individual from one culture, the culture of origin, develops competence in another culture, often the dominant majority culture. Each model has a slightly different emphasis and set of assumptions and focuses on different outcomes for the individual. We describe each one, identify its underlying assumptions, and review a number of hypotheses about the psychological impact of biculturalism that each appears to generate. We present, when available, examples from research literature that clarify the hypotheses implicit within each model.

Assimilation Model

One model for explaining the psychological state of a person living within two cultures assumes an ongoing process of absorption into the culture that is perceived as dominant or more desirable. Gordon (1964, 1978) outlined a number of subprocesses constituting various stages of the assimilation process: (a) cultural or behavioral assimilation, (b) structural assimilation, (c) marital assimilation, (d) identificational assimilation, (e) attitudinal receptional assimilation, (f) behavioral receptional assimilation, and (g) civic assimilation. Ruiz (1981) emphasized that the goal of the assimilation process is to become socially accepted by members of the target culture as a person moves through these stages. The underlying assumption of all assimilation models is that a member of one culture loses his or her original cultural identity as he or she acquires a new identity in a second culture.

This model leads to the hypothesis that an individual will suffer from a sense of alienation and isolation until he or she has been accepted and perceives that acceptance within the new culture (Johnston, 1976; Sung, 1985). This person will experience more stress, be more anxious, and suffer more acutely from social problems such as school failure or substance abuse than someone who is fully assimilated into that culture (Burnam, Telles, Karno, Hough, & Escobar, 1987; Pasquali, 1985). The gradual loss of support derived from the original culture, combined with the initial inability to use the assets of the newly acquired culture, will cause stress and anxiety.

Kerchoff and McCormick (1955) found that the greatest incidence of marginal personality characteristics (e.g., low self-esteem, impoverished social relationships, negative emotional states) among Ojibwa Indians occurred in individuals who were inclined to identify with the dominant group but encountered a relatively impermeable barrier to assimilation with that group. Chance (1965) found an overall lack of serious psychological impairment in most subjects of either sex during a period of rapidly increasing bicultural contact. However, subjects having relatively little contact with Western society, but who strongly identified with that society, showed more symptoms of personality maladjustment. Neither the contact index nor the identification index alone revealed significant differences with respect to emotional disturbance. Only the combination of the lower contact rank and high identification rank produced a situation conducive to emotional difficulties in the individual. Demographic factors such as age or education failed to delineate consistent differences in emotional disturbance.

Chadwick and Strauss (1975) found that American Indians living in Seattle maintained a strong sense of Indian identity during periods of economic and interpersonal rejection by the majority group. Even though they were able to achieve marital assimilation and perceived an absence of prejudice against them, they experienced value and power conflicts with the dominant power structure over public or civic issues. A substantial number of American Indians living their entire life in the city were perceived by the researchers to be as traditional as those who had recently left the reservation.

By contrast, Fordham's (1988) study of academically successful African-American students identified many of the problems associated with the process of assimilation. According to her findings, successful students felt that they had to reject the values of the African-American community in order to succeed in school. This seemed to be a less psychologically complicated task for women, but both sexes found that they had substantial conflict in their social and academic roles. Those choosing to become "raceless" suffered more stress and personal confusion than did those who maintained their African-American identification. On the other hand, those who did not become raceless failed to meet the standards imposed by the majority group. In this case, social success in the African-American community was associated with school failure, followed by economic failure. According to Fordham, as long as the choice is between one's ethnicity and school success, the latter will be a Pyrrhic victory.

Assimilation is the process by which an individual develops a new cultural identity. Acquiring this new identity, however, involves some loss of awareness and loyalty to one's culture of origin. Three major dangers are associated with assimilation. The first is the possibility of being rejected by members of the majority culture. The second is the likelihood of being rejected by members of the culture of origin. The third is the likelihood of experiencing excessive stress as one attempts to learn the new behaviors associated with the assimilative culture and to shed the inoperable behaviors associated with the culture of origin.

Acculturation Model

The acculturation[1] model of bicultural contact is similar to the assimilation model in three ways. They both (a) focus on the acquisition of the majority group's culture by members of the minority group, (b) emphasize a unidirectional relationship between the two cultures, and (c) assume a hierarchical relationship between the two cultures. What differentiates the two models is that the assimilation approach emphasizes that individuals, their offspring, or their cultural group will eventually become full members of the majority group's culture and lose identification with their culture of origin. By contrast, the acculturation model implies that the individual, while becoming a competent participant in the majority culture, will always be identified as a member of the minority culture.

Smither (1982) stated that one of the distinguishing characteristics of the acculturation process is its involuntary nature. Most often, the member of the minority group is forced to learn the new culture in order to survive economically. Smither presented five models for understanding the process of acculturation. The first is the multivariate model, in which a quantitative approach is used to understand the factors that influence successful acculturation. The focus of this method is on measuring the interactions among premigration characteristics; conditions, such as income; class status; and various situational determinants in the majority society, such as length of stay, education, or occupation. Supposedly, an understanding of new social, political, cultural, and economic patterns, as well as of personal experience such as identification, internalization, and satisfaction, will emerge from this interaction (Pierce, Clark, & Kaufman, 1978).

Using the multivariate model, Prigoff's (1984) study of the self-esteem, ethnic identity, job aspirations, and school stress of Mexican-American youth in a Midwest urban barrio indicated that subjects' use of the Spanish language and ethnic life-style varied inversely with the length of time spent in the United States. He found a significant relationship between ethnic pride and length of stay. In a multivariate study of ethnic migration and adjustment in Toronto, Goldlust and Richmond (1974) concluded that the influence of ethnicity on acculturation was small compared with length of stay and that level of education had a positive influence on acculturation but was negatively associated with an immigrant's primary cultural identification.

When Richman, Gaviria, Flaherty, Birz, and Wintrob (1987) explored the relationship between acculturation and perceptions of discrimination among migrants in Peru, they found that age at the time of migration was closely associated with both level of acculturation and perceptions of discrimination. The advantage of the multivariate model used in these studies is its flexibility in addressing varying situational and other conditions involved in adapting to a new culture.

The second model of cultural acquisition is the communications theory model developed by Kim (1979), which focuses on four areas of communication: intrapersonal, interpersonal, mass media behavior, and the communication environment. In this model, level of acculturation is determined by the degree of facility one has in these various methods of communication in the language of the majority culture.

The third model, put forth by Szapocznik and his colleagues (Szapocznik & Kurtines, 1980; Szapocznik, Kurtines, & Fernandez, 1980; Szapocznik, Scopetta, Kurtines, & Arandale, 1978; Szapocznik, Santisteban, Kurtines, Perez-Vidal, & Hervis, 1984; Szapocznik et al., 1986), focuses on the behavior and values of the individual to assess his or her level of acculturation. This model suggests that individuals will learn the behaviors needed to survive in a new culture before they acquire the values of the majority group. Like the multivariate model, this one views acculturation as being a function of the time an individual is exposed to the majority culture. Sex and age are other factors. It also assumes that exposure to the majority culture will produce cultural competence.

The fourth model, articulated by Padilla and his colleagues, focuses on the cultural awareness and ethnic loyalty of the individual to determine his or her status of acculturation (Olmedo & Padilla, 1978; Padilla, 1980). This model suggests that an individual's preference for the minority, versus the majority, culture provides a measure of acculturation. It posits that the acculturation process exists in five dimensions: language familiarity, cultural heritage, ethnic pride and identity, interethnic interaction, and interethnic distance. This model argues for a multidimensional understanding of the cultural acquisition process.

Many authors combine these dimensions of the cultural awareness and ethnic loyalty model in their conceptual frameworks for studying acculturation. An example is Thompson's (1948) review of the Dakota Sioux, Northern Ojibwa, Navajo, Tohono O'odham (Papago), and Hopi beliefs in immanent justice. According to this belief, the universe is inherently just and sickness arises in retribution for one's failure to fulfill proper tribal roles or adhere to sacred proscriptions. Notably, regardless of the various kinds of social organization or levels of acculturation, tribal members did not display a significant decrease in the belief in immanent justice. This review did not substantiate the deleterious impact of acculturation on cultural beliefs or values. Spindler's (1952) study of belief in witchcraft among Menomini Indians showed that this belief prevailed among subjects of differing acculturation levels. She described the function of this belief as one supporting a social system invested in retaining traditional culture and providing an adaptive response to the hostilities encountered when interacting with members of the encroaching culture.

In her study of interethnic interaction among American Indians relocated to the San Francisco Bay Area, Ablon (1964) found that most Indian relationships with Anglo-Americans were relatively superficial, consisting of necessary communication with workmates and neighbors. Rather than strive for reciprocal relationships with Anglo-Americans, or positions within Anglo-American organizations, relocated Indians continuously strove to reaffirm their tribal orientation and maintain their identification with other Indians through Pan-Indian organizations. The control these subjects exerted in selecting Anglo-Americans with whom to associate offset the tension surrounding the need to interact with them.

Barger's (1977) comparative study of Inuit (Eskimo) and Cree Indians in Great Whale River, Quebec, Canada, demonstrates the need to consider case-specific factors in the statistical approach to studying the acculturation process. Inuits and Crees who resided in the same town in which Anglos were in the minority for 14 years were compared on a number of behavioral and material integration indexes. It was found that the Inuit demonstrated greater levels of acculturation and became more fully integrated into the town life than did the Crees, who were more selective in their participation in town activities. The association between culture change and presumed deviancy among Cree subjects occurred with certain individuals or families rather than with the tribe as a whole. There were, however, no differences between the two groups in overall psychosocial adjustment.

Similarly, when Boyce and Boyce (1983) studied the relationship between cultural background and the report of illness among Navajo students during their first year at a reservation boarding school (the primary mechanism for acculturating Indian people until the 1970s), they found a significant positive association between the number of clinic visits, referrals for health or psychosocial problems, and the degree of cultural incongruity (dissonance between family and community cultural identities). This finding suggests that externally imposed acculturation does have a deleterious impact on one's health.

Smither (1982) argued that the four models reviewed earlier provide insight into the processes of acculturation at the group level but cannot explain or predict individual differences in acculturation. He supported yet another multidimensional framework, a socioanalytic approach to the study of "the personality processes of the individual which facilitate or retard acculturation" (Smither, 1982, p. 62) to explain individual variation in acculturation. He asserted that an individual must expand his or her role repertoire to meet the demands of the majority culture. In the socioanalytic model, acculturation "is a function of the size of the difference between those qualities of character structure which affect role structure in the majority culture and the same qualities of character structure in the minority compared to the majority role structure" (Smither, 1982, p. 64).

Burnam et al. (1987), in a study of the prevalence of eight psychiatric disorders among Los Angeles adults of Mexican ethnicity, used socioanalytic assumptions to help explain the finding that immigrant Mexican Americans had a lower risk factor for these disorders than their native-born peers. They hypothesized that one of the reasons for the difference between the groups was that the individual who chooses to migrate may have a stronger sense of self (e.g., be more ambitious or capable) and may therefore be better equipped to cope with acculturative stress (defined by Williams & Berry, 1991, as anxiety, depression, feelings of marginality and alienation, heightened psychosomatic symptoms, and identity confusion).

Berry and Annis (1974) applied the socioanalytic approach in their investigation of psychological adaptation to culture change among individuals from the James Bay, Carrier, and Tsimashin communities. They found that the greater the cultural discontinuities between the Indian community and the Anglo communities surrounding them, the greater the acculturation stress on the individual. Individuals attaining a degree of separateness from their fellow tribal members and acquiring an independent cognitive style in interactions with their environment were less susceptible to the stresses of sociocultural change. These studies emphasize the importance of examining the role of individual development when studying the process of second-culture acquisition. However, they do not address the stress associated with any sense of isolation or loss of community ties and approval.

A series of studies by Ekstrand (1978) revealed evidence for the importance of personality factors in the acquisition of bicultural competence. The studies were designed to determine the optimal age for acquisition of a second language. Ekstrand found that personal factors (e.g., motivation, or personal circumstances) were more salient in the acquisition of language than were social factors (e.g., socioeconomic status, immigrant status, teaching method). This supports the assertion that personality factors must be considered in explaining the variation by which individuals develop competence in a new culture.

According to the socioanalytic approach, role structure, character structure, and psychological differentiation need to be understood in relation to constant variables such as age, race, level of education, or degree of cultural discontinuity because they serve to modify expression of personality and role performance. The socioanalytic model of acculturation concentrates on the individual's personality and how it constrains or facilitates learning and the expression of culturally and situationally appropriate behavior.

These studies lend credence to the conclusion that minority individuals attempting to acculturate will often do so antagonistically (Vogt, 1957) or resign themselves to accepting second-class citizenship within the majority group. Most studies of minority groups do seem to indicate that minorities are often relegated to lower status positions within the majority group. This phenomenon seems to hold true for divergent groups such as ethnic minorities in the United States, Finns in Sweden, Turks in Germany, and Koreans in Japan. These studies also suggest that the most active agent in this process may be the discriminatory behavior of the majority culture. However, the role of minority group members' economic resources has been relatively unexplored in acculturation studies, prohibiting conclusions about the role of socioeconomic status in second-culture acquisition.

Collectively, these studies indicate that acculturation can be a stressful experience, reinforcing the second-class citizenship and alienation of the individual acclimating to a new culture. These studies do support the conjecture that the primary feature of the acculturation model rests on the notion that the individual will never be allowed to lose identification with the culture of origin. Furthermore, this can have negative economic and psychological effects on the individual. This observation led Taft (1977) to argue that the detrimental effects of acculturation can be ameliorated by encouraging biculturalism. Taft (1977) suggested that "the mature bicultural individual may rise above both cultures by following superordinate social proscriptions that serve to integrate the individual's behavior relative to each culture" (p. 146). Several of the studies cited support the hypothesis that the more control people have over their relationship with the majority culture, the less likely they are to experience the negative effects of acculturation stress.

Alternation Model

The alternation model of second-culture acquisition assumes that it is possible for an individual to know and understand two different cultures. It also supposes that an individual can alter his or her behavior to fit a particular social context. As Ogbu and Matute-Bianchi (1986) have argued, "it is possible and acceptable to participate in two different cultures or to use two different languages, perhaps for different purposes, by alternating one's behavior according to the situation" (p. 89). Ramirez (1984) also alluded to the use of different problem-solving, coping, human relational, communication, and incentive motivational styles, depending on the demands of the social context. Furthermore, the alternation model assumes that it is possible for an individual to have a sense of belonging in two cultures without compromising his or her sense of cultural identity.

Rashid (1984) defined this type of biculturalism for African Americans as the ability to function effectively and productively within the context of America's core institutions while retaining a sense of self and African ethnic identity. LaFromboise and Rowe (1983) defined this type of biculturalism for American Indians as involving dual modes of social behavior that are appropriately used in different situations.

The alternation model is an additive model of cultural acquisition parallel to the code-switching theories found in the research on bilingualism. Saville-Troike (1981) called this code switching the "sensitive process of signalling different social and contextual relations through language" (p. 3). This hypothesis implies that individuals who can alternate their behavior appropriate to two targeted cultures will be less anxious than a person who is assimilating or undergoing the process of acculturation. Furthermore, some authors (Garcia, 1983; Rashid, 1984; Rogler, Cortes, & Malgady, 1991) have speculated that individuals who have the ability to effectively alternate their use of culturally appropriate behavior may well exhibit higher cognitive functioning and mental health status than people who are monocultural, assimilated, or acculturated. This complements other research (Lambert, 1977; McClure, 1977; Peal & Lambert, 1962) on the positive effects of bilingualism. In similar fashion, Martinez (1987) found that bicultural involvement was the best predictor of esteem and well-being when studying the effects of acculturation and racial identity on self-esteem and psychological well-being among Puerto Rican college students living on the mainland. Although this theoretical perspective still needs to be explored systematically, it may point to the affective or cognitive mechanism that facilitates a bicultural individual's ability to manage the process of alternation.

The alternation model differs from the assimilation and acculturation models in two significant ways. First, it posits a bidirectional and orthogonal relationship between the individual's culture of origin and the second culture in which he or she may be living rather than the linear and unidirectional relationship of the other two models. In fact, the alternation model suggests that it is possible to maintain a positive relationship with both cultures without having to choose between them. Second, this model does not assume a hierarchical relationship between two cultures. Within this framework, it is possible for the individual to assign equal status to the two cultures, even if he or she does not value or prefer them equally.

The alternation model postulates that an individual can choose the degree and manner to which he or she will affiliate with either the second culture or his or her culture of origin. Sodowsky and Carey (1988) described certain dual characteristics of first-generation Asian Indians that appear paradoxical yet support this assumption.

Although the groups as a whole reported a high level of proficiency in reading and speaking English, they preferred thinking in an Indian language (e.g., Hindi, Tamil). Many preferred Indian food and dress at home but American food and dress outside of the home.

Early attempts to define American Indian biculturalism, although nonempirical, adhered to the suppositions of the alternation model. Polgar (1960) studied the behavior of gangs of Mesquakie boys in Iowa as they interacted within their own community and the surrounding Anglo-American community. Polgar found that biculturation was most prominent in the area of recreational activities, in which there was a persistent dualism conditioned by geographical location. Subjects were more active when they were in town than when within the Mesquakie community. Bilingual by the age of 7, they had alternative modes of expression available to them to be used as the situation demanded. They also exerted choice in the gangs with which they chose to affiliate. Of the three gangs profiled in Polgar's study, one in particular illustrated the alternation model of biculturalism. When in town, members of this gang adapted to Anglo-American norms, but while they were in the Mesquakie community they adapted to roles expected by the traditional, political, and religious leaders of the community. Polgar found it convenient, and effective, when analyzing the results of biculturation to view the gangs formed by the boys as transitional patterns in a multilineal scheme of cultural change.

McFee (1968), in studying the selective use of roles and situations by tribal members on the Blackfeet reservation, presented two prototypes of bicultural individuals. One type was Indian in psychological orientation and often included full-blood members of the tribe. Subjects in this category knew Blackfeet culture well, having learned it in their childhood homes and practiced it as adults. They were also educated in Anglo-American schools, had a wide range of experiences in various aspects of Anglo culture, and displayed many characteristics required for effective interactions with Anglo-Americans. Their ambition was to remain Indian but to do so by combining the best of the Indian way with the best of the Anglo way. The second type included subjects raised in Anglo-American families but knowledgeable of Blackfeet culture through early experience prior to removal from the home. Subjects in this latter category were situationally Indian oriented, having maintained enough contact with the Blackfeet community to learn and speak the language, know the beliefs and rituals, and appropriately use these skills during Blackfeet events. Even though these individuals retained their involvement with the Anglo-American culture, they also did things with and for the Blackfeet community that gained them respect and acceptance by that community.

As Pertusali (1988) discussed in his study of the Akwasasne Mohawk in both segregated and desegregated schools, the alternation model is nonlinear in its emphasis. The Akwasasne Mohawk reported their attempt to develop bicultural competence in their children through an educational program involving academic segregation in the reservation school up to the fourth grade, then a transfer to a desegregated school that delivered a bicultural academic program. This transition sequence would ideally help Mohawk children to develop a positive sense of cultural identity and build a strong academic foundation prior to attending Anglo-American schools. Data obtained from in-depth interviews with administrators and faculty members at both the segregated and desegregated schools and an analysis of the retention rates indicated that the bicultural curriculum was beneficial for both the Mohawk and non-Indian students. Results revealed that the non-Indian students were differentially and more positively influenced by the bicultural curriculum than the Indian students. Cantrall and Pete (1990) also described a curriculum that was based on the alternation model at Greasewood School entitled "Navajo culture: A bridge to the rest of the world" that emphasized decision-making, problem-solving, reflective and critical thinking, valuing, concept formation, and information-processing skills needed to deal with the social order change occurring on the Navajo reservation and internationally. The focus of both of these programs was not on movement from competence in the minority group to competence in the majority group but on ways students maintain competence in their culture of origin while simultaneously acquiring competence in the majority (or more global) culture.

A study of biculturalism and adjustment of Ramallah-American adolescents by Kazaleh (1986) showed that although identity conflict was indeed present, many of the adolescents had acquired an array of mechanisms for dealing with the dissonance and were adept at alternating between both cultural orientations with minimal anxiety. Those who had more difficulty adjusting were the youth whose parents and clan members reacted with greater anxiety to rapid change and resisted mainstream influences.

The alternation model implies that individuals learning to alternate their behavior to fit into the cultures in which they are involved will be less stressed and less anxious than those who are undergoing the process of acculturation or assimilation. Guzman (1986) emphasized the importance of maintaining a behavior-preference distinction in the assessment of Mexican-American adolescents from a bicultural-model-of-acculturation perspective. Furthermore, Adler (1975) suggested that one outcome of the alternation model may well be an enhanced intuitive, emotional, and cognitive experience. The views are again similar to assertions about the positive effects of bilingualism.

What we see as the essential strength of the alternation model is that it focuses on the cognitive and affective processes that allow an individual to withstand the negative impact of acculturative stress. It also looks at the role the individual has in choosing how he or she will interact with the second culture and the person's culture of origin. This model forces us to consider the bidirectional impact of cultural contact. In other words, it allows us to consider the impact that individuals from both cultures have on each other.

Multicultural Model

The multicultural model promotes a pluralistic approach to understanding the relationship between two or more cultures. This model addresses the feasibility of cultures maintaining distinct identities while individuals from one culture work with those of other cultures to serve common national or economic needs. In this model it is recognized that it may not be geographic or social isolation per se that is the critical factor in sustaining cultural diversity but the manner of multifaceted and multidimensional institutional sharing between cultures. Berry (1986) claimed that a multicultural society encourages all groups to (a) maintain and develop their group identities, (b) develop other-group acceptance and tolerance, (c) engage in intergroup contact and sharing, and (d) learn each other's language.

The multicultural model generates the hypothesis that an individual can maintain a positive identity as a member of his or her culture of origin while simultaneously developing a positive identity by engaging in complex institutional sharing with the larger political entity comprised of other cultural groups. In this model it is assumed that public and private identities need not become fused and that the tension of solving internal conflicts caused by bicultural stress need not have a negative psychological impact but could instead lead to personal and emotional growth. Kelly's (1971) finding, that with little difficulty the Tohono O'odham (Papago) in Tucson could occupy roles in the urban Tohono O'odham community parallel to their status in the wider Tucson social structure, supports the feasibility of this hypothesis.

Berry and his colleagues (Berry, 1984; Berry, Kim, Power, Young, & Bujaki, 1989; Berry, Poortinga, Segall, & Dasen, 1992), in their consideration of the acculturation literature, have developed a model that focuses on the process of group and individual adaptation within plural societies. They argued that there are four choices that the group or individual can make in such a situation: assimilate, integrate, separate, and marginalize. Berry and his colleagues argued that individuals and groups in plural societies have to manage two issues. One involves the decision to maintain one's culture of origin and the other is to engage in intergroup contact. Like Ogbu and Matute-Bianchi (1986), Berry and his colleagues proposed a strategy—the integration approach—that allows the individual or ethnic group to both engage in the activities of one culture while maintaining identity and relationships in another. Where the integration model differs from the alternation model is the former's emphasis on the relationship between the two cultural groups and its implicit assumption that they are tied together within a single social structure. The alternation model addresses this relationship and includes relationships that do not necessarily evolve within a larger multicultural framework.

It is questionable, however, as to whether such a multicultural society can be maintained. As Fishman (1989) suggested, cultural separation of groups demands institutional protection and ethnocultural compartmentalization. He suggested that there is little evidence for such structures surviving more than three generations of cross-cultural contact. Examples of this separation being maintained include groups making that choice for ideological reasons, such as the Old Amish and the Hasidim, or groups actively discriminated against by the majority group, such as American Indians, African Americans, or Australian aborigines. In lieu of active discrimination or self-selected separation, it may be difficult to maintain a truly multicultural society over time (Mallea, 1988). Instead, it is more likely that the various groups will intermingle, leading to the evolution of a new culture.

Fusion Model

The fusion model of second-culture acquisition represents the assumptions behind the melting pot theory. This model suggests that cultures sharing an economic, political, or geographic space will fuse together until they are indistinguishable to form a new culture. The respectful sharing of institutional structures will produce a new common culture. Each culture brings to the melting pot strengths and weaknesses that take on new forms through the interaction of cultures as equal partners. Gleason (1979) argued that cultural pluralism inevitably produces this type of fusion if the various cultures share a common political unit. The fusion model is different from the assimilation or acculturation model in that there is no necessary assumption of cultural superiority. The psychological impact of this model is unclear because there are few successful examples of such a new culture. It seems that minority groups become assimilated into the majority group at the price of their ethnic identity. This would suggest that an individual who is a member of a minority group undergoing fusion would have experiences similar to one undergoing assimilation. Once fused, however, the individual's psychological reality would be indistinguishable from a member of the majority group.

On the other hand, the psychological impact that contact with members of the minority group has on those of the majority group has been rarely discussed. Jung (cited in Hallowell, 1957) alluded to the American Indian influence on the U.S. majority group when he described the American Indian component in the character of some of his American clients. Hallowell also pointed out the need to explore the psychological effects of frontier contacts with American Indians in studying the historical development of the American national character. Weatherford (1988) chronicled how the cultural, social, and political practices of American Indians have influenced the way life is lived throughout the world. The idea that minority groups may have a positive impact on the majority culture also has been discussed in the popular press. For instance, a recent issue of *Ebony* (Bennett, 1991) focused on the African-American contributions to

American culture in style, politics, entertainment, sports, gender relations, and religion. This view needs to be explored in greater detail by social scientists.

Summary

Each of these models has its own assumptions concerning what happens to a person as he or she undergoes the process of second-culture acquisition. This does not mean, however, that the models are mutually exclusive. Depending on the situation and person, any one of these models may represent an adequate explanation for a person's experience as he or she acquires competency in a new culture. An example would be of an African-American family that has moved from the rural South to an urban area. One member of the family may assimilate into the dominant Anglo-oriented culture, whereas another's attempt to acquire competence in that culture may better be described using the acculturation model. Yet a third member of the same family may choose to actively alternate between the two cultures, and a fourth may seek to live in an environment in which the two cultures exist side by side as described by the multicultural model or have amalgamated as described in the fusion model.

What separates these models are the aspects of the process that they emphasize in their description of second-culture acquisitions. We assume that there are seven process variables related to second-culture acquisition. We believe that some models more readily facilitate the effective functioning of individuals operating in dual cultures. In

TABLE 1

Extent of Attention on Select Process Variables Associated with Models of Second-Culture Acquisition

Model	1	2	3	4	5	6	7
Assimilation	Low	Low	Low	Low	High	High	High
Acculturation	Low	Low	Low	High	Low	Low	Low
Alternation	High	High	High	High	High	High	High
Multicultural	High	High	High	High	Moderate	Low	Low
Fusion	Low	Low	Low	Low	High	High	High

Note. 1 = Contact with culture of origin; 2 = loyalty to culture of origin; 3 = involvement with culture of origin; 4 = acceptance by members of culture of origin; 5 = contact with the second culture; 6 = affiliation with the second culture; 7 = acceptance by members of the second culture.

Table 1, each of the models described earlier is rated on the emphasis it places on the variables of contact, loyalty, and involvement with one's culture of origin and with the second culture. This table demonstrates that most of the models assume that an individual will lose identification with his or her culture of origin, a process that can be stressful and disorienting. What seems clear from the literature we have reviewed, however, is that the more an individual is able to maintain active and effective relationships through alternation between both cultures, the less difficulty he or she will have in acquiring and maintaining competency in both cultures.

BICULTURAL COMPETENCE

The construct of bicultural competence as a result of living in two cultures grows out of the alternation model. Although there are a number of behaviors involved in the acquisition of bicultural competence (e.g., shifts in cognitive and perceptual processes, acquisition of a new language) the literature on biculturalism consistently assumes that an individual living within two cultures will suffer from various forms of psychological distress. Although it is clear that ethnic minorities in the United States and elsewhere experience high levels of economic and social discrimination as well as other disadvantages, it is inappropriate to assume that this sociological reality produces a predictable negative psychological outcome. Research suggests that individuals living in two cultures may find the experience to be more beneficial than living a monocultural life-style. The key to psychological well-being may well be the ability to develop and maintain competence in both cultures.

Like Schlossberg's (1981) model for analyzing human adaptation to transition, we recognize that there are a number of individual characteristics that may be considered significant in the development of bicultural competence. These include personal and cultural identity, age and life stage, gender and gender role identification, and socioeconomic status, among others. Not all of these characteristics have an equal impact on an individual's ability to develop and refine the necessary skills. The relative influence of each has yet to be determined.

Sameroff (1982) suggested that personal identity is organized around an individual's concept of self and his or her estimates of his or her personal impact in a given social role within particular cultural relationships. He referred to the degree to which an individual has developed a well-formed sense of his or her own identity as distinct from his or her social organization. The potential criticism of this position is that it reflects the individualistic ideology of Anglo-American society. Without promoting this ideology, we suggest that the ability to develop bicultural competence is affected by one's ability to operate with a certain degree of individuation.[2] Furthermore, we suggest that bicultural competence requires a substantial degree of personal integration for one to avoid the negative consequences of a bicultural living situation (Burnam et al., 1987). Triandis (1980) suggested that two factors determining one's effective adjustment to the majority culture are self-awareness and the ability to analyze social behavior. This points to the importance of individual personality in the development of bicultural competence.

In relation to bicultural competence, it is important to focus on two facets of identity development. The first involves the evolution of an individual's sense of self-sufficiency and ego strength. This identity is the subject of concern for developmentalists such as Erikson (1950, 1968), Spencer, Brookins, and Allen (1985). Except for radical behaviorists, most psychologists theorize an internal sense of self that is separate from a person's environment. This sense develops, in relationship to the individual's psychosocial experience, to the point where a psychologically healthy individual has a secure sense of who he or she is or is not (De La Torre, 1977). This sense of self interacts with the individual's cultural context in a reciprocally deterministic manner to develop an ethnic identity (Mego, 1988). We hypothesize that the strength or weakness of this identity will affect the development of a person's ability to acquire bicultural competence.

The other facet of identity development involves the development of cultural identity. This refers to the evolution of a sense of self in relation to a culture of origin and who one is within and without that cultural context. This type of identity involves the manner in which an individual interprets and internalizes his or her sociological reality. One's cultural identity and the individual's relative commitment to that identity is the focus of the acculturation studies discussed earlier and of those authors (Atkinson, Morten, & Sue, 1989; Cross, 1971; Helms, 1990; Sue & Sue, 1990) who have developed models of ethnic identity development. With some variation, all of these models emphasize a similar process through which a minority individual proceeds in order to develop a coherent and healthy sense of self within a bicultural context.

These models imply that one's stage of ethnic identity development will affect the manner in which the individual will cope with the psychological impact of biculturalism. The more integrated the individual's identity, the better he or she will be able to exhibit healthy coping patterns (Gonzalez, 1986; Murphy, 1977; Rosenthal, 1987). These stage models seem to indicate that the highest level of development includes the ability to be biculturally competent (Gutierrez, 1981). Furthermore, these models generate the hypothesis that a minority individual who is monocultural, either in the minority or majority groups, will experience the negative psychological effects of bicultural contact. However, as that person develops a stronger personal identity, he or she can become biculturally competent, thereby reducing the negative psychological impact of biculturalism (Zuniga, 1988).

Oetting and Beauvais (1990–1991) have recently identified an orthogonal model of cultural identification that includes these four categories: (a) high bicultural identification, (b) high identification with one culture and medium identification with another, (c) low identification with either culture, and (d) monocultural identification. They advocated the independent assessment of identification with multiple cultures (e.g., culture of origin and American Indian, Mexican American, Asian American, African American or Anglo-American). A series of studies with American Indian youth (Beauvais, 1992; Oetting, Edwards, & Beauvais, 1989) indicated that most children and adolescents on reservations showed medium identification with both Anglo and Indian cultures. Their research with Mexican-American youth living in Southwestern towns and cities containing substantial Hispanic populations, however, showed a different pattern of high Hispanic identification and moderate Anglo identification. This line of research in minority adolescent drug use supports the contention that identification with *any* culture may serve as an individual's source of personal and social strength and that such an identification will correlate with one's general well-being and positive personal adjustment. Oetting and Beauvais concluded that it is not mixed but weak cultural identification that creates problems.

This component of bicultural competence suggests the need to maintain a distinction between social variables, such as class and ethnicity, and psychological variables, such as identity development and affective processes. It is important to remember that individuals, not groups, become biculturally competent. This suggests that each person will proceed in the process of cultural acquisition at his or her own rate. Researchers can, and should, make group predictions concerning the process, but they must be cautious when applying these findings to individuals (Murphy, 1977; Zuniga, 1988). As such, to understand the psychological impact of becoming or being competent in two cultures, researchers must look at both individual psychological development and the context in which that development occurs (Baker, 1987; LaFromboise, Berman, & Sohi, 1993).

From our reading of the literature, we suggest the following dimensions in which an individual may need to develop competence so as to effectively manage the process of living in two cultures: (a) knowledge of cultural beliefs and values, (b) positive attitudes toward both majority and minority groups, (c) bicultural efficacy, (d) communication ability, (e) role repertoire, and (f) a sense of being grounded.

Knowledge of Cultural Beliefs and Values

Cultural awareness and knowledge involves the degree to which an individual is aware of and knowledgeable about the history, institutions, rituals, and everyday practices of a given culture. This would include an understanding of the basic perspectives a culture has on gender roles, religious practices, and political issues, as well as the rules that govern daily interactions among members of the culture.

A culturally competent person is presumed to be one who knows, appreciates, and internalizes the basic beliefs of a given culture. This would require an acceptance of a particular culture's basic worldview and the ability to act within the constraints of that worldview when interacting with members of that culture. For example, a study of elementary-age Sioux children living on reservations and in a neighboring boarding school (Plas & Bellet, 1983) showed that the older the children were, the more they differed culturally from younger respondents.[3] More pointedly, on the Native American Value-Attitude Scale (NAVAS; Trimble, 1981), younger children tended to provide the expected Indian response, whereas the older children both maintained a preference for the Indian values of community importance and deference to an indirect style of relating yet adopted a more Anglicized attitude toward school achievement and interpersonal involvement. This finding suggests that differences in worldview and value conflicts may be primary sources of stress for bicultural individuals. If the values and beliefs of the two cultures are in conflict, the individual may internalize that conflict in an attempt to find an integrated resolution, but the difficulty in finding this resolution may well be what motivates the individual to fuse the two cultures as a stress-reducing solution. Future research on bicultural competence must continue to examine these phenomena as being central to identifying an individual's psychological well-being.

Schiller's (1987) study lends support to considering cultural awareness and knowledge as an important component of cultural competence. In a survey study investigating the impact of biculturalism, she examined the academic, social, psychological, and cultural adjustment of American Indian college students. Schiller found that bicultural Indian students were better adjusted, particularly in the academic and cultural domains, than were their nonbicultural counterparts. They had higher grade point averages (GPAs), more effective study habits, and demonstrated a stronger commitment to using resources for academic success. Participation in cultural activities and enrollment in American-Indian-oriented courses was significantly higher for bicultural students. Finally, these students perceived their Indian heritage to be an advantage, more so than did nonbicultural students. A number of recent studies on the relationship between acculturation and the counseling process (Atkinson & Gim, 1989; Curtis, 1990; Gim, Atkinson, & Whiteley, 1990; Hess & Street, 1991; Hurdle, 1991; Ponce & Atkinson, 1989) support the hypothesis that knowledge of the second culture's values and practices facilitates an ethnic minority's willingness to use available psychological services.

Positive Attitudes toward Both Groups

This aspect of the construct assumes that the individual recognizes bicultural competence as a desirable goal in its own right, holds each cultural group in positive but not necessarily equal regard, and does not endorse positions that promulgate hierarchical relations between two cultural groups.

The inclusion of this component is based on certain theoretical assumptions. Without positive attitudes toward both groups, an individual will be limited in his or her ability to feel good about inter-acting with a group that is the target of negative feelings. Arguably, the process of interacting with individuals from a culture one does not respect will result in negative psychological and behavioral out-comes. We hypothesize that one reason for the tremendous rate of conduct disorders among ethnic minority adolescents is a result of the negative attitudes those adolescents have toward the dominant Anglo group. This hypothesis is supported by Palleja's (1987) find-ing that monocultural-affiliated Hispanic young men exhibited more rebellious behavior than did bicultural or Anglo-affiliated monocul-tural peers and Golden's (1987) finding that Korean-American high school students practicing biculturalism displayed more positive edu-cational outcomes and self-concepts than monoculturally affiliated Korean-American students. Mullender and Miller (1985) initiated a group for Afro-Caribbean children living in White families who were experiencing discomfort or limited support to help them deal with negative feelings associated with racism from the dominant group. Both the White caregivers and the Afro-Caribbean youth benefited from increased knowledge of Caribbean culture and recognition of the importance of the youth having more involvement with the Black community.

One study of Navajo children from five elementary schools in northeastern Arizona by Beuke (1978) did reveal that students in the high Indian-high Anglo cultural identification category had sig-nificantly higher self-esteem scores than did those in the low Indian-low Anglo category, regardless of which school they attended. This study on cultural identification initially supports the hypothesis that positive attitudes toward both groups may be an important compo-nent in reducing the stress of bicultural contact.

Contact itself is an essential element in one's ability to develop a positive attitude toward both groups. For example, some American Indians come from tribes that maintained considerable autonomy from the encroaching majority culture but then experienced contact at a later point. Individuals from these tribes were less often faced with the contradictions that can result from ongoing contact between different cultures. Of course, there is considerable variation between and within tribal groups regarding the amount and nature of contact with the U.S. majority and other surrounding cultures. Even today, an individual's proximity to a reservation or city influences the bicul-tural experiences that person has (Little Soldier, 1985). As Berry,

Padilla, and Szapocznik and their colleagues have suggested, the length and type of contact individuals from one culture have with the other cultures have a significant impact on their attitudes toward the majority and their own culture.

Information is also an essential element in developing a positive attitude toward both groups. Cultural translators, individuals from a person's own ethnic or cultural group who have successfully undergone the dual socialization experience, can help others in the personal integration process (Brown, 1990). He or she can interpret the values and perceptions of the majority culture in ways that do not compromise the individual's own ethnic values or norms.

Bicultural Efficacy

Rashid (1984) asserted that "biculturalism is an attribute that all Americans should possess because it creates a sense of efficacy within the institutional structure of society along with a sense of pride and identification with one's ethnic roots" (p. 15). As Bandura (1978) has demonstrated, the belief, or confidence, that an individual can perform an action has a hierarchical relationship to the actual performance of that action. In this article, we posit that bicultural efficacy, or the belief that one can develop and maintain effective interpersonal relationships in two cultures, is directly related to one's ability to develop bicultural competence.

We define *bicultural efficacy* as the belief, or confidence, that one can live effectively, and in a satisfying manner, within two groups without compromising one's sense of cultural identity. This belief will support an individual through the highly difficult tasks of developing and maintaining effective support groups in both the minority and the majority culture. It will also enable the person to persist through periods when he or she may experience rejection from one or both of the cultures in which he or she is working to develop or maintain competence (Rozek, 1980).

A study by Kazaleh (1986) showed that the Ramallah-American youth who were afforded more outlets for social expression, whether in the ethnic community or outside of it, presented the image of being more confident in their abilities and tolerant of the ethnic lifestyle than did those who were overprotected by their families and restricted in their activities with peer groups. In a study of French

Canadian adolescent boys learning English, Clement, Gardner, and Smythe (1977) found two factors that were associated with the motivation to learn English. One involved a positive attitude toward the Anglophone community and the other involved the awareness that learning English had an instrumental function in terms of academic achievement and future job performance. These factors, however, were not as predictive of actual competence in English as a student's confidence in his ability to learn the second language. In a study of Asian-American assertion, Zane, Sue, Hu, and Kwon (1991) found that self-efficacy predicted the ability of Asian Americans to be as assertive, in a situationally appropriate manner, as their Anglo-American peers. These findings support the thesis that efficacy is an important factor in the development of bicultural skills.

We hypothesize that an individual's level of bicultural efficacy will determine his or her ability to (a) develop an effective role repertoire in a second culture, (b) perform effectively within his or her role, (c) acquire adequate communication skills, (d) maintain roles and affiliations within his or her culture of origin, and (e) cope with acculturation stress. Furthermore, encouraging the development of an individual's bicultural efficacy is a vital goal of any program (e.g., therapy or skills training) that is designed to enhance his or her performance in a bicultural or multicultural environment. We believe that this statement is as true for ethnic minority people developing competence in a majority culture institution as it is for the majority person developing competence in a bicultural or multicultural environment.

Communication Ability

Communication ability refers to an individual's effectiveness in communicating ideas and feelings to members of a given culture, both verbally and nonverbally.[4] Language competency, in fact, may be a major building block of bicultural competence. As Northover (1988) suggested, "each of a bilingual's languages is the mediator between differing cultural identities within one and the same person" (p. 207). It is vital, however, to distinguish between the language-acquisition processes, which have the goal of transferring competency from the minority group's language to the majority group's language, and processes oriented toward an individual maintaining the language of origin as well as the acquisition of a second language. Bilingual programs that encourage the maintenance, rather than the transfer, of language skills promote bicultural competence rather than assimilation or acculturation (Edwards, 1981; Fishman, 1989; Thomas, 1983).

Fisher's (1974) study is a good example of the potentially positive impact of a maintenance-oriented program. He examined the effects of a bilingual-bicultural program on the self-concepts, self-descriptions, and stimulus-seeking activities of first graders. He found a highly positive effect for the Mexican-American girls on all three measures, no effect on the Mexican-American boys, no effect on the Anglo girls, and a negative effect on the Anglo boys. The drop in self-concept scores among Anglo boys during the school year was attributed to anxiety from having to learn new cultural competencies in addition to their school work. Fisher did not attempt to explain the sex difference among Anglo students in the change of their self-concept scores. The results of this study suggest that communication competency may have a direct effect on self-concept and other nonintellectual attributes. In a comparative study of Hispanic public community college students in a bilingual program and those who received only English as a second language, Tormes (1985) found that those in the bilingual program consistently performed better on most of the criterion measures (e.g., number of credits attempted and earned, GPAs, and progress toward a degree). Therefore, if a program is designed to maintain one's cultural competence, as well as one's language, it will most likely have a positive impact. If the program does not serve in this capacity, it may have a negative effect, as it did for the Anglo boys in the Fisher study and most minority children in mainstream schools or transfer language programs.

Young and Gardner (1990) found that ethnic identification and second-language proficiency were closely related. Their study of ethnic identification, perceptions of language competence, and attitudes toward mainstream and minority cultures among Chinese Canadians highlights the role of attitude in the development of communication competence. They found that the greater a participant's fear of losing his or her cultural identification, the weaker was his or her language proficiency. Participants who had that fear also had more negative attitudes toward language study. These attitudes were bidirectional, meaning that those Chinese who were identified with Canadian culture thought their Chinese language skills were weak and that their desire to improve these skills was also weak. Those who were proficient in Chinese and fearful of assimilation in Canadian culture were not eager to improve their English-language skills. Participants who had a positive attitude toward both cultures or identified with both cultures were proficient in both languages or were eager to improve their skills in the second language. These studies suggest that both attitude and ethnic identification have an impact on the development of communication competence.

McKirnan and Hamayan (1984), in a study of the ways speech norms are used to identify in-group and out-group membership, confirmed the importance of communication ability as a factor in bicultural competence. They found that Anglo in-group members in a Spanish bilingual program ascribed negative characteristics to Hispanic students on the basis of variations in their style of speech. Although the amount of intergroup contact also contributed to the in-group members' attitudes, the Anglo in-group often used the speech pattern as a trigger for making judgments about the Hispanic speaker. This suggests that communication skills are a cue for the majority group in accepting a member of the minority group. Dornic (1985) pointed out that the stress of using the second language inhibits the performance, in a wide variety of roles, of individuals who are recent immigrants to a new culture. The work of McKirnan and Hamayan and of Dornic, although reinforcing the notion that communication ability is an essential building block of bicultural competence, underscores the important function of various contact situations during formative years on acquiring that ability.

In a study of bicultural communication, Simard and Taylor (1973) found that cross-cultural dyads were able to communicate as effectively as were homogeneous dyads. If there was a difference in the effectiveness of communication, it was determined by the nature of the task rather than the cultural composition of the dyad. Those authors used their findings to suggest that cross-cultural communication is a function of both motivation and capability.

LaFromboise and Rowe (1983) evaluated an assertion training program for bicultural competence with urban Indians in Lincoln, Nebraska. The key instructional focus of this program was on the situation-specific nature of assertiveness and language style differences in the assessment of Indian and non-Indian target people prior to delivery of assertive messages. Feedback during training involved the appropriateness of American Indians being assertive with one another and ways for Indians to be succinct and more forceful when being assertive with Anglo-Americans. Behavioral measures of assertiveness, rated by both Indian and Anglo peer observers, revealed a positive training effect. The actual language form (e.g., conventional English, Indian-style English, and bilingual English and Omaha) was not evaluated here; instead, the perceptions of communicative competence derived from message content and sociolinguistic cues were examined. The results of this study reinforce the importance of defining communication competency within the context of specific situations. As such, bicultural communication competency involves one's ability to communicate in a situationally appropriate and effective manner as one interacts in each culture.

In a 1985 study of acculturative stress among 397 high school students in an urban and multiethnic school, Schwarzer, Bowler, and Rauch found that the more acculturated students who spoke English at home had higher levels of self-esteem and less experience with racial tension and interethnic conflict. Other variables (i.e., length of stay in the United States and ethnic group membership) were related to the findings, but the families' facility with the majority group's language appeared to be the primary factor that ameliorated the stress of living in a bicultural environment (see also Bettes, Dusenbury, Kerner, James-Ortiz, & Botvin, 1990).

When Robinson (1985) analyzed census data to determine background characteristics associated with language retention among Canadian Indians, she found that educational advancement reduced the probability of native-language retention but increased the probability of participation in the labor force. This suggests that attempts to improve the economic conditions of Indians by increasing their education may have a detrimental effect on the maintenance of their native-language skills. However, economic and linguistic acculturation, as described by Robinson, does not necessarily imply complete acculturation of Canadian Indian people. It does suggest that gaining majority group language competency may increase majority culture competency, but it does not suggest that majority group language competency ameliorates acculturative stress. In other words, as important as communication competency is in developing cultural competency, it is not the only skill that relieves the stress of becoming biculturally competent.

Role Repertoire

Role repertoire refers to the range of culturally or situationally appropriate behaviors or roles an individual has developed. The greater the range of behaviors or roles, the higher the level of cultural competence.

In a study of individuals who were working and living in Kenya for 2 years, Ruben and Kealey (1979) found that particular interpersonal and social behaviors led to greater effectiveness at role performance and ease in adjustment. The authors looked at (a) displays of respect, (b) interaction posture (e.g., judgmental or not), (c) orientation to knowledge or worldview, (d) empathy, and (e) role behavior. Coinciding with Smither's (1982) assertions, they found that individuals who had the personal resources to use their social skills in a situationally appropriate manner suffered less cultural shock and were more effective in their vocational duties and social interactions than were those whose behavioral repertoire within the second culture was more limited.

In McFee's (1968) study of acculturation among the Blackfeet tribe, he found that individuals knowledgeable about both Blackfeet and Anglo-American cultures and able to interact easily with members of each by applying this knowledge in a situationally appropriate manner had an important role in both cultures. McFee suggested that such individuals perform an important and valued role for both communities as cultural translators, or mediators, as long as they are not perceived by the minority group as being overidentified with the majority group.

In a study of the complexity of parental reasoning about child development in mothers who varied in ethnic background and biculturalism, Gutierrez and Sameroff (1990) found that the bicultural Mexican-American mothers were better skilled at developing an objective understanding of their child's behavior than were monocultural Mexican-American or Anglo-American mothers. Their ability to interpret child development as the result of the dynamic interplay between the child's temperament and his or her environment over time and to see that developmental outcomes could have multiple determinants enhanced their parenting role. Those researchers did not, however, examine how bicultural competence originates or elaborate on the psychological results of this form of biculturalism. Determining the psychological impact of this balancing act is an important area of concern for future research. The processes by which these bicultural skills are developed needs to be delineated, and a close look needs to be taken at the individual psychology of those who have developed these skills.

Cuellar, Harris, and Naron (1981), in a study of Mexican-American psychiatric patients, found that the patient's level of acculturation was highly correlated with diagnosis and treatment outcome. The more acculturated individuals received less severe diagnostic labels than less acculturated individuals. In that study, they were looking at the impact of providing bilingual staff and culturally appropriate decor on treatment outcome. They found that the less acculturated patients in the experimental groups were positively affected by the treatment. The treatment had little effect on more highly acculturated patients. The results of this study support the hypothesis that the minority individual who does not have a sufficient role repertoire in either the majority or minority culture receives differential treatment. It also suggests that treatment keyed to the individual's level of cultural identification is more effective than interventions using a monocultural approach.

Further support for the importance of role repertoire comes from Szapocznik, Kurtines, et al. (1980) and Szapocznik et al. (1984), who determined that the development of bicultural social skills facilitated the adjustment of Hispanic youth. The intervention used with Hispanic families in conflict — bicultural effectiveness training — consisted of the analysis of Hispanic and Anglo cultural conflicts and the presentation of information concerning biculturalism. They found that those who could develop a bicultural repertoire were less likely to experience family or school conflict or become involved in illegal drug use. This line of work reinforces the importance of focusing on bicultural social skills when delivering services to members of the minority group experiencing problems within the majority culture (see also Comer, 1980, 1985; LaFromboise, 1983).

In a study of the psychocultural characteristics of college-bound and non-college-bound Chicanas, Buriel and Saenz (1980) found that the family income and ability to perform masculine behaviors, as measured by the Bem Sex Role Inventory, were the major distinctions between the two groups. The results of this study suggest that knowing the behaviors that have traditionally led to economic success within the American culture, and the ability to be assertive in the majority culture, are aspects of the role repertoire that determine college attendance among Chicanas. Buriel and Saenz also found that family income and sex role identification were positively correlated with biculturalism, defined in their study as "an integration of the competencies and sensitivities associated with two cultures within a single individual" (p. 246). They did not find a causal relation between biculturalism and college attendance; however, they concluded that biculturalism may be an associated factor, particularly as it relates to behavior that leads to college attendance.

When developing programs to facilitate the introduction of ethnic minorities into institutions that are dominated by the majority culture (e.g., universities or corporations), it is vitally important to take the minority individual's dual focus into account (Akao, 1983). Failure to facilitate the maintenance of the minority person's role within his or her culture of origin will lead to either poor retention within the program or aggravate his or her acculturative stress (Fernandez-Barrillas & Morrison, 1984; Lang, Muñoz, Bernal, & Sorensen, 1982; Mendoza, 1981; Van Den Bergh, 1991; Vasquez & McKinley, 1982).

Groundedness

"Every culture provides the individual some sense of identity, some regulation or belonging and some sense of personal place in the school of things" (Adler, 1975, p. 20). The literature indicates that the person most successful at managing a bicultural existence has established some form of stable social networks in both cultures. This suggests that the positive resolution of stress engendered by bicultural living cannot be done on one's own (Hernandez, 1981). One must have the skill to recruit and use external support systems. We have labeled the experience of having a well-developed social support system "a sense of being grounded."

Baker (1987) supported this position when she argued that African Americans are best able to avoid the major problems that affect mental health facing their communities (e.g., Black-on-Black homicide, teenage pregnancy, attempted suicide, substance abuse, postincarceration adjustment) when they can call on the resources of the African-American extended family. Both nuclear and extended family models in American Indian communities facilitate this sense of being grounded (Red Horse, 1980). We argue that it is the sense of being grounded in an extensive social network in both cultures that enhances an individual's ability to cope with the pressures of living in a bicultural environment and that acquiring that sense in the second culture is an important outcome of second-culture acquisition (Lewis & Ford, 1991). Murphy (1977) suggested that the ability to become grounded inoculates against the development of psychopathology among immigrants.

Beiser's (1987) study of depression in Southeast Asian refugees underscores the importance of being grounded within one's culture as a coping mechanism for dealing with the psychological impact of entering a new culture. He found that immigrants who either came with other family members, or entered cities with a sizable population of individuals from their home culture, were less depressed after a year's time than were those who came alone or were not involved with people from the home culture. Fraser and Pecora (1985–1986) echoed this finding, discovering that refugees who coped best with the natural reactions to dislocation were those who had "weak ties" in a community. These weak ties are extended family acquaintances, such as an uncle's best friend, who can play an important role in the fabric of daily living by providing support such as childcare or employment information. These networks serve to increase an individual's sense of being grounded in time and space.

Porte and Torney-Purta (1987) demonstrated the positive impact that maintaining a bicultural environment had on the academic achievement and level of depression among Indochinese refugee children entering the United States as unaccompanied minors. They found that children placed in foster care with Indochinese families performed better in school and were less depressed than children placed in foster care situations with non-Indochinese families. The results of this study highlight the importance of providing a culturally relevant environment for individuals learning a second culture.

In a study of the impact of the Chinese church on the identity and mental health of Chinese immigrants, Palinkas (1982) reinforced the perspective that a solid social network, one that simultaneously grounds an individual in parts of his or her home culture while facilitating the acquisition of a new culture, sharply reduces the negative impact of acculturation. Topper and Johnson's (1980) study of the effects of relocation on members of the Navajo tribe provides a graphic example of the psychological impact of losing one's groundedness. They found that relocated individuals were eight times more likely to seek mental health services than were Navajos who had not been forced to relocate. They also reported that 70% of the relocatees were found to be suffering from depression or related disorders.

Rodriguez (1975), in a study of the subjective factors affecting assimilation among Puerto Ricans in New York City, found that Puerto Ricans living in the ghetto had more positive attitudes about succeeding in the mainstream economic system than did Puerto Ricans living in Anglo-dominated suburbs. Those living in the ghetto also claimed to experience less discrimination. As Rodriguez (1975) suggested, "the ghetto . . . provides a psychologically more supportive environment than does the middle class area" (p. 77). These findings highlight the role that being grounded plays for the individual living in two cultures. We believe that groundedness joins behavioral effectiveness and personal well-being as key characteristics of mental health.

Summary

Research suggests that there is a way of being bicultural without suffering negative psychological outcomes, assimilating, or retreating from contact with the majority culture. We recognize that bicultural competence requires a difficult set of skills to achieve and maintain. We do not doubt that there will be stress involved in the process of acquiring competence in a second culture while maintaining affiliation with one's culture of origin. The question we have for future research is whether these difficulties lead to personal growth and greater psychological well-being, or inevitably lead to the type of psychological problems posited by Stonequist (1935) and Park (1928).

MODEL OF BICULTURAL COMPETENCE

The goal of this essay was to develop an understanding, on the basis of social science research, of the psychological impact of biculturalism. We wanted to understand which factors facilitate a bicultural role and which ones impede the development of that role. We were particularly interested in identifying the skills that would make it possible for an individual to become a socially competent person in a second culture without losing that same competence in the culture of origin. To focus our exploration, we organized our search around a behavioral model of culture that would allow us to better identify the skills of bicultural competence. We also felt that it was important to describe the different models of second-culture acquisition so that our use of the alternation model could be understood in relation to other theories of biculturalism.

Our exploration of the psychological impact of biculturalism was seriously constrained by the fact that research in this area is spread across several disciplines and represents a wide range of methodologies. This fact made it difficult to derive a composite statement about the results of different studies that appeared to be examining similar aspects of biculturalism. The lack of controlled or longitudinal research compounded this difficulty. As a result, our discussion of biculturalism is speculative in nature. We have, however, been able to identify skills that we hypothesize are central to being a socially competent person in two cultures.

At this point, we want to emphasize that we do not know whether these are the only skills of biculturalism, or whether a person needs to be equally competent in all or a particular subset, in order to be biculturally competent. We do think, however, that the dimensions outlined in this essay provide a much needed focus to the research on this phenomenon. We believe that identifying these acquirable skills will allow researchers to focus on the relationship between these skills and an individual's sense of psychological well-being, as well as his or her effectiveness in his or her social and work environments. We also believe that these dimensions can be used as the framework for developing programs designed to facilitate the involvement of minority people in majority institutions such as colleges and corporations (Van Den Bergh, 1991).

Initially, each of the skills needs to be subjected to empirical examination. Reliable methods of assessment need to be developed, and construct validity needs to be established (Sundberg, Snowden, & Reynolds, 1978). Subsequently, the relationship between possessing each skill and school and work performance will have to be identified. Finally, the question as to which skills, or set of skills, are necessary in order to be functionally biculturally competent will have to be answered. In other words, these dimensions appear to describe the skills of a biculturally competent individual. Further research using this framework needs to be conducted to determine the degree to which they are normative or optimal for a person involved in two cultures.

To facilitate that process, we have developed a hypothetical model of the relationships among these skills of bicultural competence. After lengthy consideration, we have come to speculate that these skills may have a rational relationship to each other. We believe that some may be more important than others or that some may have to be developed before others. Furthermore, we developed the assumption that one or more of these skills may be the linchpin between monocultural and bicultural competence. In response to these speculations, in the model we have developed it is assumed that there are hierarchical relations among these skills, not linear ones. By this we mean that some of these skills may be developed before others but that the process of skill acquisition does not have an invariant order. Only empirical study can resolve this issue.

The primary emphasis of the model is on the reciprocal relationship between a person and his or her environment. The model becomes complex when considering the acquisition of second-culture competence because one must include two environments, both the culture of origin and the second culture. An individual's personal and cultural identities are primarily developed through the early biosocial learning experiences that an individual has within his or her culture of origin. These identities will also be influenced by the nature and amount of contact the person has with the second culture. For example, if a person lived in rural El Salvador and had no contact with American culture until forced to emigrate in early adulthood, that person's sense of personal and cultural identity would be much different from his or her U.S.-born child, who has attended public schools since kindergarten. It is our contention that in addition to having a strong and stable sense of personal identity, another affective element of bicultural competence is the ability to develop and maintain positive attitudes toward one's culture of origin and the second culture in which he or she is attempting to acquire competence. In addition, we speculate that an individual will also need to acquire knowledge of both cultures in order to develop the belief that he or she can be biculturally competent, which we have labeled *bicultural efficacy.*

We speculate that these attitudes and beliefs about self, what we think of as the affective and cognitive dimension of the model, will facilitate the individual's acquisition of both communication skills and role repertoire, which are the two facets that make up the behavioral aspect of the model. We hypothesize that the individual who has acquired the attitudes and beliefs in the affective and cognitive

TABLE 2
Degree to Which Models of Second-Culture Acquisition Facilitate
Acquisition of the Skills Related to Bicultural Competence

Model	1	2	3	4	5	6
Assimilation	Low	Low	Low	Low	Low	Low
Acculturation	Low	Low	Moderate	Moderate	Low	Low
Alternation	High	High	High	High	High	High
Multicultural	Moderate	Moderate	Moderate	Moderate	Moderate	Moderate
Fusion	Moderate	Moderate	Moderate	Low	Low	Moderate

Note. 1 = Knowledge of cultural beliefs and values; 2 = positive attitude toward both groups; 3 = bicultural efficacy; 4 = communication competency; 5 = role repertoire; 6 = groundedness.

dimension and the skills of the behavioral aspect of this model will also be able to develop the effective support systems in both cultures that will allow him or her to feel grounded. Being grounded in both cultures will allow the individual to both maintain and enhance his or her personal and cultural identities in a manner that will enable him or her to effectively manage the challenges of a bicultural existence.

This model represents a departure from previous models in that it focuses on the skills that a person needs to acquire in order to be successful at both becoming effective in the new culture and remaining competent in his or her culture of origin. This difference is represented in Table 2, which rates the five models of second-culture acquisition discussed earlier, on the degree to which the assumptions of each model facilitate the acquisition of these skills.

Table 2 shows that the alternation model, on which our model of bicultural competence is based, is the one that best facilitates the acquisition of these skills. It appears that the multicultural model would also be useful in this area, but as mentioned before, there is little evidence of a multicultural perspective being maintained over more than three generations.

CONCLUSION

We suggest that the ethnic minority people who develop these skills will have better physical and psychological health than those who do not. We also think that they will outperform their monoculturally competent peers in vocational and academic endeavors.

There is widespread agreement that failure to achieve equal partnership for minorities in the academic, social, and economic life of the United States will have disastrous effects for this society. A vital step in the development of an effective partnership involves moving away from the assumptions of the linear model of cultural acquisition, which has a negative impact on the minority individual, to a clearer understanding of the process of developing cultural competence as a two-way street. This will require that members of both the minority and majority cultures better understand, appreciate, and become skilled in one another's cultures. We hope that the ideas expressed here will serve to facilitate that process.

NOTES

This essay was prepared at the request of the National Center for American Indian and Alaska Native Mental Health Research and was partially supported by the National Institute of Mental Health Grant 1R01MH42473. We are indebted to the following colleagues: Clifford Barnett, Raphael Diaz, Martin Ford, Amado Padilla, and Wayne Rowe for their constructive feedback on earlier versions of this essay.
1. We realize that many individuals will disagree with our use of the term *acculturation*. Many have used the term to refer to the multidimensional phenomena that an individual experiences when he or she lives within or between two or more cultures. This term, when used to describe that phenomena, is not meant to imply a directional relationship. We believe, however, that the term *acculturation* is often used in a manner that does imply a directional relationship. In this work we have labeled the general phenomena of developing competence in another culture *second-culture acquisition* and use the term *acculturation* to identify a particular model of second-culture acquisition.
2. See Sampson (1988) for a discussion of the different forms of individualism. We suggest that an ensembled individual, or one who has strong sense of oneself in relation to others, would be able to become biculturally competent. We are arguing that it is the individual who is enmeshed in his or her social context who will have a difficult time developing his or her bicultural competence.
3. Specific Sioux tribal affiliations and names of reservations were not reported in this study.
4. We are not necessarily referring to an individual's ability to communicate in written form. It is certainly possible to be fluent in a language and not be literate.

REFERENCES

Ablon, G. (1964). Relocated American Indians in the San Francisco Bay Area: Social interaction and Indian identity. *Human Organization, 23,* 296–304.

Adler, P. S. (1975). The transitional experience: An alternative view of cultural shock. *Journal of Humanistic Psychology, 15,* 13–23.

Akao, S. F. (1983). Biculturalism and barriers to learning among Michigan Indian adult students. *Dissertation Abstracts International, 44,* 3572A. (University Microfilms No. DA8407162)

Atkinson, D. R., & Gim, R. H. (1989). Asian-American cultural identity and attitudes toward mental health services. *Journal of Counseling Psychology, 36,* 209–212.

Atkinson, D. R., Morten, G., & Sue, D. W. (1989). Proposed minority identity development model. In D. R. Atkinson, G. Morten, & D. W. Sue (Eds.), *Counseling American minorities: A cross-cultural perspective* (pp. 35–52). Dubuque, IA: William C. Brown.

Baker, F. M. (1987). The Afro-American life cycle: Success, failure, and mental health. *Journal of the National Medical Association, 79,* 625–633.

Bandura, A. (1978). The self system in reciprocal determinism. *American Psychologist, 33,* 344–358.

Bandura, A. (1986). *The foundations of social thought and action.* Englewood Cliffs, NJ: Erlbaum.

Barger, W. K. (1977). Culture change and psychological adjustment. *American Ethnologist, 4,* 471–495.

Beauvais, F. (1992). Characteristics of Indian youth and drug use. *American Indian and Alaskan Native Mental Health Research: The Journal of the National Center, 5*(1), 51–67.

Beiser, M. (1987). Influences of time, ethnicity, and attachment on depression in Southeast Asian refugees. *American Journal of Psychiatry, 145,* 46–51.

Bennett, L. (Ed.). (1991). How Black creativity is changing America [Special issue]. *Ebony, 66*(10).

Berry, J. W. (1984). Cultural relations in plural societies: Alternatives to segregation and their sociopsychological implications. In N. Miller & M. Brewer (Eds.), *Groups in contact* (pp. 11–27). San Diego, CA: Academic Press.

Berry, J. W. (1986). Multiculturalism and psychology in plural societies. In L. H. Ekstrand (Ed.), *Ethnic minorities and immigrants in a cross-cultural perspective* (pp. 37–51). Lisse, The Netherlands: Swets & Zeitlinger.

Berry, J. W., & Annis, R. C. (1974). Acculturation stress: The role of ecology, culture and differentiation. *Journal of Cross-Cultural Psychology, 5,* 382–406.

Berry, J. W., Kim, U., Power, S., Young, M., & Bujaki, M. (1989). Acculturation attitudes in plural societies. *Applied Psychology: An International Review, 38,* 185–206.

Berry, J. W., Poortinga, Y. P., Segall, M. H., & Dasen, P. R. (1992). *Cross-cultural psychology: Research and applications.* New York: Cambridge University Press.

Bettes, B. A., Dusenbury, L., Kerner, J., James-Ortiz, S., & Botvin, G. J. (1990). Ethnicity and psychosocial factors in alcohol and tobacco use in adolescence. *Child Development, 61,* 557–565.

Beuke, V. L. (1978). The relationship of cultural identification to personal adjustment of American Indian children in segregated and integrated schools. *Dissertation Abstracts International, 38,* 7203A. (University Microfilms No. 7809310)

Boyce, W., & Boyce, T. (1983). Acculturation and changes in health among Navajo boarding school students. *Social Science and Medicine, 17,* 219–226.

Brown, P. M. (1990). Biracial identity and social marginality. *Child and Adolescent Social Work Journal, 7,* 319–337.

Buriel, R., & Saenz, E. (1980). Psychocultural characteristics of college-bound and noncollege-bound Chicanas. *Journal of Social Psychology, 110,* 245–251.

Burnam, M. A., Telles, C. A., Karno, M., Hough, R. L., & Escobar, J. I. (1987). Measurement of acculturation in a community population of Mexican Americans. *Hispanic Journal of Behavioral Sciences, 9,* 105–130.

Cantrall, B., & Pete, L. (1990, April). *Navajo culture: A bridge to the rest of the world.* Paper presented at the annual meeting of the American Educational Research Association, Boston.

Chadwick, B. A., & Strauss, J. H. (1975). The assimilation of American Indians into urban society: The Seattle case. *Human Organization, 34,* 359–369.

Chance, N. A. (1965). Acculturation, self-identification, and personality adjustment. *American Anthropologist, 67,* 372–393.

Clement, R., Gardner, R. C., & Smythe, P. C. (1977). Motivational variables in second language acquisition: A study of francophones learning English. *Canadian Journal of Behavioral Science, 9,* 123–133.

Comer, J. P. (1980). *School power.* New York: Free Press.

Comer, J. P. (1985). Social policy and mental health of Black children. *Journal of the American Academy of Child Psychiatry, 24,* 175–181.

Cross, W. E. (1971). The Negro-to-Black conversion experience: Toward a psychology of Black liberation. *Black World, 20,* 13–27.

Cuellar, I., Harris, L. C., & Naron, N. (1981). Evaluation of a bilingual treatment program for Mexican American psychiatric inpatients. In A. Barron (Ed.), *Explorations in Chicano psychology* (pp. 165–186). New York: Praeger.

Curtis, P. A. (1990). The consequences of acculturation to service delivery and research with Hispanic families. *Child and Adolescent Social Work, 7,* 147–159.

De La Torre, M. (1977). Towards a definition of Chicano mental disorder: An exploration of the acculturation and ethnic identity process of Chicano psychiatric outpatients. *Dissertation Abstracts International, 39,* 4025B. (University Microfilms No. 7901909)

Dornic, S. M. (1985). Immigrants, language and stress. In L. H. Ekstrand (Ed.), *Ethnic minorities and immigrants in a cross-cultural perspective* (pp. 149–157). Lisse, The Netherlands: Swets & Zeitlinger.

DuBois, W. E. B. (1961). *The soul of black folks: Essays and sketches.* New York: Fawcett.

Edwards, J. R. (1981). The context of bilingual education. *Journal of Multilingual and Multicultural Development, 2,* 25–44.

Ekstrand, L. H. (1978). Bilingual and bicultural adaptation. In *Educational and psychological interactions* (pp. 1–72). Malmo, Sweden: School of Education.

Erikson, E. (1950). *Childhood and society.* New York: Norton.

Erikson, E. (1968). *Identity, youth, and crisis.* New York: Norton.

Fernandez-Barillas, H. J., & Morrison, T. L. (1984). Cultural affiliation and adjustment among male Mexican-American college students. *Psychological Reports, 55,* 855–860.

Fisher, R. I. (1974). A study of non-intellectual attributes of Chicanos in a first grade bilingual-bicultural program. *Journal of Educational Research, 67,* 323–328.

Fishman, J. A. (1989). Bilingualism and biculturalism as individual and societal phenomena. *Journal of Multilingual and Multicultural Development, 1,* 3–15.

Fordham, S. (1988). Racelessness as a factor in Black students' school success: Pragmatic strategy or pyrrhic victory. *Harvard Educational Review, 58,* 54–84.

Fraser, M. W., & Pecora, P. J. (1985–1986). Psychological adaptation among Indochinese refugees. *Journal of Applied Social Sciences, 10,* 20–39.

Garcia, H. S. (1983). Bilingualism, biculturalism and the educational system. *Journal of Non-White Concerns in Personnel and Guidance, 11,* 67–74.

Gim, R. H., Atkinson, D. R., & Whiteley, S. (1990). Asian-American acculturation, severity of concerns, and willingness to see a counselor. *Journal of Counseling Psychology, 37,* 281–285.

Gleason, P. (1979). Confusion compounded: The melting pot in the 1960's and 1970's. *Ethnicity, 6,* 10–20.

Goldberg, M. M. (1941). A qualification of the marginal man theory. *American Sociological Review, 6,* 52–58.

Golden, J. G. (1987). Acculturation, biculturalism and marginality: A study of Korean-American high school students. *Dissertation Abstracts International, 48,* 1135A. (University Microfilms No. DA8716257)

Goldlust, J., & Richmond, A. H. (1974). A multivariate model of immigrant adaptation. *International Migration Review, 8,* 193–225.

Gonzalez, M. (1986). A study of the effects of strength of ethnic identity and amount of contact with the dominant culture on the stress in acculturation. *Dissertation Abstracts International, 47,* 2164B. (University Microfilms No. DA8616648)

Gordon, M. M. (1964). *Assimilation in American life.* New York: Oxford University Press.

Gordon, M. M. (1978). *Human nature, class, and ethnicity.* New York: Oxford University Press.

Green, A. W. (1947). A re-examination of the marginal man concept. *Social Forces, 26,* 167–171.

Gutierrez, F. J. (1981). A process model of bicultural personality development. *Dissertation Abstracts International, 42,* 3871B. (University Microfilms No. DA8203892)

Gutierrez, J., & Sameroff, A. (1990). Determinants of complexity in Mexican-American mother's conceptions of child development. *Child Development, 61,* 384–394.

Guzman, M. E. (1986). Acculturation of Mexican adolescents. *Dissertation Abstracts International, 47,* 2166B. (University Microfilms No. DA8617666)

Hallowell, A. I. (1957). The impact of the American Indian on American culture. *American Anthropologist, 59,* 201–217.

Helms, J. E. (1990). *Black and White racial identity theory, research, and practice.* Westport, CT: Greenwood Press.

Hernandez, S. M. (1981). Acculturation and biculturalism among Puerto Ricans in Lamont, California. *Dissertation Abstracts International, 42,* 428B. (University Microfilms No. 8113419)

Hess, R. S., & Street, E. M. (1991). The effect of acculturation on the relationship of counselor ethnicity and client ratings. *Journal of Counseling Psychology, 38,* 71–75.

Hurdle, D. E. (1991). The ethnic group experience. *Social Work with Groups, 13,* 59–68.

Johnston, R. (1976). The concept of the "marginal man": A refinement of the term. *Australian and New Zealand Journal of Science, 12,* 145–147.

Kazaleh, F. A. (1986). Biculturalism and adjustment: A study of Ramallah-American adolescents in Jacksonville, Florida. *Dissertation Abstracts International, 47,* 448A. (University Microfilms No. DA8609672)

Kelly, M. C. (1971). Las fiestas como reflejo del order social: El caso de San Xavier del Bac. *America Indigena, 31,* 141–161.

Kerchoff, A. C., & McCormick, T. C. (1955). Marginal status and marginal personality. *Social Forces, 34,* 48–55.

Kim, Y. Y. (1979). Toward an interactive theory of communication-acculturation. In D. Nimmo (Ed.), *Communication yearbook 3* (pp. 435–453). New Brunswick, NJ: Transaction Books.

LaFromboise, T. D. (1983). *Assertion training with American Indians.* Los Cruces, NM: ERIC Clearinghouse on Rural Education.

LaFromboise, T. D., Berman, J. S., & Sohi, B. K. (1993). American Indian women. In L. Comas-Diaz & B. Green (Eds.), *Mental health and women of color*. New York: Guilford Press.

LaFromboise, T. D., & Rowe, W. (1983). Skills training for bicultural competence: Rationale and application. *Journal of Counseling Psychology, 30,* 589–595.

Lambert, W. E. (1977). The effects of bilingualism in the individual. In P. W. Hornby (Ed.), *Bilingualism: Psychological, social and educational implications* (pp. 15–27). San Diego, CA: Academic Press.

Lang, J. G., Muñoz, R. F., Bernal, G., & Sorensen, J. L. (1982). Quality of life and psychological well-being in a bicultural Latino community. *Hispanic Journal of Behavioral Sciences, 4,* 433–450.

LeVine, R. A. (1982). *Culture, behavior, and personality* (2nd ed.). Chicago: Aldine.

Lewis, E. A., & Ford, B. (1991). The network utilization project: Incorporating traditional strengths of African-American families into group work practice. *Social Work with Groups, 13,* 7–22.

Little Soldier, L. (1985). To soar with the eagles: Enculturation and acculturation of Indian Children. *Childhood Education, 61,* 185–191.

Mallea, J. (1988). Canadian dualism and pluralism: Tensions, contradictions and emerging resolutions. In J. Berry & R. Annis (Eds.), *Ethnic psychology: Research and practice with immigrants, refugees, Native peoples, ethnic groups and sojourners* (pp. 13–37). Berwyn, PA: Swets North America.

Martinez, A. R. (1987). The effects of acculturation and racial identity on self-esteem and psychological well-being among young Puerto Ricans. *Dissertation Abstracts International, 49,* 916B. (University Microfilms No. DA8801737)

McClure, E. (1977). Aspects of code-switching in the discourse of bilingual Mexican-American children. In M. Saville-Troike (Ed.), *Linguistics and anthropology* (pp. 93–115). Washington, DC: Georgetown University Press.

McFee, M. (1968). The 150% man, a product of Blackfeet acculturation. *American Anthropologist, 70,* 1096–1107.

McKirnan, D. J., & Hamayan, E. V. (1984). Speech norms and attitudes toward outgroup members: A test of a model in a bicultural context. *Journal of Language and Social Psychology, 3,* 21–38.

Mego, D. K. (1988). The acculturation, psychosocial development and Jewish identity of Soviet Jewish emigres. *Dissertation Abstracts International, 49,* 4605B. (University Microfilms No. DA8821946)

Mendoza, A. P. (1981). Responding to stress: Ethnic and sex differences in coping behavior. In A. Baron (Ed.), *Explorations in Chicano psychology* (pp. 187–211). New York: Praeger.

Mullender, A., & Miller, D. (1985). The Ebony group: Black children in white foster homes. *Adoption and Fostering, 9* (1), 33–40, 49.

Murphy, H. B. M. (1977). Migration, culture and mental health. *Psychological Medicine, 7,* 677–684.

Northover, M. (1988). Bilingual or "dual linguistic identities"? In J. Berry & R. Annis (Eds.), *Ethnic psychology: Research and practice with immigrants, refugees, Native peoples, ethnic groups and sojourners* (pp. 207–216). Berwyn, PA: Swets North America.

Oetting, E. R., & Beauvais, F. (1990–1991). Orthogonal cultural identification theory: The cultural identification of minority adolescents. *International Journal of the Addictions, 25,* 655–685.

Oetting, E. R., Edwards, R. W., & Beauvais, F. (1989). Drugs and Native American youth. In B. Segal (Ed.), *Perspectives on adolescent drug use* (pp. 1–34). New York: Haworth Press.

Ogbu, J. U. (1979). Social stratification and the socialization of competence. *Anthropology and Education Quarterly, 10,* 3–20.

Ogbu, J. U., & Matute-Bianchi, M. A. (1986). Understanding sociocultural factors: Knowledge, identity, and social adjustment. In California State Department of Education, Bilingual Education Office, *Beyond language: Social and cultural factors in schooling* (pp. 73–142). Sacramento: CA: California State University — Los Angeles, Evaluation, Dissemination and Assessment Center.

Olmedo, E. L., & Padilla, A. M. (1978). Empirical and construct validation of a measure of acculturation for Mexican Americans. *Journal of Social Psychology, 105,* 179–187.

Padilla, A. M. (1980). *Acculturation: Theory, models and some new findings.* Boulder, CO: Westview Press.

Palinkas, L. A. (1982). Ethnicity, identity and mental health: The use of rhetoric in an immigrant Chinese church. *Journal of Psychoanalytic Anthropology, 5,* 235–258.

Palleja, J. (1987). The impact of cultural identification on the behavior of second generation Puerto Rican adolescents. *Dissertation Abstracts International, 48,* 1541A. (University Microfilms No. DA8715043)

Park, R. E. (1928). Human migration and the marginal man. *American Journal of Sociology, 5,* 881–893.

Pasquali, E. A. (1985). The impact of acculturation on the eating habits of elderly immigrants: A Cuban example. *Journal of Nutrition for the Elderly, 5,* 27–36.

Peal, E., & Lambert, W. (1962). The relation of bilingualism to intelligence. *Psychological Monographs, 76* (27).

Pertusali, L. (1988). Beyond segregation or integration: A case study from effective Native American education. *Journal of American Indian Education, 27,* 10–20.

Pierce, R. C., Clark, M., & Kaufman, S. (1978). Generation and ethnic identity: A typological analysis. *International Journal of Aging and Human Development, 9,* 19–29.

Plas, J. M., & Bellet, W. (1983). Assessment of the value-attitude orientations of American Indian children. *Journal of School Psychology, 21,* 57–64.

Polgar, S. (1960). Biculturation of Mesquakie teenage boys. *American Anthropologist, 62,* 217–235.

Ponce, F. Q., & Atkinson, D. R. (1989). Mexican-American acculturation, counselor ethnicity, counseling style, and perceived counselor credibility. *Journal of Counseling Psychology, 36,* 203–208.

Porte, Z., & Torney-Purta, J. (1987). Depression and academic achievement among Indochinese refugee unaccompanied minors in ethnic and nonethnic placements. *American Journal of Orthopsychiatry, 57,* 536–547.

Prigoff, A. W. (1984). Self-esteem, ethnic identity, job aspiration and school stress of Mexican American youth in a Midwest urban barrio. *Dissertation Abstracts International, 45,* 2257A. (University Microfilms No. DA8420403)

Ramirez, M., III. (1984). Assessing and understanding biculturalism — Multiculturalism in Mexican-American adults. In J. L. Martinez & R. H. Mendoza (Eds.), *Chicano psychology* (pp. 77–94). San Diego, CA: Academic Press.

Rashid, H. M. (1984). Promoting biculturalism in young African-American children. *Young Children, 39,* 13–23.

Red Horse, J. (1980). Family structure and value orientation in American Indians. *Social Casework, 61,* 462–467.

Richman, J. A., Gaviria, M., Flaherty, J. A., Birz, S., & Wintrob, R. M. (1987). The process of acculturation: Theoretical perspectives and an empirical investigation in Peru. *Social Science and Medicine, 25,* 839–847.

Robinson, P. (1985). Language retention among Canadian Indians: A simultaneous model with dichotomous endogenous variables. *American Sociological Review, 50,* 515–529.

Rodriguez, C. (1975). A cost-benefit analysis of subjective factors affecting assimilation: Puerto Ricans. *Ethnicity, 2,* 66–80.

Rogler, L. H., Cortes, D. E., & Malgady, R. G. (1991). Acculturation and mental health status among Hispanics. *American Psychologist, 46,* 585–597.

Rosenthal, D. A. (1987). Ethnic identity development in adolescents. In J. S. Phinney & M. J. Rotheram (Eds.), *Children's ethnic socialization* (pp. 156–179). Newbury Park, CA: Sage.

Rozek, F. (1980). The role of internal conflict in the successful acculturation of Russian Jewish immigrants. *Dissertation Abstracts International, 41,* 2778B. (University Microfilms No. 8028799)

Ruben, B. D., & Kealey, D. J. (1979). Behavioral assessment of communication competency and the prediction of cross-cultural adaption. *International Journal of Intercultural Relations, 3,* 15–47.

Ruiz, R. (1981). Cultural and historical perspectives in counseling Hispanics. In D. Sue (Ed.), *Counseling the culturally different* (pp. 186–215). New York: Wiley.

Sameroff, A. J. (1982). Development and the dialectic: The need for a systems approach. *Minnesota Symposia on Child Psychology, 15,* 83–103.

Sampson, E. E. (1988). The debate on individualism: Indigenous psychologies of the individual and their role in personal and societal functioning. *American Psychologist, 43,* 15–22.

Saville-Troike, M. (1981). *The development of bilingual and bicultural competence in young children.* Urbana, IL: Clearinghouse on Elementary and Early Childhood Education. (ERIC Document Reproduction Service No. ED 206 376)

Schiller, P. M. (1987). Biculturalism and psychosocial adjustment among Native American university students. *Dissertation Abstracts International, 48,* 1542A. (University Microfilms No. DA8720632)

Schlossberg, N. K. (1981). A model for analyzing human adaptation to transition. *The Counseling Psychologist, 9,* 2–36.

Schwarzer, R., Bowler, R., & Rauch, S. (1985). Psychological indicators of acculturation: Self-esteem, racial tension and inter-ethnic contact. In L. Ekstrand (Ed.), *Ethnic minorities and immigrants in a crosscultural perspective* (pp. 211–229). Lisse, The Netherlands: Swets & Zeitlinger.

Segall, M. M. (1986). Culture and behavior: Psychology in global perspective. *Annual Review of Psychology, 37,* 523–564.

Simard, L. M., & Taylor, D. M. (1973). The potential for bicultural communication in a dyadic situation. *Canadian Journal of Behavioral Science, 5,* 211–255.

Smither, R. (1982). Human migration and the acculturation of minorities. *Human Relations, 35,* 57–68.

Sodowsky, G. R., & Carey, J. C. (1988). Relationship between acculturation-related demographics and cultural attitudes of an Asian-Indian immigrant group. *Journal of Multicultural Counseling and Development, 16,* 117–136.

Spencer, M. B., Brookins, G. K., & Allen, W. R. (Eds.). (1985). *Beginnings: The social and affective development of Black children.* Hillsdale, NJ: Erlbaum.

Spindler, L. S. (1952). Witchcraft in Menomoni acculturation. *American Anthropologist, 54,* 593–602.

Stonequist, E. V. (1935). The problem of marginal man. *American Journal of Sociology, 7,* 1–12.

Sue, D. W., & Sue, D. (1990). *Counseling the culturally different* (2nd ed.). New York: Wiley.

Sundberg, N. D., Snowden, L. R., & Reynolds, W. M. (1978). Toward assessment of personal competence and incompetence in life situations. *American Review of Psychology, 29,* 174–221.

Sung, B. L. (1985). Bicultural conflicts in Chinese immigrant children. *Journal of Comparative Family Studies, 16,* 255–269.

Szapocznik, J., & Kurtines, W. (1980). Acculturation, biculturalism and adjustment among Cuban Americans. In A. M. Padilla (Ed.), *Psychological dimensions on the acculturation process: Theory, models, and some new findings* (pp. 139–159). Boulder, CO: Westview Press.

Szapocznik, J., Kurtines, W., & Fernandez, T. (1980). Bicultural involvement and adjustment in Hispanic-American youths. *International Journal of Intercultural Relations, 4,* 353–365.

Szapocznik, J., Rio, A., Perez-Vidal, A., Kurtines, W., Hervis, O., & Santisteban, D. (1986). Bicultural effectiveness training (BET): An experimental test of an intervention modality for families experiencing intergenerational/intercultural conflict. *Hispanic Journal of Behavioral Sciences, 8,* 303–330.

Szapocznik, J., Santisteban, D., Kurtines, W., Perez-Vidal, A., & Hervis, O. (1984). Bicultural effectiveness training: A treatment intervention for enhancing intercultural adjustment in Cuban American families. *Hispanic Journal of Behavioral Sciences, 6,* 317–344.

Szapocznik, J., Scopetta, M. A., Kurtines, W., & Arandale, M. A. (1978). Theory and measurement of acculturation. *Interamerican Journal of Psychology, 12,* 113–120.

Taft, R. (1977). Coping with unfamiliar cultures. In N. Warren (Ed.), *Studies in cross-cultural psychology* (Vol. 1, pp. 121–153). San Diego, CA: Academic Press.

Thomas, G. E. (1983). The deficit, difference, and bicultural theories of Black dialect and nonstandard English. *Urban Review, 15,* 107–118.

Thompson, L. (1948). Attitudes and acculturation. *American Anthropologist, 50,* 200–215.

Topper, M. D., & Johnson, L. (1980). Effects of forced relocation on Navajo mental patients from the former Navajo-Hopi joint use area. *White Cloud Journal, 2*(1), 3–7.

Tormes, Y. (1985). Bilingual education, English as a second language and equity in higher education. *Dissertation Abstracts International, 46,* 3314A. (University Microfilms No. DA8601699)

Triandis, H. C. (1980). A theoretical framework for the study of bilingual-bicultural adaption. *International Review of Applied Psychology, 29,* 7–16.

Trimble, J. (1981). Value differentials and their importance in counseling American Indians. In P. Pedersen (Eds.), *Counseling across cultures* (pp. 203–226). Honolulu: University of Hawaii Press.

Van Den Bergh, N. (1991). Managing biculturalism at the workplace: A group approach. In K. L. Chau (Ed.), *Ethnicity and biculturalism* (pp. 71–84). New York: Haworth Press.

Vasquez, M. J., & McKinley, D. L. (1982). Supervision: A conceptual model — reactions and extension. *The Counseling Psychologist, 10,* 59–63.

Vogt, E. Z. (1957). The acculturation of American Indians. *Annals of the American Academy of Political and Social Science, 311,* 137–146.

Weatherford, J. (1988). *Indian givers: How the Indians of the Americas transformed the world.* New York: Fawcett Columbine.

Williams, C. L., & Berry, J. W. (1991). Primary prevention of acculturative stress among refugees: Application of psychological theory and practice. *American Psychologist, 46,* 632–641.

Young, M. C., & Gardner, R. C. (1990). Modes of acculturation and second language proficiency. *Canadian Journal of Behavioural Science, 22,* 59–71.

Zane, N., Sue, S., Hu, L., & Kwon, J. (1991). Asian-American assertion: A social learning analysis of cultural differences. *Journal of Counseling Psychology, 38,* 63–70.

Zuniga, M. E. (1988). Assessment issues with Chicanas: Practice implications. *Psychotherapy, 25,* 288–293.

22. Disability beyond Stigma: Social Interaction, Discrimination, and Activism

Michelle Fine and Adrienne Asch

• Between 1981 and 1984, the Eastern Paralyzed Veterans Association, Disabled in Action of New York City, and other organizations of people with disabilities fought a court battle with the New York City Metropolitan Transit Authority to gain architectural access to the city's mass transit system. The MTA opposed modifying the system, claiming that the expense would never be made up by rider fares of those mobility-impaired people then denied transit access. The *New York Times* ("Editorial," 1983; "The $2,000 Subway Token," 1984), along with most other sectors of the community, generally favoring progressive social change, supported the Transit Authority in the fight it eventually lost (Katzmann, 1986).

• In 1982 and 1983, the national media described two cases where the parents and doctors of infants with disabilities denied the infants medical treatment based on their impairments. In the first case, an infant with Down syndrome died of starvation six days after birth; in the second case, the parents finally consented to the surgery. The impairments of the infants were used as the basis for denying them treatment that could have alleviated certain of their medical problems but left them with permanent disabilities that no treatment would cure. Virtually the only supporters of the infants' right to treatment over parental objections were those commonly associated with the right-wing and right-to-life sectors of society, and perhaps also people with disabilities themselves (*Disability Rag*, 1984). (For

Editors' Note: This chapter was originally published as the introduction to a special issue of *Journal of Social Issues* on the topic of disability. References in this chapter to "this issue" indicate *Journal of Social Issues* 44, no. 1 (1988).

Reprinted with permission of the authors and the Society for the Psychological Study of Social Issues from *Journal of Social Issues* 44, no. 1 (1988): 3–21. © 1988 Journal of Social Research.

a discussion of these cases and their meaning for notions of "community," see Sarason, 1986; and for a civil libertarian supporter of Baby Doe, see Hentoff, 1987).

• In 1983 and 1984, and again in 1986, Elizabeth Bouvia, a young woman whose cerebral palsy made it impossible for her to control any of her limbs save some functions of one hand, sought to get California hospitals to allow her to die by starvation. The Americal Civil Liberties Union (ACLU), generally regarded as championing the progress of many social causes, wrote a brief in her behalf describing her disability as causing her "pitiful existence," referring to her "affliction" as "incurable and . . . intolerable," and commenting on the "indignity and humiliation of requiring someone to attend to her every bodily need" (ACLU Foundation of Southern California, 1983, pp. 14, 17, 35). The entire tone of the brief implied that it was not at all surprising that someone with her level of disability would wish to end her life. The ACLU was not dissuaded from its line of argument by testimony of the Disability Rights Coordinating Council (DRCC), including a psychologist who was also a quadriplegic, suggesting that Ms. Bouvia's situation was complicated by a host of stresses apart from her disability: "death of a sibling, marriage, pregnancy, multiple changes in residence, financial hardship, miscarriage, increased physical pain, terminal illness of a parent, and dissolution of marriage" (DRCC, 1983, p. 3). The DRCC did not dispute that people had the right to take their own lives. It disputed the unquestioned assumption that disability was a reason to end life.

The Superior Court of California, unmoved by those who sought to disentangle Ms. Bouvia's request from the situation of people with disabilities generally, endorsed her request saying, among other things: "She, as the patient, lying helplessly in bed, unable to care for herself, may consider her existence meaningless. She cannot be faulted for so concluding." Later, in describing her, it stated: "Her mind and spirit may be free to take great flights, but she herself is imprisoned, and must lie physically helpless, subject to the ignominy, embarrassment, humiliation, and dehumanizing aspects created by her helplessness" (*Bouvia v. Superior Court of California,* 1986, pp. 19, 21).

In this issue of *JSI,* we wish to resurrect the challenge to social psychology posed by Meyerson, Barker, and others in their 1948 *JSI* issue on disability. In this first article, we review the ways that disability has been viewed by social psychology over the past decades, trying to do for the study of disability what Sampson (1983) has done for the view of justice: namely, to offer some challenges to the assumptions that have guided theory and research, to speculate on the bases for these assumptions, and to suggest how alternative assumptions would alter the study of disability. We conclude by previewing the remaining articles in this issue as they reflect theory and research grounded in both old and new assumptions about the social nature of physical and mental disabilities.

DEFINING THE POPULATION OF INTEREST

Although other articles in this issue elaborate upon the problem of accurately defining and describing the current situation of people with disabilities in 1987, it is essential to specify briefly whom this issue is about. In 1980 Bowe estimated the total population of people with disabilities in the United States to be 36 million, or perhaps 15% of the nation's people. In 1986 ("Census Study"), the *New York Times* reported some 37 million people over 15 years of age with disabling conditions. As Asch (1984) has discussed elsewhere, the mere attempt to define and enumerate the population shows that disability is a social construct. The Rehabilitation Act of 1973, as amended in 1978, defines a handicapped individual as "any person who (i) has a physical or mental impairment which substantially limits one or more of such person's major life activities, (ii) has a record of such an impairment, or (iii) is regarded as having such an impairment" (Section 7B).

We can say the following with assurance: The nation's population includes some 10% of school-aged children classified as handicapped for the purposes of receipt of special educational services (Biklen, this issue); somewhere between 9 and 17% of those between 16 and 64 years of age report disabilities that influence their employment situation (Haber & McNeil, 1983); nearly half of those over 65 indicate having one or more disabilities that interfere with their life activities or are regarded by others as doing so (DeJong & Lifchez, 1983).

Laws governing the provision of educational and rehabilitation services, and prohibiting discrimination in education, employment, and access to public programs, all stress the similarities in needs and in problems of people with a wide variety of physical, psychological, and intellectual impairments. (Scotch, this issue, discusses the benefits to the disability rights movement of such a legislative approach.) In this space, however, it is important to acknowledge the *differences* among disabling conditions and their varied impact on the lives of people in this group.

First, different conditions cause different types of functional impairment. Deafness, mental retardation, paralysis, blindness, congenital limb deficiencies, and epilepsy (all taken up in greater detail in this issue) may pose common social problems of stigma, marginality, and discrimination, but they also produce quite different functional difficulties. Several of these disabilities obviously interfere with functions of daily life, but the last, epilepsy, may not. Some persons with epilepsy have no inherent limitations whatever. Nevertheless, they are likely to be regarded as having an impairment.

Furthermore, people with disabilities have different degrees of impairment: Amounts of hearing and visual loss differ; some people with impairment of mobility can walk in some situations while others cannot. Mental retardation ranges from profound to mild—so mild that many out of school never get the label. In addition, some disabilities are static, while others are progressive. Multiple sclerosis, muscular dystrophy, cystic fibrosis, some vision and hearing impairments, some types of cancer and heart conditions represent progressive disabilities that cause ever-changing health and life situations. Some conditions are congenital, others are acquired. All of these factors that distinguish the origin, experience, and effects of disability must be kept in mind in social science research on disability.

Researchers (Davis, 1961; Goffman, 1963; Ladieu, Adler, & Dembo, 1948) have long been aware that the degree of visibility of the impairment or the age at which it was acquired (Barker, 1948; von Hentig, 1948) may influence the psychological consequences and the social situation of people with disabilities. More recently, scholars have addressed the impact of ethnicity, class, and gender upon the experience of disability (Fine & Asch, 1981, 1988). In this issue, Schneider focuses on the social-psychological situation of people with a relatively invisible condition (epilepsy), and Mest analyzes the ways in which living and work contexts affect persons with retardation. Most of the other authors discuss the situations of people whose conditions are manifested by appearance or behavior. Ainlay and

Frank (both in this issue) consider the different social-psychological impact of age of onset, and their conclusions contrast with the prevailing clinical and social-psychological views that acquiring a disability later is less damaging to the self and to social interaction than is growing up with an impairment. (See Asch and Rousso, 1985, for a review of psychoanalytic literature on disability.)

DISABLED PEOPLE AS A MINORITY

Having acknowledged differences among these more than 36 million people in terms of their diagnoses, their social contexts, and their experiences of disability, it is important to return to the analysis that informs this essay and this issue as a whole: disabled people comprise a minority group and most of their problems can and must be understood in a minority-group framework. This view is neither novel nor exclusively a post-Civil Rights Era position. Roger Barker in 1948 advanced thinking about disability in minority-group terms. Lee Meyerson, in his introduction to the 1948 *JSI* (1948a), opened by commenting, "There is general agreement in the literature on physical disability that the problems of the handicapped are not physical, but social and psychological" (p. 2). Our own analysis owes much to the Lewinian person-in-environment thinking of the 1948 *JSI* contributors, and to the thoughtful work of Wright (1960/1983), herself a frequent collaborator with Barker, Meyerson, and Dembo. These authors acknowledged that people with disabilities must be understood as having psychological responses to their impairments themselves, but they went on to point out the following: environmental factors posed many barriers of discrimination, marginality, and uncertain social acceptance; people with disabilities faced ambiguous, if not rejecting, social responses; and these people responded psychologically and socially to such situations.

Our analysis expands on this significant work and the 40 intervening years of social and legislative change. In the last 15 years, the movement for disability rights has embraced a minority-group perspective. Scholars of disability outside of social psychology such as Gliedman and Roth (1980), Hahn (1983, this issue), and Scotch (1984, this issue) have attempted to elaborate a minority-group analysis of disability issues and the disability experience. Unfortunately, as seen from the ensuing discussion, much of the frequently cited social-psychological work on disability has not learned all it could from the 1948 *JSI* contributors, nor from others in the emerging field of disability studies.

The minority-group perspective that frames this volume accepts Dworkin and Dworkin's (1976) definition of a minority group, applying it to people with disabilities. The criteria include "identifiability, differential power, differential and pejorative treatment, and group awareness" (p. viii).

While disabled people as a group may fit these criteria, they nevertheless face many obstacles in developing a minority-group consciousness, as Hahn (this issue) and Scotch (this issue) discuss in some detail. Not the least of these obstacles is the inaccessibility of the built environment, rendering transportation and public facilities unusable for people with many impairments, and disrupting potential efforts at organizing. While many people with disabilities have not developed a minority-group consciousness, a recent Louis Harris survey of disabled Americans reported that 74% of people with disabilities do feel some common identity with one another and that 45% see themselves as a minority in the same sense as people who are black or Hispanic (Hill, Mehnert, Taylor, Kagey, Leizhenko et al., 1986). As a footnote to Dworkin and Dworkin, we begin with the premise that a lack of shared consciousness *by some* does not negate the importance of understanding the social, structural, and psychological situation of people with disabilities in minority-group terms. As Hahn (1983 issue) argues, the consequences of any impairment cannot be understood or appreciated without giving due weight to the environment — physical, structural, social, economic, psychological, and political — of the person with the disability. Just how disabling would deafness be if 20th-century urbanites, like Groce's (1985) rural villagers of Martha's Vineyard in the 19th century, all practiced sign language? How disabling would paraplegia be if all cities were barrier free? (See Scheer & Groce, this issue.) How limiting would mental retardation be if nearly all labeled children received their educations in settings with the nonlabeled, as Biklen (this issue) discusses?

Barker (1948) was right when he reminded us that not all of the disabled person's situation can be explained by prejudice and discrimination. It is true that some activities are foreclosed merely because of the biological impairment itself. But the articles in this issue expand upon his thinking by demanding that we cease considering the environment — whether physical or attitudinal — as given. The *JSI* contributors of 1948 and this issue contrast sharply with much of the social-psychological writing about disability in the intervening decades, which assumes that the issues of disability reside in the person and tends to minimize or neglect the environment.

ASSUMPTIONS ABOUT DISABILITY

Considered below are a set of common assumptions about what disability means. For each, there have been important methodological and theoretical consequences:

1. *It Is Often Assumed That Disability Is Located Solely in Biology, and Thus Disability Is Accepted Uncritically as an Independent Variable.* The disability and the person are assumed synonymous, and the cause of others' behaviors and attitudes. Several experimental social psychologists (Katz, 1981; Kleck, 1969; Kleck, Ono, & Hastorf, 1966) have simulated disability in the laboratory to verify Goffman's reports that handicapped people arouse anxiety and discomfort in others and are socially stigmatized. In these experiments, researchers have simulated disability by using a confederate who in one experimental condition appeared disabled and in another appeared nondisabled. The experiments did support the hypothesis that nondisabled people react differently to people with disabilities than they do to people without them. Nevertheless, it should be remembered that the confederate, whose only experience of having a disability may have been simulating it by sitting in a wheelchair, employed none of the strategies commonly used by disabled people to ease the discomfort of strangers in first meetings (Davis, 1961; Goffman, 1963). By focusing on initial encounters with strangers and by using a confederate whose only experience with disability might be simulating it, these experiments tell us nothing about how disabled people *actually* negotiate meaningful social interactions. Reports by Davis (1961) and Goffman (1963) acknowledge that obvious disability is generally prominent in initial social encounters. However, the extent to which an experimental confederate's naiveté about living with a disability can contribute to the prominence and the awkwardness of disability has not been recognized as an intervening variable. In these experiments, disability is viewed as an independent variable, much as gender had been considered prior to the early 1970s (Unger & Denmark, 1975). Disability is portrayed as the variable that predicts the out-

come of social interaction when, in fact, social contexts shape the meaning of a disability in a person's life.

Most social-psychological work using disability to examine the concept of stigma takes the experience as equivalent regardless of such factors as the disabled person's race, culture, class, and gender. Scheer and Groce (this issue), Becker and Arnold (1986), and Solomon (1986) provide valuable correctives by viewing the situation of disabled people through the disciplines of anthropology and history.

2. *When a Disabled Person Faces Problems, It Is Assumed That the Impairment Causes Them.* In their very thoughtful expansion of Goffman's notion of stigma, Jones et al. (1984) elaborate on the consequences for the "marked" person of being singled out by others. Throughout their discussion of marking and its social-psychological consequences for disabled and nondisabled alike, however, these authors never question the extent to which disability per se poses difficulties in social participation, as contrasted with difficulties caused by the environment—architectural, social, economic, legal, and cultural. For example, in their discussion of changes in the life situations of people who became disabled, the authors never question that *the disability* keeps the person from continuing in employment or from going to restaurants or other recreational facilities. The entire discussion of stigma and marked relationships assumes as "natural" what Hahn aptly terms a *disabling environment;* it views obstacles as being solely the person's biological limitations rather than the human-made barriers of architecture or discriminatory work practices.

Even Barker's (1948) early work went only part way to indicting the environment as an obstacle to the disabled person's participation. Far ahead of his time, he called for antidiscrimination laws in education and employment, although he failed to challenge the architecture, the transportation, and the communication methods that confronted people with disabilities and hampered full participation. Barker's concluding comments took social arrangements as given, urging counseling and psychotherapy for people with disabilities, so that they could come to accept "the fact that the world in which [they] live] presents serious restrictions and frustrations." He went on to say that education and antidiscrimination laws cannot "remove all restrictions on the physically deviant in a world constructed for the physically normal. The ultimate adjustment must involve changes in the values of the physically disabled person" (p. 37).

Barker's (1948) view is understandable 25 years before the passage of federal legislation to modify public-sector physical environments. Jones and his colleagues' (1984) obliviousness to environmental issues is not. Their otherwise valuable work on the social-psychological consequences of disability and stigma suffers seriously from such omissions. We can contrast these omissions of attention to environmental effects with Sampson's (1983) work on justice. Sampson urges students of justice and of resource allocation to attend to and be critical of current systems rather than merely to accept them and their consequences. We urge the same for students of disability.

3. *It Is Assumed That the Disabled Person Is a "Victim."* In a great deal of social-psychological research on attribution, the disabled person is seen as a victim who copes with suffering by self-blame (Bulman & Wortman, 1977), by reinterpreting the suffering to find positive meaning (Taylor, Wood, & Lichtman, 1983), or by denying that he or she is really suffering (Taylor et al., 1983). Bulman and Wortman studied 29 people paralyzed in accidents. Lerner (1980) describes these people as "young people who had been recently condemned to spend the rest of their lives crippled" (p. 161). In order for Lerner to make sense of why Bulman and Wortman's respondents were not displaying a sense of victimization, he posits their belief in a just world and suggests that their interpretations of the disabling events are constructed so as to retain a strong belief that the world is a just place and that bad things only happen to people for reasons. The psychological experiences of the persons with disabilities are thus examined *not* on their own terms, but instead as a form of denial. Disability is used as a synonym for victimization in this theoretical analysis.

Taylor et al.'s (1983) article, "It Could Be Worse," also illustrated the unchecked presumption of disabled-person-as-victim. The researchers examined the responses of people with cancer shortly after the onset of their condition and discovered that the interviewees consistently maintained that their situations "could be worse." To explain this finding, five "strategies" used by these "victims" to make sense of their situations were described. It is disturbing to us that these authors, who were interested in the rich qualitative ways that people describe their coping experiences, minimized informants' consistently expressed view that the trauma was not as severe as it could have been.

As Taylor et al. argued, people diagnosed as having cancer are surely traumatized, and they actively generate coping strategies. However, our concerns arise with respect to the authors' a priori assumptions. First, it should be noted that Bulman and Wortman, and Taylor and her colleagues, studied people quite shortly after the onset of disability, before they had a chance to discover what would or would not be problematic about their lives. Their findings that self-blame (Bulman & Wortman, 1977) and making downward comparisons (Taylor et al., 1983) occurred within the first months or years after disability differ dramatically from those of Schulz and Decker (1985) in their study of people with spinal cord injuries 5–20 years after disability. The former authors can be read as suggesting, if inadvertently, that the experience of disability is static in a person's life and that "coping" is the same at any point in time or in one's life situation. The work of Schulz and Decker (1985), and Ainlay (this issue), correct this prevailing assumption and enrich our understanding of disability by demonstrating that responses at a specific time may not be the ones people retain after living with a disability for several years.

There are two more problems with the interpretations of disabled-person-as-victim put forward by Bulman and Wortman (1977), Janoff-Bulman and Frieze (1983), Lerner (1980), and Taylor et al. (1983). First, in contrast to Ladieu et al.'s (1948) report on the reactions of disabled veterans after World War II, these later researchers seem to discount the experiences described by the people they interviewed. Taylor et al., for example, view their respondents as having strategies for managing or camouflaging what must be truly tragic. To the "outsider," the researcher, the "objective situation" is that a diagnosis of cancer is primarily a tragedy. That "insiders," those with cancer, overwhelmingly state that they had fared better than they would have expected is not used self-reflectively by the researchers to reframe their notions about how people think about traumatic life events (cf. Frank, this issue). Rather, the statement is interpreted to illustrate psychological defenses that disabled people mobilize in order to manage what researchers feel is not really manageable. What needs to be stated is that disability—while never wished for—may simply not be as wholly disastrous as imagined.

Second, these authors presume that the disability itself constitutes the victimizing experience. None of them emphasize the subsequent reactions or deprivations that people experience because of social responses to their disability or environmentally imposed constraints. While Janoff-Bulman and Frieze (1983) recognize discrimination based on sex or gender to be a societal injustice, disability is assumed a biological injustice and the injustices that lie in its social treatment are ignored.

4. *It Is Assumed That Disability Is Central to the Disabled Person's Self-Concept, Self-Definition, Social Comparisons, and Reference Groups.* Taylor and her colleagues (1983) describe their respondents as having to make downward social comparisons, lest they come face to face with how bad their situations really are. Jones et al. (1984), in their discussion of stigma, assume that the recently disabled paraplegic compares herself to others who are also paralyzed. She may, but perhaps only when it comes to assessing her capacity to perform certain activities from a wheelchair. Gibbons (1986) claims that while such severely stigmatized people as those labeled retarded must make only downward social comparisons to preserve self-esteem, more "mildly stigmatized" people such as those using wheelchairs seek out similarly disabled people with whom to compare themselves, and avoid social interactions and social comparisons with nondisabled people. Because disability is clearly salient for the nondisabled, it is assumed that the marked person incorporates the mark as central to a self-definition.

The above authors forget that the woman who is paralyzed may be as likely to compare herself with other women her age, others of her occupation, others of her family, class, race, or a host of other people and groups who function as reference groups and social comparison groups for her. Disability may be more salient to the researchers studying it than to the people being studied, who may define themselves as "similar to" or worthy of comparison with people without disabilities. Gurin (1984) reminds researchers in social comparison and relative deprivation to pay more attention to the conditions under which people choose particular groups with whom to compare themselves, and she stresses that social comparison may have nothing to do with gender, race, or disability.

Clearly contrasting with the above discussions of social comparison, Mest (this issue) demonstrates that their "mark" or stigma may be irrelevant to how mentally retarded persons define themselves and each other, particularly if they work and live in supportive contexts.

5. *It Is Assumed That Having a Disability Is Synonymous with Needing Help and Social Support.* People with disabilities are perceived to be examples of those ever in need of help and social support (Brickman et al., 1982; Deutsch, 1985; Dunkel-Schetter, 1984; Jones et al., 1984; Katz, 1981; Krebs, 1970; Sarason, 1986). Such an assumption is sustained both by what researchers study and write about those with disabilities and by their omission of disabled people in their discussions as providers of support.

The assumption that disability is synonymous with helplessness is not surprising when we remember that "the handicapped role" in the United States has been seen as one of helplessness, dependence, and passivity (Gliedman & Roth, 1980; Goffman, 1963). Brickman et al. (1982), in their excellent discussion of different models of helping and coping, review the essence of the medical model: The person is responsible for neither the problem encountered nor the solution required. The handicapped role, like the sick role of which it is an extension, compels the occupant to suspend other activities until recovered, to concentrate on getting expert therapy, to follow instructions, to get well, and only then to resume normal life. The nonhandicapped person equates having a disability with a *bad and eternal* flu, toothache, or broken leg. When such conditions are temporary, it may be acceptable to entrust oneself to helpers and to forego decision making briefly; but when forced to confront a moment of weakness, unsteadiness, or limitations in the capacity to see, hear, or move, people experience grave difficulty in adjusting. However, it is erroneous to conclude that their difficulties mirror those of the person who has a long-term disability and who has learned to use alternative methods to accomplish tasks of daily living and working.

That disability is assumed tantamount to incompetence and helplessness has been investigated, and supported, in laboratory research. Unfortunately, the writing that has been generated *accepts* rather than *challenges* this stereotype. Katz (1981), who found that whites gave more help to competent blacks than to ones they perceived to be less competent and enterprising, expected that the same help-giving pattern would be true for nondisabled subjects when confronting a person with a disability. Contrary to his hypothesis, however, he found that nondisabled people gave *less* help to disabled persons perceived as competent and friendly than to those perceived as incompetent and unfriendly. They also gave less help to the "disabled persons" (simulated) than to nondisabled persons. To explain this, Katz relied on Goffman (1963) and Gliedman and Roth (1980) in asserting that nondisabled persons are relatively offended or uncomfortable when confronting a person with an impairment who manages life competently! As Jones and his colleagues (1984) remind us, the able-bodied deny the reality of successful adaptation by the disabled person. They perceive it as the disabled person "making the best of a bad job," and this view supports their conviction that their own health and capacities are as important, and infallible, as they think (p. 87).

Even while we wonder whether Katz would have gotten the same finding had he used a person who actually had a disability rather than one who had simulated an impairment, it is valuable to have this experimental support for what Goffman, Gliedman and Roth, and untold numbers of people with disabilities have described. Unfortunately, Jones et al. (1984) fall prey to their own unchallenged assumptions in thinking about ongoing relationships between people with and without disabilities: Throughout their book, and especially in the chapter by French (1984), it is assumed that the person with the disability is in constant need of help and support, rather than being a victim of nondisabled persons' projections or fantasies. Thereby, three problems arise: First, that the person with a disability may need assistance with certain acts is generalized to all aspects of the relationship between a person with a disability and one without. Second, if the person does need assistance, it is assumed that a previous reciprocal relationship will change, rather than that new methods or relationships will develop to provide it. Concurrently, it is assumed that the biological condition rather than the environment and social context makes one-way assistance inevitable. Third, it perpetuates the idea that the impaired person is forever the recipient, rather than ever the provider, of help and support. If disabled people are mentioned, they are mentioned as only on the receiving end of a helping transaction.

In French's (1984) chapter on marriages between disabled and nondisabled people, the assumptions are never challenged that the disability causes marital roles to change fundamentally, that blindness or quadriplegia per se will make resuming a work role difficult or impossible, that recreation will have to be curtailed. The spouse who performs certain amounts of physical caretaking is seen not only as a physical caretaker but as a generous intellectual and emotional caretaker as well. Physical incapacities are perceived as leading inevitably to incapacities in other spheres of life. Wright's (1960/1983) notion that disability "spreads" throughout a relationship is embedded unchallenged in this entire discussion.

Moreover, it is the disability, not the institutional, physical, or attitudinal environment, that is blamed for role changes that may occur. The person with a disability may (initially, or always) need physical caretaking, such as help in dressing, household chores, or reading. It must be asked, however, whether such assistance would be necessary if environments were adapted to the needs of people with disabilities—if, for example, more homes were built to accommodate those who used wheelchairs, if technological aids could be developed to assist in performing manual tasks, if existing technology to convert the printed word into speech or braille were affordable to all who needed it. Thus, again, the physical environment as an obstruction remains an unchallenged given. In addition, the author is assuming that the role of human assistant for all these tasks will automatically fall to the "significant other" rather than considering whether such activities could be performed by others, including public sector employees, thus permitting the primary relationship to function in its primary spheres of intimacy, sharing, and emotional nurturance for both participants. If the partners reorganize their roles after the impairment of one member, such reorganization may result from a variety of factors: the way they think about disability, their relational obligations, the way that health care professionals inform them about the implications of disability, or the difficulties faced in affording appropriate assistance in the United States. These are consequences of how people think about disability and of current national disability policy, not of disability per se. As with all too much of this literature, as Wright (1960/1983) points out, researchers who are outsiders make attributions to persons and thus neglect the powerful role of the environment.

The third problem mentioned above—that disabled people are always seen as recipients—may stem not only from distortions about people with disabilities but also from using disability as a metaphor to illustrate theory rather than to reveal more about the lives of people with impairments. Deutsch (1985) may be correct in speculating that, at least temporarily, resources would or should go to a sick child rather than to a well one; Dunkel-Schetter (1984) may plausibly learn about the mechanisms of social support by studying what people with cancer find valuable and supportive from others after such a diagnosis; Krebs (1970) makes an important point in discussing how assumptions of legitimacy of others' dependency influence the helping process. Nonetheless, by staying with questions about theories of distributive systems (Deutsch, 1985), social support (Dunkel-Schetter, 1984); or altruism (Krebs, 1970), and by not focusing on ongoing reciprocal transactions, the person with a disability is never imagined or shown to be a provider of support. As Shumaker and Brownell (1984) remind us, those who receive support also commonly seek to provide it, if not to those who gave it to them, then to others. It is regrettable that people with disabilities, when studied or considered at all in most social-psychological literature, are examined only in ways that reinforce and perpetuate existing stereotypes rather than in ways that question and challenge them. In this manner, the literature fails to enrich our understanding of the lives of people with handicapping conditions.

Particularly disturbing, as an illustration of disability-as-metaphor, is Sarason's (1986) discussion of the Baby Jane Doe case. Unfortunately, his laudable effort to call for a renewed commitment to the "public interest" and a lessening of individualism is flawed by uncritically accepting the assumption that the infant with a disability can never be expected to make a valuable contribution to family or society. He consistently refers to the existence of the severely disabled child as a problem to both family and society. Sarason's examination of the public interest and of the search for community continues in this "disabled-as-helpless" vein. He refers only to "afflicted children"; finds that families who adopt disabled children were "managing their situations in surprisingly adaptive, stable, and inspiring ways" (p. 903); and describes the child only as a "problem," without any consideration of the possible contributions, benefits, or pleasures the infant born with a disability might bring to its family and society.

THE ROLE OF THESE ASSUMPTIONS FOR SOCIETY AND FOR SOCIAL SCIENCE

It is worth speculating on how these assumptions get made, why they persist, and what functions they serve for researchers and society. It remains a task for future research to discover the plausibility of these speculations.

Jones and his colleagues (1984) contend that the thought or awareness of disability evokes feelings of vulnerability and death. They suggest that the nondisabled person almost wants the one with the disability to suffer so as to confirm that the "normal" state is as good and as important as the "normal" thinks it is. Because disability can be equated with vulnerability to the uncontrollable, observing someone with a disability forces all of us to wonder about the consequences of what one cannot control. In a society seeking to control ever more of life, is there a leap to the assumption that one cannot live with the consequences of what one cannot control? Or is there a desire to view disability as a fundamental loss of control, in order to obscure the fact that many aspects of our lives are "out of our control"? Social researchers are in the business of expanding knowledge of the world and trying to optimize prediction and control. As researchers, we highly prize knowledge and the control it can provide. Does such a commitment to control suggest that social scientists may view disability as fearful, unacceptable, and different because the person with the disability is a reminder that we cannot control all life events?

As discussed earlier, perceptions of disability have been the repository and projection of human needs. How much do the social and psychological problems that many people associate with disability actually pervade all of human life? If one can think of a person with a disability as needy, in contrast, one can view those without impairments as strong and as not having needs. By thinking of the disabled person as dependent in a given situation, and the one without disabilities as independent and autonomous, one can avoid considering how extensively people without disabilities too are dependent and "out of control." As members of a social group, we are all sometimes dependent and sometimes not. Rather than the world being divided into givers and receivers of help, we are all actually interdependent. Attributing neediness and lack of control to people with disabilities permits those who are not disabled to view themselves as having more control and more strength in their lives than may be the case.

Last, perceiving a person with a disability as a suffering victim, as a stimulus object, as in need, or as different and strange, all reinforce what Goffman (1963) describes as perception of the stigmatized as "not quite human" (p. 6). In discussing the scope of justice, Deutsch (1985) comments, "Justice is not involved in relations with others . . . who are perceived to be outside one's potential moral community or opposed to it. . . . The narrower one's concept of community, the narrower will be the scope of situations in which one's actions will be governed by considerations of justice" (pp. 36–37). Deutsch goes on to contend that it has been a

> too-common assumption of victimizers, even those of good will, as well as of many social scientists, that the social pathology has been in the ghetto rather than in those who have built the walls to surround it, that the disadvantaged are the ones who need to be changed rather than the people and institutions who have kept the disadvantaged in a submerged position. . . . It is more important to change educational institutions and economic and political systems so that they will permit those groups who are now largely excluded from important positions of decision-making to share power than to try to inculcate new attitudes and skills in those who are excluded (p. 61).

These words apply as much to the situation of people with disabilities as to that of people with economic disadvantages whom Deutsch considered. By concentrating on cure or on psychological and physical restoration of the impaired person, society and the discipline of psychology have avoided the need to focus on essential changes in the environmental side of the "person-in-environment" situation. If the person with a disability is "not quite human," then that person can remain outside the community of those who must receive just distributions of rewards and resources (Deutsch, 1985). In contrast, if people with disabilities were perceived as having the same rights to mobility and life's opportunities as people without impairments, we would inevitably be compelled to rethink the view that transportation for people with mobility impairments, or access to treatment for infants or adults with disabilities, are gifts or charities that can be withdrawn when times are tight. Once people with disabilities are admitted inside the human and moral community, the task becomes one of creating an environment where all humans—including those with impairments—can truly flourish.

AIMS OF THIS ISSUE

We conclude by discussing what research might look like without the five assumptions described above and by posing questions for future study.

Although we do not see the influence of the 1948 *JSI* issue on disability in much of contemporary research, we believe it has influenced social policy in the intervening decades and has informed much of the research found in the present volume. Many of the 1948 policy recommendations have been realized: Children with disabilities are now entitled to a free, appropriate public education alongside their nondisabled counterparts (Cain, 1948). Many state civil rights laws now provide people with disabilities the same protection against discrimination in employment, housing, and public accommodations as is afforded to other minority groups. Federal law now mandates that disabled people have equal access to employment and services in all programs that receive federal money (Barker, 1948; Meyerson, 1948b,c). As laws, institutional arrangements, and social relationships begin to change, so too must the social psychology of disability change to reflect the altered experience of people with disabilities — and of persons without disabilities — as members of a common moral community.

Having been critical of the picture of disability portrayed in much of the social-psychological research previously discussed, we must ask what has kept so much research locked into the narrow assumptions about people with disabilities. As Asch (1984) has described, the focus of much social-psychological research on disability has been to determine the impact of contact with disability upon people without impairments. Such a question, particularly when framed by a researcher outside the disability experience, makes the person with the disability the object, not the subject, of study and distances the research from the disabled person's life experience. Furthermore, much of this research was undertaken primarily to bolster particular theoretical notions about stigma, victimization, social comparison processes, justice, altruism, or social support. Not surprisingly, but regrettably, the authors have used notions of disability as a metaphor to advance social theories rather than to advance our knowledge of the experience of disability.

We wonder what keeps researchers from imagining a context in which disability would not be handicapping. Major reasons may be that most research has not focused on the lives and experiences of people with disabilities, and it has often been conducted without substantial contact with people with disabilities. By contrast, the research presented in this issue, like that of the 1948 *JSI,* stems from the authors' interest in people with disabilities. The articles adopt varying disciplinary perspectives, and they demonstrate that disability often functions as an independent variable, but that reactions to and consequences of disability are dependent upon multiple variables in the social and psychological contexts of disabled and nondisabled persons. (Similarly, several essays in the collection by Ainlay, Becker, and Coleman (1986) demonstrate how much historical and cultural variation exists in just who is stigmatized, who becomes a deprived minority.)

In this issue, both Hahn and Biklen examine the ways in which having a disability contributes to minority status. As Dworkin and Dworkin (1976, p. 18) have pointed out, "selection of the relevant characteristics upon which identifiability is based is neither fixed nor self-evident; rather, it is variable and socially defined and interpreted." Hahn looks at what he classifies as nondisabled persons' "existential" and "aesthetic" anxieties as the bases for labeling, and Biklen focuses on educational finances as the primary *raison d'être* for classifying schoolchildren into categories—disabled or not.

The paper by Ainlay examines the experience of becoming disabled, for elderly men and women, while Schneider discusses the experience of persons with disabilities in their interpersonal relationships over time. These two articles demonstrate how time with an impairment modifies its lived experience. In the spirit of Schulz and Decker (1985), they challenge the notions of Bulman and Wortman (1977) and Taylor et al. (1983).

The articles by Frank and Mest examine interactions among disabled people, and between disabled people and the nondisabled who are in their intimate worlds, to discover how both members of any transaction are influenced by the presence of a known impairment in one or both of them. These reports lead us to question the way disability has been viewed in the stigma and social support literatures. Makas contributes to this analysis by advancing a methodology that distinguishes between "good" and "bad" disability attitudes.

Scheer and Groce, Darling, and Scotch all portray how different cultures and different political climates reshape the experience of having a disability. Impairment may be a ubiquitous "human constant," but response to it is not. Scheer and Groce carry on in the tradition of Hanks and Hanks (1948) to examine how different cultures, eras, institutions, and social structures influence the social integration of people with disabilities in 19th-century rural and 20th-century urban U.S. society.

Darling and Scotch each address the political responses generated by persons with disabilities and/or their advocates. Darling traces how families of disabled people have transformed a medical view of disability into a minority-group and political one. Scotch similarly analyzes the disability rights movement of the 1970s, focusing on the experience of disabled people themselves. These papers demonstrate that while the biological fact of disability may be a given, the environment need not be.

As a collection, these articles reframe disability as a minority-group issue in which a set of socially negotiated meanings of the body are played out psychologically, socially, and politically. They force reanalysis along several dimensions, pointing out the following:

1. How the experience of disability is influenced by professionals (Biklen), and how it can be studied by nondisabled researchers (Hahn; Frank; Makas).
2. That disability needs to be studied over time and in context, as a socially transforming and changing process, not a static characteristic of an individual (Ainlay; Becker; Mast; Schneider).
3. That a social-constructivist view of disability (Gergen, 1985) enables a reassessment of previously taken-for-granted views of the nature and consequences of life with impairment (Darling; Scheer & Groce; Scotch).
4. That accepting a minority-group perspective on disability and attending to all the aspects of the life space that extend beyond the person with the impairment causes social psychologists to raise new questions for research. Examples of such questions include the following: What sustains the belief that having a child with a disability is predominantly burdensome and tragic? What would make possible a different outcome? What does the experience of being close to someone with a disability do to broaden one's sense of moral community or to shrink it? What are the consequences and costs, for both disabled and nondisabled people, of an increasingly integrated society? Under what conditions, and with what consequences, does the independent-living movement or the disability-rights movement promote notions of individualism over notions of community? What are the psychological

barriers to a person with a disability getting involved in the disability-rights movement? What barriers keep progressives without disabilities from involving themselves in the disability-rights movement?

5. That quality-of-life judgments underpinning public and professional views of individuals like Baby Doe and Elizabeth Bouvia deserve serious reevaluation. Similarly, accepting the powerful role of environment as a mediating variable in outcomes for people with disabilities forces us to reexamine what a just allocation of resources would be.

This *JSI* volume is presented as an interdisciplinary, provocative exploration of an already existing literature on disability and a rapidly emerging transformed perspective on the topic. The 1948 *JSI* issue influenced social policy and the field of rehabilitation psychology. We hope that the ensuing pages will stimulate further development in social psychology and social policy.

NOTES

The authors wish to note their equal contributions to this article.

REFERENCES

ACLU Foundation of Southern California. (1983). *Elizabeth Bouvia v. County of Riverside* (Memorandum of points and authorities in support of application for temporary restraining order and permanent injunction). Los Angeles: Author.

Ainlay, S., Becker, G., & Coleman, L. (Eds.) (1986). *The dilemma of difference: A multi-disciplinary view of stigma.* New York: Plenum.

Asch, A. (1984). The experience of disability: A challenge for psychology. *American Psychologist, 39,* 529–536.

Asch, A., & Rousso, H. (1985). Therapists with disabilities: Theoretical and clinical issues. *Psychiatry, 48,* 1–12.

Barker, R. G. (1948). The social psychology of physical disability. *Journal of Social Issues, 4*(4), 28–37.

Becker, G., & Arnold, R. (1986). Stigma as a social and cultural construct. In S. Ainlay, G. Becker, & L. Coleman (Eds.), *The dilemma of difference: A multi-disciplinary view of stigma* (pp. 39–58). New York: Plenum.

Bouvia v. Superior Court of the State of California. Court of Appeal of the State of California. Second Appelate District, Division Two, 2nd Cir. No. B019134 (1986, April 16).

Bowe, F. (1980). *Rehabilitating America.* New York: Harper & Row.

Brickman, P., Rabinowitz, V. C., Karuza, J., Coates, D., Cohn, E., & Kidder, L. (1982). Models of helping and coping. *American Psychologist, 37,* 368–384.

Bulman, R., & Wortman, C. (1977). Attributions of blame and coping in the "real world": Severe accident victims react to their lot. *Journal of Personality and Social Psychology, 35,* 351–363.

Cain, L. F. (1948). The disabled child in school. *Journal of Social Issues, 4*(4), 90–93.

Census study reports one in five adults suffers from disability. (1986, December 23). *New York Times,* p. 67.

Davis, F. (1961). Deviance disavowal: The management of strained interaction by the visibly handicapped. *Social Problems, 9,* 120–132.

DeJong, G., & Lifchez, R. (1983). Physical disability and public policy. *Scientific American, 48,* 240–249.

Deutsch, M. (1985). *Distributive justice.* New Haven, CT: Yale University Press.

Disability Rag. (1984, February–March). Entire issue.

Disability Rights Coordinating Council (1983). *Elizabeth Bouvia v. County of Riverside* (Declaration of Carol Gill). Los Angeles: Author.

Dunkel-Schetter, C. (1984). Social support and cancer: Findings based on patient interviews and their implications. *Journal of Social Issues, 40*(4), 77–98.

Dworkin, A., & Dworkin, R. (Eds.) (1976). *The minority report.* New York: Praeger.

Editorial. *New York Times,* (1983, June 17).

Fine, M., & Asch, A. (1981). Disabled women: Sexism without the pedestal. *Journal of Sociology and Social Welfare, 8,* 233–248.

Fine, M., & Asch, A. (Eds.) (1988). *Women with disabilities: Essays in psychology, culture, and politics.* Philadelphia: Temple University Press.

French, R. de S. (1984). The long-term relationships of marked people. In E. E. Jones et al., *Social stigma: The psychology of marked relationships* (pp. 254–295). New York: Freeman.

Gergen, K. (1985). The social constructivist movement in modern psychology. *American Psychologist, 40,* 266–275.

Gibbons, F. X. (1986). Stigma and interpersonal relations. In S. Ainlay, G. Becker, & L. Coleman (Eds.), *The dilemma of difference: A multi-disciplinary view of stigma* (pp. 123–144). New York: Plenum.

Gliedman, J., & Roth, W. (1980). *The unexpected minority: Handicapped children in America.* New York: Harcourt, Brace, Jovanovich.

Goffman, E. (1963). *Stigma: Notes on the management of spoiled identity.* Englewood Cliffs, NJ: Prentice-Hall.

Groce, N. (1985). *Everyone here spoke sign language: Hereditary deafness on Martha's Vineyard.* Cambridge, MA: Harvard University Press.

Gurin, P. (1984). Review of *Relative deprivation and working women. Contemporary Psychology, 29,* 209–210.

Haber, L., & McNeil, J. (1983). *Methodological questions in the estimation of disability prevalence.* Washington, DC: Population Division, U.S. Bureau of the Census.

Hahn, H. (1983, March–April). Paternalism and public policy. *Society,* pp. 36–46.

Hanks, J. R., & Hanks, L. M. (1948). The physically handicapped in certain non-Occidental societies. *Journal of Social Issues, 4*(4), 11–19.

Hentoff, N. (1987). The awful privacy of Baby Doe. In A. Gardner & T. Joe (Eds.), *Images of the disabled: Disabling images* (pp. 161–180). New York: Praeger.

Hill, N., Mehnert, T., Taylor, T., Kagey, M., Leizhenko, S., et al. (1986). *The ICD survey of disabled Americans: Bringing disabled Americans into the mainstream.* New York: International Center for the Disabled.

Janoff-Bulman, R., & Frieze, I. H. (1983). A theoretical perspective for understanding reactions to victimization. *Journal of Social Issues, 39*(2), 1–17.

Jones, E. E., Farina, A., Hastorf, A. H., Markus, H., Miller, D. T., Scott, R. A., &

French, R. de S. (1984). *Social stigma: The psychology of marked relationships.* New York: Freeman.

Katz, I. (1981). *Stigma: A social-psychological analysis.* Hillsdale, NJ: Erlbaum.

Katzmann, R. A. (1986). *Institutional disability: The saga of transportation policy for the disabled.* Washington, D.C.: Brookings Institute.

Kleck, R. (1969). Physical stigma and task-oriented interactions. *Human Relations, 22,* 53–59.

Kleck, R., Ono, H., & Hastorf, A. (1966). The effects of physical deviance upon face-to-face interaction. *Human Relations, 19,* 425–436.

Krebs, D. L. (1970). Altruism: An examination of the concept and a review of the literature. *Psychological Bulletin, 73,* 258–302.

Ladieu, G., Adler, D. L., & Dembo, T. (1948). Studies in adjustment to visible injuries: Social acceptance of the injured. *Journal of Social Issues, 4*(4), 55–61.

Lerner, M. J. (1980). *The belief in a just world: A fundamental delusion.* New York: Plenum.

Meyerson, L. (1948a). Physical disability as a social psychological problem. *Journal of Social Issues, 4*(4), 2–9.

Meyerson, L. (1948b). A fair employment act for the disabled. *Journal of Social Issues, 4*(4), 107–109.

Meyerson, L. (1948c). Social action for the disabled. *Journal of Social Issues, 4*(4), 111–112.

Rehabilitation Act of 1973, Pub. L. No. 93–112, 87 Stat. 357 (1973).

Roth, W. (1983, March–April). Handicap as a social construct. *Society,* pp. 56–61.

Sampson, E. (1983). *Justice and the critique of pure psychology.* New York: Plenum.

Sarason, S. B. (1986). And what is the public interest? *American Psychologist, 41,* 899–906.

Schulz, R., & Decker, S. (1985). Long-term adjustment to physical disability: The role of social support, perceived control, and self-blame. *Journal of Personality and Social Psychology, 48,* 1162–1172.

Scotch, R. K. (1984). *From good will to civil rights: Transforming federal disability policy.* Philadelphia: Temple University Press.

Shumaker, S., & Brownell, A. (1984). Toward a theory of social support: Closing conceptual gaps. *Journal of Social Issues, 40*(4), 11–36.

Solomon, H. M. (1986). Stigma and Western culture: A historical approach. In S. Ainlay, G. Becker, & L. Coleman (Eds.), *The dilemma of difference: A multi-disciplinary view of stigma* (pp. 59–76). New York: Plenum.

Taylor, S. E., Wood, J. V., & Lichtman, R. R. (1983). "It could be worse": Selective evaluation as a response to victimization. *Journal of Social Issues, 39*(2), 19–40.

The $2,000 subway token. *New York Times,* (1984, June 23).

Unger, R. K., & Denmark, F. L. (1975). *Woman: Dependent or independent variable?* New York: Psychological Dimensions.

von Hentig, H. (1948). Physical desirability, mental conflict and social crisis. *Journal of Social Issues, 4*(4), 21–27.

Wright, B. A. (1960/1983). *Physical disability: A psychological approach.* New York: Harper & Row.

23. New Voices, New Visions: Toward a Lesbian/Gay Paradigm for Psychology

Laura S. Brown

VOICES LOST AND FOUND

What does it mean for psychology if the experiences of being lesbian and/or gay male, in all the diversity of meanings that those experiences can hold, are taken as core and central to definitions of reality rather than as a special topic tangential to basic understandings of human behavior, particularly human interactions? After all, just as there is no American Psychological Association division of the psychology of men or of white people, there is no special topic area called heterosexual studies in psychology. "Psychology," the official entity, values those experiences that are white, male, heterosexual, young, middle class, abled-bodied, and North American; thus has the universe of "human behavior" been defined. "Special topics," including lesbian and gay issues, have traditionally been defined as of special interest only, not in the core curriculum in reality or emotionally.

My raising of this essentially feminist question has roots both in personal experience and in a developing line of feminist theory. The personal experience, which was the catalyst for my thinking, has been both primary and most powerful and illustrates the feminist adage that the personal is political as well as theoretical. In 1987, I developed a supposedly untreatable neurological disorder of the voice called spastic dysphonia that left me literally speechless. For 3 months I had no voice; I experienced in an embodied way the powerlessness of the often-used metaphor of being unable to be heard. But

Reprinted by permission of the author and Cambridge University Press from *Psychology of Women Quarterly* 13 (1993): 445–58. © 1989 Cambridge University Press.

rather than accepting the verdict of Western medical science that my disorder, because neurological, was untreatable. I pursued non-Western medical care: acupuncture and Chinese herbal medicine, cranial osteopathic manipulation, spiritual healing. By deciding to change the point of view from which I understood my disorder, I regained a voice: a new and often fragile one, but a voice, nonetheless. It was a jarring reminder of the importance of not taking the view from the mainstream as the only one there is, and one that intuitively led me to develop the thought process represented in this work. If I could have a new voice by changing the point from which I understood my problem, could such a new voice not also be raised within psychology, a voice that would reflect another set of my experiences in the world, those of a white North American lesbian?

Concurrent with my personal experiences, a developing line of feminist theory has raised questions about the nature of the observer's perspective in science. Such theory suggests that the pretensions of mainstream science to objectivity, or to encompassing the universe of knowledge and meaning, are in fact evidence of white, androcentric ways of understanding (Harding, 1986; Rose, 1983). Rose and Harding have joined other authors in attempting to redefine the conditions of discourse within the sciences, including psychology and other social sciences, so as to make central and visible the previously excluded experiences of women. These theorists have argued not only for the simple inclusion of women in the discourse, but also that the terms of the discourse be changed, be reinvented, in order to move from an androcentric to a feminist science. Sandra Harding (1986), in particular, has argued that a feminist science would be one in which categories of discourse and understanding would of necessity become destabilized in order to move beyond the deeply internalized structures of Western thinking. Feminist science and social science would ask questions from the female experience.

But let us move beyond that. What happens if what has previously been a conceptual ghetto, even within feminist psychology, is redefined as the center of the universe of understanding? If the ways of knowing and of legitimizing knowledge are opened to understandings that are rooted in the phenomenology of being gay or lesbian in the world, what new voices and visions become available? Does the way in which psychologists explore lesbian and gay issues become transformed by asking such questions? How has psychology so far been shaped through the distorted lens of heterosexist psychological science and practice? Beyond that, what happens if a lesbian/gay paradigm is used as core to psychological science and practice in general? How do psychologists change their understandings of such phenomena as intimacy, parenting, attraction, relationships, or gender, if they make assumptions based in experiences of being lesbian or gay?

In order to begin the process of answering such questions, the assumptions that lie within the questions themselves must be explored. Such questions assume first that current paradigms reflect a heterosexual reality, and second that it is possible to identify what is meant by lesbian/gay reality in such a way as to address issues from that perspective.

HETEROSEXISM IN PSYCHOLOGY

The first assumption is based on the notion that the worldview of North American psychology, besides being biased by sexism, racism, and other exclusionary modal perspectives, views human behavior through the lens of heterosexual experience and is thus inherently heterosexist. What do I mean by that assertion? Concretely, this takes a number of forms. Our knowledge base is heterosexist. That is, it assumes heterosexuality and heterosexual forms of relating as the norm. More precisely, white, middle class, North American, married, Christian, able-bodied heterosexuality is defined as the norm. All other forms of experience are viewed in contrast to the norm. This non-conscious heterosexism manifests in myriad subtle ways: there are "couples," meaning heterosexual couples, and then there are "lesbian and gay couples." There are "families," meaning nuclear, two-heterosexual-parent families, and "lesbian and gay families." And so on, ad nauseam. Even in the field of psychology of women, which has probably contributed more than any other field of psychology toward the movement to deconstruct psychology and dethrone the god of logical positivism (Hare-Mustin & Marecek, 1988), there are "women," and then there are "lesbians," tucked away in our own chapters of the textbooks. Lesbian experiences are seen as unique, offering little to the understanding of the norm. What occurs instead is that we are compared to the norm, in the past to demonstrate our pathology and, more recently, to affirm our normalcy. Or we are simply categorized as an interesting variant of human experience, equal but still separate and always marginal.

This tendency to perceive lesbian and gay issues within the broadest scope of that term as tangential "special topics" robs psychology of much of its ability to understand human behavior. There are certain aspects of lesbian and gay experience which, if made central to all psychological inquiry, would change and expand the ability to comprehend both the intrapsychic and the interpersonal. But to use such a universe as core to hypothesis generation requires answering my second question regarding the definition of lesbian and gay experience.

DEFINING A LESBIAN AND GAY REALITY

In some ways, this is more complex and problematic than establishing the presence of heterosexism in psychology. This complexity exists largely because there is not one unitary lesbian and gay reality. Instead, there are multiple realities. The experience of being a white lesbian or gay man will be different from that of a lesbian or gay man of color and different within each ethnic group. The lesbian or gay man who comes from an orthodox religious background will be different from those who grew up in more religiously liberal settings. Also, a person's age cohort has a profound impact on the experience of being a sexual minority person, as does age of coming out and past history of overt heterosexual identity such as marriage. Class plays a powerful role in defining the experience and expression of being lesbian or gay. Moreover, North American lesbians and gay men live different realities than do our peers in other countries and cultures. Furthermore, constructions and parameters of gender separate the experiences of lesbians from those of gay men.

Even the concept of sexual orientation is one that is not clearly defined. Although, for the purpose of lesbian and gay rights, we may adhere to the notion that sexual orientation is a fixed and relatively immutable phenomenon, clinically and experientially we are aware that it is a fluid, continuous one, with the words "lesbian" and "gay" encompassing a range of internal experiences and social constructions of attraction, arousal, identity, and affection (Greenberg, 1988; Kitzinger, 1987). Although there is a seductive pull to see ourselves as a unitary, and thus a united group, lesbians and gay men are more diverse than my own first minority group, Jews, where we joke that, "if there are two Jews, there are three schuls" (i.e. three opinions). Anyone who has been active in the lesbian and gay community will bear testimony to our variability and the challenges that this can present to the well-meaning gay pride parade organizer. Yet we are a nation of sorts: 10% of the U.S. population is larger than the total population of my partner's native country of The Netherlands. And all nations contain a certain amount of diversity.

So, with all that diversity, are there within this "country" of internal experience those elements of being lesbian or gay male that are common to all and can be said to form a "lesbian and gay reality" from which to reconceptualize our study of human behavior? I would like to suggest that those common elements do exist cross-situationally, and that they are in fact central to my movement toward a new vision.

Biculturalism

The first among these common elements is the experience of biculturalism. Lesbians and gay men are always simultaneously participants in both heterosexual experience and lesbian and gay experiences. Our families of origin are usually comprised of heterosexual persons who participate in the privileges and rituals of the dominant heterosexual majority. Many of us have behaved heterosexually during our lifetimes, although we often revise the meaning of these aspects of our histories when we embrace a lesbian or gay identity. We are often very much in the position to "pass" for heterosexual and may experience discomfort with those aspects of ourselves or our peers that conform to cultural stereotypes of the "obvious" lesbian or gay man, while simultaneously cultivating certain aspects of those behaviors in more secure settings (Nestle, 1987). With rare exceptions, all lesbians and gay men must be in both cultures most of the time.

Marie Root (1988), writing on biracial identity development, pointed out that the experiences of the biracial person include having both minority and dominant cultures as part of one's family of origin. She suggested that this can lead to a sense of confusion and of non-fit in any context. While a person who is purely one minority group or another may feel free in the process of minority identity development to reject dominant culture. Root pointed out that for the biracial individual such a rejection also implies a rejection of a part of oneself. Biracial individuals are also often in the position of being able to choose to "pass" as members of the dominant culture and may feel ambivalence or distaste for those family members, often siblings and one parent, who are more physically like the devalued minority group and who threaten their passing status. In order to develop a functional biracial identity, the biracial person must develop ways to live within this matrix of complexity, to balance and value the differences that lie within.

Extrapolating from Root's model, it may be that living and developing biculturally, while not unique to lesbian and gay men, is an experience that may create different ways of knowing and understanding oneself and one's reality. A healthy resolution of such conflicts of identity is one that must eschew either/or perspectives on who one is and embrace what is "other" within oneself. Such a successful resolution of a bicultural identity may create a propensity to view things on continua rather than in a polarized fashion. Being able to operate within grey areas and on middle grounds and balancing the demands of two divergent groups that are now internalized self-representations are characteristic of the experience of being gay or lesbian. Walter Williams's (1987) work on sexual identity among Native American cultures provides some confirmation for this idea. He noted that in many Native nations, the persons who occupied the interim space between the genders and whose behavior might be identified as gay or lesbian within white American culture, were perceived as seers, shamans, capable of greater wisdom than their clearly heterosexually defined peers. Different external factors may operate to influence the felt and lived experiences of this bicultural existence, and some lesbians and gay men, for example, lesbians or gay men of color in North America, actually may have multicultural identities.

This experience, like that of the biracial person, is distinct from that of members of racial and ethnic minorities in that even at the most intimate level of family relationships, there will be cultural differences and pulls to participate in the dominant culture in ways that do not exist for members of racial and ethnic minorities whose families share their group membership. The experience of having both self and other within one's identity development creates a singular and potentially powerfully heuristic model for self-understanding. The constant "management of difference" (deMonteflores, 1986) can lead to a rich and distinctive perspective on reality if we are willing to embrace and value it, rather than stigmatize it as not conforming to the dominant norm. The bicultural perspective of lesbians and gay men facilitates an understanding of the rules by which the mainstream culture operates, while simultaneously being able to envision new forms by which the same tasks might be accomplished.

Marginality

A second experience that informs a lesbian and gay reality is that of marginality. Even in the most supportive and accepting of settings, we carry the experience of existential "otherness." For many lesbians and gay men, the first awareness of who we were was simply that vague sense of difference and distance from the rituals of the heterosexual culture, of not understanding what our friends saw in the opposite gender, of watching to see how heterosexual courtship rituals were played out so that we could imitate them and fit in (Adair & Adair, 1978).

Mary Daly long ago pointed out how this "otherness" can allow women to see what is not seen, to know what is forbidden to know, because they are not sanctified as knowers (Daly, 1973). Harding (1986) argued that a feminist epistemology depends upon the valuing of "alienated," "bifurcated," or "oppositional" consciousnesses in theory making. Lesbian and gay male experience reflects this alienated, marginal worldview, no matter how well an individual lesbian or gay man appears to be integrated into the dominant social context.

It is no coincidence that one of the ways that political and religious conservatives attempt to undermine the movement against violence against women and children is to "lesbian-bait" its leadership (Schechter, 1982). In essence, what they are saying is that only a woman who is, as Adrienne Rich (1979) puts it, "disloyal to civilization" will be able to continue to break the patriarchy's silence on its crimes. It's no wonder that any man who attempts to analyze and move beyond the defined male gender roles is called "faggot": who else is enough outside the definition of the role to see alternate possibilities for male existence (Grahn, 1984)? In the catcalls of those who would annihilate lesbians and gay males lie germs of the truth; our experience of the world as outsiders may allow us to see differently, hear differently, and thus potentially challenge the conventional wisdom. We may be freer to see, speak and act other truths, to have, as Judy Grahn says, "another mother tongue."

These other truths can be powerful affirmations of our experience; they can also be frightening challenges to the culture of the mainstream and even to lesbians and gay men who are struggling with our own conflicting desires to both fit in and be who we are. One striking example of the outcomes of empowering our alienated lesbian and gay knowing has been in how we have created our families.

As asked by Dykewomon (1988) in a society caught up in sanctification of "The Family," can there be such a thing as a functional family under patriarchy? While this is also an essential feminist question found early in this wave of the U.S. women's movement in the work of Firestone (1970), lesbians and gay men have put that question into practice by the creation of families that are not patriarchal. Likewise, there may be a specifically lesbian way to raise children (Cooper, 1987), different from the power-unequal norms of the heterosexist family in which age differences are assumed inherently to connote power imbalance. Also challenged is the assumption that biological parents of both genders are necessary for the creation of emotionally healthy children, and the assumption that the only appropriate number of parents is two (Pollack & Vaughn, 1987). These challenges have not been without a price to the lesbian and gay male parents who have lost access to their children of blood or spirit for daring to raise such questions. Yet, many continue to raise them, knowing by looking in from the outside that the current paradigm of "family" cannot be the only one.

Normative Creativity

A final common theme is that of being normatively different and thus creative. In other words, by lacking clear rules about how to be lesbian and gay in the world, we have made up the rules as we go along. For example, in their recent book on lesbian couples, Merilee Clunis and Dorsey Green (1988), discuss how they decided what was normative for lesbian couples. They put it rather simply: if a lot of lesbians seemed to be doing it, this must be the norm. And these norms challenge the dominant notions about what occurs in intimate interpersonal relationships; they question notions about how agency and communion function within a couple, about the healthy expression of dependency needs between adult partners. Simply *being* lesbian or gay has been something we have had to invent for ourselves (Grahn, 1984), since whatever roadmaps the dominant culture offered have been full of wrong turns and uncharted territories. This need to invent for ourselves has been equal parts terrifying and exhilarating (*vide* the common theme of works on lesbian-and-gay-affirmative therapy regarding the problems due to the lack of clear models for lesbians and gay men). However, those who claim this as a positive and possibly unique aspect of our experience as lesbians and gay men begin to embrace the possibilities for actively deconstructing and re-creating our visions of human behavior far beyond the field of lesbian and gay studies.

In summary, there are three intertwined themes that define, cross-situationally, the experience of being lesbian and gay: biculturalism, with its requirements of juggling, balance, and living in and with ambiguity; marginality, with its perspective that is both outside and within the mainstream; and normative creativity, the ability to create boundaries that will work where none exist from tools that may be only partially suited to the task. If psychologists adopt these as guiding principles for their work, where can and does this lead?

TOWARD A LESBIAN AND GAY PARADIGM FOR PSYCHOLOGY

A first and, for those in academic settings, somewhat risky step is to reevaluate the methodologies by which the knowledge base is generated. Mary Ballou (1988) has identified five epistemological perspectives that might be available for studying human behavior and pointed out how they lead to very different types of "revealed truths" when applied to inquiry. If scholars attempt to work from a valuing of the mixed, the ambiguous, the marginal, then it becomes extremely difficult to fit themselves solely within the logical positivist framework dominant in psychology. After all, such a framework assumes that phenomena are either A or B, and that if enough rigor is used in the design and test of a hypothesis, one truth can be found. This has a seductive flavor to it; as Harding (1986) pointed out, the tendency to perceive the universe in logical positivist terms is supported by such a wide variety of institutional and cultural structures that it "cannot be shucked off by mental hygiene and willpower alone" (p. 662). But this tendency must be continuously questioned since an exclusionary paradigm would not fit well with an application of lesbian and gay reality to the study of human behavior.

An alternative approach that draws upon lesbian and gay experience must allow for the use of many methodologies and the possibility of many, even conflicting, answers. A lesbian/gay psychology would be one of many truths, one in which a dialectical tension would constantly operate in such a manner as to stimulate new and wider inquiry. Rather than endless replications of the old, researchers would begin asking the questions not yet raised in the first place and then question further the answers received. If they allow their scholarship to live in as many realities as they do themselves, they find the possibility of many shades of meaning.

This has certainly been the case with my work in the area of psychotherapy ethics. By working from my lived experience as a white lesbian therapist practicing in the context of diverse lesbian communities, I've come to see ethical action as a continuous variable. One is not either ethical or nonethical, but changing and varying degrees of ethical at various levels of affective, cognitive, and behavioral expression during different periods of one's work as a therapist (Brown, 1985, 1987, 1988). I've found that simply having rules about what to do narrowed my thinking and excluded that which had never been considered, thus making it invisible. I've also learned that lesbian and gay male therapists, faced with situations unpredicted and unenvisioned by the ethics codes, have had to be creative in the development of norms that would allow us to behave ethically and yet still live within the realities of our communities (Gonsiorek, 1987; Hayden, 1987; Moss, 1987). For instance, the ethical principle regarding dual relationships (APA, 1981) gives little guidance about what to do when a therapist's former lover becomes lovers with a current client; notwithstanding, if that's what one has to deal with, and more than a few lesbian and gay male therapists have, the ethical principles for it are created along the way. The paradigms for ethical therapy evolving from lesbian and gay experience stress, not rules and regulations, but the relationship of the therapist to her or his community, and the relational context in which therapy takes place. This different perspective has allowed lesbian and gay therapists to both ask and answer questions that cannot even be raised in the conceptual universe of mainstream psychology ethics.

A second implication of adopting a paradigm for psychology that would embrace the themes of lesbian and gay experience would be a continuous reevaluation of taken-for-granted concepts in all aspects of psychology. For example, psychologists usually hold heterosexual couples as a norm simply because of their majority status. But it might be possible that what is normative for lesbian couples is in fact healthy for any intimate pair. In a paper written since her book was published, Dorsey Green (1988) raised this possibility when she discussed the issues of merger, fusion, and contact boundaries in relationships, suggesting that perhaps the merger that a healthy lesbian couple experiences is more normative and functional for intimate pairs than the illusion of autonomy and distance within a relationship that exists, she believed, in heterosexual couples simply as an artifact of gender roles. In other words, by taking the position of outsider and suggesting that the emperor in fact has no clothes, we may move psychology toward a deeper and more complex understanding of interpersonal relationships. This movement would have particular significance for the study of behaviors related to sexuality, gender role and identity, intimacy and bonding, and the development of family dynamics. While feminist psychology has commented at length on the problems of the "patriarchal, father-absent family" (Luepnitz, 1988), how might inquiries be expanded by looking first at the functioning of healthy lesbian and gay families?

An analogy can be made here to work that develops non-North American cultural versions of psychology and that generates norms and hypotheses about development from within those cultural contexts. Carla Bradshaw (1988), in a paper on the interface between Japanese psychology and feminist therapy theory, pointed out how even the basic process of personality development is quite different when viewed through the lens of Japanese experience. Bradshaw pointed out that the concepts of dependence and individuation carry strikingly different meaning in Japanese culture from that in North American society and noted how behavior that would be considered pathological or pathogenic here represents normative and functional ways of being.

Similar work is under way in the Philippines to create a "Sikolohiyang Pilipino," Philippine psychology from within a Philippine cultural context (Protacio-Marcelino, 1988). The explicit aim of this work is to strip away North American concepts and ways of seeing from psychological theory and practice. It uses Philippine language and experience to develop an entirely new and different way of seeing and knowing human behavior. For example, Protacio-Marcelino analyzed the notion of "personality" in Western psychology, contrasting it with the eight different terms in Tagalog, one of the primary indigenous languages of the Philippines, that can define "personality" in terms of the context in which the person is found and the relationship of one actor to another. From the point of view of Philippine culture, a person has not one personality, but many, each deter-mined by the relational context in which she or he is acting.

Clearly the diversity that exists within the lesbian and gay popula-tion makes the explication of a lesbian and gay psychology a chal-lenging task. Or perhaps not; within any culture, however defined, there must be levels of difference to be accounted for by a psychology of that culture. However, the analogies hold in many ways. Protacio-Marcelino and her colleagues (1988) spoke of how psychology in the Philippines was intellectually colonized by Americans; so, too, is American psychology colonized and dominated by heterosexual expe-rience. By defining norms and terms from within lesbian and gay realities, psychologists ask themselves how these new paradigms might broaden the understanding of heterosexual realities as well.

Finally, by working from within lesbian and gay realities, the study of lesbian and gay issues will and must change. This new approach in no way denigrates that which has been done before and will continue to be done by way of research and practice in the field. Everything that has come before has allowed for the conceptual leaps in this essay. But scholars have been constrained by working within the dominant paradigm so that only certain kinds of knowledge are pursued or revealed. To quote Audre Lorde (1984): "The master's tools will never dismantle the master's house," and such a renovation is what many lesbians and gay men in psychology had in mind when, a decade or more ago, we began to challenge the notion of homosexuality as psychopathology.

In challenging that one dearly held tenet of one branch of the tree of the behavioral sciences, we were, in the end, also challenging the whole structure, all of the assumptions that went into creating that idea. It's not certain that we realized that or even would have admit-ted how radical in fact this apparently simple goal was. To take the word out of the *Diagnostic and Statistical Manual* was simply one aspect of challenging the entire system of thinking that had allowed it to be placed there at all. Thus, the ideas suggested in this essay are simply a carrying forward of that action. At the very first APA program on lesbian and gay issues, Barbara Love (1975) suggested that lesbians might be the model of healthy female development. Her paper appealed intuitively to many, but few have yet to follow concretely the direction in which this non-psychologist lesbian activ-ist was pointing: that is, to rearrange the norms and then to go about the business of seeking greater self-knowledge.

Some initial steps have been taken, both in psychology and in related fields of endeavor; the volume *Lesbian Psychologies* (Boston Lesbian Psychologies Collective, 1987) provides an example of what is needed in the behavioral sciences. Some of the most exciting work developing from lesbian and gay paradigms is occurring in philosophy (Hoagland, 1988) and theology (Heyward, 1989). Both Sarah Lucia Hoagland and Carter Heyward proposed epistemologies that flow from the embodied experience of living as lesbians (Hoagland, 1988) or either lesbians or gay men (Heyward, 1989) and provide models that could be used for psychological inquiry as well.

In a paper I gave at APA in 1986 in a symposium on the state of the art in lesbian and gay affirmative psychotherapy (Brown, 1986), I suggested that lesbian and gay therapists were at a point where we needed to ask more complex questions about our work. I believe now that in order to ask those questions in satisfying ways, we need to use a lesbian/gay paradigm to construct the process of inquiry. For instance, one question raised in that earlier paper is "Why are so many lesbians in therapy?" It is now known, thanks to the National Lesbian Health Care Survey, just how high the numbers are: 78% of their respondents were current or former therapy clients (Bradford & Ryan, 1987).

To avoid quick and easy answers to this question or answers that reflect the perspectives of the dominant culture on either lesbians or psychotherapy, the questions inside the questions must be asked, that is, create a dynamic tension within psychology. What does therapy mean in a lesbian and gay context? What associations arise to the word, what does it suggest to the sexual minority speaker and hearer, the sentence, "I'm in therapy." Who are the therapists and how do they see their work? Is the therapist, particularly the lesbian or gay male therapist working within their own communities, meaning something different at non-conscious levels by her or his choice of work than does the heterosexual therapist? What is the interaction of being in therapy with other experiences in the world as lesbians or gay men? Are we defining being in therapy as evidence of pathology, which has traditionally been the case? Or have lesbians and gay men re-visioned the meaning of therapy as prima facie evidence of health and health-seeking behaviors, as one useful and appropriate strategy for sanely managing to live in the ambiguity, which, in the final analysis, is the situation for most late 20th century Americans, not only those of us on the official margin?

This last question is one that quite directly flows from the lesbian/ gay paradigm proposed here; that is, it is an outsider question, one that sees strength in what has been called weakness, one that questions that which is taken for granted about the meaning of therapy in society. It is a question about the ritual of therapy that emphasizes how the context gives that ritual place and meaning. These are questions that go beyond the statistics and encourage a search for the meaning given to the experience by culture, context, and living in a particular way. And those are the sorts of questions that psychologists need to ask in all of their work.

In proposing this new voice and vision, I am raising more questions here than I am able to provide answers to. I'm not entirely certain myself of all the concrete implications of the paradigm that I'm suggesting; in writing this essay, I have discovered just how much this idea still exists within me preconsciously, felt but unformed. Audre Lorde (1978), in *The Uses of the Erotic,* said that "in order to perpetuate itself every oppression must corrupt or distort those various sources of power within the culture of the oppressed that can provide energy for change." One such source of power is the process of owning and valuing as central one's experience even when the words are lacking in the dominant reality to describe it. My own thinking is still struggling through the muck of that distortion. It is my hope that by taking you with me as I continue that journey, I have set you to thinking, too, and that between us we will give form to what is still only a vague imagining on my part. We can pursue the comfort of the mainstream, or we can search for new voices and visions as psychology moves past its centenary with lesbian and gay psychology finally in place.

NOTES

An initial version of this article was given as the Division 44 Presidential Address at the Convention of the American Psychological Association, August 1988. For her invaluable help in making that first version come to life, I would like to thank my partner, Miriam Vogel, who got me through the first stage of my illness with love and courage, put up with my obsessing about writing this article for many months, then read the first draft and pointed out that which was still missing from my discussions. I'm also indebted to all of the presenters at the 1988 Advanced Feminist Therapy Institute, whose papers gave form and substance to my ideas. This version of the article owes a debt of gratitude to Jeanne Marecek, who invited its presence, and to two anonymous reviewers who made extremely helpful comments that allowed me to tie my own thinking into the feminist theoretical mainstream.

The use of full names in this article reflects a stylistic tradition of the Feminist Therapy Institute, which is to make the gender of a source visible to my readers. It is essential, in knowing how I came to my way of thinking, to know the perspectives of those who have influenced me.

The use of first-person pronouns to refer to lesbians and gay men is also a reflection of the feminist model of referring to one's own membership in a group about which one is writing.

REFERENCES

Adair, N., & Adair, C. (1978). *Word is out: Stories of some of our lives.* New York: New Glide/Delta.

American Psychological Association [APA]. (1981). Ethical principles of psychologists. *American Psychologist, 36,* 633–638.

Ballou, M. (1988, May). *Building feminist theory through feminist principles.* Paper presented at the Seventh Advanced Feminist Therapy Institute Conference, Seattle, WA.

Boston Lesbian Psychologies Collective (Eds.). (1987). *Lesbian psychologies: Explorations and challenges.* Urbana: University of Illinois Press.

Bradford, J., & Ryan, C. (1987). *National lesbian health care survey: Mental health implications.* Richmond: Virginia Commonwealth University Survey Research Laboratory.

Bradshaw, C. (1988, May). *Japanese psychology: What can Eastern thought contribute to feminist theory and therapy?* Paper presented at the Seventh Advanced Feminist Therapy Institute Conference, Seattle, WA.

Brown, L. S. (1985). Power, responsibility, boundaries: Ethical concerns for the lesbian feminist therapist. *Lesbian Ethics, 1,* 30–45.

Brown, L. S. (1986, August). A time to be critical: Directions and developments in lesbian-affirmative therapy. In B. Sang (Chair), *Lesbian and gay affirmative psychotherapy: State of the art.* Symposium presented at the Convention of the American Psychological Association, Washington, DC.

Brown, L. S. (1987, August). Beyond thou shalt not: Developing conceptual frameworks for ethical decision-making. In L. Garnets (Chair), *Ethical and boundary issues for lesbian and gay psychotherapists.* Symposium presented at the Convention of the American Psychological Association, New York, NY.

Brown, L. S. (1988). From perplexity to complexity: Thinking about ethics in the lesbian therapy community. *Women and Therapy, 8,* 13–26.

Clunis, D. M., & Green, G. D. (1988). *Lesbian couples.* Seattle: Seal Press.

Cooper, B. (1987). The radical potential in lesbian mothering of daughters. In S. Pollack & J. Vaughn (Eds.), *Politics of the heart: A lesbian parenting anthology* (pp. 233–240) Ithaca, NY: Firebrand Books.

Daly, M. (1973). *Beyond God the father: Toward a philosophy of women's liberation.* Boston: Beacon Press.

deMonteflores, C. (1986). Notes on the management of difference. In T. S. Stein & C. J. Cohen (Eds.), *Contemporary perspectives on psychotherapy with lesbians and gay men* (pp. 73–104). New York: Plenum Medical.

Dykewomon, E. (1988). Notes for a magazine. *Sinister Wisdom: A Journal for the Lesbian Imagination in the Arts and Politics* [Special Issue on Surviving Psychiatric Assault]. *36,* pp. 2–6.

Firestone, S. (1970). *The dialectic of sex.* New York: William Morrow.

Gonsiorek, J. (1987, August). Ethical issues for gay male therapists. In L. Garnets (Chair) *Ethical and boundary issues for lesbian and gay psychotherapists.* Symposium presented at the Convention of the American Psychological Association, New York, NY.

Grahn, J. (1984). *Another mother tongue: Gay words, gay worlds.* Boston: Beacon Press.

Green, G. D. (1988, May). *Is separation really so great?* Paper presented at the Seventh Advanced Feminist Therapy Institute Conference, Seattle, WA.

Greenberg, D. (1988). *The construction of homosexuality.* Chicago: University of Chicago Press.

Harding, S. (1986). The instability of the analytical categories of feminist theory. *Signs: Journal of Women in Culture and Society, 11,* 645–664.

Hare-Mustin, R. T., & Marecek, J. (1988). The meaning of difference: Gender theory, post-modernism, and psychology. *American Psychologist, 43,* 455–464.

Hayden, M. (1987, January). *Clinical issues in boundary setting and maintenance.* Paper presented at a conference, Boundary Dilemmas in the Client-Therapist Relationship, Los Angeles, CA.

Heyward, C. (1989). *Touching our strength: The erotic as power and the love of god.* New York: Harper & Row.

Hoagland, S. L. (1988). *Lesbian ethics: Toward new value.* Palo Alto: Institute of Lesbian Studies.

Kitzinger, C. (1987). *The social construction of lesbianism.* London: Sage.

Lorde, A. (1978). *Uses of the erotic: The erotic as power.* Trumansburg, NY: Crossing Press.

Lorde, A. (1984). *Sister outsider.* Trumansburg, NY: Crossing Press.

Love, B. (1975, August). *A case for lesbians as role models for healthy adult women.* Paper presented at the convention of the American Psychological Association, Chicago, IL.

Luepnitz, D. A. *The family interpreted: feminist theory in clinical practice.* New York: Basic Books.

Moss, L. E. (1987, January). *The problem of overlapping relationships with clients.* Paper presented at a conference, Boundary Dilemmas in the Client-Therapist Relationship, Los Angeles, CA.

Nestle, J. (1987). *A restricted country.* Ithaca, NY: Firebrand Books.

Pollack, S., & Vaughn, J. (Eds.). (1987). *Politics of the heart: A lesbian parenting anthology.* Ithaca, NY: Firebrand Books.

Protacio-Marcelino, E. (1988, May). *Toward understanding the psychology of the Filipino.* Paper presented at the Seventh Advanced Feminist Therapy Institute, Seattle, WA.

Rich, A. (1979). *On lies, secrets, and silences.* New York: Norton.

Root, M. P. P. (1988, May). *Resolving "other" status: The process of identity development in biracial individuals.* Paper presented at the Seventh Advanced Feminist Therapy Institute, WA.

Rose, H. (1983). Hand, brain, and heart: A feminist epistemology for the natural sciences. *Signs: A Journal of Women in Culture and Society, 9,* 73–90.

Schechter, S. (1982). *Women and male violence: The visions and struggles of the battered women's movement.* Boston: South End Press.

Williams, W. (1987). *Spirit and the flesh: Sexual diversity in American Indian culture.* Boston: Beacon Press.

24. Resolving "Other" Status: Identity Development of Biracial Individuals

Maria P. P. Root

Half-breed, mulatto, mixed, eurasian, mestizo, amerasian. These are the *"others,"* biracial individuals, who do not have a clear racial reference group (Henriques, 1975; Moritsugu, Foerster, & Morishima, 1978) and have had little control over how they are viewed by society. Because of their ambiguous ethnic identity and society's refusal to view the races as equal, mixed race people begin life as *marginal people.* Freire (1970) observes that *marginality is not a matter of choice, but rather a result of oppression of dominant over subordinate groups.*

The challenge for a nonoppressive theory and therapy, as feminist perspectives attempt, is twofold. First, racism must be recognized and challenged within the therapist's and theorist's world. Without meeting this challenge, it is unlikely that nonpathological models of mental health for mixed race persons can be developed. Second, theoretical conceptualization and application to therapy must become multiracial and multicultural to accurately reflect the process of more than a single racial group. New templates and models for identity development are needed which reflect respect for difference. Necessarily, these theories will need to deviate from traditional linear or systemic models which both have singular endpoints to define mental health. These models are based upon male mental health or, more recently, alternative models define white women's mental health. Current models of mental health do not accommodate the process by which individuals who have "other" identities, such as biracial and or gay/lesbian, arrive at a positive sense of

Reprinted with permission of The Haworth Press, Inc. from *Women and Therapy* 9 (1990): 185–205 © 1990 The Haworth Press, Inc.

self-identity or maintain a positive identity in the face of oppressive attitudes.

In this essay, the phenomenological experience of "otherness" in a biracial context is described and its socio-political origins explored. The integration of biracial heritage into a positive self-concept is complicated and lengthy. An alternative model for resolution of ethnic identity is offered which takes into account the forces of socio-cultural, political, and familial influences on shaping the individual's experience of their biracial identity. The uniqueness of this essay's approach is that several strategies of biracial identity resolution are offered with no inherent judgment that one resolution is better than another. Instead, the problems and advantages inherent with each type of resolution are discussed. It is proposed that individuals may shift their resolution strategies throughout their life-time in order to nurture a positive identity.

While early sociological theory might suggest that such a model as proposed here describes a "marginal personality" (Stonequist, 1935), or in DSM-III-R nosology inadequate personality or borderline personality, recent research suggests that biracial young adults are generally well adjusted (Hall, 1980; Pouissaint, 1984). Thus, the resolution of major conflicts inherent in the process of racial identity development may result in a flexibility to move between strategies which may reflect positive coping and adaptive abilities and be independent of the integrity of the individual's personality style.

ASSUMPTIONS ABOUT THE HIERARCHY OF COLOR IN THE UNITED STATES

Several general assumptions are made throughout this essay which are important for understanding the origins and dynamics of conflict surrounding the biracial individual. These dynamics further influence the developmental process of identity resolution.

First, in the United States, despite our polychromatic culture, we are divided into white and non-white. The positive imagery created by the "melting-pot" philosophy of the United States is relevant to white ethnic groups of immigrants such as the Irish, French, and Scandinavian people and not Africans, Asians, Hispanics, or even on home territory, American Indians. Cultural pluralism is neither appreciated nor encouraged by the larger culture.

Second, white is considered superior to non-white: the privileges and power assumed by whites are desired by non-whites. It is from this assumption attempts are made to prevent racial mixing because free interaction assumes equality. A corollary of this assumption is that mixed race persons who are part white and can pass as such will be very likely to strive for this racial identity in order to have maximum social power and to escape the oppression directed towards people of color.

The third assumption is that there is a hierarchy of racial/cultural groups based upon their similarity to middle-class white social structure and values. Thus, in general, Asian Americans have a higher social status than Black Americans in white America.

The hierarchical social status system based upon color has oppressed biracial people in two major ways. Both reasons stem from American society's fear of "racial pollution" (Henriques, 1975) (an attitude that was acutely reflected in Hitler's Germany). First, biracial persons have been given little choice in how they are identified. Any person with non-white ethnic features or traceable non-white blood is considered non-white (cf. Henriques, 1975). As a result, Poussaint (1984) notes than any individual with one black and one non-black parent is considered black. Because Asian ethnic groups can be equally oppressive in their fear of "racial pollution" (cf. Murphy-Shigematsu, 1986; Wagatsuma, 1973), a child that is half Asian and half anything else, particularly black, is identified by the blood of the non-Asian parent. Mixed race persons from two minority groups are likely to experience oppression from the racial group of heritage which has higher social status. This method of "irrational," incomplete racial classification has made identity resolution for the biracial individual very difficult and oppressive.

The second source of oppression stems from society's silence on biracialism as though if it is ignored, the issue will go away. It was only as recently as 1967 that the Supreme Court ruled in the *Lovings* case of Virginia that anti-miscegenation laws were unconstitutional, a ruling based on an interpretation of the 14th amendment (1868) to the Constitution that could have been made any time in the previous 100 years (Sickels, 1972). Subsequently, the last 12 states with anti-miscegenation laws were forced to overturn them. However, this ruling does not change attitudes. Society still prohibits interracial unions (Petroni, 1973).

The last assumption about the hierarchy of color is necessary for understanding the marginality of biracial persons who are part white. Because whites have been the oppressors in the United States, there is a mistrust by people of color of those accepted by or identified as white. Subsequently, those biracial individuals who are part white (and look white) will at times find it harder to gain acceptance by people of color by virtue of the attitudes and feelings that are projected onto them because of their white heritage and the oppression it symbolizes to people of color (Louise, 1988).

Being mixed race, like interracial marriages, has meant different things at different times (e.g., whether it reflects sexual oppression of a minority group, or equity and similarity of racial groups). Nevertheless, mixed race persons have always had an ambiguous ethnic identity to resolve. *It is the marginal status imposed by society rather than the objective mixed race of biracial individuals which poses a severe stress to positive identity development.* There are few if any role models due to the lack of a clear racial reference group. Friends, parents, and other people of color usually do not comprehend the unique situation and intrapersonal conflict inherent in the resolution of an ambiguous ethnic identity for mixed race persons.

THE BEGINNINGS OF "OTHERNESS"

The themes described in the development of awareness of otherness in biracial persons have been highlighted in several recent research reports, e.g., Asian-White (Murphy-Shigematsu, 1986), Black-Asian (Hall, 1980), and Black-White mixes (Pouissaint, 1984). The themes of the early years are around race, family, acceptance, difference, and isolation. It is suggested that the intrapersonal and interpersonal conflicts which emerge out of these themes are circular and transitory. They reemerge at different points in development with a chance for a greater depth of resolution and understanding with each cycle.

The awareness of "otherness," or ambiguous ethnicity begins early when a child starts to be aware of color around age three (Goodman, 1968) but before a sense of racial identity is formed. An ethnic name or non-ethnic name, which may not be congruent with how a child is perceived, can intensify this awareness. Initially this awareness develops from being identified as different from within any ethnic community. Questions and comments such as, "Where are you from?" "Mixed children are so attractive," and "You are so interesting looking," heighten the feeling of otherness. This acknowledgment of a child's ethnic mix or differentness is natural and not in and of itself harmful or particularly stressful. In fact, the special attention initially may feel good. It is the combination of inquisitive looks, longer than passing glances to comprehend unfamiliar racial-ethnic features (an "unusual or exotic look"), and comments of surprise to find out that the child is one or the other parent's biological child *along with* disapproving comments and nonverbal communication that begin to convey to the child that this otherness is "undesirable or wrong." Suddenly, previously neutral acknowledgment or special attention is interpreted as negative attention. It is with these reactions that the child in her or his dichotomous way of knowing and sorting the world may label her or his otherness as bad. The child's egocentrism can result in assuming blame or responsibility for having done something wrong related to their color; subsequently, one may notice in young children peculiar behaviors to change racial characteristics such as attempts to wash off their dark color. Because the child is not equipped to resolve this conflict at such an early age, the conflict in its complexity is suppressed. It emerges only when negative experiences force the conflict to the surface.

During the early grade school years, children start comprehending racial differences consciously (Goodman, 1968). Self-concept is in part internalized by the reflection of self in others' reactions. Subsequently, a significant part of identification of self in reference to either racial group is influenced by how siblings look, their racial identification, and people's reactions to them. Racial features can vary greatly among the children of the same parents; for example in a Black-White family, one child may look white, one may look black, and one may look mixed.

They are teased by their schoolmates, called names, and/or isolated—all the result of the prejudice that is transmitted by relatives, the media, and jokes. For those children who are products of interracial unions during foreign wars (i.e., WW II, Korean War, Vietnam War), fear of the "enemy," translated into national hatred towards the "enemy," may be projected onto interracial families and their children.

Once the child comprehends that there is a concept of superiority by color, she or he may attempt to achieve acceptance by embracing membership in the "hierarchically superior" racial group of their heritage, and rejecting the other half of their heritage. For example, Black-White children may want their hair straightened if it is kinky; Asian-White children may want blue eyes.

A teacher's oppressive assumptions and projections can also contribute to the marginality of the biracial child. This child may be singled out in ways that set her or him apart from peers. Unrealistic expectations of the child may be assumed, and misperceptions of the child's environment perpetuated. For example, in assuming that the child identifies with a culture unfamiliar to the teacher, she or he may be asked to "teach" the class about their racial/cultural group (while other children are not asked to do the same). By her or his action, the teacher is likely to project stereotypes onto the child with which they may not identify.

During the process of ethnic identity development, the biracial child from mid-grade school through high school may be embarrassed to be seen with one or both parents. This embarrassment reflects internalized oppression of societal attitudes towards miscegenation, possible internalized family oppression, as well as more typical American adolescent needs to appear independently functioning of their parents.

The Role of Family

The family environment is critical in helping the child and teenager to understand their heritage and value both races. A positive self-concept and view of people is promoted in interracial partnerships and extended families in which a person's value is independent of race though race is not ignored. This environment, whether it be as a single- or two-parent household, gives the individual a security that will help them weather the stress of adolescence. It is this unusual objectivity about people which determines the options the biracial person has for resolving their identity.

Unfortunately, the stress that has been experienced by interracial families, particularly those that have developed during wartime (e.g., Vietnam and the Korean War), has often resulted in a lack of discussion of race, discrimination, and coping strategies for dealing with discriminatory treatment. This silence has perhaps reflected these families' needs for a sanctuary from the painful issue of racial differences. Similar to issues of sexuality, the silence may also reflect the difficulty most people appear to have in discussing race issues.

Being identified with a minority group that is oppressed can generate feelings of inferiority within the biracial person, particularly if this parent is treated as such in the extended family. If the extended family is primarily composed of the socially dominant racial group, overt or covert prejudicial remarks against the parent with less racial social status will increase the child's insecurity about their acceptance. He or she may subsequently also devalue cultural and racial features associated with this parent in an attempt to be accepted.

Outright rejection of the parent with less racial social status, in the aspiration of being conditionally accepted by the dominant cultural group, reflects internalization and projection of discriminatory, oppressive attitudes towards one's own racial heritage (Sue, 1981) and creates tremendous intrapersonal conflict in resolving racial identity. Rejection at this age stems from the awareness that one is judged by those with whom they affiliate; color is a social issue that regulates acceptance and power.

In general, the intensity of the child's reaction is mediated by the racial diversity present in the community, the amount of contact the individual has with other biracial individuals, and the presence of equity among racial groups in their community (Allport, 1958). A child is much less likely to be embarrassed or to reject that part of their heritage that is judged negatively by society if there are ethnic communities which live side by side, if the parent with less racial social status has pride in themselves, and if parents have equal social status within the family. (It is important to be aware that persons of different races in relationships are not exempt from acting prejudicially or in an oppressive manner towards each other.) Based upon the pervasiveness of racism and the widespread oppression of women in American culture, it hard to imagine equity in an interracial, heterosexual marriage.

Some families have a difficult start when an interracial relationship results in the severing of emotional and physical ties by the extended family such as in refusals to visit or accept a marriage or the children. It is a type of abandonment which contributes to mixed race children feeling more different and insecure from other children. Emotional cutoffs are more subtle than physical ones and can be equally damaging, e.g., biracial grandchildren are treated negatively compared to the rest of the grandchildren. This type of discrimination can be very subtle such as loving treatment of biracial child combined with a simultaneous refusal to acknowledge biracial features. Cutoffs can also occur by non-white families and communities. For example, more traditional Japanese grandparents may refuse to accept grandchildren who are any other race *and* ethnic background (e.g., Chinese). Rigid, impermeable physical, emotional, and psychological boundaries communicate hatred and judgment; they mirror to a greater or lesser extent community feelings.

The estrangement and isolation described above encourage denial and rejection of the part of self that has been unaccepted by the extended family; it is very difficult not to internalize this oppression and rejection. As in the case of people who are emotionally deprived of acceptance, some mixed race persons will subsequently try to obtain the approval or acceptance of those persons who are least willing to give it. In the case of biracial children, they may place extra importance on the opinions of persons whose race is the same as their grandparents who initiated the cutoff. Alternately, they may displace anger towards the extended family onto strangers of the same race.

Summary

The process of identity development so far mirrors what Atkinson, Morten, and Sue (1979) describe in their first two stages of minority identity development. In the first stage (Conformity Stage), there is a preference for the dominant culture's values (which in the case of the biracial person may be part of their heritage). In the second stage (Dissonance Stage), information and experiences are likely to create confusion and challenge the individual's idealization of the dominant culture. It is at this point that the individual is usually reaching the end of elementary school and entering junior high school.

Due both to the adolescent's motivation to belong to a community or group and to the adolescent's reaction to a sense of injustice, the biracial individual may seek refuge and acceptance with the group that represents the other half of their heritage. The Minority Identity Development Model predicts that in the third stage (Resistance and Immersion) there will be a simultaneous rejection of the other part of their racial heritage, e.g., being angry and distrustful towards whites (Atkinson et al., 1979) or the racial-social group with greater status. However, this is where models for identity development are not adequate for the biracial individual's unique situation.

For the biracial individual to reject either part of their racial heritage continues an internalized oppression. In reality, it appears that some biracial persons attempt to do this, but the attempts are likely to be very shortlived due to powerful reminders of both sides of their racial heritage. To reject the dominant culture is to reject one parent and subsequently, an integral part of themselves that is unchangeable, particularly if it is the same sex parent. And because racial groups other than white have their prejudices and fears, biracial individuals may feel neither fully accepted nor fully privileged by their other reference group. The individuals are harshly reminded of their ambiguous ethnic/racial status; they are an *other*. They are *marginal* until they achieve a unique resolution for themselves that accepts both parts of their racial heritage. In order to move out of marginal status they need to place less importance on seeking social approval and even move beyond the dichotomy of thinking about the world and self as white versus non-white, good versus bad, and inferior versus superior. This strategy towards resolution requires the child to do something that in all likelihood they have few models to emulate.

FACING RACISM: THE END OF CHILDHOOD

In retrospective reports, biracial adults report differing degrees of awareness of the extent to which their biracial heritage increased the stress of adolescence (Hall, 1980; Murphy-Shigematsu, 1986; Seattle Times, April 1988). This awareness seems to be affected by the communities in which they have lived, parental support, acceptance by the extended family, racial features, and friends.

Junior high and high school are difficult developmental years as teenagers seek a balance between establishing a unique identity while pursuing conformity to peer values. For many biracial individuals, the teenage years appear to be encumbered by a more painful process than the monoracial person. Racial identity conflict is forced to the surface through increased peer dependence, cliques, dating, and movement away from the family.

Turmoil is generated when acceptance at home is not mirrored in the community. At an age that one depends on peers' reactions as the "truth," the teenager may be angry at their parents for failing to prepare them, or for leading them to believe that they are wonderful, lovable, and likable. This inconsistency results in confusion, grief, and anger. Subsequently, conflicts of vague origin increase between children and parents; the adolescent sentiment, "You don't understand; no one understands!" takes on added meaning. Teenagers feel increasingly isolated when they do not know who to trust and as a result may become vulnerable to interpreting environmental cues. For those biracial individuals who feel a tremendous amount of alienation, they may dismiss the positive feedback about self and become extra sensitive to negative feedback. They may overcompensate academically and or in social relationships in order to prove their worth.

A dual existence may be reported by the biracial person; they may appear to be accepted and even popular, but may simultaneously continue to feel different and isolated. Morishima (1980) suggests there may be more identity conflicts for Asian/White children because of their ambiguous appearance. Many White-Asians reflect feeling different regardless of growing up in predominantly white or Asian neighborhoods (Murphy-Shigematsu, 1986). In contrast, Black-White and Black-Asian persons' racial identities appear to be more influenced by their neighbors' color (Hall, 1980), though this difference may simply reflect the continuing, strong oppression of Blacks leading to less freedom of choice for persons who are part Black. However, the biracial adolescent may not relate their feelings of alienation to their biracial status, particularly in the case of those persons who have appeared to move well between and among racial groups. For therapists working with biracial persons, this source of alienation should always be kept in mind, especially with vague complaints of dissatisfaction, unhappiness, and feelings of isolation.

Dating brings many of the subtle forms of racism to the surface. For mixed race persons, all dating is interracial and can be fraught with all the tensions that have historically accompanied it (Petroni, 1973). For the teenager who has seemingly been accepted by different racial groups and has friends of different races they may be confronted with the old slur, "It's okay to have friends who are Black (Asian, White, etc.), but it's not okay to date one, and definitely not okay to marry one." A more subtle form of this racism occurs with parental encouragement of interracial friendships and even dating. However, more covert communication imparts the message, "you can date one, but don't marry one." For those biracial persons who can "pass" as white on the exterior, but do not identify as such, their attraction to non-whites may be met with statements such as, "You can do better than that." This statement is interpreted as a prejudicial comment towards their internal perception and identification of themselves. For some biracial persons this will be the first time that they experience barriers because of color or their socially perceived ambiguous race. For the child who has grown up in an extended white family and has been encouraged to act white and identify white, dating is painful. The teenager or young adult may avoid much dating and or continue in their activities in which these conflicts are absent.

A form of racism which surfaces during adolescence and may continue throughout life is "tokenism," which occurs both personally and vocationally. The biracial person's racial ambiguity and partial similarity by values or appearance may be used by a dominant group as a way of satisfying a quota for a person of color who is less threatening than a monoracial person of color (despite how the biracial person identifies). What makes this type of recruiting oppressive is that the group is using this person to avoid dealing with their racism; furthermore, they are assigning racial identity for the person and not informing her or him of their purpose. The group or organization subsequently uses their association with this person as evidence of their affirmative action or antiracist efforts. As a result, they have actually made this person marginal to the group.

Gender Issues

Like women, non-white persons have had to work harder to prove themselves equal by white, male standards. This observation is true for mixed race persons who may have to fight misperceptions that mixed race persons may be abnormal. The arenas in which biracial men and women have particular difficulties are different. Non-white men, because they have more social, economic, and political power than most women, are particularly threatening to White America. It is hypothesized that mixed race men will have a more difficult time overcoming social barriers than mixed race women; they will have to work harder to prove themselves and experience an oppression, which while shared by other minority group men, may exist also within their minority reference groups towards them.

On the other hand, because women in general are less threatening to the mainstream culture than men, mixed race women may not experience as much direct oppression as mixed race men. Biracial women may in fact be perceived as less threatening than monoracial women of color. They are likely to have difficulty comprehending, and then subsequently coping with pervasive myths that mixed race women are "exotic" and sexually freer than other women (Petroni, 1973; Wagatsuma, 1973). These myths appear to stem from myths that interracial relationships are based upon sex (cf. Petroni, 1973). Coupled with a lack of acceptance, some biracial women become sexually promiscuous in a search for acceptance (Gibbs, 1987). Mixed race women may also have more difficulty in relationships because of intersections of myths, lower status as women, and their search for an identity.

Summary

Racism challenges adolescent optimism. The young person's sensitivity to social approval and the human need for belonging make the resolution of biracial identity a long, uncharted journey. The path is determined by family, community, and peer values and environments. Racial features including skin color of self and family members also shape one's sense of racial identity.

To assume that the biracial person will racially identify with how they look is presumptive, but pervasive. Besides, the biracial person is perceived differently by different people. *Many persons make the mistake of thinking that the biracial person is fortunate to have a choice; however, the reality is that the biracial person has to fight very hard to exercise choices that are not congruent with how they may be visually and emotionally perceived.* She or he should have options to go beyond identifying with one or the other racial group of their heritage; the limitations of this dichotomy of options is oppressive and generates marginal status. To be able to have an expanded slate of options may shorten the journey and reduce the pain involved in resolution of biracial identity.

STRATEGIES FOR RESOLUTION OF "OTHER" STATUS

Several models for identity development exist both in the psychological and sociological bodies of literature. Minority models for identity development share in common the rejection of white values in order to appreciate minority values. However, as pointed out in the Atkinson et al.'s (1979) model, there is an inherent difficulty in rejecting "whiteness" if one is part white. In fact, the author proposes that for those individuals who are part white to manifest hatred towards whiteness probably reflects oppression within the nuclear and extended family system. For biracial persons who are a minority-minority racial mix, it is not clear how to apply this model.

A Beginning Schematic for Identity Development

I am proposing a schematic metamodel that might be used to understand the process of identity development for persons with different types of "other" status. This model is schematically a spiral where the linear force is internal conflict over a core sense of definition of self, the importance of which is largely determined by socialization (e.g., race, gender). Different sources of conflict may move the individual forward. It is proposed, however, that in each person's life there are at least one or two significant conflicts during critical developmental periods that move them forward. The circular or system forces encompass the political, social, and familial environments.

I suggest that in the identity development of the biracial person, the strongest recurring conflict at critical periods of development will be the tension between racial components within oneself. Social, familial, and political systems are the environments within which the biracial person appears to seek a sense of self in a circular process repeatedly throughout a lifetime. Themes of marginality, discrimination, and ambiguity are produced by these systems.

At all times, biracial persons contend with both parts of their racial heritage. Early in the process of identity development, after the child has become aware of race, she or he is likely to compartmentalize and separate the racial components of their heritage. The attention they give to aspects of their heritage may alternate (though not necessarily equally) over time. This alternating represents conflict and lack of experience and strategies for integrating components of self. Resolution reflects the lack of need for compartmentalizing the parts of their ethnic heritage.

The rest of this essay is dedicated to outlining four general resolutions of biracial identity. That there is more than one acceptable outcome confronts the limitations of traditional psychological theory which allow for only a single healthy endpoint. If there is another step in the contribution that feminist theory can make to personality development, it might be to provide flexibility and tolerance for more than a single definition of mental health.

The factors and criteria that determine each resolution are outlined. All resolutions are driven by the assumption that an individual recognizes both sides of their heritage. The resolutions that are proposed are an articulation of what appears on the surface: acceptance of the identity society assigns; identification with a single racial group; identification with both racial groups; and identification as a new racial group.

Acceptance of the Identity Society Assigns. Biracial people growing up in more racially oppressive parts of the country are less likely to have freedom to choose their racial identity. They are likely to be identified and identify as a person of color which will be equated with subordinate status. This strategy reflects the case of a passive resolution that is positive but may stem from an oppressive process. However, it is possible for it to be a positive resolution if individuals feel they belong to the racial group to which they are assigned. Affiliation, support, and acceptance by the extended family is important to this resolution being positive.

Individuals who have largely been socialized within an extended family, depending on them for friendship as well as nurturance are likely to racially identify with this group regardless of their visual similarity or dissimilarity to the extended family. One will tend to identify with the ethnic identity with which society views the family. The advantage of this identification is that the extended (well-functioning) family is a stable, secure reference group whose bonds go beyond visual, racial similarity.

This resolution is the most tenuous of the strategies outlined in that the individual may be perceived differently and assigned a different racial identity in a different part of the country. Because one's self-image in the mind's eye is stable across significant changes, the conflict and subsequent accumulated life experience would need to be tremendous to compel the individual to change their internally perceived racial identity. In the event of this challenge, the biracial person may work towards a more active resolution process. However, it is likely that she or he will still racially identify the same way but based on a different process such as identification with the extended family. Evidence of a positive resolution is that the individual would educate those persons with whom they interact of their chosen identity.

Identification with Both Racial Groups. Some biracial persons identify with both racial groups they have inherited. When asked about their ethnic background, they may respond, "I'm part Black and part Japanese," or "I'm mixed." This resolution is positive if the individual's personality remains similar across groups and they feel priv i-leged in both groups. They may simultaneously be aware that they are both similar and different compared to those persons around them. However, they view their otherness as a unique characteristic of self that contributes to a sense of individuality.

This may be the most idealistic resolution of biracial status, and available in only certain parts of the country where biracial children exist in larger numbers and mixed marriages are accepted with greater tolerance by the community such as on the West coast. This strategy does not change other people's behavior; thus, the biracial person must have constructive strategies for coping with social resistance to their comfort with both groups of their heritage and their claim to privileges of both groups.

Identification with a Single Racial Group. The result of this strategy sometimes looks identical to the strategy of assuming the racial identity that society assigns. It is different, however, by the process being active rather than passive and not the result of oppression. In this strategy, the individual *chooses* to identify with a particular racial/ethnic group regardless if this is the identity assumed by siblings, assigned by society, or matching their racial features. This is a positive strategy if the individual does not feel marginal to their proclaimed racial reference group and does not deny the other part of their racial heritage. This is a more difficult resolution to achieve in parts of the country which have the strongest prohibitions against crossing color lines (e.g., the South).

A major difficulty may be faced with this strategy when there is an incongruous match between how an individual is perceived by others and how they perceive themselves. With this strategy, the biracial person needs to be aware and accept the incongruity and have coping strategies for dealing with questions and suspicion by the reference group. Some individuals will need to make a geographic move to be able to live this resolution more peacefully.

Identification as a New Racial Group. This person most likely feels a strong kinship to other biracial persons in a way that they may not feel to any racial group because of the struggle with marginal status. Identification as a new race is a positive resolution if the person is not trying to hide or reject any aspect of their racial heritage. This individual may move fluidly between racial groups but view themselves apart from these reference groups without feeling marginal because they have generated a new reference group. There are few examples of biracial groups being recognized in a positive way. Hawaii perhaps sets one of the best examples with the Hapa Haole (White-Asian) (Yamamoto, 1973).

A clear problem with this resolution is that society's classification system does not recognize persons of mixed race. Thus, this individual would continually experience being assigned to a racial identity and would need to inform people of the inaccuracy when it felt important to them.

Summary

I suggest that these strategies are not mutually exclusive and may coexist simultaneously, or an individual may move among them. Such movement is consistent with a stable, positive sense of identity if the individual does not engage in denial of any part of their heritage (internalized oppression). Two themes are common to the resolutions listed above. First, it is important that biracial persons accept both sides of their racial heritage. Second, biracial persons have the right to declare how they wish to identify themselves racially — even if this identity is discrepant with how they look or how society tends to perceive them. Third, biracial persons develop strategies for coping with social resistance or questions about their racial identity so that they no longer internalize questions as inferring that there is something wrong with them. Rather, they attribute questions and insensitivities to ignorance and racism.

Resolution of biracial identity is often propelled forward by the internal conflict generated by exposure to new people, new ideas, and new environments. Subsequently, it is not uncommon that many individuals emerge out of college years with a different resolution to their racial identity than when they graduated high school. Furthermore, geography plays a large part in the options the individual has.

Living in more liberal parts of the country may be necessary to exercise a wider range of options with less social resistance.

CONCLUSION

The multiple strategies for resolution of other status in this essay constitute a proposal, challenge, and appeal to theorists of human personality development to be more flexible in considering the range of positive psychological functioning. Psychological theories have been oppressive by their narrow range of tolerance and allowance for positive mental health. As a result, many different types of people can relate to the search for a resolution of other status, though not necessarily based on racial/ethnic ambiguity. If theories of identity development allowed for a slate of equally valid resolutions of conflict around basic components of identity, fewer people may struggle with "identity crises." Because of the role that feminist theory has played in attempting to validate the experience of persons with "other" status by sexual orientation, religious/ethnic identity, etc., *it seems that feminist theorists and therapists may be the persons most able to develop flexible models of mental health that truly allow for diversity.* But first, more feminist theorists and therapists will have to reach out beyond their boundaries of cultural safety to understand issues of race.

Although it appears that the biracial person may have the best of both worlds, this is a naive assumption which presumes that she or he has unopposed freedom to choose how she or he wishes to be perceived. In reality all racial groups have their prejudices which when projected onto the biracial person are the creators of marginal status. The biracial person does not have a guaranteed ethnic reference group if they leave it to the group to determine if they can belong.

The key to resolving other status derived from ethnic ambiguity requires an individual to move beyond the dichotomous, irrational categorization of race by white versus non-white, which in turn has been equated with degrees of worth and privilege in our culture. Towards this goal, three significant assumptions can be made about the experience of the biracial person which subsequently affects their process of identity resolution.

First, the biracial person does not necessarily racially identify with the way she or he looks (Hall, 1980). Because self-image is an emotionally mediated picture of the self, one's perception of self is governed by more than racial features. One's image of self is shaped by the presence or absence of other people similar to them, the racial features of siblings, exposure to people of both races which they inherit, identification with one parent over another, peer reactions, and how the extended family has perceived them as children.

Second, unlike monoracial people of color, the biracial person does not have guaranteed acceptance by any racial reference group. Thus, minority models of identity development do not reflect the resolution of this situation which is the crux of the biracial person's marginal status. *Looking for acceptance from others keeps the biracial person trying to live by the "irrational" racial classification rules which may keep her or him marginal to any group.*

The third assumption is that there is more than one possible, positive resolution of racial identity for biracial persons. This assumption reflects a departure from traditional European, male originated identity models which have a single, static, positive outcome. Furthermore, the *resolution strategies for biracial identity can change during a lifetime.* It is this ability to be flexible that may indeed determine both self-acceptance and constructive, flexible coping strategies.

Marginality is a state created by society and not inherent in one's racial heritage. *As long as the biracial person bases self-acceptance on complete social acceptance by any racial reference group, they will be marginal.* Freire (1970) clearly articulates the origin and subsequently difficult resolution of marginality:

marginality is not by choice, (the) marginal (person) has been expelled from and kept outside of the social system. . . . *Therefore, the solution to their problem is not to become "beings inside of," but . . . (people) . . . freeing themselves; for, in reality, they are not marginal to the structure, but oppressed . . . (persons) . . . within it* (author's emphasis). (pp. 10–11)

NOTES

Maria P. P. Root is half Asian (Filipino) and half white, born in the Philippines and raised in California. This bicultural context has been the catalyst for many interests which appear diverse but are related through integration of the diversity represented in her cultural background, e.g., psychosomatic symptomatology, family therapy, identity development, and issues of underserved populations.

The author wishes to acknowledge feedback from Carla Bradshaw, PhD, Laura

Brown, PhD, Christine C. Iijima Hall, PhD, and Christine Ho, PhD which helped shape revisions of this paper.

REFERENCES

Allport, Gordon W. (1958). *The nature of prejudice.* Reading, MA: Addison-Wesley.

Atkinson, D., Morten, G., & Sue, Derald W. (1979). *Counseling American minorities: A cross cultural perspective.* Dubuque, IA: Brown Company.

Dien, D. S., & Vinacke, W. E. (1964). Self-concept and parental identification of young adults with mixed Caucasian-Japanese parentage. *Journal of Abnormal Psychology, 69* (4), 463–466.

Freire, Paolo (1970). *Cultural action for freedom.* Cambridge: Harvard Educational Review Press.

Gibbs, Jewelle Taylor (1987). Identity and marginality: Issues in the treatment of biracial adolescents. *American Journal of Orthopsychiatry, 57* (2), 265–278.

Goodman, M. E. (1968). *Race awareness in young children.* New York: Collier Press.

Hall, Christine C. Iijima (1980). *The ethnic identity of racially mixed people: A study of Black-Japanese.* Doctoral Dissertation, University of California, Los Angeles.

Henriques, Fernando (1975). *Children of conflict: A study of interracial sex and marriage.* New York: E. P. Dutton & Co., Inc.

Louise, Vivienne (1988). Of Color: What's In a Name? *Bay Area Women's News, 1* (6), 5, 7.

Morishima, James K. (1980). *Asian American Racial Mixes: Attitudes, Self-Concept, and Academic Performance.* Paper presented at the Western Psychological Association convention, Honolulu.

Moritsugu, John, Foerster, Lynn, & Morishima, James K. (1978). *Eurasians: A Pilot Study.* Paper presented at the Western Psychological Association convention, San Francisco, 1978.

Murphy-Shigematsu, Stephen (1986). *The voices of amerasians: Ethnicity, identity, and empowerment in interracial Japanese Americans.* Doctoral Dissertation, Harvard University.

Petroni, Frank A. (1973). Interracial Dating—The Price is High. In I. R. Stuart and L. Edwin (Eds.), *Interracial marriage: Expectations and Realities.* New York: Grossman Publishers.

Poussaint, Alvin F. (1984). Benefits of Being Interracial. In the Council on Interracial Books for Children, *Children of interracial families, 15* (6).

Sickels, Robert J. (1972). *Race, marriage, and the law.* Albuquerque, NM: University of New Mexico Press.

Stonequist, Everett (1935). The problem of the marginal man. *The American Journal of Sociology, 41,* 1–12.

Sue, Derald W. (1981). *Counseling the culturally different: Theory and practice.* New York: John Wiley & Sons.

Wagatsuma, Hiroshi (1973). Some Problems of Interracial Marriage for the Japanese. In I. R. Stuart and L. Edwin (Eds.), *Interracial Marriage: Expectations and Realities.* New York: Grossman Publishers.

Yamamoto, George (1973). Interracial Marriage in Hawaii. In I. R. Stuart and L. Edwin (Eds.), *Interracial Marriage: Expectations and Realities.* New York: Grossman Publishers

C. PERSONAL NARRATIVES AND CULTURE TALES

This is a special section of "culture tales" (Howard 1991)—very powerful and moving first-person accounts of the identity concerns, power negotiations, and political and social realities of being bicultural and biracial. As we have argued in our introduction, the voices and personal narratives of individuals who are not part of the dominant (power) center of our society can speak to us from the margins (bell hooks 1984) and can alert us, as Cherríe Moraga calls it, to "the specificity of oppression." Each of the following essays is a challenge to theory which oversimplifies the relationships between psyche and culture, ignores the issue of power, or attempts to explain away the reality, pain, and promise of people who grow up biculturally. Except for a brief introduction to each of the authors, we want to let them speak for themselves.

Cherríe Moraga, the author of chapter 25, is a Latina feminist well known for her pioneering anthology (which she edited with Gloria Anzaldua), *This Bridge Called My Back: Radical Writings by Women of Color* (1983). She is a poet and playwright as well as an essayist.

June Jordan, who wrote chapter 26, is a professor of Afro-American Studies and Women's Studies at University of California at Berkeley, and draws the personal into her extensive political and academic writings.

Arturo Madrid, a Spanish professor and social critic and commentator, served as President of the Tomás Rivera Center, a national institute for policy studies on Latino issues. He contributed chapter 27.

REFERENCES

hooks, bell. 1984. *Feminist theory: From margin to center.* Boston: South End Press.
Howard, G. S. 1991. Culture tales: A narrative approach to thinking, cross-cultural psychology, and psychotherapy. *American Psychologist* 46: 187–97.
Moraga, C., and G. Anzaldua, eds. 1983. *This bridge called my back: Radical writings by women of color.* New York: Kitchen Table Press.

25. La Güera

Cherríe Moraga

It requires something more than personal experience to gain a philosophy or point of view from any specific event. It is the quality of our response to the event and our capacity to enter into the lives of others that help us to make their lives and experiences our own.

Emma Goldman[1]

I am the very well-educated daughter of a woman who, by the standards in this country, would be considered largely illiterate. My mother was born in Santa Paula, Southern California, at a time when much of the central valley there was still farm land. Nearly thirty-five years later, in 1948, she was the only daughter of six to marry an anglo, my father.

I remember all of my mother's stories, probably much better than she realizes. She is a fine story-teller, recalling every event of her life with the vividness of the present, noting each detail right down to the cut and color of her dress. I remember stories of her being pulled out of school at the ages of five, seven, nine, and eleven to work in the fields, along with her brothers and sisters; stories of her father drinking away whatever small profit she was able to make for the family; of her going the long way home to avoid meeting him on the street, staggering toward the same destination. I remember stories of my mother lying about her age in order to get a job as a hat-check girl at Agua Caliente Racetrack in Tijuana. At fourteen, she was the main support of the family. I can still see her walking home alone at 3 a.m., only to turn all of her salary and tips over to her mother, who was pregnant again.

The stories continue through the war years and on: walnut-crack-

"La Güera" by Cherríe Moraga from *This Bridge Called My Back: Radical Writings by Women of Color* © Copyright 1983 by Cherríe Moraga. Used by permission of the author and of Kitchen Table Women of Color Press, P.O. Box 908 Latham, NY 12110.

ing factories, the Voit Rubber factory, and then the computer boom. I remember my mother doing piecework for the electronics plant in our neighborhood. In the late evening, she would sit in front of the T.V. set, wrapping copper wires into the backs of circuit boards, talking about "keeping up with the younger girls." By that time, she was already in her mid-fifties.

Meanwhile, I was college-prep in school. After classes, I would go with my mother to fill out job applications for her, or write checks for her at the supermarket. We would have the scenario all worked out ahead of time. My mother would sign the check before we'd get to the store. Then, as we'd approach the checkstand, she would say — within earshot of the cashier — "oh honey, you go 'head and make out the check," as if she couldn't be bothered with such an insignificant detail. No one asked any questions.

I was educated, and wore it with a keen sense of pride and satisfaction, my head propped up with the knowledge, from my mother, that my life would be easier than hers. I was educated; but more than this, I was "la güera": fair-skinned. Born with the features of my Chicana mother, but the skin of my anglo father, I had it made.

No one ever quite told me this (that light was right), but I knew that being light was something valued in my family (who were all Chicano, with the exception of my father). In fact, everything about my upbringing (at least what occurred on a conscious level) attempted to bleach me of what color I did have. Although my mother was fluent in it, I was never taught much Spanish at home. I picked up what I did learn from school and from over-heard snatches of conversation among my relatives and mother. She often called other lower-income Mexicans "braceros," or "wet-backs," referring to herself and her family as "a different class of people." And yet, the real story was that my family, too, had been poor (some still are) and farmworkers. My mother can remember this in her blood as if it were yesterday. But this is something she would like to forget (and rightfully), for to her, on a basic economic level, being Chicana meant being "less." It was through my mother's desire to protect her children from poverty and illiteracy that we became "anglocized"; the more effectively we could pass in the white world, the better guaranteed our future.

From all of this, I experience, daily, a huge disparity between what I was born into and what I was to grow up to become. Because, (as Goldman suggests) these stories my mother told me crept under my "güera" skin. I had no choice but to enter into the life of my mother. *I had no choice.* I took her life into my heart, but managed to keep a lid on it as long as I feigned being the happy, upwardly mobile heterosexual.

When I finally lifted the lid to my lesbianism, a profound connection with my mother reawakened in me. It wasn't until I acknowledged and confronted my own lesbianism in the flesh, that my heartfelt identification with and empathy for my mother's oppression — due to being poor, uneducated, and Chicana — was realized. My lesbianism is the avenue through which I have learned the most about silence and oppression, and it continues to be the most tactile reminder to me that we are not free human beings.

You see, one follows the other. I had known for years that I was a lesbian, had felt it in my bones, had ached with the knowledge, gone crazed with the knowledge, wallowed in the silence of it. Silence *is* like starvation. Don't be fooled. It's nothing short of that, and felt most sharply when one has had a full belly most of her life. When we are not physically starving, we have the luxury to realize psychic and emotional starvation. It is from this starvation that other starvations can be recognized — if one is willing to take the risk of making the connection — if one is willing to be responsible to the result of the connection. For me, the connection is an inevitable one.

What I am saying is that the joys of looking like a white girl ain't so great since I realized I could be beaten on the street for being a dyke. If my sister's being beaten because she's Black, it's pretty much the same principle. We're both getting beaten any way you look at it. The connection is blatant; and in the case of my own family, the difference in the privileges attached to looking white instead of brown are merely a generation apart.

In this country, lesbianism is a poverty — as is being brown, as is being a woman, as is being just plain poor. The danger lies in ranking the oppressions. *The danger lies in failing to acknowledge the specificity of the oppression.* The danger lies in attempting to deal with oppression purely from a theoretical base. Without an emotional, heartfelt grappling with the source of our own oppression, without naming the enemy within ourselves and outside of us, no authentic, non-hierarchical connection among oppressed groups can take place.

When the going gets rough, will we abandon our so-called comrades in a flurry of racist/heterosexist/what-have-you panic? To whose camp, then, should the lesbian of color retreat? Her very presence violates the ranking and abstraction of oppression. Do we merely live hand to mouth? Do we merely struggle with the "ism" that's sitting on top of our own heads?

The answer is: yes, I think first we do; and we must do so thoroughly and deeply. But to fail to move out from there will only isolate us in our own oppression —will only insulate, rather than radicalize us.

To illustrate: a gay male friend of mine once confided to me that he continued to feel that, on some level, I didn't trust him because he was male; that he felt, really, if it ever came down to a "battle of the sexes," I might kill him. I admitted that I might very well. He wanted to understand the source of my distrust. I responded, "You're not a woman. Be a woman for a day. Imagine being a woman." He confessed that the thought terrified him because, to him, being a woman meant being raped by men. He *had* felt raped by men; he wanted to forget what that meant. What grew from that discussion was the realization that in order for him to create an authentic alliance with me, he must deal with the primary source of his own sense of oppression. He must, first, emotionally come to terms with what it feels like to be a victim. If he —or anyone —were to truly do this, it would be impossible to discount the oppression of others, except by again forgetting how we have been hurt.

And yet, oppressed groups are forgetting all the time. There are instances of this in the rising Black middle class, and certainly an obvious trend of such "unconsciousness" among white gay men. Because to remember may mean giving up whatever privileges we have managed to squeeze out of this society by virtue of our gender, race, class, or sexuality.

Within the women's movement, the connections among women of different backgrounds and sexual orientations have been fragile, at best. I think this phenomenon is indicative of our failure to seriously address ourselves to some very frightening questions: How have I internalized my own oppression? How have I oppressed? Instead, we have let rhetoric do the job of poetry. Even the word "oppression" has lost its power. We need a new language, better words that can more closely describe women's fear of and resistance to one another; words that will not always come out sounding like dogma.

What prompted me in the first place to work on an anthology by radical women of color was a deep sense that I had a valuable insight to contribute, by virtue of my birthright and background. And yet,

I don't really understand first-hand what it feels like being shitted on for being brown. I understand much more about the joys of it — being Chicana and having family are synonymous for me. What I know about loving, singing, crying, telling stories, speaking with my heart and hands, even having a sense of my own soul comes from the love of my mother, aunts, cousins . . .

But at the age of twenty-seven, it is frightening to acknowledge that I have internalized a racism and classism, where the object of oppression is not only someone outside of my skin, but the someone inside my skin. In fact, to a large degree, the real battle with such oppression, for all of us, begins under the skin. I have had to confront the fact that much of what I value about being Chicana, about my family, has been subverted by anglo culture and my own cooperation with it. This realization did not occur to me overnight. For example, it wasn't until long after my graduation from the private college I'd attended in Los Angeles, that I realized the major reason for my total alienation from and fear of my classmates was rooted in class and culture. CLICK.

Three years after graduation, in an apple-orchard in Sonoma, a friend of mine (who comes from an Italian Irish working-class family) says to me, "Cherríe, no wonder you felt like such a nut in school. Most of the people there were white and rich." It was true. All along I had felt the difference, but not until I had put the words "class" and "color" to the experience, did my feelings make any sense. For years, I had berated myself for not being as "free" as my classmates. I completely bought that they simply had more guts than I did — to rebel against their parents and run around the country hitch-hiking, reading books and studying "art." They had enough privilege to be atheists, for chrissake. There was no one around filling in the disparity for me between their parents, who were Hollywood filmmakers, and my parents, who wouldn't know the name of a filmmaker if their lives depended on it (and precisely because their lives didn't depend on it, they couldn't be bothered). But I knew nothing about "privilege" then. White was right. Period. I could pass. If I got educated enough, there would never be any telling.

Three years after that, another CLICK. In a letter to Barbara Smith, I wrote:

> I went to a concert where Ntosake Shange was reading. There, everything exploded for me. She was speaking a language that I knew — in the deepest parts of me — existed, and that I had ignored in my own feminist studies and

even in my own writing. What Ntosake caught in me is the realization that in my development as a poet, I have, in many ways, denied the voice of my brown mother—the brown in me. I have acclimated to the sound of a white language which, as my father represents it, does not speak to the emotions in my poems—emotions which stem from the love of my mother.

The reading was agitating. Made me uncomfortable. Threw me into a week-long terror of how deeply I was affected. I felt that I had to start all over again. That I turned only to the perceptions of white middle-class women to speak for me and all women. I am shocked by my own ignorance.

Sitting in that auditorium chair was the first time I had realized to the core of me that for years I had disowned the language I knew best—ignored the words and rhythms that were the closest to me. The sounds of my mother and aunts gossiping—half in English, half in Spanish—while drinking cerveza in the kitchen. And the hands— I had cut off the hands in my poems. But not in conversation; still the hands could not be kept down. Still they insisted on moving.

The reading had forced me to remember that I knew things from my roots. But to remember puts me up against what I don't know. Shange's reading agitated me because she spoke with power about a world that is both alien and common to me: "the capacity to enter into the lives of others." But you can't just take the goods and run. I knew that then, sitting in the Oakland auditorium (as I know in my poetry), that the only thing worth writing about is what seems to be unknown and, therefore, fearful.

The "unknown" is often depicted in racist literature as the "darkness" within a person. Similarly, sexist writers will refer to fear in the form of the vagina, calling it "the orifice of death." In contrast, it is a pleasure to read works such as Maxine Hong Kingston's *Woman Warrior,* where fear and alienation are described as "the white ghosts." And yet, the bulk of literature in this country reinforces the myth that what is dark and female is evil. Consequently, each of us — whether dark, female, or both—has in some way *internalized* this oppressive imagery. What the oppressor often succeeds in doing is simply *externalizing* his fears, projecting them into the bodies of women, Asians, gays, disabled folks, whoever seems most "other."

> call me
> roach and presumptuous
> nightmare on your white pillow
> your itch to destroy
> the indestructible
> part of yourself
>   Audre Lorde[2]

But it is not really difference the oppressor fears so much as similarity. He fears he will discover in himself the same aches, the same longings as those of the people he has shitted on. He fears the immobilization threatened by his own incipient guilt. He fears he will have to change his life once he has seen himself in the bodies of the people he has called different. He fears the hatred, anger, and vengeance of those he has hurt.

This is the oppressor's nightmare, but it is not exclusive to him. We women have a similar nightmare, for each of us in some way has been both oppressed and the oppressor. We are afraid to look at how we have failed each other. We are afraid to see how we have taken the values of our oppressor into our hearts and turned them against ourselves and one another. We are afraid to admit how deeply "the man's" words have been ingrained in us.

To assess the damage is a dangerous act. I think of how, even as a feminist lesbian, I have so wanted to ignore my own homophobia, my own hatred of myself for being queer. I have not wanted to admit that my deepest personal sense of myself has not quite "caught up" with my "woman-identified" politics. I have been afraid to criticize lesbian writers who choose to "skip over" these issues in the name of feminism. In 1979, we talk of "old gay" and "butch and femme" roles as if they were ancient history. We toss them aside as merely patriarchal notions. And yet, the truth of the matter is that I have sometimes taken society's fear and hatred of lesbians to bed with me. I have sometimes hated my lover for loving me. I have sometimes felt "not woman enough" for her. I have sometimes felt "not man enough." For a lesbian trying to survive in a heterosexist society, there is no easy way around these emotions. Similarly, in a white-dominated world, there is little getting around racism and our own internalization of it. It's always there, embodied in some one we least expect to rub up against.

When we do rub up against this person, *there* then is the challenge. *There* then is the opportunity to look at the nightmare within us. But we usually shrink from such a challenge.

Time and time again, I have observed that the usual response among white women's groups when the "racism issue" comes up is to deny the difference. I have heard comments like, "Well, we're open to *all* women; why don't they (women of color) come? You can only do so much . . ." But there is seldom any analysis of how the very nature and structure of the group itself may be founded on racist or classist assumptions. More importantly, so often the women seem to feel no loss, no lack, no absence when women of color are not involved; therefore, there is little desire to change the situation. This has hurt me deeply. I have come to believe that the only reason women of a privileged class will dare to look at *how* it is that *they* oppress, is when they've come to know the meaning of their own oppression. And understand that the oppression of others hurts them personally.

The other side of the story is that women of color and working-class women often shrink from challenging white middle-class women. It is much easier to rank oppressions and set up a hierarchy, rather than take responsibility for changing our own lives. We have failed to demand that white women, particularly those who claim to be speaking for all women, be accountable for their racism.

The dialogue has simply not gone deep enough.

I have many times questioned my right to even work on an anthology which is to be written "exclusively by Third World women." I have had to look critically at my claim to color, at a time when, among white feminist ranks, it is a "politically correct" (and sometimes peripherally advantageous) assertion to make. I must acknowledge the fact that, physically, I have had a *choice* about making that claim, in contrast to women who have not had such a choice, and have been abused for their color. I must reckon with the fact that for most of my life, by virtue of the very fact that I am white-looking, I identified with and aspired toward white values, and that I rode the wave of that Southern California privilege as far as conscience would let me.

Well, now I feel both bleached and beached. I feel angry about this—the years when I refused to recognize privilege, both when it worked against me, and when I worked it, ignorantly, at the expense of others. These are not settled issues. That is why this work *[This Bridge Called My Back: Radical Writings by Women of Color]* feels so risky to me. It continues to be discovery. It has brought me into contact with women who invariably know a hell of a lot more than I do about racism, as experienced in the flesh, as revealed in the flesh of their writing.

I think: what is my responsibility to my roots—both white and brown, Spanish-speaking and English? I am a woman with a foot in both worlds; and I refuse the split. I feel the necessity for dialogue. Sometimes I feel it urgently.

But one voice is not enough, nor two, although this is where dialogue begins. It is essential that radical feminists confront their fear of and resistance to each other, because without this, there *will* be no bread on the table. Simply, we will not survive. If we could make this connection in our heart of hearts, that if we are serious about a revolution—better—if we seriously believe there should be joy in our lives (real joy, not just "good times"), then we need one another. We women need each other. Because my/your solitary, self-asserting "go-for-the-throat-of-fear" power is not enough. The real power, as you and I well know, is collective. I can't afford to be afraid of you, nor you of me. If it takes head-on collisions, let's do it: this polite timidity is killing us.

As Lorde suggests in the passage I cited earlier, it is in looking to the nightmare that the dream is found. There, the survivor emerges to insist on a future, a vision, yes, born out of what is dark and female. The feminist movement must be a movement of such survivors, a movement with a future.

NOTES

1. Alix Kates Shulman, "Was My Life Worth Living?" *Red Emma Speaks.* (New York: Random House, 1972), p. 388
2. From "The Brown Menace or Poem to the Survival of Roaches," *The New York Head Shop and Museum* (Detroit: Broadside, 1974), p. 48.

26. Report from the Bahamas

June Jordan

I am staying in a hotel that calls itself The Sheraton British Colonial. One of the photographs advertising the place displays a middle-aged Black man in a waiter's tuxedo, smiling. What intrigues me most about the picture is just this: while the Black man bears a tray full of "colorful" drinks above his left shoulder, both of his feet, shoes and trouserlegs, up to ten inches above his ankles, stand in the also "colorful" Caribbean salt water. He is so delighted to serve you he will wade into the water to bring you Banana Daquiris while you float! More precisely, he will wade into the water, fully clothed, oblivious to the ruin of his shoes, his trousers, his health, and he will do it with a smile.

I am in the Bahamas. On the phone in my room, a spinning complement of plastic pages offers handy index clues such as CAR RENTAL and CASINOS. A message from the Ministry of Tourism appears among these travelers' tips. Opening with a paragraph of "WELCOME," the message then proceeds to "A PAGE OF HISTORY," which reads as follows:

New World History begins on the same day that modern Bahamian history begins—October 12, 1492. That's when Columbus stepped ashore— British influence came first with the Eleutherian Adventurers of 1647. After the Revolutions, American Loyalists fled from the newly independent states and settled in the Bahamas. Confederate blockade-runners used the island as a haven during the War between the States, and after the War, a number of Southerners moved to the Bahamas . . .

There it is again. Something proclaims itself a legitimate history and all it does is track white Mr. Columbus to the British Eleutherians through the Confederate Southerners as they barge into New World surf, land on New World turf, and nobody saying one word about the

Copyright controlled by June Jordan, African American Studies, Dwinelle Hall, University of California, Berkeley, CA 94720. Copyright © 1985 by June Jordan.

Bahamian people, the Black peoples, to whom the only thing new in their island world was this weird succession of crude intruders and its colonial consequences.

This is my consciousness of race as I unpack my bathing suit in the Sheraton British Colonial. Neither this hotel nor the British nor the long ago Italians nor the white Delta airline pilots belong here, of course. And every time I look at the photograph of that fool standing in the water with his shoes on I'm about to have a West Indian fit, even though I know he's no fool; he's a middle-aged Black man who needs a job and this is his job—pretending himself a servile ancillary to the pleasures of the rich. (Compared to his options in life, I am a rich woman. Compared to most of the Black Americans arriving for this Easter weekend on a three nights four days' deal of bargain rates, the middle-aged waiter is a poor Black man.)

We will jostle along with the other (white) visitors and join them in the tee shirt shops or, laughing together, learn ruthless rules of negotiation as we, Black Americans as well as white, argue down the price of handwoven goods at the nearby straw market while the merchants, frequently toothless Black women seated on the concrete in their only presentable dress, humble themselves to our careless games:

"Yes? You like it? Eight dollar."

"Five."

"I give it to you. Seven."

And so it continues, this weird succession of crude intruders that, now, includes me and my brothers and my sisters from the North.

This is my consciousness of class as I try to decide how much money I can spend on Bahamian gifts for my family back in Brooklyn. No matter that these other Black women incessantly weave words and flowers into the straw hats and bags piled beside them on the burning dusty street. No matter that these other Black women must work their sense of beauty into these things that we will take away as cheaply as we dare, or they will do without food.

We are not white, after all. The budget is limited. And we are harmlessly killing time between the poolside rum punch and "The Native Show on the Patio" that will play tonight outside the hotel restaurant.

This is my consciousness of race and class and gender identity as I notice the fixed relations between these other Black women and myself. They sell and I buy or I don't. They risk not eating. I risk going broke on my first vacation afternoon.

We are not particularly women anymore; we are parties to a transaction designed to set us against each other.

"Olive" is the name of the Black woman who cleans my hotel room. On my way to the beach I am wondering what "Olive" would say if I told her why I chose The Sheraton British Colonial; if I told her I wanted to swim. I wanted to sleep. I did not want to be harassed by the middle-aged waiter, or his nephew. I did not want to be raped by anybody (white or Black) at all and I calculated that my safety as a Black woman alone would best be assured by a multinational hotel corporation. In my experience, the big guys take customer complaints more seriously than the little ones. I would suppose that's one reason why they're big; they don't like to lose money anymore than I like to be bothered when I'm trying to read a goddamned book underneath a palm tree I paid $264 to get next to. A Black woman seeking refuge in a multinational corporation may seem like a contradiction to some, but there you are. In this case it's a coincidence of entirely different self-interests: Sheraton/cash June Jordan's short run safety.

Anyway, I'm pretty sure "Olive" would look at me as though I came from someplace as far away as Brooklyn. Then she'd probably allow herself one indignant query before righteously removing her vacuum cleaner from my room; "and why in the first place you come down you without your husband?"

I cannot imagine how I would begin to answer her.

My "rights" and my "freedom" and my "desire" and a slew of other New World values; what would they sound like to this Black woman described on the card atop my hotel bureau as "Olive the Maid"? "Olive" is older than I am and I may smoke a cigarette while she changes the sheets on my bed. Whose rights? Whose freedom? Whose desire?

And why should she give a shit about mine unless I do something, for real, about hers?

It happens that the book that I finished reading under a palm tree earlier today was the novel, *The Bread Givers,* by Anzia Yezierska. Definitely autobiographical, Yezierska lays out the difficulties of being both female and "a person" inside a traditional Jewish family at the start of the 20th century. That any Jewish woman became anything more than the abused servant of her father or her husband is really an improbable piece of news. Yet Yezierska managed such an unlikely outcome for her own life. In *The Bread Givers,* the heroine also manages an important, although partial, escape from traditional Jewish female destiny. And in the unpardonable, despotic father, the Talmudic scholar of that Jewish family, did I not see my own and hate him twice, again? When the heroine, the young Jewish child, wanders the streets with a filthy pail she borrows to sell herring in order to raise the ghetto rent and when she cries, "Nothing was before me but the hunger in our house, and no bread for the next meal if I didn't sell the herring. No longer like a fire engine, but like a houseful of hungry mouths my heart cried, 'herring—herring! Two cents apiece!' " who would doubt the ease, the sisterhood of conversation possible between that white girl and the Black women selling straw bags on the streets of paradise because they do not want to die? And is it not obvious that the wife of that Talmudic scholar and "Olive," who cleans my room here at the hotel, have more in common than I can claim with either one of them?

This is my consciousness of race and class and gender identity as I collect wet towels, sunglasses, wristwatch, and head towards a shower.

I am thinking about the boy who loaned this novel to me. He's white and he's Jewish and he's pursuing an independent study project with me, at the State University where I teach whether or not I feel like it, where I teach without stint because, like the waiter, I am no fool. It's my job and either I work or I do without everything you need money to buy. The boy loaned me the novel because he thought I'd be interested to know how a Jewish-American writer used English so that the syntax, and therefore the cultural habits of mind expressed by the Yiddish language, could survive translation. He did this because he wanted to create another connection between us on the basis of language, between his knowledge/his love of Yiddish and my knowledge/my love of Black English.

He has been right about the forceful survival of the Yiddish. And I had become excited by this further evidence of the written voice of spoken language protected from the monodrone of "standard" English, and so we had grown closer on this account. But then our talk shifted to student affairs more generally, and I had learned that this student does not care one way or the other about currently jeopardized Federal Student Loan Programs because, as he explained it to me, they do not affect him. He does not need financial help outside his family. My own son, however, is Black. And I am the only family help available to him and that means, if Reagan succeeds in eliminating Federal programs to aid minority students, he will have to forget about furthering his studies, or he or I or both of us will have to hit the numbers pretty big. For these reasons of difference, the student and I had moved away from each other, even while we continued to talk.

My consciousness turned to race, again, and class.

Sitting in the same chair as the boy, several weeks ago, a graduate student came to discuss her grade. I praised the excellence of her final paper; indeed it had seemed to me an extraordinary pulling together of recent left brain/right brain research with the themes of transcendental poetry.

She told me that, for her part, she'd completed her reading of my political essays. "You are so lucky!" she exclaimed.

"What do you mean by that?"

"You have a cause. You have a purpose to your life."

I looked carefully at this white woman; what was she really saying to me?

"What do you mean?" I repeated.

"Poverty. Police violence. Discrimination in general."

(Jesus Christ, I thought: Is that her idea of lucky?)

"And how about you?" I asked.

"Me?"

"Yeah, you. Don't you have a cause?"

"Me? I'm just a middle-aged woman: a housewife and a mother. I'm a nobody."

For a while, I made no response.

First of all, speaking of race and class and gender in one breath, what she said meant that those lucky preoccupations of mine, from police violence to nuclear wipe-out, were not shared. They were mine and not hers. But here she sat, friendly as an old stuffed animal, beaming good will or more "luck" in my direction.

In the second place, what this white woman said to me meant that she did not believe she was "a person" precisely because she had fulfilled the traditional female functions revered by the father of that Jewish immigrant, Anzia Yezierska. And the woman in front of me was not a Jew. That was not the connection. The link was strictly female. Nevertheless, how should that woman and I, another female connect, beyond this bizarre exchange?

If she believed me lucky to have regular hurdles of discrimination then why shouldn't I insist that she's lucky to be a middle-class white Wasp female who lives in such well-sanctioned and normative comfort that she even has the luxury to deny the power of the privileges that paralyze her life?

If she deserts me and "my cause" where we differ, if, for example, she abandons me to "my" problems of race, then why should I support her in "her" problems of housewifely oblivion?

Recollection of this peculiar moment brings me to the shower in the bathroom cleaned by "Olive." She reminds me of the usual Women's Studies curriculum because it has nothing to do with her or her job: you won't find "Olive" listed anywhere on the reading list. You will likewise seldom hear of Anzia Yezierska. But yes, you will find, from Florence Nightingale to Adrienne Rich, a white procession of independently well-to-do women writers. (Gertrude Stein/Virginia Woolf/Hilda Doolittle are standard names among the "essential" women writers.)

In other words, most of the women of the world — Black and First World and white who work because we must — most of the women of the world persist far from the heart of the usual Women's Studies syllabus.

Similarly, the typical Black History course will slide by the majority experience it pretends to represent. For example, Mary McLeod Bethune will scarcely receive as much attention as Nat Turner, even though Black women who bravely and efficiently provided for the education of Black people hugely outnumber those few Black men who led successful or doomed rebellion against slavery. In fact, Mary McLeod Bethune may not receive even honorable mention because Black History too often apes those ridiculous white history courses which produce such dangerous gibberish as The Sheraton British Colonial "history" of the Bahamas. Both Black and white history courses exclude from their central consideration those people who neither killed nor conquered anyone as the means to new identity, those people who took care of every one of the people who wanted to become "a person," those people who still take care of the life at issue: the ones who wash and who feed and who teach and who diligently decorate straw hats and bags with all of their historically unrequired gentle love: the women.

Oh the old rugged cross
on a hill far away
Well I cherish the old rugged cross

It's Good Friday in the Bahamas. Seventy-eight degrees in the shade. Except for Sheraton territory, everything's closed.

It so happens that for truly secular reasons I've been fasting for three days. My hunger has now reached nearly violent proportions. In the hotel sandwich shop, the Black woman handling the counter complains about the tourists; why isn't the shop closed and why don't the tourists stop eating for once in their lives. I'm famished and I order chicken salad and cottage cheese and lettuce and tomato and a hard boiled egg and a hot cross bun and apple juice.

She eyes me with disgust.

To be sure, the timing of my stomach offends her serious religious practices. Neither one of us apologizes to the other. She seasons the chicken salad to the peppery max while I listen to the loud radio gospel she plays to console herself. It's a country Black version of "The Old Rugged Cross."

As I heave much chicken into my mouth tears start. It's not the pepper. I am, after all, a West Indian daughter. It's the Good Friday music that dominates the humid atmosphere.

Well I cherish the old rugged cross

And I am back, faster than a 747, in Brooklyn, in the home of my parents where we are wondering, as we do every year, if the sky will darken until Christ has been buried in the tomb. The sky should darken if God is in His heavens. And then, around 3 p.m., at the conclusion of our mournful church service at the neighborhood St. Phillips, and even while we dumbly stare at the black cloth covering the gold altar and the slender unlit candles, the sun should return through the high gothic windows and vindicate our waiting faith that the Lord will rise again, on Easter.

How I used to boy my head at the very name of Jesus: ecstatic to abase myself in deference to His majesty.

My mouth is full of salad. I can't seem to eat quickly enough. I can't think how I should lessen the offense of my appetite. The other

Black woman on the premises, the one who disapprovingly prepared this very tasty break from my fast, makes no remark. She is no fool. This is a job that she needs. I suppose she notices that at least I included a hot cross bun among my edibles. That's something in my favor. I decide that's enough.

I am suddenly eager to walk off the food. Up a fairly steep hill I walk without hurrying. Through the pastel desolation of the little town, the road brings me to a confectionary pink and white plantation house. At the gates, an unnecessarily large statue of Christopher Columbus faces me down, or tries to. His hand is fisted to one hip. I look back at him, laugh without deference, and turn left.

It's time to pack it up. Catch my plane. I scan the hotel room for things not to forget. There's that white report card on the bureau.

"Dear Guests:" it says, under the name "Olive." "I am your maid for the day. Please rate me: Excellent. Good. Average. Poor. Thank you."

I tuck this momento from the Sheraton British Colonial into my notebook. How would "Olive" rate *me?* What would it mean for us to seem "good" to each other? What would that rating require?

But I am hastening to leave. Neither turtle soup nor kidney pie nor any conch shell delight shall delay my departure. I have rested, here, in the Bahamas, and I'm ready to return to my usual job, my usual work. But the skin on my body has changed and so has my mind. On the Delta flight home I realize I am burning up, indeed.

So far as I can see, the usual race and class concepts of connection, or gender assumptions of unity, do not apply very well. I doubt that they ever did. Otherwise why would Black folks forever bemoan our lack of solidarity when the deal turns real. And if unity on the basis of sexual oppression is something natural, then why do we women, the majority people on the planet, still have a problem?

The plane's ready for takeoff. I fasten my seatbelt and let the tumult inside my head run free. Yes: race and class and gender remain as real as the weather. But what they must mean about the contact between two individuals is less obvious and, like the weather, not predictable.

And when these factors of race and class and gender absolutely collapse is whenever you try to use them as automatic concepts of connection. They may serve well as indicators of commonly felt conflict, but as elements of connection they seem about as reliable as precipitation probability for the day after the night before the day.

It occurs to me that much organizational grief could be avoided if people understood that partnership in misery does not necessarily provide for partnership for change: *When we get the monsters off our backs all of us may want to run in very different directions.*

And not only that: even though both "Olive" and "I" live inside a conflict neither one of us created, and even though both of us therefore hurt inside that conflict, I may be one of the monsters she needs to eliminate from her universe and, in a sense, she may be one of the monsters in mine.

I am reaching for the words to describe the difference between a common identity that has been imposed and the individual identity any one of us will choose, once she gains that chance.

That difference is the one that keeps us stupid in the face of new, specific information about somebody else with whom we are supposed to have a connection because a third party, hostile to both of us, has worked it so that the two of us, like it or not, share a common enemy. *What happens beyond the idea of that enemy and beyond the consequences of that enemy?*

I am saying that the ultimate connection cannot be the enemy. The ultimate connection must be the need that we find between us. It is not only who you are, in other words, but what we can do for each other that will determine the connection.

I am flying back to my job. I have been teaching contemporary women's poetry this semester. One quandary I have set myself to explore with my students is the one of taking responsibility without power. We had been wrestling ideas to the floor for several sessions when a young Black woman, a South African, asked me for help, after class.

Sokutu told me she was "in a trance" and that she'd been unable to eat for two weeks.

"What's going on?" I asked her, even as my eyes startled at her trembling and emaciated appearance.

"My husband. He drinks all the time. He beats me up. I go to the hospital. I can't eat. I don't know what/anything."

In my office, she described her situation. I did not dare to let her sense my fear and horror. She was dragging about, hour by hour, in dread. Her husband, a young Black South African, was drinking himself into more and more deadly violence against her.

Sokutu told me how she could keep nothing down. She weighed 90 lbs. at the outside, as she spoke to me. She'd already been hospitalized as a result of her husband's battering rage.

I knew both of them because I had organized a campus group to aid the liberation struggles of Southern Africa.

Nausea rose in my throat. What about this presumable connection: this husband and this wife fled from that homeland of hatred against them, and now what? He was destroying himself. If not stopped, he would certainly murder his wife.

She needed a doctor, right away. It was a medical emergency. She needed protection. It was a security crisis. She needed refuge for battered wives and personal therapy and legal counsel. She needed a friend.

I got on the phone and called every number in the campus directory that I could imagine might prove helpful. Nothing worked. There were no institutional resources designed to meet her enormous, multifaceted, and ordinary woman's need.

I called various students. I asked the Chairperson of the English Department for advice. I asked everyone for help.

Finally, another one of my students, Cathy, a young Irish woman active in campus IRA activities, responded. She asked for further details. I gave them to her.

"Her husband," Cathy told me, "is an alcoholic. You have to understand about alcoholics. It's not the same as anything else. And it's a disease you can't treat any old way."

I listened, fearfully. Did this mean there was nothing we could do?

"That's not what I'm saying," she said. "But you have to keep the alcoholic part of the thing central in everybody's mind, otherwise her husband will kill her. Or he'll kill himself."

She spoke calmly. I felt there was nothing to do but to assume she knew what she was talking about.

"Will you come with me?" I asked her, after a silence. "Will you come with me and help us figure out what to do next?"

Cathy said she would but that she felt shy: Sokutu comes from South Africa. What would she think about Cathy?

"I don't know," I said. "But let's go."

We left to find a dormitory room for the young battered wife.

It was late, now, and dark outside.

On Cathy's VW that I followed behind with my own car, was the sticker that reads BOBBY SANDS FREE AT LAST. My eyes blurred as I read and reread the words. This was another connection: Bobby Sands and Martin Luther King Jr. and who would believe it? I would not have believed it; I grew up terrorized by Irish kids who introduced me to the word "nigga."

And here I was following an Irish woman to the room of a Black South African. We were going to that room to try to save a life together.

When we reached the little room, we found ourselves awkward and large. Sokutu attempted to treat us with utmost courtesy, as though we were honored guests. She seemed surprised by Cathy, but mostly Sokutu was flushed with relief and joy because we were there, with her.

I did not know how we should ever terminate her heartfelt courtesies and address, directly, the reason for our visit: her starvation and her extreme physical danger.

Finally, Cathy sat on the floor and reached out her hands to Sokutu.

"I'm here," she said quietly, "Because June has told me what has happened to you. And I know what it is. Your husband is an alcoholic. He has a disease. I know what it is. My father was an alcoholic. He killed himself. He almost killed my mother. I want to be your friend."

"Oh," was the only small sound that escaped from Sokutu's mouth. And then she embraced the other student. And then everything changed and I watched all of this happen so I know that this happened: this connection.

And after we called the police and exchanged phone numbers and plans were made for the night and for the next morning, the young South African woman walked down the dormitory hallway, saying goodbye and saying thank you to us.

I walked behind them, the young Irish woman and the young South African, and I saw them walking as sisters walk, hugging each other, and whispering and sure of each other and I felt how it was not who they were but what they both know and what they were both preparing to do about what they know that was going to make them both free at last.

And I look out the windows of the plane and I see clouds that will not kill me and I know that someday soon other clouds may erupt to kill us all.

And I tell the stewardess No thanks to the cocktails she offers me. But I look about the cabin at the hundred strangers drinking as they fly and I think even here and even now I must make the connection real between me and these strangers everywhere before those other clouds unify this ragged bunch of us, too late.

27. Diversity and Its Discontents

Arturo Madrid

My name is Arturo Madrid. I am a citizen of the United States, as are my parents and as were my grandparents and my great-grandparents. My ancestors' presence in what is now the United States antedates Plymouth Rock, even without taking into account any American Indian heritage I might have.

I do not, however, fit those mental sets that define America and Americans. My physical appearance, my speech patterns, my name, my profession (a professor of Spanish) create a text that confuses the reader. My normal experience is to be asked, "And where are *you* from?" My response depends on my mood. Passive-aggressive, I answer, "From here." Aggressive-passive, I ask, "Do you mean where I am originally from?" But ultimately my answer to those follow-up questions that will ask about origins will be that we have always been from here.

Overcoming my resentment I try to educate, knowing that nine times out of ten my words fall on inattentive ears. I have spent most of my adult life explaining who I am not. I am exotic, but—as Richard Rodriguez of *Hunger of Memory* fame so painfully found out—not exotic enough . . . not Peruvian, or Pakistani, or whatever. I am, however, very clearly the *other,* if only your everyday, garden-variety, domestic *other.* I will share with you another phenomenon that I have been a part of, that of being a missing person, and how I came late to ьhat awareness. But I've always known that I was the *other,* even before I knew the vocabulary or understood the significance of otherness.

I grew up in an isolated and historically marginal part of the

Reprinted with permission of the author and the American Association of University Professors from *Academe* 76 (1990): 15–20. Arturo Madrid is Murchison Distinguised Professor of the Humanities at Trinity University. From 1984 until 1993 he served as Founding President of the Tomás Rivera Center, a national institute for policy studies on Latino issues.

United States, a small mountain village in the state of New Mexico, the eldest child of parents native to that region, whose ancestors had always lived there. In those vast and empty spaces people who look like me, speak as I do, and have names like mine predominate. But the *americanos* lived among us: the descendants of those nineteenth-century immigrants who dispossessed us of our lands; missionaries who came to convert us and stayed to live among us; artists who became enchanted with our land and humanscape and went native; refugees from unhealthy climes, crowded spaces, unpleasant circumstances; and, of course, the inhabitants of Los Alamos, whose sociocultural distance from us was accentuated by the fact that they occupied a space removed from and proscribed to us. More importantly, however, they—*los americanos*—were omnipresent (and almost exclusively so) in newspapers, newsmagazines, books, on radio, in movies, and, ultimately, on television.

Despite the operating myth of the day, school did not erase my otherness. It did try to deny it, and in doing so only accentuated it. To this day what takes place in schools is more socialization than education, but when I was in elementary school—and given where I was—socialization was everything. School was where one became an American, because there was a pervasive and systematic denial by the society that surrounded us that we were Americans. That denial was both explicit and implicit.

Quite beyond saluting the flag and pledging allegiance to it (a very intense and meaningful action, given that the United States was involved in a war and our brothers, cousins, uncles, and fathers were on the frontlines), becoming American was learning English, and its corollary: not speaking Spanish. Until very recently ours was a proscribed language, either *de jure*—by rule, by policy, by law—or *de facto*—by practice, implicitly if not explicitly, through social and political and economic pressure. I do not argue that learning English was not appropriate. On the contrary. Like it or not, and we had no basis to make any judgments on that matter, we were Americans by virtue of having been born Americans and English was the common language of Americans. And there was a myth, a pervasive myth, to the effect that if only we learned to speak English well—and particularly without an accent—we would be welcomed into the American fellowship.

Sam Hayakawa and the official English movement folks notwithstanding, the true text was not our speech, but rather our names and our appearance, for we would always have an accent, however perfect our pronunciation, however excellent our enunciation, however divine our diction. That accent would be heard in our pigmentation, our physiognomy, our names. We were, in short, the *other*.

Being the *other* involves contradictory phenomena. On the one hand being the *other* frequently means being invisible. Ralph Ellison wrote eloquently about that experience in his magisterial novel, *Invisible Man*. On the other hand, being the *other* sometimes involves sticking out like a sore thumb. What is she/he doing here?

For some of us being the *other* is only annoying; for others it is debilitating; for still others it is damning. Many try to flee otherness by taking on protective colorations that provide invisibility, whether of dress or speech or manner or name. Only a fortunate few succeed. For the majority of us otherness is permanently sealed by physical appearance. For the rest, otherness is betrayed by ways of being, speaking, or doing.

The first half of my life I spent downplaying the significance and consequences of otherness. The second half has seen me wrestling to understand its complex and deeply ingrained realities; striving to fathom why otherness denies us a voice or visibility or validity in American society and its institutions; struggling to make otherness familiar, reasonable, even normal to my fellow Americans.

I spoke earlier of another phenomenon that I am a part of: that of being a missing person. Growing up in northern New Mexico I had only a slight sense of us being missing persons. *Hispanos,* as we called (and call) ourselves in New Mexico, were very much a part of the fabric of the society, and there were *hispano* professionals everywhere about me: doctors, lawyers, schoolteachers, and administrators. My people owned businesses, ran organizations, and were both appointed and elected public officials.

My awareness of our absence from the larger institutional life of the society became sharper when I went off to college, but even then it was attenuated by the circumstances of history and geography. The demography of Albuquerque still strongly reflected its historical and cultural origins, despite the influx of Midwesterners and Easterners. Moreover, many of my classmates at the University of New Mexico were *hispanos,* and even some of my professors. I thought that would obtain at UCLA, where I began graduate studies in 1960. Los Angeles had a very large Mexican population and that population was visible even in and around Westwood and on the campus. Many of the groundskeepers and food-service personnel at UCLA were Mexican. But Mexican-American students were few and mostly invisible, and I do not recall seeing or knowing a single Mexican-American (or, for that matter, African-American, Asian, or American Indian) professional on the staff or faculty of that institution during the five years I was there. Needless to say, people like me were not present in any capacity at Dartmouth College, the site of my first teaching appointment, and of course were not even part of the institutional or individual mind-set. I knew then that we—a we that had come to encompass American Indians, Asian-Americans, African-Americans, Puerto Ricans, and women—were truly missing persons in American institutional life.

Over the past three decades the *de jure* and *de facto* types of segregation that have historically characterized American institutions have been under assault. As a consequence, minorities and women have become part of American institutional life. Although there are still many areas where we are not to be found, the missing persons phenomenon is not as pervasive as it once was. However, the presence of the *other*, particularly minorities, in institutions and in institutional life resembles what we call in Spanish a *flor de tierra* (a surface phenomenon): we are spare plants whose roots do not go deep, vulnerable to inclemencies of an economic, or political, or social, nature.

Our entrance into and our status in institutional life are not unlike a scenario set forth by my grandmother's pastor when she informed him that she and her family were leaving their mountain village to relocate to the Rio Grande Valley. When he asked her to promise that she would remain true to the faith and continue to involve herself in it, she asked why he thought she would do otherwise. "Doña Trinidad," he told her, "in the Valley there is no Spanish church. There is only an American church." "But," she protested, "I read and speak English and would be able to worship there." The pastor responded, "It is possible that they will not admit you, and even if they do, they might not accept you. And that is why I want you to promise me that you are going to go to church. Because if they don't let you in through the front door, I want you to go in through the back door. And if you can't get in through the back door, go in the side door. And if you are unable to enter through the side door I want you to go in through the window. What is important is that you enter and stay."

Some of us entered institutional life through the front door; others through the back door; and still others through side doors. Many, if not most of us, came in through windows, and continue to come in through windows. Of those who entered through the front door, some never made it past the lobby; others were ushered into corners and niches. Those who entered through back and side doors inevitably have remained in back and side rooms. And those who entered through windows found enclosures built around them. For, despite the lip service given to the goal of the integration of minorities into institutional life, what has frequently occurred instead is ghettoization, marginalization, isolation.

Not only have the entry points been limited, but in addition the dynamics have been singularly conflictive. Gaining entry and its corollary, gaining space, have frequently come as a consequence of demands made on institutions and institutional officers. Rather than entering institutions more or less passively, minorities have of necessity entered them actively, even aggressively. Rather than waiting to receive, they have demanded. Institutional relations have thus been adversarial, infused with specific and generalized tensions.

The nature of the entrance and the nature of the space occupied have greatly influenced the view and attitude of the majority population within those institutions. All of us are put into the same box; that is, no matter what the individual reality, the assessment of the individual is inevitably conditioned by a perception that is held of the class. Whatever our history, whatever our record, whatever our validations, whatever our accomplishments, by and large we are perceived unidimensionally and dealt with accordingly. I remember an experience I had in this regard, atypical only in its explicitness. A few years ago I allowed myself to be persuaded to seek the presidency of a well-known state university. I was invited for an interview and presented myself before the selection committee, which included members of the board of trustees. The opening question of that brief but memorable interview was directed at me by a member of that august body. "Dr. Madrid," he asked, "why does a one-dimensional person like you think he can be the president of a multi-dimensional institution like ours?"

Over the past four decades America's demography has undergone significant changes. Since 1965 the principal demographic growth we have experienced in the United States has been of peoples whose national origins are non-European. This population growth has occurred both through birth and through immigration. A few years ago discussion of the national birthrate had a scare dimension: the high — "inordinately high" — birthrate of the Hispanic population. The popular discourse was informed by words such as "breeding." Several years later, as a consequence of careful tracking by government agencies, we now know that what has happened is that the birthrate of the majority population has decreased. When viewed historically and comparatively, the minority populations (for the most part) have also had a decline in birthrate, but not one as great as that of the majority.

There are additional demographic changes that should give us something to think about. African-Americans are now to be found in significant numbers in every major urban center in the nation. Hispanic-Americans now number over 15 million people, and although they are a regionally concentrated (and highly urbanized) population, there is a Hispanic community in almost every major urban center of the United States. American Indians, heretofore a small and rural population, are increasingly more numerous and urban. The Asian-American population, which has historically consisted of small and concentrated communities of Chinese-, Filipino-, and Japanese-Americans, has doubled over the past decade, its complexion changed by the addition of Cambodians, Koreans, Hmongs, Vietnamese, et al.

Prior to the Immigration Act of 1965, 69 percent of immigration was from Europe. By far the largest number of immigrants to the United States since 1965 have been from the Americas and from Asia: 34 percent are from Asia; another 34 percent are from Central and South America; 16 percent are from Europe; 10 percent are from the Caribbean; the remaining 6 percent are from other continents and Canada. As was the case with previous immigration waves, the current one consists principally of young people: 60 percent are between the ages of 16 and 44. Thus, for the next few decades, we will continue to see a growth in the percentage of non-European-origin Americans as compared to European-Americans.

To sum up, we now live in one of the most demographically diverse nations in the world, and one that is increasingly more so.

During the same period social and economic change seems to have accelerated. Who would have imagined at mid-century that the prototypical middle-class family (working husband, wife as homemaker, two children) would for all intents and purposes disappear? Who could have anticipated the rise in teenage pregnancies, children in poverty, drug use? Who among us understood the implications of an aging population?

We live in an age of continuous and intense change, a world in which what held true yesterday does not today, and certainly will not tomorrow. What change does, moreover, is bring about even more change. The only constant we have at this point in our national development is change. And change is threatening. The older we get the more likely we are to be anxious about change, and the greater our desire to maintain the status quo.

Evident in our public life is a fear of change, whether economic or moral. Some who fear change are responsive to the call of economic protectionism, others to the message of moral protectionism. Parenthetically, I have referred to the movement to require more of students without in turn giving them more as academic protectionism. And the pronouncements of E. D. Hirsch and Allan Bloom are, I believe, informed by intellectual protectionism. Much more serious, however, is the dark side of the populism which underlies this evergoing protectionism—the resentment of the *other*. An excellent and fascinating example of that aspect of populism is the cry for linguistic protectionism—for making English the official language of the United States. And who among us is unaware of the tensions that underlie immigration reform, of the underside of demographic protectionism?

A matter of increasing concern is whether this new protectionism, and the mistrust of the *other* which accompanies it, is not making more significant inroads than we have supposed in higher education. Specifically, I wish to discuss the question of whether a goal (quality) and a reality (demographic diversity) have been erroneously placed in conflict, and, if so, what problems this perception of conflict might present.

As part of my scholarship I turn to dictionaries for both origins and meanings of words. Quality, according to the *Oxford English Dictionary,* has multiple meanings. One set defines quality as being an essential character, a distinctive and inherent feature. A second describes it as a degree of excellence, of conformity to standards, as superiority in kind. A third makes reference to social status, particularly to persons of high social status. A fourth talks about quality as being a special or distinguishing attribute, as being a desirable trait. Quality is highly desirable in both principle and practice. We all aspire to it in our own person, in our experiences, in our acquisitions and products, and of course we all want to be associated with people and operations of quality.

But let us move away from the various dictionary meanings of the word and to our own sense of what it represents and of how we feel about it. First of all we consider quality to be finite; that is, it is limited with respect to quantity; it has very few manifestations; it is not widely distributed. I have it and you have it, but they don't. We associate quality with homogeneity, with uniformity, with standardization, with order, regularity, neatness. All too often we equate it with smoothness, glibness, slickness, elegance. Certainly it is always expensive. We tend to identify it with those who lead, with the rich and famous. And, when you come right down to it, it's inherent. Either you've got it or you ain't.

Diversity, from the Latin *divertere,* meaning to turn aside, to go different ways, to differ, is the condition of being different or having differences, is an instance of being different. Its companion word, diverse, means differing, unlike, distinct; having or capable or having various forms; composed of unlike or distinct elements. Diversity is lack of standardization, of regularity, of orderliness, homogeneity, conformity, uniformity. Diversity introduces complications, is difficult to organize, is troublesome to manage, is problematical. Diversity is irregular, disorderly, uneven, rough. The way we use the word diversity gives us away. Something is too diverse, is extremely diverse. We want a little diversity.

When we talk about diversity, we are talking about the *other,* whatever that other might be: someone of a different gender, race, class, national origin; somebody at a greater or lesser distance from the norm; someone outside the set; someone who possesses a different set of characteristics, features, or attributes; someone who does not fall within the taxonomies we use daily and with which we are comfortable; someone who does not fit into the mental configurations that give our lives order and meaning.

In short, diversity is desirable only in principle, not in practice. Long live diversity . . . as long as it conforms to my standards, my mind set, my view of life, my sense of order. We desire, we like, we admire diversity, not unlike the way the French (and others) appreciate women; that is, *Vive la différence!* —as long as it stays in its place.

What I find paradoxical about and lacking in this debate is that diversity is the natural order of things. Evolution produces diversity. Margaret Visser, writing about food in her latest book, *Much Depends on Dinner,* makes an eloquent statement in this regard:

Machines like, demand, and produce uniformity. But nature loathes it: her strength lies in multiplicity and in differences. Sameness in biology means fewer possibilities and therefore weakness.

The United States, by its very nature, by its very development, is the essence of diversity. It is diverse in its geography, population, institutions, technology; its social, cultural, and intellectual modes. It is a society that at its best does not consider quality to be monolithic in form or finite in quantity, or to be inherent in class. Quality in our society proceeds in large measure out of the stimulus of diverse modes of thinking and acting; out of the creativity made possible by the different ways in which we approach things; out of diversion from paths or modes hallowed by tradition.

One of the principal strengths of our society is its ability to address, on a continuing and substantive basis, the real economic, political, and social problems that have faced and continue to face us. What makes the United States so attractive to immigrants is the protections and opportunities it offers; what keeps our society together is tolerance for cultural, religious, social, political, and even linguistic difference; what makes us a unique, dynamic, and extraordinary nation is the power and creativity of our diversity.

The true history of the United States is one of struggle against intolerance, against oppression, against xenophobia, against those forces that have prohibited persons from participating in the larger life of the society on the basis of their race, their gender, their religion, their national origin, their linguistic and cultural background. These phenomena are not consigned to the past. They remain with us and frequently take on virulent dimensions.

If you believe, as I do, that the well-being of a society is directly related to the degree and extent to which all of its citizens participate in its institutions, then you will have to agree that we have a challenge before us. In view of the extraordinary changes that are taking place in our society we need to take up the struggle again, irritating, grating, troublesome, unfashionable, unpleasant as it is. As educated and educator members of this society, we have a special responsibility for ensuring that all American institutions, not just our elementary and secondary schools, our juvenile halls, or our jails, reflect the diversity of our society. Not to do so is to risk greater alienation on the part of a growing segment of our society; is to risk increased social tension in an already conflictive world; and, ultimately, is to risk the survival of a range of institutions that, for all their defects and deficiencies, provide us the opportunity and the freedom to improve our individual and collective lot.

Let me urge you to reflect on these two words—quality and diversity—and on the mental sets and behaviors that flow out of them. And let me urge you further to struggle against the notion that quality is finite in quantity, limited in its manifestations, or is restricted by considerations of class, gender, race, or national origin; or that quality manifests itself only in leaders and not in followers, in managers and not in workers, in breeders and not in drones; or that it has to be associated with verbal agility or elegance of personal style; or that it cannot be seeded, nurtured, or developed.

Because diversity—the *other*—is among us, will define and determine our lives in ways that we still do not fully appreciate, whether that other is women (no longer bound by tradition, house, and family); or Asians, African-Americans, Indians, and Hispanics (no longer invisible, regional, or marginal); or our newest immigrants (no longer distant, exotic, alien). Given the changing profile of America, will we come to terms with diversity in our personal and professional lives? Will we begin to recognize the diverse forms that quality can take? If so, we will thus initiate the process of making quality limitless in its manifestations, infinite in quantity, unrestricted with respect to its origins, and more importantly, virulently contagious.

I hope we will. And that we will further join together to expand—not to close—the circle.

NOTES

The original version of this essay was delivered as the Tomás Rivera lecture at the 1988 meeting of the American Association for Higher Education.

PART IV

Diagnostic Assessment, Treatment, and Cultural Bias

A. DIAGNOSIS, CLASSIFICATION, AND LABELING

Many of the issues raised elsewhere in this collection, concerning the effects of scientific epistemology on methodology, also appear when one examines the underlying assumptions of psychological classification and assessment theory. When psychologists categorize and diagnose men and women from culturally diverse backgrounds and use theoretically or empirically derived standardized measurement scales and instruments, the first question of culture theorists is: Whose behaviors, values, interpersonal expectations and intentions, and expressive and cognitive styles are presumed to be the standard?

Arthur Kleinman, the influential cultural psychiatrist, examines the theoretical assumptions and methodological fallacies behind the search for universals in human pathogenesis and mental illness in chapter 28. By calling into question the "tacit professional ideology that exaggerates what is universal in psychiatric disorder and deemphasizes what is culturally particular," he exposes how research strategies which decontextualize human behaviors and exclude cultural variation as a source of error can lead to findings that are an artifact of methodology. Lack of appreciation for what he calls "cultural idioms of distress" leads psychiatric researchers to accept models of human mental illness that emphasize biology as the etiological bedrock whereas cultural specificity is minimized as epiphenomenal.

The "political innocence" of mental health workers, when it comes to matters of professional hegemony and policy that protect the status quo in theory and treatment, is the center of Isaac Prilleltensky's critique of the field of abnormal psychology in chapter 29. Even though the field has moved from models of human development and pathology that conceive of individuals as essentially asocial (sources of suffering located within the individual) to microsocial and macrosocial models which attend to family, community, and cultural contexts (sources of suffering located in the environment), many psychologists still avoid confronting sociopolitical realities and complexities; thus, intervention is focused on coping with what is rather than on social change. Of particular interest in this paper is Prilleltensky's critique of psychological models which are presumed to be progressive, for example, Szasz's labeling theory, family systems theory, and community psychology. Not so, says Prilleltensky, not when you look closely.

One of the strongest voices among Afro-American psychologists who write about racial and ethnic group differences in cognitive ability test performance is that of Janet Helms. Arguing persuasively for a culturalist perspective (as superior to a biological or environmentalist perspective) in the interpretation of group differences, Helms looks in chapter 30 at cultural equivalence fallacies that can invade psychometric theory, sampling strategies, and other measurement procedures. It is not a simple matter of correcting standard tests for culture bias or of constructing new cultural equivalency tests, she argues; it is necessary that practitioners and researchers alike confront the effects of white European-centered values and beliefs on cognitive ability testing and examine their implicit assumption of the superiority of white cognitive strategies.

In chapter 31, Enrico Jones and Avril Thorne bring to our attention what they call "the primacy of the subjective." We cannot understand people from diverse communities by relying on comparative studies of people grouped by large and problematic social categories (e.g., race or gender) or normed tests which reflect a static view of society. People and societies are constantly changing; cultural interpenetration is more common in the United States than intact cultural groups with distinctive boundaries; many American citizens are more bicultural or multicultural than monocultural. Jones and Thorne believe that, in order to understand persons in their historical and cultural context, we must move beyond positivist empirical methods which emphasize group differences to a study of within-group differences, subjective realities, and personal meaning-making. This is better accomplished, they claim, by interpretive methods, narrative accounts, and the verification of scientific interpretations through the involvement of informants and other members of the minority community as research collaborators. This strategy will require the researcher to relinquish his or her status as the "sole expert who brings findings together and draws conclusions."

28. Do Psychiatric Disorders Differ in Different Cultures? The Methodological Questions

Arthur Kleinman

. . . but where truth is too finicky, too uneven, or does not fit comfortably with other principles, we may choose the nearest amenable and illuminating lie. Most scientific laws are of this sort: not assiduous reports of detailed data but sweeping Procrustean simplifications.

—Nelson Goodman, *Ways of World Making*

THE ANATOMY OF CROSS-CULTURAL RESEARCH IN PSYCHIATRY

An anthropologist reading the literature in cross-cultural psychiatry will quickly convince himself that psychiatrists maintain a strong bias toward discovering cross-cultural similarities and "universals" in mental disorder.[1] This bias should not surprise us. Much cross-cultural research in psychiatry has been initiated with the desire to demonstrate that psychiatric disorder is like any other disorder and therefore occurs in all societies and can be detected if standardized diagnostic techniques are applied. In the late 1960s the WHO began a series of international comparisons of schizophrenics in a wide range of societies with precisely this motive.

The first of these studies, the International Pilot Study of Schizophrenia (IPSS), funded principally by the National Institute of Mental Health, set out to show that there are core symptoms of schizophrenia that cluster into more or less the same syndromal pattern in Western and non-Western, industrialized and nonindustrialized societies (WHO 1973, 1979). The accounts of clinicians working in

Reprinted with permission of The Free Press, a Division of Macmillan, Inc. from *Rethinking Psychiatry: From Cultural Category to Personal Experience* by Arthur Kleinman. Copyright © 1988 by The Free Press.

different parts of the world had repeatedly suggested this hypothesis. To prove it required a methodology in which groups of patients in participating research centers in India, Nigeria, Colombia, Denmark, the United Kingdom, the Soviet Union, and the United States were assessed by psychiatrists who were rigorously trained in the use of the same diagnostic instrument (the Present State Examination (PSE), a psychiatric interview schedule developed at the Institute of Psychiatry of the University of London), which had been carefully translated into the local languages. The psychiatrists' assessments showed a high degree of reliability within the centers and across the centers.

The IPSS clearly demonstrated that at each center, using strict inclusion and exclusion criteria, samples of psychotic patients could be assembled who displayed similar symptoms. The IPSS had run into several difficulties, however. First, most of the psychiatric patients who presented at the different clinical centers had to be excluded, since they did not fit the criteria. This suggested the possibility that what the study had accomplished was to use a template to stamp out a pattern of complaints that produced a more or less homogeneous sample whose similarity was an artifact of the methodology. The patients who were excluded from the study were precisely those who demonstrated the most heterogeneity. From an anthropological viewpoint, it is this very group—those who were excluded from IPSS sample—who would be expected to demonstrate the greatest cultural difference. Second, in spite of the homogenizing template approach there were still important cross-cultural divergences. One finding was expected based on the clinical literature: certain symptoms differed in prevalence across the centers. For example, most of the cases of catatonia were in India and Nigeria.

But a rather unexpected finding emerged that ran counter to conventional psychiatric reasoning of the time: the *course* of schizophrenia was better for patients in the less developed societies and worse for those in the industrially most advanced societies. This striking difference between countries, however, took a back seat to the finding that core schizophrenic symptoms could be demonstrated in all the centers. The latter was interpreted as further evidence for the biological basis of schizophrenia, which was invoked to explain the similar pattern in spite of greatly different sociocultural contexts. This, by the way, is a quite typical example of the invocation of biological explanations in psychiatry. Ironically, it is the reverse of the argument evolutionary biologists advance to explain the great diversity of species worldwide (Mayr 1981). There biology is viewed as the major source of variation.[2]

Following the IPSS, the WHO launched, again with quite substantial NIMH support, the far more ambitious Determinants of Outcome Study (Sartorius and Jablensky 1983). This study attempted to begin with a more representative sample of schizophrenic patients in the general population who made their first contact with a health or mental health agency—a measurement of so-called first-contact incidence of schizophrenia. That is, patients were assembled from various professional, administrative, and folk healing agencies in well-surveyed catchment areas, who were attending for the first time during an episode of psychotic disorder that met inclusion and exclusion criteria for schizophrenia. Patients and family members were then interviewed as in the IPSS with the PSE, but also with a more elaborate menu of forms assessing symptomatology, various risk factors, and course of disorder over several years.

This study is important enough to examine the findings in detail, because it is the most rigorous and systematic multicultural comparison ever undertaken to study mental illness (Sartorius and Jablensky 1983). More than 1,300 cases were studied in twelve centers in ten countries, including three centers in India (one being the only rural center in the study) and centers in Japan, Nigeria, Colombia, Denmark, the United Kingdom, and the United States (Rochester and Honolulu). The authors' summary of findings includes the following statement: "The frequency of the use of individual ICD [the WHO's International Classification of Disease, Ninth Revision] subtype rubrics varied from 0 to 65% of the cases in the different centers. Overall, paranoid schizophrenia was the most commonly diagnosed subtype followed by that of 'other' (undifferentiated) and acute schizophrenic episodes. However, in the developing countries the acute subtype diagnosis was used almost twice as often (in 40% of the cases) as the diagnosis of the paranoid subtype (in 23% of the cases). Catatonic schizophrenia was diagnosed in 10% of the cases in developing countries but in only a handful of cases in the developed countries. In contrast, the hebephrenic subtype was diagnosed in 13% of the patients in the developed countries and in only 4% of the patients in developing countries" (p. 16). Here we have three important instances of cross-cultural differences, yet the authors' chief conclusion is, "Patients with diagnosis of schizophrenia in the different popula-

tions and cultures share many features at the level of symptomatology . . ." (p. 24). They add that, "Once the existence of broad similarities or manifestations of schizophrenia across the centers was
established . . ." (p. 25). The authors are of course correct, they do
have evidence of "broad similarities," evidence they choose to highlight. But they also have evidence of substantial differences, evidence
they choose to deemphasize.

Take, as another example, the data on annual incidence of schizophrenia. The authors make two calculations—one for a "broad" diagnostic definition of schizophrenia that includes virtually all cases in
the sample, and another for a "restrictive" definition based on a
computer program (CATEGO) classification of a subtype called S+.
For the former, the rates of new cases of schizophrenia per year per
10,000 population range from 1.5 in Aarhus, Denmark, to 4.2 in
the rural catchment area of the Chandighar center in India. For
the latter, the more restrictive computer-based definition, the range
narrows impressively; it now is from 0.7 in Aarhus to 1.4 in Not-
tingham (pp. 18–19). The authors interpret these findings by arguing that the application of the restrictive definition is valid because
it does not result in such a decreased sample size that there is a loss
of statistical significance. They do not address the question of the
epistemological significance of scrapping most of a sample that shows
heterogeneity in order to work with the most homogeneous subsample. They conclude later in the paper that there is a relatively uniform rate of incidence for schizophrenia across the ten societies. From
the perspectives of psychiatric epidemiology and biostatistics this
may be a valid conclusion, but from a cultural point of view, it is
not. The broad sample, again from the cross-cultural perspective, is
the valid one, since it includes all first-contact cases of psychosis
meeting the diagnostic criteria. The restricted sample is artifactual,
since it places a clinical template on the original population that
excludes precisely those cases that demonstrate the most cultural
heterogeneity. This analytic methodology effectively transforms population-based data into clinic-based data, just the distortion in the
IPSS the Determinants of Outcome Study was meant to correct.

To be sure, the restrictive sample demonstrates that a core schizophrenic syndrome can be discovered among cases of first-contact psychosis in widely different cultures. This is an important finding,
frequently repeated by clinicians in single-culture studies. It is not,
however, evidence of a uniform pattern of incidence. Indeed, the

broader sample is the appropriate one to use to make that determination, and it demonstrates the pattern of incidence is not uniform. The restrictive sample is of most interest to psychiatrists because it demonstrates a narrow range of cultural difference; the broader sample is of most interest to anthropologists because it demonstrates a wide range of cultural variation. The biases of the two disciplines (psychiatry and anthropology) are inverse; and therefore it might be argued that both perspectives are essential complements in cross-cultural research. Other epidemiological studies of schizophrenia exhibit a much more substantial range of difference in incidence and prevalence around the globe, as would be expected of a disorder that appears to have a significant genetic basis (given the wide range of human genetic patterns around the world). The WHO findings based on the restricted sample are atypical and suggest the possible influence of an administrative or methodological artifact.

Several other key instances could be adduced in which the authors of the WHO report review findings that disclose both important similarities and important differences; yet Drs. Sartorius et al. elect to focus principally on the former, the "universals." Finally, these influential investigators reassess the data that support better outcome for schizophrenia in centers in developing societies. They report the crucial fact that this finding holds up even when mode of onset (acute versus insidious), which differs significantly across centers with many more acute onset cases in the developing world, is taken into account.

For several decades this finding has been the single most provocative datum to emerge in cross-cultural research in psychiatry (see Lambo 1955; Rin and Lin 1962; Jilek and Jilek-Aall 1970; Murphy and Raman 1971; Waxler 1977). Enormous effort has gone into research methods to verify it. At each stage, leading psychiatric researchers have played down its significance and expressed the expectation that it would turn out to be an artifact of the methodology. The WHO group is to be greatly commended for establishing the validity of this finding. Readers will be profoundly disappointed, however, if they hope to learn more about its sources or implications. The authors are silent on these points, which strangely enough do not appear to have received detailed investigation in this project called "Determinants of Outcome." That is to say, the most important finding of cross-cultural difference receives scant attention compared to that devoted to the findings of cross-cultural similarity.

Hypotheses have been generated about the causes of differential outcome since the late 1960s (Murphy 1968, 1982; Cooper and Sartorius 1977; Waxler 1977). Yet none of these seems to have been
tested. In the paper's conclusion, the other findings of cultural differences in mode of onset, symptomatology, and help seeking are deemphasized as well.

In all fairness to the authors, this is the first of the final reports
from this long-term outcome study, and later reports may well review the data on cross-cultural differences in more detail. Nonetheless, it would seem appropriate to ask why there is such a systematic
bias in interpretation. This question is especially appropriate, since
we are not dealing with a single instance of such bias, but rather
with a pattern repeated time and again in cross-cultural psychiatric
research. The WHO's cross-cultural study of depressive disorders
(Sartorius and Jablensky 1983) does much the same thing as do
the vast majority of reports by other groups of leading psychiatric
investigators.

There is, then, a tacit professional ideology that exaggerates what
is universal in psychiatric disorder and deemphasizes what is culturally particular. The cross-cultural findings for schizophrenia, major
depressive disorder, anxiety disorders, and alcoholism disclose both
important similarities *and* equally important differences. Hence the
chief anthropological question (how do psychiatric disorders differ
across cultures?) is a necessary addition to the main psychiatric question (how are psychiatric disorders similar across cultures?). Psychiatric research increasingly tends to be dominated by epidemiological
and survey assessments which involve large samples and achieve
statistically significant results. But compared to traditional clinical
assessments and anthropological field work, this research employs
relatively superficial assessments of patients. Epidemiologists conduct interviews once or at most several times for a total of no more
than an hour or two. Ethnography, in contrast, like psychotherapy,
places the anthropologist in very intensive long-term relations with
a small number of informants. Also like psychotherapy, it involves
relations of trust which, over the course of many months and years of
research, lead to the uncovering of deeply personal, subtle, and difficult to obtain findings. Those findings make up in validity for what
they lack, because of small sample size and informal interview methods, in reliability. What we need are studies that combine both methodologies; a few such studies, which I will review later on, have

already been completed, but they account for a very small proportion of cross-cultural research in psychiatry.

In order to illustrate the difficulties that beset cross-cultural psychiatric studies which lack an anthropological component, let us look at a recent and remarkably frank discussion of problems in the assessment of expressed emotion (EE)—an index particularly of critical comments, hostility, and emotional overinvolvement (excessive protectiveness and intrusive concern), but including positive feelings as well expressed by family members toward the patient—in the WHO's Determinants of Outcome Study. High level of negative expressed emotion in the families of schizophrenic patients, as I have already noted, has been found in England and the U.S. to be a strong predictor of relapse of schizophrenic patients (Vaughn and Leff 1976; Karno et al. 1987). The WHO study sought to corroborate this finding as well as to determine if EE plays a similar role in non-Western cultures. Wig et al. (1987) tested whether EE could be rated for the relatives of schizophrenics in the Chandighar center (India) of the Determinants of Outcome project. The senior author, one of India's preeminent psychiatric researchers, and his colleagues note that there indeed were problems in the evaluation of the quality and intensity of "positive remarks" and "warmth" on the taped record of the Camberwell Family Interview (CFI), the British instrument used in these studies in the West, but none affected the assessment of "critical comments" and "hostility." The interpretation of "overinvolvement" had some problems in the Indian sample, but these were ascribed to technical, not cultural difficulties.

Wig and his coworkers operationalized culture as linguistic differences in content and tonal quality of Hindi and English. Verification was defined as the measure of inter-rater reliability between London and Chandighar centers, and also between individual raters. The authors conclude, "It is evident from these results that the rating of critical comments can be transferred satisfactorily from English to Hindi."

These authors have established the reliability of measuring EE in India. They have not established its validity for Indian culture. Validity, as we have seen, is verification of concepts, not observations. Establishing the validity of this measurement requires the study of what EE—negative and positive, high and low—means in an Indian context. Inasmuch as anthropologists have shown, moreover, that emotion in India (as well as other societies) is communicated nonverbally through posture, gait, facial movements, and dress as well as subtle, indirect verbal displays of etiquette and other salient social metaphors such as offering food and receiving gifts (Nichter 1982; Shweder 1985), can an analysis of EE based entirely on direct expression of "critical," "hostile," or "negative" verbal terms be an adequate method of assessment? Culture creates alternative channels for communicating and distinctive idioms for expressing negative feelings. Evaluation of only the verbal channel and the direct idiom may well underestimate the extent to which Indian families communicate negative EE. In fact, Wig et al. (1987) have found that EE measured solely in the verbal mode is lower in Indian than in British or Danish families. (Jenkins, in press, has determined much the same for Mexican Americans, but she reasons that to understand this difference requires interpretation of fundamental differences in the family structure and interpersonal communication styles in societies.) The question remains, is the finding that EE can be measured in India with an instrument developed in London valid? The answer to that question cannot come from a coefficient of interrater reliability, but must await a much wider-angled ethnographic study of the context of emotional expression and its meaning in the families of schizophrenic patients in Indian culture. In the meantime, research such as the study we have reviewed may result in misleading conclusions.

WHAT IS THE TACIT MODEL IN PSYCHIATRY THAT EXAGGERATES BIOLOGICAL DIMENSIONS OF DISEASE AND DEEMPHASIZES THE CULTURAL DIMENSIONS OF ILLNESS?

Many psychiatrists, when they interpret the findings of international and cross-ethnic studies, draw on a usually tacit model of pathogenicity/pathoplasticity which has become close to a professional orthodoxy. In this model, biology is presumed to "determine" the cause and structure of what McHugh and Slavney (1986) call the "forms" of mental disease, while cultural and social factors at most "shape" or "influence" the "content" of disorder. The paradigmatic example given to illustrate this ideological view is paranoid delusions in schizophrenia: the biologically based disease is said to cause the *structure* of delusional thought processes; the system of cultural beliefs is said to organize the *content* of paranoid thinking, here as fear that the CIA is out to harm one, there as fear that the KGB is the culprit. In other words, the structure is the same; only the content changes.

Another classical case recounted by psychiatric researchers is the finding that bodily complaints predominate over psychological complaints in depressive and anxiety disorders among members of non-Western societies, among traditionally oriented ethnic minorities, and among less educated members of the lower socio-economic classes (Leff 1981; Kirmayer 1984). This finding is taken to mean that the biology of depression and anxiety disorders underwrites the inner form of these disorders, but cultural beliefs and values so shape the "expression" of the disease that the bodily complaints come to "mask" the "real" psychiatric disease "underlying" them. Indeed, at one point the term "masked depression" was widely used to indicate this phenomenon.

In this stratigraphic version of the mind/body dichotomy, biology is bedrock (the source of pathogenesis), and psychological and especially social and cultural layers of reality are held to be epiphenomenal (i.e., they are said to exert "merely" pathoplastic effects). They need to be stripped away to disclose the "real" disease underneath. As expressed by the illness/disease distinction, the disease is an entity or object hidden by the illness, which is a cultural dressing: catatonic or somatic or hysterical manifestations of the underlying causal process. Diagnosis, as we have already seen, becomes reductionism, the downward semiotic interpretation of the "signs" of the infrastructure of disease out of "the blooming, buzzing confusion" of illness symptoms. The same old wine in another bottle is the distinction between *endogenous* depression, which is supposed to occur independent of social and psychological influences as an inherited biological disorder, and *reactive* depression, which is supposed to be a response to environment and personal experience. This turns out to be an untenable dichotomy for anyone who examines the evidence, since environmental and personal sources of depression are to be found, if carefully looked for, regardless of the severity of the depression or the burden of genetic predisposition.

The anthropological gaze picks out an alternative model. Depression experienced entirely as low back pain and depression experienced entirely as guilt-ridden existential despair are such substantially different forms of illness behavior with distinctive symptoms, patterns of help seeking, and treatment responses that although the disease in each instance may be the same, the illness, not the disease, becomes the determinative factor. And one might well ask, is the disease even the same?

There is overwhelming evidence in North American society that the social and psychological components of the illness experience of chronic pain are more powerful determinants of disability and return to work than the biological abnormalities, which are nonetheless real enough (Yelin et al. 1980; Stone 1984; Osterweis et al. 1987). For these reasons, a more useful model is one in which biological and cultural processes dialectically interact. At times one may become a more powerful determinant of outcome, at other times the other. Most of the time it is the interaction, the relationship, between the two which is more important than either alone as a source of amplification or damping of disability in chronic disorder. That dialectic transforms the physiology of pain and suffering, which becomes inseparable from personal perception and social interaction, just as it alters the perception of social relationships, which become part of the neurology of pain (Lewontin, Rose and Kamin 1984).

The tacit pathogenetic/pathoplastic model is also inadequate for understanding the culture-bound syndromes. The tendency once again is to interpret these syndromes, which are either unusually conspicuous or actually specific to a culture area, as exotic (the viewpoint is always that of the homespun Westerner) illness manifestations of particular underlying diseases, e.g., *susto* ("soul loss") in Mexico is taken to be a culturally dressed-up version of good old depressive disorder; semen loss syndromes, once abstracted from their unusual constellation of South Asian cultural beliefs, are basically anxiety disorders; *amok* in Malaysia is merely a homicidal version of the brief reactive psychoses seen in emergency rooms in London and New York; and so forth (cf. Kiev 1972).

The picture is a great deal more complex than these reductionistic equations make it out to be. Carr (1978; Carr and Vitaliano 1985) shows, for example, that amok is a *final common pathway of behavior* along which are shunted various kinds of problems: acute and chronic psychoses of various kinds, to be sure, but also alcohol and drug intoxications, criminal behavior without psychopathology, and the like. Guarnaccia et al. (in press) and Low (1985), among others, demonstrate that *ataques de nervios* among Hispanics—pseudo-seizures, syncopes, and other dissociation states—are not simply conversion disorders as a generation of psychoanalytically oriented Caucasian psychiatrists treating Puerto Rican patients paternalistically claimed when they renamed *ataques* "the Puerto Rican Syndrome." Instead, these culturally approved behaviors may be anything from a medical disease to a normal aspect of bereavement.

Anthropologists suggest that a more accurate mapping of the experience of culture-bound syndromes is provided by regarding such behaviors as idioms of distress. Nichter (1982) has shown that South Havik Brahmin women in India express distressed emotions, family tensions, and other social problems not through a discursive jargon of psychologically minded terms, but rather through traditional cultural idioms such as dietary preference for certain foods, religious metaphors, and the traditional tropes of Ayurvedic medicine (e.g., humoral imbalance in the body). Good (1977), working in a Turkish town in Iran, describes how the idiom "heart distress" condenses key sources of frustration (e.g., typical conflicts in marriage and family) in a culturally sanctioned mode of expression, heart complaints, that communicates distress in both the sick person's body and social relations. The complaint of heart distress opens up negotiations for change, in marriage, family, and work, among protagonists whose troubling life circumstances are metaphorically articulated by this local idiom. The medical anthropological literature contains accounts of cultural idioms of distress for many of the world's cultures.

Not surprisingly, bodily metaphors predominate (Douglas 1970; Needham 1979). In all societies, the body appears to represent both a rich source of symbols for communicating about the social group or the individual person and a way to express the brute materiality of the experience of many forms of misery, much of it socially caused. Bodily complaints can be metaphors of personal, social, and even political distress (Comaroff 1985; Taussig 1980; Turner 1984). The body expresses social status and relationships through patterns of mutilation, adornment, and socially learned styles of gait, posture, and movement. That culture-bound syndromes represent communicative or rhetorical idioms—which, for instance, alert an inattentive husband or sensitize an overly demanding mother-in-law to the personal plight of a long-suffering wife/daughter-in-law or which give the sufferer a little more leverage in negotiating for a less difficult work situation or help in managing household responsibilities in a time of great pressure—does not mean the complaints are without biological significance. Rubel et al. (1984), for example, demonstrate that victims of *susto* in Oaxaca have higher rates of mortality than matched controls. Again, models of culture-biology interactions relating biomedical and anthropological analyses best account for the data.

Heretofore, theory in cross-cultural psychiatry has been impressively underdeveloped. There is no tradition of critical analysis of alternative models. There has been a tendency to avoid engaging the pertinent scholarly context of ideas in a critical colloquy. Avoidance of theoretical issues may have been useful at an earlier stage in psychiatry, when grand theories abounded and there was little agreement on diagnostic criteria. But it can no longer be justified. Anthropology's contribution is to press for a more theoretically sophisticated and conceptually critical approach to cross-cultural studies, an approach that develops midrange concepts to explain how culture affects mental illness. Translation is a seemingly prosaic but in fact particularly significant issue for advancing a cultural critique of psychiatric research; it suggests alternative concepts and methods of inquiry.

HOW DOES TRANSLATION INFLUENCE THE STUDY OF MENTAL ILLNESS IN DIFFERENT CULTURES?

Medical, including psychiatric, research often proceeds as if translation was a nuisance to be managed in much the same way as one controls the demographics in matched samples. For psychologists, translation looms as a larger concern but one that is reduced to a technical problem in research methods. It can be managed through a rigorous process of translation by one set of bilingual key informants; back translation into the original language of the psychometric instrument by yet another set of bilingual informants; negotiation of the differences in order to restructure the questionnaire to be semantically (not merely lexically) accurate; and testing of its reliability compared to other measures of the same phenomena that have already been used in the recipient society and by different investigators. Quantitative standards, such as a correlation coefficient for reliability, once met, relieve the psychologist's concern about the translatability and utility of her questionnaire in another culture.

For the ethnographer, in contrast, translation is neither a nuisance nor a strictly technical question. Rather, translation is the essence of ethnographic research. In anthropological studies, description of indigenous categories of thought, modes of communication, and patterns of behavior is at heart the translation from one cultural system into another. That translation is what the ethnographer spends her days doing—i.e., getting it right from the native point of view. Having achieved a valid understanding of the local context in its own terms, the ethnographer then undertakes another type of translation in which she puts her findings into terms and categories appropriate for transcultural comparison. That kind of translation is the final, not as in psychiatry the first, step in research. Therefore, the cultural challenge to psychiatry is to take a much more strenuous, systematic, and contextual approach to translation. Ethnographers insist that psychiatrists recognize translation as the central issue in cross-cultural research. A few examples of a cultural orientation to methods of translation used in psychiatric research should clarify why this subject is so important.

Most psychiatric assessment instruments are developed in a vernacular that is quite difficult to translate into other languages. North American diagnostic instruments, for example, frequently depend on colloquial terms like "feeling blue" or "feeling down" to evaluate depressive affect. A strictly lexical translation of these terms would have no meaning in most non-Western languages. Manson et al. (1985) translated the widely used and NIMH-sponsored Diagnostic Interview Schedule (DIS) into Hopi, an American Indian language. One of the DIS questions includes the concepts of guilt, shame, and sinfulness in the same sentence. Each of these concepts was clearly understood to convey distinctive meaning by 23 bilingual Hopi health professionals. They indicated to Manson and his colleagues that three separate questions were required to render this questionnaire item into Hopi without confounding potentially different responses. Kinzie and his coworkers (1982) experienced a similar problem in developing a Vietnamese-language depression scale for use with Vietnamese refugees in the United States. They found that "shameful and dishonored" but not "guilt" discriminated depressed from nondepressed Vietnamese Americans.

When Gaviria et al. (1984) translated the DIS into Spanish for research in Peru, many of the substances listed in the substance-abuse section of the questionnaire were unavailable in Peru; on the other hand, coca paste, a major drug in Peru, did not appear in the North American-oriented DIS. For some of their informants who were illiterate and who had no prior experience filling out a questionnaire, the responses elicited represented a misunderstanding of intentions more than an accurate reflection of their mental state. Gaviria et al. also note that in their experience the responses to an interview relate to theoretical constructs within the local culture. Neurasthenia, as we have seen, is a salient cultural category in the popular culture in China, though it no longer forms a coherent category for most North Americans. For a research interview to be conceptually valid in China, it needs to operationalize this category, turn neurasthenia into a series of linked questions that explore its phenomenology and meaning, not simply list its symptoms. In their entirety, several of the leading symptom checklists commonly used in psychiatric research include the symptoms that appear in the neurasthenic syndrome. Because these are not organized into a syndromal cluster, however, the symptom checklists fail to elicit subjects' informed response. Thus, Chinese research subjects suffering from neurasthenia could not convey, through responses to items in such Western-based questionnaires, either that they had neurasthenia or the full range of their experience of that condition (Kleinman 1982; Cheung et al. 1981). This is true in all non-Western contexts. Unless questionnaires add operationalized symptom clusters for locally salient illness experience, they fail to validly register cultural differences in the symptomatology of mental illness.

Intracultural diversity makes the task of developing culturally meaningful translations even more complex. Canino et al. (1987) used the Spanish-language version of the DIS (developed at UCLA for use with Mexican Americans) in a study of Puerto Ricans. They had to change 67 percent of the questions in order to adapt the instrument to the colloquial Spanish spoken by Puerto Ricans. Level of acculturation, history of migration, education, class, sex, age cohort, and urban/rural residence further influence the process of effective translation. Yet few psychiatric studies go to the trouble to systematically consider these variables. Indeed, I have reviewed grant applications by psychiatrists proposing research with rural populations in South America in which they translated their questionnaires from English into Spanish even though most of their subjects were Indians who were likely to speak Spanish poorly if at all.

To assess cultural differences adequately, it is essential to translate local idioms of distress and add them to standard questionnaires, while deleting those that make no sense in the local culture. This may seem obvious, but it is not routinely done. For example, Ebigbo (1982) has demonstrated that Nigerian psychiatric patients have a unique set of somatic complaints — "things like ants keep on creeping in various parts of my brain" and "I feel heat in my head" — which are not represented in standard symptom screening scales, including those used in most research with Nigerian patients; yet they are robust predictors of mental illness. Kinzie et al. (1982) found that among Vietnamese Americans, the concept "sadness" was represented by three different terms and "discouragement" by two. Among Latinos, Guarnaccia (personal communication) points out, headaches are described as *dolor de cabeza* ("headache") and *dolor del cerebro* ("brainache"), and these two expressions may be associated with different experiences and disorders. In a number of African cultures, anxiety is expressed as fear of failure in procreation or in dreams or complaints about witchcraft. To adequately evaluate psychopathology among members of these cultures, it is necessary to ask about these fears, dreams, and complaints.

During the 1950s and 1960s, a number of multiethnic psychiatric studies were carried out in New York City (Srole et al. 1962; Dohrenwend 1966; Haberman 1970, 1976) using the 22 Item Scale (22IS), a symptom checklist containing primarily somatic symptoms of anxiety and depression. These studies consistently found that of the ethnic groups in the sample, Puerto Ricans reported the highest number of symptoms. In the Midtown Manhattan Study this finding was especially striking (Srole et al. 1962). Although the Puerto Rican subsample was quite small, 61 percent of the Puerto Rican subjects reported experiencing impairing levels of symptoms compared with 31 percent of the non-Puerto Ricans. Not one of the 27 Puerto Ricans was rated as "well"! Dohrenwend (1966) demonstrated that the differences in reported levels of symptoms were better explained by attitudes toward the social desirability of reporting psychosomatic symptoms than by different levels of psychopathology (see p. 31). Guarnaccia (personal communication) argues that the symptoms of the 22IS fit closely with the category *nervios* ("nerves") among Puerto Ricans, a folk complaint associated with headaches, trembling, palpitations, difficulty concentrating, insomnia, worries, and gastrointestinal symptoms. He suggests what made Puerto Ricans respond so readily to the scale is that the instrument inadvertently tapped a salient cultural category associated with the stress of acculturation of recent Puerto Rican immigrants to New York

City—a problem hardly ever mentioned in psychiatric investigations.

There are other means by which culture influences psychiatric research. One of those concerns the repeated finding that bodily states and psychological experiences are monitored (i.e., perceived), assessed, and reported differently by members of different cultural groups. In Zborowski's (1952) classical account of difference in reporting pain among Irish, Italian, Jewish, and Anglo-Saxon Americans, ethnicity correlated highly with degree of expressivity, pain tolerance, and worries over the sigificance of the experience. Angel and Thoits (1987) review evidence indicating that Mexican Americans focus their concern on different parts of the body and different symptoms than the mainstream North American population. "Nerves," for example, is no longer a common complaint among middle-class members of North American society, whereas it is still an important idiom of distress among Hispanics and natives of Appalachia. "Falling out," "high blood," and "pressure" are complaints of lower-socioeconomic-class Southern blacks, based on folk medical beliefs, which are not routinely assessed by psychiatrists or epidemiologists (Snow 1974; Weidman 1977; Nations et al. 1985) even though they are important expressions of distress in this population.

There is evidence, to which I have alluded, that the social undesirability (stigma) of reporting distressing symptoms when asked in questionnaire-based studies is less among Hispanics than among blacks or Northern European Americans (see also, Haberman 1976; Krause and Carr 1978; Vernon et al. 1982). This difference appears to increase the likelihood that Hispanic subjects will be defined as suffering more distress and disease on epidemiological scales. Gaines and Farmer (1986) show that complaining about health and personality problems among impoverished members of Southern European cultures has a long history of providing the status of cynosure to so-called visible saints, individuals who become moral exemplars of the burden of life's difficulties and the obdurate grain of martyrdom in human nature. Complaining in this cultural context is positively valued and rewarded. This is in strong contrast to Northern European traditions that emphasize austerity, continence and understatement of personal troubles and that attach great stigma to the open expression of complaints as an indication of personal "weakness." Thus, different cultural norms influence how individuals in different societies respond to questionnaires. The repeated finding on psychiatric epidemiological surveys that blacks report fewer complaints in spite of suffering high levels of distressing social conditions appears to be a part of a long-standing and understandable response strategy by means of which blacks have tried to deflect the prying attention of social agencies. Not surprisingly, then, black respondents give more information to black interviewers (Dohrenwend 1966).

The social setting of research also influences the findings. Subjects interviewed in a medical clinic—where much of the cross-cultural research has been conducted that discloses more somatization of psychological problems in the non-Western world—are more likely to express physical complaints than subjects interviewed in their homes. After all, their expectation is likely to be that physical complaints are what physicians want to hear. Mitchell et al. (1985) report another common problem in cross-cultural research. A North American interview schedule which they used with Peruvian Indians was insistent to the point of violating the reticent style of response of Indians when talking to non-Indian professionals. Cultural convention sometimes makes it virtually impossible to ask questions in surveys about sexuality and other highly charged topics. For example, surveys in China frequently drop items about sexuality from the Western questionnaires they employ, for this reason. Yet such information can often be obtained by ethnographers, who develop relationships of trust over long stretches of time with informants that enable them to probe intimate meanings.

From an anthropological vantage point, these potentially confounding cultural influences on the determination of whether a patient in another society or a member of an ethnic minority group should be assessed as ill, and if so with what specific diagnosis, should make psychiatrists extremely cautious in interpreting the results of past surveys and in planning new research. This is an especially important caution for clinicians, since misdiagnosis is commonplace in cross-cultural settings of health care. Nonetheless, in spite of the difficulties I have reviewed, some recent studies have systematically taken into account cultural differences in a way that is a model for future research.

Manson and his colleagues (1985) organized a combined psychiatric epidemiology and ethnography of depressive illness among Hopi Indians. A team of anthropologists and psychiatrists first carried out a systematic translation of a standard psychiatric assessment interview (DIS) into Hopi based on a detailed anthropological understanding of the local context. They then elicited Hopi categories of sickness that are believed to affect people's minds or spirits. From this list they identified five categories of illness which intersected in different ways with the North American category of depressive neurosis. The English translations of these indigenous categories of disorder include "worry sickness," "unhappiness," "heartbroken," "drunken like craziness with or without alcohol," and "disappointment; pouting." The symptoms for these Indian disease concepts were included in the diagnostic instrument developed by Manson, who is himself a Native American anthropologist, and his psychiatric coworkers. "Unhappiness" correlated strongly with depressed affect on the DIS; it did not correlate with any of the other symptoms of depression. "Heartbroken," on the other hand, correlated strongly with a number of the concomitant symptoms of depression. Thus, this interdisciplinary team was able to demonstrate important local expressions of disorder that are not subsumed by existing North American psychiatric categories and that would be missed if research was conducted by following only the standard North American research criteria. Their work is also an excellent model of how to translate and adapt clinical diagnostic interviews and questionnaires so that they are valid in a very different cultural setting. In an earlier study, Carstairs and Kapur (1976), a Scottish psychiatrist raised in India and an Indian psychiatrist trained in Scotland, developed a sensitive psychiatric interview schedule for use in a local area of Karnataka in south India, based on their extensive review of clinical records of patients from that area and knowledge of local idioms of distress. These local symptom clusters and idioms were then built into their diagnostic interview. These studies indicate that culturally sensitive and anthropologically informed psychiatric research is feasible. The extreme relativism of some antipsychiatry anthropologists is as outrageously ideological as is the universalistic fundamentalism of some card-carrying biological psychiatrists. [3]

NOTES

1. Sections of this chapter are adapted and expanded from Kleinman (1987). The review of the methodological issues benefited greatly from collaboration with Professors Peter Guarnaccia and Byron Good.
2. "There are good biological reasons to question the idea of fixed universal categories. In a broad sense, they run counter to the principles of the Darwinian theory of evolution. Darwin stressed that populations are collections of unique individuals.

In the biological world there is no typical plant. . . . Qualities we associate with human beings and other animals are abstractions invented by us that miss the nature of the biological variation." (Rosenfeld, 1986, p. 22).
3. An interesting collection of illustrations of the value of combining anthropological and epidemiological methods can be found in Janes et al. (1986). That volume should convince even diehard defenders of ethnography that it can be combined with quantitative epidemiological techniques to the benefit of both disciplines.

REFERENCES

Angel, R., and P. Thoits. 1987. The impact of culture on the cognitive structure of illness. *Culture, Medicine and Psychiatry* 2:465–94.

Canino, G. J., et. al. 1987. The Spanish DIS: Reliability and concordance with clinical diagnoses in Puerto Rico. *Archives of General Psychiatry* 44:420–26.

Carr, J. 1978. Ethnobehaviorism and the culture-bound syndromes: The case of amok. *Culture, Medicine and Psychiatry* 2:269–93.

Carr, J., and P. Vitaliano. 1985. Theoretical implications of converging research on depression and culture-bound syndromes. In A. Kleinman and B. Good, eds., *Culture and depression.* Berkeley: University of California Press; pp. 244–66.

Carstairs, M., and R. Kapur. 1976. *The great universe of Kota: Change and mental disorder in an Indian village.* Berkeley: University of California Press.

Cheung, F., et al. 1981. Somatization among Chinese depressives in general practice. *International Journal of Psychiatry in Medicine* 10:361–74.

Comaroff, J. 1985. *Body of power, spirit of resistance.* Chicago: University of Chicago Press.

Cooper, Jr., and N. Sartorius. 1977. Cultural and temporal variations in schizophrenia. *British Journal of Psychiatry* 130:50–55.

Dohrenwend, B. 1966. Social status and psychological disorder. *American Sociological Review* 31:14–34.

Douglas, M. 1970. The healing rite. *Man* 5:302–08.

Ebigbo, P. O. 1982. Development of a culture specific (Nigeria) screening scale of somatic complaints indicating psychiatric distress. *Culture, Medicine and Psychiatry* 8:29–44.

Gaines, A., and P. Farmer. 1986. Visible saints: Social cynosures and dysphoria in the Mediterranean tradition. *Culture, Medicine and Psychiatry* 10:295–330.

Gaviria, M., et al. 1984. Developing instruments for cross-cultural research. Paper presented at the American Psychiatric Association Annual Meeting.

Good, B. 1977. The heart of what's the matter: The semantics of illness in Iran. *Culture, Medicine and Psychiatry* 1:25–28.

Goodman, N. 1978. *Ways of world making.* New York: Hackett.

Guarnaccia, P., et al. In press. *Nervios* in Puerto Ricans. *Medical Anthropology.*

Haberman, P. W. 1970. Ethnic differences in psychiatric symptoms reported in community surveys. *Public Health Reports* 85:495–502.

———. 1976. Psychiatric symptoms among Puerto Ricans in Puerto Rico and New York City. *Ethnicity* 3:133–44.

Janes, C. R., et al. 1986. *Anthropology and epidemiology.* Dordrecht, Holland: D. Reidel.

Jenkins, J. H. In press. Conceptions of schizophrenia as a problem of nerves: A cross-cultural comparison of Mexican-Americans and Anglo-Americans. *Social Science and Medicine.*

Jilek, W. G., and L. Jilek-Aall. 1970. Transient psychosis in Africans. *Psychiatric Clinics* 3:337–64.

Karno, M., et al. 1987. Mental disorder among Mexican-Americans and non-Hispanic whites in Los Angeles. In *Health and behavior: Research agenda for Hispanics*. Chicago: University of Illinois at Chicago, Simon Bolivar Hispanic Research Program, ed. M. Gaviria and J. D. Arand; pp. 110–26.

Kiev, A. 1972. *Transcultural psychiatry*. Hammondsworth, England: Penguin.

Kinzie, D., et al. 1982. Development and validation of a Vietnamese language depression rating scale. *American Journal of Psychiatry* 139:1276–81.

Kirmayer, L. 1984. Culture, affect and somatization, Parts 1 and 2. *Transcultural Psychiatry Research Review* 21:159–88, 237–62.

Kleinman, A. 1982. Neurasthenia and depression. *Culture Medicine and Psychiatry* 6:117–90.

———. Anthropology and Psychiatry. *British Journal of Psychiatry* 151:447–54.

Krause, N., and L. G. Carr. 1978. The effects of response bias in the survey assessment of the mental health of Puerto Rican migrants. *Social Psychiatry* 13:167–73.

Lambo, T. 1955. The role of cultural factors in paranoid psychosis among the Yoruba. *Journal of Mental Science* 101:239–66.

Leff, J. 1981. *Psychiatry around the globe*. New York: Marcel Dekker.

Lewontin, R. C., S. Rose, and L. J. Kamin. 1984. *Not in our genes*. New York: Pantheon.

Low, S. 1985. *Nervios in Costa Rica*. Philadelphia: University of Pennsylvania Press.

Manson, S., et al. 1985. The depressive experience in American Indian communities. In *Culture and depression*, ed. A. Kleinman and B. Good. Berkeley: University of California Press; pp. 331–68.

Mayr, E. 1981. *The growth of biological thought*. Cambridge, MA: Harvard University Press.

McHugh, P., and A. Slavney. 1986. *The perspectives of psychiatry*. Baltimore: Johns Hopkins University Press.

Mitchell, T., et al. 1985. The DIS in Latin America. Paper presented at Annual Meeting of the American Psychiatric Association.

Murphy, H. B. M. 1968. Cultural factors in the genesis of schizophrenia. In *The transmission of schizophrenia*, eds. D. Rosenthal and S. Kety. Elmsford, NY: Pergamon.

———. *Comparative psychiatry: The international and intercultural distribution of mental illness*. New York: Springer-Verlag.

Murphy, H. B. M., and A. C. Raman. 1971. Chronicity of schizophrenia and indigenous tropical peoples. *British Journal of Psychiatry* 118:489–97.

Nations, M., et al. 1985. "Hidden" popular illnesses in primary care: Residents' recognition and clinical implications. *Culture, Medicine and Psychiatry* 9:223–40.

Needham, R., ed. 1979. *Right and left: Essays on dual symbolic classification*. Chicago: University of Chicago Press.

Nichter, M. 1982. Idioms of distress. *Culture, Medicine and Psychiatry* 5:379–408.

Osterweis, M., et al. eds. 1987. *Pain and disability*. Washington, DC: National Academy Press.

Rin, H., and T. Y. Lin. 1962. Mental illness among Formosan aborigines as compared with Chinese in Taiwan. *Journal of Mental Science* 108:134–46.

Rosenfield, I. 1986. Neural Darwinism: A new approach to memory and perception. *New York Review of Books* 33, no. 15:21–27.

Rubel, A., et al. 1984. *Sussto*. Berkeley: University of California Press.

Sartorius, N., and A. Jablensky. 1983. *Depressive disorders in different cultures*. Geneva: WHO.

————. 1986. Early manifestations and first contact incidence of schizophrenia. *Psychological Medicine* 16:909–28.

Shweder, R. A. 1985. Menstrual pollution, soul loss, and the comparative study of emotions. In *Culture and depression,* eds. A. Kleinman and B. Good. Berkeley: University of California Press; pp. 182–215.

Snow, L. 1974. Folk medical beliefs and their implications for care of patients. *Annals of Internal Medicine* 81:82–96.

Srole, L., et al. 1962. *Mental health in the metropolis: The Midtown Manhattan Study.* New York: McGraw-Hill.

Stone, D. 1984. *The disabled state.* Philadelphia: Temple University Press.

Taussig, M. 1980. *The devil and commodity fetishism in South America.* Chapel Hill: University of North Carolina Press.

Turner, B. 1984. *The body and society.* Oxford: Basil Blackwell.

Vaughn, C., and J. Leff. 1976. The measurement of expressed emotion in the families of psychiatric patients. *British Journal of Social and Clinical Psychology* 15:157–65.

Vernon, S., et al. 1982. Response tendencies, ethnicity and depression scores. *American Journal of Epidemiology* 116:484–95.

Waxler, N. 1977. Is outcome for schizophrenia better in non-industrialized societies? *Journal of Nervous and Mental Disease* 167:144–58.

Weidman, H. H. 1977. Falling out. *Social Science and Medicine* 13B:95–112.

WHO. 1973. *The international pilot study of schizophrenia.* Geneva: WHO.

————. 1979. *Schizophrenia: An international follow-up study.* Chichester: John Wiley.

Wig, N. N., et al. 1987. Expressed emotional schizophrenia in North India, I. The cross-cultural transfer of ratings of relatives' expressed emotion. *British Journal of Psychiatry* 151:156–59.

Yelin, E., et al. 1980. Toward an epidemiology of work disability. *Milbank Memorial Fund Quarterly* 58, no. 3:385–414.

Zborowski, M. 1952. Culture components in responses to pain. *Journal of Social Issues* 8:16–30.

29. The Politics of Abnormal Psychology: Past, Present, and Future

Isaac Prilleltensky

INTRODUCTION

At a time when the ability of North American society to promote human welfare for the population at large is questioned on numerous accounts (e.g., Edwards, *et al.*, 1986; George and Wilding, 1976; Sennett and Cobb, 1972), psychologists of various orientations have become increasingly and justifiably concerned with psychology's witting or unwitting strengthening of the societal status quo (Albee, 1989; Anderson and Travis, 1983; Braginsky, 1985; Buss, 1979; Holland, 1978; Larsen, 1986; Prilleltensky, 1989; Sampson, 1981; Sarason, 1981a; Sullivan, 1984). Psychologists need to be alert to the appropriation of psychological formulations by policy-makers who extrapolate from the realm of *psycho*pathology to *socio*pathology. The risk involved in such extrapolation is the explanation of social ills in purely psychological and individualistic terms, a stratagem bound to result in a narrow conceptualization of social predicaments. Hence, professionals in the field of abnormal behavior should be cognizant of the sociopolitical repercussions of their theorizing.

The purpose of this inquiry is twofold. First, to examine the implications of models of abnormal psychology for social change or support for the present social order. Second, to propose some directions for a paradigm shift is psychopathology in which (a) the analysis and treatment of abnormal behavior would not facilitate inadvertent endorsement of undesirable social conditions, and in which (b) these undesirable social conditions could be addressed in order to

Reprinted by permission of the author and Plenum Publishing Corporation from *Political Psychology* 11 (1990): 767–785 © Plenum Publishing Corporation.

alleviate human suffering, psychological and otherwise. Through a dialectical approach, the suggested blueprint should deal with social and psychological concerns at once.

In the area of psychopathology, political ramifications derive mainly from the effect attributed to societal factors in the etiology, emergence, and reproduction of problems usually referred to as psychological. In most cases, the lesser the concern with and for societal variables, the greater the likelihood that the political message will be a conservative one, simply because social adversities such as poverty and crime are likely to be attributed to personal—as opposed to structural—deficiencies. Conversely, as the concern with and for societal variables increases, so does the likelihood that the political message will be a progressive one (e.g., Wineman, 1984).

If one were to schematically depict the sociopolitical history of the field in the last 40 years, one would notice a progression from an *asocial* approach, through an enhanced awareness of its *microsocial* elements, to an increased alertness of *macrosocial* variables. The medical model, either in its organic or psychodynamic version, captures the essence of the asocial stage, the political implications of which appear to be fairly conservative. Theories with a salient interpersonal and transactional component such as labeling and family therapy are representative of the microsocial phase. Highly progressive and conservative interpretations can be given to these models of abnormal behavior. An effort will be made to elucidate their political repercussions. Community psychology, prevention, and the ecological approach are examples of the macrosocial paradigm. Inasmuch as these target the social aspects of psychopathology and direct intervention efforts at social reform, they contain a strong progressive element. However, their efforts seem to have been undermined by the fact that they have not gone far enough in addressing the ideological and political context. The latter will be dealt with in the paradigm termed *macro-sociopolitical.*

None of these, it should be noted, entirely superseded the rest. Rather, they *dynamically coexist* in a state of tension in which different approaches momentarily dominate the field. Currently, in terms of its derivatives for social reform, the field of abnormal psychology is at a crossroads. With a growing "movement to 'remedicalize' psychiatry" (Reiser, 1988 and "cognitive" (i.e., "internalize," "endogenize") abnormal psychology, there is a distinct possibility of a retreat into the original conservative apolitical stance. On the other hand, there is an effort to expand the understanding of its events and their impact on the mental health of the population.

ABNORMAL PSYCHOLOGY I: ASOCIAL

Albee (1981) has aptly conceptualized the asocial approach to the study of abnormal behavior as the *defect* model. The defect method, also known as medical (Braginsky and Braginsky, 1976) or mental medicine (Foucault, 1954/1987), analyzes "inappropriate" behavior in terms of an internal organic or psychological malfunction. Whatever inability the person may suffer from is located *within* the individual. As a result, etiological reasoning and intervention strategies are predominantly directed at the single identified patient (e.g., Nelson *et al.*, 1985). While environmental factors are not entirely disregarded, they are given second priority and remain largely in the background. At best, these are variables to be thought of but not acted upon.

The defect model bifurcates into an organic and psychological branch (e.g., Braginsky and Braginsky, 1976; Foucault, 1954/ 1987). Its organic or biochemical form, mostly espoused by psychiatrists but by psychologists as well, contends that conduct deemed "irrational" is largely determined by biological, neural, or chemical abnormalities. It follows, then, that most mental diseases would ultimately be cured by biochemical methods. "In recent years, a multitude of psychopharmacological preparations have been advanced as *the* treatment, if not the cure, for a variety of mental diseases" (Braginsky and Braginsky, 1976, p. 72). This is not to devalue the contribution made by pharmacotherapy in the alleviation of suffering in certain cases, but simply to highlight the fact that a single-minded search for organic cures diverts resources from much needed improvements in the social ecology.

The expression *Homo psychologicus* (Foucault, 1954/1987, p. 74) represents the immense importance ascribed to the individual psyche in the psychological version of the defect model. As a supposedly autonomous entity, the person carries within him/herself the causes of his/her own malady, and is therefore to be modified to be returned to the community as a well-adjusted citizen. Unprecedented impetus for this treatment modality was furnished by applied—as opposed to theoretical—psychoanalysis. It is important to distinguish between the political implications of psychoanalytic theory and practice. While the former criticizes oppressive elements of social entities, such as the family and religion and advocates for change (e.g., Abramson, 1984; Caruso, 1964; Englert and Suarez, 1985; Freud, 1927/1964; Marcuse, 1966), the latter tends to reinforce existing social institutions by focusing exclusively on the malfunctions of the individual psyche (Brooks, 1973: Jacoby, 1983). To be sure, there have been attempts to pursue the practice of a radical psychoanalysis in North America (Kovel, 1981), but those have been overshadowed by the more widely spread conservative branch of psychoanalysis (Jacoby, 1983; Thomas and Sillen, 1972). The diversity of trends within the pyschoanalytic movement precludes a conclusive and categorical statement about the political effects of psychoanalysis in general. However, like Jacoby (1983), I would argue that abnormal psychology has readily embraced the more conservative elements of psychoanalysis, while politics and other liberal arts have taken hold of its more progressive components.

In effect, applied psychoanalysis, like the biochemical approach, deemphasizes the role played by "out of the skin" elements in the genesis and reproduction of the person's actions. This trend has begun to gain renewed vigor through cognitive therapy, whereby a mind cure is primarily called for, often at the expense of careful consideration of societal solutions (Prilleltensky, 1990; Stoppard, 1989).

Inadvertently, the defect paradigm promoted the notion that maladapted persons are the sole product of a less able organism and/or a genetic handicap. As a result, preventive social action is not deemed crucial. Such an attitude, voiced by Lamb and Zusman (1979) is highly symptomatic of the resurgence of the asocial model in abnormal psychology. Their attack on preventive programs translates into fewer efforts at advancing our understanding and treatment of social constellations of factors affecting the mental health of the population. While Lamb and Zusman's views have been refuted on numerous accounts (Albee, 1986; Nelson et al., 1985), they have managed to influence the policies of at least one province in Canada: British Columbia has adopted their propositions in its mental health planning report (see Nelson et al., 1985).

In each of these modalities, biochemical, psychodynamic or cognitive, there is a tendency to portray the individual as dissociated from the wider systems of society, thus creating an ahistorical and asocial image of persons (Sarason, 1981a, b). When human suffering is interpreted in terms of a deficient organism, a distinct conforming message emerges quite clearly: poor nutrition, detrimental living conditions, unemployment, and poverty in general are "determined" by the inability of those people to help themselves (e.g., Gross, 1980; Ryan, 1971, 1981). "To blame the problems of those who are most severely affected by destructive conditions *primarily* on the deficits of 'character disorder' or 'pathology' of individuals is a classic case of blaming the victim" (Wineman, 1984, pp. 44–45).

Albee (1986) has cogently argued that as long as psychologists, psychiatrists, and, most importantly, social policy legislators continue to believe that mental illness, criminal tendencies, and low intelligence derive mainly from a deficient psyche or organism, early compensatory education programs and primary prevention programs in general never will be satisfactorily implemented.

ABNORMAL PSYCHOLOGY II: MICROSOCIAL

The microsocial approach refers to a number of theories and studies whose primary concern has been the identification of pathological and/or iatrogenic interpersonal processes in the immediate context of a specific setting such as the psychiatric hospital or the family. Unlike the almost uniform conservative stance of the asocial model, the political repercussions of the microsocial are quite ambiguous. Both strong progressive and conservative messages can be found in the latter. The microsocial approaches to abnormal psychology that I have chosen to present are *labeling* and *family therapy*. The former has been selected for discussion primarily because of the vast confusion surrounding the political views of Szasz. Contrary to popular perceptions, his beliefs appear to embody highly conservative principles (cf. Sedgwick, 1982; Vatz and Weinberg, 1983). Family therapy is worth examining because of its ambiguous political repercussions. Though allegedly progressive when compared to asocial models, its preoccupation with the family unit militates against a comprehensive analysis of structural forces in the genesis of abnormal behavior. Other microsocial conceptualizations of abnormal psychology, such as behavior modification and humanism, can be found in Holland (1978) and Prilleltensky (1989), respectively.

The Politics of Labeling

By now a well-known body of literature has been devoted to examining the iatrogenic aspects of psychological and psychiatric practices in mental health settings [for reviews see books by P. Brown (1985), Grusky and Pollner (1981), and Dean *et al.* (1976)]. A salient theme in that literature is the contribution to and solidification of mental illnesses through labeling.

Two sharply contrasting political uses have been made of labeling theory and research. Left-wing interpretations indict the mental health establishment as a sophisticated means of social control. Right-wing interpretations indict the establishment on charges of furnishing an "excuse" for deviant individuals. According to the latter, the mental health system is too liberal. It helps criminals go unpunished by classifying them as mentally ill. Both interpretations will be briefly explored.

Labeling is intimately related to social control. The proliferation of the term "disease" and the medicalization of social deviance for purposes of social control are widely documented phenomena in our culture (e.g., Conrad, 1981; Glenn and Kunnes, 1973; Pearson, 1975; Scheff, 1976). The notion of mental illness has been strategically utilized as a nonjudicial mode of treating social deviants, political dissidents, and nonconformists not only in the communist block (Fireside, 1979; Medvedev and Medvedev, 1971) but also in the North American society (e.g., Bayer, 1981; Foucault, 1985; Halleck, 1971; Nahem, 1981; Schacht, 1985; Spiers, 1973).

Furthermore, left-wing readings contend that labeling theory has demonstrated quite convincingly that mental ilnesses are not the sole product of intrapsychic mechanisms but also of interpersonal transactions based on inequality of power. Expectations placed on helpless individuals by mental health professionals, relatives, friends, and society at large greatly determine the behavior of the former. In exposing these transactions, labeling theory has been instrumental in undermining the hegemony exercised by the medical model and its concomitant conservatism. Simply put, "the community response is critical in shaping and organizing the nature and extent of what will come to be seen as pathology" (Grusky and Pollner, 1981, p. 40).

The broad political repercussions of labeling as a means of social control have been succinctly articulated by Scheff (1976). He claimed that "to the extent that medical (and psychiatric) science lends its name to the labeling of nonconformity as mental illness, it is giving legitimacy to the social status quo" (p. 215).

Psychiatrists Szasz (1963, 1965, 1974, 1984) and Wood (1986) also oppose the use of labels, but for entirely different reasons. In their view (a) they are supposedly "myths" concocted by professionals, and (b) provide an excuse for people who engage in deviant behavior and/or lack moral fiber. In advancing the former proposition they have at least theoretically and potentially deprived of services individuals requiring help. The risks involved in the "myth" argument have been cogently expressed by Coulter:

> That there are economic, political, juridical, temporal and ideological pressures to which some clinicians succumb is a well-documented and socially important fact; but to conclude from a documentation of abuses to the non-discriminability of mental illness or to its "non-existence" is to indulge in a distracting and potentially harmful metaphysics. (Coulter, 1979, p. 149)

Yet, the "myth" position keeps strengthening (Wood, 1986). Perhaps the most conservative derivation of this notion is that if mental illness is basically a myth, then there is no such thing as committing a crime due to mental illness. By promoting that postulate, Szasz, who has been erroneously regarded as a progressive and even a radical, has been acting as a protector of the status quo; for in avoiding the issue of mental illness, he also eludes placing society on the stand. Vatz and Weinberg are quite correct in noting that indeed "a basic conservatism is central to Szasz's work" (1983, p. 17) (see also Sedgwick, 1982). Consider for example Szasz's desire to abolish the insanity plea:

> Should people also be free to be a danger to others? This problem disappears once we recognize that criminals cannot be divided into two categories — that is, persons who break the law because they choose to and persons who break it because their "mental illness" compels them to do so. All criminal behavior should be controlled by means of the criminal law, from the administration of which psychiatrists ought to be excluded. (Szasz, 1984, p. 31)

Szasz completely avoids the question of intention and possible environmental precipitating factors. Much like Szasz, Wood (1986) perceives deviant behavior not as madness but rather as badness.

> The view is taken here that such people are bad rather than mad, and should be treated as such, being far better off in prison than in a hospital if they

have broken the law. . . . The deficiency in sociopathy is a moral deficiency. The individual exhibits no conscience, cannot hear, or chooses to ignore, its dictates. He chooses to be bad in exactly the same way as others choose consistently to be good. He represents the inferior end of the good-bad continuum. (Wood, 1986, p. 41)

Both Szasz and Wood appear to oversimplify an intricate issue in terms of a hardly defensible dichotomy between good civilians and bad civilians. By vehemently espousing the politico-legal postulates of individual responsibility and individualistic solutions, they seem to overlook the possibility that some individuals might engage in criminal behavior in large part due to societal precipitating facts, however distant and complex. As a psychiatrist recently pointed out, it must be remembered that some criminal patterns, "are due not to individual psychopathology per se, but to basic institutional factors that make such behavior almost inevitable under certain circumstances . . . our society is so structural that many people are driven to destroy, impair or threaten the interests of other people" (Marmor, 1988, pp. 489–490).

The Politics of Family Therapy

Since the late 50s, family processes have been identified as a source of major psychological disorders such as schizophrenia. Through elaborate interactions among family members, one person is subjected to a particular kind of treatment that may be referred to as *psychological oppression* (Bateson *et al.*, 1956; Bowen, 1978; Laing and Esterson, 1974). This insight was historically highly relevant in the evolution of the family therapy movement, a trend whose often contradictory political implications need to be spelled out.

Founded primarily on the principles of general systems theory, originally postulated by Bertalanffy (1968), family therapy became an essential tool in analyzing and modifying family dynamics. The notion of a system as a "complex of interacting elements" (Bertalanffy, 1968, p. 55), was readily applicable to the family situation. The introduction of general systems theory into the field of abnormal psychology represented a shift from mechanistic, linear cause-and-effect reasoning to a more global, interactive, and circular mode of thinking (Goldenberg and Goldenberg, 1985; Hoffman, 1981; Karpel and Strauss, 1983; Levant, 1984; Tomm, 1980). The adoption of a systemic frame of reference cultivated the aspiration that not only would the individual be studied in the context of the family, but also that the family would be investigated in the larger context of society. That very expectation, which contained the progressive seed of family therapy, appears to remain largely unfulfilled (Busfield, 1974; Jacoby, 1975; Mannino and Shore, 1984; Poster, 1978; Wineman, 1984).

A minimalist reading of systems theory has led the field to perceive the family as the ultimate system to be concerned with, and to pay only lip service to wider societal systems. Systems family therapy has been operating under the working (not theoretical) assumption that intervention is with *all* the family, and *nothing but* the family (e.g., Mannino and Shore, 1984; Pearson, 1974). Pearson's (1974) observation that family therapy "rips *family structure* out of wider *social structure* and proceeds to lay the fault at the door of the family itself, labeling it a 'sick' family" (p. 147) describes the situation quite well. Mannino and Shore (1984) have summarized the truncated evolution of family therapy. Their account is worth quoting at length:

Recent writings on the family, especially in the area of family therapy, place great emphasis upon systems theory and the importance of interactions, communications, and patterns of relationships. Too often, however, family therapists tend to concentrate their efforts entirely on the 'family,' to the neglect of . . . the environmental context of the family's activities. . . . Thus, it appears that we may have moved (not in a sense of growth) from the boundaries of the individual personality structure unrelated to the environment, to the boundaries of the family unrelated to the environment. . . . The latter substitutes a family orientation for the individual. Thus, we look to the family system for indications of the problem and, when found, direct treatment on this relationship system as the intervention target. In both of these approaches the ecological context is ignored and either the individual or the family, depending upon the orientation, is viewed as the only level necessary to focus upon for diagnosis and intervention. Disregarded in these approaches is the concept that the problem could lie at the level of the ecological system, of which the individual and the family are component parts. (Mannino and Shore, 1984, pp. 76–77)

Hence, the transition effected by family therapists from an individualistic model to a systemic one has been rather limited. As James and McIntyre (1983) pointed out, "despite family therapy's claim to a broader perspective, it is a perspective which is itself limited by its failure to take account of powerful and pervasive social forces" (p. 123). By depicting the family as a central perpetrator in the infliction of psychological distress, attention is deflected from social conflicts that may actively shape and perpetuate the mental health of the population.

ABNORMAL PSYCHOLOGY III: MACROSOCIAL

We have witnessed the progression from individualistic to microsocial conceputalizations of abnormal psychology. This third paradigm represents a much broader perception of the role played by society in contributing to mental health/illness. This position, furthered through community psychology (e.g., Heller and Monahan, 1977; Rappaport, 1977) and the ecological approach (O'Conner and Lubin, 1984), has gathered impetus in the last 20 years. Rather than rejecting the two paradigms previously presented, community psychology endeavors to integrate their accomplishments with the firmly held view that psychological disorders can be neither understood nor treated in isolation from social factors.

While "on paper" community psychology endorses a discernment of human behavior that incorporates personal, communal, and global forces such as economy and politics, in practice it appears to have fallen short of properly addressing a key constituent in the sociogenesis of psychopathology: The unequal distribution of power in society and its concomitant fragmentation into markedly opposed interest groups. That is to say that in principle community psychology promotes the politicization of abnormal behavior, a much-needed emphasis. However, when they become involved in the political arena, the kind of politics advocated by community psychologists is not a radical one. In other words, it is a politics that does not threaten the status quo. Consequently, its implications are not as effectual as desired. An elaboration of these propositions is in order.

Declarative statements about the purposes of community psychology contain explicit mention of dissatisfaction with the status quo and a clear desire to alter it.

Community psychology is interested in social change, particularly in those systems of society where psychologists are active participants. Change in society involves relationships among its component parts, encompassing those of individuals to social systems such as schools, hospitals, and courts, as well as to other individuals. *Change toward a maximally equitable distribution of psychological as well as material resources is sought.* (Rappaport, 1977, p. 3) [emphasis added]

To eliminate any doubts about the scope of its endeavor, Rappaport asserts that "community psychology is by its very nature dedicated to a challenge of the status quo" (1977, p. 29). These words clearly illustrate the *intent* to change societal structures. This aspiration emanates from the realization that "an ecological perspective, focusing on the match or 'fit' between persons and environments, rather than on 'fixing up' those who are seen as inferior . . . is the most sensible" (Rappaport, 1977, p. 3).

Political activity, then, is an inherent part of this paradigm, for environments and social structures cannot otherwise be transformed to suit the needs of individuals. Community psychologists have, at least in principle, "overstepped the limits of the available psychological paradigms and are now interested in social change, social justice, politics, economics and social systems as well as individuals" (Rappaport, 1977, p. 19). This paradigm was to address the human experience in a global and integrative, as opposed to fragmentary fashion.

As envisioned by Rappaport in 1977, community psychology was indeed very promising. However, as evaluated by Sarason in 1984 (Sarason, 1984), the field was at best making its very first steps in the political scenario; at worst, it was still too attached to the comfort of the academic world to venture into the uncertainties of the political arena. Sarason's (1984) observations gain further support from the lack of political awareness and activity recently observed in the literature on ecological (Jason and Glenwick, 1984; O'Connor and Lubin, 1984) as well as social and community interventions (Gesten and Jason, 1987). Gesten and Jason (1987) conclude their review stating that *"Psychologists in the past have largely avoided participation in public policy matters. The concerns of the future may render such involvement on the part of a significant subgroup far more essential"* (p. 451).

To be sure, community psychologists have taken into account the influence of systemic variables such as social classes and institutions, but by and large their analyses have stopped there. This factual consideration has not been accompanied by a serious challenge of these very structures. The term *coping* more than *changing* typifies social and community interventions. Though too few to be very meaningful, attempts at the latter are beginning to emerge. Examples of empowerment-projects testify to that effect.

I would propose that if meaningful social action is to take place, an adjustment in community psychology's priorities and vision of the political world is called for. These are presented in the next and last paradigm to be discussed.

ABNORMAL PSYCHOLOGY IV: MACRO-SOCIOPOLITICAL

This model commences where community psychology stops, that is, in the enhancement of critical political awareness. It is not intended to substitute the macrosocial perspective endorsed by community psychology but rather to complete its task. The following is primarily an outline for a paradigm that, though already advocated by many psychologists, still needs considerable strengthening.

Proposed here is a coalition between community psychology and community politics. While the former brings the scientific and research background necessary for understanding the impact of societal structures on the human experience, the latter may provide the insight required not only for scrutinizing the social system but also for modifying it. Community politics is differentiated here from conventional politics in that it may question the effectiveness of the current political process itself in bringing about meaningful reforms, not the least of which is equality for all sectors of the population (Ryan, 1981). When the conventional political process, as well as most major endeavors affecting public life, are manipulated by the rich and powerful (Domhoff, 1986; Gross, 1980; Reich and Edwards, 1986; Schwartz, 1987), it is not at all certain that the interests of underrepresented constituencies such as the mentally ill or the poor will be meaningfully served (Wineman, 1984). Community politics seeks to empower the underpriviledged to affirm their rights and interests.

Power is a key element in the preservation or change of the social order. Consequently, community psychologists ought to be more appreciative of its crucial role. Such need may be satisfied by the proposed unification between community psychology and community politics. These two enterprises are highly compatible in that both pursue social changes to better serve the needs of particularly vulnerable populations. The infusion of activism which would be attained by this model may revitalize important community psychology practices which have been dormant or unduly relegated to a second place.

In order to further the advocated amalgamation of forces, a few directions are outlined below. These implications for action are not necessarily innovative. Rather, they represent an effort to establish new priorities in practices that are either already in existence, or have been waiting to be articulated. In either case, the suggestions made below are believed to be entirely congruent with the paradigm which community psychology has been attempting to promote.

From Public Policy to Political Public

Currently, community psychologists become in involved in politics mostly through the legislative process—a process whereby decisions are made by individuals who are too removed from the vicissitudes of the suffering population, be that population mental patients, visible minorities, women, or the poor. Public-policy-makers are not necessarily in touch with these people's shared plight unless the latter loudly voice their concerns. This will be accomplished by politicizing the public.

Individuals should be educated to assert their needs, instead of having professionals do that for them. Professionals, too, are many times quite removed from the suffering of their clients. Rather than going up to the legislators to advocate for the people, community psychologists ought to go down to the people to help them in affirming their interests. Empowerment projects of this sort have been conducted with promising results (Bermant and Warwick, 1978; Gesten and Jason, 1987). A fruitful cross-fertilization may occur by learning from empowerment projects conducted by political scientists and mental-health workers not only in North America but in other countries as well [for an example of work in the Italian mental-health system, see Basaglia (1981); for empowerment of a small Peruvian peasant community, see Dobyns et al. (1971)].

Public policy may be at present the most important catalyst for change, but a more political public may be even more important in that it may set the tone not only for the policies to be legislated but also for pursuing alternate means of social change (cf. Wineman, 1984).

From Interdisciplinary to Interclass Thinking and Action

The need to engage professionals from other disciplines in the solution of community problems (e.g., Bechtel, 1984) is heard far more often than the equally important need to involve community members themselves. This may entail a shift from expert advice to interclass dialogue. The professional helper, who usually belongs to the middle class, needs to be educated about the plight of community members who in many cases belong to the lower class. This interclass communication may be more fruitful than more interdisciplinary communication. This is not to devalue the opinions of experts but rather to convey a change in priorities.

From Single-Issue to Systemic-Political Thinking and Action

Although concentration of energies on a single issue, such as deinstitutionalization, is useful in that it helps gather momentum for much needed changes or at least palliatives; it is also dangerous in that it promotes a very fragmentary view of systemic complexities. Piecemeal action is constantly under the threat of being undermined by overwhelming structural impositions.

A few examples should suffice to illustrate this point. In a typical primary prevention example, "efforts to reduce the incidence and management of diarrhea in infants through parent education in simple health care practices were constrained by the fact that many families had limited access to uncontaminated water" (Halpern, 1988, p. 257). By the same token, it is becoming increasingly obvious that poverty will not be eradicated by a few more jobs or the acquisition of a few more skills, but by a large-scale modification of a system which perpetuates inequality (Ryan 1981). That large numbers of discharged mental patients are exploited by landlords, live in subhuman conditions, lack any shelter whatsoever, and have less access to psychiatric services (Bassuk and Gerson, 1985; Capponi, 1985; Levine, 1981) are not unpreventable natural disasters; they are primarily the consequences of a tradition of trying to solve social problems without thinking through their full ramifications. In reviewing the implementation of the 1963 American Community Mental Health Centers Act (PL 88-164), Levine (1981) concludes:

The problem of caring for mental patients is part of the larger problem of welfare in a capitalistic and individualistic society, and funds to implement programs for assistance to the elderly and the handicapped depend upon welfare economics and health care economics and politics. Programs and policies that interacted with mental health programs and shaped them devel-

oped without any apparent consideration for the effect of one piece of legislation on another, and without regard for the tendency of bureaucracies to
pursue their own ends, almost independently of legislative intent or authori-
zation. Everything is connected to everything else, ideas to politics, politics
to economics, economics to bureaucratic organizational dynamics. One cannot understand one without looking at all the others. (p. 77)

Remedial action at one level without concomitant modifications at
all levels leads to assimilation without accommodation, to invoke
Piaget. It should not be concluded from this that local changes are
irrelevant until all of society changes. What should be concluded is
that local changes are to be considered initial steps in an effort to
reform larger societal structures that interfere with the solution of
the specific problem at hand. In other words, local changes should be
accompanied by gradual and larger reforms to facilitate accommodation and eventual adaptation.

From Psychological to Environmental Prevention

As an offspring of clinical psychology (Sarason, 1984), it may be
only natural that many of community psychology's most successful
preventive efforts be psychological par excellence: Witness, for instance, the progress made in the areas of social support and competence building (Gesten and Jason, 1987; Nelson et al., 1985; Saulnier, 1985). While the psychoeducational focus of prevention projects
is vital, it may not be as essential as environmental prevention.
Environment "in this context is interpreted in its broadest sense,
and includes not only our physical surroundings, both natural and
artificial, but also the social, cultural, regulatory and economic conditions and influences that impinge on our everyday lives" (Health
and Welfare Canada, 1988, pp. 4–5).

As illustrated above in the prevention program reported by Halpern (1988), attempts to minimize infants' diarrhea by psychoeducational measures were severely hindered by an overbearing environmental condition: lack of access to uncontaminated water. This is
but one example of incidents where psychological prevention should
take a back seat to the reduction of pernicious systemic variables.

Recently, this proposition has been elequently argued in *Mental
Health for Canadians: Striking a Balance,* a document published by
Health and Welfare Canada (1988). The paper incisively pinpoints

structural deficiencies conducive to psychological vulnerability in general and mental illness in particular. Based on the assumption that "whatever makes it difficult for the individual, the group and the environment to interact effectively and justly (for example, poverty, prejudice or poor coordination of resources) is a threat or barrier to mental health" (Health and Welfare Canada, 1988, p. 8), the document addresses the imperative needs to reduce social inequality, discriminatory social attitudes, and to enhance social justice. Though somewhat lacking in specific recommendations, the document does a much better job than recent scholarly reviews of social factors affecting psychopathology (Kessler et al., 1985; Strauss, 1979) in stating that the "distribution of power among individuals, groups and their environments is a crucial determinant of mental health" (Health and Welfare Canada, 1988, p. 10) (only time will tell whether the government is seriously committed to changing these societal adversities).

As Halpern (1988) has lately observed, the factors that a primary prevention program, such as early intervention, "can influence directly (parent childrearing behavior, knowledge, and attitudes) are themselves strongly influenced by other factors much more difficult to alter in a discrete social program (e.g., economic insecurity, limited access to services, dilapidated housing)" (p. 253).

Attitudes, coping strategies, education, and interpersonal support are indeed unquestionably important parts of preventive projects. Yet efforts in reshaping the psychological world of persons may be wasted if the environmental world, as broadly defined above, is not concurrently reshaped. This notion may be foreign to many psychologists, but it certainly should not be to community psychologists; for they are committed to promoting the *fit* between persons and environments.

From Scientific to Political Activities

A move from scientific to political activities is not intended to detract from the scientific base of community psychology. Rather, it is designed to convey the message that, at this juncture, political awareness may be restricted by too scientific-academic an approach. According to Levine (1981), professional helpers are considerably myopic about the political context in which their endeavors take place. Unfortunately, it would seem that this situation has been at least partially created by the unbalanced priority given to more "credible" enterprises such as science.

Levine (1981) has documented at length the political innocence of mental-health workers in the United States for most of this century. His indictment is followed by this conclusion:

> The field of mental health by no means belongs exclusively to the professional mental health workers no matter how fervently we wish it. The reality is that public mental health services are necessarily influenced by their social, political and economic context. . . . It may be that it is our task as professionals, and as teachers of the next generation of professionals, to engage in consciousness raising so that political science, law, and economics become as much parts of the mental health curriculum . . . as abnormal psychology or psychotherapy. We should not give up the scientist-professional model, nor should we depart from our service ideal, but the needs of the future, both of the profession and of its clients, will depend upon a much more sophisticated and self-conscious appreciation of the contexts within which we live and work that has characterized our fields in the past. (Levine, 1981, p. 206)

These implications for action are regarded as important first steps in training mental health workers to perceive and modify political complexities which extend much beyond the individual patient. The implementation of those initial small steps will undoubtedly generate new and unanticipated problems to contend with, but their emergence will be considered a sign of growing pains.

CONCLUSION

The purpose of this essay has been to examine the political repercussions of different models of abnormal psychology. Although the plethora of theories and trends within trends in the field of psychopathology preclude simple categorization, an attempt has been made to arrange them on the basis of their sociopolitical implications. The analysis resulted in four distinct paradigms. Whereas the first three are widely practiced, the last one constitutes more of a desideratum than an existing model. The fourth paradigm was outlined with the clear intent of activating dormant tenets of community psychology, one of the branches of psychology with the most potential to reshape the environment in order to make it more suitable for the promotion of well-being. Unless community psychology enacts a new set of priorities to vivify its seeds of political activism, it might regress to the stage where preoccupation with psychological dimensions inter-feres with the rectification of social adversities.

Countless obstacles will be encountered by those willing to invigo-rate the field of abnormal psychology by entering the turbulent polit-ical scene of community life. Psychologists prepared to give up some of the comfort afforded by the scientist-professional model to question existing social structures are likely to risk severe opposition from their employing institutions, as well as isolation from colleagues who may perceive their activities as derogating the painfully gained scientific reputation of psychology. This embroilment is occasioned by a model whose chief goal is the promotion of human welfare, as opposed to paradigms designed primarily to dissect the human experience in the hope of finding replicable laws of behavior. The latter may be conducted without disrupting the social order. The former is bound to perturb the status quo.

ACKNOWLEDGMENT

This essay is based on a chapter of a doctoral dissertation submitted by the author to the University of Manitoba. I am most grateful to Frederick L. Marcuse for his valuable suggestions on earlier drafts of the manuscript.

REFERENCES

Abramson, J. B. (1984). *Liberation and Its Limits: The Moral and Political Thought of Freud*, Free Press, New York.

Albee, G. W. (1981). Politics, power, prevention, and social change. In Joffe, J. M., and Albee, G. W. (eds.), *Prevention Through Political Action and Social Change*, University Press Hanover, N.H., pp. 3–24.

Albee, G. W. (1986). Toward a just society: Lessons from observations on the primary prevention of psychopathology. *Am. Psychologist* 41(8): 891–898.

Albee, G. W. (June 1989). *Suffer the Little Children*. Invited opening address to The International Council of Psychologists, Halifax, Nova Scotia.

Anderson, C. C., and Travis, L. D. (1983). *Psychology and the Liberal Consensus*, Wilfried Laurier University, Waterloo, Ontario.

Basaglia, F. (1981). Breaking the circuit of control. In Ingleby, D. (ed.), *Critical Psychiatry*, Penguin, New York, pp. 184–192.

Bassuk, E. L., and Gerson, S. (1985). Deinstitutionalization and mental health ser-vices. In Brown, P. (ed.), *Mental Health Care and Social Policy*, Routledge and Kegan Paul, London, pp. 127–144.

Bateson, G., Jackson, D. D., Haley, J., and Weakland, J. (1956). Toward a theory of schizophrenia. *Behav. Sci.* 1: 251–264.

Bayer, R. (1981). *Homosexuality and American Psychiatry: The Politics of Diagnosis,* Basic Books, New York.

Bechtel, R. B. (1984). Patient and community, the ecological bond. In O'Conner, W. A., and Lubin, B. (eds.), *Ecological Approaches to Clinical and Community Psychology,* Wiley, New York, pp. 216–231.

Bermant, G., and Warwick, D. P. (1978). The ethics of social intervention: Power, freedom, and accountability. In Bermant, G., Kelman, H. C., and Warwick, D. P. (eds.), *The Ethics of Social Intervention,* Wiley, New York, pp. 327–417.

Bertalanffy, L. V. (1968). *General System Theory: Foundations, Development, Applications,* George Braziller, New York.

Bowen, M. (1978). *Family Therapy in Clinical Practice,* Jason Aronson, New York.

Braginsky, B. M., and Braginsky, D. D. (1976). The myth of schizophrenia. In Magarao, P. A. (ed.), *The Construction of Madness,* Pergamon, New York, pp. 66–90.

Braginsky, D. D. (1985). Psychology: Handmaiden to society. In Koch, S., and Leary, D. E. (eds.), *A Century of Psychology in Science,* McGraw-Hill, New York, pp. 880–891.

Brooks, K. (1973). Freudianism is not a basis of Marxist psychology. In Brown, P. (ed.), *Radical Psychology,* Harper and Row, New York, pp. 315–374.

Brown, P. (ed.), (1985). *Mental Health Care and Social Policy,* Routledge and Kegan Paul, London.

Busfield, J. (1974). Family ideology and family pathology. In Armistead, N. (ed.), *Reconstructing Social Psychology,* Penguin, Middlesex, pp. 157–173.

Buss, A. R. (ed.), (1979). *Psychology in Social Context,* Irvington, New York.

Capponi, P. (1985). How psychiatric patients view deinstitutionalization. In Canadian Council on Social Development (ed.), *Deinstitutionalization: Costs and Effects,* Ottawa; Author, pp. 7–10.

Caruso, I. A. (1964). How social is psychoanalysis? In Ruitenbeek, H. M. (ed.), *Psychoanalysis and Contemporary Culture,* Delta, New York, pp. 263–281.

Conrad, P. (1981). On the medicalization of deviance and social control. In Ingleby, D. (ed.), *Critical Psychiatry: The Politics of Mental Health,* (Penguin, New York, pp. 102–119.

Coulter, J. (1979). *The Social Construction of Mind,* Rowman and Littlefield, Totowa, N.J.

Dean, A., Kraft, A. M., and Pepper, B. (eds.) (1976). *The Social Setting of Mental Health,* Basic Books, New York.

Dobyns, H. F., Doughty, P. L., and Lassell, H. D. (eds.), (1971). *Peasants, Power, and Applied Social Change,* Sage, London.

Domhoff, W. (1986). Capitalist control of the state. In Edwards, R. C., Reich, M., and Weisskopf, T. E. (eds.), *The Capitalist System* (third edition), Prentice-Hall, Englewood Cliffs, N.J., pp. 191–200.

Edwards, R. C., Reich, M., and Weisskopf, T. E. (eds.), (1986). *The Capitalist System* (third edition), Prentice-Hall, Englewood Cliffs, N.J.

Englert, E. H., and Suarez, A. (eds.), (1985). *El psicoanalisis como teoria critica y la critica politica al psicoanalisis* [Psychoanalysis as critical theory and the political critique of psychoanalysis], Siglo Veintiuno, Mexico.

Fireside, H. (1979). *Soviet Psychoprisons,* Norton, New York.

Foucault, M. (1985). *Un dialogo sobre el poder* [A dialogue on power]. Alianza Editorial, Madrid.

Foucault, M. (1987). *Mental Illness and Psychology* (A. Sheridan, trans.). University of California Press, Berkeley (Original work published 1954).

Freud, S. (1964). *The Future of an Illusion* (W. D. Robson-Scott, trans.), Anchor, New York [Original work published 1927).

George, V., and Wilding, P. (1976). *Ideology and Social Welfare,* Routledge and Kegan Paul, Boston.

Gesten, E. L., and Jason, L. A. (1987). Social and community interventions. *Annu. Rev. Psychol.* 38: 427–460.

Glenn, M., and Kunnes, R. (1973). *Repression or Revolution,* Harper and Row, New York.

Goldenberg, I., and Goldenberg, H. (1985). *Family Therapy: An Overview* (second edition), Brooks/Cole, Calif.

Gross, B. (1980). *Friendly Fascism,* Black Rose, Montreal.

Grusky, O., and Pollner, M. (eds.) (1981). *The Sociology of Mental Illness,* Holt, Rinehart and Winston, New York.

Halleck, S. (1971). *The Politics of Therapy,* Science House, New York.

Halpern, R. (1988). Action research for the late 1980s. *J. Commun. Psychol.* 16: 249–260.

Health and Welfare Canada (1988). *Mental Health for Canadians: Striking a Balance,* Author, Ottawa.

Heller, K., and Monahan, J. (1977). *Psychology and Community Change,* Dorsey, Homewood, Ill.

Hoffman, L. (1981). *Foundations of Family Therapy: A Framework for Systems Change,* Basic Books, New York.

Holland, J. G. (1978). Behaviorism: Part of the problem or part of the solution? *J. Appl. Behav. Anal.* 11: 163–174.

Jacoby, R. (1975). *Social Amnesia,* Beacon, Boston.

Jacoby, R. (1983). *The Repression of Psychoanalysis,* Basic Books, New York.

James, K., and McIntrye, D. (1983). The reproduction of families: The social role of family therapy? *J. Marit. Fam. Ther.* 9(2): 119–129.

Jason, L. A., and Glenwick, D. S. (1984). Behavioral community psychology. In Hersen, M., Eisler, R. M., and Miller, P. M. (eds.), *Progress in Behavior Modification: Vol. 18,* Academic Press, New York, pp. 85–121.

Karpel, M. A., and Strauss, E. S. (1983). *Family Evaluation,* Gardner Press, New York.

Kessler, R. C., Price, R. H., and Wortman, C. B. (1985). Social factors in psychopathology. *Ann Rev. Psychol.* 36: 531–572.

Kovel, J. (1981). *The Age of Desire: Care Histories of a Radical Psychoanalyst,* Pantheon, New York.

Laing, R. D., and Esterson, A. (1974). *Sanity, Madness and the Family.* Tavistock, London.

Lamb, H. R., and Zusman, J. (1979). Primary prevention in perspective. *Am. J. Psychiat.* 136: 12–17.

Larsen, K. S. (ed.) (1986). *Dialectics and Ideology in Psychology,* Ablex, Norwood, N.J.

Levant, R. (1984). *Family Therapy: A Comprehensive Overview,* Prentice-Hall, N.J.

Levine, M. (1981). *The History and Politics of Community Mental Health,* Oxford, New York.

Mannino, F. V., and Shore, M. F. (1984). An ecological perspective on family intervention. In O'Conner, W. A., and Lubin, B. (eds.), *Ecological Approaches to Clinical and Community Psychology,* Wiley, New York, pp. 75–93.

Marcuse, H. (1966). *Eros and Civilization: A Philosophical Inquiry into Freud,* Beacon Press, Boston.

Marmor, J. (1988). Psychiatry in a troubled world. *Am. J. Orthopsychiat.* 58(4): 484–491.

Medvedev, Z., and Medvedev, R. (1971). *A Question of Madness,* Vintage Books, New York.

Nahem, J. (1981). *Psychology and Psychiatry Today,* International Publishers, New York.

Nelson, G., Potasznik, H., and Bennet, E. M (1985). Primary prevention: Another perspective. In Bennet, E. M. and Tefft, B. (eds.), *Theoretical and Empirical Advances in Community Mental Health,* Edwin Mellen, Queenston, Ontario, pp. 11–20.

O'Conner, W. A., and Lubin, B. (eds.) (1984). *Ecological Approaches to Clinical and Community Psychology,* Wiley, New York.

Pearson, G. (1974). The reification of the family in family therapy. In Armistead, N. (ed.), *Reconstructing Social Psychology,* Penguin, Middlesex, pp. 137–156.

Pearson, G. (1975). *The Deviant Imagination: Psychiatry, Social Work and Social Change,* Holmes and Meier, New York.

Poster, M. (1978). *Critical Theory of the Family,* Seabury, New York.

Prilleltensky, I. (1989). Psychology and the status quo. *Am. Psycholog.* 44(5): 795–802.

Prilleltensky, I. (1990). On the social and political implications of cognitive psychology. *J. Mind Behav.* 11(2): 127–136.

Rappaport, J. (1977). *Community Psychology,* Holt, Rinehart and Winston, New York.

Reich, M., and Edwards, R. C. (1986). Liberal democracy, political parties, and the capitalist state. In Edwards, R. C., Reich, M., and Weisskopf, T. E. (eds.). *The Capitalist System* (third edition), Englewood Cliffs, Prentice-Hall, N.J. pp. 200–211.

Reiser, M. F. (1988). Are psychiatric educators losing the mind? *Am. J. Psychiat.* 145(2): 148–149.

Ryan, W. (1971). *Blaming the Victim,* Pantheon, New York.

Ryan, W. (1981). *Equality,* Pantheon, New York.

Sampson, E. E. (1981). Cognitive psychology as ideology. *Am. Psycholog.* 36(7): 730–743.

Sarason, S. B. (1981a). *Psychology Misdirected,* Free Press, New York.

Sarason, S. B. (1981b). An asocial psychology and a misdirected clinical psychology. *Am. Psycholog.* 36(8): 827–836.

Sarason, S. B. (1984). Community psychology and public policy: Missed opportunity. *Am. J. Commun. Psychol.* 12(2): 199–207.

Saulnier, K. (1985). Networks, change and crisis: The web of support. In Bennet, E. M., and Telft, B. (eds.), *Theoretical and Empirical Advances in Community Mental Health,* Edwin Mellen, Queenston, Ontario, pp. 21–40.

Schacht, T. E. (1985). DSM-III and the politics of truth. *Am. Psycholog.* 40(5): 513–521.

Scheff, T. J. (1976). Schizophrenia as ideology. In Dean, A., Kraft, A. M., and Pepper, B. (eds.), *The Social Setting of Mental Health,* Basic Books, New York, pp. 209–215.

Schwartz, M. (ed.) (1987). *The Structure of Power in America: The Corporate Elite as a Ruling Class,* Holmes and Meier, New York.

Sedgwick, P. (1982). *Psychopolitics,* Harper and Row, New York.

Sennett, R., and Cobb, J. (1972). *The Hidden Injuries of Class,* Vintage, New York.

Spiers, H. (1973, Winter). Psychiatric neutrality. *The Body Politic.*

Stoppard, J. M. (1989). An evaluation of the adequacy of cognitive/behavioural theories for understanding depression in women. *Canad. Psychol.* 30(1): 39–47.

Strauss, J. S. (1979). Social and cultural influences on psychopathology. *Ann. Rev. Psychol.* 30: 397–415.

Sullivan, E. V. (1984). *A Critical Psychology,* Plenum, New York.

Szasz, T. (1963). *Law, Liberty, and Psychiatry,* Collier, New York.

Szasz, T. (1965). *The Ethics of Psychoanalysis: The Theory and Method of Autonomous Therapy,* Delta, New York.

Szasz, T. (1974). *The Myth of Mental Illness* (revised ed.), Harper and Row, New York.

Szasz, T. (1984). *The Therapeutic State,* Prometheus, Buffalo.

Thomas, A., and Sillen, S. (1972). *Racism and Psychiatry,* Citadel, Secaucus, N.J.

Tomm, K. (1980). Towards a cybernetic systems approach to family therapy at the University of Calgary. In Freeman, D. S. (ed.), *Perspectives on Family Therapy,* Butterworth, Vancouver, pp. 3–18.

Vatz, R. E., and Weinberg, L. S. (eds.) (1983). *Thomas Szasz: Primary Values and Major Contentions,* Prometheus, Buffalo, N.Y.

Wineman, S. (1984). *The Politics of Human Services,* Black Rose, Montreal.

Wood, G. (1986). *The Myth of Neurosis: Overcoming the Illness Excuse,* Harper and Row, New York.

30. Why Is There No Study of Cultural Equivalence in Standardized Cognitive Ability Testing?

Janet E. Helms

In the area of so-called *standardized* cognitive ability testing, U.S. psychologists and psychometricians, particularly those whose specialization is the construction and validation of cognitive ability tests (CATs), seemingly have no clear understanding of what scores on such devices really mean about the intelligence or intellectual abilities of different racial and ethnic groups in this society. In this essay, CATs refers to those measures designed to assess intelligence, mental abilities, cognitive abilities, and scholastic aptitude because, as Graham and Lily (1984) pointed out, these terms are virtually synonymous.

In the psychometric literature (e.g., Cleary, 1968; Jensen, 1980; Samuda, 1975; Scarr, 1981; Temp, 1971) it has become a virtual truism that the average performance of racial and ethnic groups (especially Blacks and Whites) on CATs differs, sometimes by as much as a standard deviation. However, the question of whether such differences have any practical implications for how the tests should be used with different groups remains mired in controversy. The most recent version of this controversy within society, as well as among psychometricians themselves, concerns the ongoing debate over the fairness of using separate norms for different racial and ethnic groups—in other words, "race-norming," (R. Cohen, 1990; "Department of Labor Inundated," 1991; Duke, 1991; Welsh, 1990). Unfortunately, because of their own confusion regarding how best to construct and validate CATs for use with racial and ethnic

Reprinted by permission of the author and the American Psychological Association from *American Psychologist* 47 (1992): 1083–1101. Copyright © 1992 by the American Psychological Association.

groups, psychologists and psychometricians have contributed to intensifying the controversy rather than resolving it. In addition, they have been unable to provide clear guidelines as to how to interpret racial and ethnic group differences in CAT performance or evidence that these assessment devices have comparable meaning or equivalence within the various racial and ethnic groups.

Primarily, two philosophical perspectives, the implicit biological and the environmental, have been used to explain racial and ethnic group differences in CAT performance. I suggest that each of these perspectives is characterized by its own set of assumptions and research traditions that have influenced the manner in which racial and ethnic group differences in test performance are interpreted by psychologists and psychometricians as well as society more generally. Each approach also uses some version of the concept of culture to explain variations in average performance between groups, although their manner of defining culture ostensibly differs. The differing definitions of culture are related to use of different strategies for investigating the effects of culture on test performance.

Nevertheless, I argue that neither approach has been operationally defined adequately enough to permit valid interpretations of racial and ethnic group differences in CAT performance nor to justify the extensive use of such measures across racial and ethnic groups other than for research purposes. In addition, I argue that neither perspective offers culture-specific models, principles, or definitions that can be used for examining issues of how culture per se influences the content of CATs as well as the performance of respondents on these tests.

A third perspective, culturalist, will be proposed as a more viable alternative for examining the cultural equivalence of CATs, that is, the comparative meaning of CAT scores when race or ethnicity of respondents is an issue. Some suggestions for using the culturalist perspective to analyze cultural influences on existing CATs as well as to develop alternative culture-specific measures of intellectual abilities will also be presented. In addition, recommendations for culture-focused CAT research and management of cultural factors are discussed.

The primary focus of this essay will be cultural influences on the CAT performance of Black Americans, although it will be recognized that these issues cannot be addressed independently of test construction and validation issues more generally. In this presentation, cultural equivalence concerns of Black Americans will be addressed most specifically, inasmuch as this is the racial-ethnic group that has been most denigrated in psychometric literature. Nevertheless, many of the issues raised conceivably pertain, to some extent, to other racial and ethnic minorities—henceforth, visible racial or ethnic groups (VREGs)—as well (cf. Bernal, 1990).

IMPLICIT BIOLOGICAL PERSPECTIVE

The implicit biological or genetic view of cognitive ability test construction and validation equates quantity of cognitive or intellectual ability with test scores derived from CATs, as previously defined, virtually regardless of the cultural origins or the sociopolitical experiences of test takers. The perspective is implicit because proponents of biological explanations of racial-group CAT performance rarely explicitly state the differences in CAT performance are due to biological or genetic characteristics. Rather, they permit that inference by not offering alternative explanations of essentially correlational data and by treating racial and ethnic group classifications as biological categories ipso facto rather than merely convenient socially created categories (e.g., Jensen, 1969, 1976, 1981). Furthermore, with few exceptions (cf. Scarr, 1981), racial and ethnic group comparison studies subsumed under this perspective typically have used race or ethnicity and culture synonymously.

The most blatant example of a research methodology associated with the implicit biological perspective is the use of pseudo-racial or pseudo-group comparisons to explain racial and ethnic group differences in CAT performance. Perhaps less obvious versions involve the implicit attribution of between-group differences to genetic or biological deficits in Black (in this instance) test takers.

Pseudo-Racial Group Comparisons

The pseudo-racial methodology, which is intended to demonstrate that Blacks are not as intellectually developed as Whites, typically involves comparing Black children's CAT performance with younger (differing in age by two or more years) White children's CAT performance. Using this procedure, for example, item difficulty indices obtained within groups are correlated across the racial-age groups. Similarity in correlations with respect to the pseudo-racial groups is taken as evidence of a developmental lag in the Black group rather than a manifestation of cultural differences.

So, for example, Jensen (1980) reported the results of his research, in which he found greater similarity in item-difficulty correlations between White fourth graders and Black sixth graders ($r = .98$) than between White fourth graders and White sixth graders ($r = .81$). He argued that

This result seems much less consistent with the hypothesis of a *cultural difference* [italics added] than with the hypothesis of *a difference in rates of intellectual development* [italics added] unless we make the *unlikely* [italics added] assumption that the test manifestations of cultural differences are indistinguishable from the test manifestations of general developmental difference within a *culturally homogeneous group* [italics added]. (p. 572)

From this and several similar conclusions, presumably, one is intended to infer a racial, group-linked lag in cognitive development for Black children. However, the implicit biological perspective seems inadequate for explaining these particular between-group findings because to support a racially linked biological explanation of these findings one would need to suppose that younger Whites are racially identical to their older Black counterparts and, conversely, that Black children are as White as White children two years younger than themselves; that is, they share racial genotypes. Yet, somehow this racial similarity disappears when the White and Black children are the same age. This does seem unlikely!

A more plausible explanation of Jensen's (1980) pseudo-race studies from environmental and cultural perspectives is that when one compares White groups with one another, environmental quality and culture of origin are fortuitously controlled. Consequently, differences and similarities within the White group may actually reflect differences in their intellectual abilities. It is also possible that within White groups, older children are more proficient in their own culture than are younger children, hence, the imperfect correlation between item difficulty rankings between age groups within the White race.

However, when comparisons are made across racial groups, environmental quality and exposure to White culture are no longer controlled. In fact, the differences with respect to these factors may be exaggerated. Consequently, the developmental lag that Jensen (1980) interpreted as a difference in intellectual ability may instead be a difference in acculturation or the learning of White culture. Maybe White children learn their own culture two or more years sooner than Black children vicariously learn White culture, but then, presumably, White children have more direct exposure to their own culture (and, parenthetically, the culture of CATs). Because Black test takers as a group are unlikely to have the same depth of exposure to White culture as Whites have, then it is plausible that a cultural lag of some degree might be present throughout the life span.

Note that this acculturation explanation signifies nothing about the rate at which Black children learn their own culture or, for that matter, the rate at which White children learn Black culture. Support for the cultural equivalence of CATs seems to require investigation of each of these possibilities. Again, however, to the extent that Black children learn White culture at all, then their White cultural knowledge should be related to White-culture-laden criteria in the same direction as such cultural knowledge is related when White children manifest it. Therefore, in such instances, when one compares groups' performance with respect to factor structure and correlation matrices, then one should find similarities because one is, in effect, examining the relationships among various indicants of proficiency in White culture.

A more general variant of the pseudo-racial approach (called pseudo-group) involves using total CAT score distributions to select different ability groups to represent the typical response patterns of selected racial groups and then comparing CAT performance between groups with respect to the internal structure of tests (cf. Bernal, 1990). Of course, lack of evidence of cultural equivalence of CATs makes this procedure equally problematic. If the CATs indeed are heavily loaded with White cultural influences, then total CAT test scores are a proxy for level of mastery of White culture. Under such circumstances, selection or matching according to overall test scores is tantamount to selecting samples who have mastered White culture (arguably) equivalently. However, such mastery may have little or no meaning with respect to equivalence of intellectual ability because it can be argued that Black individuals who perform at the same level as Whites are intellectually superior to the extent that they are functioning so well in a "foreign" cultural context.

Group Classifications. The most popular version of this approach involves comparing average CAT scores of Black and White test takers on the basis of their racial or ethnic classifications rather than on their biological characteristics. Thus, one does not often find attempts to define and assess either between or within groups the particular biological characteristics hypothesized to alter a racial or ethnic group's CAT performance relative to that of other groups. Yet considerable heterogeneity may exist within biological (racial) characteristics. The Black and White populations in this country are not "pure" because of (a) voluntary and involuntary interracial procreation, (b) the tendency of researchers to assign subjects to one group or another on the basis of physical appearance, (c) the decision of some VREGs who appear White to disappear into White society (a process called *passing* in Black culture), and (d) the possibility that immigrants who would be considered Black if they were born of similar parentage in this country classify themselves as White or other than Black.

Thus, in the absence of the specification and measurement of the alleged racial characteristics of participants in CAT research, claims of genetic differences in CAT performance because of racial characteristics are insupportable. Nevertheless, one does not often find attempts to define and assess the particular biological characteristics (e.g., melanin levels, blood groupings) hypothesized to alter a racial or ethnic group's CAT performance relative to that of other groups. Moreover, in the few studies (cf. Scarr, 1981; Scarr, Pakstis, Katz, & Barker, 1977) that have actually attempted to identify and measure race-related biological correlates of CAT performance, no significant correlations between measured biological markers and test scores have been found when VREGs have been studied. Thus, insofar as one can tell, the strong belief in the inheritability of intellectual ability (as assessed by CATs) within and across racial groups primarily rests on inferences from racial-membership-group classification studies rather than on measurement of racial characteristics; it also relies on heritability studies of (presumably) White test takers of unknown racial or genetic and cultural composition.

Both physical appearance (e.g., skin color), from which racial membership is usually inferred, and CAT performance are complex phenotypes. That is, there is likely to be no direct correspondence between genetic composition of test takers and either their racial appearance or their behavior (e.g., CAT performance). Scarr (1981) noted,

Under different conditions the same genotype [genetic trait] can become
different phenotypes; under the same environmental conditions different
genotypes can become different phenotypes; and under uniform environmental conditions different genotypes may result in the same phenotype. . . . A
large number of genetic-environmental combinations will yield the [same or
different skin colors and] the same [or different] IQ score. (pp. 17–18)

Because a detailed critique of the limitations of attempted biological investigations of race and CAT performance is beyond the scope
of this essay, the reader is referred to Scarr (1981) for examples of
this approach as well as extensive commentaries about the strengths
and weaknesses of current methodologies. Of particular concern here
is that none of these biological studies has attempted to operationally
define culture per se, although a few have resorted to proxies for
cultural variables such as socioeconomic status (e.g., Scarr & Weinberg, 1976).

General Ability Testing. Perhaps the most sophisticated implicit biology methodology makes use of the common observation that test
scores on various kinds of CATs tend to be positively correlated
with one another. Dating as far back as Spearman (1927), many
psychometricians have postulated that the mechanism underlying
this pattern of intercorrelations is an index of general ability, commonly called a g or general ability factor (Cattell, 1963). This factor
is assumed to have a physiological basis and to be assessed by various
CATs in differing amounts. One's test scores relative to a comparison
group are assumed to provide information about one's level of g or
general ability.

In arguing for the universality of g and, therefore, the appropriateness of inferring a deficit in general cognitive ability from Blacks'
performance on CATs, Jensen (1980) argued,

As for the ubiquity of g across the time span of human history, it seems most
unlikely that a different kind of intelligence from that defined by our present
conception of g was involved in the architectural and engineering feats of the
ancient Egyptians. (p. 248)

Because Jensen, presumably, was not contending that ancient Egyp-
tian culture or environment can be equated with that of contemporary society, a logical inference is that he was arguing that some
CAT-related genetic material has been passed down from ancient
Egyptians to Whites in this country, but not to Blacks.

However, whole-hearted acceptance of Jensen's contention requires one to ignore the treatises of historians, anthropologists, and Egyptologists, which suggest that all people are descended from Africans and that ancient Egyptians were probably black (ben-Jochannan, 1981; Browder, 1989; Diop, 1974; Mourant, 1983; Weaver & Brill, 1985; Zuckerman, 1990). The significance of this observation is that it allows consideration of the possibility that g may have been inherited by all humankind through mutual ancestry but that environmental circumstances may have conspired to influence its manners of expression or phenotypes among various subgroups of peoples. In that case, the breadth of intellectual ability would not be assessed to the extent that traditional CATs are assessing only a small portion of the potential human cognitive abilities.

The hypothesis of restricted assessment of g does not seem so far-fetched if one recognizes that the g factor as we know it is a hypothetical construct inferred from intercorrelations among CATs of similar content, format, and perhaps cultural loadings. Thus, perhaps the nature of g could be changed by altering the kinds of devices from which it is inferred. For instance, interactive methods of assessment such as "test[s] that teach" (Moses, 1990) might contribute to their own patterns of intercorrelations and, therefore, a broader definition of g.

The hypothesis of alternative g makes it possible to maintain (if one must) primarily biological explanations of racial differences in CAT performance without also assuming the innate inferiority of either group. Consider, for example, three findings that have been used to buttress the argument of innate inferiority of Blacks as evidenced by their CAT performance. They are as follows: (a) There are between-racial-group differences in average scores across a wide variety of CATs that favor Whites over Blacks, (b) individual items seem equivalently difficult to test takers of both races, and (c) validity coefficients are similar across racial groups. Data relevant to each of these points are summarized in Jensen (1980).

Suppose, for the sake of discussion, we call the type of g allegedly assessed by contemporary CATs "White g" and the type of g that these tests might be unable to assess "African g." One could argue that recessive in the population of Black Americans, either because of the common African ancestry of humankind or the admixture of White and Black genetic material in recent history (cf. Mourant,

1983; Weaver & Brill, 1985, Zuckerman, 1990), reside whatever biological characteristics are responsible for the expression of White g within the White population. If the genotype responsible for expression of White g by Blacks is recessive in the Black population as a whole, then one might expect the White g phenotype to be manifested in the same direction for both groups, but not necessarily at the same level. Consequently, individuals of any racial group who have the capacity to express White g might express it in a similar manner (e.g., perceive the same test items as difficult) without it being their primary means of thinking or otherwise behaving. Also, given that White g would likely operate in the same direction within groups, one would expect similar correlations between CATs and criteria.

Thus far, this argument sounds much akin to what Franklin (1991) contended was the gist of the mulatto hypothesis, that is, higher percentages of White ancestry contribute to improved CAT performance among Blacks. The argument apparently diverges because advocates of the superiority of White genes do not seem to acknowledge the possibility of a phenotype of African g whose genotype is dominant among Blacks but is perhaps recessive among Whites or the possibility that if the relevant phenotype were adequately assessed, it might be the crosscultural equivalent of what is measured by standardized CATs. In other words, as Grubb and Dozier (1989) have pointed out, current CATs can provide some information about "what is salient to each [VREG culture] on tests *and* [italics added] within the [White] culture, and what is not. *The tests, however, are not responsive to what is salient to the [VREG culture] but absent in the [White] culture"* [italics added] (p. 24).

Nevertheless, as mentioned earlier, existing evidence involving actual measurement of biological characteristics does not support the existence of a recessive or dominant genotype for differential levels of expression of White g within Black or White samples (cf. Scarr, 1981). To my knowledge, similar biologically based efforts to validate the construct of African g are not readily available for examination (cf. Schiele, 1991; Willis, 1989). Furthermore, it is conceivable that some combinations of environmental and cultural perspectives may offer more parsimonious explanations of each of the three proposed "crucial" issues than are likely to be provided by the implicit biological perspective.

ENVIRONMENTAL PERSPECTIVE

None of the philosophical approaches to interpretation of racial or ethnic differences in CAT performance is entirely independent of the others. Rather, the difference among the perspectives is one of emphasis. The environmental philosophical perspective emphasizes the effects of factors external to individuals on their CAT performance. In particular, where Black-White differences in CAT performance are concerned, it stresses the injurious effects of environmental factors on Blacks' performance and the salubrious effects of environmental factors on Whites' performance.

The environmental and implicit biology perspectives share the assumption that differences in Black-White test scores reflect deficits where Blacks are concerned. However, the environmental perspective argues that these deficits in Blacks' performance on CATs are due to their oppression or deprivation and intellectual skill (rather than physiological) deficiencies resulting therefrom. This perspective has been most forcefully presented by the judicial system, usually in response to VREG parental objections to CAT usage in selection and placement in educational settings or management-personnel discord within employment settings (e.g., Bersoff, 1981; Bernal, 1990; Weinberg, 1989).

The environmental perspective uses quality of environment and culture virtually equivalently. Implicit in this equation is the assumption that White-American culture defines the most intellectually rich environment. Immersion in the environment, so defined, is assumed to be an ideal toward which members of every racial and ethnic group in this country should aspire. Concepts such as *culturally deprived* and *culturally disadvantaged,* when used to explain CAT performance, imply inadequate exposure or access to the best environment for facilitating CAT performance and intellectual development.

Research efforts to demonstrate qualitative differences in the environment(s) of Black test takers relative to that of White test takers usually have been of two types. One relies largely on the impressionistic cultural analysis of test content for the purpose of identifying items that might be biased because of environmental factors. The second type attempts to identify the relevant environmental factors that might impede performance.

Through both research strategies, psychologists and psychometricians infer relationships between environmental factors and CAT scores. The environmental factor most often used in such inferences has been socioeconomic status (SES; Eckland, 1979; Gordon & Rudert, 1979; Guterman, 1979). Although the manner of operationally defining SES variables differs, both research strategies are based on the assumption that differences in CAT performance are attributable to differences in socioeconomic levels, with higher levels performing better than lower levels. Lower levels are assumed to be more culturally deprived than upper levels as a consequence of having had less access to the environmental resources needed to develop adequate intellectual skills or to comprehend the content of CATs.

Item Quality

On the basis of personal experiences or intuitive or logical analyses, users of this approach attempt to select items that should elicit different responses from test takers reared in deficient environments than from those reared in the "standard" environment. In theory, racial or ethnic differences in overall CAT scores occur if the tests consist of an excess of environmentally biased items. An example of an allegedly biased item, frequently cited by proponents and opponents of the environmental perspective, concerns Black children's typical response to the Wechsler Intelligence Scale for Children (WISC; Wechsler, 1949) item, "What is the thing to do if a fellow (girl) much smaller than yourself starts to fight with you?" In discussing "this favorite example of test critics," Gordon and Rudert (1979) asserted that environmentalists contend that Black children are taught that the appropriate response to this item is "hit him back" (p. 179). They use empirical evidence from several studies (e.g., Doppelt, 1977 [cited in Gordon & Rudert, 1979]; Jensen, 1976) to show that Black children do not give this incorrect answer any more frequently than do their White counterparts and may, in fact, give the correct answer somewhat more often. Such evidence, Gordon and Rudert asserted, refutes the environmental perspective inasmuch as no strong race by item interaction is present.

However, what Gordon and Rudert (1979) have apparently overlooked in their argument is the likelihood that environmentalists who predict such findings are generally predicting the responses of Blacks of lower SES, and even in these instances, it is not clear that their predictions are based on empirical analyses of social class variability within the Black group rather than on mere speculation. In other words, both opponents and proponents of the environmental perspective often make the mistake of relying on myth to support or dismiss assumptions concerning culture by item interactions on CATs.

Environmental Impediments

Cultural deprivation is often equated with alleged qualitative environmental deficits such as quantity and quality of educational materials present in one's home environment, parental education, or income (i.e., SES), or personality characteristics (anxiety, lack of motivation) elicited by submersion in an unfamiliar (testing) environment, although these deficits are rarely measured.

Environmental quality. The underlying logic in the environmental-deficit hypothesis is that differential access to information (e.g., rarity of item content) would be the source of nonequivalence, if it exists. However, in the absence of a theoretical formulation of distinctive cultural context(s), it is difficult to operationally define rarity. For instance, Jensen (1974) operationally defined rarity by rank ordering the frequency of occurrence of stimulus words in "American" newspapers, magazine, and books. Yet, it is not at all clear that his selections included African-American sources or that he obtained evidence concerning the prevalence of, presumably, White-American resources in VREG homes. Thus, it is entirely possible that rarity of usage may have been defined according to a particular cultural context, but one that was irrelevant to the cultural question at hand. Again, it is not surprising that correlations with respect to item difficulty and rarity are similar within racial groups as well as between them, given the culturally laden definition of rarity. Familiarity with White culture should operate in the same direction.

This type of cultural analysis presumably had led researchers to generalize their findings concerning CAT performance across racial groups, regardless of whether the findings included race-related analyses of any sort (cf. Guterman, 1979; Jensen, 1980). In other words, Blacks are often considered to derive from culturally deficient environments, regardless of whether or not they do. Thus, in studies of cultural deprivation, race, and cognitive abilities, the first two factors' influence on the latter is assumed to be interchangeable. Consequently, what has meaning for Whites of "deprived" status is assumed to have analogous meaning for Blacks, regardless of their cultural status.

Socioeconomic Status

Efforts to offer socioeconomic status as a plausible explanation for Black-White environmental differences in CAT performance have been characterized by a number of conceptual and related methodological flaws, in addition to those previously discussed. Major conceptual flaws are the imposition of White cultural definitions of SES on Black samples and the assumption of socioeconomic homogeneity within the population of Black Americans.

Imposed Definitions. Considering the matter of definition, much of the existing CAT literature apparently has used indicators that have meaning in White culture (e.g., income) as the criteria for membership in various strata and, consequently, for exploring hypothesized differences in CAT performance (cf. Jensen, 1980; Scarr, 1981). This approach might be called an environmental exosystem approach for operationally defining SES, inasmuch as the focus is on the larger environment's characteristics rather than on the local environment or the individual. Often, census tract data are sued to assess socioeconomic status via this conceptualization. Yet, it also is the case that relatively restricted access to income-generating and educational opportunities may have contributed to different cultural definitions of SES among Blacks. At least from a historical perspective, factors such as generation in the country and stability of income, as opposed to the level of income, have contributed to within-group and self-perceptions of social class that do not necessarily conform to the standards of White culture (cf. Gatewood, 1990).

It seems conceivable that one's perceptions of one's socioeconomic status (an individual characteristic) would have at least as great and perhaps greater influence on the types of cultural characteristics one develops as extraneous (out-of-culture) definitions of one's status. If this observation concerning phenomenological definitions of SES is accurate, then it may also be true that in past studies of CAT performance in which Black and White samples were ostensibly matched or selected on the basis of socioeconomic characteristics, in actuality they were selected for quantity of assimilation or the extent to which members of the respective samples were equivalently exposed to White (middle-to-upper-class) culture.

Socioeconomic Homogeneity. In addition to assuming that social-class effects on CAT scores observed within White samples necessarily generalize to Black samples, investigators also have often been guilty of either ignoring social class or focusing excessively on the lower stratum when Black test-takers' responses are examined, presumably because they assume that this stratum accurately represents the Black population. Nevertheless, although it is true that a much greater percentage of Blacks than Whites in this country are and have been poor, it is also true that since 1959, the majority of Blacks have not been poor even when one uses environmental indicants from White culture to operationally define class (cf. Ruiz, 1990). For example, Axelson (1985) reported that whereas 55.1% of Blacks as compared with 18.1% of Whites were poor in 1959, by 1969 the poverty rates had decreased to 32.2% and 9.5% for Blacks and Whites, respectively. These rates varied by from one to three percentage points during the successive three decades. In her examination of fluctuations in socioeconomic status of various racial and ethnic groups between 1978 and 1986, Ruiz reported a national poverty level varying from 31% to 36% for Blacks and 9% to 12% for Whites. Thus, together, these data support an interpretation of a positively skewed distribution of wealth for Blacks, but they do not support an interpretation of mono-SES. Nor do they support use of SES as a stable cultural variable because it seems possible that fluctuations in rates could be attributed to upward or downward mobility of some of the same people. Therefore, it is difficult to figure out why researchers assume that models of poverty permit an adequate examination of the operation of environmental factors on the CAT performance of Black test takers.

Perhaps it is evident that the limited attention given to the interactions between racial group membership and SES variables presupposes homogeneity of racial groups in two ways. First, lack of attention to SES variability across racial groups assumes an equivalence of life experience that is not moderated at all by racial group membership. Second, obliviousness to variability of socioeconomic statuses within Black racial groups assumes a lack of heterogeneity of social class among Black people, so that any evidence concerning membership in one class stratum (especially deprived classes) necessarily describes the others. This homogeneity assumption in its various forms may have contributed to measurement myths that have obsfucated the search for cultural influences on CAT performance.

Here, one major concern is that racial comparison groups may not have been adequately matched on characteristics ostensibly extraneous to intellectual functioning, such as SES. Adequate matching requires use of matching variables of comparable meaning rather than identical physical properties. Considering that Black Americans, regardless of how SES is defined, usually have not had the range of exposure to White culture as have Whites of either gender, it is conceivable that it might not be possible to identify equivalent samples at any phase of the CAT construction and validation process. Also, in the rare instances, such as those in the study by Scott and Shaw (1985), in which VREGs and Whites have been matched (if that is even remotely possible) with respect to extraneous characteristics, conflicting relationships between predictors and criteria have been found. For example, Scott and Shaw found that the relationship between Graduate Record Examination (GRE) scores and grade point averages (GPA) was negative for Blacks and positive for a matched sample of Whites.

Moreover, considering the environmental perspective more generally, a basic cornerstone of this perspective is that differences in race-related oppression account for racial differences in CAT performance. Yet, no models for conceptualizing and assessing the effects of exposure to oppression (cf. Landrum-Brown, 1990) on CAT performance are apparent in the psychometric literature. Instead, exposure to oppressive environments is inferred from racial group membership or social class by both proponents and opponents of the environmentalist perspective.

CULTURAL BIAS IN COGNITIVE ABILITY TESTING

Neither the implicit biological nor environmental philosophical perspectives offer explicit models for examining issues of cultural equivalence or the practical significance of CATS, particularly as they involve different racial and ethnic groups. Nor are the investigations that purport to examine cultural (racial) influences on CAT performance driven by race-specific models.

The absence of clearly articulated, theoretically based models for examining the influence of race-related cultural factors on cognitive ability is reflected in the ambiguous language used to discuss racial factors and CATs. Two concepts that apparently require greater differentiation within the context of racial and ethnic group CAT performance are cultural bias and cultural equivalence. Cultural bias, when used to compare racial and ethnic groups' CAT performance, commonly refers to whether tests appear to yield comparable scores across racial groups or whether usage of tests results in disparate treatment (e.g., selection, placement) of members of different racial and ethnic groups. Cultural equivalence in standardized CATs has generally been inferred from studies of cultural bias, suggesting that the two constructs have become confused in the literature. Cultural equivalence is supposed to refer to whether constructs have similar meaning within and across cultural groups and requires some thoughtful analysis of the meaning of events.

Cultural bias is generally examined through psychometric statistical analyses of measures and selection procedures. A typical study of racial bias involves administering the same test to groups of Blacks and Whites and comparing their average scores or patterns of response in some manner. To the extent that selected statistical indicators (e.g., regression lines, intercepts, means, cutoff scores, factor patterns) appear to be similar across groups, then between-group equivalence is assumed. Although they are too extensive to be covered here, a myriad of studies and reviews of studies can be found in which the psychometric or statistical approach to demonstrating equivalence across racial groups has been used in some manner (e.g., Cleary, 1968; Cleary, Humphreys, Kendrick, & Wesman, 1975; N. S. Cole, 1981; Humphreys & Taber, 1973; Jensen, 1980; Linn, 1982).

In their interpretation of the psychometric approach for assessing cultural bias in testing, Walsh and Betz (1985) viewed content bias and selection bias as the crucial indicators of whether tests should be used with VREGs in the same manner as they are used with Whites. They define content bias as the extent to which test content is more familiar to White middle-class examinees than to Blacks (in this instance), uses pictorial or linguistic materials that numerically or otherwise favor Whites over Blacks, and results in different factor structures when the test items are compared between groups. They define selection bias as the extent to which test scores result in differential predictions of criteria (e.g., grades, job performance) when the two groups are compared. Thus, one of the basic assumptions of the environmental perspective (universality of White culture) is embedded in the definition of bias and racial group (i.e., implicit biological) statistical comparisons are virtually dictated by the operational definitions of cultural bias.

Consequently, from a psychometric perspective, when comparing Blacks and Whites, tests are assumed to have the same internal structure and, consequently, to lack cultural bias (and therefore to be culturally equivalent) if the two racial groups' CAT responses result in similar factor patterns when they are factor analyzed (Humphreys & Taber, 1973; Jensen, 1980). Similarly, tests are assumed not to result in selection bias if analyses of the relationship of test scores to predictors result in regression lines that do not differ significantly between groups (N. S. Cole, 1981) or if a single regression line, based on the test scores and criteria of both racial groups, results in differential prediction that seemingly favors (i.e., "overpredicts" the criterion scores of) Blacks (Boehm, 1972; Jensen, 1980, 1981; Hunter, Schmidt, & Hunter, 1979).

Statistical evidence notwithstanding, none of these statistical strategies necessarily demonstrates the presence of cultural equivalence in either standardized CATs or the criteria that the tests are used to predict. Of particular relevance here is the observation that the psychometric-statistical approach has been used without regard to how cultural factors might influence the statistics themselves. Naroll's (1970) work, for example, raises questions concerning psychometric equivalence that should be addressed when Blacks and Whites are compared. He argued that cultural groups may not be entirely independent if geographic proximity makes it possible for cultural borrowing or cultural diffusion to occur. If the groups being compared are not truly independent, then, Naroll asserted, the assumptions underlying most statistical procedures are weakened or violated. One consequence of such violations can be that what appears to be a significant correlation between a predictor and criterion across racial groups might instead reflect overlap on a third unmeasured factor resulting from cross-group exposure.

A hypothetical example involving 12 Black and 12 White college students might illustrate Naroll's (1970) point. Suppose that their exposure to racism in the educational system could be assessed by summing respondents' "yes" responses to questions such as the following: (a) Have you ever received an essay back from an instructor of a race other than your own with a low grade, but no explanation for the grade? (b) Has an instructor ever told you that you were inferior in some way because of your racial or ethnic group membership? (c) Has an instructor ever told you not to waste your time studying racial and ethnic issues? (d) Have you ever attended a lecture in which an instructor portrayed all members of your race or ethnicity as intellectually inferior? (e) Have you ever participated in a class in which the instructor expected you to explain why all members of your racial or ethnic group think or behave as they do?

Exposure to racially or ethnically oppressive situations of this sort are extremely common for Black students in predominantly White educational institutions at all levels (cf. Webster, Sedlacek, & Miyares, 1979). Other authors hypothesize that some Whites, particularly White ethnics, might now or historically have experienced similar discrimination (Bond, 1980). Thus, in this example, it seems reasonable to hypothesize skewed distributions of racial experiences between the two racial groups, with Blacks ($M = 3.83$, $SD = 1.03$) experiencing on average more of these incidents than Whites ($M = 0.50$, $SD = 0.67$), although the number per individual might vary, with Whites experiencing some but not many of these incidents. Thus, the range of scores on this variable for both groups is restricted, but not necessarily in the same manner. In this instance, responses to the racism experience scale would represent Naroll's (1970) third variable. The other two imaginary variables in this example are participants' cumulative GPA (Black $M = 1.98$, $SD = 0.62$; White $M = 2.22$, $SD = 0.81$) and IQ test scores (Black $M = 99.75$, $SD = 14.17$; White $M = 103.67$, $SD = 17.19$).

If one examines the simple correlations between IQ and GPA, disregarding race ($r = .34$, $p < .05$), then it appears that the two are positively correlated. Thus, one might reasonably conclude that IQ test scores similarly predict GPA for both racial groups. However, partialing out the variance due to racism experiences increases somewhat the correlation between IQ and GPA for the combined group ($r = .36$, $p = .04$). Yet, this significant relationship is attributable to a higher correlation for Whites ($r = .37$, $p = .13$) than for Blacks ($r = .21$, $p = .26$) when racism is controlled. Thus, consistent with Naroll's (1970) hypothesis, exposure to racism represents a third unmeasured factor that might influence the quality of performance on predictors and criteria for Blacks and Whites. Of course, this example does not "prove" that this particular or any third variable does intrude between CAT scores and criteria. It does suggest that investigators, particularly those who endorse the environmental perspective, might search for more inventive measures of environment.

Conclusions based on common statistical patterns between racial groups must also be questioned if one takes into account methodological issues such as the following: (a) Black and White samples are generally drawn from populations that differ markedly in size and diversity of educational and occupational experiences (Scott & Shaw, 1985); (b) restriction of range issues may occur differently for Blacks and Whites, particularly if the measures involved are not culturally equivalent in actuality (i.e., if the CATS are measuring different characteristics in each group); (c) the influence of differential race-related contextual factors (e.g., racial oppression) on criteria is rarely examined, particularly in educational settings; (d) the content of tests and criteria are determined by Whites and White culture; and (e) because psychometric and statistical studies are not theory driven, virtually any results one obtains can be interpreted as support for one's hypothesis. In the absence of consideration of the impact of racial-group interdependence and these other methodological problems on the psychometrics of standardized cognitive ability testing, it is impossible to ascertain what the statistics really mean. Therefore, it is not reasonable to conclude that existing procedures *have* demonstrated lack of cultural bias and, by implication, to infer that they *can* demonstrate cultural equivalence.

Even if the methodological concerns did not exist with respect to previous investigations of cultural bias, it would still be possible for CATs to lack cultural bias as statistically defined but also to lack cultural equivalence. For instance, if current CATs assess White g rather than African g or levels of acculturation and assimilation to White culture as postulated in earlier sections of this essay then it might be possible to use these measures to assess general intellectual ability in Whites quite well without their necessarily performing the same function for Blacks. In other words, Whites would be expressing their abilities in the modal biological or environmental styles of their group, whereas Blacks would not. Perhaps in such an instance the CAT performance of Black test takers would be more indicative of level of acculturation or assimilation to White culture than of level of cognitive ability.

If such disparity in conceptual meaning of the tests did exist, then (unless acculturation and intellectual ability are synonyms) when CATs were used for selection or placement purposes, Whites potentially would be selected on the basis of greater intellectual ability in White culture, whereas Blacks would not be selected on the basis of greater intellectual ability as represented in Black culture. Because the construct being assessed would not be equivalent within each racial group, then identical interpretation of test responses for Blacks and Whites would be inappropriate. Moreover, use of CATs in such a manner would result in cultural bias, according to which the most intellectually qualified Whites, but not necessarily the most intellectually qualified Blacks, would be selected. Potential disparity in the meaning of CATs for different racial groups—that is, questionable cultural equivalence—is essentially the unresolved issue underlying the controversy concerning use of separate norms for different racial groups.

In the area of standardized cognitive ability testing, cultural equivalence per se has not been investigated empirically. Unfortunately, there seem to be no commonly accepted alternatives to the statistical approaches for instigating such investigations. Yet what is even more distressing than the lack of explicit alternatives is an apparent inability of psychologists and psychometricians to articulate the relevant issues as they affect test takers from various racial and ethnic groups within the United States. Therefore, the conclusion that whatever construct is measured by standardized CATs constitutes universal intelligence or general cognitive ability for all racial and ethnic groups in this country is dubious at best.

CULTURALIST PERSPECTIVE

Culture-specific theories, or the *culturalist* perspective, requires the specification of those race-related (in this instance) psychological characteristics hypothesized to describe and perhaps differentiate individual racial groups (e.g., Grubb & Dozier, 1989). Although there is no universally accepted definition of *culture* in American psychology, in general, the term seems to refer to learned or acquired behaviors or to traits attributable to the socialization experiences resulting from membership in particular systems or institutions within a society. D. W. Sue and Sue (1990), for example, proposed that culture "consists of all those things that people have learned to do, believe, value, and enjoy in their history. It is the totality of ideals, beliefs, skills, tools, customs, and institutions into which each member of a society is born" (p. 35).

Theorists who propose different cultures for different racial and ethnic groups generally locate the foundations of these cultures in older civilizations. Thus, Black styles of cognitive functioning are thought to emanate from classic African civilizations (Schiele, 1991); the roots of White styles are generally located in ancient Western European civilizations (Katz, 1985). Culturalists propose that contemporary expression of these respective cultural dimensions is influenced by persons' environmental contexts but that the original dimensions have not been obliterated by environment. Therefore, valid investigation of cultural influences on test performance across racial groups requires the specification and assessment of dimensions thought to characterize each (racial) cultural group, such as behaviors, beliefs, and values. Variables of these types usually are what one means by *psychological* characteristics. It should be possible to specify and assess these dimensions independently of CAT performance, and it is necessary to do so if one intends to make a convincing cultural difference argument.

In their discussion of the culturalist perspective with respect to Asian-American educational achievement, S. Sue and Okazi (1990) proposed that the culturalist perspective requires (a) specification of the psychological dimensions hypothesized to typify members of a racial or ethnic group, (b) assessment of these dimensions, and (c) demonstrations of how the presence or absence of these cultural dimensions influences the target behavior across racial and ethnic groups. In addition, Grubb and Dozier (1989) argued that cultural influences on CAT performance must be conceptualized and analyzed on four levels: (a) individual (i.e., What are relevant characteristics of the person being assessed?), (b) microsystem (What variables within the immediate setting predispose the person to perform in one way rather than another?), (c) exosystem (What characteristics in the larger social structure influence cognitive development and performance?), and (d) macrosystem (What cultural beliefs, attitudes, and values prevail in society defined more globally?).

Grubb and Dozier's (1989) perspective illustrates the complexity of operationally defining culture. The complexity is increased if one takes into consideration the multiple culturally diverse environments or settings in which VREGs function, in contrast to their White counterparts. Needless to say, a culturalist perspective with anywhere near the theoretical sophistication required has been all but invisible in traditional psychometric literature. Be that as it may, what is clear from the various definitions of culture is that it is not a static entity. Nor is it uniform. Therefore, a person does not either have culture or not have culture. Rather, acculturation, or the learning of culture, is a dynamic process that individuals undoubtedly accomplish at different rates, even within the same ostensible environment. Consequently, knowledge of a person's racial group membership reveals nothing about the amount or type of culture the person has absorbed.

Although many CAT developers have attempted to reduce cultural influences on CATs through construction of culture-fair tests (e.g., Cattell, 1940), these devices represent attempts to control the influences of different cultures rather than to measure them. Also, there has been at least one attempt to develop a culture-specific intelligence test for Blacks (R. Williams, 1975). One can argue that the latter attempt apparently was unsuccessful because the test developers' confusing of the environmental and culturalist perspectives resulted in items that were probably biased in favor of specific social class and regional groups rather than Blacks as a cultural group. With respect to both efforts to construct more culturally equivalent CATs, it seems reasonable to ask whether it is possible to control something that one has not conceptualized adequately.

By encouraging consideration of the idea that many intact cultures can exist within the same national (e.g., the U.S.) environment, the culturalist perspective may offer at least the rudiments of a framework for formulating testable hypotheses concerning the impact of test constructors' cultural orientations on the content of their products. The perspective may also suggest different explanations for what are ostensibly racial or ethnic group differences in CAT performance, but may be cultural differences in actuality.

In culture-specific psychology, the insistence that White-American culture is universal and superior and should be absorbed by every racial and ethnic group in the country is often referred to as an assimilation or melting-pot norm (Duran, 1988; Jones & Korchin, 1982). In testing, as well as in other areas of psychology, rigid adherence to such a norm adversely impacts the groups for whom the norm is foreign, in that it devalues their unique and special cultural characteristics. It also adversely impacts American culture more broadly, in that it potentially deprives the society of the kinds of diversity in intellectual functioning that might lead to a better society. As it is, to the extent that the average performance of Blacks on such tests deviates from that of Whites, Blacks are assumed to be inferior, less bright, and incapable of performing in educational and work settings that theoretically require the presence of "brighter" people (Gottfredson, 1988). Few investigators have asked what Black people might be contributing to society apart from scores on traditional CATs.

It is interesting that if one checks the reference lists of authors who apparently ascribe to the melting-pot norm in testing (Gottfredson, 1988; Jensen, 1980; Scarr & Weinberg, 1976), one rarely finds any references from the cross-cultural personality assessment or cognitive developmental literature (M. Cole, Gay, Glick, & Sharp, 1971; Lonner, 1981, 1985; Thompson, 1989; Weinberg, 1989). Yet, it is this literature that should be most useful in helping one avoid committing the fallacy of cultural equivalence. When comparing racial or ethnic groups, one commits the cultural equivalence fallacy by assuming that cultural equivalence in CATs exists across racial and ethnic groups rather than by demonstrating that it does. In testing, there are potentially many aspects of cultural equivalence. However, these aspects rarely have been extrapolated to the study of racial and ethnic group cultures in the United States.

Cultural Equivalence in Tests

Various definitions of cultural equivalence from the personality assessment literature can be adapted to permit examination of the equivalence of CATs for racial or ethnic cultural groups. Lonner (1981) discussed four kinds of equivalence: (a) functional equivalence, the extent to which test scores have the same meaning in different cultural groups and measure psychological characteristics that occur with equal frequency within these groups; (b) conceptual equivalence, whether groups are equally familiar or unfamiliar with the content of test items and consequently assign the same meaning to them; (c) linguistic equivalence, whether the language used in tests has been equalized so that it has the same meaning to different cultural groups; and (d) (psycho)metric equivalence, the extent to which tests measure the same things at the same levels across cultural groups.

From Butcher's (1982) list of potential sources of nonequivalence in cross-cultural research, the following kinds of equivalence can be added: (a) testing condition equivalence, assurance that the idea of testing as a means of assessing ability and the testing procedures are equally familiar and acceptable to Blacks and Whites; (b) contextual equivalence, evidence that in the various environments in which the person functions, the to-be-assessed cognitive ability is evaluated similarly; and (c) sampling equivalence, determination that samples of subjects representing each racial or ethnic group are comparable at the test development, validation, and interpretation stages. Failure to consider any of the aforementioned forms of equivalence can contribute to committing the cultural equivalence fallacy.

Earlier in this essay, I have attempted to illustrate that the cultural equivalence fallacy has been committed repeatedly with respect to equivalence of concept, psychometrics, and sampling. In particular, the discussions of item quality and environmental impediments illustrate that assumptions of conceptual and sampling equivalence have remained unproven, as does the discussion of cultural bias with respect to psychometric equivalence. Other forms of cultural equivalence (testing condition, functional, and linguistic) have received so little attention that one must suppose that psychologists and psychometricians do not recognize that the lack of evidence concerning these forms of equivalence should severely restrict the usage of CATs across racial groups.

Testing Condition. The equivalence of testing conditions has been examined primarily by comparing the CAT performance of Black children tested by a White examiner with the performance of Black children tested by an examiner of their own race (cf. Sattler, 1970). Of course, this investigative strategy begs the question of equivalence by assuming that (a) racial group category and culture are equivalent, (b) CATs have no cultural characteristics apart from those of the test administrator, and (c) whatever culture the administrator and the test taker might have in common supersedes the culture of CATs themselves.

Functional Equivalence. Functional equivalence concerns the extent to which cognitive ability, as defined by the researcher, operates in the same manner within racial and ethnic groups — that is, is universal. Cause for questioning the universality of CATs for different racial and ethnic cultural groups comes from many sources. Glick (1975) reported that Kpelle natives could demonstrate the same level of conceptual problem-solving skills as college undergraduates when instructed to perform sorting tasks as a "fool" would do them. Miller-Jones (1989) provided a charming excerpt from an assessment interview in which a Black child expressed her incredulity at the assessor's request that she give obvious responses to intelligence test questions. Rogoff and Morelli (1989) pointed out that supplying known answers in order to satisfy an adult's request to do so rather than to accomplish a functional goal violates the norms of everyday life for many cultural groups. Moreover, a number of studies have provided evidence suggesting that Blacks with the same or lower *measured* levels of cognitive ability (as indicated by CAT scores) actually function at higher levels than do their White counterparts (cf. Gerstein, Brodzinsky, & Reiskind, 1976; Grubb & Ollendick, 1986; Lemkan & Imre, 1969).

Linguistic Equivalence. Linguistic equivalence has not received even cursory attention using Black adult samples and has generated only minimal attention where Black children are concerned (cf. Williams & Rivers, 1972 [cited in Scott & Shaw, 1985]). It should be obvious that equivalence cannot exist unless the percepts of a construct are communicated in a language that is equally comprehensible to both groups. I could locate no study in which the linguistic equivalence of cognitive ability tests was investigated using native English-speaking middle-class Black Americans as the standard. For that matter, insofar as one can tell, investigators have not even attempted to determine whether the familial language of test takers labeled "Black" is the language of the tests. How are the test scores of African Americans whose families speak French, Amharic, Spanish, Portuguese, and so forth treated in racial comparative studies?

In general, Black Americans are the descendants of linguistically pluralistic African ancestors. These ancestors, in the United States, created languages by which people who originally belonged to linguistically different ethnic groups could communicate with each other as well as with Whites. Furthermore, these ancestors developed subtle and elegant modifications of English language in order to circumvent racial oppression. All of these linguistic accomplishments occurred in an environment in which written communication was forbidden. It seems unlikely that remnants of this linguistic diversity did not survive in their descendants in some form. One might expect, for instance, that African language patterns persist in African-American groups to the extent that they have not acculturated or have not been assimilated into White culture or to the extent that they are linguistically bicultural (Bernal, 1990; Brislin, 1970; Lein, 1975; Tharp, 1989).

It is also unlikely that most Blacks in the United States exist without being exposed to some versions of Black *and* White English. Thus, even in those instances of acculturation or assimilation, cross-cultural psychotherapy literature suggests that language switching — that is, "unconscious" communicating in the language that feels most comfortable — may occur during times of stress, which might include testing and assessment situations (Malgady, Rogler, & Constantine, 1987; Marcos, Alpert, Urcuyo, & Kesselman, 1973).

Best (1986) further pointed out that even when a person is considered to be bilingual, there are 32 language dimensions that must be mastered for the individual to be equivalently fluent in both languages. The individual's manner of acquiring knowledge and competence in both languages may also influence her or his proficiency in the language. In this instance, individuals could be (a) monolingual in Black standard English; (b) coordinate bilinguals who may have learned Black and White standard English in two completely different settings, from different speakers, and at different times; (c) bilinguals who have learned Black and White standard English from the same people, in the same setting, at the same time; or (d) monolingual in White standard English.

These four categories, of course, become even more varied if one includes Blacks for whom English of any variety is not their first language. Be that as it may, because White standard English is the language of the tests, monolinguals in Black standard English and coordinate bilinguals might operate under a greater language disadvantage than monolinguals in White standard English and compound bilinguals. Nevertheless, instead of empirically investigating the rival hypothesis that language differences may effect performance on tests that are written entirely in White-American language, without necessarily implying anything about the linguistic ability or aptitude of Black-American examinees, researchers have assumed a rather ethnocentric stance, in which White-American English is assumed to be *the* standard to which other Americans must conform in order to prove that they are intelligent. Insofar as language equivalence is considered at all, psychologists and psychometricians argue that Black test takers are deficient to the extent that they use "slang" or "nonstandard English" rather than "standard" (i.e., White) English. These scientists rarely seem to realize that it is (many) English people rather than (most) White Americans who speak "standard" English (many of these English people think that White Americans speak slang rather than standard English). Therefore, what makes White-American English "the best" in this country, in general, and in the testing process, more specifically, is that White Americans who have been the numerical majority in the United States define "standard" English and write the tests in the language that is most familiar to them.

If language is a contributing factor in performance on CATs, then it clearly operates in a direction that favors Whites over Blacks. Given this possibility, one runs the risk of committing the cultural equivalence fallacy in the absence of evidence that test items do in fact have the same linguistic meaning across racial groups. Again, mere statistical evidence demonstrating similarity in patterns of response is not necessarily sufficient, because if one understands White English at all, one might be able to respond to it "correctly" on some of the 32 dimensions discussed by Best (1986), but better-than-average performance on current versions of CATs likely requires that one have an intimate knowledge of English language subtleties (e.g., connotations as well as denotations) as defined by Whites rather than Blacks.

Be that as it may, questions about the quality of tests and, for that matter, criteria are not likely to be raised until psychometricians are at least willing to acknowledge that cognitive tests may be measuring something other than, or in addition to, general ability in VREGs, and one cannot determine what the other thing(s) might be merely by replicating studies in which Whites and White cultural standards are used as the exclusive criteria for determining intelligence or general ability. However, development of more sophisticated CATs requires more sophisticated conceptualizations and operational definitions of culture(s), particularly as it influences the CAT process broadly defined. The culturalist perspective suggests that generalization of culture-specific models to the CAT process may increase psychologists' and psychometricians' levels of cultural sophistication.

Eurocentricism in Cognitive Ability Testing

Perhaps White cultural influences on CATs can be investigated by studying the dimensions and values that comprise Eurocentricism.

Helms (1989b) defined Eurocentricism as "a perceptual set in which European and/or European American values, customs, traditions and characteristics are used as exclusive standards against which people and events in the world are evaluated and perceived" (p. 643). Some theorists (Helms, 1989b; Katz, 1985; Stewart, 1971) have attempted to delimit the characteristics of Eurocentric culture that distinguish it from other worldviews as well as from other cultures such as Afrocentricism (Asante, 1988; Nobles, 1991) and Asiatic perspectives (Pedersen, 1977).

Several of the values and beliefs of the Eurocentric worldview may have particular relevance to the area of test construction and validation. Some of these are summarized in Table 1. Of these, the following may have the most pervasive detrimental effects on those for whom this perspective is inappropriate: (a) dualistic linear or rational thinking, (b) the White superiority assumption, and (c) the emphasis on the scientific method or logical positivism as the modus operandi for "discovering" intellectual ability (see also Helms, 1989a; Hoshmand, 1989). Each of these values or beliefs potentially influences test construction (e.g., content), procedures (e.g., administration), and test interpretation (e.g., validation) as well as the "research designs" (e.g., testing situations and procedures) from which support for tests and their usage emerges.

Dualism in Testing. Prevalent in European-American philosophical thought is the principle that life events can be dichotomized: The mind and body are separate, as are one's environmental context and expressed intelligence; answers are either right or wrong; a person is either intellectually inferior or superior, and so forth. This dualism is inherent in the scientific method and permeates every aspect of the testing process, although perhaps it is most evident in those aspects of cultural equivalence involving the meaning of test content or conceptual equivalence.

One manifestation of dualistic thinking in testing is the belief that one can devise standardized tests, in which each test question has only one right answer, the rightness of which is determined by the normative White response. It is assumed that the intelligent person, virtually regardless of race or ethnicity and related socialization experiences, can retrieve from memory or discover these answers through linear, rational (i.e., nonemotional), time-limited thinking. That is, the intelligent individual is operationally defined as the one

TABLE 1

White Cultural Components in Cognitive Ability Testing (CAT):
Effects of European-Centered Values and Beliefs

Dimension/General Description	Cultural Influence on Test Response
Rugged individualism	
The wants, needs, and characteristics of the individual are more important than those of the group.	"Correct" answers to test items often require reasoning independent of social context.
Individual achievement is most highly valued.	The person(s) with the highest test scores is (are) entitled to the most privileges.
The individual is primarily responsible for his or her success or failure.	The person(s) with low test scores is (are) intellectually defective.
Action orientation	
Everyone can control his or her own life and environment.	All test takers can choose to be exposed to "correct" life experiences.
A person should resolve problems by taking action.	A person should take action to maximize his or her test score.
Status and power	
White cognitive strategies are best.	Performance on White cognitive ability tests determines intellectual level.
Experts with credentials determine merit.	Test scores are valued more highly than behavior in selection and placement.
Communication	
White English is best.	Tests are written in White English.
People who use White English are better than others.	Test takers' facility with White English influences evaluation of their general ability levels.
Competition	
There is not enough for everyone, so each person must compete for her or his share.	Test scores influence the quality of one's subsequent educational and employment opportunities.
One is either a winner or a loser.	High test scores mean that a person is intelligent and meritorious; low scores mean the converse.
Time	
Time is a valuable commodity.	The faster one obtains "right" answers, the brighter one is.
The best people adhere to rigid time schedules.	Tests are timed.

Dimension/General Description	Cultural Influence on Test Response
History Anything worth knowing has its basis in the experience of European immigrants in the United States.	Test content is often derived from European history, culture, and so forth, but rarely includes experiences of non-Europeans.
History European history is to be emulated. European experiences are valued universally.	Test content portrays European experiences as "heroic." The "right" answer often requires the test taker to interpret the world as Whites do.
Family structures The nuclear family is the ideal and normative social unit.	Test questions pertaining to family, genetics, and so forth often assume a nuclear family "Low" test scores may be attributed to deviations from the nuclear family structure.
Aesthetics The best music and art come from European culture. The best people "look" European.	Test content is likely to reflect European culture. Racial group differences in which Whites have the "highest" test scores mean that they are brightest; the same assumption does not hold for non-European groups. The right answer to test questions can require that one recognize people of European appearance as best.
Emphasis on scientific method Objective and rational evaluation is highly valued.	Tests are supposed to be administered in an objective and neutral manner.
The best people use rational and logical thought.	"Correct" responses often require the test taker to separate "facts" from their social context.
Linear problem solving is valued.	"Correct" answers to test items require one to apply "rational" thinking.
Dichotomies can be used to understand and predict life's events.	Every test question has only one right answer; everything else is wrong.
Everything can be quantified.	A number accurately describes a person's intelligence.

Note: Dimensions are adapted from Katz's (1985) taxonomy.

who can apply Eurocentric rules most efficiently. However, to the extent that non-Eurocentric worldviews lead members of a racial or ethnic group to "see" alternative right answers, or to the extent that they do not have equivalent access to Eurocentric rules of proceeding, tests lack cultural equivalence for the differently advantaged group.

One occasionally hears of instances in which White test takers discover test items with alternative correct answers. A case in point involves two White prelaw students who convinced the Law School Admissions Services that a Law School Admissions Test (LSAT) question had two correct answers (Mathews, 1989). Presumably, these young men were socialized in White culture. However, it is quite possible that alternate cultural backgrounds might also lead one to choose more intelligent or more creative answers than the test constructors intended. Such persons are likely to be severely penalized on two fronts. Not only will they be deemed less intelligent than the person who chose the White culturally appropriate answer, but they will be considered less deserving of the rewards and benefits that are often associated with high CAT scores.

Needless to say, lack of cultural equivalence of response alternatives is rarely offered as an explanation for VREGs' test performance. Yet, most cognitive ability tests have been developed by (presumably) White psychologists and psychometricians who have been socialized interpersonally and professionally in Eurocentric environments. The tests have been standardized on predominantly White samples, most of whom have been similarly socialized. Given this differential favoritism, it *should* be the case that CATs favor Whites and other groups who naturally use or are willing to develop a similar belief system, and others who have intimate access to White culture (Scarr, 1988). This advantage occurs not necessarily because Whites are more intelligent than any other group but because the measurement devices cannot help but maintain the status quo (cf. Prilleltensky, 1989).

Until investigators begin to investigate cultural issues through a broader array of conceptual as well as statistical analyses of existing measures, the cultural equivalence fallacy cannot be ruled out as an explanation for between-racial-group differences on cognitive ability tests, regardless of whose score is higher. Moreover, use and monocultural (i.e., White cultural) interpretation of scores resulting from such testing devices devalues intelligence as expressed in other cultures and perpetuates the myth of White intellectual superiority.

White Superiority Assumption. Judging the cognitive abilities of VREGs exclusively on the basis of command of White English, history, aesthetics, and so forth suggests an implicit orientation on the part of test constructors in which White culture is assumed to be superior to VREG cultures. Yet, because Black test takers may not use the strategies of White culture as their cognitive strategies of first choice does not necessarily mean they cannot use them. Whether one uses a biological or an environmental definition, there is evidence to suggest that White culture has its origins in African civilizations (e.g., ben-Jochannan, 1981; Diop, 1974). For Whites to have evolved their dominant style, Black Africans were undoubtedly capable of using such a style at one time, and therefore, it is likely that Black African Americans *can* demonstrate the Eurocentric style now. However, the question of cultural (conceptual and functional) equivalence here has to do with whether the thinking style, for example, has the same meaning, that is, is equally dominant and serves the same purposes in both groups.

Furthermore, it is quite possible that the normative strategies for processing information in White culture, rational and dualistic thinking, are not the ingredients that are most or exclusively important in the successful performance of work or education for any group. Yet, cultural and environmental analyses of criteria, to the extent that they exist, do not typically take into account the possibility that different kinds of equally intelligent strategies might lead to the same or better outcomes. For example, it would be interesting if African culturally laden cognitive strategies turned out to be more useful constructs for predicting performance than White culturally laden cognitive strategies as assessed by CATs. Be that as it may, until investigators examine this and other possibilities, then CATs should not be assumed to have any of the previously mentioned kinds of equivalence when they are used with Black Americans.

Scientific Method. Where test usage, criteria, and research design involving quantification of cognitive abilities are concerned, Eurocentricism likely is often intrinsic to the criteria or evaluations thereof as well as to the tests themselves. When Eurocentricism mutually characterizes tests and criteria, then significant test-criteria correlations should occur. However, the meaning of the correlations may not be that intelligence (as measured by CATs) is predictive of performance (as variously measured). Instead, they might merely indicate that a Eurocentric cognitive style is correlated with itself wherever one measures it. At best, such correlations demonstrate that one can quantify similar thinking styles among Blacks and Whites, and to the extent that these styles are also a part of the criteria, one should find similar (perhaps small) validity coefficients, which has usually been the case (e.g., Hunter et al., 1979).

In the absence of alternative strategies for operationally defining intelligent thinking in test construction, usage, and interpretation, the dilemma of cultural equivalence cannot be resolved through exclusive reliance on statistical analyses as currently conducted. Walsh and Betz (1985) explained that psychometricians are attempting to eliminate cultural bias in existing tests by allowing panels of experts representative of various racial and ethnic, gender, and social-class groups to assist in constructing test items. Such procedures may be better than none. However, they probably will not resolve the issues of cultural equivalence as long as these consultants are restricted by the Eurocentricism inherent in the construction and validation process as it is currently construed.

Afrocentricism in Cognitive Ability Testing

Eventual resolution of the cultural equivalence issues raised so far requires that researchers begin to examine other cultural theoretical models for their implications to the cognitive ability testing process. Several authors have proposed various dimensions of African culture, that is, Afrocentricism, (Boykin, 1983; Heath, 1989; Nobles, 1991; Shade, 1983; Tharp, 1989; Thompson & Fretz, 1991; Tracey & Sedlacek, 1984, 1985, 1987) that might be applicable to the testing process. Table 2 summarizes eight African-American intellectual dimensions proposed by Boykin and Toms (1985). In Table 2, I also present some hypotheses about how these dimensions might be expressed in traditional CATs. Note that these authors, contrary to what critics assert about culture-specific perspectives, are not proposing a nonintellectual or relationship-dominant form of intelligence. Rather they are asserting that efficient use of Africa-centered cognitive abilities requires awareness and integration of social contextual factors into one's thinking processes. In other words, African-centered information-processing strategies might be implicit unmeasured aspects of CATs as well as the criteria CATs are used to predict.

TABLE 2
African Cultural Components in Cognitive Ability Testing:
Hypothesized Effects of African-Centered Values and Beliefs

Dimension	General Description	Influence on Test Responses
Spirituality	Greater validity of the power of immaterial forces in everyday life over linear, factual thinking.	It may be difficult to separate relevant aspects of the test stimuli from factors caused by luck or circumstance.
Harmony	The self and one's surroundings are interconnected.	The ambience in which one takes the test may influence one's responses.
Movement	Personal conduct is organized through movement.	Active test-taking strategies may result in better performance than sedentary ones.
Affect	Integration of feelings with thoughts and actions.	Feelings may facilitate or hinder test performance; respondent may find it difficult to "understand" persons in test stimuli who act without feeling.
Communalism	Valuing of one's group(s) more than individuals.	Performance may be influenced when person perceives that it represents the group.
Expressive	Unique personality is expressed through one's behavioral style.	Test taker may choose the more imaginative response alternative.
Orality	Knowledge may be gained and transmitted orally and aurally.	Test performance may differ when the person is tested orally and aurally.
Social time	Time is measured by socially meaningful events and customs.	The belief that obtaining a "good" answer is more important than finishing on time may lead the test taker to "waste" time.

Note: Dimensions are adapted from Boykin's (1983) list.

Consider the following sample GRE question, presented by Walsh and Betz (1985):

Old Mother Hubbard went to the cupboard
To get her poor dog a bone
But when she got there her cupboard was bare
And so the poor dog got none.

If the above is an accurate report of an event, which of the following headline versions gives an account that does not add to the given facts?

(A) Mother H Refuses Bone to Hungry Dog
(B) Mealtime Brings Only Bare Cupboard for Mrs. Hubbard and Dog
(C) Mother Hubbard Seeks Bone for Dog, Finds Empty Cupboard
(D) Dog Lover Unable to Continue Support of Pet
(E) Bone Missing From Hubbard Cupboard—Mystery Unsolved.
    (p. 174)

The correct answer is supposed to be C. Yet one can make an argument for at least one of the other alternatives.

Take E, for example. If we assume that Mother Hubbard was expecting to find a bone in her cupboard (otherwise, she would not have gone there looking for one), then indeed the whereabouts of the bone is (without going beyond the facts) an unsolved mystery to her (and probably to her dog as well). The point here is not to resolve the bone crisis for Mother Hubbard, but to suggest that if it is true, as Heath (1989) argued, that many Blacks are not socialized to believe that authority figures (parents, teachers, etc.) reward obvious answers, but do reward expansive or creative answers, then they might choose an alternative other than C.

Heath (1989) argued that from childhood, Black Americans are socialized in Black communities to develop spontaneous, creative, interactive, and expansive thinking skills. Consequently, upon reaching testable age, it is difficult for them to reconcile the contrasting socially oriented worldviews of their communities with the ascetic Eurocentric view that presumably underlies test construction, particularly when they are bombarded with information to the effect that test scores and intelligence are synonymous. Nevertheless, non-White rational skills (Africa g?) have been functional in helping Black people survive in actually and potentially hostile racial environments. Moreover, it does not take much extrapolation to suppose that these might well have been the same sort of intellectual skills that allowed Black Africans to develop many of the valued aspects of civilizations, including language, math, science, and universities (Browder, 1989; C. Williams, 1987), when there were no preexisting rules to apply.

Yet, to my knowledge, no standardized CAT has attempted to incorporate the "original" thinking style, although variants of this style are apparently more common in the world than is the dualistic rational style (cf. Cole et al., 1971; Kluckhohn & Strodtbeck, 1961; Stewart, 1971). In fact, considerable evidence exists concerning differential usage (and perhaps prominence) of cognitive strategies of Blacks relative to Whites — at least among children (e.g., H. G. Cohen, 1985; Hale, 1982; Shade, 1983; Thompson & Fretz, 1991). Although this research area has been plagued by negatively biased language when referring to styles that seemingly are more typical of Black examinees (e.g., use of *field dependent* rather than *contextually sensitive* or *contextually aware*), it is still sufficient to suggest that if the testing procedures do not take into account the varied cultural experiences of the involved groups, then the results of the assessment procedures may not have the same meaning for Blacks as they do for Whites.

Instead, when alternative styles of intellectual functioning have been proposed or observed in Black people in the United States, their existence has been taken as prima facie evidence of intellectual deficiency caused by personal inadequacies, and therefore, they become characteristics to be remediated by modifying the Black individual (rather than the tests by which the individual is judged). Consequently, one does not know whether currently existing tests actually measure general intelligence or merely a particular minority (i.e., White) thinking style.

CONCLUSIONS AND IMPLICATIONS

By way of summary, in the case of cognitive ability testing and Black versus White samples, questions concerning cultural equivalence of tests might be conceptualized as follows: (a) Is there evidence that the culturally conditioned intellectual skills used by Blacks and Whites generally differ and that these differences have been equivalently incorporated into the measurement procedures? (b) Do Blacks and Whites use the same test-taking strategies when ostensibly responding to the same material, and do these strategies have equivalent meaning? (c) If different strategies are used by the racial groups, to what extent are these differences an aspect of predictors and criteria? (d) How does one measure the cultural characteristics of CATs? Until such questions have been seriously and systematically investigated, it seems injudicious to use pejorative language (e.g., lower standards, brighter) that implies resolution of the between-racial-groups cultural equivalence quandaries.

The implication of these questions for the practitioner is that when differences in performance on cognitive ability tests are attributed to racial or ethnic differences, the practitioner must recognize this explanation for the non sequitur that it is. Instead of continuing to use such measures until something better comes along, practitioners must challenge the scientists on whose work their test usage is based to find culturally defined psychological explanations (e.g., culture-specific attitudes, feelings, or behaviors) for why such racial and ethnic differences exist.

Perhaps by now it has become more evident why existing research designed to investigate cultural bias in CATs cannot answer questions of cultural equivalence between racial and ethnic groups. Eliminating this lacuna in testing literature requires a greater diversity of conceptualizations of culture and psychometric methodologies than is currently present in the cultural bias literature. Diversification means that existing tests ought to be modified to include greater cultural variety, new types of cognitive assessment must be developed and standardized, and instead of using race as a proxy for other factors (e.g., attitudes, environments), explicit principles, hypotheses, assumptions, and theoretical models for investigating these other factors must be proposed. Moreover, the existing frameworks—implicit biological, environmental, and cultural—must be operationally defined in manners that are consistent with their basic premises.

I offer two working hypotheses and some ideas about how alternatives to implicit biological (racial) explanations can be investigated empirically through explicit environmental or cultural perspectives: (a) Acculturation and assimilation to White Euro-American culture should enhance one's performance on currently existing cognitive ability tests, and (b) inclusion of Black African-American culture in cognitive ability assessment procedures should result in fairer (more equivalent) assessment of Black Americans' general cognitive ability levels. Systematic examination of either of these hypotheses could lead to multiple methods of assessing ability across Black and White racial and ethnic groups. Use of these (or some) guiding principles would move the field of cognitive ability testing beyond the strategy of piecemeal comparisons of Blacks and Whites on individual items, regression lines, and so forth that are likely skewed to favor White culture. Moreover, the attempt to substitute theory-driven culture-specific psychometric research for statistically driven research could move psychology toward a more proactive way of examining African (and other VREG) cultural components of intelligence.

The following are preliminary ideas for how such research might be implemented:

1. Develop and make use of measures for determining interracial group cultural dependence (Naroll, 1970), individuals' level of acculturation (e.g., levels of Eurocentric values, beliefs) and Afrocentricity (e.g., levels of Afrocentric values, beliefs) as well as the level of assimilation (e.g., integration) implied by the content of items.

To control for intergroup dependence, Berry (1979) recommended the use of *ethunits,* specifying the demographic, typological, and psychological dimensions that make groups distinct. His and analogous methodologies could be used to adjust responses so that the scores of acculturated and assimilated persons (be they Black or White) might be given less weight (on Eurocentric tests) than the same "correct" responses given by persons who had less or qualitatively different exposure to White culture. Perhaps the person who can use his or her imagination to select the "right" answer is more "intelligent" than the person whose cognitive socialization experiences have been saturated with White culture. Which task is easier, successfully manipulating unfamiliar signs and symbols of another culture or successfully manipulating the symbols of one's own culture?

2. Modify existing test content to include test items that reflect a diversity of cultural content.

The procedures used to update the Wechsler Intelligence Scale for Children (WISC-R; Sandoval, 1989) might provide a model for this type of redevelopment. However, one could still hope that the sociocultural experiences of the various racial and ethnic groups in this country would be better balanced.

3. Explore the meaning of "wrong" answers by talking to examinees.

Occasionally, the test-takers' rationale for choosing one alternative over another should be examined from their perspective. Perhaps equally intelligent people use differing, but equally intelligent, rea-

soning strategies that remain unrecognized because of the test-mak-
ers' ethnocentric perspective.

4. Make greater use of the advances in cognitive psychology more
generally.

Use of interactive modes of assessment based on models such as
those proposed by Vygotsky (1978) and discussed by strategic learning theorists (e.g., Belmont, 1989) may offer some exciting alternatives for the assessment of cognitive abilities.

5. Use theoretical perspectives to study the "environmental" content of criteria.

Some researchers have attempted to develop alternatives for the
prediction of success in employment settings. This research has included examinations of biographical data (Reilly & Chao, 1982),
interviews (Arvey, 1979), and performance appraisal measures
(Goldstein, 1986). In spite of the overemphasis on these alternative
measures as predictors rather than criteria, there is ample evidence
that environmental factors influence scores on such measures. For
instance, White evaluators evaluate White performance more positively than they do Black performance, especially in real life settings
(Kraiger & Ford, 1985). Thus, to the extent that the quality of one's
performance is under the control of a third party's perceptions (e.g.,
supervisors, teachers) and to the extent that that party's perceptions
have been heavily influenced by Eurocentricism, it is unlikely that
alternative modes of being will be viewed with comparable favor.
Yet, conformity to Eurocentric norms may not mean the same thing
for Blacks as it does for Whites. Moreover, under many circumstances, conforming to Eurocentric norms is more likely to be seen
and reacted to favorably if a White person does it. Additional research
is needed to discover the effect of environmental bias and different
cultural socialization on quantification of the criteria and resulting
validity coefficients when CATs are used in industrial and educational settings.

6. In the absence of demonstrably culturally equivalent CATs,
make greater and more consistent use of separate racial group norms.

If one must use such devices as estimates of the abilities of VREGs,
then it is important to remember that racial and ethic group classifications are generally used as imperfect substitutes for unassessed
cultural factors, defined according to at least one of the three proposed theoretical perspectives. Therefore, whereas it is possible that
various styles of cognitive functioning may be specific to cultural

groups rather than racial groups (i.e., transcend racial group membership), until psychometricians develop more diverse methodologies for controlling and investigating the culture of CAT, it seems reasonable to proceed as though these measures generally favor White culture over the culture of Blacks (and other VREGs) and adjust test scores to compensate for the potential cultural imbalance inherent in CATs themselves.

Many of the foregoing recommendations have in common that they are differing ways of advising psychologists and psychometricians that rivals to the implicit biological and environmental perspectives predominant in the field have neither been devised nor systematically examined in the area of cognitive ability testing. Yet, even the most neophyte graduate student soon learns that correlational studies of naturally occurring phenomenon are not of much scientific merit unless alternative plausible hypotheses (e.g., other predictor or criterion variables) concerning one's finding have been ruled out (Kerlinger, 1986). Butcher (1982) further warned that "contemporary one-shot investigations without a grand scheme or sequence of related studies generally add very little to knowledge in the field" (p. 281). The critical flaw in the CAT research literature is not that a series of related studies do not exist, but rather that these studies *do* exist in the absence of adequate culturally based theoretical formulations.

With respect to the issue of cultural equivalence in intelligence tests in particular, Ibrahim (1989) expressed doubt about the ethicality of imposing a White perspective on everyone in this country. She used Scarr's (1988; Scarr & Weinberg, 1976) study of the IQs of Black transracially adopted children to support her concerns. In rebutting Ibrahim, Scarr (1989) argued "in the original article (Scarr & Weinberg, 1976), we explained at length that the [Black transracially adopted] children were being reared in the [White] culture of the tests and the [White] culture of the schools, which accounted for their [relatively high] scores" (p. 849). She further added what may be the modern-day equivalent of "let them eat cake": "We *complained* [italics added] that other measures that could sample the skills and knowledge of minority children reared in their own communities had not been well developed" (p. 849). Juxtapose Scarr's argument with Russo, Olmedo, Stapp, and Fulcher's (1981) findings that of the 3.1% of American Psychological Association members who could be identified as VREG members, none of the 19 psychometricians were Black (an anonymous reviewer pointed out that Russo et al.'s data were not entirely accurate because he or she was overlooked), and then one begins to see the problem. Surely, Scarr and those of similar ilk would not purposefully argue that the *subjects* (e.g., Black children) should provide the *scientists* with culturally equivalent measurement tools. Nor would one presumably argue that the virtually nonexistent VREG psychologists and psychometricians should assume the burden for the entire field. Who, then, will "well develop" these culturally sensitive measures of cognitive abilities if not those renowned psychologists and psychometricians whose careers have flourished under the Eurocentric tradition in testing?

NOTES

Samuel M. Turner served as action editor for this essay.

I wish to thank Anne Regan, Eric Kohatsu, Ralph Piper, Bruce Fretz, and Ray Lorion for their comments on earlier versions of this essay and Gordon Rice for his assistance in preparing the manuscript.

REFERENCES

Arvey, R. D. (1979). Unfair discrimination in the employment interview: Legal and psychological aspects. *Psychological Bulletin, 86,* 736–765.

Asante, M. K. (1988). *Afrocentricity.* Trenton, NJ: Africa World Press.

Axelson, J. A. (1985). *Counseling and development in a multicultural society.* Monterey, CA: Brooks/Cole.

Belmont, J. M. (1989). Cognitive strategies and strategic learning: The socio-institutional approach. *American Psychologist, 44,* 142–148.

ben-Jochannan, Y. (1981). *Black man of the Nile and his family.* New York: Alkebu-Ian Books.

Bernal, E. M. (1990). Increasing the interpretative validity and diagnostic utility of Hispanic children's scores on tests of achievement and intelligence. In F. C. Serafica, A. Schwebel, R. K. Russell, P. D. Isaac, & L. B. Myers (Eds.), *Mental health of ethnic minorities* (pp. 108–138). New York: Praeger.

Berry, J. W. (1979). Research in multicultural societies: Implications of cross-cultural methods. *Journal of Cross-Cultural Psychology, 10,* 415–434.

Bersoff, D. N. (1981). Testing and the law. *American Psychologist, 36,* 1047–1056.

Best, J. B. (1986). *Cognitive psychology.* St. Paul, MN: West.

Boehm, V. R. (1972). Negro-White differences in validity of employment and training selection procedures: Summary of research evidence. *Journal of Applied Psychology, 56,* 33–39.

Bond, L. (1980). Review of bias in mental testing by A. R. Jensen. *Applied Psychological Measurement, 4,* 406–410.

Boykin, A. W. (1983). The academic performance of Afro-American children. In J. T. Spence (Ed.), *Achievement and achievement motives* (pp. 322–371). San Francisco: Freeman.

Boykin, A. W. & Toms, F. D. (1985). Black child socialization: A conceptual framework. In H. P. McAdoo & J. L. McAdoo (Eds.), *Black children: Social educational and parental environments* (pp. 33–51). Beverly Hills, CA: Sage.

Brislin, R. W. (1970). Back translation for cross cultural research. *Journal of Cross-Cultural Psychology, 1,* 185–216.

Browder, A. T. (1989). *From the Browder file.* Washington, DC: Institute of Karmic Guidance.

Butcher, J. N. (1982). Cross-cultural research methods in clinical psychology. In P. C. Kendall & J. N. Butcher (Eds.), *Handbook of research methods in clinical psychology* (pp. 273–308). New York: Wiley.

Cattell, R. B. (1940). A culture free intelligence test: Part I. *Journal of Educational Psychology, 31,* 161–179.

Cattell, R. B. (1963). Theory of fluid and crystallized intelligence: A critical experiment. *Journal of Educational Psychology, 54,* 1–22.

Cleary, T. A. (1968). Test bias: Prediction of grades of Negro and White students in integrated colleges. *Journal of Educational Measurement, 5,* 115–124.

Cleary, T. A., Humphreys, L., Kendrick, A., & Wesman, A. (1975). Educational uses of tests with disadvantaged students. *American Psychologist, 30,* 15–41.

Cohen, H. G. (1985). A comparison of the development of spatial conceptual abilities of students from two cultures. *Journal of Research in Science and Teaching, 22,* 491–501.

Cohen, R. (1990, September 4). Johnny's miserable SATs. *The Washington Post,* p. A19.

Cole, M., Gay, J., Click, J. R., & Sharp, D. W. (1971). *The cultural context of learning and thinking.* New York: Basic Books.

Cole, N. S. (1981). Bias in testing. *American Psychologist, 36,* 1067–1077.

Department of Labor inundated with comments on GATB. (1991). *Science Agenda: APA, 4*(1), 6–7.

Diop, C. A. (1974). *African origin of civilization: Myth or reality?* New York: Lawrence Hill.

Duke, L. (1991). Racial politics envelop job-test scores. *The Washington Post,* pp. A1, A11.

Duran, A. (1988, Winter). Subjective experiences with dependence. *El Boletion: The National Hispanic Psychology Association Newsletter,* pp. 7–15.

Eckland, B. K. (1979). Genetic variance in the SES-IQ correlation. *Sociology of Education, 52,* 191–196.

Franklin, V. P. (1991). Black social scientists and the mental testing movement, 1920–1940. In R. L. Jones (Ed.), *Black psychology* (pp. 207–224). Berkeley, CA: Cobb & Henry.

Gatewood, W. B. (1990). *Aristocrats of color: The Black elite.* Bloomington: Indiana University Press.

Gerstein, A. I., Brodzinsky, D. M., & Reiskind, N. (1976). Perceptual integration on the Rorschach as an indicator of cognitive capacity: A developmental study of racial differences in a clinic population. *Journal of Consulting and Clinical Psychology, 44,* 760–765.

Glick, J. (1975). Cognitive development in cross-cultural perspective. In F. Horowitz (Ed.), *Review of child development research* (Vol. 4, pp. 564–595). Chicago: University of Chicago Press.

Goldstein, I. L. (1986). *Training in organizations: Needs assessment development and evaluation* (2nd ed.) Monterey, CA: Brooks/Cole.

Gordon, R. A., & Rudert, E. E. (1979). Bad news concerning IQ tests. *Sociology of Education, 52,* 174–190.

Gottfredson, L. S. (1988). Reconsidering fairness: A matter of social and ethical priorities. *Journal of Vocational Behavior, 33,* 293–319.

Graham, J. R., & Lily, R. S. (1984). *Psychological testing.* Englewood Cliffs, NJ: Prentice-Hall.

Grubb, H. J., & Dozier, A. (1989). Too busy to learn: A "competing behaviors" explanation of cross-cultural differences in academic ascendancy based on the cultural distance hypothesis. *Journal of Black Psychology, 16*(1), 23–45.

Grubb, H. J., & Ollendick, T. H. (1986). The culture-distance perspective: An exploratory analysis of its effect on learning and intelligence. *International Journal of Intercultural Relations, 10,* 399–414.

Guterman, S. S. (1979). I. Q. tests in research on social stratification: The cross-class validity of the test. *Sociology of Education, 52,* 163–173.

Hale, J. (1982). *Black children: Their roots, culture, and learning styles.* Provo, UT: Brigham Young University Press.

Heath, S. B. (1989). Oral and literate traditions among Black Americans living in poverty. *American Psychologist, 44,* 367–373.

Helms, J. E. (1989a). At long last—Cultural paradigms for counseling psychologists. *The Counseling Psychologist, 17,* 98–101.

Helms, J. E. (1989b). Eurocentricism strikes in strange places and in unusual ways. *The Counseling Psychologist, 17,* 643–647.

Hoshmand, L. T. (1989). Alternative research paradigms: A review and teaching proposal. *The Counseling Psychologist, 17,* 3–79.

Humphreys, L. G., & Taber, T. (1973). Ability factors as a function of advantaged and disadvantaged groups. *Journal of Educational Measurement, 10,* 107–115.

Hunter, J. E., Schmidt, F. L., & Hunter, R. (1979). Differential validity of employment tests by race: A comprehensive review and analysis. *Psychological Bulletin, 86,* 721–735.

Ibrahim, F. A. (1989). Response to "psychology in the public forum" on socially sensitive research. *American Psychologist, 44,* 847–848.

Jensen, A. R. (1969). How much can we boost IQ and scholastic achievement? *Harvard Educational Review, 39,* 1–123.

Jensen, A. R. (1974). How biased are culture-loaded tests? *Genetic Psychology Monographs, 90,* 185–244.

Jensen, A. R. (1976). Test bias and construct validity. *Phi Delta Kappa, 58,* 340–346.

Jensen, A. R. (1980). *Bias in mental testing.* New York: Free Press.

Jensen, A. R. (1981). *Straight talk about mental tests,* New York: Free Press.

Jones, E. E., & Korchin, S. J. (1982). (Eds.). *Minority mental health.* New York: Praeger.

Katz, J. H. (1985). The sociopolitical nature of counseling. *The Counseling Psychologist, 13,* 615–624.

Kerlinger, F. N. (1986). *Foundations of behavioral research.* New York: Holt, Rinehart & Winston.

Kluckhohn, F. R., & Strodtbeck, F. L. (1961). *Variations in value orientations.* New York: Harper & Row.

Kraiger, K., & Ford, J. K. (1985). A meta-analysis of ratee race effects in performance ratings. *Journal of Applied Psychology, 70,* 56–65.

Landrum-Brown, J. (1990). Black mental health and racial oppression. In D. S. Ruiz (Ed.), *Handbook of mental health and mental disorder among Black Americans,* (pp. 113–132). New York: Greenwood Press.

Lein, L. (1975). "You were talkin' though, oh yes, you was." Black American migrant children: Their speech at home and school. *Council on Anthropology and Education Quarterly, 6*(4), 1–11.

Lemkan, P. V., & Imre, D. P. (1969). Results of a field epidemiologic study. *American Journal of Mental Deficiency, 73,* 858–863.

Linn, R. (1982). Ability testing: Individual differences, prediction, and differential prediction. In A. K. Wigdor & W. R. Garner (Eds.), *Ability testing: Uses, consequences, and controversies: Part 2. Documentation section* (pp. 335–388). Washington, DC: National Academy Press.

Lonner, W. J. (1981). Psychological tests and intercultural counseling. In. P. B. Pedersen, J. G. Draguns, W. J. Lonner, & J. E. Trimble (Eds.), *Counseling acr ss cultures* (pp. 275–303). Honolulu: East-West Center and University of Hawaii.

Lonner, W. J. (1985). Issues in testing and assessing in cross-cultural counseling, *The Counseling Psychologist, 13,* 599–614.

Malgady, R. G., Rogler, L. H., & Constantine, G. (1987). Ethnocultural and linguistic bias in mental health evaluations of Hispanics. *American Psychologist, 42,* 228–234.

Marcos, L. R., Alpert, M., Urcuyo, L., & Kesselman, M. (1973). The effect of the interview language on the evaluation of psychopathology in Spanish-American schizophrenic patients. *American Journal of Psychology, 130,* 549–553.

Mathews, J. (1989, March 25). Aspiring lawyers already finding a way to make a point. *The Washington Post,* p. A3.

Miller-Jones, D. (1989). Culture and testing. *American Psychologist, 44,* 360–366.

Moses, S. (1990, November). Assessors seek test that teaches. *APA Monitor,* pp. 1, 37.

Mourant, A. E. (1983). *Blood relations: Blood groups and anthropology.* New York: Oxford University Press.

Naroll, R. (1970). The culture-bearing unit in cross-cultural surveys. In R. Naroll & R. Cohen (Eds.), *A handbook of method in cultural anthropology* (pp. 721–765). New York: Natural History Press.

Nobles, W. (1991). African philosophy: Traditions of Black psychology. In R. Jones (Ed.), *Black psychology* (pp. 47–63.) Berkeley, CA: Cobb & Henry.

Pedersen, P. (1977). Asian theories of personality. In R. Corsini (Ed.), *Contemporary theories of personality* (pp. 367–397). Itasca, IL: Peacock.

Prilleltensky, I. (1989). Psychology and the status quo. *American Psychologist, 44,* 795–802.

Reilly, R. R., & Chao, G. R. (1982). Validity and fairness of some alternative employee selection procedures. *Personnel Psychology, 35,* 1–62.

Rogoff, B., & Morelli, G. (1989). Perspectives on children's development from cultural psychology. *American Psychologist, 44,* 343–348.

Ruiz, D. S. (1990). Social and economic profile of Black Americans, 1989. In D. S. Ruiz (Ed.), *Handbook of mental health and mental disorder among Black Americans* (pp. 1–52). New York: Greenwood Press.

Russo, N. F., Olmedo, E. L., Stapp, J., & Fulcher, R. (1981). Women and minorities in psychology. *American Psychologist, 36,* 1315–1365.

Samuda, R. J. (1975). *Psychological testing of American minorities.* New York: Harper & Row.

Sandoval, J. (1989). The WISC-R and internal evidence of test bias with minority groups. *Journal of Counseling and Clinical Psychology, 47,* 919–927.

Sattler, J. M. (1970). Racial "experimenter effects" in experimentation, testing, interviewing, and psychotherapy. *Psychological Bulletin, 73,* 137–160.

Scarr, S. (1981). *Race, social class, and individual differences in I.Q.* Hillsdale, NJ: Erlbaum.

Scarr, S. (1988). Race and gender as psychological variables. *American Psychologist, 43*, 56–59.

Scarr, S. (1989). Constructivism and socially sensitive research. *American Psychologist, 44*, 849.

Scarr, S., Pakstis, A. J., Katz, S. H., & Barker, W. B. (1977). Absence of a relationship between degree of White ancestry and intellectual skills with a Black population. *Human Genetics, 39*, 69–86.

Scarr, S., & Weinberg, R. A. (1976). IQ test performance of Black children adopted by White families. *American Psychologist, 31*, 726–739.

Schiele, J. H. (1991). An epistemological perspective on intelligence assessment among African-American children. *Journal of Black Psychology, 17*(2), 23–36.

Scott, R. R., & Shaw, M. E. (1985). Black and White performance in graduate school and policy implications of the use of Graduate Record Examination scores in admissions. *Journal of Negro Education, 54*(1), 14–23.

Shade, B. J. (1983). Cognitive strategies as determinants of school achievement. *Psychology in the Schools, 20*, 488–493.

Spearman, C. (1927). *The abilities of man.* New York: Macmillan.

Stewart, E. C. (1971). *American cultural patterns: A cross-cultural perspective.* Pittsburgh, PA: Regional Council for International Understanding.

Sue, D. W., & Sue, D. (1990). *Counseling the culturally different.* New York: Wiley.

Sue, S., & Okazi, S. (1990). Asian-American educational achievements: A phenomenon in search of an explanation. *American Psychologist, 45*, 913–920.

Temp, G. C. (1971). Validity of the SAT for Blacks and Whites in thirteen integrated institutions. *Journal of Educational Measurement, 8*, 245–251.

Tharp, R. G. (1989). Psychocultural variables and constants, effects on teaching and learning schools. *American Psychologist, 44*, 349–359.

Thompson, C. E. F. (1989). *Towards a person-environment model of retention: The relationship of field independence-dependence to Black student retention at a predominantly White university.* Unpublished doctoral dissertation, University of Maryland, College Park.

Thompson, C. E. F., & Fretz, B. R. (1991). Predicting the adjustment of Black students at predominantly White institutions. *Journal of Higher Education, 62*, 437–450.

Tracey, T., & Sedlacek, W. E. (1984). Noncognitive variables in predicting academic success by race. *Measurement and Evaluation in Guidance, 16*, 171–178.

Tracey, T., & Sedlacek, W. E. (1985). The relationship of non-cognitive variables to academic success: A longitudinal comparison by race. *Journal of College Student Personnel, 26*, 405–410.

Tracey, T., & Sedlacek, W. E. (1987). Prediction of college graduation using noncognitive variables by race. *Measurement and Evaluation in Counseling and Development, 19*, 177–184.

Vygotsky, L. S. (1978). *Mind in society.* Cambridge, MA: Harvard University Press.

Walsh, W. B., & Betz, N. E. (1985). *Tests and assessment.* Englewood Cliffs, NJ: Prentice-Hall.

Weaver, K. F., & Brill, D. L. (1985). The search for our ancestors. *National Geographic, 168*, 560–623.

Webster, D. W., Sedlacek, W. E., & Miyares, J. (1979). A comparison of problems perceived by minority and White university students. *Journal of College Student Personnel, 20*, 165–170.

Wechsler, D. (1949). *Wechsler Intelligence Scale for Children.* New York: Psychological Corporation.

Weinberg, R. A. (1989). Intelligence and IQ: Landmark issues and great debates. *American Psychologist, 44,* 98–104.

Welsh, P. (1990, September 16). Fast-track trap: How 'ability grouping' hurts our schools, kids and families. *The Washington Post,* pp. B1, B4.

Williams, C. (1987). *The destruction of Black civilization.* Chicago: Third World Press.

Williams, R. (1975). The BITCH-100: A culture-specific test. *Journal of Afro-American Issues, 3,* 103–106.

Willis, M. G. (1989). Learning styles of African-American children: A review of the literature and interventions. *Journal of Black Psychology, 16*(1), 47–61.

Zuckerman, M. (1990). Some dubious premises in research and theory on racial differences. *American Psychologist, 45,* 1297–1303.

31. Rediscovery of the Subject: Intercultural Approaches to Clinical Assessment

Enrico E. Jones and Avril Thorne

In recent years, the many problems attendant to the psychological assessment of cultural and ethnic minority groups have been widely acknowledged (Butcher, 1982; E. E. Jones & Korchin, 1982). For a number of decades, psychology and the social sciences in general have labored within the confines of the assumption that ethnic minorities are frequently deficient in important ways. The 'deficit hypothesis' (Katz, 1974), briefly stated, posits that minority communities have historically experienced isolation and continued economic and cultural deprivation and that impoverishment, powerlessness, and disorganization find expression in psychological deficits in such realms as intellectual performance (Guthrie, 1976; Kamin, 1974), personality functioning (Proshansky & Newton, 1974), and mental health (Baughman & Dahlstrom, 1972; Kardiner & Ovesey, 1951). Deficit conceptions of the psychological and social functioning of cultural minorities arose in part from a "psychology of race differences" tradition. Studies in this tradition typically compared minority and majority groups on measures standardized on White samples. Cultural, linguistic, and social-status differences were typically minimized or overlooked, and in these and other ways the psychological import of obtained differences was obscured.

By now, of course, serious questions have been raised concerning the methodological adequacy of ethnic and multicultural research in the United States (Cole & Bruner, 1971; Gynther, 1972). An important step forward occurred when traditional research strategies

Reprinted by permission of the authors and the American Psychological Association from *Journal of Consulting and Clinical Psychology* 55 (1987): 488–95. Copyright © 1987 by the American Psychological Association.

and assessment techniques began to be seriously applied cross-culturally. The obvious linguistic and cultural differences between researchers their assessment methods, and indigenous target populations evoked an appreciation for context and for local meanings that had been missing from efforts at studying minority groups within our society. There has been a growing awareness that ethnic minorities, although physically proximate to the majority culture, cannot be readily or effectively compared with dominant culture group members on conventional assessment measures. Increasingly, inquiry into the psychological functioning of minority group members has been recast in a cross-cultural paradigm that is sensitive to the cultural loading in our measures and to problems in the interpretation of information derived from such assessment methods.

A pivotal issue for intercultural assessment is construct definition (Irvine & Carroll, 1980), that is, what it is that our procedures and measures actually allow us to know and understand. A case in point is the study of personality in Black populations, an important focus of which has been the construct *self-concept.* Inquiry about Black self-concept has centered on the notion of White preference, the hypothesis being that especially Black children reject themselves and express self-identification and evaluative preference for physical characteristics (represented by dolls, puppets, drawings, or photographs) that are not Black. This research was initially undertaken to substantiate the deleterious effect of school segregation among Black children (Clark & Clark, 1950), but it has subsequently been impugned by minority social scientists as a damaging example of the deficit hypothesis. The construct validity of the White-preference paradigm and the assumptions underlying it were subjected to an important critique by Banks (1982), who argued that preference for dominant culture artifacts among some Black children has not been convincingly linked to a tendency toward self-rejection and low self-esteem. This view has recently been supported by McAdoo's (1985) work demonstrating that measures of racial attitude are unrelated to Black children's self-concept and that, among many Black youth, an outgroup orientation is directly related not to self-hatred but to positive self-concept. It is quite possible that in a multicultural society such as ours, a too exclusive own-group preference among minorities may reflect a defensive use of ethnic identity (DeVos, 1982).

Another instructive example is the construct, Internal-External Locus of Control, (I-E scale; Rotter, 1966), which measures the extent to which people report they exercise control over their lives and destinies. The I-E scale has become a frequently used measure in studies of minority populations and of gender differences as well as in cross-cultural investigation. The scale is popular in this kind of research because the control construct intersects social, clinical, and political realms with its relevance to such experiences as social alienation, feelings of powerlessness, lack of personal control, and desire for self-determination. Cross-cultural studies have found differences among samples from a variety of nations and cultures. The most consistent findings have shown a higher degree of externality among women than among men and among people from developing nations than those from industrialized societies (McGinnies, Nordholm, Ward, & Bhanthumnavin, 1974; Nagelschmidt & Jakob, 1977). However, important inconsistencies have also emerged. Several studies of United States Blacks, for example, found that young, non-college-educated, lower-class samples tended to score more externally than White samples (Battle & Rotter, 1963; Lefcourt, 1965). The meaning of this difference was called into question by Gurin, Gurin, Lao, and Beattie's (1969) study of Black college students. Contrary to what might be predicted on the basis of Rotter's theory, it was discovered that Blacks who were willing to participate in social protest action obtained low scores on internal control, suggesting that external scorers believed they could influence their destinies.

Factor analytic studies, considered an important means for establishing a measure's validity, have also raised serious questions about the meaning of the I-E scale in different populations. Studies of I-E scale item responses among Brazilians, Jamaicans, United States Blacks, and women (E. E. Jones & Zoppel, 1979; Nagelschmidt & Jakob, 1977; Sanger & Alker, 1972) have not supported Rotter's (1975) claim that the scale is unidimensional; instead they have suggested that attitude structures in these groups vary and that the comparison of summary I-E scale scores across samples is consequently inappropriate. This tendency for the factor structure of the I-E scale to differ as a function of the population under study leaves few researchers at ease when confronted with the problem of understanding the meaning and implications of differences across population groups. The use of the locus of control construct cross-culturally or with minority groups may constitute an *imposed etic* (Berry, 1969), a culture-specific schema erroneously presumed to be universal in nature.

NEW NORMS FOR MINORITY GROUPS?

The pitfalls in intercultural assessment are also illustrated in the evaluation of psychological dysfunction, especially as measured through inventory-type indices. Minority status or ethnicity as an important source of variance on such assessment instruments has been well-documented, especially in relation to the Minnesota Multiphasic Personality Inventory (MMPI; E. E. Jones, 1978). Subgroup differences on the MMPI were, until relatively recently, construed as demonstrating lower levels of personal adjustments among Blacks, or Chicanos, or Native Americans (e.g., Baughman & Dahlstrom, 1972). Gynther's (1972) comprehensive review and reinterpretation of such data suggest a number of alternate explanations to the old deficit hypothesis, primary among them being the impact of cultural differences on values, perceptions, and expectations. Although Blacks and other United States minorities, for example, tend to score quite a bit higher on the MMPI Schizophrenia (Sc) scale, recent cross-cultural work has demonstrated that subjects from countries ranging from Israel to Japan have similarly elevated Sc scale scores (Butcher & Pancheri, 1976).

Fairly extensive cross-national and cross-cultural work has been conducted with the MMPI. Butcher and Pancheri (1976) argued for the cross-language generality and comparability of the MMPI factor structure. It appears that conventional inventory-type measures can be adapted to different cultural groups if careful work is carried out to determine such matters as equivalence of factor structures and intercultural generality of test constructs, and if renorming and validation studies are conducted. There is also some evidence that the diagnostic classification system, from which the MMPI scales are derived, is applicable cross-culturally (Dohrenwend & Dohrenwend, 1974), although this remains a controversial topic. Because new norms are being developed for the MMPI in several nations, the call for renorming the instrument for United States ethnic groups (e.g., Gynther, 1972) appears to be a natural application of an increasingly accepted cross-cultural framework for psychological inquiry.

Still, the problems in adapting such measures for minority groups are far from being thoroughly worked out, and it is difficult to imagine that they ever entirely will be. One persistent problem is the percentage of items endorsed differently by ethnic and dominant culture groups. Studies have consistently shown that the endorsement rate for MMPI items among, for example, Black and White subjects is different for a very high percentage (40%–80%) of items and that the content of these items suggests that they are culturally sensitive (E. E. Jones, 1978). Indeed, there is evidence that the well-known MMPI scale score differences between Blacks and Whites would be even greater if it were not for a cancelling-out process within scales. The effect of item-endorsement differences of such magnitude remains a serious problem for the validity of traditional clinical interpretations.

It may be more difficult to adapt conventional standardized measures to United States ethnic minority populations than to foreign populations contained within national boundaries because minority groups can be extraordinarily heterogeneous, and they reside within an ever-changing sociocultural context. Renorming the MMPI for Blacks would require, at the very least, an adequate sampling of regional differences (e.g., north vs. south, urban vs. rural). But would the new norms be valid for distinct subgroups, such as Jamaican and Haitian immigrants? The problem is an even larger one for Hispanics, who include sizable populations of Puerto Ricans and Cubans as well as Mexican Americans and Central Americans. Although some Hispanics are recent arrivals, many have resided in the United Stated for generations, and there are important differences in language use, culture, and ethnic identity among the various groups (Muñoz, 1982). Should such variation be recognized, we would be confronted with an array of new norms for many different population subgroups and with a growing proliferation of a psychotechnology that places us at an ever-increasing distance from the subject of our inquiry.[1]

It is true that the construction of new norms acknowledges the pluralistic nature of our society. However, it also reflects a kind of static view of society and rests on the assumption that ethnic communities maintain their culture in a stable, enduring fashion. It fails to consider important processes of acculturation or, as some prefer, cultural interpenetration; nor does it reflect the dynamic, changing nature of our social world in whose continuing evolution minority groups play an important role. Individuals are considered only as members of a category, and the extent to which they share the values and perceptions of their particular ethnic group is obscured. Such a strategy must ultimately run afoul of an important egalitarian ethos in American society that views formal recognition of questionable distinctions among individuals with distaste.

CULTURE-SPECIFIC MEASURES: REMEDY OR IDEOLOGICAL REACTION?

Another proposal for remedying the problems of assessment of cultural minorities goes beyond establishing different norms and instead advocates the construction of entirely new, culture-specific measures. This solution foregoes intercultural assessments entirely and, indeed, challenges the soundness of applying any assessment procedure in culture comparisons. A recent volume (R. L. Jones, in press), for example, provided tests and measures expressly developed for Black populations. Instruments included personality assessment questionnaires, self-esteem scales, and ethnic identity measures. The rationale behind the construction of these new, culture-specific instruments is that they more accurately reflect minority experiences, values, and personality characteristics than do conventional measures. Such instruments are still in nascent form and, admittedly, require a great deal more work to establish their validity and utility.

There is a question, though, whether these culture-specific instruments are truly useful remedies to the problem of etic instruments or whether they are primarily products of an ideology. There has been a tendency among minority social scientists to emphasize the differences, cultural and otherwise, between the majority group and ethnic minorities. Their motives have been influenced, at least in part, by social movements of recent decades that have had as important themes ethnic identity and pride and a renewed interest in cultural and historical roots. Minority researchers have often been at the forefront in recognizing the importance of cultural diversity for psychological inquiry and of challenging the inequity associated with the deficit hypothesis. A parallel development has occurred among some feminist scholars, who emphasize differences between the male-dominated culture and women's culture.

Such thinking, motivated by concern for social justice and human equality, has contributed to an appreciation of the cultural pluralism of our society and has defined the ways in which psychological theories and procedures can contribute to the maintenance of an inequitable status quo. The question remains, however, whether ethnic-specific measures enlarge our understanding of personality functioning and psychopathology. Communities of scholars will find it difficult to develop comprehensive understandings if assessment procedures are highly specialized and are not comparable across samples and if they obstruct communication and inquiry across cultural boundaries.

In some ways, these culture-specific methods seem to repeat the problems of the conventional measures they will presumably supplant. To date, such measures have considered a given ethnic group as homogeneous, without consideration of geographic, religious, generational or social-status differences. There are undeniably common qualities in the experience of ethnicity: certain mutually shared experiences that are the result of more-or-less shared culture and like conditions. However, there are also important differences within ethnicity, and for that matter, within gender. Such differences have perhaps more often been recognized by feminist scholars than by minority researchers. Feminist scholars, for example, have called for a more refined understanding of women of color and women of working class background, whose experiences are not well-represented in prevailing psychological theories (Eisenstein, 1983). What all members of a minority group share and what is likely to be different (and in what degree) remains largely unspecified; within-group variability is enormous.

There has been a longstanding debate about whether ethnic groups in the United States have separate and distinct cultures. The case for Spanish-speaking and Asian Americans is, at least for the more recently arrived, readily made, although the argument for distinct cultural elements among Black Americans has also been advanced (DuBois, 1980; Herskovitz, 1958; Price-Williams, 1975). The question of whether or not minorities have distinct cultures can in part be addressed through the notion of *subjective culture* (Osgood, 1965; Triandis, 1972). Subjective culture is a group's characteristic way of perceiving its social environment. People who live near one another speak the same dialect, and engage in similar activities are likely to share the same subjective culture. Particularly relevant to the discussion here is that the assumption of heterogeneity (what is similar and what is different) is essential even to the concept of subjective culture.

An instructive example of inattention to in-group variability by those who are keen on culture-specific instruments is the disregard of education or socioeconomic status as an important mediator of cultural experience. Any analysis of ethnic culture must, in fact, address socioeconomics because it is not always clear whether the characteristics presumed to be distinctive are attributable to cultural differences or to social status and educational level. Although some ethnic characteristics may persist as minority group members advance educationally and economically, others may not. It is likely that standard assessment instruments are more valid for minorities who have achieved middle-class status than for those who are working class or poor (E. E. Jones & Zoppel, 1979), and one wonders whether those researchers who advocate culture-specific instruments are actually referring to the latter subgroup, significant as it may be within the minority population. Education is closely associated with acculturation processes, and the concern in many minority communities that school curricula include ethnic history or related topics can be understood in this light. It is clear that some of the same problems attending the creation of new norms for ethnic groups on conventional measures — group heterogeneity and acculturation — also apply to the construction of culture-specific assessment procedures.

We must seriously question whether culture-specific methods really provide an answer to the problems of psychological inquiry with ethnic minority populations in a society as diverse as our own, where cultures transform one another and where minority individuals often aspire strongly to educational and economic advancement and not infrequently reside long distances from their communities of origin. With the exclusionary note they strike, such methods reflect in part an attempt to assert the existence of ethnic culture, which is sometimes perceived as in danger of being devitalized, and reflect in part an expression of a need among minority group individuals to maintain a distinctive identity.

PRIMACY OF THE SUBJECTIVE IN CLINICAL ASSESSMENT

The problems of intercultural and multiethnic assessment and research readily direct attention to a larger problem concerning the nature of psychological and social inquiry itself. Traditional positivist and empiricist methods of inquiry have been targets of a growing crescendo of criticism, with chords struck by interpretive or hermeneutic approaches (Packer, 1985; Rabinow & Sullivan, 1979), feminist commentary on science (Keller, 1985; Vickers, 1982), and social constructionist perspectives (Gergen, 1985b). Although these critical analyses differ in interesting ways among themselves, they have joined with longstanding phenomenological critiques of research methods in psychology (Giorgi, 1976; Valle & King, 1978).

These various perspectives challenge the often-held view that scientific theory and empirical method serve to reflect or map reality in a direct and transparent manner. The interpretive critique, for example, posits that the web of meaning that constitutes human existence cannot be meaningfully or accurately reduced to narrow categories such as "behaviors" or "act" or, for that matter, personality test scores. This approach recognizes that issues of understanding and interpretation arise in the very construction of categories and in the identification of data (Packer, 1985). Not incidentally, those who attempt to apply psychological methods interculturally have long grappled with these very concerns.

Traditional assessment relies on documenting the co-occurrences of observables. In contrast, the interpretive approach attempts to elucidate and make explicit understandings of observed actions. The approach uses a detailed, progressive description of episodes of social interchange and gradually articulates more of their organization. Accounts are given by both the subject and the observer of events and actions, principally in a narrative, natural language form. Especially relevant to intercultural assessment, interpretations are rendered in the context of the historical and cultural situation under study. The co-occurrences that are often presumed to be universal in traditional research are viewed as being more temporary, situated in the vicissitudes of particular social processes. Constructionism's affinity with hermeneutic approaches is clear in its concern with elaborating human system meanings. Of particular importance for the present discussion is the considerable ethnomethodological work that has been carried out from this perspective, especially the emphasis on methods used by persons in various cultures to render the world sensible (Geertz, 1979).

Many contemporary social scientists have not found the empiricist orientation a congenial perspective because it advocates manipulation of, and removal from, the persons one wishes to understand. Indeed, both minority (E. E. Jones & Korchin, 1982) and feminist (e.g., Wittig, 1985) investigators have struggled with the tension between scholarly inquiry and advocacy and with the tension between scientific and humanistic values in the choice of methods and procedures. Feminists have searched for alternative methods of inquiry and have occasionally noted the extent to which other perspectives share their concern for more contextualized and intersubjectively valid processes of interpretation (Vickers, 1982). Minority scholars, on their part, have largely overlooked the interpretive, constructionist alternative and have instead either confined themselves to all-out attacks on conventional methods (c.f. Banks's, 1982, "deconstructive falsification") or have attempted to develop ever more careful, and questionable, culture-specific refinements and adaptations of existing empirical methods (see R. L. Jones, in press). This is an unfortunate oversight because constructionism invites the view that prevailing categories of understanding are historically and culturally situated and are therefore subject to critique and transformation. In contrast with the claimed moral neutrality of the empiricist tradition, constructionism is sensitive to moral criteria for scientific practice. Gergen (1985b), for example, argued that the extent to which psychological theory and practice enter into the life of a culture to sustain certain patterns of conduct and alter others, it must be evaluated in terms of its social benefits: "The practitioner can no longer justify a socially reprehensible conclusion on the ground of being a victim of facts; the pragmatic implications of such a conclusion within society must be confronted" (p. 273). It is this kind of ethically accountable vision of psychological research and practice that many in our field have sought.

The phenomenological tradition within psychology shares with the relatively more recent interpretive, feminist, and constructionist perspectives a critique of experimentation and of its deemphasis of the subject's experience (Colaizzi, 1978). The focus of the phenomenological perspective is the subject's apprehension and understanding of his or her own world. Phenomena and situations are defined principally by the subject rather than by the investigator. The emphasis is on describing a phenomenon rather than imposing what we presume to know about it; in the language of cross-cultural psychology, this is akin to emic exploration. The investigator not only obtains information about the subject's understanding of the objective situation but also, and more important, obtains a shared experience to which the subjects of the study have contributed as communication partners (Giorgi, 1976).

Few would argue with the proposition that clinical assessment must in some way be oriented toward understanding the understandings of individuals: how they construe their experiences, their predicaments, their lives. All theoretical frameworks concede that one cannot adequately comprehend psychological disturbances through exclusive reliance on procedures that remain outside the disturbance as it is lived and experienced. Psychological problems cannot be studied, let alone treated, without a fundamental respect for the person and without a constant effort to grasp the experience of the person. This is true even for medically oriented approaches, despite their emphasis on diagnostic signs and symptomatology. Behavioral approaches, especially the newer cognitive-behavioral treatments, have increasingly emphasized the importance of the inner thought processes of the subject. Psychodynamically oriented practitioners have traditionally understood the importance of personal interviews to provide background data that will contextualize and personalize the results of other, often more structured, tests and procedures. Although clinical assessment must somehow be grounded in experience and introspection, subjective experience is often deemphasized in contemporary procedures. And although neglect of personal meanings is pervasive in much standardized assessment, the problem is even more critical in intercultural assessment. Especially here there is a need to move beyond form, for example, diagnostic category or scale score, and to reemphasize underlying meaning.

SUBJECT AS COLLABORATOR: NARRATIVE ACCOUNTS

Interpretive, constructionist, and experiential methods all favor obtaining some form of introspective, narrative account from the subject. In particular, they emphasize the elaboration of meaning through joint inquiry with the subject. The inquiry is open-ended and reflective and has the quality of critical dialogue (Von Eckartsberg, 1971). An example is Levinson's (1978) biographical interviewing methods, which aimed to reconstruct an individual's life story. The biographical interview combined aspects of the research interview, the clinical interview, and a conversation between acquaintances. As a research interview, certain topics had to be covered; however, the interviewer was also sensitive to the feelings expressed by the subject and followed themes through diverse topics. As a conversation between acquaintances, the relationship was egalitarian, and the interviewer could respond with his or her personal experiences. The result was not "simply an interviewing technique or procedure, but a relationship of some intimacy, intensity, and duration; significant work [was] involved in forming and maintaining and terminating the relationship" (Levinson, 1978, p. 15). Oakley's (1981) discussion of her interviews with pregnant women provided another example. Whereas traditional textbook formulas for interviewing define the interview situation as a one-way process in which the interviewer asks questions and the respondent provides answers, Oakley revealed the poverty of this framework through a study of the questions that respondents asked back. These questions signified a good deal about important concerns of the respondents, including their unanticipated need for medical information and psychological support. This kind of assessment approach construes the investigative encounter as an unfolding relationship, in process rather than static. Its effectiveness relies in large part on the capacity of the examiner to ask discerning questions, to interpret responses skillfully, and to perspicaciously decide which responses should be further pursued. Its success also depends in part on the capacity of the subject, with the help of the interviewer, to begin to elaborate or articulate what is meant by a particular response.

The more psychometrically oriented investigator or clinician might ponder how such concepts as test validity and reliability, which have long anchored traditional assessment techniques, are to be considered within approaches that view the subject as collaborator. Validity (in the sense of how we know we are identifying and assessing that which we wish) and reliability (the extent of unsystematic variation of a subject's responses or scores from one assessment occasion to another) have, at least in their technical meaning, a more direct reference to empirical models. These models are formal, quantitatively oriented systems of description and explanation that use categorization and operations by which categories are established and related to one another (as with personality inventories). They make use of procedures to assure a verifiable reference and are regulated by requirements of consistency (e.g., test reliability) and non-contradiction. As we have already discussed briefly (see Bruner, 1986, for a more complete statement of this important topic), constructivism, and related work in theories of meaning, has shifted the focus in our scientific dialogue away from the products of scientific inquiry toward the processes of inquiry themselves. Social science, especially, has begun to move away from the traditional positivist stance toward a more interpretive stance in which meaning becomes the central focus (e.g., how speech is interpreted and by what codes meaning is regulated; Bruner, 1986). The emphasis in narrative accounts, then, is not on procedures for establishing formal and empirical proof but on verisimilitude (or face validity). The narrative method attempts to achieve believable accounts that involve action, intention, and goals. Language is viewed as an expression of culture, and narratives are conceptualized as constituting a psychological and cultural reality that is alive. We should not lose sight of the fact that it is precisely a deep disquiet about the validity (in the broad sense) of conventional assessment methods cross-culturally that has led to efforts at developing alternative procedures.

ACCOUNTS METHOD: INTERCULTURAL APPLICATIONS

One approach in which the subject-as-collaborator has a central role has been termed the *accounts method* (Harré & Secord, 1972). This method is in some ways a hybrid of the critical-incidents technique in industrial psychology, the Thematic Apperception Test in personality-clinical psychology, and ethnographic methods in sociology (Thorne, 1985). Although information from the accounts can be subsequently systematized in various ways (e.g., Cacioppo & Petty, 1981), the accounts themselves are free-flowing or semistructured through the use of probes. The collection of subjects' narrative accounts holds real promise for intercultural assessment and research. A study by Ball (1983) provided a useful example of an application of the accounts method in the assessment of psychological functioning and community needs in an ethnic minority group. The work was done with a Samoan population in San Francisco and focused on failures in psychosocial adaptation that resulted in emotional disorder. Narrative accounts were first obtained from Samoan subjects about their process of adaptation to the new culture; these accounts were collected both from those who had made successful adaptation and from those who had not. A small group of Samoans then studied the accounts and identified key factors affecting level of well-being, major problem categories, and human service needs. The data in this reduced form were then presented to a larger group at a community forum for open discussion that aimed at verifying the data. The accounts method, as applied in this study, helped to narrow the gap between the minority group members being assessed and the scientist-practitioner and helped to resolve problems of bias and accountability in the interpretation and use of assessment data.

Regardless of the strategy of application, the elicitation of subjects' accounts cannot help but enhance ecological validity. Peterson (1979), for example, commented that he has yet to show anyone a set of accounts and not hear some remark about the sense of authenticity they convey. Because accounts are in narrative form, subjects render their experience in their own language; they are not asked to express their experience in the language of the investigator or to adapt it to a preexisting format. This kind of ecological validity is particularly important for intercultural assessment, where the extent to which a meaning code is shared or a common language exists is always a central issue. The accounts method is sufficiently flexible to be useful in many aspects of intercultural assessment and inquiry. We will discuss several strategies for the application of participants' accounts in such endeavors (a) to construct measures, (b) to provide postassessment narratives to complement more structured measures, and (c) to verify previously obtained interpretations.

Using Target Groups to Help Construct Measures

One variant of the accounts method involves enlisting target group members to help construct questionnaires or other assessment instruments. The measures are developed inductively and are used for the purpose at hand. They are not culture specific in that they purport to be valid not for the whole minority population but only for the limited sample under investigation. What these measures may lack in the formal validation possible with large samples or in empirical criterion keying is made up for in ecological validity: They are not applied from an entirely different context and set of experiences, and they are not an imposed etic.

Triandis's (1976) method of constructing critical incidents representing social interactions between individuals of different ethnic groups illustrates this approach. The incidents and potential attributions about them were submitted for criticism by target group members and were refined until they were credible and culturally congruent. Related examples involved asking a group of subjects from a lower socioeconomic urban environment to translate assessment measures into Black ghetto English (E. E. Jones, 1979; Landis, McGrew, Day, Savage, & Saral, 1976). Another study (Triandis, Malpass, & Feldman, 1976) asked representatives of contrasting groups within an ethnic community to provide attributes that are commonly used in thinking about particular stereotypes and roles. These elicited attributes were subsequently used in scales on which target group members could make judgments. The latter method resembles the use of Kelly's Role Construct Repertory Test in cross-cultural studies (E. E. Jones & Zoppel, 1979), in which each respondent provides an idiographic description of the framework used to construe the personal social world. All of the strategies described here represent the constructive use of subjects as collaborators in developing appropriate and focused assessment measures. In addition, the methods recognize the reality that minority groups are not homogeneous by including subjects who represent contrasting groups.

Postassessment Narratives

Obtaining postassessment narratives is particularly useful when the usual, more-or-less etic instruments have been used. Narrative accounts help to reconceptualize the data by providing access to subjects' impressions about what they believed the instrument was attempting to assess, what the items or questions meant to them, and what meaning the test-taking situation held for them; in short, what motives, expectations, and understandings they brought to the assessment situation. This contextual information can play a decisive role in the researcher's interpretation of the meaning of subjects' responses, especially responses to pencil-and-paper measures, and can help ascertain the face validity of items, that is, whether the subjects' understandings of items corresponded with those intended by the investigator. For example, Cowan and Goldman (1974) informally interviewed subjects, including ethnic minority subjects, after they had completed the Internal-External Locus of Control Scale (I-E scale). In asking what the items meant to the subjects, what they thought the measure was trying to get at, and how they felt about completing the scale, the investigators found that subjects were responding as much to whether an item was phrased in absolute (I always, I never) or qualified (I sometimes, I rarely) terms as they were to an item's content. Gergen (1985a) similarly examined the range of meanings that could potentially underlie responses to the I-E scale. Subjects had little difficulty interpreting responses to certain items in terms of fear, shyness, narrow-mindedness, or other attributes that fall outside the theoretical frame of locus of control. For instance, agreement with the item "There is a direct connection between how hard I study and the grades I get" could be interpreted as an expression of shyness because "such a rationale excuses the shy person from too much socializing and allows him to secrete himself in his room" (Gergen, 1985a, p. 124). It is precisely this kind of variability in interpreting the meaning of particular test items that has concerned cross-cultural researchers. Studies such as these highlight the value of allowing subjects to account for the meaning of their responses in order to ensure that the understandings of the investigator or practitioner coincide with those of the subjects.

This strategy can actually be used in conjunction with any kind of investigative or experimental procedure. Sardello (1971), for example, recommended obtaining transcripts of the entire encounter with the subject. Not only is the transcript then used by the experimenter to discern the meaning of the experience for the subject, but the transcript is also reviewed collaboratively with the subject to determine if the explicated meaning of the phenomenon can also be seen by the subject. A form of the accounts method can be applied in more purely clinical assessment procedures as well. Hendricks et al. (1983) demonstrated that clinical diagnostic procedures, such as the Diagnostic Interview Schedule (DIS), yield different rates of disorders across ethnic groups. In particular, they reported a low rate of agreement for schizophrenia between the DIS and clinician judgments based on open-ended interviews. After conducting a more formal, structured interview (such as the DIS), it may be valuable to obtain more information through the use of open-ended probes of the patient's responses that are considered indicative of a particular disorder. Especially with those patients from different subcultures, such accounts may lead to new interpretations of their responses and hence to new diagnostic implications.

Verification of Interpretations

The accounts or narrative method can also be used to obtain verification of findings from other members of the target population. This application is essentially for the purpose of cross-validation. The procedure differs from the previously described strategy in that it is not the initial subjects from whom accounts are obtained but rather a second group with whom there is mutual identification. For example, in the previously cited study by Ball (1983), an open community forum discussed the interpretations rendered by one group of subjects to determine whether the initial conclusions adequately represented the concerns of the community at large. This strategy, in particular, requires a shift in attitude on the part of the evaluator or a partial relinquishing of the status of sole expert who brings findings together and draws final conclusions. A reliance on what the subject can tell us, even at the final stages of inquiry, decisively shifts the role of the subject from passive object to active collaborator in the investigative enterprise. By asking subjects to more fully participate at various stages of inquiry, assessment and research are grounded in, and accountable to, the experiences and understandings of those we are trying to understand. Assessment theory and procedures necessarily become more adequate because they are more intersubjectively valid.

CONCLUSION

Many problems of clinical assessment and research with cultural and ethnic minorities stem from the tendency of psychologists and others interested in social inquiry to presume that a priori hypotheses and standard measures adequately map the experience, reality, and meanings of a particular people. Proposed alternatives to conventional assessment procedures—renorming standard measures or constructing entirely new, culture-specific instruments—attempt to move closer to particular populations. Such approaches, however, do not focally address one of the most difficult and persistent problems in intercultural assessment: how to ensure that assessment techniques adequately reflect the experience of a cultural group and at the same time facilitate the cross-communication of findings to other groups. The collaborative and flexible nature of narrative accounts promotes ecologically valid interpretations and invites attempts to replicate and verify findings with other populations. The collection of accounts furthers an appreciation of the understandings subjects of cultural minority groups have about their behavior and their world. As a method, it encourages a suspension of skepticism about subjects' willingness to communicate their experience. A genuine interest in the individual is a precondition for the successful use of this collaborative method, as is the establishment of trust and rapport. By failing to include the subject's viewpoint in various aspects of assessment and psychological inquiry, we have often obscured the meaning of our findings and have promoted the attitude that cultural differences are boundaries to be crossed rather than relationships to be entered into.

NOTES

1. A project to restandardize the MMPI has been undertaken by the test publisher over the past 3 years. New norms that include representative samples of Blacks, Hispanics, and American Indians will appear in the near future.

REFERENCES

Ball, F. L. J. (1983). *Psychosocial issues in a West Coast Samoan community and the role of community mental health services.* Unpublished manuscript, University of California, Berkeley.

Banks, W. C. (1982). Deconstructive falsification: Foundations of a critical method in Black psychology. In E. E. Jones & S. J. Korchin (Eds.), *Minority mental health* (pp. 59–73). New York: Praeger.

Battle, E., & Rotter, J. (1963). Children's feelings of personal control as related to social class and ethnic group. *Journal of Personality, 31,* 482–491.

Baughman, E., & Dahlstrom, W. G. (1972). Racial differences on the MMPI. In S. Guterman (Ed.), *Black psyche: The modal personality pattern of Black Americans* (pp. 166–188). Berkeley, CA: Glendessary Press.

Berry, J. W. (1969). On cross-cultural comparability. *International Journal of Psychology, 4,* 119–128.

Bruner, J. (1986). *Actual minds, possible worlds.* Cambridge, MA: Harvard University Press.

Butcher, J. N. (1982). Cross-cultural research methods in clinical psychology. In P. C. Kendall & J. N. Butcher (Eds.), *Handbook of research methods in clinical psychology* (pp. 273–308). New York: Wiley.

Butcher, J. N., & Pancheri, P. (1976). *A handbook of cross-national MMPI research.* Minneapolis: University of Minnesota Press.

Cacioppo, J. T., & Petty, R. E. (1981). Social psychological procedures for cognitive response assessment: The thought-listing technique. In T. V. Merluzzi, C. R. Glass, & M. Genest (Eds.), *Cognitive assessment* (pp. 309–342). New York: Guilford Press.

Clark, K. B., & Clark, M. P. (1950). Emotional factors in racial identification and preference in Negro children. *Journal of Negro Education, 19,* 341–350.

Colaizzi, P. F. (1978). Psychological research as the phenomenologist views it. In R. S. Valle & M. King (Eds.), *Existential-phenomenological alternatives for psychology* (pp. 48–71). New York: Oxford University Press.

Cole, M., & Bruner, J. S. (1971). Cultural differences and inferences about psychological processes. *American Psychologist, 26,* 867–876.

Cowan, P. A., & Goldman, R. K. (1974). *A discovery of confounding in Rotter's measure of locus of control.* Unpublished manuscript, University of California, Berkeley.

DeVos, G. A. (1982). Adaptive strategies in U.S. minorities. In E. E. Jones & S. J. Korchin (Eds.), *Minority mental health* (pp. 74–117). New York: Praeger.

Dohrenwend, B. P., & Dohrenwend, B. S. (1974). Social and cultural influences on psychopathology. *Annual Review of Psychology, 25*, 417–453.

DuBois, W. E. B. (1908). *The Negro American family.* Atlanta, GA: Atlanta University Press.

Eisenstein, H. (1983). *Contemporary feminist thought.* Boston: Hall.

Geertz, C. (1979). From the native's point of view: On the nature of anthropological understanding. In P. Rabinow & W. M. Sullivan, (Eds.), *Interpretive social science: A reader* (pp. 225–241). Berkeley: University of California Press.

Gergen, K. J. (1985a). Social pragmatics and the origins of psychological discourse. In K. J. Gergen & K. E. Davis (Eds.), *The social construction of the person* (pp. 111–127). New York: Springer-Verlag.

Gergen, K. J. (1985b). The social constructionist movement in modern psychology. *American Psychologist, 40*, 266–275.

Giorgi, A. (1976). Phenomenology and the foundations of psychology. In W. J. Arnold (Ed.), *1975 Nebraska symposium on motivation* (pp. 281–348). Lincoln: University of Nebraska Press.

Gurin, P., Gurin, R., Lao, R., & Beattie, M. (1969). Internal-external control in the motivational dynamics of Negro youth. *Journal of Social Issues, 25*, 29–53.

Guthrie, R. (1976). *Even the rat was white.* New York: Harper & Row.

Gynther, M. (1972). White norms and black MMPIs: A prescription for discrimination? *Psychological Bulletin, 78*, 386–402.

Harré, R., & Secord, P. F. (1972). *The exploration of social behavior.* Oxford, England: Blackwell.

Hendricks, L. E. Bayton, J. A., Collins, J. L., Mathura, C. B., McMillan, S. R., & Montgomery, T. A. (1983). The NIMH diagnostic interview schedule: A test of its validity in a population of black adults. *Journal of the National Medical Association, 75*, 667–671.

Herskovitz, M. L. (1958). *The myth of the Negro past.* Boston: Beacon Press.

Irvine, S. H., & Carroll, W. K. (1980). Testing and assessment across cultures. In H. C. Triandis & J. W. Berry (Eds.), *Handbook of cross-cultural psychology: Methodology* (Vol. 2, pp. 181–244). Boston: Allyn & Bacon.

Jones, E. E. (1978). Black-white personality differences: Another look. *Journal of Personality Assessment, 42*, 244–252.

Jones, E. E. (1979). Personality characteristics of black youth: A cross-cultural investigation. *Journal of Youth and Adolescence, 8*, 149–159.

Jones, E. E., & Korchin, S. J. (1982). Minority mental health: Perspectives. In E. E. Jones & S. J. Korchin (Eds.), *Minority mental health* (pp. 3–36). New York: Praeger.

Jones, E. E., & Zoppel, C. L. (1979). Personality differences among blacks in Jamaica and the United States. *Journal of Cross-Cultural Psychology, 10*, 435–456.

Jones, R. L. (Ed.). (In press). *Handbook of tests and measurements for Black populations* (Vols. 1–2). Richmond, CA: Cobb & Henry.

Kamin, L. (1974). *The science and politics of IQ.* Potomac, MD: Erlbaum.

Kardiner, A., & Ovesey, L. (1951). *The mark of oppression.* Cleveland, OH: The World.

Katz, I. (1974). Alternatives to a personality-deficit interpretation of Negro underachievement. In P. Watson (Ed.), *Psychology and race* (pp. 377–391). Chicago: Aldine.

Keller, E. F. (1985). *Reflections on gender and science.* New Haven, CT: Yale University Press.

Landis, D., McGrew, P., Day, H., Savage, J., & Saral, T. (1976). Word meanings in black and white. In H. C. Triandis (Ed.), *Variations in black and white perceptions of the social environment* (pp. 45–80). Urbana: University of Illinois Press.

Lefcourt, H. (1965). Risk-taking in Negro and white adults. *Journal of Personality and Social Psychology, 2,* 765–770.

Levinson, D. J. (1978). *The seasons of a man's life.* New York: Knopf.

McAdoo, H. P. (1985). Racial attitude and self-concept of young black children over time. In H. P. McAdoo & J. L. McAdoo (Eds.), *Black children: Social, educational and parental environments* (pp. 213–242). Beverly Hills, CA: Sage.

McGinnies, E., Nordholm, L. A., Ward, C. D., & Bhanthumnavin, D. L. (1974). Sex and cultural differences in perceived locus of control among students in five countries. *Journal of Consulting and Clinical Psychology, 42,* 451–455.

Mūnoz, R. F. (1982). The Spanish-speaking consumer and the community mental health center. In E. E. Jones & S. J. Korchin (Eds.), *Minority mental health* (pp. 362–398). New York: Praeger.

Nagelschmidt, A., & Jakob, R. (1977). Dimensionality of Rotter's I-E Scale in a society in the process of modernization. *Journal of Cross-Cultural Psychology, 8,* 101–111.

Oakley, A. (1981). Interviewing women: A contradiction in terms. In H. Roberts (Ed.), *Doing feminist research* (pp. 30–61). London: Routledge & Kegan Paul.

Osgood, C. E. (1965). Cross-cultural comparability in attitude measurements via multilingual semantic differentials. In I. D. Steiner & M. Fishbein (Eds.), *Current studies in social psychology* (pp. 95–107). Chicago: Holt, Rinehart & Winston.

Packer, M. J. (1985). Hermeneutic inquiry in the study of human conduct. *American Psychologist, 40,* 1081–1093.

Peterson, D. R. (1979). Assessing interpersonal relationships in natural settings. *New Directions for Methodology of Behavioral Science, 2,* 33–54.

Price-Williams, D. R. (1975). *Explorations in cross-cultural psychology.* San Francisco: Chandler & Sharp.

Proshansky, H., & Newton, P. (1974). Colour: The nature and meaning of Negro self-identity. In P. Watson (Ed.), *Psychology and race* (pp. 176–212). Chicago: Aldine.

Rabinow, P., & Sullivan, W. M. (1979). The interpretive turn: Emergence of an approach. In P. Rabinow & W. M. Sullivan (Eds.), *Interpretive social science: A reader* (pp. 1–21). Berkeley, University of California Press.

Rotter, J. (1966). Generalized expectancies for internal versus external control of reinforcement. *Psychological Monographs, 80* (1, Whole No. 609).

Rotter, J. B. (1975). Some problems and misconceptions related to the construct of internal versus external control of reinforcement. *Journal of Consulting and Clinical Psychology, 43,* 56–67.

Sanger, S., & Alker, H. (1972). Dimensions of internal-external locus of control and the women's liberation movement. *Journal of Social Issues, 28,* 115–129.

Sardello, R. J. (1971). A reciprocal participation model of experimentation. In A. Giorgi, W. F. Fischer, & R. von Eckartsberg (Eds.), *Duquesne studies in phenomenological psychology* (Vol. 1, pp. 58–65). Pittsburgh, PA: Duquesne University Press.

Thorne, A. (1985, August). The use of interactants' accounts for interpersonalizing personality theory. In P. F. Secord (Chair), *Uses of interactants' accounts in interpersonal research.* Symposium conducted at the meeting of the American Psychological Association, Los Angeles.

Triandis, H. C. (1972). *The analysis of subjective culture.* New York: Wiley.

Triandis, H. C. (1976). The culture assimilator: An approach to cultural training. In H. C. Triandis (Ed.), *Variations in black and white perceptions of the social environment* (pp. 26–40). Urbana: University of Illinois Press.

Triandis, H. C., Malpass, R. S., & Feldman, J. (1976). Method and a sample of results. In H. C. Triandis (Ed.), *Variations in black and white perceptions of the social environment* (pp. 81–117). Urbana: University of Illinois Press.

Valle, R. S., & King, M. (Eds.). (1978). *Existential-phenomenological alternatives for psychology.* New York: Oxford University Press.

Vickers, J. M. (1982). Memoirs of an ontological exile: The methodological rebellions of feminist research. In G. Finn & A. Miles (Eds.), *Feminism in Canada* (pp. 27–46). Montreal, Quebec, Canada: Black Rose Books.

Von Eckartsberg, R. (1971). On experiential methodology. In A. Giorgi, W. F. Fischer, & R. von Eckartsberg (Eds.), *Duquesne studies in phenomenological psychology* (Vol. 1, pp. 66–79). Pittsburgh, PA: Duquesne University Press.

Wittig, M. A. (1985). Metatheoretical dilemmas in the psychology of gender. *American Psychologist, 40,* 800–811.

B. CULTURAL MEANINGS AND TREATMENT APPROACHES

Beneath all clinical theory and concepts of normalcy, psychopathology, and psychotherapy lie culturally determined assumptions about the nature of the self. Hope Landrine, in an essay rich with clinical detail and culture wisdom (chapter 32), demonstrates how Western notions of the self have led to the misunderstanding, misdiagnosis, and failed treatment of minority group members. The bounded, independent, active Western self (Landrine calls this the "referential self") acts as a free agent in the world and seeks primary control over nature, people, and situations to meet one's needs; the "indexical self" of sociocentric cultures (such as African, Asian, and Latino cultures and communities) is constituted by social interactions, contexts, and relationships, thus has no enduring cross-situational characteristics or aims. Landrine insists that clinicans must understand these contrasting self-systems in order to fathom cultural differences in meanings, "the metaphors [people] live by" (Lakoff and Johnson 1980), and what is taken for granted as "what everybody knows." Only then can we draw conclusions about what is culturally considered normal and what is not.

Given their low utilization and high drop-out rates, "there is ample evidence that ethnic minorities are not faring well in our mental health system [in the U.S.]," say Stanley Sue and Nolan Zane, prominent critics of American mental health services and therapists. Therapists tend to have insufficient knowledge of cultural differences or they apply what little cultural knowledge they have in inappropriate ways. Part of the problem, they say, is the missing link between knowledge of a client's culture group and the transformation of this knowledge into effective treatment practices and strategies. In chapter 33 Sue and Zane present a model for treatment with ethnic minorities that emphasizes credibility (the perception of the therapist as effective) and gift giving (the client's perception that something was received in the therapeutic encounter).

In response to the increasing multiculturalism in the United States, there have been a number of efforts to counteract the ethnocentrism of American psychology (Pedersen 1989; American Psychological Association 1991) and to develop ethnically sensitive models of clinical diagnosis and treatment. In chapter 34, Forrest Tyler, Deborah Ridley Sussewell, and Janice Williams-McCoy present an "ethnic validity model" as an alternative framework for psychotherapeutic work within and across ethnic groups. Recognizing that many American citizens are shaped in part by the cultural views and ethos of the dominant culture group and in part by what may be divergent or even conflicting worldviews and ways of knowing that arise out of their minority group membership, Tyler and his colleagues insist that, in psychotherapeutic relationships, personal understanding and rapport are not enough; "the racial/ethnic social context (of therapist and client) and its effects must be incorporated as an integral component" of therapeutic theory and transaction.

The family theorists and researchers of Hispanic youth — José Szapocznik and William Kurtines — provide a new contextualist model for understanding children, families, and culture in chapter 35. Building on Bronfenbrener's ecological theory (1979, 1986), they propose that a contextualist paradigm promotes the complex notion of "embeddedness of the individual within the context of the family within the context of culture." Before we can develop appropriate educational and treatment interventions for troubled minority youth, we must reexamine, they say, how multiple cultural forces and realities filter down through families and affect family process. Culture conflicts (or culture collisions in our terms) are added to generational conflicts and directly affect communication and alliance problems in bicultural families. The authors end with an explication of their bicultural effectiveness training (BET) approach which grew out of family systems theory and the authors' knowledge of the role of culture in family conflict.

REFERENCES

American Psychological Association. 1991. *Guidelines for providers of psychological services to ethnic, linguistic, and culturally diverse populations.* Washington, DC.

Bronfenbrenner, U. 1979. *The ecology of human development.* Cambridge: Harvard University Press.

————. 1986. The ecology of the family as a context for human development. *Developmental Psychology* 22: 723–42.

Lakoff, G., and M. Johnson. 1980. *Metaphors we live by*. Chicago: University of Chicago Press.

Pedersen, P. B. 1989. Developing multicultural ethical guidelines for psychology. *International Journal of Psychology* 24: 643–52.

32. Clinical Implications of Cultural Differences: The Referential versus the Indexical Self

Hope Landrine

As the percentage of ethnic minorities in the population increases, the need for clinicians to be increasingly sensitive to their many culturally constituted psychological and psychiatric differences becomes salient. The task of increasing cross-cultural understanding is made difficult by the fact that cultural differences are not primarily differences in behavior, but rather in the meanings attached and attributed to "the same" behaviors. Because culture is a set of shared (intersubjective), unconscious definitions and assumptions, it is a cognitive variable (Shore, 1991) that cannot be observed but is nonetheless powerful; culture is the unwritten social and psychiatric dictionary that we have each memorized and then repressed. Increasing cross-cultural understanding, then, becomes the two-part task of bringing our own dictionary to the level of full conscious awareness, and then memorizing the dictionaries of others, so that we can shift easily from one to another.

The definitions that fill the cultural dictionary of many White Americans (based upon the great Western-European cultural tradition) differ significantly from those of ethnic-cultural minorities. Among the entries for which significant cultural differences in meaning have been discovered by anthropologists and cross-cultural psychologists are time (Hall, 1983); control (Weisz, Rothbaum, & Blackburn, 1984); mind, body, health, and healing (Fabrega, 1974); and the self or person (Gaines, 1982; Shweder & Bourne, 1982; Shweder & Miller, 1985; Strauss, 1977, 1982). These meanings and

Reprinted with permission of the author and *Clinical Psychology Review* from *Clinical Psychology Review* 12 (1992):401–15. Elsevier Science Ltd, Pergamon Imprint, Oxford, England.

understandings, it must be emphasized, are fundamental, unconscious assumptions; they are taken for granted as "the way things are," as "what everybody knows," and so constitute a psychological, symbolic universe or canopy in and through which members of any culture exist. For example, those who participate in the Western-European cultural tradition assume that time "flows" from past to future; that the past is "behind" and "backward" while the future is "ahead" and "forward"; that time is marked by clocks and so "marches on" with or without them; and that time is a "valuable" natural resource that should be "saved" and "used wisely" rather than "wasted," that should be "managed" (therapists can teach "time management"), and that ought to be "stolen" for intimate purposes. These unconscious, Western cultural definitions and meanings are no "mere" metaphors, but are instead cultural "metaphors we live by" (Lakoff & Johnson, 1980). As such, these meanings form the basis of a plethora of clinical concepts regarding punctuality; delay of gratification; impulsivity (the failure to plan "ahead"); laziness; goal-directedness; reality-testing; orientation (to time and place), as well as countless clinical assumptions about termination and its vicissitudes; and about the type of influence the "past" can and should have on the "present." Such assumptions are alien to those who take it for granted—equally unwittingly—that time flows backward (things start in the present and then become past), that the future does not exist (because it's the present when one "arrives" there), and that time is constituted and marked not by a clock, but by their own behavior (see Hall, 1983). Such fundamental, unconscious assumptions, definitions, and meanings are the substance of the culture of ethnic-cultural minorities and American Whites alike, and ostensible behavioral differences are the mere shadows cast by these meanings.

Of the many definitions and meanings cultures take for granted, those regarding the self are the most basic, the "deepest," the furthest from awareness, and are thus rarely ever made explicit. Simultaneously, while assumptions about what a self is are furthest from our conscious awareness, they also are the most powerful and significant assumptions behind and beneath our behavior (Strauss, 1982, p. 112). This is because what we assume a self is by and large predicts our assumptions about how a self relates to others, takes control, develops, "ought" to behave, think and feel, and "goes wrong." Thus, culturally determined assumptions about the self are beneath all Western cultural, clinical concepts and understandings of normalcy, psychopathology, and psychotherapy. Lack of awareness of the Western cultural definition of the self, of the manner in which such cultural beliefs shape clinical psychology, as well as of the radically different way in which the self is understood by many ethnic-cultural minorities, can lead to misdiagnosis and failed treatment of minority groups.

THE REFERENTIAL SELF OF THE WESTERN-CULTURAL TRADITION

The basic, unconscious assumption of Western culture is that there is an unequivocal, irrevocable distinction between that which is the self on the one hand, and that which is nonself on the other. From this tacit assumption it follows that Western culture defines the failure to construct and maintain a distinction between self and nonself as psychopathology (i.e., failure to maintain ego boundaries, enmeshment, identity diffusion, delusion, or psychosis).

The separated, encapsulated self of Western culture is conceptualized as a god, in the sense that it is presumed to be the originator, creator, and controller of behavior. Thus, the belief that one's behavior is controlled by someone/something other than the self is defined as psychopathology—as externalization, projection, and delusion. This self is presumed to be prototypically human (to possess all of the attributes that constitute humanity or person-ness) and indeed, to define these. Thus, to experience this self as nonhuman, as an automaton, as more dead or machine than alive and human also is defined in Western culture as a symptom or type of psychopathology (e.g., as derealization, depersonalization, delusion, depression, or schizotaxia). Nonhumanness is defined, a priori, as all that is not self or does not possess a self of its own; conversely, whatever lacks a self of its own is unconsciously represented as not humanlike, and as thereby akin to an "it," an object. The nonself realm includes plants, the natural environment, emotions, time, work, and a variety of other phenomena. Each element of the nonself realm is assumed to differ fundamentally from the self and to exist independently of the self. The nonself realm is assumed to function on its own, by virtue of its own principles and processes, and largely independent of the self. Thus, to believe that events within the separated, encapsulated self (e.g., wishes or feelings) created changes in the nonself realm (e.g., cause others to die, cause storms, drought, accidents, or plagues) is also defined in Western culture as a symptom of psychopathology—viz., as "magical" or "superstitious" ideation, thought disorder, or delusion.

As an object or objectlike, the nonself realm is unconsciously represented as that which must be mastered, controlled, managed, conquered, and "dealt with" by the self, to the self's advantage. People from Western culture speak of "using," "saving," "wasting," "spending," and "managing" their time; of "controlling," "regulating," and "dealing with" their emotions; of "exploiting" situations, "dealing with" interpersonal issues, "mastering" people, and "managing" others, emotions, and patients. Such colloquialisms speak to the unconscious representation of the nonself as a lifeless yet threatening object. Thus, the failure to construe the nonself as lifeless and threatening—the tendency instead to imbue the physical world with thoughts, feelings, and goals—is construed as thought disorder, delusion, or magical thinking. Likewise, the failure to endeavor to master and manage the nonself realm (e.g., to master situations, manage one's time, or control one's emotions) is defined as psychopathology, viz., as learned helplessness, passivity, or as deficits in social skills, self-control, and self-efficacy.

The self is presumed to be an entity; a bounded, unique, singular, encapsulated, noncorporeal, ghostlike, and godly entity somewhere within the body. The self is seen as contiguous with but not synonymous with the body. The self is the mind side of a mind/body dualism in which the body is an object or entity belonging more to the realm of nonself than self. Because the self is unconsciously construed to be a singular and integrated entity, experiencing the self as fragmented, as not bounded, or as multiple is defined as a symptom or a type of psychopathology in Western culture (e.g., as multiple personality disorder, or psychotic delusion). *The self is presumed to be a cognitive and emotional universe, the center of awareness, emotion, judgment, and action.* The self is said to think, feel, observe, and possess all sorts of cognitive processes. Thus, psychopathology is also defined in Western culture as experiencing one's thoughts and feelings as emanating from somewhere other than the self, and as experiencing these as controlled by someone/something other than the self; such beliefs are said to be thought disorder, delusion, or obsession-compulsion.

The self is represented as existing free of any and all contexts: The self is here; the context is there. Given that the self is seen as an emotional and cognitive universe above, beyond, and without a context, the self is believed to possess attributes of its own, in isolation from other selves, over time, and across situations. Thus, this *referential self,* as Crapanzano (1981) and Gaines (1982) call it, has cross-situational and longitudinal traits: It has abilities, preferences, needs, desires, and a "style" of its own that describe it, refer to it (hence, referential), and differentiate it from other selves. The referential self can be described without reference to others or to a context: The self can be reflected upon; it can be thought about, analyzed, and discussed in isolation. Therefore, one can be aware of it, and conscious of it. Self-awareness, self-criticism, self-consciousness, self-reflection, self-determination, self-actualization, self-fulfillment, and self-change are all possible, permissible, and, indeed, expected in Western psychotherapy. An inability to reflect upon the self and describe what it is like, what it wants, what it experiences, and what it has done independent of others and of contexts is defined as a symptom of psychopathology—as resistance, lack of insight or intelligence, concrete thinking, and other deficits, and as a sign of defense mechanisms, psychopathy, or brain damage.

The referential self of Western culture is construed as an autonomous entity defined by its distinctiveness and separateness from the natural and social world. It is construed to be a unit, a region, and a universe unto itself that is inviolate, protected within the body, and, a priori, free. In other words, *the referential self is presumed to be a free agent—to be an agent that does what it wishes. Thereby, the self has rights*—the right to privacy, autonomy, and to be protected from intrusions from others being foremost among these. Thus, the failure of a family to respect the privacy and autonomy of its members is defined as a type of family pathology, and various family members are construed as enmeshed, victimized, domineering, smothering, and the like. As a free agent, the self is unconsciously presumed to make all sorts of choices and decisions of its own, based upon its various whims and wants. Thus, the self alone, in the final analysis, is construed as determining the actions—the behaviors—of the body in the world. *The self is unconsciously assumed to be morally responsible: The self in Western culture is the final explanation for behavior, and is responsible for behavior.* It is taken for granted that the self will claim responsibility for its actions and for the consequences of its actions in the world. Behavior is construed to be a mere consequence—the superficial, external, outward signs, symptoms, and symbols—of the activities, decisions, choices, preferences, whims, and processes of an independent, free self within the body. Western culture, and the clinical psychology and psychiatry based upon it, assumes that all behavior begins with, ends with, and is mediated by the self. Thus, attributing one's thoughts and actions to forces or persons other than the self, and attributing control of or responsibility for one's behavior to anyone/anything other than the self, are symptoms of a variety of psychopathologies — ranging from psychopathy, delinquency, and brain damage to compulsive, paranoid, and psychotic disorders.

The referential self is unconsciously assumed to seek to maintain and develop itself. Ideally, it ought to undertake personal projects that are designed to further develop, fulfill, enhance, and actualize itself. Thus, the failure to seek to maintain, develop, differentiate, and/or actualize the self and its needs is considered a symptom of psychopathology. In the process of seeking to develop, fulfill, or actualize itself, the referential self seeks *primary control*. While control in general refers to actions designed to decrease punishment and increase the gratification of the self's needs, *primary control* refers to changing others and situations to meet one's needs, and *secondary control* refers to changing oneself to fit with others and situations and thereby meet one's needs (Rothbaum, Weisz, & Snyder, 1982; Weisz et al., 1984). In Western culture, control is understood in primary control terms. Thus, *the referential self is expected to act upon the world and others in order to meet its needs,* avoid punishment, and further itself. Ideally, the self takes steps to make things happen. Thus, in Western culture, the failure to seek primary control is construed as helplessness, passivity, lack of assertiveness and self-efficacy, submissiveness, low self-esteem, inadequacy, and depression.

Finally, *relationships for the referential self are derivative:* They are secondary to and presume the prior existence of the self. It is unconsciously assumed that selves exist first — indeed, must exist first — and relationships are then the billiard-ball interaction of these selves. "We" is the association and interaction of "I's," where each "I" is autonomous and unique, has needs and traits of its own, and so may have trouble getting along with other "I's."

In summary, the encapsulated, unique referential self of Western culture is a god that creates, explains, and takes responsibility for its free actions. It is "a very big thing in this country," one of my Japanese-American students said. "That must be why Americans capitalize 'I' even in the middle of a sentence." Although a discussion of the genesis of this understanding of the self is beyond the scope and purpose of this review, a few remarks can be offered. This construction of the self is said to be rooted in the Protestant tradition of Western culture (Gaines, 1982) and in Western sociocultural practices and institutions such as privacy (Shweder & Bourne, 1982). Such an understanding of the self is almost unknown in cultures where privacy is virtually absent (e.g., Japan), as well as Buddhist and other non-Protestant cultures.

Westerners may pay psychological "costs" for this referential conception of the self. Among these is a "lack of a meaningful orientation to the past. We come from nowhere, the product of random genetic accident. . . . Cut adrift from any larger whole the self has become the measure of all things" (Shweder & Bourne, 1982, p. 132). The self in Western culture is cut off from community, family, and nation; it is adrift in a land of strangers — of other autonomous selves — with which it longs to establish lasting and meaningful attachments. Community, nation, family, roles, and relationships are all secondary to the self, and are conceptualized as an "instrumentality" for the self (Sampson, 1989, p. 915). *Each of these larger social units is presumed to exist in order to meet the self's needs, and will be rejected if it fails to do so.* The self thereby chooses its values, roles, politics, and religion, as well as the forms of relationship and community in which it will participate (Sampson, 1989). Consequently, many in America — conceptualized as free from family and tradition — often suffer chronic, psychological, and existential crises characterized by conflict and anxiety about the meaning and purpose of their lives in the larger scheme of things; about their self-determined politics, values, and careers; and their alienation from neighbors, family, and community.

This referential construction of the self is buttressed by the social and political ideology of individualism that characterizes Western culture, as well as by the psychology and psychiatry of those cultures. The referential self is explained and justified by our psychological theories of moral and personal development, in which the referential self is said to be the normal outcome of normal development. It is further justified by our concepts of psychopathology (mentioned previously) in the sense that these *psychiatric "symptoms" and "disorders" are violations of Western cultural assumptions about how the self ought to be experienced.* This concept and experience of the self is limited to a few Western cultures (and may be pronounced in America) as well as to White, *male,* middle-class Americans. It does not describe the experience or understanding of the self in the many cultures that do not "socialize autonomy or redundantly confirm the right of the individual to projects of personal expression, to a body, mind, and room of his own" (Shweder & Bourne, 1982, p. 132). The referential conception of the self is unknown among most Asians and Asian-Americans (Marsella, DeVos, & Hsu, 1985); among most Black-Americans (Nobles, 1976); Native-Americans (Strauss, 1977), Hispanic-Americans (Marsella & White, 1982), Mediterranean-Americans (Gaines, 1982), Hindu-Americans (Bharati, 1981), and, indeed, among most White-American women (Lykes, 1985), as well as among the vast majority of the world's peoples (Bateson & Mead, 1942; Geertz, 1973; Gergen & Davis, 1985; Hardman, 1981; Heelas & Locke, 1981; Lee, 1982; Levy, 1973; Miller, 1984; O'Connor, 1982; Read, 1955; Rosaldo, 1980; Shweder & LeVine, 1984; Shweder & Miller, 1985; Smith, 1981). The alternative concept of the person understood by many American ethnic-cultural minorities, the *indexical self,* is not the product of deficits or psychopathologies, but is instead, "mediated by the world premise to which one is committed (e.g., holism) and by the metaphors by which one lives" (Shweder & Bourne, 1982, p. 133). The indexical self, like the referential self, "is the product of collective imagination" (Shweder & Bourne, 1982, p. 132).

THE INDEXICAL SELF OF SOCIOCENTRIC CULTURES

The cultures of many American minorities do not begin or end their dictionary entry for "self" with a self vs. nonself distinction. "The self" in these cultures is not an entity existing independently from the relationships and contexts in which it is presented. The self (for lack of any other term) is not discrete, bounded, fully separate, or unique. Rather, to the extent that one is or has a self at all, this self is seen as constituted by social interactions, contexts, and relationships. The self is created and re-created in interactions and contexts, and exists only in and through these. One might argue that sociocentric (as opposed to Western, individualistic, or egocentric) cultures fail to reify the self, and so construe the self as an ongoing sociocultural process or phenomenal encounter.

Gaines (1982) has labeled the self of sociocentric cultures as *indexical,* because such a self "is perceived as constituted or 'indexed' by the contextual features of social interaction in diverse situations" (Gaines, 1982, p. 182). Because the indexical self exists only in and through interactions, it cannot be described per se, without reference to specific, concrete encounters with others. Thus, *the indexical self has no enduring, trans-situational characteristics, no traits or desires or needs of its own in isolation from its relationships and contexts.* In order to describe the self, many ethnic-cultural minorities may present several concrete, detailed descriptions of their most recent or proto-typical interactions in specific situations, meant to *characterize* rather than to describe the self. Typically, several different, contrasting presentations are given in an effort to demonstrate the various faces of a self that changes from relationship to relationship. Thus, in answer to the common clinical query, "Tell me something about yourself," the client from a sociocentric culture presents a few long, detailed, concrete descriptions of encounters with others and fails, from a Western perspective, to give the "simple facts." Yet, the "facts" cannot be given when the self is not an entity to which one can refer. Such stories in response to a (ostensibly) simple question about the self can be misinterpreted as circumstantial, tangential speech—a sign of underlying thought disorder—by therapists from Western culture. This misinterpretation of the sociocentric presentation of the self may well contribute to the frequent (mis) diagnosis of minorities as schizotypal or schizophrenic. In addition, Western-cultural clini-cians may often view the indexical presentation as resistance to treat-ment, and the failure to reflect on the self in isolation as lack of "insight." The presentation of several contrasting encounters that are meant to explicate the many faces of the indexical self also can be misinterpreted by Western-cultural clinicians as a contradiction. The sociocentric client's (ostensibly) contradictory description of the self is further misinterpreted as a sign of psychopathology (e.g., as a symptom of borderline personality organization, a manifestation of "splitting," or evidence of the compartmentalization seen in the vari-eties of paranoia). These misinterpretations may also contribute to the (mis) diagnosis of minorities (and women) as paranoid or border-line personality disorders. The typical mode of presentation of the indexical self also can be misinterpreted as "concrete thinking," and so as a sign of the lack of intelligence with which this pejorative term is associated. Thus, within the first 10 minutes of a session with an ethnic-cultural minority client, Western-cultural clinicians may view the client as an unintelligent, concrete thinker who lacks "insight," verbal ability (after all, they cannot even describe themselves), and is not "ready" for psychotherapy. The effects of this construction on therapists' expectations of treatment are obvious. *The indexical self is not a separate entity that can be referred to or reflected upon in isolation.* Instead of self-awareness there is a keen awareness of one's situation and relationships. Reflection is on these, and self-reflection — on an abstract entity — is virtually impossible for the client. Thus, the client persists in describing situations, or simply responds with genuine confusion to questions regarding what he or she "really" feels, wants, and wishes from therapy, and regarding his/her symptoms as well as personal history. This presentation can be misinterpreted as externalization, immaturity, projection, resistance, or evidence of not being "ready" for psychotherapy. To complicate matters, the lines between the indexical self, others, and the natural and supernatural are blurred. These lines are semipermeable membranes rather than brick walls, such that *the self includes other people and portions of the natural and supernatural world.* The self includes persons and things that Western clinicians ordinarily construe to be separate from the external to the self; the boundaries of the self are drawn not around an individual but around a "foyer" (Gaines, 1982) that includes family members, deceased relatives, and deities. Thus, gods, ghosts, family members, and significant others are parts of, and powerful competing voices within, the self. *Their* desires, *their* demands are felt as one's own, and indeed often cannot be distinguished from one's own. The self then consists of persons and forces over which the individual has little control. These persons, forces, and immaterial beings, rather than the self, are seen as responsible for the self's actions.

The Western clinician's quest to assist sociocentric clients in separating their needs from those of family, or to assist these clients in asserting their needs against those of the family, are misguided insofar as family and self are a single, internal unit. Such construction of the self (as containing family and significant others) can be misinterpreted as enmeshed, helpless, passive, and in need of assertiveness training and differentiation. Sociocentric clients' tendency to attribute responsibility for their choices to family may be misinterpreted as externalization, and as an immature failure to take responsibility. Finally, sociocentric clients' tendency to view the self as determined by fate, god, or gods, and as pushed and pulled by immaterial, anonymous community and spiritual forces may be misunderstood as delu-

sional, or simply as backward, superstitious, unintelligent, uneducated, and impossible to work with.

The indexical self may be manifested in one of two ways. The first
and more common manifestation is the *self-as-social-role;* the second,
less common, manifestation is *self-as-receptacle* of immaterial forces
or (therefore) *the self-as-an-illusion.*

The Indexical Self as Social Role

In many sociocentric cultures (e.g., Latino, African, and Asian cultures, and hence, Latino-American, Afro-American, and Asian-
American communities), the indexical self takes the form of social
roles: *The self and the roles it occupies are unconsciously presumed to be
synonymous.* In these cultures,

persons are defined by their particular social contexts. Persons [are] fundamentally citizens of the *polis,* members of their religious communities,
spouses, soldiers, and so forth, not merely individuals as such. Unlike [Amer-
ican] current understanding, which distinguishes between real persons and
the roles they must play, in [sociocentric cultures] roles [are] not appended to
the 'real' person who somehow continues to dwell authentically somewhere
behind them. There [is] no stepping outside one's community and one's roles
within the community and in its behalf. To be outside [is] in effect to be nonexistent, a stranger, or dead. . . . Persons are seen as creatures whose very
identities are constituted by their social locations. There are no subjects who
can be defined apart from the world; persons are constituted in and through
their attachments, connections, and relationships . . . persons do not choose
the ends or purposes they will select to follow, but rather they engage in a
shared, common process of discovery in which their goals and purposes are
revealed in a never-ending process of living with others. . . . In effect [from
a sociocentric point of view], there is no meaningful way to speak about
persons abstracted from the particular community that is an essential ingredient of their identities as persons. . . . [A]ttachments within a community
do not describe mere attributes of a person's identity but are in effect constituents of their identities. (Sampson, 1989, pp. 914–915, 918)

As noted earlier, Western culture construes persons as prior to community and family, and construes these larger units as an instrumentality for persons: Roles are understood to be occupied by choice
rather than necessity; the "person" dwells behind a role chosen to
fulfill the self, and she or he can and should relinquish that role if it
fails to actualize or meet the needs of the self. In contrast, in sociocentric cultures, the person is the role he or she occupies because family
and community are prior to individuals. Families and communi-

ties—rather than individuals—have goals, desires, and needs. Individuals are an instrumentality for these larger units—individuals are seen as existing to meet the needs of these units, rather than the other way around. Thus, *these social-role-selves do not have rights (to privacy, autonomy, and self-determination), but duties and obligations* to perform their role well for the larger units. Such a self is, by definition, social and commonplace rather than individualized and unique; and it exists only to the extent that it performs its role. Consequently, *the failure to perform one's role as wife, mother, father, husband, daughter, or son is a failure to be a person at all: Role failure or violation is the loss of the self in sociocentric cultures;* it is the existential, social, and psychological death of the individual.

As a result of this unconscious understanding of the self as the roles it occupies, specific and peculiar forms of psychopathology can be seen in minority clients. The most common of these is the bizarre and severe state of agitation and panic seen in minority clients who are failing in their roles (e.g., a Chinese father who loses his job), or who are considering rejecting their roles (e.g., a Japanese student considers a career that violates the vocation that the family has dictated). This odd set of symptoms can defy DSM classification, yet often has a folk diagnosis in the culture in question—e.g., *susto* for Mexican-Americans (Rubel, 1964), or "falling out" for Black and Puerto-Rican Americans (Weidman, 1978). This rather common presentation of agitation and chronic, diffuse anxiety as a result of actual or fantasized role violations can be misdiagnosed as depression, or misunderstood as a histrionic overreaction to the simple, "developmental" issue of autonomy. It is neither. The minority client who violates or considers violating role expectations, whether by choice or by accident (e.g., job loss or physical injury), is facing a serious crisis—the loss of a sense of identity—where the degree of panic exhibited correlates with the level of desperation and fear. The client's issue is thus a complex, dynamic one for which standard diagnoses, interventions, and understandings are woefully inadequate. Clinicians who attempt to assist such clients in finding a "true self" (presumed to exist behind the role, independent of the role and family, and yearning to express itself) are engaging in an extremely inappropriate intervention—one that may precipitate a severe, iatrogenic depression or even a suicide attempt.

The sociocentric client who fails in or violates his or her role is "dead" not only from the client's perspective but also from that of the family. Thus, these clients may report that they have been or fear that they will be disowned, rejected, and exiled permanently from their families. These reactions on the part of the sociocentric family do not stem from their pathology, rigidity, or cruelty, but instead from their understanding of what a person or self is. Likewise, the client's report of, or fears of, these reactions from the family are not histrionic but accurate appraisals of what is at stake—and what's at stake is not the loss of mere "approval" but the loss of being, existence, and life itself.

The culturally sensitive treatment of minorities presenting this specific problem entails assisting the client in finding not a referential self, but a new *social identity,* a new role, a new *self-for-family or being-for-others.* This treatment goal works within, rather than against, the grain of the culture's understandings. Such treatment necessitates treating the family or relationship in which the new role will exist, and will inevitably entail a redefinition and renegotiation of the needs and goals of the socially and culturally constituted relationship of relevance. Alternatively, therapy may entail or necessitate a renegotiation of the construction of the self *by all members of the relationship, for all members of the relationship.* Caution in the latter type of intervention is crucial to assure that the relationship has chosen to adopt a more referential conception of the self, and that the Western clinician is not imposing one culture's construction upon another. Western clinicians must incessantly ask themselves these *cross-cultural ethical questions:* Is my intervention a pernicious form of missionary work? Are my therapeutic goals mere proselytization? Does my effect on this family—on this culture—differ significantly from that of colonialism?

Because the self is often defined as its roles and exists for the good of the family and community, the culturally appropriate treatment of minorities includes treatment of the socially defined family, kin, community, or network. This view has been echoed by clinicians who specialize in treating Native-Americans (e.g., Everett, Proctor, & Cartmell, 1989; Lewis & Ho, 1989), Asian-Americans (e.g., Root, 1985; Sue, 1989), Afro-Americans (e.g., Grevious, 1985), and Latino-Americans (e.g., Christensen, 1989; Padilla, Ruiz, & Alvarez, 1975). Treating the minority client in isolation is perhaps the most frequent cross-cultural, psychotherapeutic error. This error is based on unconscious Western cultural assumptions about the primacy of the person as an autonomous entity possessing problems, needs, and symptoms of their own. This implies that clinical psychology Ph.D. and internship programs that fail to train students in family and/or community interventions (irrespective of theoretical orientation) are failing to prepare them for treating clients effectively in our multicultural society. The priority that clinical training (historically) has given to individual psychotherapy reflects the primacy that Western culture has offered the individual; in this sense, clinical training, like clinical concepts, is a product of Western-European culture, and so it too needs to be culturally diversified.

Clearly, the indexical self-as-social-role easily can be misunderstood as psychopathology. Western therapists may view the self-as-role as a sign that the sociocentric client lacks autonomy; is controlled by others; is dependent and enmeshed; is deficient in self-reflection, self-reliance, self-respect, and self-esteem; is lacking social skills; and is nonassertive and developmentally arrested. Each of these misunderstandings is not only a failure to understand the indexical self-as-role: *These conceptualizations also are cross-cultural projections in that they represent what the problem would be and what the behaviors would mean if Westerners were behaving in such a manner.* Treating those who understand the self in this specific form of indexical framework thereby necessitates violating "what everybody knows" and takes for granted; suspending the culturally determined definitions and meanings we ordinarily would attribute to behavior; and adopting a radically different dictionary of personhood.

The Indexical Self as Illusion or Receptacle

An alternative manifestation of the indexical self appears in Indonesian, Polynesian, many Asian (e.g., Hindu), several Southeast-Asian, and many Native-American cultures; such an unconscious understanding of the self may be held by American minorities who belong to these cultural traditions. In these cultures, the self is not an entity to which one can refer, nor a social role, nor an index of relationships, nor even a "foyer" that includes the family. Instead, the self is understood as a mere vessel for immaterial forces and entities; the individual is understood as a more or less irrelevant and dead shell through which the spirits of ancestors and a multitude of immaterial entities pass, thereby lending the appearance or illusion that the individual has characteristics. Like the referential and the indexical-self-as-role constructions, this understanding of the self is unconscious and implicit for those who hold it, and so it can lead to significant cross-cultural misdiagnosis and misunderstanding.

For example, for the Lohorung of East Nepal (see Hardman, 1981), the self, person, or *lawa* within anyone's body is conceptualized as nothing more than an entity-force that is shared by the community and links individuals to ancestors. This shared self is construed as something that travels from person to person and place to place, belonging to no one in particular. Symptoms are understood as appearing when the shared self has been away from any one person for too long. Therapy consists of finding the self and returning it to the symptomatic individual. The Maori of New Zealand (Smith, 1981), on the other hand, view individual behavior and experience as originating not from a self within the body, but from outside. One's behavior and experience are not only construed to be beyond one's control and responsibility, but are also viewed as an *attack* upon a person, and thereby associated with intense fear. For the Maori, much of the emotion that Westerners would construe as deeply internal and personal is seen as external, alien, and ego-dystonic, whether "pleasant" or not. Likewise, at the extreme sociocentric end of a cultural continuum of constructions of the self are the Balinese, who see the individual as

a receptacle within which several supernatural forces interact as integral components of the individual's personality. The most important of these are the personified spiritual forces referred to as the 'four siblings'—*kanda mpat* . . . they are referred to familiarly in everyday conversation as 'my siblings'. (O'Connor, 1982, p. 257)

An individual's behavior and personality are seen as a function of the activities of these four siblings as well as of the spirits of deceased relatives. Because the self is understood as a mere (but infinite!) stage upon which such immaterial forces act, Balinese socialization consists of learning to destroy anything unique to the individual to assure an unadulterated presentation of the immaterial beings. It is these beings—not the self—that are believed to truly exist (Geertz, 1975).

Likewise, the Hindu religion views the referential self as an illusion (if not as a delusion) that the wise and "enlightened" transcend. Such understandings of the self in each of these cultures are held by everyone—they are "what everybody knows" (just as the referential self is what Westerners know). These constructions and understandings are not limited to priests, shamans, or the intellectual elite. Thus, the ordinary Hindu-American believes that only one being exists, the *brahman,* who is formless.

The multitude of other beings, souls, selves, gods . . . beasts, stars, and planets, etc., are erroneous superimpositions on the . . . *brahman.* The task of the wise is to break through this delusion of multiplicity. . . . One might think that such abstruse thoughts could only have been relevant . . . to an intellectual or religious elite, [in fact, however] . . . Hindu thoughts and perceptions, Hindu value—*all* Hindu values—have been thoroughly informed by these seemingly recondite concepts. (Bharati, 1981, pp. 187–189)

Clearly, clients who understand the self as a receptacle or illusion may not be discussing what we think they are discussing when they present problems to us. For example, a Balinese-American who speaks for what his or her "siblings" have been doing lately may not be speaking of biological siblings and that may never be clear to the clinician; a Native-American may refer to having been advised to seek treatment by someone else, and unbeknownst to the clinician, that someone died 200 years ago. Treatment of these clients necessitates considerable cognitive flexibility; an openness to the idea that gods, ghosts, and spirits may be as real (even more real) to the client as the clinician's chairs; and a willingness to admit to the very real possibility that one simply may not know what's going on. Treatment may necessitate reading anthropology texts and/or consultation with indigenous healers, scholars, or "elders" of the cultural community in question to assure that diagnosis and treatment are appropriate. Therapists may want to consider employing what I call the *cultural triage model* of intervention. In this approach, a Western clinician, a folk healer from the culture and/or an authority from the community in question, and the family consult, agree upon several conceptualizations of the problem and a multicultural/multilevel treatment by the Western clinician, the indigenous healer, and the family alike. This kind of approach was effective in a disaster in Stockton, California, in August 1990. A sniper shot Southeast-Asian children in a schoolyard, killing several and wounding others. Most of the children refused to return to school after this, and many would not or could not eat, sleep, or speak, because they could see the "spirits" of their murdered peers wandering the schoolyard (see *Los Angeles Times,* August 1990, special series). The interventions of

American clinicians failed repeatedly and the children would not return to school. In the end, a Southeast-Asian folk healer and an expert from the community, along with the parents of the children, were consulted, and the indigenous healer "removed" the spirits from the schoolyard through a culturally sanctioned ritual. The children's symptoms simply disappeared, and they returned to school, monitored carefully by Western clinicians.

This implies that irrespective of whether the sociocentric client construes the indexical self as a role or as receptacle and illusion, the effective cross-cultural clinician seeks to understand these constructions, and works within—rather than against—their framework. In the final analysis, an openness to radically different meanings, definitions, and assumptions, rather than some specific therapeutic technique or theoretical orientation, facilitates success.

In both of these indexical constructions of the self or person, *the self is not construed to be the center of cognition, affect, or action, and so is not the explanation for behavior.* One's thoughts, goals, and feelings can be synonymous with those of others, can be caused by forces or persons that are ostensibly external to the self, and can be controlled by these external forces and persons. Behavior does not begin with, end with, or is mediated by an abstract, isolated self. Instead, relationships, situations, and immaterial entities and forces are the culturally constituted and culturally acceptable explanations for one's "own" thoughts, feelings, goals, fears, and behaviors. Thus, *in sociocentric cultures, the self tends to be seen as not responsible for behavior.* As White and Marsella (1982) explained,

> . . . the 'loose' or 'permeable' boundaries of the 'sociocentric' person [result in viewing the self] as a passive . . . agent, whose actions are [responses] to the moral demands . . . of others. . . . [Behavior is understood] as the result of socio-moral conflict or strained relations within a significant social group (e.g., family, village), rather than within an individual psyche. . . . [This view] may require that treatment or cure be focused on mending social relations. (pp. 21, 24)

Once again, it is clear that effective psychotherapy with people from sociocentric cultures must entail treating the relationship—the marriage, the family, the relationship between the person and various immaterial beings—through which the individual has or is a self at all. Appropriate therapeutic goals include assisting the group or relationship in its sense of harmony and fulfillment.

Finally, in sociocentric cultures, relationships, family and community are construed to exist first—before selves—and selves exist only by virtue of these. Thus, relationships and community are not derivative but are primary, and the self is derivative. The indexical self therefore seeks to maintain, fulfill, actualize, and develop not itself, but the relationships and community through which it exists. One seeks to advance the family rather than the self, to assure the achievement and happiness of the relationship rather than the self, to please the gods, or to assure the autonomy of the relationship, not of the self. Thus, the indexical self engages in *secondary control:* The individual is changed, adjusted, and acted on until he or she fits more harmoniously within the family, relationship, or community; or, the entire group is changed to improve the quality of life of all of its members, rather than for any individual. This radically different understanding of control can be misinterpreted by Western clinicians as submissiveness, passivity, and helplessness, and results in the frequent urge to provide assertiveness training, in particular, for Asian-American clients. *Increasing the secondary—not the primary—control of all members of the relationship of relevance may be a more culturally sensitive, appropriate, and acceptable treatment goal,* unless the client indicates an interest in primary control.

The indexical construction of the person may appear to Westerners to be a confining and unhappy existence. Much of the unconscious urge to shape a referential self in minorities stems from the culturally determined assumption that the minorities would be "better off" if they experienced themselves and the world as Westerners do. Yet, frequently, those who construct the self in a referential framework are anxious, lonely, and isolated in their autonomy. Thus, to "members of sociocentric cultures the concept of the autonomous individual, free to choose and mind his own business, [seems] alien, a bizarre idea of cutting the self off from the interdependent whole, dooming it to a life of isolation and loneliness" (Shweder & Bourne, 1982, p. 132). Although members of sociocentric cultures relinquish primary control and autonomy through the indexical understanding of the person, they gain a sense of purpose, meaning, belonging, and security in their families and communities. Whether or not the client would benefit from a more referential understanding of the self must finally be the client's rather than the clinician's decision.

CLINICAL IMPLICATIONS AND QUESTIONS

Diagnosing Minorities

Clearly, all Western psychiatry, psychology, and psychotherapy is predicated on the assumption that normal persons experience the self in a referential framework (Gaines, 1982). Thus, *those who construe the self in an indexical framework are at risk, a priori, to be misdiagnosed as psychiatrically disturbed—and as borderline, schizotypal, or schizophrenic in particular* (diagnoses minorities frequently receive). Thus, in addition to highlighting the need for therapy that is more sensitive to the indexical self, this review must raise questions about the meaning of the diagnoses minorities often receive. The diagnosis of schizophrenia is one obvious source of concern because it (more so than any other diagnosis) is based on the unconscious assumption that the self is and should be experienced in a referential framework. If the self is not experienced in a referential framework but, instead, is understood as lacking boundaries and being controlled by immaterial forces and family members, then

how will the "basic lesion" of schizophrenia show itself behaviorally? In short, which of the behavioral descriptors of schizophrenia is one likely to see? . . . [T]he claim here is not that unusual psychological experiences or social behaviors are not part of "schizophrenia" but rather that [the *unusualness* of these experiences, and] the form and meaning which they take in Western culture are . . . an outcome of the way "selves" are constructed here . . . (Fabrega, 1989, pp. 57–58)

Can those who understand the self as a receptacle be schizophrenic, and if so, how would we know that they are? Are those who hear or see their deceased ancestors hallucinating, and if so, are they psychotic? Can those who understand the self as a role-for-others be passive or nonassertive, and if so, how would we discriminate between such "symptoms" and the indexical self? Are minorities who can neither describe, reflect upon, nor take responsibility for the behavior of the self lacking "insight" or a sense of guilt? If minorities believe that their thoughts and feelings emanate from elsewhere and are controlled by others and external forces, how will we decide if this is pathological or cultural? Can those who view the self as containing family members be "enmeshed"? Can those who view the self as including the demands of others have compulsions? Can those who do not view the self as a mentalistic entity somewhere within the body but as synonymous with the body engage in somatization? How many psychological processes (e.g., projection, externalization, introjection, somatization) are based on the presumption of the referential self? If these processes are the culturally constituted by-products of the referential self and its mind/body dualism, do these apply to minorities—do these concepts describe any aspects of minority behavior (e.g., "physical" complaints)? Is the entire DSM taxonomy an inappropriate categorization scheme for the diagnosis of psychopathology in those who lack—and always have lacked—a referential understanding of the person?

These questions are serious and difficult ones whose answers have not been provided by research. Until the relevant data are available, these questions imply that we clinicians need to be far more cautious in diagnosis, assessment, and clinical conceptualization of minority clients' difficulties. Indeed, in light of our current understanding (or lack of it) of the role of culture in the behavior and the experience of our steadily increasing (and increasingly diverse) minority population, it may be that *the only culturally sensitive and professionally appropriate diagnosis we can give to minorities is "Adjustment Disorder."* This diagnosis may have to suffice until an alternative taxonomy is constructed.

Psychotherapy with Minorities

Concepts of psychotherapy are similarly based upon the referential concept of the self. As Gaines (1982) put it,

Talk and insight therapies are clearly based upon some notion of self as an alterable yet consistent and coherent *entity* which is self-reflective. . . . [These therapies] entail an implicit . . . conception of the person as an empirical being always in the process of becoming or, for that matter, unbecoming. (p. 182)

If the client lacks an understanding of and/or a belief in the self-as-an-entity that can gain insight, then *what* should our therapeutic goals be, and *how* will we know that the client has "improved"? If the client believes his or her behavior is controlled by immaterial forces and beings, then how can we shape new behaviors or modify existing ones? How do we treat the client who believes that his or her symptoms are punishment from god(s), or the manifestations of the activities of dead ancestors? The answers to these questions appear to be that our treatment goals, diagnoses, yardsticks for measuring psychotherapeutic change, and our interventions must be more culturally diverse if we are to provide effective therapy for the diversity of minorities who now constitute one third of the population. Such diversity and change might begin with an awareness and appreciation of the indexical self and its vast clinical implications.

REFERENCES

Bateson, G., & Mead, M. (1942). *Balinese character: A photographic analysis.* New York: New York Academy of Sciences.

Bharati, A. (1981). The self in Hindu thought and action. In A. J. Marsella, G. Devos, & F. L. K. Hsu, *Culture and Self: Asian and Western perspectives* (pp. 185– 230). New York: Tavistock.

Christensen, E. W. (1989). Counseling Puerto Ricans: Some cultural considerations. *Personnel and Guidance Journal, 55,* 412–415.

Crapanzano, V. (1981). Text, transference, and indexicality. *Ethos: The Journal of Psychological Anthropology, 9,* 122–148.

Everett, F., Proctor, N., & Cartmell, B. (1989). Providing psychological services to American Indian children and families. In D. R. Atkinson, G. Morten, & D. W. Sue (Eds.), *Counseling American minorities.* Dubuque, Iowa: Wm. C. Brown.

Fabrega, H. (1974). *Disease and social behavior.* Cambridge, MA: MIT Press.

Fabrega, H. (1989). On the significance of an anthropological approach to schizophrenia. *Psychiatry, 52*(1), 45–65.

Gaines, A. (1982). Cultural definitions, behavior, and the person in American psychiatry. In A. J. Marsella & A. White (Eds.), *Cultural conceptions of mental health and therapy.* London: Reidel.

Geertz, C. (1973). Person, time, and conduct in Bali. In C. Geertz (Ed.), *The interpretation of cultures.* New York: Basic Books.

Geertz, C. (1975). On the nature of anthropological understanding. *American Scientist, 63,* 47–53.

Gergen, K., & Davis, K. (1985). *The social construction of the person.* New York: Springer-Verlag.

Grevious, C. (1985). The role of the family therapist with low-income Black families. *Family Therapy, 12,* 115–122.

Hall, E. (1983). *The dance of life.* New York: Anchor/Doubleday.

Hardman, C. (1981). The psychology of conformity and self expression among the Lohorung Rai of East Nepal. In P. Heelas & A. Locke (Eds.), *Indigenous psychologies: The anthropology of the self.* New York: Academic Press.

Heelas, P., & Locke, A. (1981). *Indigenous psychologies: The anthropology of the self.* New York: Academic Press.

Lakoff, G., & Johnson, M. (1980). *Metaphors we live by.* Chicago: University of Chicago Press.

Lee, B. (1982). *Psychosocial theories of the self.* New York: Plenum.

Levy, R. R. (1973). *Tahitians: Mind and experience in the Society Islands.* Chicago: University of Chicago Press.

Lewis, R. G., & Ho, M. K. (1989). Social work with Native Americans. In D. R.

Atkinson, G. Morten, & D. W. Sue (Eds.), *Counseling American Minorities.* Iowa: Wm. C. Brown.

Lykes, M. B. (1985). Gender and individualistic vs. collectivist bases for notions about the self. *Journal of Personality, 53*, 356–383.

Marsella, A. J., DeVos, G., & Hsu, F. L. K. (1985). *Culture and self: Asian and Western perspectives.* New York: Tavistock.

Marsella, A. J., & White, G. M. (1982). *Cultural conceptions of mental health and therapy.* London: Reidel.

Miller, J. G. (1984). Culture and the development of everyday social explanation. *Journal of Personality and Social Psychology, 46*, 961–978.

Nobles, W. W. (1976). Extended self: Rethinking the so-called "Negro" self concept. *Journal of Black Psychology, 2*, 2–8.

O'Connor, L. (1982). The unbounded self: Balinese therapy in theory and practice. In A. J. Marsella & G. M. White (Eds.), *Cultural conceptions of mental health and therapy* (pp. 251–267). London: Reidel.

Padilla, A. M., Ruiz, R. A., & Alvarez, R. (1975). Community mental health services for the Spanish-speaking/surnamed population. *American Psychologist, 30*, 892–905.

Read, K. E. (1955). Morality and the concept of the person among the Gahuku-Gama. *Oceania, 25*, 233–282.

Root, M. P. P. (1985). Guidelines for facilitating therapy with Asian-American clients. *Psychotherapy, 22*, 349–356.

Rosaldo, M. (1980). *Knowledge and passion: Ilongot notions of self and social life.* New York: Cambridge University Press.

Rothbaum, F., Weisz, J. R., & Snyder, S. S. (1982). Changing the world and changing the self: A two-process model of perceived control. *Journal of Personality and Social Psychology, 42*, 5–37.

Rubel, A. J. (1964). The epidemiology of a folk illness: *Susto* in Hispanic America. *Ethnology, 3*, 268–283.

Sampson, E. E. (1989). The challenge of social change for psychology: Globalization and psychology's theory of the person. *American Psychologist, 44*(6), 914–921.

Shore, B. (1991). Twice born, once conceived: Meaning construction and cultural cognition. *American Anthropologist, 93*(1), 9–27.

Shweder, R., & Bourne, E. J. (1982). Does the concept of the person vary cross-culturally? In A. J. Marsella & G. M. White (Eds.), *Cultural conceptions of mental health and therapy* (pp. 97–137). London: Reidel.

Shweder, R., & LeVine, R. (1984). *Culture theory: Essays on mind, self, and emotion.* Cambridge: Cambridge University Press.

Shweder, R., & Miller, J. (1985). The social construction of the person: How is it possible? In K. Gergen & K. Davis (Eds.), *The social construction of the person* (pp. 41–69). New York: Springer-Verlag.

Smith, J. (1981). Self and experience in Maori culture. In P. Heelas & A. Locke (Eds.), *Indigenous psychologies: The anthropology of the self.* New York: Academic Press.

Strauss, A. S. (1977). Northern Cheyenne ethnopsychology. *Ethos, 5*, 326–357.

Strauss, A. S. (1982). The structure of the self in Northern Cheyenne culture. In B. Lee & K. Smith (Eds.), *Psychosocial theories of the self.* New York, NY: Plenum.

Sue, D. W. (1989). Ethnic identity: The impact of two cultures on the psychological development of Asians in America. In D. R. Atkinson, G. Morten, & D. W. Sue (Eds.), *Counseling American minorities.* Iowa: Wm. C. Brown.

Weidman, H. (1978). Falling-out. *Social Science and Medicine, 13B*, 95–112.

Weisz, J. R., Rothbaum, F. M., & Blackburn, T. C. (1984). Standing out and standing in: The psychology of control in America and Japan. *American Psychologist,* 39(9), 955–969.

White, G. M., & Marsella, A. J. (1982). Cultural conceptions in mental health research and practice. In A. J. Marsella & G. M. White (Eds.), *Cultural conceptions of mental health and therapy* (pp. 3–38). London: Reidel.

33. The Role of Culture and Cultural Techniques in Psychotherapy: A Critique and Reformulation

Stanley Sue and Nolan Zane

For nearly two decades research has been devoted to the investigation of the adequacy of psychotherapeutic services and treatment practices for ethnic-minority populations. Yet clinical and community psychologists continue to be perplexed by the problem of how to increase the effectiveness of mental health services to these populations. Although it can be legitimately argued that much more research is needed in order to address this problem, perhaps our efforts need to be redirected to some basic issues that have been overlooked.

This essay examines the principles underlying attempts to develop effective psychotherapy with ethnic-minority groups. Several points are made. First, investigators have been remarkably consistent in offering recommendations or suggestions for improving the relationship between therapists and ethnic-minority clients. These recommendations typically involve therapists' knowledge of culture and specific techniques based on this knowledge. Second, the suggestions raise problems for therapists. Third, in order to resolve these problems, research and practice should be redirected to two key processes involving therapist credibility and giving. Fourth, by focusing on these processes, guidelines for therapy, training, and research can be more adequately specified. Although these four points are illustrated primarily with Asian Americans in this article, they have direct relevance to other ethnic or cultural groups.

Reprinted by permission of the authors and the American Psychological Association from *American Psychologist* 42 (1987): 37–45. Copyright © 1987 by the American Psychological Association.

PROBLEMS IN PROVIDING
EFFECTIVE SERVICES

The research and clinical literature on the delivery of mental health services to ethnic-minority populations has been quite consistent in drawing attention to inadequacies in the provision of services. For example, in summarizing the work of its Asian/Pacific-American, Black-American, Hispanic-American, and Native-American/Alaska-Native subpanels, the Special Populations Task Force of the President's Commission on Mental Health (1978) concluded that ethnic minorities "are clearly underserved or inappropriately served by the current mental health system in this country" (p. 73). The first author (Sue, 1977) studied nearly 14,000 clients in 17 community mental health centers in the greater Seattle area. Results indicated that Blacks and Native Americans were overrepresented in the centers, whereas Asian Americans and Hispanics were underrepresented. The disturbing finding was that regardless of utilization rates, all of the ethnic-minority groups had significantly higher dropout rates than Whites. About half of the ethnic-minority clients failed to return for treatment after one session, compared to the 30% dropout rate of Whites. Without belaboring the point, we believe that there is ample evidence that ethnic minorities are not faring well in our mental health system.

How can these problems be explained? Again, researchers and practitioners exhibit remarkable agreement about the reasons for the inadequacies in mental health services. Some of these reasons include the lack of bilingual therapists, stereotypes therapists have of ethnic clients, and discrimination. However, the single most important explanation for the problems in service delivery involves the inability of therapists to provide culturally responsive forms of treatment. The assumption, and a fairly good one, is that most therapists are not familiar with the cultural backgrounds and life-styles of various ethnic-minority groups and have received training primarily developed for Anglo, or mainstream, Americans (Bernal & Padilla, 1982; Chunn, Dunston, & Ross-Sheriff, 1983; Wyatt & Parham, 1985). Consequently, therapists are often unable to devise culturally appropriate forms of treatment, and ethnic-minority clients frequently find mental health services strange, foreign, or unhelpful. Szapocznik, Santisteban, Kurtines, Hervis, and Spencer (1982) argued that Hispanic Americans in contrast to Anglo Americans value linearity (i.e., role-structured rather than egalitarian relationships) and a present-time orientation in therapy. They believe that failure to recognize and utilize these values in treatment is an impediment to effective psychotherapy. Similarly, Nobles (1980) delineated several Black-American cultural traditions including group identification and collectivity, spirituality, and a flexible concept of time. These traditions, along with reactions to racial oppression, must be understood by psychotherapists working with Black Americans (Jones, 1985). The need to appreciate the cultural values of Native-American (Attneave, 1984; Manson & Trimble, 1982) and Asian-American (Kim, 1985) groups has also been emphasized. The Special Populations Task Force of the President's Commission on Mental Health (1978) recommended that "services to be provided for the special populations should be delivered, again with a view toward the best possible of worlds, by persons who share the unique perspective, value system and beliefs of the group being served" (p. 732).

NEW ISSUES RAISED BY CONTEMPORARY STRATEGIES

Because of the unresponsiveness of services to the needs of ethnic minorities, researchers and practitioners advocated changes in the mental health system. The changes had to do with the process of match, or fit: Treatment should match, or fit, the cultural life-style or experiences of clients. Otherwise, ethnic-minority clients would continue to underutilize services, prematurely terminate, or fail to show positive treatment outcomes. Modifications were deemed important at the system level and at the face-to-face, client-therapist level.

At the system level several policy recommendations were made (Sue, 1977). First, existing mental health services were urged to hire bilingual/bicultural personnel who could work with ethnic-minority clients. The continuing education of current staff through seminars, workshops, and lectures on various cultural groups was also deemed important. Indeed, many mental health centers developed continuing education programs on ethnic issues. Second, the initiation of parallel services was necessary in areas where a large ethnic community existed. These services included the creation of mental health centers or sections of mental hospitals that specialized in treating these ethnic clients. Finally, nonparallel services for ethnic-minority clients were advocated. For example, because of the stigma attached to the use of mental health services, new means of delivering such services were needed. Some communities organized multiservice centers where mental health programs could be embedded within legal, social service, and language programs.

There is evidence that these three recommendations are being implemented (see Snowden, 1982; Uba, 1982) and that structural changes have been made in the service delivery sector. We are not implying that newly formed programs are sufficient to meet the needs of ethnic-group populations. The main point is that research and the concept of match have played important roles in influencing system changes.

Applying the concept of match, or fit, at the client-therapist level has generally meant that (a) more ethnic therapists who presumably are bilingual or are familiar with ethnic cultural values should be recruited into the mental health field, (b) students and therapists should acquire knowledge of ethnic cultures and communities, and (c) traditional forms of treatment should be modified because they are geared primarily for mainstream Americans. These tasks have been difficult and problematic to achieve. For example, it can be difficult to recruit Hispanics who are fluent in Spanish because graduate programs are often reluctant to admit students if their English verbal skills are low. Another problem is that few training programs offer courses in ethnicity or cultural diversity, as mentioned earlier.

Perhaps the most difficult issue confronting the mental health field is the role of culture and cultural techniques in psychotherapy. We believe that cultural knowledge and techniques generated by this knowledge are frequently applied in inappropriate ways. The problem is especially apparent when therapists and others act on insufficient knowledge or overgeneralize what they have learned about culturally dissimilar groups. This is illustrated in the following situations:

One of our colleagues conveyed the following story to us. His daughter's fourth-grade teacher had just returned from a human relations workshop where she had been exposed to the necessity of incorporating "ethnicity" into her instructional planning. Since she had a Japanese American student in her class, she asked the child to be prepared to demonstrate to the class how the child danced at home. When the child danced in typical American fashion on the following Monday, the teacher interrupted and said, "No! No! I asked you to show the class the kinds of dances you dance at home." When the child indicated she had done just that, the teacher said, "I wanted you to show the class how you people dance at the *Bon Odori*" (a Japanese festival celebrated in some Japanese American communities at which people perform Japanese folk dances).

Obviously, the teacher was looking for a dance which would be different and which she could use to demonstrate that in a pluralistic society there are many forms of dance. (Mizokawa & Morishima, 1979, p. 9)

A similar effect can be seen in clinical practice. Years ago when one of the authors was a clinical intern, a case conference was held concerning a Chinese-American client. The person presenting the case contrasted Chinese and American cultures and proceeded to apply the contrast to the client in a literal and stereotypic fashion, despite the fact that the client was a fourth-generation American. The point is that in working with ethnic-minority groups, no knowledge of their culture is detrimental; however, even with this knowledge, its application and relevance cannot always be assumed because of individual differences among members of a particular ethnic group.

Other issues are raised by the match, or fit, concept. Is it not impossible to gain sufficient knowledge of the different ethnic groups? If traditional forms of treatment should be modified, does this mean that popular forms of Western treatments such as psychoanalysis, gestalt therapy, humanistic approaches, and behavior modification are inappropriate? In what ways should therapy be modified? If match is important, should not therapists be ethnically similar to their clients? The notion of match brings forth a whole host of problems and issues.

The inability to fully address the problems concerning match, or fit, resulted in technique-oriented recommendations. Rather than simply advocating the necessity for therapists to be culturally sensitive and to know the cultural background of clients, some investigators began to specify intervention strategies to use with ethnic clients. For example, Asian Americans tend to prefer counselors who provide structure, guidance, and direction rather than nondirectedness in interactions (Atkinson, Maruyama, & Matsui, 1978). They are presumably more culturally familiar with structured relationships. Therapists are therefore advised to be directive. Ponce (1974) recommended that mental health workers treating Filipinos avoid approaches that emphasize communications, interpersonal feelings, feeling-touching maneuvers, or introspections. At least in the initial stages, an authoritative as opposed to egalitarian therapist role is more consistent with the helper-helpee relationship that Filipino Americans expect.

Recommendations for conducting psychotherapy with other ethnic groups have also appeared. In working with Hispanics, therapists have been advised to reframe the client's problems as medical ones in order to reduce resistance (Meadow, 1982) and to deemphasize the necessity for self-disclosure (Cortese, 1979). In the case of Black clients, Calia (1966) suggested that therapists use an action-oriented and externally focused (as opposed to intrapsychic) approach.

The implications are that therapists should be structured, authoritarian, and surface-problem oriented in working with ethnic-minority clients. Although these suggestions for the role of the therapist may, indeed, be more culturally consistent with certain groups such as Asian Americans, they raised difficulties. First, individuals who developed a theoretical style or orientation found problems in adopting a different style. Psychoanalytic or client-centered therapists would have to abandon to some extent insight or reflective techniques. Second, many Asian-American clients who were unacculturated seemed quite willing to talk about their emotions and to work well with little structure. Third, and most important, these technique-oriented suggestions were distal to the goal of effective therapy.

Distal Nature of Contemporary Strategies

The major problem with approaches emphasizing either cultural knowledge or culture-specific techniques is that neither is linked to particular processes that result in effective psychotherapy. In the case of cultural knowledge, therapists assume that it enables them to more accurately understand and assess clients and to develop treatment strategies that result in positive outcomes. In actuality, therapists' knowledge of the culture of clients is quite distal to therapeutic outcomes, in the sense that the knowledge must be transformed into concrete operations and strategies. This is why recommendations for knowledge of culture are necessary but not sufficient for effective treatment. That is, given knowledge of clients' culture, what should therapists do?

As mentioned previously, the need for concrete suggestions on how to conduct therapy with ethnic-minority clients stimulated recommendations for culturally specific forms of intervention. However, these intervention approaches are also distal to the outcome of psy-

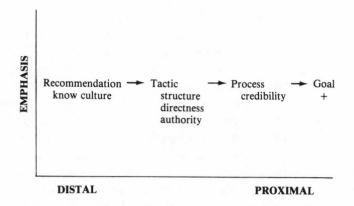

FIGURE 1
Relationship between Therapeutic Emphasis and Distance from the
Goal of Treatment

chotherapy. Let us imagine the following dialogue between an advocate and a skeptic of culturally specific techniques for Asian-American clients:

ADVOCATE: "Therapists need to be directive and structured in their interactions with Asian clients."
SKEPTIC: "Why?"
ADVOCATE: "Because the roles are more consistent with Asian cultures."
SKEPTIC: "Why is it important to be culturally consistent?"
ADVOCATE: "There are probably many reasons. Clients do not find therapy so strange. They believe that therapists understand them and can appropriately relate to them. Therapy and therapists become more meaningful to clients. Also, with a knowledge of the cultural background of clients, therapists are in a better position to assess, understand, and facilitate change in clients."
SKEPTIC: "Then, being directive and culturally responsive are means to another end. That is, certain therapy strategies enhance the credibility of therapists and therapies to clients. This enhancement facilitates positive outcomes in treatment."
ADVOCATE: "Yes."

As indicated in Figure 1, the recommendations can be placed on a continuum of distance from the goal of positive outcomes. Knowledge of culture is the most distal. It leads to formulations of culturally consistent tactics such as providing structure to clients. These tactics occupy an intermediate distance because they do not magically lead to effective therapy. Rather, they presumably result in a process such as increased therapist credibility. Therefore, it may be wiser to focus on the proximal process of therapist credibility than on the more distal techniques. Instead of learning how to be authoritarian, directive, or structured with Asian-American clients, we should learn how to become credible with clients.

Perhaps these issues can be illustrated by reversing the situation. Let us imagine that an Anglo-American client seeks treatment from a therapist in Taiwan who has had little contact with Americans. The therapist knows that compared to Chinese, Americans are individualistic, self-disclosing, assertive, and expressive. From this knowledge, how should the therapist conduct psychotherapy? Is the client a simple caricature of American values? Let us now assume that the therapist is given culturally specific techniques to use. Because Americans value insight into personal problems and insight-oriented treatment is still a predominant approach (Korchin, 1976), the therapist uses psychoanalysis in working with the client. Undoubtedly, many Americans would object to this "cookbook" technique as the culturally appropriate form of therapy for Americans.

We are not implying that knowledge of culture and the formulation of culturally consistent techniques are unnecessary or unimportant. They have been necessary and valuable in the attempts to provide more adequate services for ethnic-minority groups. However, as noted by Rappaport (1981), today's solutions often become tomorrow's problems, and psychology must continually strive to devise new paradigms and practices.

A REFORMULATION

The field of cross-cultural therapy has reached the point where it is necessary to review current practices and suggest recommendations for the future. We would like to reinterpret some of the research findings in an attempt to distill two basic processes (i.e., credibility and giving) that are important to consider in working with ethnic-minority clients. These two processes are not the only ones that are important in treatment; nor are they important only for ethnic minorities. Rather, credibility and giving are *particularly* relevant considerations in working with culturally diverse groups. Credibility refers to the client's perception of the therapist as an effective and trustworthy helper. Giving is the client's perception that something was received from the therapeutic encounter. The client has received a "gift" of some sort from the therapist. Credibility and giving are not new concepts in treatment. They are related to the much-discussed notions of expectancy, trust, faith, and effectiveness in therapy. The purpose in discussing these two concepts is to show how they are especially relevant to ethnic minorities and how they can be goals for training programs. For discussion purposes we have drawn examples relevant to Asian Americans.

Credibility

Many investigators have noted the critical role of therapist credibility in treatment. Frank (1959) stated,

Expectancy of benefit from treatment in itself may have enduring and profound effects on his (the patient's) physical and mental state. It seems plausible, furthermore, that the successful effects of all forms of psychotherapy depend in part on their ability to foster such attitudes in the patient. (p. 36)

Phares (1984) maintained that outcomes for clients are better when clients believe in their therapists and in the methods being employed.

How do ethnic-minority clients come to believe in therapists or therapeutic methods? At least two factors are important in enhancing credibility: ascribed and achieved status. *Ascribed* status is the position or role that one is assigned by others. In the case of Asian Americans, Shon (1980) argued that communication patterns are often governed by factors such as age, expertise, and sex. In traditional Asian cultures, the youth is subordinate to the elder, the woman to the man, the naive person to the authority, and so on (Bodde, 1957; Kim, 1985). These role patterns, of course, are not true of all Asians, nor are they always desirable (such as the male-female roles). But these patterns generally exist in traditional Asian cultures. Status, or credibility, can also be *achieved.* Achieved credibility refers more directly to therapists' skills. Through the actions of therapists, clients come to have faith, trust, confidence, or hope. These actions may involve culturally consistent interventions and general therapeutic skills such as empathic understanding, ability to accurately assess clients, and so on.

The focus on the process of credibility also allows for an analysis of potential problems such as the following: (a) A nationally renowned psychotherapist is perceived by a client as being effective for Caucasians but not for Asians (perceived cultural difference in ascribed credibility); (b) A young female therapist is perceived as having expertise but low status because of her age and sex (discrepancy between ascribed credibility characteristics); (c) An older, mature expert in psychotherapy fails to be effective with an Asian client (high ascribed credibility but low achieved credibility), or (d) A client who is skeptical of therapy and of the therapist's training is pleasantly surprised that the therapist is quite skilled and helpful (low ascribed credibility but high achieved credibility).

Many other possibilities can be generated. The main point is that by analyzing credibility, we can begin to break the processes related to therapeutic effectiveness into components that can serve to direct our efforts in treatment and training. Ascribed and achieved credibility are related to one another. However, the lack of ascribed credibility may be the primary reason for underutilization of therapy, whereas the lack of achieved credibility may better explain premature termination. Many Asian Americans believe that therapists in the mental health system cannot help them (Root, 1985). They avoid services because of low ascribed credibility. Once in treatment, clients will drop out if therapists do not achieve credibility. Jenkins (1985) also argued that Black clients tend to "size up" therapists and to be wary of them. Credibility and a treatment relationship must be established within two to three sessions. In general, if therapists lack certain aspects of credibility with clients, other aspects must be strengthened. This will be illustrated later in a case example. Table 1 shows the two types of credibility and their consequences for clients.

TABLE 1
Factors in Credibility

Ascribed Credibility	Achieved Credibility	
	Low	High
Low	Client avoids treatment; if already in treatment, premature termination likely.	Client avoids treatment; if in treatment, expectations exceeded and may stay in treatment.
High	Client likely to enter treatment; high expectations are not realized so may terminate prematurely.	Client likely to enter treatment; high expectations are realized by skills of therapist.

Achieved credibility can be examined in terms of three areas in which cultural issues are important. These are stated as hypotheses

1. *Conceptualization of the problem.* If the client's problems are conceptualized in a manner that is incongruent with the client's belief systems, the credibility of the therapist is diminished. Directly or indirectly, therapists often convey their understanding or conceptualization of the causal links in the problems or situation of clients. If these are antagonistic to clients, credibility may not be achieved.

2. *Means for problem resolution.* If the therapist requires from the client responses that are culturally incompatible or unacceptable, the achieved credibility of the therapist is diminished. For example, a therapist may encourage an Asian client to directly express anger to his or her father in family therapy. The response (expression of anger to father) may be quite ego dystonic because of cultural values.

3. *Goals for treatment.* If the definitions of goals are discrepant between therapist and client, credibility of the therapist will be diminished. D. W. Sue (1981) cited the example of an Asian-American client who saw a counselor for vocational information. The counselor's goal in working with the client was to facilitate insight into deep underlying dynamics concerning motives and decisions. This was not the goal of the client, who felt extremely uncomfortable in the session. In such situations, the therapist and client tend to judge the effects of treatment on different criteria. One may feel treatment is successful; the other, unsuccessful.

These three hypotheses are not intended to imply that therapists should simply strive to match clients. At times, the client's belief systems may be inappropriate; he or she may need to learn new and (previously considered) incompatible responses. The client may hold inappropriate goals or the therapist may have to define other goals in order to address the client's primary problem. Nevertheless, therapists should realize that incongruities in conceptualization, problem resolution, or goals often reduce credibility. This diminished credibility needs to be restored or increased by demonstrating the validity of the therapist's perspective. Moreover, the incongruities should alert the therapist to the need to reexamine treatment strategies. For example, are the treatment decisions guided by the therapist's limitations in understanding the culture and context of the client or by well-thought-out outcome considerations for this client?

The role of cultural knowledge is to alert therapists to possible problems in credibility. Without knowing the cultural values of an ethnic-minority group, therapists would have to assess their credibility on a case-by-case basis. They would be unprepared to deal with possible cultural discrepancies in conceptualizing the problem, finding means to resolve problems of the client, and setting goals for treatment. On the other hand, because of the link between cultural knowledge and the process of credibility, therapists can avoid confounding the cultural values of the client's *ethnic group* with those of the *client.* The knowledge is used in the service of developing credibility. Because credibility is the central process of interest, it remains the focal point even when the client may be quite acculturated and Anglo American in perspective.

The role of culture-specific techniques is also influenced by the consideration of credibility. As indicated in the dialogue between the advocate and the skeptic, these techniques have been used to facilitate credibility. By focusing on credibility, therapists may be less likely to use culture-specific approaches for those ethnic clients who would not benefit from them.

Giving

In one way or another, clients often wonder how talking about problems to psychotherapists can result in the alleviation of emotional and behavioral distress. In response to clients' uncertainties, therapists often resort to the explaining of the treatment process: Clients should not expect immediate resolution of problems, talking about emotional difficulties results in greater insight and control of these difficulties, alternative causes of action to alleviate problems may be generated, the sharing of problems with another person is often helpful, one can learn better ways of dealing with crises, and so on. Explanations of treatment are intended to provide a rationale and to alter clients' expectations so that they fit the therapy process. In other words, we attempt to change their expectations to match our form of treatment. Such a strategy is needed in order to deal with clients who do not understand the treatment process. Nevertheless, explanations of therapy should be viewed as necessary but not sufficient to maintain the involvement and motivation of clients.

Almost immediately, clients need to feel a direct benefit from treatment. (We have called this benefit a "gift" because gift giving is a ritual that is frequently a part of interpersonal relationships among

Asians.) The therapist cannot simply raise the client's expectations about outcomes. Direct benefits must be given as soon as possible. These are needed because of (a) the high dropout rate from treatment, (b) the need to demonstrate the achieved credibility of the therapist (and of therapy), and (c) the skepticism toward Western forms of treatment on the part of many Asian Americans. Gift giving demonstrates to clients the direct relationship between work in therapy and the alleviation of problems. Providing a gift is difficult, particularly in the initial session, because the therapist may be interested in gathering information for assessment purposes.

What kinds of gifts can be given in therapy? Depending on the client and situation, the therapist can strive to provide certain benefits. For example, clients who are depressed or anxious will perceive gains in therapy if there is an alleviation or reduction of these negative emotional states. For clients in a state of crisis and confusion, the therapist frequently helps clients to develop cognitive clarity or a means of understanding the chaotic experiences these clients encounter. Such a technique is often used in crisis intervention.

S. Sue and Morishima (1982) advocated normalization in work with Asian clients. Normalization refers to a process by which clients come to realize that their thoughts, feelings, or experiences are common and that many individuals encounter similar experiences. The purpose is not to deny unique experiences or to make trivial the client's problems. Rather, it is intended to reassure clients who magnify problems and who are unable to place their experiences in a proper context because of a reluctance to share thoughts with others.

Gift giving does not imply short-term treatment or even the necessity of finding quick solutions. However, it does imply the need for attaining some type of meaningful gain early in therapy. The process of giving, of course, can be conceptualized as a special case of building rapport or establishing a trusting relationship, and cultural factors may influence whether a gift is actually a gift. Our central argument is that therapists should focus on gift giving and attempt to offer benefits from treatment as soon as possible, even in the first session. Some of the gifts (immediate benefits) that the therapist can offer include anxiety reduction, depression relief, cognitive clarity, normalization, reassurance, hope and faith, skills acquisition, a coping perspective, and goal setting.

In our analysis of the importance of credibility and giving, several features are apparent. First, the concepts of credibility and giving are not new. What we have tried to do is argue their particular relevance for ethnic minorities in general and Asian Americans in particular. These concepts should be the initial focal point of therapists. It may be wise for therapists to address some questions such as the following: What is my level of ascribed credibility with this client? How can I enhance my ascribed/achieved credibility? What kind of gift is important to provide? How can I offer this gift? Second, the two concepts are not limited to any particular therapeutic orientation. They cut across different approaches such as gestalt, psychoanalytic, client centered, and behavioral treatment. Third, credibility and giving are viewed as necessary but not sufficient ingredients for positive treatment outcomes. Long-term client changes are influenced by a variety of other therapist, client, and situational factors. However, we believe that the mental health profession, in its attempts to find effective means of treatment, has lost sight of some basic processes that are crucial. Most investigators have focused on distal considerations (e.g., knowledge of culture or culturally consistent tactics) rather than on the processes that underlie these considerations. Fourth, credibility and giving provide more specific targets for our intervention and training efforts than notions of cultural responsiveness, match or fit, therapeutic flexibility, cultural sensitivity, and so forth. Cultural knowledge is necessary, but if we have erred, it has been in the direction of ignoring therapeutic processes in favor of abstract admonishments to know culture. A balance between the two is needed.

A Case Example

We will now present an example case of a client and then discuss the issues it raises concerning credibility and giving. The case is taken from S. Sue and Morishima (1982) and was selected not because it neatly illustrates the processes of credibility and giving, but because the treatment raises issues relevant to the processes.

At the advice of a close friend, Mae C. decided to seek services at a mental health center. She was extremely distraught and tearful as she related her dilemma. An immigrant from Hong Kong several years ago, Mae met and married her husband (also a recent immigrant from Hong Kong). Their marriage was apparently going fairly well until six months ago when her husband succeeded in bringing over his parents from Hong Kong. While not enthusiastic about having her parents-in-law live with her, Mae realized that her husband wanted them and that both she and her husband were obligated to help their parents (her own parents were still in Hong Kong).

After the parents arrived, Mae found that she was expected to serve them. For example, the mother-in-law would expect Mae to cook and serve dinner, to wash all the clothes, and to do other chores. At the same time, she would constantly complain that Mae did not cook the dinner right, that the house was always messy, and that Mae should wash certain clothes separately. The parents-in-law also displaced Mae and her husband from the master bedroom. The guest room was located in the basement, and the parents refused to sleep in the basement because it reminded them of a tomb.

Mae would occasionally complain to her husband about his parents. The husband would excuse his parent's demands by indicating, "They are my parents and they're getting old." In general, he avoided any potential conflict; if he took sides, he supported his parents. Although Mae realized that she had an obligation to his parents, the situation was becoming intolerable to her. (pp. 76–77)

Mae's ambivalence and conflict over entering psychotherapy were apparent. On the one hand, she had a strong feeling of hopelessness and was skeptical about the value of treatment. Mae also exhibited an initial reluctance to discuss her family problems. On the other hand, she could not think of any other way to address her situation. Then, too, her friend had suggested that she see me because I (S. Sue) had experience with Asian-American clients. In retrospect I realize that my ascribed credibility with Mae was suspect. I was an American-born Chinese who might not understand her situation; furthermore, her impression of psychotherapy was not positive. Mae did not understand how "talking" about her problem could help. She, as well as her close friend, was unable to think of a solution, and she doubted a therapist could help. My age was probably an advantage—too young to be considered a parental figure (who might be an ally of her parents-in-law) and old enough to have experience in working with clients. The sex difference did not seem to matter.

In such a situation, achieving credibility is critical. I wanted to demonstrate that I understood her conflict and would not adopt the position of her in-laws. I attempted to reflect and to occasionally summarize her feelings of anger at her in-laws for their demands (and at her husband for not helping her) and of her failure to act as an ideal daughter-in-law and wife in fulfilling obligations. These attempts were somewhat successful judging by her progressive openness in detailing her problems and by her emotional reactions (e.g., crying) when summaries of her problems were verbalized to her. Unlike many Asian Americans, Mae seemed willing to self-disclose as long as I did not do anything to reduce my credibility. That is, the task was to avoid mistakes rather than to find means of drawing her out. I believe that had I defined Mae's problem as her lack of assertiveness and suggested assertiveness training as a goal, my credibility would have been diminished.

Toward the end of the first session, I also wanted to provide Mae with some gifts — normalization and hope. I indicated that conflicts with in-laws were very common, especially for Chinese, who are obligated to take care of their parents. I attempted to normalize the problems because she was suffering from a great deal of guilt over her perceived failure to be the perfect daughter-in-law. I also conveyed my belief that in therapy we could try to generate new ideas to resolve the problem — ideas that did not simply involve extreme courses of action such as divorce or total submission to the in-laws (which she believed were the only options).

I discussed Mae during a case conference with other mental health personnel. It is interesting that many suggestions were generated: Teach Mae how to confront the parents-in-law; have her invite the husband for marital counseling so that husband and wife could form a team in negotiation with his parents; conduct extended family therapy so that Mae, her husband, and her in-laws could agree on contractual give-and-take relationships. The staff agreed that working solely with Mae would not change the situation. However, these options entailed extreme response costs. Confronting her in-laws was discrepant with her role of daughter-in-law, and she felt very uncomfortable in asserting herself in the situation. Trying to involve her husband or in-laws in treatment was ill-advised. Her husband did not want to confront his parents. More important, Mae was extremely fearful that her family might find out that she had sought psychotherapy. Her husband as well as her in-laws would be appalled at her disclosure of family problems to a therapist who was an outsider.

We are not implying that these strategies would have failed. There is no a priori way of knowing their effectiveness. What is known is that Mae would have found these means for resolving the problem unacceptable. Urging her to adopt these strategies might have reduced the credibility of the therapist (he does not understand Chinese role relationships, he is not aware of the situation, and so on) and might have resulted in her termination of treatment.

How could Mae's case be handled? During the case conference, we discussed the ways that Chinese handle interpersonal family conflicts, which are not unusual to see. Chinese often use third-party intermediaries to resolve conflicts. The intermediaries obviously have to be credible and influential with the conflicting parties.

At the next session with Mae, I asked her to list the persons who might act as intermediaries, so that we could discuss the suitability of having someone else intervene. Almost immediately, Mae mentioned her uncle (the older brother of the mother-in-law), whom she described as being quite understanding and sensitive. We discussed what she should say to the uncle. After calling her uncle, who lived about 50 miles from Mae, she reported that he wanted to visit them. The uncle apparently realized the gravity of the situation and offered to help. He came for dinner, and Mae told me that she overheard a discussion between the uncle and Mae's mother-in-law. Essentially, he told her that Mae looked unhappy, that possibly she was working too hard, and that she needed a little more praise for the work that she was doing in taking care of everyone. The mother-in-law expressed surprise over Mae's unhappiness and agreed that Mae was doing a fine job. Without directly confronting each other, the uncle and his younger sister understood the subtle messages each conveyed. Older brother was saying that something was wrong and younger sister acknowledged it. After this interaction, Mae reported that her mother-in-law's criticisms did noticeably diminish and that she had even begun to help Mae with the chores.

Our intent in presenting Mae's case is not to illustrate the appropriateness or inappropriateness of certain techniques. The purpose is to demonstrate how credibility and giving should be relevant *processes* to consider in working with ethnic minorities. We believe that therapist credibility and giving are important processes that have implications for treatment, training, and research.

IMPLICATIONS

Treatment

It could be argued that credibility and giving are important in working with any client—so why emphasize these in the treatment of ethnic-minority individuals? Granted credibility and the importance of giving are salient issues even with a Caucasian client who is naive about or distrustful of psychotherapy. However, such issues are dealt with in a sociocultural context in which the client and therapist frequently share common values, attitudes, norms, patterns of communication, and language. This situation is less prevalent for many Asian-American or ethnic-minority clients. Outcome in therapy is the *cumulative* product of many discrete dynamics between client and therapist. For example, we doubt that an ethnic-minority client prematurely terminates solely because he or she may be ashamed of seeking help or unfamiliar with psychotherapy. He or she leaves after a series of frustrations, misunderstandings, disappointments, and defensive reactions on his or her part that combine to create a poor response to treatment. For many ethnic clients, language problems, role ambiguities, misinterpretations of behavior, differences in priorities of treatment, and so forth occur in conjunction with one another to produce a rapidly accelerating negative process in therapy. Viewed in this context, credibility and gift giving become all the more important because they can either exacerbate or help reverse this process.

Although it would be ideal to maximize both credibility and giving in treatment, our clinical experience suggests a more realistic objective in working with ethnic-minority clients: to minimize problems in credibility while maximizing gift giving. In essence, ascribed credibility and the three aspects of achieved credibility can be seen as marker areas for potential cultural problems in therapy. Gift giving, on the other hand, represents a potential positive force in treatment. In this framework both cultural problems as well as constructive solutions become salient foci in treatment.

Minimization of cultural problems does not imply that treatment should always match cultural expectations and norms. The primary purpose of therapy is to provide clients with new learning experiences. Often these involve prescriptions that run counter to cultural beliefs and/or accepted patterns of behavior. For example, a therapist working with a depressed Black woman may want her to become more self-disclosing, especially in expressing her feelings about certain problems she is having with her husband. Given that extensive self-disclosure of negative feelings and the focus on negative thoughts may be culturally incongruent means of problem solving for the client, the therapist must decide whether this decrement in credibility is offset by other perceived gains in treatment. A gift may involve agreeing to help the client arrange for an intermediary to talk with her husband, as in Mae's case. The point is that cultural incongruities are often unavoidable and at times are necessary. However, by being knowledgeable of issues of credibility and giving, therapy proceeds in a more systematic manner toward handling these incongruities, with an emphasis on producing constructive benefits.

Training

Culturally responsive problem conceptualization, means for problem solving, goals for evaluating progress, and gift giving constitute specific clinical tasks that must be undertaken in the treatment of ethnic-minority clients. Training can be conceptualized as a program for developing skills in each of these areas. In this way, the diffuse concept of cultural sensitivity is transformed into a set of meaningful operational objectives for the development of skilled therapists.

By using this model it becomes apparent why simply imparting knowledge of different cultures was insufficient in the past. Such knowledge often involved very general and abstract concepts. More important, few training programs offered explicit guidelines for the application of these concepts to the specific clinical tasks of therapy.

Trainees working with clients can be videotaped, and evaluations can be made of credibility and gift-giving effectiveness; or therapist-client role playing situations can be created whereby the person adopting the role of client can provide the therapist-trainee with feedback on these skills. We have reached a point where innovative training practices must be found if we are to respond to ethnic-minority groups.

Research

The reformulation of the role of culture and the two processes we have identified suggest areas of clinical research. An interesting line of investigation would be to test the hypotheses proposed earlier: Do therapist-client discrepancies in problem conceptualization, means for problem resolution, and goals for treatment reduce therapist credibility and positive outcomes? Previous research has largely focused on therapeutic outcomes as a function of clients' expectancies about the value of treatment (Weiner & Bordin, 1983) and as a function of client-therapist match on global characteristics (e.g., race, social class, sex, general personal constructs, or personality characteristics; Berzins, 1977; Ivey & Simek-Downing, 1980; Phares, 1984). By specifying those discrepancies that may be important in the therapeutic endeavor, we more precisely test and understand the significance of client-therapist match. Furthermore, Greenberg (1986) pointed out that

particular processes occur at different times in therapy and have different meanings in different contexts. It is more the occurrence of a particular pattern of variables than their simple presence or frequency of occurrence that indicates the therapeutic significance of what is occurring in therapy. (p. 7)

Given the complexity of therapeutic processes, it is important to investigate the relative significance of the three aspects of achieved credibility, the influence of one aspect on another, and the critical time periods that may exist in developing these aspects of credibility.

In the gift-giving process, we need to determine the kinds of gifts that are effective and the method by which gifts can be delivered. Here again, knowledge of culture can be used in the service of the process. Although gift giving may be a simple idea, its simplicity is more apparent than real. For example, we know that by providing a reward after the occurrence of a behavior, the frequency of that behavior often increases. Many Chinese offer gifts (i.e., rewards) first, in order to control the behavior of others. That is, an implicit obligatory relationship is created. Although this gift-giving procedure does not run counter to the principle of operant conditioning (e.g., the gift can be seen as a stimulus rather than a consequence of the behavior), it does point to the complexities that need to be addressed in research.

Another aspect to consider is the interaction between credibility and the effectiveness of a particular gift-giving action. Whether an action is perceived or experienced as a gift may be a function of the level of credibility. For instance, if therapists succeed in conceptualizing their clients' problems in a manner consistent with the clients' world view, clients may be more likely to "accept" reassurance from the therapist. On the other hand, clients who feel that their therapists do not understand them and their problems may perceive attempts at reassurance as condescending or pro forma gestures. Research examining the interaction between the various components of credibility and the gift-giving process may make significant contributions toward the development of effective treatment strategies for ethnic minorities.

NOTES

The first author presented an earlier version of this essay as an invited address at the Asian American Psychological Association Convention, August 1985, in Los Angeles.

REFERENCES

Atkinson, D. R., Maruyama, M., & Matsui, S. (1978). The effects of counselor race and counseling approach on Asian Americans' perceptions of counselor credibility and utility. *Journal of Counseling Psychology, 25,* 76–83.

Attneave, C. L. (1984). Themes striving for harmony: Conventional mental health services and American Indian traditions. In S. Sue & T. Moore (Eds.), *The pluralistic society: A community mental health perspective* (pp. 149–166). New York: Human Services Press.

Bernal, M. E., & Padilla, A. M. (1982). Status of minority curricula and training in clinical psychology. *American Psychologist, 37,* 780–787.

Berzins, J. I. (1977). Therapist-patient matching. In A. S. Gurman & A. M. Razin (Eds.), *Effective psychotherapy* (pp. 124–139). New York: Pergamon Press.

Bodde, D. (1957). *China's cultural tradition.* New York: Holt, Rinehart & Winston.

Calia, V. F. (1966). The culturally deprived client: A reformulation of the counselor's role. *Journal of Counseling Psychology, 13,* 100–105.

Chunn, J. C., Dunston, P. J., & Ross-Sheriff, F. (Eds.). (1983). *Mental health and people of color: Curriculum development and change.* Washington, DC: Howard University Press.

Cortese, M. (1979). Intervention research with Hispanic Americans: A review. *Hispanic Journal of Behavioral Sciences, 1,* 4–20.

Frank, J. P. (1959). The dynamics of the psychotherapeutic relationship. *Psychiatry, 22,* 17–39.

Greenberg, L. S. (1986). Change process research. *Journal of Consulting and Clinical Psychology, 54,* 4–9.

Ivey, A. E., & Simek-Downing, L. (1980). *Counseling and psychotherapy.* Englewood Cliffs, NJ: Prentice-Hall.

Jenkins, A. H. (1985). Attending to self-activity in the Afro-American client. *Psychotherapy, 22,* 335–341.

Jones, A. C. (1985). Psychological functioning in black Americans: A conceptual guide for use in psychotherapy. *Psychotherapy, 22,* 363–369.

Kim, S. C. (1985). Family therapy for Asian Americans: A strategic-structural framework. *Psychotherapy, 22,* 342–348.

Korchin, S. J. (1976). *Modern clinical psychology.* New York: Basic Books.

Manson, S. M., & Trimble, J. E. (1982). American Indian and Alaska Native communities: Past efforts, future inquiries. In L. R. Snowden (Ed.), *Reaching the underserved: Mental health needs of neglected populations* (pp. 143–164). Beverly Hills, CA: Sage.

Meadow, A. (1982). Psychopathology, psychotherapy, and the Mexican-American patient. In E. E. Jones & S. J. Korchin (Eds.), *Minority mental health* (pp. 331–361). New York: Praeger.

Mizokawa, D. T., & Morishima, J. K. (1979). The education for, by, and of Asian/Pacific Americans. *Research Review of Equal Education, 3,* 1–33.

Nobles, W. (1980). Extended self: Rethinking the so-called Negro self-concept. In R. L. Jones (Ed.), *Black psychology* (pp. 99–105). New York: Harper & Row.

Phares, E. J. (1984). *Clinical psychology.* Homewood, IL: Dorsey.

Ponce, D. (1974). The Filipinos in Hawaii. In W. S. Tseng, J. F. McDermott, & T. W. Maretzki (Eds.), *People and cultures in Hawaii* (pp. 34–43). Honolulu: University Press of Hawaii.

Rappaport, J. (1981). In praise of paradox: A social policy of empowerment over prevention. *American Journal of Community Psychology, 9,* 1–25.

Root, M. P. (1985). Guidelines for facilitating therapy with Asian American clients. *Psychotherapy, 22,* 349–356.

Shon, S. (1980). The delivery of mental health services to Asian and Pacific Americans. In U.S. Commission on Civil Rights (Ed.), *Civil rights issues of Asian and Pacific Americans: Myths and realities* (pp. 724–733). Washington, DC: U.S. Government Printing Office.

Snowden, L. R. (Ed.). (1982). *Reaching the underserved: Mental health needs of neglected populations.* Beverly Hills, CA: Sage.

Special Populations Task Force of the President's Commission on Mental Health. (1978). *Task panel reports submitted to the President's Commission on Mental Health: Vol. 3.* Washington, DC: U.S. Government Printing Office.

Sue, D. W. (1981). *Counseling the culturally different: Theory and practice.* New York: Wiley.

Sue, S. (1977). Community mental health services to minority groups: Some optimism, some pessimism. *American Psychologist, 32,* 616–624.

Sue, S., & Morishima, J. K. (1982). *The mental health of Asian Americans.* San Francisco: Jossey-Bass.

Szapocznik, J., Santisteban, D., Kurtines, W. M., Hervis, O. E., & Spencer, F. (1982). Life enhancement counseling: A psychosocial model of services for Cuban elders. In E. E. Jones & S. J. Korchin (Eds.), *Minority mental health* (pp. 296–330). New York: Praeger.

Uba, L. (1982). Meeting the mental health needs of Asian Americans: Mainstream or segregated services. *Professional Psychology, 13,* 215–221.

Weiner, I. B., & Bordin, E. S. (1983). Individual psychotherapy. In I. B. Weiner (Ed.), *Clinical methods in psychology* (pp. 333–388). New York: Wiley.

Wyatt, G. E., & Parham, W. D. (1985). The inclusion of culturally sensitive course materials in graduate school and training programs. *Psychotherapy, 22,* 461–468.

34. Ethnic Validity in Psychotherapy

Forrest B. Tyler, Deborah Ridley Sussewell, and Janice Williams-McCoy

Over the past two decades researchers and practitioners representing a variety of interests and perspectives have criticized the paradigms of American Psychology as being ethnocentric and as representing Anglo-American male values and world views (Caplan & Nelson, 1973; Lorion, 1978; Nobles, 1976; President's Commission on Mental Health, 1978; Sampson, 1977). Collectively, these criticisms highlight the need for a paradigmatic shift in at least three ways. First, psychological paradigms must incorporate the importance of culture, race, and ethnicity in defining its constructs, concepts, and parameters. Second, psychological paradigms must fully acknowledge their clients as "knowing" individuals who shape their worlds and destinies through conceptual frameworks which they develop about the world and their lives. Third, psychological paradigms must acknowledge the role of system and individual interactions in their formulations about how people function and organize their lives.

We have presented an extensive review of conceptual perspectives and empirical research which have implications for cross-racial ethnic psychotherapy in another context (Tyler *et al.*, unpublished manuscript). In it are presented the rationales and evidence for advocating an Ethnic Validity Model (EVM) as an alternative psychological paradigm which is responsive to the general considerations mentioned above. We have indicated that the literature on cross-racial/ethnic psychotherapy represents three distinct perspectives: universalism, particularism, and transcendism.

Proponents of a universalist perspective stress that all people, regardless of race, ethnicity, or culture, develop along uniform psycho-

Reprinted by permission of the authors and *Psychotherapy* from *Psychotherapy* 22 (1985): 311–20. © 1985 *Psychotherapy*.

logical dimensions. Their writings have espoused that there are universal laws which govern behavior, that there is a nonbiased set of scientific concepts and methods, and that unique ethnic characteristics are products of social conditions and learning (Griffith & Jones, 1979; Jones, 1978; Korchin, 1980). Research consistent with the universalist perspective has shown that therapist variables such as degree of warmth and understanding are necessary to determine client satisfaction (Kaduchin, 1972) and that there are no black/white differences with respect to therapist preference (Cimbolic, 1972); client willingness to explore with a white therapist (Alston, 1974); or resistance and length of treatment (Stevens, 1945; Weiss & Dlugokinski, 1974).

The particularist perspective stresses that there are salient factors in an individual's experience which significantly impact his or her world view and development. Culture, ethnicity, race, and sex are examples of such variables. There are numerous writers who espouse this perspective and who stress that persons from different ethnic/racial backgrounds cannot understand or effectively assist each other therapeutically (Dixon, 1976; Jackson, 1976; White, 1970). Studies consistent with their view have shown client preference for, more positive therapeutic experiences with, more self-exploration, and better therapy attendance with same race/ethnic versus different race/ethnic pairs (Acosta, 1980; Acosta & Sheehan, 1976; Banks, 1972; Carkhuff & Pierce, 1967; Griffith, 1977; Li, 1980; Sue et al., 1974).

The transcendist perspective stresses that persons from different ethnic/racial backgrounds are psychosocially different but that under some circumstances those differences can be transcended in therapy. The ethnic validity model has been developed as a framework for integrating these diverse views and findings in a transcendist perspective as one which more effectively encompasses all of them. This article provides a detailed formulation of the EVM and outlines for psychotherapists a framework within which to conceptualize their cross-race/ethnic activities from a nondeficit and nonblaming perspective for both client and therapist.

Specifically, the ethnic validity model of human understanding and interaction is defined by its recognition, acceptance, and respect for the presence of commonalities and differences in psychosocial development and experiences among people with different ethnic or cultural heritages. It also incorporates the related assumptions that people's distinctive ethnic perspectives each embody some unique truths but that they are not disparate enough to prohibit communication or interaction. Rather they may provide a basis for constructive interchange and growth.

The EVM is built in part on three sets of assumptions. The first is that there are a variety of ways of being human. Further, those ways of being human are not directly translatable into each other. Rather, these ways of being human have characteristic forms, lead to the development of characteristic life-styles, and have characteristic strengths *and* limitations. Tyler's psychosocial competence conception (1978) provides an initial framework for formulating such a model of ethnic validity. In that model emphasis is placed on defining people's general competence/effectiveness in living in terms of a configural sense of self-efficacy and sense of self-world relationships, plus a characteristic pattern of coping. Emphasis is also placed on how those factors are shaped by engagement with life's ongoing events and circumstances. Within that framework research to date (Pargament *et al.*, 1982; Tyler *et al.*, 1979; Tyler & Pargament, 1981) has suggested that ethnic circumstances (racial, religious, sexual) contribute to those events and psychosocial patterns. The model presented here is a step toward a more complete formulation of the concepts needed to account for such findings. It also directs attention to relevant questions about the interrelations among individual and ethnic factors as they influence people's functioning in relation to their own and other cultural contexts.

Second, it is assumed that there are characteristic patterns of relationship and exchange among people who differ with regard to race and ethnicity. That is, a person's life experiences and life conditions are, in part, a reflection of that person's unique individuality and, in part, a function of the social milieu and historical context in which the person is socialized. That milieu and context include the person's ethnic or cultural identity, other historical contexts, ethnic identities, and individual identities. We are all confronted with evolving our lives in such a heterogeneous context. Consequently the ethnic validity model we formulate must enable us to understand and transcend these many facets of our diverse existences.

Heterogeneous civilizations tend to be shaped or dominated by one of the ethnic groups within them. From a power position point of view that group functions as a culture-defining group (CDG). Its heritage and its members are preeminent in shaping the ethos of the culture. Our relationship to ourselves and to others are in part defined, supported, and constrained by how that CDG views our race, culture, sex, age, socioeconomic status, physical characteristics, place of birth, or other attributes. This point is not meant in any way to suggest that non-culture-defining group (NCDG) individuals are totally defined by the dominant cultural views. They, of course, are not. However, by virtue of their living in such a culture, they are exposed to its impact on the form of their lives and life options. Further, it impacts on how they are likely to be viewed and treated within the available therapeutic models and by most culturally congruent psychotherapists.

Adopting an ethnic validity model leads us to view a person as constructing a psychosocial identity by combining individual, ethnic, and cultural perspectives. For example, in the culture of the United States a person at one extreme embodies individual characteristics (good health, attractive appearance, secure childhood) plus racial/ethnic (upper-class white, male, Protestant) and cultural characteristics (sense of self-efficacy as an unquestioned member of the culture-defining elite), interpersonal trust (that others will be benign and supportive), and a direct, masterful, planful approach to life (as it has been responsive). Part of such a pattern of being human is frequently an unexamined sense of one's own reality as universal and just.

A person at another extreme may be endowed with poor health, physical unattractiveness, a traumatic personal history, and inclusion in an ethnic group defined by that same culture as undesirable. That person is likely to have a sense of his or her personal and ethnic identity and of the culture as embodying contradictory values. For that person reality is by no means universal. Its inequity and injustice are seen as quite selective. Further, that person is confronted with the high probability of needing to deal with an unlike reference group which is culture defining.

The third set of assumptions concerns pluralism. Specifically, the integrity of an individual's diverse heritage and identity must be acknowledged and respected at both an individual and a group level. That model must also provide a means for incorporating and understanding the potential of reciprocal interchange and cross-ethnic understanding. It must provide for individual and social change in a fashion which respects that diversity, builds on the unique strengths of those various ways of being, and neither systematically advantages nor subjugates any particular heritage.

An ethnic validity concept must also incorporate the perspective that individuals create their life space and life events as they develop as persons and in turn form their own natures out of their life experiences and life conditions. Thus it follows that individuals will be somewhat unique and somewhat a reflection of their life conditions. Just as it is important to respect diversity in ethnic life-styles, it is also important to respect diversity in individual ways of being. An ethnic validity model must also permit conceptualization of the uniqueness, the integrity, and the relative strengths of individual life-styles. It must acknowledge that all individuals are "knowers" and create and develop their life spaces from their unique experiences and life conditions. That is, each individual has a conception of a reference group and of validity within that group. Each individual also has a conception of self, self-world relationships, and coping skills that stem from direct or indirect relationships with various like and unlike reference groups. We must therefore address the notion of ethnic validity within and across reference groups to have a basis for a full understanding of individuals.

The patterns of ethnic validity for different groups may reflect convergence, divergence, or conflict with each other. *Convergent* ethnic validity pertains to patterns of interaction in which some or all of the criteria of psychological well-being transcend culture, race, and other ethnic considerations. *Divergent* ethnic validity pertains to patterns of interaction in which some or all of the patterns of well-being are unique to each of the persons involved because their patterns are unique to their culture, race, or group. *Conflicting* ethnic validity pertains to patterns of interaction in which the criteria of psychological well-being in different ethnic groups are not only different but also in conflict.

These possibilities of convergence, divergence, and conflict also suggest that the life-styles in different reference groups may provide different patterns of well-being and different patterns of disintegration in response to varying kinds of conditions. To the extent that such differences exist, members of any group are limited in their ability to understand or assist members of other groups. Further, those limitations present the most difficulties for members of NCDGs because of their negative power position and in part underlie questions such as whether it is appropriate in the United States for black clients to go to white therapists. For example if black and white conceptions of well-being are in conflict, then in order to "improve" in the eyes of white therapists, black clients must suffer some violations of their own senses of self, or self-world relationships, or of their manner of coping.

In contrast, to the extent that each ethnic world view is necessarily somewhat limited, people can also potentially gain from understanding the strengths of divergent and conflicting life-styles. Consequently, it is also possible that cross-racial/ethnic interchanges can be beneficial. In fact, these interchanges may go through phases in which they move from being convergent to divergent, divergent to convergent, divergent to conflicting, and so on. It is only from an ethnic validity framework that this range of interchanges between individuals from similar or different backgrounds can be described, understood, and utilized constructively.

The patterns of exchange involved in therapy are not only inherently important, but they also provide a prototype of cross-ethnic exchanges, including their often asymmetrical nature. An important part of that asymmetry is the gain-and-risk pattern involved for the participants. If we look at individuals from a minority or NCDG, which is discriminated against, their relation to CDG members (particularly those with authority) is crucial to our understanding of that interaction. Most NCDG individuals have had to work with those who constrain them in order to survive and have been forced to do so within the CDG framework. They bear a far greater risk in cross-ethnic interacting than the CDG members. They have far more to lose by risking openness because they become even more vulnerable. In fact, they become particularly vulnerable if their openness focuses on the inequity in their relationship, resentment about it, or desires to redress it. Further, their efforts to come to a broader understanding of self, of the culture, or of relationships with CDG individuals may make them more likely to act against those inequities. Yet paradoxically when they do act in their own behalf they become even more endangered.

In contrast, CDG therapists do not have to understand NCDG frameworks to survive and prosper. CDG persons may encounter different risks from their interactions. They risk sacrificing their own privileges and self-justifying world view as superior. They have to deal with the resentments of NCDG individuals as well as the rejection of their CDG associates. In doing so, CDG individuals have to give up control and status, admit the possibility of someone else being able to define them, and accept the legitimacy of that definition even though it is a disquieting one.

Yet to some extent people's ways of being human rest on ethnic heritages which offer different perspectives on life. Each of us is limited in fundamental ways if we cannot transcend our own ethnic validity. Each of us needs to confront the broader perspective that has here been labeled the EVM. Specifically, that model embodies the assumption that there is some truth in each of the conceptions underlying points of convergent validity, divergent validity, and conflicting validity. Our task is to sort out those truths and learn to work with them in ways that enrich the convergence and divergence and reduce or contain the conflict among us.

TABLE 1
Therapist-Client Patterns

CDG Client	CDG Therapist
I. *Gains*	
Reaffirm Culture. Shared Experience and Identity. View of Effective CDG Coper.	Reaffirm Culture. Shared Experience and Identity. View of Ineffective CDG Coper.
Losses	
Opportunity to Learn More Options and Transcend Biases. Sense of Worth, Hope, Identity.	Opportunity to Grow Beyond Cultural Limitations and Transcend Biases. Credibility-Self and Client

NCDG Client	CDG Therapist
II. *Gains*	
Richness of Cultural Diversity. Different View of Self and Culture's Options.	Richness of Cultural Diversity. Sense of: Cultural Inequities. Need to Work for Change.
Losses	
Communication. Opportunity to Grow. Perspective for Evaluation.	Communication. Opportunity to Grow. Sensitivity to Own Poor Work and Investment. If Ineffective: Sense of Integrity.

NCDG Client	NCDG Therapist
III. *Gains*	
Shared Experience and Identity. View of Self and Culture from Effective NCDG Coper.	Shared Experience and Identity. View of Self and Culture from Ineffective NCDG Coper.
Losses	
Opportunity to Transcend Biases. Focus on Role. Credibility to Self and Therapist. Loss of hope.	Opportunity to Transcend Biases. Focus on Role Credibility to Self and Client. Sensitivity to Own Poor Work and Investment.
CDG Client	NCDG Therapist
IV. *Gains*	
Broader View of Culture. Better Validation of Solutions.	Broader View of Culture and Needed Social Change.
Losses	
Communication. Opportunity to Grow. Perspective for Evaluating.	Communication. Opportunity to Grow. If Ineffective: Sense of Worth. If Effective: Sense of Integrity.

We arrive, given these assumptions, at the conclusion that all therapeutic pairings involve tradeoffs. They involve somewhat distinctive gains and losses for both therapist and client as can be seen in Table 1. It highlights the four interchange possibilities involving therapist-client pairings within and between cultural defining group members and non-members.[1] The table is intended to provide for both the therapist and the client a framework for understanding the social and individual implications of ethnic factors in the therapeutic context. The following examples are illustrative and intended to provide a further basis for exploration and elaboration by the reader.

CDG THERAPIST AND CDG CLIENT

This pairing is most exemplified in the United States by a white Anglo-Saxon middle- or upper-middle-class male therapist and client.

From the similarities of their backgrounds, as can be seen from section I in Table 1, they both gain a reaffirmation of the basic truths and values of the culture. They also gain from their relatively high sense of shared experience and identity. Further, the therapist may gain a fuller sense of himself and of the culture from the perspective of a much less effective coper. The client may gain a fuller sense of self and of the culture from a CDG member who has presumably coped with situations more effectively.

A white male therapist working with a white male client is constantly in direct and subtle ways experiencing a familiar shared sense of possibilities and meanings. The opportunities for mastery, for creation and elaboration of relationships emerge almost effortlessly from the flow of therapeutic interchange. The therapist can identify readily with the flow of the client's life. He can also see himself leading that life more masterfully. As he does so and responds to the client's struggles with interpretations as well as with empathy and understanding, the client participates in those affirmations. Specifically he too affirms that the status in life into which he was born has enriched possibilities and that the therapist can see and experience them more fully than he.

A hospitalized talented young white male art student had a personal history which was quite deviant. His father was an alcoholic who had consistently turned positive cultural and family events such as Christmas and birthdays into nightmare horrors. His mother in her own instability had focused on overcontrol of her children as a way of affirming her own adequacy—her marriage might be a failure but she was a good mother as evidenced by the fact her children were well adjusted and successful. The student's creativity had taken him into an artistically rich and rewarding fantasy life which served as the wellspring of his art but also as the basis of his interpretation of reality. It all got expressed in terribly drunken and decadent Santa Clauses and Christ figures as well as in a very idiosyncratic and ineffective way of interacting with teachers and other establishment figures.

The white male therapist found it relatively easy to enter his world and follow through it with him. The therapist was even useful to him in sorting out artistic fantasy from personally and interpersonally disturbing fantasies. Beyond that he was able to help the student acquire more effective ways of relating to the ward and the rest of his environment. The therapist had an interest in art, a personal history of somewhat similar struggles, and their interactions affirmed shared personal and cultural identities and experiences.

In this instance the CDG therapist and client found convergence within a broad base of historical, cultural, and societal expectations.

For example, they had a shared understanding and expectation about what it means to be a "white male," and they each had experienced childrearing and educational expectations based on this aspect of self. Also, they shared somewhat similar understandings of family composition, functioning, and responsibility. Artists may seldom get rich or be fully understood, but the student was a young white male and the world lay before him if he could get it together. It was only in retrospect that the therapist realized how smug and accepting they both were of a world that decreed that the student's problems were only those of individual creativity and identity.

There are also potentially important losses in such a pairing. Because of their shared embeddedness in the culture-defining group, both therapist and client as white males lose an opportunity to transcend their cultural biases and grow beyond their cultural limitations. That loss may be particularly acute for the client. In this particular case, for example, the client lost the possibility of learning about a broader range of options for dealing with life than the options which are familiar to white middle-class Anglo-Saxon males. Further, for both the white male therapist and the client there are additional losses unique to their homogeneous pairing if the therapeutic interchange is unsuccessful. The therapist may lose credibility to himself and to the client as a member of the elite who is unable to help a fellow member. The client is particularly vulnerable to a loss of sense of worth, hope, and identity. As a member of the elite seeking help from a therapist of the elite and then still failing to overcome his difficulties, the client may indeed despair.

CDG THERAPIST AND NCDG CLIENT

Probably the most publicized pairing for the interchange pictured in section II of Table 1 is that of a white therapist and a black client. It could of course involve a white therapist and a client who is Hispanic, Asian, Native American, etc. To a somewhat lesser extent this pattern also depicts the relation between a white middle-class therapist and a white lower-class client, and between a male therapist and a female client. However, the focus here is on the general characteristics of this type of interaction, not the particulars of those different pairings.

In this type of interchange both therapist and client potentially can gain a much greater sense of the richness of cultural diversity. In addition the therapist can gain a fuller sense of the presence and nature of the culturally based inequities in our society and of the need to work for social as well as individual change. The client can learn a different and potentially more helpful view of himself and of the culture's options for him.

A white male therapist was working with a black male psychology graduate student. The student was enraged with the faculty, other students, and himself. He alternated between servility and outbursts of aggression toward them, toward the therapist, and toward himself. He spent two stormy years in which he skirted dropping out, academic dismissal (by refusing to complete course requirements or by writing examinations that he knew were unacceptable), and potentially destructive alliances with exploitive faculty members (by choosing to work with faculty whom he knew had betrayed students in the past and he knew he did not trust). The therapist kept working to focus on his own belief in the student and to avoid being drawn into these maneuvers. He emphasized his inability to live the student's life and his belief that it was the student's responsibility to work out his own life. He stuck as well as he could with his position that it was self-defeating for the student to destroy his career by creating problems to show that the graduate program was imperfect and that the therapist, the faculty, and other students were imperfect and in some ways prejudiced. Finally the student began to evolve a more stable sense of himself, his capabilities, and ways to cope with his graduate school world. As therapy began to terminate the student commented, "What you've taught me is to be myself and be proud of who I am."

In this dyad, convergence focused on the therapist's and client's shared value concerning the importance of "being understood." The therapist's ability to empathize with the client was of utmost importance. In the psychotherapy literature the success of this type of convergence in cross-racial pairings has been attributed to therapist characteristics (e.g., degree of empathy and warmth). A black client can have a therapeutically helpful and unique learning experience from working with a white therapist if his or her racial/ethnic uniqueness can be valued and appreciated without condescension by someone who is white. However the therapist's growth was also important to the success of the therapy. It enabled him to recognize and support the nature of the internal and external battles the client was fighting and the often unique resources that the client could call on to deal with them. He in turn gained a far deeper and less intellectually contained sense of the pain and destructiveness of discrimination, of the ways psychologists use their theories to rationalize their prejudices, and of the strengths this black client brought to his struggle with racism and with himself. That is, the convergence grew out of the interchange and mutual growth, not just out of the characteristics of the therapist or the uniqueness of the experience for the client.

On the other side of the picture, such therapist and client pairs may not be able to surmount their perceptions of their differences. They may lose their capacity to communicate with each other and consequently also lose an opportunity to grow in individual and social stature. Therapists may lose their sensitivity to their own poor work and their investment in it. If ineffective, therapists may also lose their sense of integrity and question their capacity to understand others with obvious needs. Clients may lose their perspective for evaluating differentially the contributions and perspectives of the therapist and end up unselectively accepting or rejecting everything offered.

NCDG THERAPIST AND NCDG CLIENT

This pairing, prototypically the black therapist–black client, is outlined in section III of Table 1. In this context also, the potential gains derive from the comparable backgrounds of the participants. Potentially they do gain from getting in touch with their sense of shared experiences and identity and from mutual reaffirmation of the strengths and positive components of that heritage. In addition the therapist may gain a fuller sense of self and of the culture from the perspective of a much less effective NCDG coper. In contrast, the client may gain a fuller sense of self and of the culture from an NCDG member who has coped with that situation much more effectively. On the loss side of their interchange, as was true with the CDG therapist-CDG client pairing, both may lose an opportunity to transcend their own biases stemming from their common heritage. Further, therapists may lose credibility to themselves and their clients if, in spite of their common background, they still cannot be successful helpers. For similar reasons clients may lose their sense of belief in themselves and their therapists if they cannot gain in working with their problems. Finally, both may potentially lose focus on their individual roles and become totally focused on the social inequities they both confront (Griffith, 1977). If so, they become unable to work effectively within the range of individual discretion available to them.

A black female client was referred to therapy with a black female therapist. She was experiencing racial identity difficulties and those difficulties had not been adequately addressed in therapy with a white therapist. As the therapy progressed similar relationship difficulties evolved (e.g., feeling not understood, anger). Upon exploration it was discovered that racial identity issues were secondary to those with people in general. When this finding was agreed upon by therapist and client the client began to make substantial progress in working out her feelings and relationships in and out of therapy.

In this instance race provided a vehicle of convergence for therapist and client. Consequently they could eliminate the racial factor that had blocked the previous therapeutic relationship and acknowledge their areas of divergence (experiences leading to very different ways of viewing and relating to people). It was the open acknowledgment of both their differences and their sharing of a historical and racial history that allowed them to develop additional constructive interactions and contain their potentially destructive conflicts.

NCDG THERAPIST AND CDG CLIENT

In this final pairing presented in section IV of Table 1 the prototypic situation of a black therapist and white client arises. Again we face the possibility that both may gain from their diversity a richer and broader view of the culture. In addition the therapist can gain a fuller sense of the needs for social change since social inequities also impact on CDG individuals. The client may gain a better or stronger sense of validation of solutions to problems worked out in therapy from the knowledge that the therapist, from an NCDG group, knows they work. On the loss side of the interchange, ironically, therapists may also lose if effective. That outcome may raise the question of whether they have sold out and violated their own sense of integrity. Further, neither therapist nor client may be able to transcend their ethnic barriers, and thus both lose their chance to communicate and to grow from their interaction. Therapists, if ineffective, may lose even more of a sense of their worth for not being able to help a CDG member. Clients, on the other hand, if they are unable to overcome their biases, may overvalue or devalue their therapists and lose their perspective for evaluating differentially the relevance and worth of the contributions the therapist is making.

A black female therapist was working with a schizophrenically disturbed young adult white female. She had been told by other staff that the client's family was bigoted and that the client had been reprimanded for racial slurs in the treatment setting. In the therapist's interactions with the client she had been called "nigger" on one occasion and had been told that the only reason she had a job was because she was black. She found that cultural/racial issues were impairing her ability to treat this client. She tried several strategies to develop a relationship with the client. They included limit setting around verbal abuse, not reacting defensively to statements implying that she lacked competence, and ventilating her anger and frustration in sessions with her supervisor.

Eventually the effort that the therapist was investing in maintaining these strategies became an issue in itself. She began to ask why she should work so hard to help someone as abusive as this client. Consequently she ceased her efforts to form a relationship with this client and with her family. She took on a role that focused primarily on managing the verbal abuse and interacting with the client around concrete tasks such as daily activities.

This example highlights several aspects of an interaction in which both therapist and client lost due to their inability to manage their conflicting views of their own ethnic validities. The therapist lost because this experience rekindled and fostered a more ethnocentric perspective of treatment. Thus it served to limit her desire to explore the cultural and psychological dynamics of this white client (and potentially of others). The client lost in that she did not receive the level and quality of therapeutic work and advocacy that she needed and that was available. Therapist and client were never able to reach a healthy acceptance of differences (an acceptance of their divergent ethnic validities). Unfortunately the level of convergence which was mutually acceptable to the client and the therapist was not one that could sustain the further development of constructive therapeutic change for the client or growth for the therapist.

SUMMARY AND CONCLUSIONS

The ethnic validity model provides a perspective on psychotherapy which endorses that there are different ways of being human which are valid and embody truths. The ethnic validity model also emphasizes incorporating the social context and its effects as integral to understanding the psychological impact of an individual's life circumstances and experiences. The therapeutic task is to optimize the convergence and divergence elements and to contain the conflicting factors in a framework of equitable solutions, not ethnocentric ones. Those issues must be worked out between the therapist and client as well as in helping that client work out meaningful problem solutions in his or her life. Further, they must be worked out within a psychosocial framework as they involve racial/ethnic as well as individual factors. In short, from an ethnic validity perspective personal understanding and rapport are important, but they are not enough. The racial/ethnic social context and its effects must be incorporated as an integral component of psychological and therapeutic theories and their applications.

Central to the ethnic validity model is acknowledging that some ways of living are valid across cultural contexts (convergence), some are different (divergence), and some are in conflict. As they manifest themselves in the therapy relationship these self- and world views carry potential benefits and risks which have been described earlier. It is particularly in instances of divergent and conflicting world views that the ethnic validity approach makes its most significant contribution to psychotherapy paradigms. That is, from an ethnic validity perspective ethnicity is a factor in therapeutic relationships, and the presence of a racial/ethnic difference may enhance as well as preclude constructive interchange.

Mapping therapeutic processes and levels of interchange through the use of the concepts of convergence, divergence, and conflict may facilitate therapeutic gains and enlighten our understanding of therapeutic processes, of how the therapist and client are relating, of helpful and stalemated points in therapy, and of the general progress of therapy. It can be especially useful in interracial/cross-ethnic therapy for tracing and identifying areas traditionally thought of as transference and countertransference. For example, a white therapist and black client (or vice versa) may begin a therapeutic relationship and find that they both have similar values and ways of understanding life events. That is, they have found common denominators around which to communicate and are experiencing convergence in their therapeutic relationship. At some point in this relationship they may find that their world views are dramatically different in conceptualizing new situations which arise in the therapy. That is, they diverge but their different views contain valid perspectives as well as limitations or destructive and conflicting elements. If therapist and client are unable to voice these differences and discuss them in a way that preserves each other's integrity, destructive conflict results. The concepts of convergence, divergence, and conflict seem particularly central to describing and analyzing therapeutic processes and outcomes in ways that will alert therapists and clients to such ethnic considerations.

A special consideration in making this model a viable one is acknowledging the salience of ethnic variables. Individuals are so shaped by their life conditions that to ignore this variable would necessarily reduce the effectiveness of therapy. For example, the models espoused by humanistically and existentially oriented psychotherapy also advocate the imparting of empathy, the unconditional acceptance of the client, and acceptance of the legitimacy of the client's world view. However, they do not emphasize the salience and importance of acknowledging and working with racial and ethnic variables as such rather than as personal/individual factors.

Another key tenet of the model is acknowledging the unique strengths and limitations of various life-styles. And finally, an ethnic validity perspective incorporates the notion that clients are knowers as well as known. They are active in shaping their worlds and creating theories about the whys, hows, and wherefores of their own lives and the lives of others.

In conclusion, the following points are highlighted for their heuristic as well as ethical, professional, and substantive importance. They impact on issues ranging from those concerning who is a good therapist, to what is good training, to what are the relationships between individual and social well-being. They also identify areas in which research as well as enlightened education and practices are sorely needed.

1. As therapists we need to learn how to learn from our clients and how to accept the validity and value of their perspectives on their lives and situations. This is especially true in regard to clients who are ethnically different from us.

Another consideration is the importance of identifying salient ethnic issues in specific concrete instances. The examples provided in this article have been chosen intentionally to highlight "ordinary" interactions. In effect we are arguing that therapy begins (or begins to go awry) with the first interactions between client and therapist. Further, the formation of their relationship and its import are not confined to abstract or unconscious issues which are evident only to therapists with advanced training and experience. They occur at the level of ordinary human interactions and they involve responses which are evident to clients as well as therapists. In fact, it is the lack of interactions with ethnically different people which limits the perspectives of many therapists. Therapists may be sensitive to mixed messages, body language, and confused thoughts and feelings but not have any idea of the social meaning and dynamics of those manifestations. It is those contextual factors that we have chosen to emphasize as we consider them of fundamental importance.

2. As therapists and evaluators of therapy we need to learn how to validate client goals, how to work toward outcomes which are different from those we prefer and how to evaluate the effectiveness of our work in relation to those outcomes.

3. As educators of therapists we need to teach ethnic validity considerations to our students.

The EVM provides a framework within which to conceptualize the psychotherapy process irrespective of a therapist's theoretical orientation. Further, it is a model which is easy to understand and to teach. It can provide the novice psychotherapist a viable framework from which to understand and evaluate the treatment process. It can also provide experienced therapists a fresh and explicit racially/ethnically oriented viewpoint from which to reevaluate their cross-racial/ethnic experiences.

4. We need to learn how our own theories can hurt or destroy other people who have valid but ethnically different ways of being human.

An ethnic validity framework provides a useful reference context from which to respond when the issue of race or ethnic difference comes up. It provides the therapist with a basis for saying, "I don't know, but I can learn and would like your help so that I can learn as we work together. Then I can be of more help to you." It provides a therapist a basis for also acknowledging "countertransference" feelings, for saying, "I feel uncomfortable about an issue and need to sort it out." Then the therapist can confront explicitly the necessity and value of learning together with the client how to sort out complex and conflicted feelings.

5. Finally, we need to confront the fact that we cannot separate our concerns about individual well-being and social well-being. That is, to confront issues of ethnic validity in therapy is also to confront the need to define and work toward a society that accepts and supports divergent as well as convergent ways of being and that contains conflicting ways of living (of being human) in an equitable, not an ethnocentric, fashion.

NOTES

Portions of this manuscript were presented at the first annual conference on Studies in Third World Psychology: Psychotherapy with American minorities. Boston, Massachussetts, November 1981. Support for this work has been provided in part by National Institute of Mental Health grants 8847 and 16744.
1. Cross-ethnic/racial psychotherapy may also involve a therapist and client who are both from minority (NCDG) groups but from different ethnic/racial groups. Their interactions will have somewhat different characteristics and involve somewhat different potential gains and losses. Those patterns are also important to understand. The authors hope that the format provided will be of value as a guide to readers for exploring the characteristics of those interactions as well. They are not discussed in detail here because of space limitations.

REFERENCES

Acosta,, F. X. (1980). Self-described reasons for premature termination of psychotherapy by Mexican American, Black American, and Anglo-American patients. *Psychological Reports,* 47(2), 435–443.

Acosta, F. X. & Sheehan, T. G. (1976). Preferences toward Mexican-American and Anglo-American Psychotherapists. *Journal of Consulting and Clinical Psychology,* 44, 272–279.

Alston, L. (1974). Minority students and the college mental health clinic. *Journal of American College Health Association,* 23, 22–29.

Banks, W. (1972). The black client and the helping professional. *In* R. Jones (Ed.), *Black Psychology.* New York: Harper & Row.

Caplan, N. & Nelson, S. (1973). On being useful: The nature and consequences of psychological research on social problems. *American Psychologist,* 28, 199–211.

Carkhuff, R. R. & Pierce, R. (1967). Differential effects of therapist race and social class upon rate and depth of self-exploration in the initial clinical interview. *Journal of Consulting Psychology,* 31, 632–634.

Cimbolic, P. (1972). Counselor race and experience effects on black clients. *Journal of Consulting and Clinical Psychology,* 39, 328–332.

Dixon, Y. (1976). World views and research methodology. *In* L. King, V. Dixon, and W. Nobles (Eds.), *African Philosophy: Assumptions and Paradigms for Research on Black Persons.* Los Angeles: Fanon Research & Development Center.

Griffith, M. S. (1977). The influences of race on the psychotherapeutic relationship. *Psychiatry,* 40, 27–40.

Griffith, M. & Jones, E. (1979). Race and psychotherapy: Changing perspectives. *In* J. Masserman (Ed.), *Current Psychiatric Therapies,* vol. 18. New York: Grune & Stratton.

Jackson, G. (1976). Cultural seedbeds of the black backlash in mental health. *Journal of Afro-American Issues,* 4, 70–91.

Jones, E. E. (1978). Effects of race on psychotherapy process and outcome: An exploratory investigation. *Psychotherapy: Theory, Research and Practice,* 15, 226–236.

Kaduchin, A. (1972). The racial factor in the interview. *Social Work,* 17, 88–98.

Korchin, S. (1980). Clinical psychology and minority problems. *American Psychologist,* 35, 262–269.

Li, R. D. (1980). Cultural influences on clinical perception: A comparison between

Caucasian and Chinese-American therapists. *Journal of Cross-Cultural Psychology*, 11(3,) 327–342.

Lin, K. M., Inui, T. S., Kleinman, A. M. & Womack, W. M. (1982). Sociocultural determinants of the help-seeking behavior of patients with mental illness. *Journal of Nervous and Mental Diseases*, 170(2,) 78–85.

Lorion, R. P. (1978). Research on psychotherapy and behavior change with the disadvantaged: Past, present, and future directions. *In* S. L. Garfield and A. E. Bergin (Eds.), *Handbook of Psychotherapy and Behavior Change: An Empirical Analysis*, 2nd ed. New York: John Wiley.

Nobles, W. (1976). Extended self: Rethinking the so-called Negro self-concept. *Journal of Black Psychology*, 2, 15–24.

Pargament, K. I., Sullivan, M. S., Tyler, F. B. & Steele, R. (1982). Patterns of attribution of control and individual psychosocial competence. *Psychological Reports*, 51, 1243–1252.

President's Commission on Mental Health (1978). *Report to the President of the President's Commission on Mental Health*. Washington, D.C.: Government Printing Office.

Sampson, E. (1977). Psychology and the American ideal. *Journal of Personality and Social Psychology*, 35(ii,), 767–782.

Stevens, M. (1945). Meeting the needs of dependent Negro children. *The Family*, 2, 176–181.

Sue, S., McKinney, H. A. & Hall, J. (1974). Delivery of community mental health services to black and white clients. *Journal of Consulting and Clinical Psychology*, 42, 794–801.

Tyler, F. B. (1978). Individual psychosocial competence: A personality configuration. *Educational and Psychological Measurement*, 38, 309–323.

Tyler, F. B., Gatz, M. & Keenan, K. (1979). A constructivist analysis of the Rotter I-E scale. *Journal of Personality*, 47, 11–35.

Tyler, F. B. & Pargament, K. I. (1981). Racial and personal factors and the complexities of competence-oriented changes in a high school group-counseling program. *American Journal of Community Psychology*, 9, 697–714.

Tyler, F. B., Sussewell, D. & Williams, J. *Universalism, particularism and transcendism: A review of racially/ethnically relevant research and conceptions of psychotherapy*. Unpublished manuscript.

Weiss, S. L. & Dlugokinski, E. (1974). Parental expectations of psychotherapy. *Journal of Psychology*, 86, 71–80.

White, J. (1970). Guidelines for black psychologists. *Black Scholar*, 1, 52–57.

35. Family Psychology and Cultural Diversity: Opportunities for Theory, Research, and Application

José Szapocznik and William M. Kurtines

There is a growing recognition that contemporary psychology is undergoing a paradigm shift. Many challenges are being raised to a psychology concerned primarily with the individual as a focus of study. One important challenge has come from the contextualist view, which has had a broad impact on the field (cf. Liddle, 1987). Contextualism generally refers to the view that behavior cannot be understood outside of the context in which it occurs. Contextualism is concerned with the interaction between the organism and its environment—explaining and understanding the changing individual in a changing world. This essay contributes to the debate by extending contextualism in a number of directions.

Our interest in extending the concept of contextualism grew out of our experience working with troubled Hispanic youths. Over the past two decades we have struggled to develop theory, conduct research, and design interventions with this population (Szapocznik & Kurtines, 1989; Szapocznik, Kurtines, Foote, & Perez-Vidal, 1983, 1986; Szapocznik, Kurtines, Santisteban, & Rio, 1990; Szapocznik et al. 1988; Szapocznik, Rio, & Kurtines, 1991). We became increasingly aware of broader movements within the field that have had substantial implications for our work. In the past decade there has been a considerable effort to define contextual issues in terms of the individual in the context of the both family (e.g., Kaslow, 1987; Liddle, 1987) and culture (e.g., Sampson, 1988; Sue & Zane, 1987). These efforts have produced an extensive body of psychological litera-

Reprinted by permission of the authors and the American Psychological Association from *American Psychologist* 48 (1993): 400–407. Copyright © 1993 by the American Psychological Association.

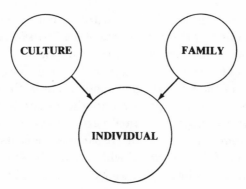

FIGURE 1
The Individual in the Context of the Family and Culture

ture that addresses the individual in the context of the family and in the context of culture; however, each literature has emerged as a relatively distinct and separate area of study, as illustrated in Figure 1.

As we learned more about developments in these areas and attempted to apply them to our work, we recognized certain limitations inherent in studying the individual in each context separately. We began to formulate a model that extended the concept of contextualism in two important ways. First, to help bridge the gap between the literatures on family and culture, we gave greater emphasis to the embeddedness of contexts themselves. That is, we extended the concept of contextualism to include the notion that the individual needs to be understood in the context of the family, and that the family in turn needs to be understood in the context of the culture. To help us understand the reality of cultural diversity in our work with troubled Hispanic adolescents, we also extended the concept of contextualism to include the notion of the individual embedded within a family that is itself embedded in a *culturally diverse context.* Our experience with these youth taught us that if we were interested in studying cultural context, we had to study it as it *really* occurs, rather than as some idealized historical concept of indigenous culture. That is, the idealized historical and homogenous concept of culture often found in the literature needs to be expanded, because in modern society most families (including ethnic minorities) are actually exposed to a context that is culturally diverse and heterogeneous.

In this essay we propose to view the individual, family, and culture in a more complete contextualist paradigm that includes the

more complex notion of individual within a family within a culturally diverse context: *the embeddedness of contexts within a diverse and
complex cultural milieu.* In the first two parts of the essay, we briefly
describe some of the emerging literature that addresses the individual
in the context of the family and the individual in the context of the
culture. In the third part, we introduce the idea of the embeddedness
of contexts. In the fourth and final part, we outline the model that
has evolved from our work with Hispanic adolescents that incorporates the notion of the individual within a family within a context in
which the cultural milieu is defined by increasing diversity and complexity.

THE INDIVIDUAL IN THE CONTEXT OF
THE FAMILY

A recognition of the importance of understanding the individual in
the context of the family is as old as the field of psychiatry itself,
beginning with Sigmund Freud's profound preoccupation with the
influence of the family on early childhood development and the development of psychopathology (Freud, 1953, 1965). More recently, the
recognition of the importance of understanding the individual in the
context of the family is reflected in the family psychology movement.
This movement has had a broad impact on the field as well as important implications for our own area of concern: conduct and behavioral disorders in children and adolescents.

Considerable research literature linking conduct disorders and behavior problems to family relational patterns has now evolved. Family interactional characteristics have been identified that place youth
at risk for conduct disorders (Alexander, 1973; Farrington, 1978;
Hanson, Henggeler, Haefele, & Rodick, 1984; Hetherington & Martin, 1979; Kazdin, 1987; Loeber & Dishion, 1984; McCord,
McCord, & Zola, 1959; Patterson, 1982, 1986; Patterson & Dishion, 1985; Rutter & Guiller, 1983). Our work with Hispanic
youths has also contributed to identifying dysfunctional family interactional patterns that impact on conduct disorders in youth (Szapocznik & Kurtines, 1989; Szapocznik et al., 1990).

There is a small but growing literature that suggests that certain
family behaviors may protect individuals from developing these disorders, even children who are otherwise in contexts that may place
them at high risk (Becerra, 1988; Jaco, 1959; Laosa, 1990; Loeber

& Dishion; 1984; Madsen, 1964; Sanchez-Ayendez, 1988; Santisteban, Szapocznik, Kurtines, & Rio, in press). We also have proposed a number of protective family characteristics that enhance the family's ability to respond to stressors (Szapocznik & Kurtines, 1989).

As illustrated in Figure 1, most of this literature focuses on the link between the individual and the family and gives relatively little attention to the role of culture.

THE INDIVIDUAL IN THE CONTEXT OF CULTURE

Culture, like family, has long been recognized as an important context for understanding the individual, and a large literature has emerged addressing concerns in cross-cultural psychology (e.g., Triandis & Brislin, 1984; Triandis et al. 1980–1981). In the mental health field there has been concern about the relationship of culture and individual psychopathology (e.g., Draguns, 1980; Marsella, 1979, 1980; Sanua, 1980), which has resulted in a significant movement to incorporate cultural concepts into mental health care (e.g., E. E. Jones & Korchin, 1982; R. L. Jones, 1980; Lefley & Pedersen, 1986; Marsella & Pedersen, 1981; Padilla, Ruiz, & Alvarez, 1975; Rogler, Malgady, Costatino, & Blumenthal, 1987; Rogler, Malgady, & Rodriguez, 1989; Sue & Zane, 1987). Most of this work has emphasized the relationship of culture and the individual. Thus, interest in culture has often reflected a profound concern with the impact of context on individual behavior, psychopathology, and mental health care, as illustrated in Figure 1.

The contextualist metaphor, however, has a more profound implication: the embeddedness of contexts themselves. Hence, the concern with the individual in a cultural macrocontext does not fully recognize the microcontext (e.g., the family) that links the individual to her or his culture. We have found it useful to extend our concern for culture to include the concept of the nesting of the individual within the family and the family within the culture.

THE EMBEDDEDNESS OF CONTEXTS

In contrast to these large bodies of work on culture and on the individual, there is an emerging interest in a new contextualist paradigm that emphasizes the notion of embeddedness: the study of the

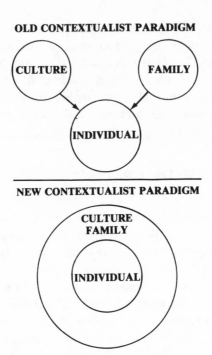

FIGURE 2
The New Contextuality Paradigm: The Embeddedness of Contexts

individual within the context of a family, which is in turn embedded in a cultural context, as illustrated in Figure 2. Perhaps the most important pioneer of this more complete view of contextualism was Urie Bronfenbrenner (1977, 1979, 1986). Bronfenbrenner's work strongly influenced our thinking, particularly in the early stages of our research. As Bronfenbrenner (1979) clearly stated "Seldom is attention paid to the person's behavior in more than one setting or to the way in which relations between settings can affect what happens within them" (p. 18). He postulated that an individual's ecological environment is composed of a complex set of nested structures that range from micro- to meso- to exosystems. A fledgling literature has built on the concept of the embeddedness of contexts and its application to work with families within larger social contexts. This includes the work of Auerswald (1971), Aponte (1974), Belsky (1980), Gable, Belsky, & Crnic (1992), Boyd-Franklin (1989), and McGoldrick, Pearce, and Giordano (1982). Empirical evidence of the impact of contextual variables in early childhood development has been reviewed by Zigler, Taussig, and Black (1992). They document the fact that interventions that target the social context in which families are embedded during the early childhood years have an impact on delinquent behavior 10–15 years later.

A MODEL FOR A CULTURALLY PLURALISTIC MILIEU

Origins

Although the contextualist tradition is concerned with a broad range of contexts, for the purposes of developing a rigorous program of systematic research, we focused on two major aspects of context: family and culture. Because our work was with Hispanic adolescents and their families, we will begin with a brief description of the origins of our research; however, as will become clear, the implications of our work extend beyond this relatively specialized population. The implications extend to all families who are confronted by a complex and pluralistic cultural milieu. In the United States, this population has increasingly included virtually all families, regardless of their cultural or ethnic origin.

Our work emerged from the clinical observations of the impact of the acculturation process on Cuban refugee families during the early 1970s (Szapocznik, Scopetta, & King, 1978; Szapocznik, Scopetta, Kurtines, & Arnalde, 1978); youngsters in these families were presenting with high rates of conduct problems (Szapocznik & Kurtines, 1980). Interestingly, in the early 1970s when the therapeutic zeitgeist for management of adolescent problems was strongly individualistic, we—coming from an Hispanic perspective—recognized the importance of studying these problems in the context of family and culture.

As we began our clinical work, it became apparent that cultural forces were impacting the way in which family interacted in very specific ways and that these changes in family dynamics appeared to underlie the conduct problems in these immigrant youth. The first step in working with these families was to understand the impact of these cultural forces on the family. It was crucial that we recognized that we could not fully explain the nature of the family changes that were taking place by viewing families strictly within the context of their culture of origin. Rather, the families that we were working

FAMILIES IN CULTURALLY PLURALISTIC CONTEXTS

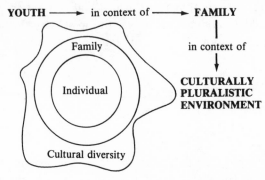

FIGURE 3
A Model for the Embeddedness of Contexts within a Culturally
Pluralistic Milieu

with were living in a multicultural context. For this reason, we had
to adjust our thinking to understanding families—no longer only
within the framework of their culture, but within the framework of
a culturally pluralistic environment, as depicted in Figure 3.

The problem that we faced then was to modify our understanding
of the concept of embeddedness to include the influence of a culturally
pluralistic environment on the family (Szapocznik, & Kurtines,
1980; Szapocznik, Kurtines, & Fernandez, 1980). Our earliest understanding of the problem was that our Cuban families were embedded in a culturally diverse context, in which parents and children
were exposed to both Hispanic and mainstream values and customs.
Following traditional learning curves, young people acculturated far
more quickly to the mainstream, whereas parents tended to remain
far more attached to their traditions (Szapocznik, Scopetta, Kurtines,
& Arnalde, 1978). As can be seen in Figure 4, this framework that
considered the effect of a culturally diverse environment not only
explained the dynamics that were occurring across the generations
but was also differentially predictive of impact by gender.

Thus, our willingness to view the individual within the context
of a family exposed to a culturally pluralistic milieu provided the
framework for explaining how family dynamics evolved within a
culturally diverse environment and how such changes were linked
to the emergence of conduct problems in youngsters (Szapocznik,
Santisteban, Rio, Perez-Vidal, & Kurtines, 1986). Families exposed

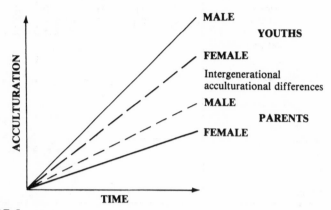

FIGURE 4
Acculturation as a Function of Time, Age, and Gender in Cuban-American Immigrants

Note: From "Theory and Measurement of Acculturation" by J. Szapocznik, M. A. Scopetta, W. Kurtines, & M. A. Aranalde, 1978, *Interamerican Journal of Psychology, 12,* p. 115. Copyright 1978 by the Interamerican Society of Psychology. Reprinted by permission.

to a culturally diverse environment developed a classic Ericksonian challenge: a family struggle in which some family members (the youth) struggled for autonomy and others (the elders) for family connectedness. As Figure 5 illustrates, this struggle usually develops in families around the time of adolescence, but in this case the magnitude of the struggle was considerably exacerbated by acculturational differences across generations. As a result of this struggle, children lost emotional and social support from their families, and parents lost their positions of leadership.

The impact of a culturally diverse environment on these families resulted in the emergence of conflict-laden intergenerational acculturational differences in which parents and youths developed different cultural alliances (Hispanic and American, respectively). These intergenerationally related cultural differences were added to the usual intergenerational conflicts that occur in families with adolescents to produce a much compounded and exacerbated intergenerational *and* intercultural conflict. As a consequence, parents became unable to properly manage youngsters who made strong claims for autonomy and who no longer accepted their parents' traditional Cu-

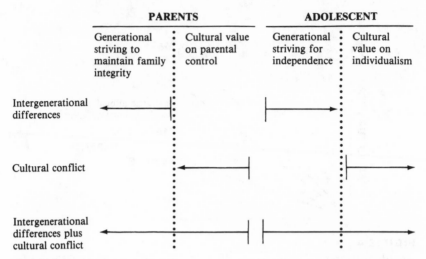

FIGURE 5

The Additive Effects of Intergenerational and Acculturational
Differences in Cuban-American Immigrant Families

Note: From "Bicultural Effectiveness Training: A Treatment Intervention for Enhancing
Intercultural Adjustment in Cuban American Families" by J. Szapocznik, D. Santisteban, W. M.
Kurtines, A. Perez-Vidal, & O. Hervis, 1984, *Hispanic Journal of Behavioral Sciences, 6*, p. 328.
Copyright 1984 by the *Hispanic Journal of Behavioral Sciences.* Reprinted by permission of Sage
Publications, Inc.

ban ways, giving rise to the emergence of conduct problems in adolescents.

From our earliest work then, we have been concerned about the embeddedness of contexts—the youth within the family within a cultural context. Our concern has been that the kind of cultural context in which our Hispanic families find themselves is not the kind of context that is usually studied, that is, a Hispanic context. Rather, our families are embedded in a culturally diverse context.

Moreover, we found it necessary to extend the conventional approach to the study of Hispanic families to permit us to study the family in a way that more truly represents the cultural reality in which it is embedded, namely, in a multicultural context. Our work thus posed a challenge not only for us but for the tradition in the research on culture that has tended to focus largely on historical or idealized aspects of culture. This challenge was to seek an understanding of the importance of culture as it occurs, which is in an increasingly multicultural and pluralistic context.

This subtle distinction between the study of culture as it occurs versus as it occurred is significant to a contextualist perspective. From a contextualist perspective, culture is important because it represents a *context* that helps to understand and explain human behavior. To that extent, it is the full range of cultural context—its history, complexity, and diversity—that is of concern within the contextualist paradigm.

Bicultural Effectiveness Training: An Intervention for Families in Culturally Pluralistic Milieus

As a result of the enhanced theoretical understanding that our model of the individual embedded within a family within a context of cultural diversity provided, we were able to make an important contribution to the development of the kinds of interventions that might address the problems that arise in multicultural contexts by formulating and successfully implementing a family-oriented intervention to enhance bicultural skills in all family members (Szapocznik, Santisteban, Kurtines, Perez-Vidal, & Hervis, 1984; Szapocznik, Santisteban, Rio, Perez-Vidal, Kurtines, & Hervis, 1986; Szapocznik, Santisteban, Rio, Perez-Vidal, Santisteban, & Kurtines, 1989). Our work focused on enhancing the bicultural skills that parents and youngsters need to develop: greater competence in managing their cultural differences within the family and successfully functioning in a culturally pluralistic milieu.

For this purpose we integrated our structural systems approach to family therapy (Szapocznik & Kurtines, 1989) with our cultural understanding of the conflicts presented by these families. We took advantage of the generic structural systems approach to changing family process while using content as a vehicle to achieve desired changes in family interactions. Because for these families the content of conflicts seemed to remain remarkably consistent with regard to differences along cultural lines or alliances, a set of psychoeducational interventions was designed restructuring the family to reduce intergenerational conflict while using culture as a standard content.

The bicultural effectiveness training (BET) approach was developed to be conducted in 12 conjoint sessions. The process that BET uses to bring about structural family change involves two change strategies developed specifically for the BET modality and derived

Initial Conflict

| HISPANIC VALUES/PARENTS | •••••| YOUTH/ACCULTURATED VALUES |

1) Detouring

(a) Creating an IP: value conflict placed in IP role, blamed for the family's ailment. The integenerational conflict is reframed by attributing all negative consequences to the cultural conflict.

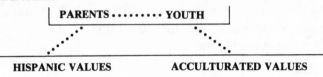

| PARENTS ••••••••• YOUTH |

| HISPANIC VALUES   ACCULTURATED VALUES |

(b) Reframing: intergenerational relationship is attributed positive consequences (enrichment available from differences), and the family is encouraged to perceive culture conflict as a common foe. Intergenerational cultural conflict between generations is detoured through culture conflict.

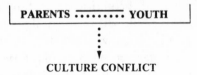

| PARENTS •••••••• YOUTH |

CULTURE CONFLICT

2) Establishing crossed alliances

(a) Family boundaries are made more permeable at this time to foment crossed alliances and encourage Parent/Acculturated Value and Youth/Hispanic Value relationships. Crossed alliances are expected to further weaken existing generational-cultural alliances.

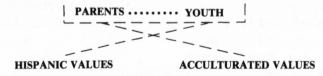

| PARENTS ••••••••• YOUTH |

HISPANIC VALUES   ACCULTURATED VALUES

(b) By viewing culture conflict as a common foe and by weakening existing generational-cultural alliances new crossed alliances are fostered, the overall level of biculturalism in families is enhanced, and parents and youth strengthen their relationship vis à vis cultural alliances.

| PARENTS ———— YOUTH |

HISPANIC VALUES ———————— ACCULTURATED VALUES

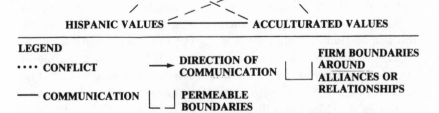

LEGEND

•••• CONFLICT

———— COMMUNICATION

→ DIRECTION OF COMMUNICATION

⌐ ⌐ PERMEABLE
⌐ ⌐ BOUNDARIES

FIRM BOUNDARIES AROUND ALLIANCES OR RELATIONSHIPS

from structural family therapy concepts (Szapocznik, Santisteban, Kurtines, et al., 1984; Szapocznik, Santisteban, Rio, et al., 1986). As can be seen in Figure 6, the initial change strategy is to temporarily detour[1] family conflict by placing the focus of both the intergenerational and the intercultural differences on the cultural conflict. Detouring is done by placing the cultural conflict in the identified patient role.[2] Placing the cultural conflict in an identified patient role is brought about by reframing the family's perception of the conflict. Reframing[3] in turn is accomplished by providing the family with a transcultural perspective that emphasizes the communality between parents and their children and by deemphasizing the intergenerational differences (e.g., by teaching that each member has a value position or point of view that is culturally determined). The purposes of this technique are to establish boundaries[4] around the family and to foster a new interactional pattern between parents and adolescents. From a process perspective, detouring is a useful means of loosening the existing rigid generational–cultural alliances (parent–Hispanic and adolescent-acculturated Americanized). The purpose of BET is to bring about more permanent structural changes in family interaction patterns, which is accomplished through the second strategy.

As can be seen from Figure 6, the second BET change strategy, establishing crossed alliances, provides a means of creating new cross alliances between family members and cultures. This is done through exercises designed to make both parents and youths more comfortable with both cultures. Through these exercises, parents are encouraged to accept and understand the value of certain aspects of the American culture represented by their child, and the adolescents are encouraged to accept and understand the value of certain aspects of the Hispanic culture represented by their parents. From a structural perspective, at a process level, enhancing biculturalism in family members is accomplished by creating cross alliances between generations and

FIGURE 6
BET: Two Basic Change Strategies

Note. BET = bicultural effectiveness training. From "Bicultural Effectiveness Training: A Treatment Intervention for Enhancing Intercultural Adjustment in Cuban American Families" by J. Szapocznik, D. Santisteban, W. M. Kurtines, A. Perez-Vidal, & O. Hervis, 1984, *Hispanic Journal of Behavioral Sciences, 6,* p. 331. Copyright 1984 by the *Hispanic Journal of Behavioral Sciences.* Reprinted by permission.

cultures. The expected outcome after the second change strategy is a reduction in intergenerational conflict and firmer boundaries around the family. Corresponding to the intrafamily change is a new set of family generational–cultural relationships with flexible alliances between parents and both cultures as well as between youths and both cultures.

CONCLUSION

We have outlined the model of the individual embedded within a family within a context of cultural diversity that we have been using in our work and have illustrated the opportunities it provides for psychological theory, research, and application. As noted, however, the implications of the model extend beyond the particular population that has been the focus of our work. The concept of embeddedness takes on an even greater urgency in view of the broader social, political, and historical trends taking place. This is especially the case as we in America become an increasingly culturally diverse society. If trends continue, the culturally diverse world of the 21st century will be dramatically different from prior eras in American history when our people were equally culturally diverse. In past eras, cultural diversity was rejected by our social, cultural, and political norms; there was pressure for culturally diverse people to blend into an idealized homogeneous stream that was called America. However, in 21st-century America, if current trends continue, culturally diversity will be respected and, perhaps, even cherished and nurtured. To the extent that we nurture cultural diversity, while promoting interethnic relations, we create a world in which families will be living increasingly at the interface between cultures and customs.

As the context changes, so must our science. Our science will be stretched and will have new opportunities for growth as it incorporates concepts such as the embeddedness of contexts, in which one of these contexts is defined as a culturally diverse society. Ultimately, not only science will benefit from the breakthroughs achieved by using a broader lens, but the vast majority of our people—who are increasingly culturally diverse—will benefit from our findings.

NOTES

Editors' note. This article was originally presented as part of a Distinguished Professional Contributions award address by José Szapocznik at the 100th Annual Convention of the American Psychological Association in Washington, DC, in August 1992. *Author's note.* This work was supported by National Institute on Drug Abuse Grant 1 RO1 DAO53341, Office of Substance Abuse Prevention Grant 1H86 SPO2350 to José Szapocznik, and National Institute on Drug Abuse Grant 1 P50 DAO7697 to Howard Liddle. We are grateful to Carl Eisdorfer for his encouragement, support, and critical review of the manuscript.

1. *Detour:* In family systems, a detour is a communication or conflict between two parties that, rather than traveling directly from one party to the next, is channeled through an indirect route or a third party.
2. *Identified patient role:* In structural family systems theory, the identified patient is the repository of blame for the family's ailment. A defense mechanism typically used by a system in conflict is to create an identified patient. The bicultural effectiveness training (BET) strategy of placing culture as the repository for the family's ailment draws on a natural proclivity of systems in conflict to create identified patients.
3. *Reframing* refers to an intervention that creates a new understanding or perspective for an old situation.
4. *Boundaries* serve to establish or denote the separation between organisms or entities. They indicate or clarify where one organism ends and another begins.

REFERENCES

Alexander, J. F. (1973). Defensive and supportive communications in normal and deviant families. *Journal of Consulting and Clinical Psychology, 40,* 223–231.

Aponte, H. J. (1974). Psychotherapy for the poor: An ecostructural approach to treatment. *Delaware Medical Journal, 46*(3), 1–7.

Auerswald, E. H. (1971). Families, change, and the ecological perspective. *Family Process, 10,* 263–280.

Becerra, R. M. (1988). The Mexican American family. In C. H. Mindel, R. W. Haberstein, & R. Wright (Eds.), *Ethnic families in America: Patterns and variations* (3rd ed., pp. 201–237). New York: Elsevier.

Belsky, J. (1980). Child maltreatment: An ecological integration. *American Psychologist, 35,* 320–335.

Boyd-Franklin, N. (1989). *Black families in therapy: A multisystems approach.* New York: Guilford Press.

Bronfenbrenner, U. (1977). Toward an experimental ecology of human development. *American Psychologist, 32,* 513–531.

Bronfenbrenner, U. (1979). *The ecology of human development.* Cambridge, MA: Harvard University Press.

Bronfenbrenner, U. (1986). The ecology of the family as a context for human development. *Developmental Psychology, 22,* 723–742.

Draguns, J. G. (1980). Psychological disorders of clinical severity. In H. C. Triandis & J. C. Draguns (Eds.), *Handbook of cross-cultural psychology: Vol. 6. Psychopathology* (pp. 99–174). Boston: Allyn & Bacon.

Farrington, D. P. (1978). The family backgrounds of aggressive youths. In L. A. Hersov, M. Berger, & D. Shaffer, (Eds.), *Aggression and antisocial behavior in childhood and adolescence* (pp. 89–106). Oxford, England: Pergamon.

Freud, S. (1953). *A general introduction to psychoanalysis.* Garden City, NY: Doubleday.

Freud, S. (1965). *New introductory lectures.* New York: Norton.

Gable, S., Belsky, J., & Crnic, K. (1992). Marriage, parenting, and child development: Progress and prospects. *Journal of Family Psychology, 5,* 276–294.

Hanson, C. L., Henggeler, S. W., Haefele, W. F., & Rodick, J. D. (1984). Demographic, individual, and family relationship correlates of serious and repeated crime among adolescents and their siblings. *Journal of Consulting and Clinical Psychology, 52,* 528–538.

Hetherington, E. M., & Martin, B. (1979). Family interaction. In H. C. Quay & J. S. Werry (Eds.), *Psycho-pathological disorders in childhood* (2nd ed., pp. 26–49). New York: Wiley.

Jaco, E. G. (1959). Mental health of Spanish Americans in Texas. In M. F. Opler (Ed.), *Culture and mental health: Cross-cultural studies* (pp. 145–163). New York: Macmillan.

Jones, E. E., & Korchin, S. J. (1982). *Minority mental health.* New York: Praeger.

Jones, R. L. (Ed.). (1980). *Black psychology.* New York: Harper & Row.

Kaslow, F. W. (1987). Trends in family psychology. *Journal of Family Psychology, 1,* 77–90.

Kazdin, A. E. (1987). *Conduct disorders in childhood and adolescence.* Newbury Park, CA: Sage.

Laosa, L. M. (1990). Psychosocial stress, coping and development of Hispanic immigrant children. In F. C. Serafica, A. I. Schuebel, R. K. Russel, P. D. Isaac, & L. Myers (Eds.), *Mental health of ethnic minorities* (pp. 42–65). New York: Praeger.

Lefley, H. P., & Pedersen, P. B. (Eds.). (1986). *Cross-cultural training for mental health professionals.* Springfield, IL: Charles C Thomas.

Liddle, H. A. (1987). Family psychology: The journal, the field. *Journal of Family Psychology, 1,* 5–22.

Loeber, R., & Dishion, T. J. (1984). Boys who fight at home and school: Family conditions influencing cross-setting consistency. *Journal of Consulting and Clinical Psychology, 40,* 223–231.

Madsen, W. (1964). Value conflict and folk psychotherapy in South Texas. In K. Ari (Ed.), *Magic, faith and healing* (pp. 420–440). New York: Free Press.

Marsella, A. J. (1979). Cross-cultural studies of mental disorders. In A. J. Marsella, R. G. Tharp, & T. J. Ciborowski (Eds.), *Perspectives on cross-cultural psychology* (pp. 233–263). San Diego, CA: Academic Press.

Marsella, A. J. (1980). Depressive experience across cultures. In H. C. Triandis & J. C. Draguns (Eds.), *Handbook of cross-cultural psychology: Vol. 6. Psychopathology* (pp. 237–289). Boston: Allyn & Bacon.

Marsella, A. J., & Pedersen, P. B. (Eds.). (1981). *Cross-cultural counseling and psychotherapy.* Elmsford, NY: Pergamon Press.

McCord, W., McCord, J., & Zola, I. K. (1959). *Origins of crime.* New York: Columbia University Press.

McGoldrick, M., Pearce, J. K., & Giordano, J. (1982). *Ethnicity and family therapy.* New York: Guilford Press.

Padilla, A., Ruiz, R., & Alvarez, R. (1975). Community mental health services for Spanish-speaking surnamed populations. *American Psychologist, 30,* 892–905.

Patterson, G. R. (1982). *Coercive family process.* Eugene, OR: Castalia.

Patterson, G. R. (1986). Performance models for antisocial boys. *American Psychologist, 41,* 432–444.

Patterson, G. R., & Dishion, T. J. (1985). Contributions of families and peers to delinquency. *Criminology, 23,* 63–79.

Rogler, L. H., Malgady, R. G., Costatino, G., & Blumenthal, R. (1987). What do culturally sensitive services mean? The case of Hispanics. *American Psychologist, 42*, 565–670.

Rogler, L. H., Malgady, R. G., & Rodriguez, O. (1989). *Hispanics and mental health: A framework for research.* Malabar, FL: Krieger.

Rutter, M., & Guiller, H. (1983). *Juvenile delinquency—Trends and perspectives.* New York: Penguin.

Sampson, E. E. (1988). The debate on individualism: Indigenous psychologies of the individual and their role in personal and societal functioning. *American Psychologist, 43*, 15–22.

Sanchez-Ayendez, M. (1988). The Puerto Rican family. In C. H. Mindel, R. W. Haberstein, & R. Wright (Eds.), *Ethnic families in America: Patterns and variations* (3rd ed., pp. 31–49). New York: Elsevier.

Santisteban, D. A., Szapocznik, J., Kurtines, W. M., & Rio, A. T. (in press). Behavior problems among Hispanic youth: The family as moderator of adjustment. In J. Szapocznik & H. Munoz (Eds.), *An Hispanic family approach to substance abuse prevention.* Washington, DC: U.S. Government Printing Office.

Sanua, V. D. (1980). Familial and sociocultural antecedents of psychopathology. In H. C. Triandis & J. C. Draguns (Eds.), *Handbook of cross-cultural Psychology: Vol. 6. Psychopathology* (pp. 175–236). Boston: Allyn & Bacon.

Sue, S., & Zane, N. (1987). The role of culture and cultural techniques in psychotherapy: A critique and reformulation. *American Psychologist, 42*, 37–45.

Szapocznik, J., & Kurtines, W. M. (1980). Acculturation, biculturalism and adjustment among Cuban Americans. In A. Padilla (Ed.), *Recent advances in acculturation research: Theory, models, and some new findings* (pp. 139–157). Boulder, CO: Westview.

Szapocznik, J., & Kurtines, W. M. (1989). *Breakthroughs in family therapy with drug abusing and problem youth.* New York: Springer.

Szapocznik, J., Kurtines, W. M., & Fernandez, T. (1980). Biculturalism and adjustment among Hispanic youths. *International Journal of Intercultural Relations, 4*, 353–375.

Szapocznik, J., Kurtines, W. M., Foote, F., & Perez-Vidal, A. (1983). Conjoint versus one-person family therapy: Some evidence for the effectiveness of conducting family therapy through one person. *Journal of Consulting and Clinical Psychology, 51*, 889–899.

Szapocznik, J., Kurtines, W. M., Foote, F., & Perez-Vidal, A. (1986). Conjoint versus one-person family therapy: Further evidence for the effectiveness of conducting family therapy through one person. *Journal of Consulting and Clinical Psychology, 54*, 395–397.

Szapocznik, J., Kurtines, W. M., Santisteban, D. A., & Rio, A. T. (1990). Interplay of advances between theory, research, and application in treatment interventions aimed at behavior problem children and adolescents. *Journal of Consulting and Clinical Psychology, 58*, 696–703.

Szapocznik, J., Perez-Vidal, A., Brickman, A. L., Foote, F., Santisteban, D., Hervis, O., & Kurtines, W. (1988). Engaging adolescent drug abusers and their families into treatment: A strategic structural systems approach. *Journal of Consulting and Clinical Psychology, 56*, 552–557.

Szapocznik, J., Rio, A. T., & Kurtines, W. M. (1991). University of Miami School of Medicine: Brief strategic family therapy for Hispanic youth. In L. E. Beutler & M. Crago (Eds.), *Psychotherapy research: An international review of programmatic studies* (pp. 123–132). Washington, DC: American Psychological Association.

Szapocznik, J., Santisteban, D., Kurtines, W. M., Perez-Vidal, A., & Hervis, O.

(1984). Bicultural effectiveness training: A treatment intervention for enhancing intercultural adjustment in Cuban American families. *Hispanic Journal of Behavioral Sciences, 6,* 317–344.

Szapocznik, J., Santisteban, D., Rio, A., Perez-Vidal, A., & Kurtines, W. M. (1986). Family effectiveness training (FET) for Hispanic families. In H. P. Lefley & P. B. Pedersen (Eds.), *Cross-cultural training for mental health professionals* (pp. 245–261). Springfield, IL: Charles C Thomas.

Szapocznik, J., Santisteban, D., Rio, A., Perez-Vidal, A., Kurtines, W. M., & Hervis, O. (1986). Bicultural effectiveness training (BET): An intervention modality for families experiencing intergenerational/intercultural conflict. *Hispanic Journal of Behavioral Sciences, 8,* 303–330.

Szapocznik, J., Santisteban, D., Rio, A., Perez-Vidal, A., Santisteban, D. A., & Kurtines, W. (1989). Family effectiveness training: An intervention to prevent drug abuse and problem behaviors in Hispanic youth. *Hispanic Journal of Behavioral Sciences, 1,* 4–27.

Szapocznik, J., Scopetta, M. A., & King (Hervis), O. E. (1978). Theory and practice in matching treatment to special characteristics of Cuban immigrants. *Journal of Community Psychology, 6,* 112–122.

Szapocznik, J., Scopetta, M. A., Kurtines, W. M., & Arnalde, M. A. (1978). Theory and measurement of acculturation. *Interamerican Journal of Psychology, 12,* 113–130.

Triandis, H. C., & Brislin, R. W. (1984). Cross-cultural psychology. *American Psychologist, 39,* 1006–1016.

Triandis, H. C., Lambert, W., Berry, J., Lonner, W., Heron, A., Brislin, R., & Draguns, J. (Eds.). (1980–1981). *Handbook of cross-cultural psychology (Vols. 1–6).* Boston: Allyn & Bacon.

Zigler, E., Taussig, C., & Black, K. (1992). Early childhood intervention preventive for juvenile delinquency. *American Psychologist, 47,* 997–1006.

Index